A CLINICAL HANDBOOK/ PRACTICAL THERAPIST MANUAL

For Assessing and Treating Adults with Post-Traumatic Stress Disorder (PTSD)

Donald Meichenbaum, Ph.D.

University of Waterloo
Department of Psychology
Waterloo, Ontario
Canada N2L 3G1

Institute Press

A CLINICAL HANDBOOK/
PRACTICAL THERAPIST MANUAL
For Assessing and Treating Adults with
Post-Traumatic Stress Disorder (PTSD)

Published by
INSTITUTE PRESS
292 Shakespeare Drive
Waterloo, Ontario, Canada N2L 2V1

Manufactured in the United States of America

PROLOGUE

This **Therapist Handbook/Manual** arose out of a **seven year** intensive period during which I have been deeply involved in work with clients (adults, adolescents, and children) who have been traumatized by natural and technological disasters and due to traumatic events of intentional human design. In various settings and in my private practice I have been called upon to assess and treat clients who experience PTSD and related distress. I have also been involved in training both inpatient and outpatient mental health staff about PTSD. In each instance, I have put together detailed handout material. These handouts constitute the basis of the present manual on work with **adults**. No review or **Handbook/Manual** can be complete, given the immense activity in this area. Hopefully, I have been able to put together a practical guidebook that can be updated on an annual basis. The **Handbook/Manual** should prove to be a valuable resource that can be referred to for many years to come.[1] It reflects all the cumulative scholarship and clinical experience that I have developed over 30 years of doing clinical work and conducting research. I hope you find it helpful and valuable. In order not to be overwhelmed, each Section has a statement of objectives, section summaries, "how to" guidelines, critical evaluations of the field as well as a test of your level of "expertise". **Enjoy!**

A brief consideration of the clinical settings in which I have consulted will make the present **Handbook/Manual** more understandable. These settings include:

Inpatient Treatment
    Adult psychiatric hospital where there is a sizable percentage of both inpatient and outpatient clients who have been "victimized" (some 40% to 60% report histories of childhood trauma).
    Dual diagnosis ward (PTSD and alcohol abuse) at a Veterans Administration Hospital.
    Child and adolescent residential programs where some 38% met PTSD criteria and over 90% had been exposed to "victimization" experiences. 29% had been victims of sexual abuse and 97% had been exposed to some type of severe community violence (e.g., being shot at, attacked with a knife, beaten up, mugged, or seen someone killed or commit suicide). These children often pose a danger to themselves or others, have severely dysfunctional families, exhibit uncontrollable behavior, are actively psychotic, or present a complicated clinical picture requiring extended observation, assessment and treatment. Irwin (1982) suggests that up to 450,000 children in the U.S. require such intensive treatment. We have been working on developing a total cognitive behavioral therapy milieu program for these children.
    Shelter program for children (from infancy to adolescence) who have been withdrawn from their families because of child sexual abuse.

---

[1] I have taken the liberty throughout this **Handbook/Manual** to include personal observations, anecdotes, and side-references. The topics to be covered are very "heavy" and can be depressing for they reflect the "evil" side of human nature (e.g., war, crime, rape, incest, domestic violence). The topic also conveys the remarkable story of courage and human resilience. For the last two years I have worked to put this **Handbook/Manual** together. At times, I felt I was a cross between two of my personal heroes. I grew up reading the weekly newsletter of the iconoclastic reporter I.F. Stone. He was the voice of conscience and reason; he used his "pen" to unmask pomposity and misrepresentation. In the wee hours when I was working on this project I had "delusions" that I was the I.F. Stone of the PTSD literature. My other hero was the French painter, George Seurat, who was the father of "pointillism". As each new article, each new journal, would cross my desk I would find "nuggets" to add to different Sections of the **Handbook/Manual**. "A bit of yellow; now a point of red!"

Outpatient Treatment

Consult on hostage taking, school shooting, police shooting, debriefing victims of natural disasters.

Supervise and consult with clinicians who treat clients who have been sexually abused.

Consult with home visitors who work with families where child abuse has been reported.

Treatment of spouse abuse in the U.S. military.

Treatment of traumatic brain injury (TBI) clients and their family members; many of the women have head injury due to spouse abuse.

Native Indian youth who experience PTSD due to "victimization" and economic distress.

Treatment of both inpatient and outpatient persons with developmental disabilities (formerly labelled persons with mental retardation). It is worth noting that Ryan (1994) has reported that the incidence of PTSD in persons with developmental disabilities was 16.5% (out of 310 subjects). Persons with developmental disabilities are more frequently abused physically, emotionally, and sexually than are nondisabled persons.

Consultation

Application of stress inoculation training for military personnel (e.g., United Nation's peace keepers) and for health care providers.

To labor unions on developing an assessment battery for PTSD -- accidents, sexual harassment, robberies, etc. (Note that claims of job-related stress "injuries" in the US rose from 5% of all occupational injury claims in 1980 to 15% in 1987. More and more claims of PTSD are emerging. See Ravin & Boal, 1989.)

To a petrochemical company for victims of technological accidents and ways to implement prevention procedures using stress inoculation training.

Testify in court on PTSD. (See Slovenko, 1994 for a discussion of the legal aspects of PTSD.)

Editorial Activities

Edit Plenum Series on Stress and Coping (See list of books in the Plenum Series in the reference section of this **Handbook/Manual**).

Private Practice

Focuses on "traumatized" clients

Training

Consult on the development of a week long Veterans Administration training program for clinicians on the assessment, diagnosis, and treatment of PTSD clients.

Conduct 2 and 5 day workshops on PTSD.

Finally, I should note that a major portion of my time is spent on training clinicians **to become more "expert"**. Thus, I have given a good deal of thought to the questions of **"What constitutes expertise?"**, and **"How can I help nurture such clinical expertise?"** In fact, much of my ongoing research is on understanding how expertise develops (see Meichenbaum & Biemiller, 1991). The research on "expertise" indicates that experts differ from their less competent colleagues in terms of:

a) knowledge (declarative -- "know what"; procedural -- "know how"; conditional -- "know when");

b) strategies (organization, automaticity, implementation, monitoring including metacognitive or executive "control" strategies);

c) motivation to persist and "stick to it" which is needed because repeated practice is required to become an "expert".

My attempt to improve the expertise of psychotherapists is consistent with the recent conclusions drawn by Ericsson and Charness (1994) who have highlighted that expertise is "acquired as a result of deliberate practice, especially when conducted in an apprenticeship relationship with a teacher or coach". What exactly do experts acquire and what are the implications for how I have put together this therapist manual? According to Ericsson and Charness, the literature on expertise indicates that experts acquire:

(1)   facts, skills and strategies;

(2)   the ability to form immediate representation of a problem that systematically cues their knowledge and permits them to reason forward or anticipate future events;

(3)   the ability to perceive meaningful relations and recognize configurations. It is not the amount of information stored per se, but rather how that information is stored, "chunked", indexed, and accessed that characterizes experts;

(4)   the ability to not just respond accurately, but also rapidly and effortlessly in dynamically changing situations, as a result of the refinement that comes with extensive repetitive practice;

(5)   the ability to recognize if and when a particular action is required.

I have put this **Handbook/Manual** together with these component processes in mind. You will find a great deal of information ("knowledge") on PTSD. In addition, I have included examples of "strategic" subroutines (e.g., how to conduct assessment and interviews, and how to ask clients to undertake "homework", how to treat specific target symptoms, how to conduct Critical Incident Stress Debriefing, and the like). With practice, one can become more expert in implementing and altering these clinical procedures. Finally, with regard to motivation, I have tried to nurture a "critical" and "open-minded" stance toward the challenging work of helping those in extreme distress. **I want to insure that mental health professionals do not revictimize clients** out of ignorance of the literature. I have also highlighted the **need to help the helpers.** In order to assess your personal level of expertise, **at the end of each section there are a set of questions and tasks** whereby you can calibrate your knowledge, strategies, and skills in working with traumatized clients. These questions and tasks reflect the central teaching objectives of each section. Note, it is possible for a group of students or clinicians to establish a study group and work through this entire Handbook/Manual, taking the Tests at the end of each Section. I can assure you that if you can answer these Test questions, you will have enhanced your clinical "expertise" substantially. I have a dream that some day you will be able to go for a job interview and indicate that one of your credentials is that you have mastered and can teach the material in this **Handbook/Manual** to others. *Please provide me with feedback on how successful I have been in helping you become "more expert.".*

My varied clinical consultations have proven to be a remarkable learning experience. I am deeply indebted to the many clients and their families who have permitted me to be part of their lives. I am also indebted to the various clinicians who have allowed me to learn and consult at the same time. In particular, I would like to express special appreciation to Drs. Nancy Price-Munn and Don Woodside, psychiatrists in practice in Hamilton, Ontario, Canada (and their colleagues) who have been fine mentors and sensitive creative clinicians in working with PTSD clients.

I am especially indebted to the many clinicians and researchers whom I cite in this **Handbook/Manual.** Their work has laid the foundation for my efforts. I have tried to provide citation and appropriate credit for their many contributions, and hopefully, this **Therapist Handbook/Manual** will further disseminate their important work. I would like to thank

Jan Wallace, Chris Schwendinger, Christy Gillin, and Theresa Schaefer for their secretarial efforts and Mary Goerzen-Sheard for both her editorial and secretarial contributions in putting this **Therapist Handbook/Manual** together. I would also like to thank Robert Guerette, Gerald Piaget and David Lima for their support in sponsoring the workshops I have given on PTSD. **This project could not have been completed without the patience and support of my wife Marianne. I am deeply in her debt.**

It should be noted that the topic of PTSD is so extensive that no one **Handbook/Manual** could adequately cover the subject matter. The interested reader should peruse the Journal of Traumatic Stress and the recent International Handbook of Traumatic Stress Syndromes by John Wilson and Beverly Raphael (1993). Also see the June, 1994 issue of Psychiatric Clinics of North America (Vol. 17, No. 2) that is devoted to PTSD, as well as an earlier edition (Ettedgui, 1985). Another useful resource is Pilots International Literature On Traumatic Stress (PILOTS) produced by Fred Lerner and Jan Clark. It is a computer-based resource and available on the Dartmouth College Library On-line System. PILOTS User guide is available from National Technical Information Service, Springfield, VA, 22161. The Veterans Administration National Center for PTSD publishes two very worthwhile newsletters on PTSD: (1) National Center PTSD Clinical Quarterly[1] and (2) National Center for PTSD Research Quarterly[2]. Also, the interested reader can contact the APA Division of Psychotherapy Task Force on Trauma Response and Research or the International Society WIMSIC[3]. Finally, Charles Figley[4] has initiated a computer Internet system on traumatic stress. In order to join the **Traumatic Stress Forum** send the following message to: MAILBASE@MAILBASE.AC.UK SEND (without a subject line): JOIN TRAUMATIC STRESS «put your first name and last name here« STOP

In addition, it should be noted that a clinical training program in PTSD is available through the National Center for PTSD in Palo Alto, CA. For further information call Caryl Polk, BCD, Clinical Training Program Coordinator (415-493-5000 ext. 2054).

I would like to extend an invitation to you, the reader, to provide feedback on the material presented in this **Handbook**. I am sure this document will continually be revised and I welcome your input. Please pass along references and clinical/research observations that you believe would be helpful.

Finally, I have taken the liberty of listing on the next two pages books and recent chapters I have written, that put the present **Handbook/Manual** in some perspective of my other work. I have also listed how I can be contacted. Order information for this **Handbook/Manual** is included on the inside cover page Thank you for your interest and your feedback.

I DEDICATE THIS HANDBOOK TO THE "VICTIMS". MAY MY WORK HELP THEM TO BECOME "SURVIVORS" AND "THRIVERS".

---

[1] Order from VAMC Palo Alto/MPD, 3801 Miranda Blvd., Palo Alto, CA 94304 (call John Aboytes at 415-493-5000 x2477).

[2] Order from National Center for PTSD, VA Medical Center (1160), White River Junction, Vermont 05009 (802-296-5132). Because of demand, a subscription can be ordered from the Superintendent of Documents (US Govt. Office) or downloaded from the Dartmouth computer.

[3] WISMIC is the World Veterans Federation and Information Center. They put out a newsletter twice a year. Order from Professor Lars Weisaeth, WISMIC, P.O. Box 39, 0320 Oslo 3, Norway.

[4] Charles Figley, Florida State University Family Center, 103 Sandels Bldg, Call Street and Ivy Way, Tallahasse Florida 32306-4094. E-Mail: CFIGLEY@GARNET.ACNS.FSU.EDU

PUBLICATIONS

Books

Meichenbaum, D. Cognitive-behavior modification: An integrative approach, 1977. Plenum Publishing Corporation, 233 Spring Street, New York, New York 10013.

Meichenbaum, D. Stress inoculation training: A clinical guidebook, 1985. (Paperback). Pergamon Press was original publisher. Now order from Neo-Data, Order Processing Center, P.O. Box 11071, Des Moines, Iowa 50336-1071. Ask for ISBN 0205-144187. Also order from Allyn & Bacon, Order Department 200, Old Tappan Road, Old Tappan, New Jersey 07675 (1-800-223-1360). In Canada order from Prentice Hall Canada, 1870 Birchmount Road, Scarborough, Ontario, Canada M1P 2J7 (416-293-3621). (Paperback $20.95, Casebound $31.95 plus shipping.)

Turk, D., Meichenbaum, D., & Genest, M. Pain and behavioral medicine, 1983. Guilford Press, Department B123, 200 Park Avenue S., New York, New York 10013.

Meichenbaum, D., & Jaremko, M. (Eds.), Stress reduction and prevention, 1983. (Plenum Press, see address above.)

Meichenbaum, D. Coping with stress, 1984. (Paperback). Facts on File, 460 Park Avenue S., New York, New York 10016 (1-800-322-8755).

Bowers, K., & Meichenbaum, D. (Eds.), The unconscious reconsidered, 1984. John Wiley, 605 Third Avenue, New York, New York 10158.

Meichenbaum, D., & Turk, D. Facilitating treatment adherence: A practitioner's guidebook, 1987. (Plenum Press, see address above.)

Meichenbaum, D., Price, R., Phares, E.J., McCormick, N., & Hyde, J. Exploring choices: The psychology of adjustment, 1989. Glenview, Illinois: Scott, Foresman & Company.

Film: Three approaches to psychotherapy. (Order from Psychological and Educational Films, 3334 East Coast Highway, #252 Corona Del Mark, California 92625). Call Sharon Shostrom 714-494-5079.

Don Meichenbaum

Department of Psychology   Phone: 519-885-1211, ext. 2551
University of Waterloo   (Secretary, ext. 2813)
Waterloo, Ontario, Canada   Fax: 519-746-8631
N2L 3G1

PUBLICATIONS

Recent Papers

Meichenbaum, D. (1992). The personal journal of a psychotherapist and his mother. In G.G. Brannigan and M.R. Merrens (Eds.), The undaunted psychologist. New York: McGraw Hill.

Meichenbaum, D. (1992). Evolution of cognitive behavior therapy: Origins, tenets and clinical examples. In J. Zeig (Ed.), The evolution of psychotherapy, Vol. II. New York: Brunner/Mazel.

Meichenbaum, D., & Biemiller, A. (1991). In search of student expertise in the classroom: A metacognitive analysis. In M. Pressley, K.R. Harris, and J.T. Guthrie (Eds.), Promoting academic competency and literacy in school. New York: Academic Press.

Meichenbaum, D. (1993). Changing conceptions of cognitive behavior modification: Retrospect and prospect. Journal of Consulting and Clinical Psychology, 61, 202-204.

Meichenbaum, D. (1993). Stress inoculation training: A twenty-year update. In R.L. Woolfolk and P.M. Lehrer (Eds.), Principles and practice of stress management. New York: Guilford Press.

Meichenbaum, D. (1993). The "potential" contributions of cognitive behavior modification to the rehabilitation of individuals with traumatic brain injury. Seminars in Speech and Language, 14, 18-31.

Meichenbaum, D., & Fitzpatrick, D. (1993). A constructivist narrative perspective on stress and coping: Stress inoculation applications. In L. Goldberger and S. Breznitz (Eds.), Handbook of stress. New York: Free Press.

Meichenbaum, D., & Fong, G. (1993). How individuals control their own minds: A constructive narrative perspective. In D.M. Wegner and J.W. Pennebaker (Eds.), Handbook of mental control. New York: Prentice Hall.

Loera, D., & Meichenbaum, D. (1993). The "potential" contribution of cognitive behavior modification to literacy training for deaf students. American Annals of the Deaf, 138, 87-95.

Turk, D., & Meichenbaum, D. (1992). A cognitive-behavioural approach to pain management. In P.D. Wall and R. Thelzack (Eds.), Textbook of pain (3rd Edition). London: Churchill Livingstone.

TABLE OF CONTENTS

HOW TO USE THIS HANDBOOK/MANUAL WITHOUT BECOMING OVERWHELMED

It is <u>not</u> expected that the reader will read this book from cover to cover, but rather this **Handbook/Manual** can be a useful reference guide. The following is a "user friendly" guide for where you can find the following items: *(Also see the Subject Index in Section VIII)*

SECTION III -- <u>ASSESSMENT OF PTSD</u>

<u>How to Assess for PTSD</u> (118)

Assessment Strategies: Long and Short Versions (122)

Open-ended Clinical Interviews: The Best Questions You Can Ask (124)

Standardized Assessment Measures for PTSD -- Review of PTSD Measures
and Ways to Assess for "Victimization Histories" (173)

Related Assessment Measures: Assessment for Specific Traumatic Events
(Combat, Abuse, Disasters) As Well As Measures of Coping (180)

Assessment of Children and Adolescents (201)

Challenge of Differential Diagnoses (201)

Assessment Measures of Comorbidity (201)

General Psychopathology (203)

Suicide -- Indicators, Assessment Procedures, Treatment Approaches (212)

Alcohol and Substance Abuse -- Assessment Approaches (229)

Family Assessment (236)

<u>Assessment of Premorbid Factors: Who is at High Risk</u>? (240)

<u>Can Traumatic Events Lead to Positive Outcomes</u>? (244)

<u>How Can I Have Clients Do Self-Monitoring and "Homework"</u>? (246)

SECTION IV -- <u>CAUTIONS ABOUT ASSESSMENT</u>

<u>What are the Dangers in Assessing Traumatic Memories</u>? (Issue of so-called False
Memories) (258)

<u>How Do Clinicians Assess the "Authenticity" of Their Clients' Memories</u>? (268)

<u>Guidelines for Handling Client's Autobiographical Memories</u> (275)

<u>How Do I Help the Helpers</u>? (278)

SECTION V -- <u>TREATMENT ALTERNATIVES: A CRITICAL ANALYSIS</u>

<u>Overview of Treatment Alternatives</u> (287)

<u>Evaluation of Treatment Outcome Studies with PTSD Clients: Critiques of</u>

<u>Pharmacological Studies with PTSD</u> (295)

SECTION VII -- POST-DISASTER INTERVENTIONS

SECTION VIII -- INFORMATION SHEETS AND REFERENCES

SECTION I
EPIDEMIOLOGICAL AND DIAGNOSTIC INFORMATION ABOUT PTSD

Goals of Section I

Since there is so much information to cover on PTSD, I will begin each Section with a brief statement of the Section goals and a statement of what the reader should be able to take away from the Section. The test that follows each section will permit you to assess whether the goals have been achieved. Hopefully, these advanced organizers will make the material more manageable. **The first objective is to insure that a core knowledge base about PTSD exists** before we consider assessment and treatment issues related to PTSD. Thus, in turn, we will consider:

1. the diversity of traumatic events;

2. the scope or widespread incidence of such traumatic events;

3. the multifarious impact of trauma;

4. the epidemiological data of PTSD for specific target populations (e.g., veterans, rape, and crime victims, victims of natural disasters, and victims of child sexual abuse).

A consideration of this epidemiological data will highlight, not only the potential toll of traumatic events, but also the **remarkable resilience, adaptability and courage** that individuals evidence. **THE STORY OF PTSD IS THE TALE OF THE INDOMITABLE AND INDEFATIGABLE HUMAN SPIRIT TO SURVIVE AND ADAPT.** As we shall see, a consideration of this data has important implications for assessment and treatment.

In addition to these topics, I will describe the diverse clientele who will be considered in this **Clinical Handbook/Manual,** including health care providers (HCPs) who work with traumatized populations. In order to put this opening discussion of PTSD in some historical context the **changing labels for PTSD** will be enumerated, followed by a discussion of the **psychiatric categories** that are now used to diagnose PTSD, including the findings of the latest DSM-IV clinical trials.

As a result of working through SECTION I of this **Clinical Handbook/Manual** the reader should be able to answer the following questions:

1. What are the different types of traumatic stressors?

2. What is the impact of traumatic events at various levels (phenomenological, physiological, and symptomatic)? What are the signs of comorbidity? (As we shall see, the majority of victims of trauma develop a range of other disorders, as well as PTSD.)

3. What are the diagnostic criteria of PTSD?

4. What is the basic epidemiological data for various specific classes of adults with PTSD (e.g., combat veterans, rape victims, crime victims, victims of child sexual abuse)? What are the implications of these descriptive data for assessment and treatment?

Overview of Section I

Basic Epidemiological Information

1. Different classes of PTSD clients

2. Different types of traumatic events

3. Scope and impact of various traumatic events: Some general epidemiological data

   How widespread are traumatic stressors and resultant PTSD and related disabilities?

   A. Natural disasters -- how widespread are such disasters?
   B. What is the impact of exposure to such natural disasters?
   C. What is the impact of technological disasters?
   D. What is the long-range impact?
   E. Automobile accidents: A more personal exposure to traumatic events
   F. Other forms of exposure
   G. Gender differences
   H. Intensity or dose effects of traumatic events
   I. "Positive" effects and Conclusions

4. What are adults' general responses to traumatic events? -- Multifarious impact

   Table 1 -- Physiological Alterations Associated With PTSD
   Table 2 -- Neurohumoral/Neuroendocrinological Abnormalities Associated With PTSD

5. What is the history of the concept of PTSD -- Changing labels?

6. DSM definitions of stress disorders

   Table 3 -- DSM-IV Post-Traumatic Stress Disorder Criteria
   Table 4 -- Disorders of Extreme Stress (DES) Scales and Categories Used In The
             DSM-IV Field Trial (van der Kolk et al., in press)

7. What is the evidence for comorbidity (or multiple diagnoses) with PTSD?

8. Examples of illustrative data on special PTSD populations:

   a)   Vietnam and other combat-related experiences

   b)   Rape victims

   c)   Victims of domestic violence (spouse abuse)

   d)   Crime victims

   e)   Victims of child sexual abuse

DIFFERENT CLASSES OF PTSD "CLIENTS"

At the outset it is important to recognize the heterogeneity of "PTSD clients". Subsumed under the heading of PTSD are **seven different classes of "clients"**, each of whom call for slightly different assessment and intervention procedures. The populations include:

1. Individuals who have been exposed to traumatic events (natural or man-made disasters) and who are seen as part of **post-disaster interventions**. These individuals and their families are **not seeking treatment** *per se*, but they can benefit from various forms of psycho-educational interventions (e.g., critical incident stress debriefings *as discussed in Section VII*).

2. Individuals who have "knowingly" been exposed **recently** to victimizing experiences and **who initiate and seek help**. These individuals may have experienced either Type I stressors (e.g., sudden, unpredictable stressors such as rape, accident, shooting, natural disaster), or Type II stressors (prolonged, sustained repeated stressors such as child sexual abuse, war experience, domestic violence). *(We will consider the differences between Type I and Type II stressors below.)*

3. Individuals who have "knowingly" experienced traumatic events **some time ago** and they evidence chronic, intermittent or delayed PTSD symptoms (e.g., combat veteran from Vietnam war, prisoners of war, Holocaust survivors).

4. Individuals who are being treated either on an inpatient or outpatient basis for other psychiatric disorders (e.g., anxiety, depression, eating disorders, personality disorders such as borderline, multiple, addictive behaviors) or medical disorder (e.g., somatizing disorders) and who **report** early "victimization experiences" during the course of treatment.

5. Individuals who enter treatment with the "goal" to determine if they have, indeed, been "abused". They enter treatment with the **wish to determine whether these "victimizing"** experiences have occurred and whether they contribute to their present difficulties. *(We will consider the challenge of working with such clients in Section IV.)*

6. Individuals who manifest classic PTSD symptoms, but "without the trauma" according to the stressor Criterion A in DSM-IV. As proposed by Scott and Stradling (1994), these individuals experience **Prolonged Duress Stress Disorder (PDSD)**. This category is usually applied to individuals who experience prolonged distress due to work or troubling interpersonal relationships, or as a result of having to cope with chronic illness, or they provide continual care to someone who is chronically ill. It is the **cumulative** impact of these **unremitting stressors** that can cause PTSD symptomatology, as well as other forms of distress. They do not meet the strict criteria of a specific "pathogenic" trauma (e.g., disaster, assault, and accident). The **PDSD** "sufferers" usually have experienced more diffuse cumulative stressors that need to be assessed and treated accordingly as discussed in the assessment and treatment Sections *(See Sections III and VI, respectively)*.

7. The **health care providers** who treat "victimized" clients. (This category raises the important issue of **"vicarious traumatization"** and **"compassion fatigue"** and the need to take care of the caretakers *(as examined in Section IV.)*

Note, many times these various classes of individuals overlap. These are not mutually exclusive categories.

We now turn our attention to a consideration of the variety of traumatic events that bring individuals into contact with health care providers.

DIFFERENT TYPES OF TRAUMATIC EVENTS

A. "Short-Term" Traumatic Events

1. Traumatic events refer to events that are so extreme or severe, so powerful, harmful and/or threatening that they demand extraordinary coping efforts. They may take the form of an unusual event or a series of continuous events that subject people to extreme, intensive, overwhelming bombardment of perceived threat to themselves or significant others. Such events may overwhelm a person's sense of safety and security. These events may be relatively brief and powerful (e.g., rape, assault, witnessing a crime, being in a disaster, or other forms of extreme personal threat), often lasting no more than a few minutes or hours. These events can leave behind long-term secondary stressors (see Kleber et al., 1992 for a fuller discussion). They may take the form of a single traumatic event (dangerous, hazardous, threatening, vivid, often sudden and overwhelming to nearly everyone). Examples include:

   a) natural disaster -- the most common natural hazards are floods, hurricanes and severe tropical storms, tornadoes and severe windstorms, earthquakes and severe tremors, as well as volcanic eruptions, and avalanches (Solomon & Smith, 1994).

   b) accidental disaster -- car, train, boat, airplane accidents[1], fires, explosion. Some accidents are what are called "communication disasters" where people are severely injured or die often far away from home where there is no available social network (e.g., airplane accidents). Other accidents are technological in nature, and may fit the category "silent disasters", as described below.

   c) deliberately caused disasters/intentional - human design (IHD) -- bombing, shooting, rape, terrorist attack, hostage taking, assault and battery, robbery, industrial accident.

2. Baum et al. (1993) have noted that these disturbing, rapidly unfolding events create terror, extreme fright, threat to life, feelings of helplessness, vulnerability, loss of control and uncertainty. These traumatic events can cause very long-term changes in "affect, stress-related behavior, physiological functioning and mental health," **but not for all victims.** For some, these short-term traumatic events may reactivate unresolved conflicts and reactions from prior victimization. As we shall consider in Section VII on **Post Disaster Interventions**, a number of mediating factors besides the proximity, intensity and duration of the stressor are important in influencing individual reactions.

   Other classes of traumatic stressors may be **prolonged** in nature, or those **experienced vicariously.**

B. "Long-Term" Traumatic Events

1. **Prolonged repeated trauma**

   a) natural and technological disasters -- chronic illness, nuclear accident, toxic spills. Those accidents that have **high levels of powerful impact** with **low levels of predictability** and **controllability** can have most devastating effects on the community, family and individual (e.g., see Erikson, 1976). "Studies of natural disasters tend to show declines in symptoms over a 1 to 2 year period, with

---

[1] In spite of the widespread possibility of airplane accidents, it is interesting to note that Butcher (1992) reports that only 24% of airports in the U.S. have conducted disaster drills in the last 3 years.

functioning often returning to normal ranges. Technological disasters also tend to indicate decreases in symptoms over time, however, the return to "normal" is not as clearly demonstrated". In fact, following technological disasters, "the symptoms related to anger and irritability may not decline, but may continue or even increase post-disaster" (Green & Solomon, 1994, p.13).

b) intentional human design -- hostage taking, political prisoner, POW, victimization such as child sexual abuse, battered syndrome, Holocaust victim, sexual harassment, refugees.

C. Vicarious exposure (especially in the case of children)

Two populations have been examined most intensely with regard to vicarious exposure. First, the long-term impact of the **Holocaust** on both survivors and their children has been studied. The second population is that of **combat veterans** (e.g., Vietnam and Israeli soldiers) and their spouses and children. A brief consideration of these groups will highlight the potential role of **vicarious exposure to traumatic events**.

a) As Weisel (1960, 1965) has repeatedly noted, words are inadequate to describe the Holocaust. Nevertheless, Bruno Bettleheim (1943) observed:

> "What characterized the Holocaust was its inescapability, its uncertainty and unpredictability ... The fact that nothing about it was predictable, that one's very life was in jeopardy at every moment and one could do nothing about it."

We have all seen the vivid pictures of concentration camps. What is the long-term impact of such a traumatic event on survivors and on their offspring? After all these years, controversy still abounds. Clinical studies are often juxtaposed with methodological critiques. Adequate studies are few. For example, Falk et al. (1994) in reviewing the literature in PTSD and Holocaust survivors notes that there is **only one study** on the topic, namely Kuch and Cox (1992).[1] They reported that **46%** of the total sample met criteria for **PTSD some 50 years after the Holocaust**. The extensive remaining studies are primarily case demonstrations on selective clinical populations. For instance Lomranz (1994) has reviewed 110 articles regarding first generation survivors of the Holocaust. He highlights the extremely small samples and the majority of clinical case studies. In spite of sampling bias, he notes that the "mere experience of the most extreme traumatic event does not necessarily result in a disorder" (p.3). Moreover, the "transmission of trauma" did not always occur. While some offspring continue to "pay the price" of their parent's traumatic exposure, **many do not**.

b) For example, children of the approximately **350,000 Holocaust survivors** may evidence "contagious" adjustment difficulties in terms of low self-esteem and affective impairment (Barocas & Barocas, 1979; Felsen & Erlich, 1990; Nadler & Ben Shushan, 1989; Rosenheck & Nathan, 1985). But these conclusions must be

---

[1] See Kuch, K., & Cox, B.J. (1992). Symptoms of PTSD in 124 survivors of the Holocaust. American Journal of Psychiatry, 149, 337-340. In considering work with Holocaust victims caution is warranted as evident in the findings by Wagnaer and Goenewed (1990) who found that approximately 25% of Holocaust survivors became significantly distressed when interviewed about their experiences. Also see Danieli (1994) for a thoughtful discussion of the challenge of working with Holocaust survivors and their families.

tempered by the variety of methodological critiques of research on Holocaust survivors and their offspring (e.g., see Krell, 1982; Peskin, 1981; Solkoff, 1991).

c) But, the conclusions about the long-term impact of a stressful event such as the Holocaust needs to be qualified, by the observation that as survivors age a variety of life events (e.g., retirement, children leaving home, death of a loved one, and other stressful events) may serve as triggers for what Danieli (1994) calls "unmasked latent PTSD" (p.21). She highlights that it is very hard to draw conclusions based on outward appearances as she points to the recent suicides of such prominent Holocaust survivors as Primo Levi, Jerzy Kosinsky and Bruno Bettleheim. Once again, however, great caution is warranted when generalizing from a few prominent cases. But as we will consider below in the discussion of POWs and aging, a pattern of prolonged disability is evident in trauma survivors. In this context, it is important to highlight Danieli's (1994, p.20) astute observation that:

> "Survivors of trauma may be both successful in their post-trauma adaptation and troubled in relation to their survival experience".[1]

Meichenbaum and Fong (1994) have noted that the same "coping mechanism", or "mind games", that can be used to facilitate coping, may also be used to foster noncompliant and antisocial behaviors. For example, while this **"doubling"** process may be used adaptively by victims of trauma, Lifton (1986) has described how Nazi doctors were able to "split" themselves into two functioning wholes, namely, an "Auschwitz self" and a "prior self". Is it possible that the "same psychological mechanisms" that the perpetrators used to "protect" themselves during the Holocaust (namely, "doubling") could have been used by the survivors after the Holocaust?

d) A factor that may contribute to long-term distress is the survivor's tendency to adopt a collective identity, namely that of a "Holocaust survivor", with the accompanying potential secondary victimization and possible stigmatization. Shalev (1994) and Lipton (1973) describe the dangers of adopting such a collective identity by Holocaust victims and by survivors of the atomic bomb in Japan. Ayalon (1982) has described such a process in the victims of terrorist attacks in Israel. It is not only the exposure to the traumatic event, but the narrative constructed around the event that influences the adaptive processes. Such narratives can be transmitted cross-generationally and can lead to vicarious exposure in the offspring.

e) In the case of **Vietnam veterans**, Rosenheck (1986) has suggested that PTSD combat veterans, especially those who have been victims of childhood abuse themselves, may be at high risk for maltreatment of their children. In the U.S., it has been estimated that **one million children are victims of "secondary victimization"** as a result of repeated exposure to a parent with chronic PTSD (Hiley-Young et al., 1993). Harkness (1991) in discussing the effects of combat-related PTSD on children notes that the impact may take various forms including the a) over-identified child, b) child as rescuer of a distressed family member, c) child as emotionally uninvolved in the family. **The level of the parents' PTSD symptoms often predict the level of the child's PTSD symptoms.** In a subsequent section we will consider the data on the spouses of Israeli soldiers with PTSD.

---

[1] In this context it is interesting to note that Herman (1992) describes the Orwellian concept of **double-think** which is the ability to hold two **contradictory** beliefs in one's mind simultaneously and accepting both of them. Thus, one might see oneself as a "survivor" and "victim", simultaneously.

f) Exposure to "near miss" traumatic experience can also lead to PTSD symptoms.

g) *In Section IV we will consider how psychotherapists of trauma clients can also be "vicariously victimized".*

D. Type I and Type II Traumatic Events: An Important Distinction

1. Terr (1991) has drawn a distinction between what she calls **short term Type I** and **prolonged Type II** traumatic events:

    a) <u>Type I traumas -- short-term, unexpected traumatic event</u>

        i)   single blow, dangerous, and overwhelming events
        ii)   isolated traumatic experiences, often rare
        iii)   sudden, surprising, devastating events
        iv)   limited duration
        v)   e.g., rape, natural disasters, car accidents, sniper shooting
        vi)   events become indelibly etched on an individual's mind (recalled in detail) and create more vivid and complete memories than does Type II trauma
        vii)   more likely to lead to typical PTSD symptoms of intrusive ideation, avoidance, and hyperarousal reactions
        viii) more likely to lead to classic reexperiencing experience
        ix)   quicker recovery more likely

    Note, however, that Type I stressors can trigger or recapitulate an earlier history of victimization, fears of abandonment, and the like.

    b) <u>Type II traumas -- sustained and repeated ordeal stressors</u> -- series of traumatic events or exposure to a <u>prolonged</u> traumatic event

        i)   variable, multiple, chronic, long-standing, repeated, and anticipated traumas
        ii)   more likely to be of intentional human design
        iii)   e.g., ongoing physical and sexual abuse, combat
        iv)   initially experienced as Type I stressors, but as trauma reoccurs, victim expects and fears its reoccurrence
        v)   feels helpless to prevent it
        vi)   memories[1] are typically "fuzzy" and "spotty" because of dissociation; over time dissociation can become a way of coping
        vii)   may lead to altered view of self and of the world and accompanying feelings of guilt, shame, and worthlessness
        viii) more likely to lead to long-standing characterological and interpersonal problems, as evident in increased detachment from others, restricted range of affect, and emotional liability
        ix)   result in attempts to protect self that may involve the use of dissociative responses, denial and numbing, withdrawal, use of addictive substances
        x)   more likely to lead to what Herman (1992) calls a Complex PTSD Reaction and what van der Kolk et al. (1993) characterize as Disorders of Extreme Stress (DES) *(see descriptions below)*. Individuals with these reactions have poorer recovery.

---

[1] "Memories tend to be retained in spots, rather than as complete wholes" (Terr, 1991, p. 14). As Lindsay and Read (1994) observe, "complete amnesia is not characteristic of either Type I or Type II abuse".

A stressor is more likely to produce PTSD if it is severe, sudden, unexpected, prolonged, repetitive and intentional (Tomb 1994).

2. Both Type I and II stressors have been researched in some detail. Consider an illustrative list of the litany of traumatic events that have been studied -- wars in Vietnam, Middle East, Ireland, and Cambodia; accidents at Three Mile Island, Chernobyl and Buffalo Creek; fires at Coconut Grove and bush fires in Australia; natural disasters such as Mt. St. Helena volcanic eruption; Hurricanes Andrew and Hugo; LA and Armenian earthquakes; the Chowchilla kidnapping; and the list goes on and on. For example, just consider the impact of a natural and a man-made disaster. In the Armenian earthquake it was estimated that between 25,000 and 100,000 people were killed and over half a million people were left homeless (Green, 1994). The industrial accident at the Union Carbide plant in Bhophal India resulted in the exposure of 200,000 people to the gas leak and the deaths of 4037 people. Approximately, 50,000 of the exposed population are estimated to be suffering from long-term health effects (Dhara & Kriebel, 1993). These natural and man-made disasters underscore the observation that PTSD is a topic of the 90's. In fact, the World Health Organization (WHO) has established a goal that by 1995 "90% of all countries will have developed master plans to deal with disaster situations".

3. There is a strong suggestion in the literature that human caused disasters and resultant victimization are worse than naturally caused disasters (Baum et al., 1983; Ursano et al., 1994). In many instances, disasters represent a combination of both natural and intentional human design (see Green & Solomon, 1994).

4. O'Donohue and Elliott (1992) have commented on the heterogeneity of traumatic events and suggested the following subcategories of PTSD: "i) war; ii) child sexual abuse; iii) physical abuse; iv) psychological abuse; v) accident; vi) adult rape; vii) natural disaster; viii) violent nonsexual crime; and ix) other" (p. 434). With serious trauma, the **lifetime prevalence rate for PTSD is approximately 30%**, whereas the **current prevalence after several years is usually below 10%** (Tomb, 1994).

5. What is critical for our discussions of PTSD is that research indicates that **victims of different traumas such as disasters, rape and combat** have **similar profiles of psychopathology**, not only PTSD and PTSD + DES (Disorders of Extreme Stress), but also other diagnoses with which PTSD is **frequently co-occurs, generalized anxiety disorder, depression, substance abuse** (Solomon et al., 1992).

6. As we consider the epidemiological data on PTSD and related sequelae, it is important to keep in mind that the likelihood of individuals experiencing distress is influenced by:

    a) characteristics of the trauma
    b) characteristics of the individual's and group's reactions to the trauma
    c) pretrauma factors
    d) posttrauma recovery factors

With this complexity in mind, we can begin by considering some basic epidemiological data on traumatic events and their impact.

SCOPE AND IMPACT OF VARIOUS TRAUMATIC EVENTS:
Some General Epidemiological Data

How Widespread Are Traumatic Stressors
and Resultant PTSD and Related Disabilities?

(See Bolin, 1988; Davidson & Fairbank, 1992; Duckworth, 1987; Green, 1991, 1994; Hartsough, 1985; Keane, 1990; Kleber & Brom, 1992; Melick et al., 1982; Smith et al., 1988; Ursano et al., 1994; Vogel & Vernberg, 1994; Wilson & Raphael, 1994; for a more complete summary.) (In particular, see Green, 1994, 1994b; Green & Solomon, 1994; and WHO, 1992 for the most succinct and comprehensive reviews. These articles should be read if you work with disaster populations.)

Before we consider the epidemiological data of the exposure rates to traumatic events and the resultant impact, it is important to recognize that there is much disagreement about the incidence and prevalence of PTSD and other psychiatric and social sequelae that follow from exposure to traumatic events. This disagreement is due in part to the fact that researchers have sampled diverse populations (general population, homeless population, clinical samples, etc.) and they have varied in both the measures used to assess exposure and impact. For example, Helzer et al. (1987) estimated that only 1% of the general population suffer from PTSD, while Norris (1992) estimated that 7% of the general population suffer from PTSD, and Regier et al. (1988) estimated a lifetime PTSD prevalence of 9.2% in an HMO population in Detroit.[1] The marked variability of the prevalence of PTSD is underscored by the authors of DSM-IV who report "community-based studies reveal a lifetime prevalence for PTSD ranging from 1% to 14%, with the variability related to methods of ascertainment and the population sampled. Studies of at-risk individuals (e.g., combat veterans, victims of volcanic eruptions, or criminal violence) have yielded prevalence rates from 3% to 58%" (p.426).

Given this variability, we will consider in this Section not only the general prevalence and incidence but also examine the incidence/prevalence of PTSD and accompanying distress and maladjusted behavior for a variety of specific populations (e.g., combat veterans, rape victims and crime victims, victims of domestic violence, and child sexual abuse).

In considering this epidemiological data it is important to pay special heed to the advice offered by Alexander (1993, p.465),

> "A major trap seems to be that helpers become pedlars of gloom and miserable statistics about the presence of post traumatic stress symptoms. However awful that the circumstances of a disaster, it is imperative that a **positive approach be maintained.** People do cope with adversity and even in the worst tragedies one can (and should) find the positive gains."

---

[1] Keane (1990) observes that even if one uses Helzer's conservative estimate, this translates into **2.4 to 4.8 million cases of PTSD in the U.S.A. alone.** Also see Weisaeth & Eitinger (1991) for a discussion of PTSD from a European perspective.

Exposure Rates and Impact: Just How Common Is Exposure to Traumatic Events Such as Natural and Technological Disasters, Accidents, War, Crime, and Abuse?

While I will attempt to answer this question for specific classes of traumatic events, it is useful to frame the answer in more general terms. The most succinct answer I have encountered has been offered by Green (1994) who has reviewed the psychosocial research on traumatic stress. Her general conclusions are worth repeating, for they set the stage for the more interested reader to examine the specific epidemiological data that I review below. As Green (1994) reports:

a) 3/4 of the general population in the US has been exposed to some event in their lives that meet the stressor criterion for PTSD,

b) **only about 1/4 of individuals who are exposed to such traumatic events go on to develop the full blown PTSD syndrome,** with rape routinely producing the highest rates of PTSD,

c) 1/2 of those who develop the PTSD disorder may continue to have it decades later without treatment,

d) the rates of PTSD usually decline over time, even without treatment. In human-caused events, this decrease may not be a return to normal levels,

e) about 1/2 of those treated may still meet full criteria for PTSD at termination,

f) other diagnoses associated with traumatic exposure include major depression, substance abuse, phobia and panic, as well as adverse medical outcomes and higher medical service utilization,

g) the intensity of exposure is a risk factor for the development of PTSD. Other risk factors include low education/social class, preexisting psychiatric symptoms or diagnosis, prior trauma, a family history of psychiatric problems, and exposure to multiple stressful events. *(In Section VII we will consider vulnerability factors in detail.)*

What is important to take away from this introductory epidemiological data is that the exposure to trauma is a necessary, but insufficient cause of PTSD. **The presence of a PTSD following a traumatic event is the exception rather than the rule.** (Yehuda and McFarlane, 1994)

For those who wish more detailed information consider the following **epidemiological data**.

A. **Natural Disasters -- How Widespread Are Such Disasters?**

1. "Between the years 1967 and 1991, nearly 8000 **natural disasters** were reported worldwide. These events killed over 3 million people and adversely affected nearly **800 million** people and resulted in immediate economic damage of $23 billion (Green, 1994b; WHO, 1992). It was the poorest countries, and those with the largest populations, which sustained the most deaths during this period -- 86% of disasters occurred in developing countries, as well as 78% of all deaths. "The actual numbers killed in disasters is estimated to be some **3 or 4 times higher** in developing countries than in the developed countries" (WHO, 1992, p.11). The ratio of affected to killed individuals was 2.9 in developed countries, but tenfold in developing countries." (Green, 1994, p. 5).

2. In North America (N.A.), **4 out of 10 people** are **exposed** to **major traumas** in their **lifetime. 7%** of the N.A. population (or approximately 17 million) is **exposed annually to traumatic events.** As many as 2 million American households experience injuries and physical damage each year from fire, floods, hurricanes, tornadoes, severe tropical storms or windstorms, and earthquakes (Rossi et al., 1983). Ursano et al. (1994) estimate that in the year 2000, over 1700 deaths will occur in the US owing to major disasters and property and income loss will total more than $17 billion.

3. Between 1974 and 1980 there were **37 major catastrophes** in the U.S. From 1970 to 1980 approximately 2 million residents in the U.S. suffered injuries or property damage due to disasters (Freedy et al., 1992).

4. Illustrative of this epidemiological research is a study by Norris (1994). She asked 1000 residents in 4 cities in Southeastern U.S. if they had been exposed to 9 traumatic events: robbery; physical assault; sexual assault (forced, unwanted sexual activity of any kind); fire; disasters of either natural or technological origin; exposure to other environmental hazards; tragic death of a close friend or family member by means of an accident, suicide or homicide; injury-causing motor vehicle crash; and combat). **69%** of the sample had **experienced one or more traumatic events.** She also assessed the incidence of PTSD. **"Age was by the far the strongest predictor of PTSD."** Only **3%** of the **older** respondents (60+) met all criteria of PTSD, compared to 9-10% of the younger (18-39) and middle-aged (40-59) respondents. **14%** of the overall population had experienced the traumatic event(s) **within the last year.** If one extrapolates from Norris' data, for just the elderly population, one can appreciate the scope of the problem. For example, among the 60+ population **"6 million older people** are **traumatized** in any given year and close to **1 million older adults now suffer from PTSD."** (Norris, 1994, p. 9). She also found that symptoms associated with disaster exposure were somewhat fewer than those associated with other types of traumatic events, such as crime victimization.

B. **What is the Impact of Exposure to Such Natural Disasters?**

1. Information from a variety of disasters indicate that the **prevalence** of psychiatric disorder in a disaster-affected community will **increase by** approximately **20%.**[1] A significant proportion of these individuals will develop a further range of stress-related symptoms such as depression, panic and generalized anxiety that may coexist with PTSD. In approximately 30% of individuals with PTSD there will be a co-occurrence of alcohol or substance abuse (McFarlane, 1993). Green (1991) notes that the overlap between depression and PTSD is higher in a clinical sample than in a community sample. Note that approximately 20% of the general population suffer from some form of general psychopathology prior to exposure to a traumatic event and they are particularly vulnerable to the impact of such traumatic events.

2. Another way to represent the **impact of natural disasters** is to consider the specific percentage of the population affected. While overall, **most individuals exposed to traumatic events and disasters do quite well and do not suffer prolonged psychiatric illness** (Ursano et al., 1994), for **some** survivors, psychiatric illness, behavior change, and alterations in physical health result. Consider the following:

---

[1] For example, after reviewing the impact of 52 disasters, Rubonis & Bickman (1991) reported **a 17% increase in the prevalence of psychopathology,** as compared to control groups, or as compared to predisaster levels of psychopathology.

a) 75% of any population of catastrophic victims will be initially dazed, stunned, bewildered, and evidence initial symptoms (e.g., absence of emotion, inhibition of activity, indecision, fear). These symptoms might last from minutes to hours before giving way to emotional expression that may be intense.

b) Responses to natural disasters may cover a wide range of symptoms including fears, phobias, anxieties, depression, grief reactions, guilt, anger, physical symptoms, interpersonal problems, as well as PTSD symptoms (Green, 1991).

c) 12-25% of the immediately affected population will remain cool and collected during the impact of the disaster. They will be effective, tense, and excited.

d) 10-25% will evidence impairment symptoms (persistent disorientation, immobilization, numbing and feeling out of control). These symptoms usually dissipate within 6 weeks (Giel, 1990). Many potent effects that arise after a disaster dissipate by the **sixth week** (Pennebaker & Harber, 1993).

e) **50%** of those initially affected by PTSD will **recover by 3 months** and adjust despite anxieties. Of the 50% of people who evidence high levels of psychological distress, half of them will have "normal" reactions within **one year** (Wortman & Silver, 1989). It is worth noting that the **initial response to traumatic events is often predictive of future adjustment** (e.g., presence of dissociative response).

f) The three types of diagnosable disorders most prevalent for adults after disaster are anxiety, depression and PTSD. PTSD is more likely to occur in disasters with sudden onset and high life threat, but PTSD is less likely than anxiety and depression after technological disasters (Vogel & Vernberg, 1994).

g) PTSD is most likely to arise not only following a sudden, unpredictable, life threatening stressor (especially of human design), but also following other traumatic events involving exposure to grotesque death, personal injury, or injury to loved ones (McNally, 1991).

h) **For children**, the most common disaster responses are specific fears, separation difficulties, sleep problems, and PTSD symptoms. The negative mental health effects occur across age groups with the exception of being exposed to "silent" technological disasters (e.g., exposure to radioactive contamination where the stressor is information rather than observable effects, Green, 1994b). With "silent" disasters younger children show less negative effects. The rates of disorder in children exposed to natural disasters have been found to range from 5% to 39% over a time period of one week to about two years. An exception to this rate is the study of children who were at the earthquake epicenter of the Armenian city of Spitak where 91% were given a PTSD diagnosis, as compared to 37% of children who resided at a more distant location (Pynoos et al., 1994). This high PTSD rate in children was maintained at a 1 year followup. *(We will consider PTSD in children in Section VII).*

It should be noted that parents and teachers often underestimate the level of a child's distress. These changes are rarely evident on general behavior problem checklists. Very high PTSD symptoms **two weeks to a month** after a disaster are a relatively good predictor of persisting high levels of PTSD symptoms a year later (Vogel & Vernberg, 1994). The most extensive followup of children who were exposed to disasters was conducted by Green and her colleagues. She assessed children who were survivors of Buffalo Creek (a dam collapse disaster) **17 years after the**

disaster. She found **no differences** between the exposed individuals and a control sample, although differences had existed at two years post-disaster (Green, 1994). **There is a low incidence of delayed PTSD reactions in children.**

C. What is the Impact of Technological Disasters?

1. **Technological disasters** or "silent disasters" such as potential radioactive leaks and chemical exposure have the added dimension of **"future orientation"** and have "no low point", in that exposure can pose future risk of cancer and birth defects. There is the possibility of disease to themselves and their children years after the exposure, providing an ongoing, chronic stressor (Baum et al., 1983). Such technological disasters can produce a combination of chronic anxiety and depression symptoms, along with alienation and mistrust, more so than PTSD (Green, 1991). Chronic uncertainty, anxiety, obsessive behavior, hypervigilance and somatoform reactions may be evident (Vyner, 1987). For example, stressful events like Three Mile Island nuclear accident can cause symptomatology that does not reach the level of diagnosable illness, but can be clinically important. Exposure to such continual stressors can contribute to apathy, resigned coping methods, and a lowered ability to deal with additional stressors, furthering the illness process (Dew et al., 1987). Green (1994b) notes that while symptoms often decline following natural disasters in subsamples of survivors of technological disasters persistent symptoms may remain, especially irritability, aggression, hostility, even when assessed a decade later. Green and Lindy (1994) observe that the impact of natural disasters seem to be no longer detectable after about 2 years, the effects of man-made events are much more prolonged.

2. For a case study of the impact of a technological disaster of toxic contamination see Green et al.'s (1994) account of a radioactive leak in Fernald, Ohio. These individuals had to deal with the ongoing future-oriented stress of toxic contamination. Many residents felt "trapped" in their contaminated homes. They could not seem to get thoughts and worries about the exposure out of their minds. They were not trusting of others (neighbors, authorities) and they felt alienated from the rest of the world. These obsessive and distrusting reactions did not diminish over time for a sizeable percentage of the population. This profile has led Green et al. (1994) to propose a specific syndrome called **Informed of Radioactive Communication Syndrome, IRCS** which is similar to, but distinguishable from PTSD and adjustment disorder, since the stressor is ongoing, future-oriented, and not confined to a single happening. This clinical description is particularly timely when we learn that in the US at the present time there are 30,000 chemical dump sites capable of causing health problems (Solomon & Smith, 1993).

3. van den Bout et al. (in press) describe the aftermath of the nuclear accident at Chernobyl in terms of the loss of trust, increased anxiety and depression, apathetic helplessness, and increased specific health problems (e.g., Thyroid cancer in children). Moreover, the survivors evidence the tendency to attribute all health problems to radiation. During the initial acute evacuation phase, they also evidenced intrusive memories, but with the absence of a high impact phase, the incidence of intrusive reaction decreased. The dominant theme focused on the question, "What will become of me?", as many families remain refugees in their own country. Given the uncertainty of the effects of radiation, major concerns involve, "What will happen to my children?, Should I have more children? Will they be normal?"

D. What is the Long Range Impact of Exposure to Such Natural and Technological Disasters?

1. Solomon and Green (1992) concluded that the effects of **natural disasters** may persist for **many years**, but **most symptoms abate within 16 months**. With children, there is a considerable decrease in symptoms by 9 to 14 months post disaster. **Three months** post disaster is usually taken as an important **dividing point** between acute versus chronic PTSD symptomatology. Vogel and Vernberg (1994) note that the steady decrease in symptoms over time may <u>not</u> occur when there have been very high levels of life threat and where there has been substantial destruction and bereavement with continuing impact on family functioning.

2. Green (1994) reports that among 120 survivors of the 1972 Buffalo Creek dam collapse, 44% experienced PTSD at 2 years following the disaster and this was reduced to 28% at 14 years post disaster. While survivors of Buffalo Creek disaster continued to show improvement at the 14 year followup, they also evidenced impairment in the form of anxiety and depressive symptoms relative to nonexposed samples. A 5 year followup at the Three Mile Island nuclear accident site revealed a similar pattern. In considering the impact of a disaster such as Buffalo Creek, it is important to keep in mind Erikson's (1976) observation. She spoke of **two traumas**, namely the traumatic event itself, and secondly, the destruction of community life and loss of social activities. Both traumas can have an impact.

3. Pathology among disaster victims **may not surface for up to 3 months**, when between 15% and 25% will need specialized assistance (Brom & Kleber, 1989).

4. **In summary**, about 80% of the victims of serious life events manage to cope with traumatic events, such as disasters (as well as violence and combat), while a minority of about **10% - 30%** develop serious, long-lasting disorders (Kleber & Brom, 1989). **Approximately $1/4$ to $1/3$ of individuals exposed to unusually traumatic events such as disasters, as well as combat, acts of violence, and accidents develop chronic PTSD and other forms of mental disorders (depression, anxiety)** (Yehuda et al., 1993).

5. Less than 25% of individuals exposed to extreme stressors develop an Axis I syndrome.

6. As noted, **lifetime prevalence** of traumatic experiences reported in epidemiological studies have varied greatly, ranging from 9% to 75%. In part, these reported differences reflect methodological differences in how traumatic events are assessed (Falsetti et al., 1994; Resnick et al., 1993). Vargas and Davidson (1993) estimate that **8% to 15% of all young U.S. adults** fulfill the diagnostic criteria of PTSD and since PTSD is often chronic, they estimate that **50% of the PTSD population has continual difficulty with symptoms** related to the trauma.

7. In subsequent sections we will consider the long-term effects of exposure to other traumatic events such as combat, abuse and crime experience. For example, when one considers the exposure to the Holocaust, Danieli (1994) and Dasberg (19487) have reported that debilitating effects can persist for a lifetime.

E.   Automobile Accidents: A More Personal Exposure to Traumatic Events

1. Thus far, we have considered traumatic events that can affect entire communities in the form of natural or technological disasters. It is also important to consider the traumatic impact of more individualized events such as automobile accidents. The impact of automobile accidents can be measured in terms of its psychological morbidity on the victims and on the surviving family members. For example, in 1992 there were 40,000 fatalities in the U.S. due to motor vehicle accidents (MVAs). Blanchard et al. (1994) report that 46% of a sample of MVA victims met the criteria for PTSD and an additional 20% met the criteria for sub-syndromal PTSD. Moreover, they found that previous traumas and previous major depressive episodes sensitized or predisposed the individuals to develop PTSD. At this point, we do not know how long such PTSD symptomatology lasts. But some suggestion comes from the work of Mayou et al. (1993) who reported on 188 road accident victims (aged 18 to 70). They were seen in emergency departments of a large general hospital in Oxford, England. 20% suffered from Acute Stress Syndromes; 10% had mood disorders 12 months later, 10% had PTSD and phobic travel anxiety. Interestingly, PTSD did not occur in survivors who had been briefly unconscious and were amnesic for the accident. This is consistent with the observations by Richard Lazarus and Susan Folkman (1984) that appraisal of threat is critical in order for the physiological and psychological stress reactions to occur.

2. A study of the long-term effects (4 to 7 years) of losing a spouse or a child in a sudden **motor vehicle crash** indicated that the bereaved spouses were virtually indistinguishable from psychiatric outpatients on a number of measures of symptomalogy. Some 30% to 85% continue to ruminate about the accident or what could have been done to prevent it and they were unable to "accept, resolve or find meaning in the loss". In the U.S. approximately 150,000 people die from sudden untimely traumatic accidental deaths each year and the impact of such losses on family members appears to be **long-term**. As Lehman et al. (1987) observe, following such traumatic losses "lasting distress is not a sign of individual coping failure but, rather, a common response to the situation" (p. 229). These results are likely compounded when the survivor feels responsible, in some way, for the accident or feels he/she could have done something to prevent it. PTSD can complicate and prolong the bereavement process. *(We will consider how guilt and shame can be treated in Section VI.)* Thus, not only do the victims suffer, but so do other survivors and family members.

3. Scotti et al. (1994) reports that persons exposed to severe accidents were also more likely to have experienced a greater number of other forms of trauma (e.g., floods, death of a significant other, physical or sexual abuse, or physical assault). Thus, there is a need to systematically assess for prior trauma exposure

4. Finally, Malt (1994) reports that in a 3 year follow-up study of adults injured in traffic accidents with some physical sequelae, 25% of close relatives reported impaired psychological health in themselves as a consequence of the injury to their loved one. This finding further underscores the value of **involving family members in treatment**.[1]

---

[1] McFarlane (1994) notes that MVA (and burn victims) require active contact during hospitalization in order to increase their participation in treatment.

F. Other Forms of Exposure to Traumatic Events

1. **War** can cause incalculable distress, including PTSD as described below. It has been estimated that since 1945 there have been 150 wars that have left 22 million people dead. At present, it has been estimated that there are 48 countries in the world where war or violent internal strife are taking place (Wilson & Raphael, 1993). One consequence of war is the large number of refugees and displaced persons which is estimated to be 18 million. Children and mothers constitute 50% to 70% of the world refugee population, especially in third world countries (de Jong, 1994). For a discussion of the mental health needs of refugees see J. de Jong and L. Clark (1992), Refugee mental health manual (Geneva: WHO/UNHER).

2. 40% to 70% of individuals in the US have been exposed to **crime**, as to be discussed below. The degree of injury received, fear of injury or death during the crime, and the relationship to the perpetrator have been associated with the incidence of PTSD.

3. **It has been estimated that 40% to 60% of psychiatric outpatients and 50% to 60% of psychiatric inpatients report histories of early childhood victimization (e.g., physical and sexual abuse) (Herman, 1992).**

4. Moreover, PTSD clients may experience a form of **"secondary victimization"** due to the negative reactions from others or from agencies (e.g., medical, legal) consisting of denial, disbelief, blaming the victim, stigmatization and denial of assistance. In some instances, victims of trauma may encounter overprotective behaviors from significant others, insulating them from everyday stressors, or what Lindy et al. (1991) metaphorically describe as the formation of a protective **"trauma membrane"**.

G. Gender Differences in Incidence and Impact of Exposure to Traumatic Events

1. Thus far we have considered epidemiological data for the population at large. When it comes to exposure and impact data it is critical to consider the role of gender.

   a) In a representative sample of women over the age of 18 in the US, Kilpatrick (1992) found that 69% had been exposed to a traumatic event some time in their lives.

   b) The remarkable array of victimization experiences (rape, sexual and physical assault, crime and noncrime traumas) that women encounter, contributes to **"estimates that 11.8 million adult women in the U.S. experienced PTSD at some point during their lives and 4.4 million currently have PTSD. ... A majority of American women (68.9%) have experienced at least one type of traumatic event during their lifetime."** (Resnick et al., 1993, p. 988).

   c) Of victims who had experienced rape, life threat and physical injury, PTSD developed in almost **80%**. The **highest rate of lifetime PTSD** is found among women who had experienced the crime of completed **rape -- 57%** (Resnick et al., 1994). Moreover, studies which measure many kinds of traumas have indicated that as many as **33% to 54% of those exposed to one trauma have also experienced another traumatic event** (Falsetti et al., 1993). *(We will consider rape, incest, crime below.)*

   d) Studies of the impact of trauma as a function of gender have been "mixed". Green (1994b) in reviewing this literature concluded that "the impact may be more dependent upon the particular type of outcome observed", with women at higher risk for anxiety and depression, while men are at higher risk for substance abuse and antisocial personality disorder"..."Gender might best be regarded as a factor that relates to the specific expression of symptoms rather than one which defines risk per se" (p.24).

e) Other investigators (Breslau et al., 1991; Norris, 1992) have speculated that males are at greater risk for exposure to traumatic events, but once exposed females are at a greater risk for developing PTSD. Males are more likely to have been in combat, motor vehicular accidents and physical assaults. Women are more likely to have been sexually assaulted (raped, child sexual abuse) or been in an abusive relationship.

f) Women are more distressed than men when witnessing violent injuries or deaths. When disasters occur women are more likely to endorse self-report statements reflecting greater fear and distress than men. Women report a higher incidence of psychological symptoms, especially anxiety and depression, while men evidence an increased number of physician visits, physical symptoms, hospital referrals, belligerence and alcohol use (Green, 1994).

g) Women also evidence greater sensitivity to the stress of others, or what is called **"network stress"** (Vrana & Lauterback, 1994). Women are more often called upon to provide emotional support. For instance, Green and Solomon (1994) observe that married women victims of Buffalo Creek disaster showed higher psychopathology than women who lived alone. Moreover, a spouse's anxiety or depression more seriously distressed women than men. For some, **"strong family ties may be more burdensome than supportive in times of extreme stress"** (p.19). In interpreting these gender differences it is important to keep in mind both the situational and cultural context. (See Banyard and Graham-Bermann's, 1993, for a critique from a feminist perspective and see Coyne et al., 1988 for a discussion of the consequences of emotional overinvolvement and miscarried helping.)

h) Another important gender difference has to do with the comfort in self-disclosing. In general, females benefit more from talking with others about personal issues than do males. Males have less desire to ventilate feelings and thoughts and are less comfortable disclosing information about intimate topics to others (Clark, 1993).

i) In the consideration of gender issues it is also important not to overlook the unique **stress of being homosexual** in essentially a homophobic environment. A survey by the National Gay and Lesbian Task Force (1984) estimated that over 90% of gays and lesbians have experienced some type of "victimization" at least once in their lives because of their sexual orientation (e.g., physical assault, verbal abuse).

H. Intensity or "Dose" Effects of Traumatic Events *(See cautionary Point (e) below)*

It is **not** only the occurrence of traumatic events that influences an individual's reactions, but rather the nature of the **"dose" of the disaster,** or the perceived severity of the exposure to the event (extent of life threat, loss, injury). *(See Section VII for an exhaustive list of the factors that influence the nature of the survivors' response.)* This dosage effect is illustrated in the results of 16 of 19 studies that have examined the **dose-response relationship** (March, 1993). In these studies, the magnitude of the stressor has been found to be directly proportionate to the subsequent risk of developing PTSD. As Green (1994b) observes, "knowing which subjects were more exposed to a disaster event gives the clinician a starting point in identifying those survivors who are most at risk for developing problems" (p.21). A few examples will illustrate this dose-response relationship.

a) In studies of combat exposure, investigators have found repeatedly that the more intense and frequent the violence (as reflected in being wounded, committing or witnessing atrocities, being a member of the special forces), the greater the risk for developing subsequent PTSD.

b) This dose-response relationship is not limited to adults. In studies of children who were exposed to a sniper attack, Pynoos (1990) found that the greater the risk involved (being exposed to the sniper on the playground as compared to being in the school building), the greater the risk of children developing PTSD.

c) In the area of sexual abuse *(to be reviewed in more detail later in this Section)*, being injured, perceiving a threat to one's life because of the presence of a weapon, sexual penetration, were each related to an increased risk of PTSD.

d) But is not just the objective features of the traumatic event, but also **the meaning that the trauma holds for the individual** that can put someone at increased risk for developing PTSD. Two examples will be offered to illustrate the important role that "meaning" plays in acting as a "filter of perception". The impact of sexual abuse (clearly one of the most high risk events for developing long-term PTSD and other problems), is influenced by the nature of the relationship between the victim and the perpetrator. Sexual abuse by a biological father or sexual abuse by a step-father is more debilitating than sexual abuse by a distant relative or by a stranger. It is not just the event, but the ascribed meaning of the stressor that is critical.

Even in the area of combat exposure, Fontana and his colleagues (1992) and Ursano and his colleagues (1992) found that the veteran's assessment of **perceived threat, risk, and responsibility** were more important in predicting outcome than the combat features of the actual event. How the soldier viewed his role, namely, as a "witness, participant, target, observer, agent" was related to PTSD outcome. Similarly, whether the soldier views his role as being responsible, as having failed, as feeling helpless, guilty or ashamed, each influenced the soldier's reactions. *(We will return to the importance of appraisal processes in Section II.)* For now, it is important to remember that the dose-response relationship is mediated in important ways by cognitive and emotional processes.

e) **Cavaet:** In considering this well-founded relationship between exposure and PTSD, a warning has been offered by McFarlane (in press). He astutely observes that the majority of studies that have demonstrated the primacy of the stressor (in the form of exposure characteristics) in influencing outcome, were conducted on patient populations. When community samples were studied, the relationship between the severity of symptoms and exposure to the stressor do not hold up.

I.   Are the Effects of Exposure Always Negative?

Potential Positive Effects: Ursano et al. (1994) highlight the need not to assume that exposure to traumatic events will always have a negative effect. For example, they report that the majority of survivors of a tornado described positive outcomes such as "learning that they could handle crises effectively"; "feeling they were better off for having met this type of challenge"; "rearranging their priorities"; "learning a lesson"; "bringing the community together". Elder and Clipp (1989) report similar data for combat veterans. *(In Section III on Assessment we will consider further evidence for other potential "salutogenic", as opposed to, the "pathogenic" impact of exposure to traumatic events, e.g., also see Antonovsky, 1974.)*

WHAT SHOULD YOU TAKE AWAY FROM THIS COLLECTION OF EPIDEMIOLOGICAL FACTS ABOUT TRAUMATIC EVENTS?

1. Trauma refers to extreme or severe events that are so powerful, harmful, and/or threatening that they demand extraordinary coping efforts. Such traumatic events are very neither rare, nor unusual.

2. "While the figures vary across situations and across types of traumas, at most, **only a substantial minority of trauma victims develop serious difficulties or are diagnosed with substantial emotional disorders**" (Davidson & Baum, 1994, p.272). As Malt (1994, p.108) observes, "it should be remembered that the **majority** of traumatized persons respond in a **controlled** and **unremarkable way.**

3. An examination of diverse "traumatic" events (natural and technological disasters, criminal assault, war, various forms of abuse) can lead to the same range of symptom patterns. Moreover, PTSD is only one sequelae that follows from exposure to "traumatic" events. Other likely consequences may include depression, anxiety, addictive behaviors, somatizing, and a number of clinical problems. This similarity, however, should <u>not</u> obscure the wide variation in individual symptomatology within the diagnostic category of PTSD.

4. While some traumatic events may last no more than a few minutes or hours (Type I stressors), they can leave behind a good deal of potential stress that can give rise to long-term debilitating responses involving changes in affect, physiological functioning, stress-related behaviors, and mental and physical health problems. Trauma-related symptoms can fade with time, but they can also be revived.

5. Although most individuals exposed to PTSD qualifying stressors do <u>not</u> develop a psychiatric disturbance, mental health workers should routinely screen for the occurrence and impact of traumatic events. Clinical assessment should inquire explicitly about the range of event types and about the particular nature of the traumatic events that have been experienced.

6. There is a sizeable minority of individuals who have been exposed to traumatic events who are significantly affected by such events, both in the short-term, and most significantly, over the course of their lives. **PTSD clients are a remarkably heterogeneous group.**

7. Acute reactions to traumatic events are related to the subsequent probability of developing PTSD and other forms of psychopathology, but <u>not</u> in all instances. Often PTSD responses may occur at a later time in individuals who did <u>not</u> evidence maladaptive responses at the time of the trauma.

8. The presence of substantial PTSD symptoms at **3 months or more** posttrauma are likely to become chronic and contribute to maladaptive behavior. Thus, active clinical intervention is required to prevent the development of PTSD. With the longevity of PTSD symptoms, the risk of comorbidity is increased.

9. The impact of traumatic stressors may remain dormant and emerge later on in life, but this is a relatively rare phenomena.

10. It is <u>not</u> only the characteristics of the stressor in terms of intensity, suddenness, duration, amount of warning, degree of physical injury and death, but also the "meaning" that such stressful events hold for individuals that influence the survivors' reactions.

11.   There is a need to assess for both recent and developmental traumatic events in psychiatric inpatients and outpatients. There is a high likelihood that individuals exposed to one trauma have also experienced another traumatic event.

12.   There is a need to be sensitive to gender differences in terms of risk of exposure, nature of impact, and in ways of coping.

13.   The effects of traumatic events are <u>not</u> always bad. There is a need <u>not</u> to have a psychopathology bias, but to assess for possible <u>positive effects</u> as well.

We now turn our attention to what form such reactions may take.

WHAT ARE ADULTS' GENERAL RESPONSES TO TRAUMATIC EVENTS?

There are several ways to cluster the <u>multifarious</u> impact of trauma. These clusters include:

A. Response categories (Hiley et al., 1993)
B. Symptomatic responses (Classen et al, 1993)
C. Cardinal symptoms according to DSM-III-R and DSM-IV (Henden & Haas, 1988; Rundell et al., 1989)
D. Phenomenological responses
E. Neurophysiological responses (Charney et al., 1993; Southwick et al., 1994)

A. <u>Response categories</u>.

Hiley et al. (1993) separate the response to traumatic events into four general categories:

1. <u>Emotional</u> -- shock, disbelief, anger, rage, terror, guilt, grief, vulnerability, irritability, helplessness, fears, anxiety, depression, sadness, disgust, hostility, despair and anguish. Fears of abandonment, fear of being alone, and wary of others. Unable or have difficulty with "loving" feelings (feel detached/estranged). Angers easily, explosive temper.

2. <u>Cognitive</u> -- impaired concentration, confusion, self-blame, disorientation, intrusive thoughts, avoidance and decreased self-esteem and lowered self-efficacy, heightened fear of losing control, and fear of reoccurrence of the trauma. In terms of memory difficulties it is not clear whether there are memory retrieval problems. More likely, input difficulties. Horowitz (1986) has highlighted the vacillation between denial/avoidance and intrusive thoughts and feelings. He has noted that **most clients seek help for intrusive symptoms that feel overwhelming.**[1] Jones and Barlow (1990) view reexperiencing as being central to PTSD since situations previously considered safe evoke alarm (a hypersensitive alarm system). This may lead to avoidance and paranoid thinking.

   Research reported by Baum et al. (1993) indicates that the **more** the individual has **intrusive memories** of the traumatic event, the **more symptoms of somatic chronic distress** he/she will experience (as evident by increased urinary cortisol and norepinephrine levels, heightened systolic blood pressure, as well as poorer attentional performance). Intrusive memories are less diagnostically significant early in post-accident situations, but become more important and **diagnostically significant as time passes.** For instance, intrusive thoughts are quite frequently experienced during the acute phase (less then 30 days) post-trauma. The presence of intrusive symptoms during the early phase may <u>not</u> predict particularly well the development of chronic PTSD (Abueg et al., 1994). Nolen-Hoeksma (1990) report that the level of rumination is highly correlated with measures of anxiety, depression and sleep disturbance. Davidson and Baum (1994) hypothesize that intrusive images and thoughts may <u>not</u> be a <u>consequence</u> of PTSD and chronic stress, **but rather a cause or facilitating agent of chronic stress.**

   Some forms of **intrusion may be adaptive.** For example, Creamer et al. (1992) found that in a study of office workers following a multiple shooting greater intrusion was associated with lower subsequent distress and that avoidance behavior was primarily a reaction to intrusion.

---

[1] PTSD symptoms can be reactivated by reminders or "triggers". I have worked with PTSD clients whose traumatic experience were made into a movie for television and replayed on the anniversary date each year.

3. <u>Biological</u> -- fatigue, sleeplessness (insomnia), nightmares, hyperarousal, startle response, and psychosomatic complaints. Research on sleep patterns of trauma survivors suggest they experience less time in deep sleep, have more awakenings, more abnormalities during rapid eye movement sleep periods and spend less total time sleeping (Engdahl, 1994; Ross et al., 1989; also see Reynolds, 1989 for a discussion of the controversy over sleep data). Page and Engdahl (1994) indicate that preliminary studies of PTSD clients show reduced time in bed, reduced sleep, reduced REM latency, and increased sleep movements, respirations and heart rate. Mild to significant sleep apnea (breathing blockage) is also evident. Some initial efforts are underway to treat sleep disturbances and assess the effects on daytime PTSD symptoms.

4. <u>Behavioral</u> -- avoidance, alienation, social withdrawal, increased stress within relationships (marital relationship suffer--less able to trust and be intimate), substance abuse, sensation-seeking behavior, vocational impairment, regressed behavior to early developmental stages in children under age 7, and conduct disorders. Symptoms will vary with the child's age. Decrements in task performance. High incidence of divorce, multiple marriages. Note that the **avoidance** that may be a response to intrusive stimuli may take various forms, for example, avoidance of feelings (numbing), avoidance of knowledge of the event (amnesia), avoidance of behavior (phobic response) and avoidance of communication about the event (Schwarz & Prout, 1991).

5. <u>Characterological</u> -- survivors of prolonged abuse develop characteristic personality changes including "deformations of relations and identity" (Herman, 1992). Kolb (1989) even goes so far as to suggest that "PTSD is to psychiatry, as syphilis was to medicine. At one time or another PTSD may appear to mimic every personality disorder." The traumatized individual may try to overcompensate by becoming a "workaholic".

B. **Symptomatic responses.**
Classen, Koopman and Spiegel (1993) observe that trauma constitutes an abrupt physical disruption in ordinary daily experience that "renders a person helpless as the world suddenly becomes unpredictable, threatening, and assaultive". **Symptoms experienced during the trauma may include:**

1. <u>Dissociation</u>[1] -- dissociation may take various forms including the survivors of the traumatic event feeling automatically detached from the traumatic event as it happens. They may see events from a distance, or the scenario of events may seem slowed down, or they may feel removed from events altogether. The impact of the trauma "splits off" from their sense of self resulting in the lack of integration of thoughts, feelings and experiences into the stream of consciousness (Bernstein & Putnam, 1986). Traumatized victims may detach themselves from overwhelming fear, pain, and helplessness. More specifically, this detachment may be evident as a form of:

   a) stupor -- dazed, state of shock
   b) derealization -- feel as though one's surroundings are unreal and dreamlike
   c) depersonalization -- feel detached or like an "automaton", an observer of one's mental and bodily processes
   d) sense of numbing -- suppress emotional response, feel detached
   e) amnesia for the event

   Psychogenic amnesia is relatively rare in persons for whom PTSD has originated in adult life experience.

---

[1] *See the discussion of the significance of dissociation symptoms in Section VII on post-disaster reactions.*

2. Anxiety -- hyperarousal, difficulty concentrating, hypervigilant, exaggerated startle response. Somatic symptoms of muscle tension, restlessness, palpitations, tachycardia, fatigue, jumpiness, and insomnia. Note, dissociative responses can often cause anxiety.

3. Other symptoms -- rage, despair, hopelessness, guilt feelings. Note that specific forms of dysfunction such as sexual difficulties vary with the type of stressor. Sexual dysfunctions are commonly associated with PTSD resulting from rape and childhood sexual abuse.

If the PTSD symptoms dissipate over time and if they have not prevented functioning in work and in interpersonal relationships, then they are viewed as a "normal" response to an abnormal situation. If symptoms last between **two days and one month**, then they may meet the criteria of Acute Stress Disorder (ASD). If the symptoms last **more than one month**, then they may meet the criteria of Post Traumatic Stress Disorder (PTSD). It is worth noting that research suggests that the level of ASD is often predictive of later PTSD (Solomon, 1993). *(See descriptions of ASD and PTSD below.)*

C. **Cardinal symptoms according to DSM-III-R and DSM-IV.** *(See detailed description of DSM-IV criteria below and Brett et al., 1988, and Green et al., 1985.)* The authors of DSM IV note that the course of PTSD symptoms and their relative predominance may vary over time. PTSD can occur at any age and the symptoms usually begin within the **first 3 months after the trauma,** although there may be a delay of months or years before symptoms appear. Frequently, the disturbance initially meets criteria of Acute Stress Disorder *(described below).* In approximately **half the cases** there is **complete symptom relief within 3 months,** with many others having **persisting symptoms** for **longer than 12 months** after the trauma. These symptoms may take various forms:

1. Reexperiencing -- intrusive remembering or reliving of the traumatic event

   a) recurrent and intrusive thoughts, dreams, and horrifying nightmares

   b) flashbacks of trauma with accompanying feelings that the trauma is reoccurring

   c) intense distress with reminders of traumatic event

   d) intensive recollections may occur spontaneously

   e) in children flashbacks occur less frequently and may take the form of repetitive play (as if the child is stuck on a specific theme)

   f) in children, horrifying nightmares may turn into bad dreams about other frightening images (e.g., ghosts, monsters)

   (It is worth repeating that intrusive symptoms are generally the chief reason for clients seeking professional help.)

2. Avoidance[1] -- of stimuli reminiscent of the trauma and numbing or loss of pleasure in usually pleasurable activities.

   a) avoid thoughts and feelings associated with trauma

   b) avoidance of reminders of the event

   c) inability (or reluctance) to recall aspects of the trauma

   d) decreased interest in significant events -- "psychic numbing"

   e) emotional withdrawal from life, not able to feel happiness

   f) feel detached, and estranged from others.

   g) restricted range of feelings, not able to feel emotions as keenly as they once did.

   h) most children do not evidence amnesia, they are able to remember the events rather vividly, although the memories are altered somewhat over time

   i) emotional withdrawal from life.

3. Hyperarousal symptoms

   a) sleep difficulties, irritability, hypervigilance, difficulty concentrating, restlessness, exaggerated startle response, outbursts of anger and increased arousal to salient cues such as news footage. (See detailed description of physiological changes below.)

D. **Phenomenological and narrative responses.**
Epstein (1991) and Janoff-Bulman (1992) report that traumatic events can have a major impact on one's belief system and feelings:

1. Traumatic events can "violate" or "shatter" basic assumptions and beliefs such as:

   a) the belief in one's own invulnerability ("It can't happen to me.")

   b) the belief that events are orderly, predictable, controllable and fair ("Why did it happen to me?"; "The world is not what I thought it was.")

   c) the belief that life is meaningful

   d) the assumption that one is a worthy person ("I am not what I thought I was.")

2. Traumatic events can lead to feeling a sense of loss -- Raphael (1986) describes the "loss of belief in oneself, in the safety of the world, and in trust of others".

---

[1] Green (1991) observed that avoidance criteria are the most difficult to diagnose. The avoidance may take different forms including avoiding reminders of the trauma, avoid thoughts or settings associated with the trauma, decreased involvement with the outside world, diminished interest in family, friends, activities. Shalev (1992) noted that avoidant symptoms tended to develop **later than** intrusive symptoms, suggesting that avoidance may be a way of coping with disturbing recollections.

3. Feel a loss of relatedness and identity (question the belief that people are trustworthy and worth relating to). ("Why am I all alone?")

4. Overwhelm a person's sense of safety and security.

5. Blame self for having been victimized (adopt the notion that people get what they deserve).

These phenomenological changes are reflected in the individual's narrative account.

While not every victim asks him/herself the following questions, it is proposed that those who experience PTSD are prone to get "stuck" in the following narrative:

"What happened to me?"; "This can't be happening to me."; "Why me?"[1]; "What if?"; "If only I had..."; "Only if I would have ..."; "I could have ..."; "I should have known better."; "I should have ..."; "Why them?"; "Why me?"; "Why did he do it?"; "Why our building?"; "Why our floor?"; "Why did I live and why did they die?"; "It could have been me."; "How did I survive?"; "It's so unfair. Why did it have to happen?"; "Why now?"; "Just when ..."; "Had I only ...?"; "What have I done?"; "How could I have been more effective?"; "What could I have done to prevent it?"; "What more could I have done?"; "What could have been done differently?"; "Where can I be safe?"; "Who is safe?"; "Whom can I count on?"; "Who can I trust?"; "How much control can I ever have? How much control do I need?"; "Why do I have to go through this?"; "Was it really rape?"; "Why me?"; "I can't stop thinking it's going to happen again. Why?"; "Why did he die at the wrong end of life?"; "What is happening to me?"; "What is going to become of me?"; "What if I don't get better?"; "Am I going crazy?"; "How could God let this happen?"; "I don't want to face anything anymore."; "I don't want to face anyone."; "It hurts so bad I don't want to deal with it."; "No one understands my pain."; "I am now a different person."; "I am not a person."; "Why do these things happen?"; "Can I ever see my life in the same way again?"; "Why won't it end?"; "What will become of me?"

Note, the way these questions are formulated usually preclude or reduce the likelihood of the individual accepting, resolving, or finding meaning in the "loss". There are few satisfactory answers to "why" questions.

For some, the traumatic event can become the defining event that marks a significant time in an individual's life story (viz., before the trauma, "BT", and after the trauma, "AT") and it colors the way events and people are viewed. PTSD clients tend to get "stuck" or "fixated" on one solution, or dwell on past difficulties, namely, to remake the past or recreate what existed before the trauma occurred. They have difficulty "moving on" with their lives. They mourn their losses (childhood, innocence, youthful optimism, sense of self, betrayal).

In their narratives, PTSD clients often include questions addressing the issues of:

Foreseeability -- Could the catastrophic event or trauma been realistically anticipated?

Controllability -- Could the catastrophic event or trauma been modified through human action?

---

[1] At a recent conference on PTSD Camille Wortman noted that a sizeable percentage of "victims" of traumatic events did not ask themselves, "Why me?" type questions. Of those who did continue to ask such self questions, 80% failed to come up with a "satisfactory response", and they were more prone to experience personal distress. In the best line of the conference she conveyed her perplexity with those who fail to ask, "Why me?" type questions. She noted that when she goes to a public restroom and runs out of toilet paper, she is likely to ask herself, "Why me?". She noted that academics are prone to search for attributions or self-centered causal explanations. She reminded her audience that a sizeable percentage of the general population do not engage in a "search for meaning", even when traumatic events occur.

Culpability and self-blame[1] -- Could I have behaved differently? Am I responsible? Why didn't I get out?

E. **Neurophysiological and biochemical responses that accompany PTSD.** (See Everly, 1994; Kolb, 1987; Mason et al., 1990; van der Kolk, 1994; Saporta & van der Kolk, 1992; Shalev & Rogel-Fuchs, 1993; Southwick et al., 1994; and Yehuda et al., 1993, for a more detailed discussion.) *(In Section III on assessment we will consider how to measure these physiological indicators.)*

1. Patients with PTSD display:

   i) greater sympathetic nervous system arousal (abnormal startle response, slower habituation to repeated presentations of stimuli) and exhibit sympathetic hyperresponsiveness to stimuli reminiscent of the traumatic events they experienced.

   ii) hypofunction of the hypothalamic-pituitary-adrenocortical (HPA) axis, enhanced sensitivity of HPA feedback

   iii) dysregulation of the endogenous opioid system.

   iv) changes in the physiology of sleep and dreaming (insomnia)

2. Individuals who are exposed to traumatic events also may evidence neuroendocrine disturbances (see Baum et al., 1993; Davidson & Baum, 1993; Friedman, 1992; and van der Kolk, 1994)

   i) cardiac reactivity

   ii) long-lasting elevations in blood pressure

   iii) changes in immune and digestive system functioning

   iv) elevations in urinary catecholamine levels, corticosteroid secretion and increased platelet aggregation

   v) elevations in symptom reporting

3. These physiological changes that accompany trauma may have a "kindling" effect, heightening hypersensitivity and vulnerability. "People with PTSD suffer from generalized hyperarousal and from physiological emergency reactions to specific reminders" (van der Kolk, 1994, p. 4). "Medications that stimulate autonomic arousal may precipitate visual images and affective states associated with prior trauma experience (e.g., panic attacks, flashbacks)." (van der Kolk, 1994, p. 18)

4. Friedman (1992) and Hiley-Young et al. (1993) provide the following list of specific physiological changes that may accompany PTSD. (See Tables 1 and 2.)

---

[1] A distinction has been drawn between behavioral self-blame which targets certain behaviors that can be changed or that are modifiable and controllable, and characterological self-blame that attributes causality to an unchangeable aspect of one's character or personality. The latter is less likely to lead to change and a sense of personal control. For instance, a rape victim might offer the behavioral attribution: "I was walking on the wrong street" versus "I am a gullible born-loser type of person" (characterological).

Table 1

PHYSIOLOGICAL ALTERATIONS ASSOCIATED WITH PTSD
(Friedman, 1992; Hiley-Young et al., 1993)

1. Sympathetic nervous system arousal

    a) Elevated baseline sympathetic indices
    b) Excessive response to neutral stimuli
    c) Excessive response to traumamimetic stimuli

2. Excessive startle reflex

    a) Lowered threshold
    b) Increased amplitude

3. A reducer pattern of cortical evoked potentials in response to neutral stimuli

4. Abnormalities in sleep physiology (Initiating and maintaining sleep.)

    a) Increased sleep latency; increased body movements; increased number of awakenings
    b) Decreased total sleep time; decreased sleep efficiency
    c) Possible disturbances in sleep architecture (controversial)
    d) Traumatic nightmares, which are unique, differing from other types of nightmares

Table 2

NEUROHUMORAL/NEUROENDOCRINOLOGICAL ABNORMALITIES ASSOCIATED WITH PTSD
(Hiley-Young et al, 1993; Vargas & Davidson, 1993)

1. Increased noradrenergic activity

    a) Increased urinary catecholamine levels
    b) Down-regulation of alpha-2 and beta receptors
    c) Reduced platelet MAO activity
    d) Yohimbine-induced panic and PTSD adrenergic flashbacks

2. Hypofunction of hypothalamic-pituitary-adrenocortical (HPA) axis

    a) Decreased urinary cortisol levels
    b) Elevated urinary catecholamine/cortisol ratio
    c) Increased sensitivity to dexamethasone suppression (DST) -- HPA suppression following DST test
    d) Blunted ACTH response to CRH

3. Opioid system dysregulation -- abnormalities of the endogeneus opioid system

    a) General lowering of pain threshold at rest
    b) Stress-induced analgesia by traumagenic stimuli
    c) Decreased endorphin levels

WHAT IS THE HISTORY OF THE CONCEPT PTSD --
CHANGING LABELS?

The discussion thus far may give the false impression that post-traumatic stress disorders are a new phenomena. Mankind has always had to cope with natural and man-made disasters. The clinical pattern of distress that is receiving so much attention has had many forerunners. For instance, what is now known as PTSD was described by Samuel Pepys in 1666 in his depiction of people's reactions to the great fire in London (Daly, 1983). This Section enumerates briefly, the recent history of PTSD and its ever changing label.

Post-traumatic Stress Disorder (PTSD) was introduced in the Third Edition of the Diagnostic and Statistical Manual of Mental Disorders (DSM-III) in 1980. Previous editions had referred to stress reactions with terms like gross stress reaction and transient situational disturbance. But these were only two of many labels that have been applied to this behavioral pattern. It is instructive to consider the wide array of terms that have been employed, each with its own implicit etiological theory (e.g., "shell shock").[1]

Historically, PTSD has been given many different names including: Hysteria, Tunnel Disease, Railway Spine Disorder (1800's), Nostalgia (in Civil War), Soldier's Heart, Psychic Trauma Neurosis, Nervous Exhaustion, Da Costa's Syndrome, Irritable Heart, Effort Syndrome, Neurocirculatory Asthenia, Traumatophobia, Shell Shock (in W.W.I), Anxiety Neurosis, Physioneurosis (Abraham Kardiner in 1941), Combat Neurosis, Combat Fatigue, Battle Exhaustion (in W.W. II), War Neurosis (Grinker & Spiegel, 1943), Stress Disorders (in Korean War), Battle Fatigue, Traumatic Neurosis, Compensation Neurosis, Nervous Shock, Gross Stress Reactions and Transient Situational Disturbance, Survivor's Syndrome, Post-Vietnam Syndrome, Rape Trauma Syndrome, Post-Sexual Abuse Syndrome, Child-Abuse Syndrome, Survivor Syndrome, Battered Wife Syndrome, and as noted, Posttraumatic Stress Disorder in DSM-III in 1980.

The inclusion of PTSD in the DSM-III represented a major step in the diagnosis of stress-related reactions. The authors of DSM-III, DSM-III-R and DSM-IV have decided to include PTSD under the diagnostic category of Anxiety Disorder because of the presence of intrusive and anxiety provoking ideation, worry over loss of control, hypervigilance, exaggerated startle response, fear of repetition of the traumatic events, and phobic-like avoidance behaviors. Also evident are various forms of denial, dissociation, numbing and blunting. As we will consider, the concept of PTSD is still evolving as the results of DSM-IV clinical trials are indicating the value of considering the concept of complex PTSD (Herman, 1992) and the category of PTSD plus Disorders of Extreme Stress (DES) (van der Kolk et al., 1993). (For intriguing discussions of the history of the concept of PTSD, see Bentley, 1991; Hartsough, 1988; Kolb, 1993; Trimble, 1981, 1985. and Wilson, 1994 who has traced the history from Freud to DSM-IV.)

With these multiple labels as background, we can now consider how the mental health community currently views PTSD.

---

[1] Falk et al. (1994) report that 40% of the published literature on the effects of trauma has focused on combat veterans and POWs. Thus, much of what we know about PTSD came from the study of verterans. How readily these findings can be generalized to other victim groups is not clear.

DSM DEFINITIONS OF STRESS DISORDERS

The diagnosis of PTSD is different from most other psychiatric diagnostic categories because it includes the presumed **cause** in the diagnostic criteria. DSM requires explicit specification of the probable cause, namely, the presence of an explicit traumatic stressor (or what is called criterion A in the DSM-III, DSM-III-R, and DSM IV systems). (Parenthetically, note that brain injury and intoxication disorders also require an explicit external etiological cause.) Thus, we begin our consideration of the diagnosis of PTSD with a brief consideration of what constitutes the **Criterion A** stressor definition of PTSD.

In order to receive a diagnosis of PTSD the individual had to experience an extreme **life-threatening** stressor according to the classification system. Such common stressors as financial loss, severe marital conflict, chronic illness, and "simple" bereavement do <u>not</u> meet the Criterion A "gatekeeping role" for PTSD. Instead, consider the definitions of the **Stressor Criterion** for PTSD diagnosis in DSM-III, DSM-III-R, DSM IV and ICD-10[1]

DSM-III Criterion A: Existence of a recognizable stressor that would evoke significant symptoms of distress in almost everyone.

DSM-III-R Criterion A: The person has experienced an event that is outside the range of usual human experience and that would be markedly distressing to almost anyone, e.g., serious threat to one's life or physical integrity; serious threat or harm to one's children, spouse, or other close relatives and friends; sudden destruction of one's home or community; or seeing another person who has recently been, or is being, seriously injured or killed as the result of an accident or physical violence.

DSM-IV Criterion A: The person has been exposed to a traumatic event in which the following were present:

(1) -- the person **experienced, witnessed,** or was **confronted** with an event or events that involved actual or threatened death or serious injury, or a threat to the physical integrity of self or others.

(2) -- the person's response **involved intense fear, helplessness or horror.** Note: In children this may be expressed instead by disorganized or agitated behavior.

(3) -- the disturbance causes clinically **significant distress** and **impairment** in **social, occupational,** or other important areas of functioning.

Thus, being confronted with an event that involved serious injury to <u>others</u> and responding with horror can meet the criterion A, thus incorporating the concept of <u>vicarious traumatization</u>.

---

[1] The International Classification of Disease (ICD-10) has drawn a distinction between Acute Stress Reaction, PTSD, Adjustment Disorder, and Enduring Personality Change After Catastrophic Experience. In the case of **Acute Stress Reaction** the symptoms typically resolve within hours or days of the causative traumatic event. With **PTSD**, symptoms rarely exceed 6 months post-event onset. In **Adjustment Disorders**, emotional distress and functional impairment usually arise within 1 month of stressful event and rarely exceeds 6 months. **Enduring Personality Change** are "profound and lasting", including hostility and mistrust, social withdrawal, feeling hopeless, anxious, threatened, and estranged.

-- Exposure to an exceptional mental or physical stressor, either brief or prolonged. Events commonly eliciting this response include military combat, sexual or other violent assault, human or natural disasters, and severe accidents. Infrequently, in the presence of heightened personal vulnerability, events that are objectively less threatening may induce the disorder.

Thus, individuals cannot receive a diagnosis of PTSD unless they have been exposed to a traumatic event(s) that meets the Stressor Criterion A.

Now let us consider the various DSM diagnostic categories of PTSD. As noted, while the concept of PTSD has a long history, it is only recently that it has been formally recognized in psychiatric nomenclature. We will consider **4 proposed diagnostic definitions** of stress disorders according to DSM-IV criteria. When considering these diagnostic categories it is important to keep in mind that the same traumatic event can trigger acute, delayed, intermittent and chronic forms of PTSD, as well as related forms of psychopathology (e.g., anxiety, depression, abuse of addictive substances, somatic complaints). For example, studies of Dutch Resistance veterans from W.W.II indicated that 30% experienced first symptoms within 5 years after W.W.II, 30% during the next 20 years, and the remainder more than 25 years later. Several patterns were noted: (sub)acute PTSD which progressed to chronic condition or remitted, delayed form of PTSD, PTSD with remissions and exacerbations (Engdahl & Eberly, 1994). Although the various diagnostic categories are described separately, it is important to recognize that they may appear within the same individual over the course of a lifetime. **It is critical to adopt a life-span perspective of PTSD.** The four diagnostic categories include:

I.   **Acute Stress Disorder** (ASD)

II. **Post Traumatic Stress Disorder** (PTSD)

III. **Partial PTSD** (as described by Classen et al., 1993)

IV. **Complex PTSD** (as proposed by Herman, 1992) and more recently labeled **Disorders of Extreme Stress** (DES) (as assessed in the DSM-IV field trials by van der Kolk et al., 1993). This diagnostic category reflects the recognition that individuals who have experienced Type II stressors are more likely to evidence a clinical picture that goes well beyond the classic PTSD symptoms of reexperiencing, avoidance and hyperarousal. Exposure to Type II stressors can engender a wide array of behavioral changes in areas of relatedness, emotional liability, and self-identity. In DSM IV these **constellation of associated symptoms** or **associated features** are seen as most commonly occurring following "exposure to interpersonal stressors such as childhood sexual or physical abuse, domestic battering, being taken hostage, incarceration as a POW or in a concentration camp, victim of torture". According to DSM IV, the descriptive features include "impaired affect modulation, self-destructive and impulsive behaviour, dissociative symptoms, somatic complaints, feelings of ineffectiveness, shame, despair or hopelessness, feeling permanently damaged, a loss of previously sustained beliefs, hostility, social withdrawal, feeling constantly threatened, impaired relationship with others, or a change from the individual's previous personality characteristics" (p.425). There may be an increased risk of associated mental disorders including panic, agoraphobia, obsessive-compulsive, social and specific phobias, major depressive disorder, somatization and substance-related disorders. These disorders may precede or follow the onset of PTSD.

"The DSM IV Field Trial for PTSD lends support to the notion that trauma, particularly trauma that is prolonged, that first occurs at an early age, and that is of an interpersonal nature, can have pervasive effects on the totality of people's personality development, resulting in chronic affect dysregulation, aggression against self and others, dissociative symptoms, somatization, alterations in the perception of self and others, and in systems of meaning" (van der Kolk et al., in press, p.13). They go on to note that these diverse symptoms are **found together**. The **impact** of trauma is likely to be **most evident** during the **first decade of life** and the effects become less pervasive in more mature individuals. **"The diagnosis of PTSD alone captures but a small part of what troubles them"**. "The **DES syndrome** is quite specifically associated with exposure to traumatic experiences, and rarely occurs in people without histories of early trauma" (p.15). The results of the Field Trial also indicated that **"overwhelming life experiences have a different impact on people at different stages of development"** (p.15). For example, early interpersonal traumatization gave rise to more complex post-traumatic psychopathology than did later interpersonal trauma. The younger the age of the first trauma, the more likely one is to endorse DES items. Also, the longer the duration of the trauma, the more likely one is to endorse more DES items.

In summary, PTSD can come in different forms. These include:

a)   acute
b)   delayed[1]
c)   chronic
d)   intermittent or recurrent

---

[1] Falk et al. (1994) comment on whether cases of **delayed onset of PTSD** are more accurately labeled **delayed recognition**. The syndrome may be present, but incomplete, disguised, or may <u>not</u> reach the criteria for a syndrome as evident by "outwardly living a normal life, but also experiencing PTSD symptoms of withdrawal, anxiety attacks, poor sleep, intrusive thoughts, and the like."

I. **Acute Stress Disorder (ASD).**
    (Proposed as a new diagnosis in DSM-IV; Classen et al, 1993) Distinguished from PTSD because the symptom pattern in ASD must **occur within 4 weeks** of the traumatic event and **resolve within that 4 week period**.

    A. The person has been exposed to a traumatic event in which **both** of the following have been present:

        1. the person has experienced, witnessed, or been confronted with an event or events that involve actual or threatened death or serious injury, or a threat to the physical integrity of oneself or others;

        2. the person's response involved intense fear, helplessness, or horror.

    B. Either while experiencing or after experiencing the distressing event, the individual has at least **three (or more)** of the following **dissociative** symptoms:

        1. a subjective sense of numbing, detachment, or absence of emotional responsiveness;

        2. a reduction in awareness of his or her surroundings (e.g., "being in a daze");

        3. derealization (i.e., the environment is experienced as unreal or dreamlike);

        4. depersonalization (i.e., an experience of feeling detached, as if one is an outside observer of one's own mental processes or body , or feeling like an automaton);

        5. dissociative amnesia (i.e., inability to recall an important aspect of the trauma).

    C. The traumatic event is persistently reexperienced in **at least one** of the following ways: recurrent images, thoughts, dreams, illusions, flashback episodes, or a sense of reliving the experience; or distress on exposure to reminders of the traumatic event.

    D. Marked avoidance of stimuli that arouse recollections of the trauma (e.g., thoughts, feelings, conversations, activities, places, people).

    E. Marked symptoms of anxiety or increased arousal (e.g., difficulty sleeping, irritability, poor concentration, hypervigilance, exaggerated startle response, motor restlessness).

    F. The disturbance causes clinically significant distress or impairment in social, occupational, or other important areas of functioning or impairs the individual's ability to pursue some necessary task,[1] such as obtaining necessary assistance or mobilizing personal resources by telling family members about the traumatic experience.

    G. **The disturbance lasts for a minimum of 2 days and a maximum of 4 weeks and occurs within 4 weeks of the traumatic event.**

    H. The disturbance is not due to the direct physiological effects of a substance (e.g., a drug of abuse, a medication) or a general medical condition, is not better accounted for by Brief Psychotic Disorder, and is not merely an exacerbation of a preexisting Axis I or Axis II disorder.

---

[1] Note, DSM IV requires that symptoms either cause significant distress or cause marked impairment in important areas of functioning.

II. Post Traumatic Stress Disorder (PTSD).[1]

According to DSM IV, PTSD includes the following criterion that covers at least **6 symptoms** --**1** or more **of 5** persistently **reexperiencing symptoms**, **3** or more **of 7** symptoms of **persistent avoidance** and **numbing of general responsiveness**, and **2** or more **of 5** persistent symptoms of **increased arousal**. Table 3 summarizes the DSM IV diagnostic criteria of PTSD.

The DSM-IV revision was based in part on a field trial of 528 adults, 400 of whom were in treatment. Among those who experienced PTSD, most lasted 3 months or more. 11% reported symptom onset 6 months or longer following exposure to the traumatic event. The onset of the first occurrence of the traumatic event was often before age 18. The exposure to traumatic events was almost always associated with strong feelings of fear, helplessness and horror. The field trial results are consistent with the general finding that **most people will experience a traumatic event at some point during their lives, often while they are still quite young. The exposure to traumatic events are neither rare, nor unusual.**

---

[1] If the criteria for a DSM diagnosis of PTSD are not met, **Adjustment Disorder** is often the default diagnosis. Note that the Adjustment Disorder can **persist for no longer than six months** and remit once the **stressor is removed.** Moreover, in PTSD the stressor must be extreme (i.e., life threatening), whereas in Adjustment Disorder the stressor can be of any severity (e.g., spouse leaving, being fired).

Table 3

DSM-IV POST-TRAUMATIC STRESS DISORDER CRITERIA

A. The person has been exposed to a traumatic event in which **both** of the following were present:

    1. the person has experienced, witnessed, or was confronted with an event or events that involved actual or threatened death or serious injury, or a threat to the physical integrity of self or others;

    2. the person's response involved intense fear, helplessness, or horror (in children, disorganized or agitated behavior).

B. The traumatic event is **persistently reexperienced** in at least **one (or more)** of the following ways:

    1. recurrent and intrusive distressing recollections of the event, including images, thoughts, or perceptions (in young children, repetitive play may occur in which themes or aspects of the trauma are expressed);

    2. recurrent distressing dreams of the event (in children, there may be frightening dreams without recognizable content);

    3. acting or feeling as if the traumatic event were recurring (includes a sense of reliving the experience, illusions, hallucinations, and dissociative flashback episodes, including those that occur upon awakening or when intoxicated) (in young children, trauma-specific reenactment may occur);

    4. intense psychological distress at exposure to internal or external cues that symbolize or resemble an aspect of the traumatic event;

    5. physiologic reactivity[1] on exposure to internal or external cues that symbolize or resemble an aspect of the traumatic event.

C. **Persistent avoidance** of stimuli associated with the trauma **and** numbing of general responsiveness (not present before the trauma), as indicated by at least **three (or more)** of the following:

    1. efforts to avoid thoughts, feelings or conversations associated with the trauma;

    2. efforts to avoid activities, places, or people that arouse recollections of the trauma;

    3. inability to recall an important aspect of the trauma;

    4. markedly diminished interest or participation in significant activities;

    5. feeling of detachment or estrangement from others;

---

[1] The symptom of physiological reactivity has been moved from the hyperarousal cluster in DSM-III-R to the reexperiencing cluster in DSM-IV.

   6. restricted range of affect (e.g., unable to have loving feelings);

   7. sense of a foreshortened future (e.g., does not expect to have a career, marriage, children, or a normal life span).

D. Persistent symptoms of **increased arousal** (not present before the trauma), as indicated by at least **two (or more)** of the following:

   1. difficulty falling or staying asleep;

   2. irritability or outbursts of anger;

   3. difficulty concentrating;

   4. hypervigilance;

   5. exaggerated startle response.

E. Duration of the disturbance (symptoms in criteria B, C, and D) is **more than one month.**

F. The disturbance causes clinically significant distress or marked impairment in social, occupational, or other important areas of functioning.

Specify if:
Acute: if duration of symptoms is **less than three months**
Chronic: if duration of symptoms is **three months or longer**

Specify if:
With **Delayed Onset:** onset of symptoms is **at least six months have passed between the traumatic event and the onset of the symptoms**

III. Partial PTSD.

   1. Meeting criterion A (stressor) and criterion E (symptoms evident for at least one month)

   2. Five or fewer of the symptoms from criterion B, C, and D (reexperiencing, avoidance, and hyperarousal); whereas PTSD requires 6 or more symptoms

IV. Complex PTSD and Disorders of Extreme Stress.

   1. Herman (1992) has offered a clinical profile of individuals who have experienced prolonged and repetitive exposure to traumatic stressors. She characterized these as **Disorders of Extreme Stress Not Otherwise Specified or DESNOS.** This clinical profile is described in Herman (1992) and in Table 4. Herman describes the consequences of an individual's subjugation to totalitarian control over a prolonged period of time (months to years). Examples include being a hostage, prisoner of war, concentration camp survivor, survivor of a religious cult, domestic battering, childhood physical and sexual abuse and organized sexual exploitation. These prolonged and repeated interpersonal traumas can lead to alterations in:

     A) Affect regulation (e.g., persistent dysphoria, explosive or extremely inhibited anger and sexuality)

    B)   Consciousness (e.g., amnesia, transitive dissociative episodes, depersonalization, ruminative preoccupation)

    C)   Self-perception (e.g., sense of helplessness, shame, guilt, self-blame, stigmatization, aloneness, specialness)

    D)   Perception of perpetrator (e.g., preoccupation with revenge, paradoxical gratitude, acceptance of perpetrator's belief system)

    E)   Relations with others (e.g., isolation and withdrawal, disruption of intimate relationships, persistent distrust, repeated failures of self-protection, search for a rescuer)

    F)   Systems of meaning (e.g., loss of faith, sense of hopelessness and despair)

V. Disorders of Extreme Stress (DES)

van der Kolk et al. (1993) have extended and translated Herman's complex PTSD into a diagnostic category DES that has recently undergone clinical trials.[1] They have noted that PTSD captures only a limited aspect of post-traumatic psychopathology. The study of victims of prolonged and severe interpersonal trauma (e.g., physical and sexual abuse, battered women, concentration camp survivors, hostages) revealed an area of symptoms that was not adequately covered by the PTSD diagnosis. To meet this need researchers have formulated a new category **Disorder of Extreme Stress** (DES) to **supplement PTSD**. The specific subcategories of DES are noted in Table 4.

In support of the concept of DES, the results of the DSM-IV clinical field trial indicated that:

1. **early** traumatization gave rise to more complex PTSD symptomatology than did later occurring interpersonal trauma;

2. **prolonged** interpersonal trauma had most pervasive effects in terms of the various subcategories of DES;

3. DES co-occurred with PTSD in **interpersonal** traumatic events and were more likely the basis for seeking treatment than were PTSD symptoms alone;

4. The results of the field trial also indicated that **"trauma had its most pervasive impact during the first decade of life and becomes less encompassing with age ... The diagnosis of PTSD alone captures but a small part of what troubles them."** (van der Kolk et al., 1993, p.13);

5. Thus, van der Kolk et al. (1993) have reframed Herman's diagnostic label of Complex PTSD as a combination of both **Disorders of Extreme Stress** and **PTSD**. It entails:

    1. Impairment of regulation of affective arousal

    2. Dissociation and amnesia

    3. Somatization

---

[1] The changes in personality resulting from exposure to traumatic catastrophic events have been recognized by the authors of the International Classification of Disease (10th Edition) who introduced a new concept of **"Enduring Personality Changes"** to describe personality changes (becoming avoidant, hostile, distrustful, hopeless).

    4. Alterations in perception of self and others

    5. Alterations in symptoms of meaning

Table 4 enumerates the DES categories. The authors of DSM IV have subsumed these indicators under the heading of **Associated Features and Disorders**.

Table 4

Disorders of Extreme Stress (DES) Scales and Categories Used in the DSM-IV Field Trial (van der Kolk et al., in press)

I.   Alteration in Regulation of Affect and Impulses (Category A plus 1 other)

    A. Chronic Affect Dysregulation
    B. Difficulty Modulating Anger
    C. Self-destructive and Suicidal Behavior
    D. Difficulty Modulating Sexual Involvement
    E. Impulsive and Risk-taking Behaviors

II. Alterations in Attention or Consciousness (1)

    A. Amnesia
    B. Transient Dissociative Episodes and Depersonalization

III. Somatization (2)

    A. Digestive System
    B. Chronic Pain
    C. Cardiopulmonary Symptoms
    D. Conversion Symptoms
    E. Sexual Symptoms

IV. Alterations in Self-perception (2)

    A. Chronic Guilt, Shame and Self-blame
    B. Feelings of Being Permanently Damaged
    C. Feeling Ineffective
    D. Feeling Nobody Can Understand
    E. Minimizing the Importance of the Traumatic Event

V.   Alterations in Perception of the Perpetrator
    (not needed for diagnosis)

    A. Adopting Distorted Beliefs
    B. Idealization of the Perpetrator
    C. Preoccupation with Hurting the Perpetrator

VI. Alterations in Relations with Others (1)

    A. Inability to Trust
    B. Revictimization
    C. Victimizing Others

VII. Alterations in Systems of Meaning (1)

    A. Despair, Hopelessness
    B. Loss of Previously Sustaining Beliefs

WHAT IS THE EVIDENCE FOR
COMORBIDITY[1] (OR MULTIPLE DIAGNOSES) WITH PTSD?

1. Traumatic events are associated with the development of multiple forms of comorbid psychopathology , both Axis I and Axis II disorders. For example, substance abuse, suicidality, depression, anxiety, (e.g., panic attacks), somatization and eating disorders, dissociative disorders (relationship and identity difficulties), antisocial and aggressive behaviors, marital problems, borderline and multiple personality disorder, each may co-occur with PTSD. **In particular, there is a high frequency of alcoholism, depression, generalized anxiety and panic attacks with PTSD.** *(Because of the high incidence of comorbidity we will consider how to assess for these clinical problems in Section III and how to treat them in Section VI.)*

2. Illustrative findings that lead to this conclusion:

    a) In studies of natural and technological disasters, Green (1994b) reports a high incidence of comorbidity of PTSD and other diagnoses, usually **depression**. For example, in studies of survivors of a dam collapse at 14 years **only 5%** of those with PTSD had that diagnosis alone. A three-and-a-half year followup study of firefighters indicated 77% who had a diagnosis of PTSD also had an additional diagnosis, usually major depression. As Green (1994b, p.12) concludes, **"...while PTSD may be the most frequent diagnosis following disaster in many cases, it rarely occurs alone"**.

    b) Pierre Janet reported that $1/3$ of the patients who had received the initial Briquet syndrome of **somatization disorder** had been abused or what he called "mistreated" before age 12. Pribor et al. (1993) have recently supported Janet's observation in noting an association between Briquet's syndrome, dissociation, and abuse in female psychiatric clinic outpatients.

    c) Falsetti and Resnick (1994) highlight the comorbidity of **panic attacks** and PTSD. They note that in DSM-IV panic attacks are listed prior to the criteria for other anxiety disorders, therefore allowing the specification of PTSD with panic attacks. Moreover, they report a high incidence of a history of criminal victimization in clients with panic disorders. Trauma histories obtained from 711 anxiety disorder patients found 35% of them reported significant traumas and 10% met PTSD DSM-III-R criteria (Fierman et al., 1993). Sheikh et al. (1994) have reported a high incidence of panic disorder in older women who have a history of childhood abuse.

    d) Studies of PTSD have suggested that **as anxiety symptoms diminish over time, depression increases.** "A relationship of PTSD to affective disorders has been

---

[1] The term **comorbidity** has been used in different ways, as Lillenfeld et al. (1994) have noted. In some instances, co-morbidity denotes **diagnostic co-occurrence** among diagnoses, a "dual diagnosis", or the simultaneous presence in an individual of two diagnoses which are not necessarily correlated to an appreciable extent within the population. Another meaning of comorbidity is **diagnostic co-variation** which is the tendency of certain diagnoses to co-occur more often than by chance. The terms **diagnostic co-occurrence** and **diagnostic co-variation** hold different implications for understanding and treating mental disorders. *(See Clinical Psychology 1994, 1, 71 to 100 for a debate about the concept of comorbidity.)* For example, when it comes to the concept of PTSD, the question emerges when does depression or Disorders of Extreme Stress constitute one and the same mental disorders, a different developmental phase of the same disorder, or some form of co-occurrence versus co-variation?

suggested by family and concurrent illness studies." (Vargas & Davidson, 1992). However, Solomon and Smith (1994) reports that disasters appeared to exacerbate preexisting depressions, rather than to initiate symptoms of the disorder in those previously symptom-free.

e) Among **crime victims** with PTSD, 41% had sexual dysfunction, 82% depression, 27% obsessive compulsive symptoms, and 18% phobias (Kilpatrick et al, 1987).

f) Somatization disorders are widespread among **Holocaust victims** and in 55% of child sexual abuse clients. Somatization disorders increase over time in rape victims. Hypochondriacal patients recall more childhood trauma than do nonhypochondriacal patients (Barsky et al., 1994). There is a strong association between chronic PTSD and physical illness and exaggerated somatic concerns and medical utilization (Shalev et al., 1990; White et al., 1989).

g) "Anywhere from 40% to 60% of women in recovery for **bulimia, anorexia**, and **compulsive overeating** report victimization experiences." (Matsakis, 1992). Gleaves and Eberenz (1994) report the high incidence of sexual abuse histories in treatment-resistant bulimia-nervosa patients.

h) Overall, PTSD sufferers have a 19% increased **suicide risk**, with 20% of rape victims attempting suicide, 42% of battered women attempting suicide. *(Thus, we will consider suicide assessment in Section III.)*

i) 75% of Vietnam veterans with PTSD also met criteria for at least one other diagnosis; the most common being depression and substance abuse (Green, 1994). The National Study of **Vietnam Veterans** (NVVRS) cites current PTSD co-morbidity rates of 15.7% for major depression and 19.8% for generalized anxiety disorder. To suppress the symptoms of hyperarousal, clients may have resorted to alcohol and other addictive substances. For example, the National Study of **Vietnam Veterans** (NVVRS) found a life-time prevalence of PTSD in Vietnam combat veterans to be over 30% at one time or another. 75% of these veterans met the criteria for alcohol abuse or dependence. Among female Vietnam veterans, a PTSD diagnosis predicts greater than a five-fold increase in alcohol abuse and dependence. **Nearly half of all veterans who have ever suffered PTSD and alcoholism still experience this dual diagnosis today.** Veterans who meet the criteria of alcohol abuse or dependence suffer more impairment and are less likely to have completed high school, less likely to be employed, evidence more occupational instability, are less likely to be married, have multiple divorces, greater parental difficulties, are socially isolated, and are more prone to use violence (Hiley-Young et al., 1993). *(We will consider alcohol assessment in Section III and treatment of addictive behaviors in Section VI.)*

j) Green et al. (1984) found that **only 13%** of a treatment seeking population of Vietnam veterans manifest a single diagnosis of PTSD. Green et al.(1989) report that among Vietnam veterans exposure to grotesque death (i.e., mutilation) was highly predictive of alcohol use and PTSD.

k) High rates of **alcohol abuse** have also been noted among W.W.II and Korean combat veterans. Davidson et al. (1990) report that on the average, major depression occurred 9 years after the development of PTSD in a sample of W.W.II soldiers and 4.8 years after PTSD in Vietnam veterans. Alcoholism preceded PTSD in Vietnam veterans, but followed PTSD in W.W.II veterans. Thus, there are important socio-historical/cohort differences. There is also a high incidence of **cigarette abuse** among individuals with PTSD (Ursano et al., 1994).

l) "Approximately 50% to 60% of women and 20% of men in **chemical dependency** recovery programs report having been victims of childhood sexual abuse. Approximately 69% of women and 80% of men in such programs report being victims of childhood physical abuse." (Matsakis, 1992).

m) "Severe trauma has also been documented among **compulsive gamblers** seeking help, among runaway and delinquent children and adolescents, and among both male and female prostitutes and actresses and models in pornographic films and magazines." (Matsakis, 1992).

n) Of the 2-3% of the general population with **borderline personality (BP)** disorders, roughly $1/3$ fulfill the criteria for PTSD, 75% of whom are women. There are high rates of traumatic childhood experiences in adolescent and adult patients with BP disorder, in the range of 60% to 75%. The traumatic experiences include physical and sexual abuse, and exposure to violence (Gunderson & Chu, 1993; Gunderson & Sabo, 1993).

o) Many, if not most, patients with **dissociative disorders** report childhood histories of abuse, neglect and deprivation. 90% of **multiple personality disorder (MPD) patients** report histories of severe physical and sexual abuse (Coons & Milstein, 1986; Putnam et al., 1986). **The causal relationship between MPD and child sexual abuse is quite controversial,**[1] *as will be discussed in Section VI.* In fact, as Spanos (1994) observes, the strong connection between child abuse and MPD is of recent origin. Case reports in the early part of the 20th century and before were much less likely than modern cases to be associated with reports of child abuse. While many MPD patients report abuse during childhood, most abused individuals do not develop MPD.

p) "Researchers have also noted increases in **alcohol consumption** among survivors of fires, floods, and other natural disasters." (Matsakis, 1992). Also, **decreases** in alcohol use have been reported (Ursano et al., 1994).

q) Women who have **chronic pelvic pain** are more likely to have been sexually assaulted before age 14 (Walker et al., 1992).

r) Finally, Williams-Keeler and Jones (1993) in a very thoughtful paper explored the relationship between PTSD and **schizophrenia**. They argue that the mental disorder of schizophrenia can exert a traumatic impact on the sufferer and that it is similar in effect to combat. Moreover, they note that PTSD sufferers may be misdiagnosed with paranoid schizophrenia (Van Putten & Emery, 1973; Domash & Sparr, 1982). Friedman (1994) observes that chronic, severe PTSD patients are often "reclusive, mistrustful, demoralized individuals who require careful **case management** and **resocialization,** as do schizophrenics."

s) **It is also worth noting that the symptomatic aftermath of being exposed to a traumatic event can, in itself, contribute to further difficulties and further distress.**

In conclusion, the cumulative data indicates that no matter what clinical population you work with, you should consider the systematic assessment of victimization experiences. The discussion thus far has addressed the problem of exposure to general traumatic events. The field of traumatology has made important advances in mapping the

---

[1] See A. Piper (1994) Multiple personality disorder. British Journal of Psychiatry, 164, 600-612.

epidemiology, impact, course, assessment, and treatment of populations who have been exposed to specific traumatic stressors. In this next section, we will consider the findings on:

a) Vietnam veterans and other combat experiences;

b) rape victims;

c) victims of domestic violence;

d) victims of child sexual abuse;

e) crime victims.

       In each of these sections, I consider the epidemiological impact and treatment implications. Because of the extensive literature reviewed, I have concluded each section with an encapsulated **summary of what you should take away from the epidemiological data**. It is critical that clinicians be knowledgeable when working with "victim" groups, so we do <u>not</u> inadvertently revictimize them. At the end of this section is a "TEST" designed to asses your general knowledge.

EXAMPLES OF ILLUSTRATIVE SPECIAL PTSD POPULATIONS: VIETNAM VETERANS AND OTHER COMBAT EXPERIENCES[1]

(See Archibald & Tuddenham, 1965; Bourne, 1990; Cavenar & Nash, 1976; Center for Disease Control, 1988; Fairbank & Nicholson, 1987; Friedman et al., 1994; Gal & Mangelsdorf, Milgram, 1986; 1991; Grinker & Spiegel, 1945; Hiley-Young et al., 1993; Jordan et al., 1991; Kulka et al., 1988; Maxwell & Sturm, 1994; Oei et al., 1990; Rosenheck & Fontana, 1994; Schlenger et al., 1992; Solomon, 1990; Veterans Administration Report, 1991 for a discussion of the enduring impact of combat trauma)

One of the most moving experiences for me was visiting the Holocaust memorial in Jerusalem and bearing witness to the death of six million Jews and other groups in concentration camps. Another very moving experience was visiting the Vietnam memorial in Washington, D.C and seeing the inscribed names of almost 60,000 soldiers who died in Vietnam. These memorials are a testimony to man's brutality and stupidity and the resultant losses. During the Vietnam war I was a graduate student at the University of Illinois. My draft board in New York City met their quota, so I was not called up. Instead, I attended sit-ins, marched, and in my feeble way tried to find a means of expression, a way of helping. The opportunity to help came many years after the Vietnam war when I was asked to consult at a Veterans Administration hospital for **dual diagnosis** (PTSD and substance abuse). In my own compulsive academic fashion, I tried to summarize what was the "cost" these brave young men and women had paid? What did the literature say about:

1) the scope of the physical and psychiatric disabilities;

2) the short-term and long-term consequences on both the Veterans and on significant others in their lives;

3) the impact of war, in general, and not just the Vietnam War;

4) what could be done to help.

My answer to these questions gave rise to this handout. An examination of this epidemiological data has many implications for assessment and treatment. One **caveat** to keep in mind in reviewing the data on combat veterans and PTSD is that there may be **differences in posttrauma responses between veteran and civilian populations.** (e.g., see North et al., 1994). While the full syndrome of PTSD may be common among Vietnam veterans (especially, if they have been exposed to a number of pre-combat, combat, and post-combat experiences described below), the general population exposed to violence may show fewer symptoms of PTSD, (Helzer et al., 1987; Resnick et al., 1993). Soldiers are trained to anticipate and expect combat. For a civilian population, as in the case of a mass shooting, the violence seems random and "shatters" beliefs of safety. These differences are evident in the symptom profile, as well. In a civilian population who were exposed to a mass shooting, intrusive recollections are most frequent and emotional numbing is least frequent. In contrast, among combat survivors with PTSD, survivor guilt and emotional numbing are more central (North et al., 1994). As Scurfield (1992) observes, "Many in our society still seem <u>not</u> to appreciate the **remarkable** and **durable**

---

[1] Garbarino (1993, p. 791) has characterized "war is a man's game. The impulse to war lies deeply embedded in the masculine psyche". While there are reports of women victimizing people, **the predominant story of PTSD is that occasioned by men victimizing people (e.g., war, rape, incest, crime, greed).** The reasons why men behave in such a fashion is beyond the scope of this **Handbook/Manual.** Interesting speculations have been offered by Pantony and Caplan (1991) and by Russell (in press).

impact that war has on our troops, and their families, and our society" (p. 509). (See Schnurr, 1991.)

Lessons from the Vietnam War

In this section we will consider the lingering impact of war. As we consider the epidemiological data, it is important to keep in mind the observations offered by Holloway and Ursano (1984) who concluded:

> "The literature suggests that if given the opportunity, most people
> who have been exposed to the extreme rigors of war and battle
> will cope well with their subsequent lives" (p.103).

Nevertheless, war can take a terrible toll as noted by Homer in the Illiad, Shakespeare in Henry IV, and by the many astute clinical observers of soldiers (see Weathers et al., 1994 for a summary of this literature). In fact, Weathers et al. (1994) highlight how similar the reactions to battle have remained throughout recorded history. Moreover, **many trauma survivors develop post-traumatic sequelae without manifesting acute disabling symptoms during the trauma exposure** (Shalev, 1994). For instance, the low number of identified stress casualties during the Vietnam war did <u>not</u> reflect the high incidence of PTSD that veterans developed in subsequent years, as documented in the following epidemiological data.

> *"If there's a lesson in this, which there is not, its*
> *very simple. You don't have to be in Nam to be in*
> *Nam."* (Tim O'Brien[1] "The Vietnam in Me", <u>New</u>
> <u>York Times Magazine</u>, Oct. 2, 1994)

1. 3.14 million men and women served in S.E. Asia during the Vietnam war. 36% were exposed to high war zone activity, 20% report having witnessed atrocities.

2. In Vietnam approximately 58,000 American soldiers died. There were 300,000 wounded, 75,000 seriously disabled.

3. O'Brien (1994) notes that while all wars are horrific events, from a psychiatric point of view the Vietnam War was particularly egregious. He compares the Gulf War and Falklands conflict with Vietnam. The former were comparatively brief, offensive, lacked direct threat to home and family, involved mostly professional soldiers and a clearly defined enemy. In contrast, the Vietnam War involved 40% draftees, an ill-defined enemy and little support at home. "Some studies of Vietnam veterans indicate that idealistic volunteers had more mental health problems than draftees" (O'Brien, 1994, p. 443). But war takes a toll on both sides. For example, Hauff & Vaglum (1993) and Scurfield (1992) report that 900,000 Vietnamese were wounded, and about 250,000 were killed, 300,000 are missing in action, and 100,000 were incarcerated, and 6 to 10 million were resettled. These statistics on the Vietnamese are not readily discussed in what Scurfield (1992) describes as the "collusion", "sanitization" and "silence" about wars.[2] The lingering impact of such multiple war traumas on the Vietnamese boat-people who escaped has been documented by the Norwegian investigators Hauff & Vaglum (1993). They observe that 1/4 of Vietnamese refugees had PTSD when they arrived

---

[1] For insightful moving accounts of the impact of war also see Tim O'Brien <u>The thing they carried; In the lake of</u> <u>the woods.</u>

[2] To put these numbers in some context, consider that as a result of WWI there was a 5% civilian casualty rate, in WWII a 50% civilian casualty rate, and in Vietnam an 80% civilian casualty rate (Kleber et al., in press).

in Norway and this was some 7 years after the end of the war. Forced separation from one's spouse and the absence of social networks in finding jobs contributed to poor adjustment 3 years later.

4.   **"15.2 percent of all male Vietnam theater veterans currently have PTSD". The incidence of PTSD was 21% among African Americans; 28% among Hispanics[1] (Kulka et al., 1990).   The lifetime rates of PTSD were essentially twice that of the current rates (Keane, 1990).** This represents about 450,000 of the estimated 3.14 million men who served in the Vietnam theater between August 5, 1964 and May 7, 1975. 2.5 per cent of non-war zone Vietnam veterans have PTSD. (It is worth highlighting Scurfield's (1992) observation that the prevalence of PTSD in Vietnam veterans is comparable to that among W.W. II U.S. veterans. As noted, the low acute psychiatric casualty rate in Vietnam did not necessarily have any relationship to the long-term chronic, or delayed psychiatric casualty rate.

5.   **8.5 percent of all female Vietnam theater veterans currently have PTSD.** This represents about 610 of the 7200 women who served. Among female high war zone Vietnam veterans the rate was 17.5 per cent, with 2.6 per cent reporting PTSD at some point in their lives. The rates of lifetime PTSD since the war in female theater veterans is 26% and among male theater veterans it is 30%. When partial and full PTSD statistics are combined nearly half (48%) of female theater veterans had at some point suffered from symptoms related to PTSD (Wolfe, 1990). PTSD in women who served outside of the Vietnam theater was 1.1%. To complicate matters, some female veterans also experienced sexual harassment and assault. See Wolfe et al. (1994) for a discussion of treatment for female veterans. (Psychotherapy, 1994, 31, 87-93).

6.   An additional **11.1** percent of male theater veterans and 7.8 percent of female theater veterans -- 350,000 additional men and women, currently suffer from **"partial PTSD"**. That is, they have clinically significant stress reaction symptoms of insufficient intensity or breadth to qualify as full PTSD, but they may still warrant professional attention. **Thus, nearly 830,000 Vietnam theatre veterans continue to have clinically significant stress reaction symptoms.** These reactions may entail heightened arousal (jumpiness, irritability, insomnia), experience current events as if "reliving" past traumas, and inability to modulate intense emotions such as anxiety and anger (Engel et al., 1993). **17% of Vietnam veterans experience flashbacks.** In fact, the intrusion subscale of the Impact Event Scale was one of the best predictors of PTSD in Vietnam veterans. Davidson and Baum (1994) report that irrespective of combat exposure, **soldiers who reported more intrusive symptoms were more likely to experience symptoms of chronic stress 14 years later.** They also may feel a sense of isolation, detachment and estrangement. Participation in atrocities were more likely to predict reexperiencing symptoms, while general combat experience was more likely to predict avoidance behaviors. The impact of intrusive ideation was conveyed by O'Brien (1994, p. 56).

> *"The hardest part, by far, is to make the bad pictures go away. On war time, the world is one long horror movie, image after image, and if its anything like Vietnam, I'm in for a lifetime of wee-hour creeps."*

7.   Negative psychological outcomes to war trauma are most likely to occur among troops exposed to the most gruesome experiences, particularly events that incorporate exposure to grotesque death, macabre stimuli and human suffering (Sutker et al., 1994).

---

[1] Friedman et al., (1994) report that the increased prevalence among African Americans was explained by their greater amount of combat exposure relative to whites; the difference between Hispanics and whites was only partially explained by increased exposure among Hispanics.

8.   Wilmer (1987) has described three categories of **disturbing war dreams** of Vietnam combat veterans. Approximately 1/2 of the nightmares may be exact replications of actual traumatic events; approximately 1/4 are images of actual trauma elaborated by credible "might-have-been experiences", and approximately 1/4 resemble hallucinatory nightmares. Such nightmares and the accompanying sleep disturbance can be quite disturbing.

9.   National Vietnam Veterans Readjustment Study (NVVRS) analyses of the **lifetime prevalence of PTSD** indicate that nearly **one-third (30.6 percent)** of male Vietnam theater veterans (over 960,000 men) and over **one fourth (26.9 percent)** of women serving in the Vietnam theater (over 1900 women) have had the full-blown disorder at some point since returning from Vietnam. **Thus, about one-half of the men and one-third of the women who have ever had PTSD still have it today.** These findings are consistent with the conceptualization of PTSD as a chronic, rather than an acute, disorder. Also, Kukla et al. (1988) reported that 50% of those with current PTSD met criteria for at least one additional Axis I or Axis II diagnosis, underscoring **the high incidence of comorbidity or dual diagnosis.** Put otherwise, **nearly 1.7 million veterans will exhibit clinically significant stress reactions at some time during their lives.** They are twice as likely to have enduring psychological problems when compared to other wars.

10.   NVVRS findings also indicate a strong relationship between PTSD and other postwar readjustment problems in virtually every domain of life. For example, Motta (1993) reports that 16% of all veterans and 29% of combat veterans have significant problems in adjusting to civilian life, as evident in occupational instability, chronic health problems and service connected physical disabilities, and familial difficulties. Veterans are 65% more likely to have died of suicide[1] and 48% more likely to die in automobile accidents than nonveterans. 53% of Vietnam veterans suffered work-related symptomatology. The Vietnam veteran's experience a 15% overall unemployment rate, with double that rate among African American veterans (Figley, 1993).

11.   The prevalence of PTSD and other postwar psychological problems is significantly higher among those who experienced **high levels of combat exposure** and other war zone stressors in Vietnam, either in comparison with their Vietnam era veteran and civilian peers, or when compared with other veterans who served in the Vietnam theater and who were exposed to low or moderate levels of war zone stress. For example, the lifetime prevalence rates were 7 times greater for males in the highest war zone stress area and 4 times greater for females in the greatest war zone stress areas. The rates of PTSD were higher for those who were **injured** (Ursano et al., 1994). Further illustrating the relationship between degree of exposure and impact is the finding that those who were shot down prior to 1969 experienced substantially worse conditions and greater maltreatment than those shot down after 1969. Those in the pre-1969 showed more psychiatric disturbance over a 5 year follow-up period (Ursano et al., 1994). The exposure to **"grotesque death"**, abusive violence and atrocities were more strongly related to PTSD (Zaida & Foy, 1994). Atrocities of war have a powerful negative effect on mental health, not only for the surviving victims, but for the perpetrators (O'Brien; 1994). Green et al. (1989, 1990) reported that the loss of a buddy, injury, and general combat predicted postwar PTSD, whereas exposure to grotesque death and exposure to dangerous special high risk missions predicted continuing or chronic PTSD. Bradshaw et al. (1993) implicated the number of comrades killed and the horror of their dying as factors affecting postwar personality changes. There is no difference in the rates of depression,

_____

[1] The recent suicide death of the Pulitzer prize winning Vietnam veteran, Lewis B. Puller Jr. underscores these numbers. The facts included in this Section cannot match the poignant account offered in Puller's book "Fortunate son: The healing of a Vietnam vet."

anxiety and alcoholism in those who served or did not serve in Vietnam. **Participation in combat was the sole risk factor for PTSD.** The exposure to grotesque stimuli is predictive of later stress response.

12. **Precombat sexually and physically abused veterans** (those with parenting and family adjustment problems) are significantly **more likely** to have **experienced PTSD** (Bremner et al., 1993, Zaidi & Foy, 1994). Engel et al. (1993) found this relationship to hold more so for female veterans, than for male veterans, who served in Operation Desert Storm. They noted that those who had a history of abuse may have been especially sensitive to feeling "unprotected, trapped, coerced, or controlled when exposed to combat" (p. 687). Male soldiers who had a troubled and/or abusive relationship with their fathers were also at "risk". Thus, there is a need to **consider the soldier's pre-combat "victimization" experiences.** This is especially true, when we learn that the pre-service psychiatric problems predicted placement in more severe combat situations (Green et al., 1990). Other **premilitary factors** indicating risk for PTSD included younger age of entry into the military, less premilitary education, prior psychiatric disorder and childhood behavior problems (Friedman et al., 1994).

13. Among the variety of PTSD symptoms that Vietnam veterans experience, a major one is **guilt.** As Kubany (1994) observes, guilt may take the form of the veteran believing he/she "could have" or "should have" done something different, done more, known better. They also may experience feelings of **shame** as they recall and recount what happened. (*See Section VII for how therapists can help clients manage feelings of guilt*).

14. Fischer (1991) reported that exposure to heavy combat in Vietnam more than doubled the risk for post-discharge substance abuse. Younger and less educated soldiers were at higher risk. The length of time to begin their first job following return from Vietnam and the length of time they held that initial job were also predictive of post-discharge substance abuse problems.

15. Robins, Helzer and Davis (1975) and Robins (1993) report on the surprisingly **low levels of re-addiction** and **rarity of addiction** to narcotics alone in returning Vietnam veterans. The addiction rate to narcotics in Vietnam was estimated to be 20%. In the first year after return, only 5% of those who had been addicted in Vietnam were addicted in the US, and after 3 years only 12% of those addicted in Vietnam were addicted at any time in the 3 years since return, and for those readdicted, the addiction had usually been very brief. Drug addiction tended to remit quickly, even in the absence of treatment. **"Drug users who appear for treatment have special problems that will not be solved just by getting them off drugs,"** (p.1051). These treated veterans who use drugs have a high relapse rate.

16. Substantial differences in current PTSD prevalence rates were also found by **minority status.** African-Americans, Hispanics, Native American theater veterans reported more overall adjustment problems than did Caucasians. Kulka et al. (1990) reported that the prevalence of PTSD was **twice as high among African-American Vietnam combat veterans** and **50% higher among Hispanic Vietnam combat veterans,** than among their Caucasian counterparts. More specifically, current PTSD is found in 20.6% of African-Americans, 27.9% of Hispanic theater veterans in contrast to 13.7% of Caucasian veterans (NVVRS study). A variety of factors including differing levels of combat exposure, discriminatory practices, developmental, sociohistorical, cultural and post-war factors may contribute to these group differences. See Parson (1985) for a discussion of African-American Vietnam veteran experience, Oreiro (1990) for a discussion Native American Indian veterans, Hamada (1991) and Loo (1994) for a discussion of Asian American-Vietnam veterans, and Marsella et al. (1990) for a general discussion of ethnocultural aspects

of PTSD in Vietnam war veterans. Marsella et al. note the role of racial stereotypes, lower social status, ridicule, inequitable treatment, conflicts deriving from fighting "on behalf of a country many considered racist", and guilt about fighting a non-white culture. On top of these differences cultural factors influence the expression of symptomatology and help-seeking attitudes and behaviors. Moreover, many of the tests and interviews used to assess PTSD are based on norms which do not include specific minority groups (Marsella et al., 1990). *(See discussion on ethnic differences in Section III.)*

17. Combat veterans with PTSD had more **marital problems** in terms of self-disclosure and expressiveness, hostility and aggression toward their partner and global marital maladjustment. Wives were less communicative, more angry and fearful of their partner than comparison groups (Figley, 1994). Social rejection and alienation following trauma is a hindrance to recovery.

18. PTSD has a substantial negative impact not only on the veterans' lives, but also on the lives of spouses, children, and others living with the veteran (Hiley-Young et al., 1993; Matsakis, 1988; Motta, 1990; Williams, 1990). For example, 38% of marriages of Vietnam veterans broke up within 6 months of homecoming (Peebles-Kleiger & Kleiger, 1994). These findings are not limited to Vietnam Veterans. For example, Solomon et al. (1992) reported that 6 years after the Lebanon war, **wives** of Israeli soldiers who experienced combat stress reactions and PTSD evidenced increased psychiatric symptoms, loneliness, impaired marital and family relations. **Any treatment that focuses exclusively on the individual soldier and fails to consider the spouse and family members will likely have limited effectiveness.**

19. **40% of homeless men are veterans and 1/2 served during Vietnam.** Rosenheck and Fontana (1994) have noted the complex pattern of influences from **premilitary** (childhood traumas, placement in foster care during childhood, conduct disorder), **military** -- being in military zone, and **post military** (social isolation, psychiatric disorder and substance abuse) on **homelessness**.

20. **Disabled veterans**[1] are among the **highest risk groups** of war-veterans to develop PTSD. For example, 3.5% of nonwounded Vietnam veterans had a history of PTSD compared to 20% in veterans wounded in Vietnam (Malt, 1994). In fact, physical disability is a high risk marker for PTSD and associated disorders for civilian accidents, as well (Malt, 1994). The prevalence of PTSD among wounded Vietnam veterans is over 30%, in contrast to the prevalence rate among all Vietnam veterans which is 15% (Scurfield & Tice, 1991). Moreover, disabled PTSD veterans are more likely to be currently unemployed, unmarried and dissatisfied with their lives. Batres (1992) report that of 346,000 Vietnam veterans who have a service connected disability, more than 74,000 have current PTSD. However, they do not suffer from other major psychological disorders than veterans without service connected disabilities. (See descriptions by Cleland, 1980, and Downs, 1984, for moving accounts of the experience of wounded Vietnam veterans.)

21. In spite of these alarming figures, it is worth noting that only 4% (40,000 out of 900,000) Vietnam veterans have applied for compensation claims for PTSD and only 10% of veterans with current PTSD and 20% with lifetime PTSD have ever used V.A. facilities (Friedman, 1991).

---

[1] Additional information on physically disabled veterans can be obtained in the Working Group's 1988 Report available from the National Office of Readjustment Counseling Service, 810 Vermont Ave., N.W. Washington, D.C. 20420. It is also important to note from Green (1994) that when the extent of injury was considered in non-combat populations it did not have consistent association with PTSD. She proposes that it may be the perceived loss of function that plays a greater role.

22. An estimated 12,000 to 40,000 Canadians enlisted in the US military and fought in Vietnam. Many years later, a survey by Stretch (1990) indicates that <u>Canadian veterans are 2.3 times more likely to experience chronic PTSD than are American veterans</u> and these problems have <u>not</u> diminished with time. The incidence of PTSD is running **20% higher** in Canadians who volunteered to fight in Vietnam than their American counterparts. Stretch suggests this is due to lack of social supports and recognition from Canadian society, isolation from other Vietnam veterans, and lack of readjustment counseling centers. Post war factors such as being ignored, shunned, unwelcomed, resented by society can have a debilitating effect on adjustment. Stretch (1991) observed that the prolonged isolation from other Vietnam veterans, lack of recognition, and no readily available treatment for PTSD in Canada contribute to these findings.

23. **Lessons from Operation Desert Storm (ODS)**[1]

While each war brings its own unique constellation of stressors, many of the lessons from the Vietnam war were replicated in ODS. Between August, 1990 and March, 1991 500,000 military personnel (40,000 women) were called to duty in the Persian Gulf. While there were few cases of combat stress reactions (CSR) and PTSD, the war, like all wars, had its cost. As Lehmann (1993) observes, "While rates of PTSD are lower in Gulf than in Vietnam veterans, there are "pockets of PTSD: individuals or units that experienced severe stress and, in consequence, report high levels of PTSD and other psychological reactions." (p. 13).

   a) Rosenheck (1993) reports on 4500 Persian Gulf veterans (mainly National Guard and Reserve Units). He found that approximately **9% of returnees** reported symptoms scoring in the **PTSD range** and **34%** appear to experience other forms of **significant psychological distress** in the months following their return. When they returned home they felt dazed, numb, agitated, estranged, had difficulty making emotional contact and difficulty participating in practical life problems. Peebles-Kleiger and Kleiger (1994) estimated that 10% - 20% evidence significant symptomatology 6 months after deployment. Friedman et al., (1994) report that "a few days after return to the US, the prevalence of current PTSD in men was 3.2% and in women 9.6%. Approximately 18 months later, these figures increased to 9.4% and 19.8%; respectively" (p. 267). It is not clear what accounts for this gender difference.

   b) Among those who conducted graves registration duties that included handling, processing and transporting human remains they evidenced current (48%) and lifetime (65%) rates of PTSD, as well as high levels of anxiety, anger and somatic complaints, 8 months following return to U.S.

   c) 19% ODS veterans experienced moderate or severe family adjustment problems (Figley, 1993); 40% of veterans reported family or marital distress 1 year after ODS which is comparable to the same level of familial distress following disasters. Ford et al (1993) found that **marital distress was a better marker of adjustment** than were measures of general distress of the veterans. Six months following deployment was a heightened marital risk period. **There is an association between family dysfunction and chronicity of PTSD.**

---

[1] See the <u>Operation Desert Storm Clinical Packet ODS-CP</u>, National Center for PTSD, Department of Veteran's Affair (1991) for a comprehensive presentation of clinical material and the <u>Journal of Social Issues</u>, 1993, <u>49</u> (4) on <u>Psychological research on the Persian Gulf war</u> (D. Lehman, Editor).

    d) Involving spouses in treatment facilitated outcome[1] -- for example, brief (2 to 6 sessions) individual and group conjoint psychoeducational meetings helped veterans and their spouses identify, explain, and "normalize" stress and fostered better adjustment (Ford et al., 1993). One aspect of the intervention was to have the couple do a **joint walk-through** of their specific trauma and stressor experiences that they each experienced during ODS. Each partner developed a parallel account of the war and home front experiences and its impact which provided a sense of their "having done it together even though they were 5000 miles apart." *(This is only one form of Critical Incident Stress Debriefing that we will discuss in more detail in Section VII.)*

    e) Research by Ford et al., Peebles-Kleiger and Kleiger, McCubbin & Figley, indicate that the accumulation or "pile up" of familial stressors can exacerbate adjustment reactions. *(See assessment Section III on the importance of measuring "hot reactions" in families, namely, those who manifest high expressed emotional behaviors, criticism, blame, intrusiveness, etc.)*

    f) There was a correlation between substance abuse and symptoms of PTSD among ODS veterans (Figley, 1993).

    g) Precombat history of sexual or physical abuse put soldiers at greater risk for PTSD (Engel et al., 1993)

24. Veterans of the Korean Conflict: An Overlooked Population

    a) "The general consensus in the literature is that PTSD currently exists in many World War II and Korean War veterans 4 or 5 decades after their actual combat experiences ... PTSD is not a constant or static condition, but a disorder that may actually wax and wane throughout a lifetime." (Falk et al., 1994, p. 395)

    b) Rosenheck and Fontana (1994) compared the long-term adjustment of combat in WWII, Korea and Vietnam veterans and concluded, **"that Korean combat veterans, more than Vietnam combat veterans, are the forgotten warriors of today"** (p.342). They note that the veterans of the Korean conflict also fought a controversial war of containment in which some 55,000 veterans died in Korea. Moreover, veterans of the Korean Conflict are least likely to use the VA health services, while the veterans from Vietnam war used the VA services more than any other veterans from other conflicts.

25. Lessons from the Israeli War Experiences[2]

    a) Solomon (1994) in her work with soldiers in the Israeli military has reported the presence of an acute syndrome of war zone stress, or what she calls **Combat Stress Reactions (CSR)**, or what has been called "shell shock", "combat exhaustion", or "war neurosis." CSR are <u>not</u> the same as PTSD. CSR represent a situational reaction of anxiety, distancing (psychic numbing, fainting), restlessness, psychomotor retardation, stuttering, withdrawal, nausea, vomiting, confusion, paranoid reactions, and guilt about functioning, increased sympathetic nervous system reactions, all contributing to an inability to function militarily that endangers both oneself and one's comrades. She has found that the occurrence of CSR's are predictive of subsequent PTSD. (Past wartime

---

[1] See the Guide to Mentally Healthy Reunion (1991) -- National Mental Health Association, Alexandria, VA.

[2] For a more detailed account see Gal, R. (1986), A portrait of the Israeli soldier. Westport CT: Greenwood Publishing Group.

research findings lead one to expect approximately 1 combat stress casualty for every 3 physical casualties, with a higher ratio in a mass casualty situation.)

b) For example, 56% of 3,553 Israeli soldiers who experienced acute CSR were diagnosed with PTSD 2 years later versus only 18% of 235 soldiers who did not have previous CSR had PTSD 2 years later. She also reported that 16% of 386 combat veterans of the 1982 Lebanon war who had not sought treatment for the psychological effects of war, suffered from PTSD one year later. Among those with delayed PTSD only 10% have sought help.

c) 74% of soldiers who broke down (CSR's) in combat and who were not returned to duty were experiencing symptoms of PTSD one year later, and 59% reached criteria for PTSD. Of those soldiers who broke down in combat and who were returned to duty, 38% were suffering from PTSD one year later. Of those who did not break down in combat, only 16% were suffering from PTSD one year later (Solomon, 1993).

d) In another study, Solomon (1993) compared 213 CSR (combat stress reaction) versus 116 unaffected matched control soldiers for 3 years after the Lebanon war. The incidence of diagnosable PTSD were as follows:

Incidence of PTSD

	Year 1	Year 2	Year 3
CSR (N = 213)	63%	57%	43%
No CSR (N = 116)	14%	17%	9%

"Approximately half of the soldiers who sustained CSR on the battlefield were still suffering from pervasive diagnosable PTSD 3 years after participation in battle." These reactions often took the form of recurrent intrusive scenes, sleep difficulties and loss of interests. **Wartime breakdowns are not transient.** Moreover, like Vietnam veterans, the Israeli veterans were **reluctant to seek help.** Such soldiers have to contend with the implications of their breakdown in terms of feelings of shame, guilt, self-esteem, feelings about violating trust, and their sense of manhood.

e) Solomon (1993, 1994) also reports that there is a **cumulative** toll of the stressors that soldiers experience. Israeli soldiers were asked which of 7 prior wars they had participated in. A study of Israeli soldiers indicated that after a soldiers' second war, every additional battle he fights makes him more susceptible to psychiatric breakdown in battle. For example, Israeli combat soldiers in the 1981 Lebanon war, showed that those who sustained combat stress reactions (CSR) on the battle front were 4 to 5 times more likely than non-CSR to develop chronic PTSD in the 3 years following the war. Soldiers who had a previous history of CSR were 57% more likely to experience CSR in the next war, 67% if they participated in 2 wars, and 83% likelihood of experiencing CSR if they participated in 3 wars. As Solomon (1993) observes, "repeated battle will eventually fell even the hardiest souls" (p. 1738).

The soldier's immediate response to stress indicated his susceptibility for long-term PTSD. Exposure to traumatic events leaves individuals more vulnerable in general. After a soldier was traumatized in war, he did not return to prewar levels of adjustment. **Moreover, reactivation of PTSD symptoms often occurred after many years of dormancy.** Solomon observes that while some stressors may strengthen a person's ability to cope, massive stressors like war and the Holocaust depletes coping ability.

f) In a unique feature that could only be examined in Israel, Solomon and her colleagues were able to examine the impact of a latent vulnerability factor on susceptibility to CSR and PTSD. The **susceptibility factor** was being the **offspring of Holocaust surviving parent(s).** The incidence of PTSD in combat veterans second generation survivors of the Holocaust lasted longer. More specifically, Solomon (1993) reported:

<u>Rates of PTSD</u>

	<u>Year 1</u>	<u>Year 2</u>	<u>Year 3</u>
Holocaust in background	70%	73%	64%
No Holocaust in background	70%	52%	39%

The PTSD symptoms lasted much longer and were also more severe in those soldiers who are second generation Holocaust survivors.

g) Analysis of the impact of the 1973 Yom Kippur War further underscores the long-range impact. Solomon compared the incidence of PTSD for 164 Israeli prisoners of war, 112 veterans who experienced combat stress reactions during the war, and 184 control veterans. The PTSD rates were respectively 23% (POWs), 37% (CSR) and 14% (controls), and at a followup assessment the rates were 13%, 13% and 3%, respectively. Almost 2/3 of the veterans with CSR and PTSD recovered and 1/2 of the POWs showed improvement.

h) Solomon and Benbenishty (1986) reported that 80% of acute military casualties treated by frontline principles of proximity, immediacy, and expectancy during the Lebanon war were <u>not</u> suffering PTSD one year later <u>versus</u> only 29% of acute psychiatric casualties treated by other modalities. (*We will consider these military interventions further in Section VII on post-disaster interventions.*)

i) Evidence from Israel and the Gulf War indicates that while 60 - 90% of combat sufferers can be treated and returned to duties if mental health teams are available in the theatre, but many have further problems after the war (O'Brien, 1994; Solomon & Shale, 1989).

j) We also learn from studies of the Israeli civilian population. For instance, Solomon (1994) reported that at the time of the first SCUD missile attack on Israel, during the Persian Gulf War, over 200 civilians reported to the emergency room having injected themselves with atropine thinking they had been exposed to chemical gas (when in fact they had not been exposed). In fact, more civilian Israelis died of fear reactions than from combat wounds.

26. Orner (1992) has reviewed PTSD in **European War Veterans.** He notes that between 1945 and 1988 approximately 15 to 20 million people were killed worldwide in wars, massacres, and revolutions. PTSD was found to be **universal.** For example, O'Brien and Hughes (1991) reported a PTSD prevalence rate of 22% in veterans of the **Falkland War** 5 years after the conflict.

27. Op den Velde (1993) highlights the varied **developmental course of PTSD** in his study of Dutch resistance fighters. Some had a subacute form of PTSD that gradually became chronic, while others had a delayed form with onset 5 to 35 years after the end of WWII, and yet others with intermittent PTSD with relapses and remissions. For a fascinating account of **how cultural factors can influence the post-recovery** environments of trauma

victims, and in turn, their adjustment see Op den Velde et al. (1994) and Keilson (1992). They describe how the trauma recovery process in Dutch war victims was influenced by the Dutch sociocultural climate after World War II. The strong societal ambivalence, the Calvinistic morals, and other institutional responses, each inhibited the trauma recovery process and retarded the nature of integration. Keilson (1992) describes how the conditions experienced by Dutch war orphans were predictive of their later level of adjustment.

28. **Prisoners of War** (POW's).[1] Much of what we have learned about the long term effects of traumatic events has come from the study of POW's. Some 40 years ago the Institute of Medicine, in collaboration with the VA, began the longitudinal study of POW's from the European and Pacific theaters in WWII, Korean POW's, Vietnam POW's (Page, 1992; Page & Englab, 1994). Similar studies have been conducted with POW 's in many countries throughout the world (see Engdehl, 1994 for a review). In the U.S. there are nearly 68,000 POW's alive. Compared to matched control groups, the WWII POW's evidence a four to five fold excess of psychiatric hospitalization, with the Pacific theater POW's who received harsher treatment evidencing more physical and psychiatric disabilities. Even at the 20 and 40 year followup, POW's had a significantly higher symptomatology (e.g., 3 to 5 times higher incidence of depression). The initial post captivity anxiety symptoms tended to decrease over time and depressive symptoms increased. Depressive symptoms were more severe among POW's who had been treated more harshly. Recurrent distressing dreams are also evident at the followup periods. The PTSD lifetime rates may be as high as 70%, with current rates of PTSD of 20% to 40%. Not only is there sleep disturbance and recurrent distressing dreams, but the POW's experienced anxiety, somatic complaints, persistent flashbacks and extreme reactions to reminders of POW experience.[2] Some physical and psychiatric symptomatology may be due to physical maltreatment while in captivity. POW's who **lost 35% of their body weight** during captivity had the poorest recovery (Eberly and Engdahl, 1991). The need to carefully assess POW's for PTSD is underscored by Schnurr (1994) who reported that in a study of geriatric patients in a VA 1/4 had current PTSD that had been missed during previous evaluations.

The data on POW's clearly indicates that **PTSD can be a chronic lifetime disorder.** For example, Goldstein et al (1987) reported that 29% of the men who had been POW's in Japan during WWII met PTSD criteria 40 years after release. **But this is only part of the story. The vast majority of former POWs successfully secured employment, married and raised families.** As Page and Engdahl (1994) observe, "Despite their persisting anxiety and depressive symptoms, a remarkable number of POW's **have adjusted well.** Indeed, many POW's used their ordeal as an organizer to move toward greater psychological health" (p. 5). A similar positive picture is evident from the 221 career military aviation officers captured and tortured by the North Vietnamese. Despite everything, they maintained their morale and are a "relatively healthy group, physically and psychologically" (Engdahl, 1994, p. 6). The age and education level at the time of captivity, the coping style during captivity (attempt to maintain some sense of control and an active coping style, attributional style following captivity (not attributing survival to luck), and the level of social supports following captivity, were found to be related to the level of adjustment (Engdahl, 1994).

29. **Children and War.** While the focus of this **Handbook** is on adults with PTSD, and on adult reactions to war, it is worth noting the significant impact of war on children (see Garbarino et al., 1991; and Rosenblatt, 1983). As we will consider in Section VII on post-

---

[1] See the March 1994 issue of Psychology and Aging (Vol. 9) for a set of papers on the military experience in adult development and aging.

[2] See VA videotape Priority POW which follows a Korean war POW as described by Lehmann (1994).

disaster interventions, children can also manifest PTSD symptoms. Interestingly, the literature also indicates that children can become "acclimated" to chronic <u>low</u> to <u>moderate</u> intensity levels of prolonged violent conflicts (see Jensen and Shaw, 1993, for a review of this literature. Also see the <u>Journal Child Abuse and Neglect</u> 1993, volume 17, which is a special edition on children and war.) However, when exposed to intense forms of war and military occupation, children can experience high levels of PTSD. For example, Nader et al. (1993) found that 70% of the children sampled in Kuwait following the Gulf War reported moderate to severe post-traumatic stress reactions. This is of the same magnitude as children who 1-1/2 years after the Armenian earthquake experienced PTSD. Interestingly, secondary re-exposure in the form of graphic television scenes influenced the severity of the reaction in the Kuwaiti children. Shaw and Harris (1994) provide a moving portrayal of child victims of terrorism in Mozambique.

30. <u>The **treatment literature** on **Vietnam veterans**</u> reflect great diversity of approaches. These interventions include acute inpatient care, short-term and long-term[1] rehabilitation, treatment programs that focus on the comorbidity of PTSD and alcohol abuse, outreach programs, self-help rap groups, individual, group and family treatment, and community-based VET centers. A number of investigators have attempted to identify the commonalities that cut across these diverse interventions (e.g., Bradshaw et al., 1993; Motta, 1993). Some of the common features include the following.[2]

   a) creation of a "place of safety" and "trust" where veterans can find and "integrate" acceptance of their sense of self and their behavior at the time of war. Establishment of a therapeutic alliance.

   b) provide an arena for veterans to "tell their stories" and confront the trauma; accept its impact for the rest of their lives and integrate their experience. Include in the telling of their "stories" the positive qualities, even those occurring during severe combat reactions.[3] Intermingled in their "stories" of death, atrocities, dread and disaster are likely to be reports of the "good times" with one's buddies, the camaraderie and feelings of prowess. Encourage veterans to indicate what they each did to "survive" and what they took away from their war experience. Highlight that their "stories" did <u>not</u> end with their return from combat; obtain the "stories" of the postcombat experiences. Discuss the impact of the rapid shift from "foxhole to front porch transition". Also, over the course of treatment obtain the "story" of their precombat experiences (note any early traumatic "victimization" experiences and ask participants what impact, if any, do they feel these earlier traumatic experiences may have played).

   c) educate veterans about PTSD -- reframe current symptoms in a more positive light. (*See Section VI on educating clients about PTSD*). Also discuss the potential chronic nature of PTSD, how to "self-monitor" for onset indicators or triggers.

   d) help the veterans mourn the loss of comrades and the loss of innocence -- some "reexposure" in a graded dose fashion may take place (*See Section VI on reexposure treatments*).

---

[1] *Inpatient programs for Vietnam veterans are described in Section V.*

[2] It is <u>not</u> being suggested that these treatment elements should be implemented in the order in which they are being enumerated.

[3] In the Assessment Section III we will consider self-report measures by Aldwich et al. (1994) and Elder & Clipp (1989) that can be used to assess possible "positive", as well as "negative", features of war experiences.

e) help veterans develop ways to control their behavior (e.g., anger control), and alter avoidance behaviors that may take the form of substance abuse and social isolation. *(See Section VI on treatment of anger control.)*

f) address issues of guilt and shame that many veterans may experience. *(See Section VI on cognitive restructuring methods to address these emotional experiences).*

g) facilitate resolution and foster integration of painful memories so veterans can come to see themselves as moving from "passive victim" to "active survivor". Integrate "wartime" and "peacetime" selves. As Williams-Keeler and Jones, (1993) observe, help veterans "learn to care about day to day events and let go of "adrenaline rush" of inappropriate behavior. Settle for a calmer existence." See Johnson et al 1994 for a discussion of what they call **"second generation"** training programs for Vietnam veterans. These **"second generation"** programs highlight focusing on "here and now" problem-solving. But the focus on "here and now" should not result in the therapist "colluding" with the veteran in "isolating" his/her war experience. Rather than "bury" his/her war experience, there is a need to assist veterans in examining the meaning of this experience for themselves. There is a need to integrate the war experience into their narrative. (See Maxwell and Sturm, 1994 for a similar discussion.)

h) redirect energies toward constructive behavior and goals -- include problem-solving skills training as discussed in Section VI discussion of anger control.

i) assess impact on the veteran's family members and involve them in treatment.

j) address issues of comorbidity , (e.g., PTSD and substance abuse) concurrently (Kofoed et al., 1993). *(See Section VI on treatment of alcohol abuse and borderline personality.)*

k) address issues of treatment noncompliance (see Burnstein, 1986)

31. Scurfield et al. (1984) in analyzing some 81 sessions with post-Vietnam rap/therapy groups noted that the groups discussed issues of anger, impulse control, Vietnam, guilt, depression and primary relationships. The therapy interventions included ventilation, identification, interpretation and peer support.

32. **"Group treatment is now seen as the treatment of choice** by many and is supplemented by one-on-one and family counseling as needed" (VA report, 199, p. 34). *We will discuss the potential advantages of group treatment in Section V.*

33. The single most important cause for failure in treatment programs was substance abuse (Boudewyns et al., 1991).

WHAT SHOULD YOU TAKE AWAY FROM THIS EPIDEMIOLOGICAL DATA ON WAR EXPERIENCE?

The clinician should appreciate:

(1) that there is clear evidence that PTSD is a long lasting disorder in many individuals. Up to $1/2$ who develop the disorder may continue to have it decades later without treatment (Green, 1994);

(2) "If the personal and interpersonal sequelae of acute traumatization are not treated preventively, both retraumatization and maladjusted coping patterns and lifestyles are likely to cause and/or exacerbate chronic PTSD" (Ford et al., 1993, p. 4).

(3) the need to assess over a prolonged period of time in multiple areas and the need to involve family members in both assessment and treatment; the need to assess for marital distress and other social adjustment indices;

(4) the need to assess for combat experience that are associated with an increased risk for mental health problems including: length and intensity of combat duty, perception of threat to life, witness or participate in abusive violence (e.g., atrocities), witness deaths and "grotesque" stimuli, being wounded, physically deprived (POW), perceived responsibility for injury and death of others, survivor guilt, perceive loss of control and meaning;

(5) the need to assess for and treat comorbidity (anxiety, depression, somatic complaints, and abuse of substances);

(6) the need to assess for developmental traumagenic events like physical and sexual abuse, harsh upbringing, and not delimit treatment exclusively to the combat trauma;

(7) the need to assess for possible salutory or "positive" effects that may follow from combat exposure.

(8) the value of employing group interventions;

(9) the need to provide outreach services and educational programs to engage reluctant populations of veterans and their families to avail themselves of treatment.

(10) the need to use case management skills-oriented interventions with veterans who have chronic PTSD.

(11) finally, the need to be careful in formulating a differential diagnosis. PTSD can be masked or confused with other diagnoses.

RAPE VICTIMS

(See Atkeson et al., 1982; Browne, 1993; Burge, 1988; Burnam et al., 1988; Burgess & Holmstrom, 1974; Calhoun & Resick, 1993; Goodman et al., 1993; Kilpatrick et al., 1985, 1992; Koss, 1993; Koss & Harvey, 1991; Lebowitz & Roth, 1994; Muran & DiGiuseppe, 1994; Roth & Lebowitz, 1988; Rothbaum et al., 1992; Steketee & Foa, 1987; and the Special Issue on Rape in the Journal of Interpersonal Violence, June 1993. Also see the biographical account of a rape victim by Scherer, 1992.)

A. **Prevalence and Incidence**[1]

1. Prevalence of rape estimates range from 5% to 22% of adult women (Foa et al., 1993). "Between 1981 and 1991 the rate of rape in the US increased 4 times as much as the overall crime rate. American women are 6 times more likely to be raped than European women (20x more likely than in Portugal, 15x Japan, 23x Italy, 46x Greece)." For instance reported rapes in US were 35.7 per 100,000 vs. 5.4 per 100,000 in Europe (Hanson et al., in press). Some 40% to 80% of college women report being assaulted by dates or friends (Matsakis, 1992). (See Koss, 1993 for a discussion of the definitional and methodological problems in measuring rape.)

2. In the US, 12.1 million adult women have been forcibly raped during their lifetime. Of these, 39% had been raped more than once. 1 in 4 females experience rape sometime in their lifetime. Every 6 minutes a women is raped in the US.

3. Approximately 680,000 adult women have been forcibly raped during a one year period in the U.S. 57% of women in a community sample who had been raped developed PTSD at some point in their lives. The incidence of rape and other traumatic events are even higher among the homeless (North et al., 1994). There is a higher incidence of rape in urban than rural areas (Winfeld et al, 1990).

4. **1.3 million** adult American women are currently estimated to have **rape-related PTSD** and approximately 211,000 will develop it each year (Calhoun & Resick, 1993).

5. **Rape victims may constitute the largest single group of PTSD sufferers** (Foa et al., 1993). While traumatic events generally led to PTSD in less than 25% of the time, **80% of rape victims** evidence PTSD symptomatoloy (Breslau et al., 1991). 31% of all rape victims develop rape-related PTSD sometimes in their lifetimes (Harvey & Herman, 1992). The degree of violence experienced during rape affected the severity of the PTSD symptoms (Sales et al., 1984). Victims who had developed PTSD **3 months** following the rape were significantly more likely to have had a prior history of sexual, aggravated assault (Yehuda et al., 1993).

6. The majority of rape victims are raped by family members and acquaintances (29% by acquaintance, 22% by a stranger, 16% by another relative, 11% by a father/stepfather, 10% by a boyfriend/exboyfriend, 9% by a husband/exhusband, and 3% unsure/refused to answer. Half of all rape of women over the age of 30 are partner rapes). (Data from FBI crime reports, as reported by Hartman and Jackson, 1994.) Little is known about men who have been victimized by sexual assault.

---

[1] See coding manual for collecting and maintaining descriptive statistics on rape. It is available from Service for Sexual Assault Victims, 6450 Young St., Halifax, Nova Scotia, Canada, B3L 2A2.

7. The majority of rapes happen in childhood and the perpertrators are know to the victims. 33% are raped between the ages 11 and 17, 38% at the age 18 and over, 29% 11 and younger. 62% of all forcible rape cases occurred when the victim was under 18 years of age (Hanson et al., in press). Approximately a half million high school girls will be raped before they graduate. 1 in 12 college women will be a victim of rape or attempted rape each year. Only 8% of college students report such rape incidents (Hartman and Jackson, 1994).

8. Only 1% of rapes are ultimately resolved by arrest or conviction of the offender. The average time served in State prisons for a rape conviction is 29 months.

B. Impact

1. Symptoms experienced by rape victims[1] -- sleep disturbance, nightmares, flashbacks, anxiety, fear and phobic avoidance of reminders and thoughts of the assault, exaggerated startle responses, hypervigilance, impaired leisure activities, sense of detachment, blunted affect, impaired memory and concentration difficulties, excessive feelings of guilt, shame, hostility, interpersonal and sexual difficulties, physical illness and posttraumatic stress. Harvey and Herman (1992) report that rape is a risk factor for depression. Rape victims are 4 times more likely than nonvictims to contemplate suicide and 13 times more likely to have made a suicide attempt.

2. Critical crime risk factors include life threat and injury (aggravated assault), a history of multiple traumatic events (e.g., an additive effect of prior crime history) and repeated exposure. For instance, the impact of rape is influenced by whether the rape victim had been previously raped or been incestuously abused as children. It is critical to **assess for prior victimization.** (See Ellis, 1983; Koss, 1993, Rothbaum et al., 1992).

3. **A Changing Symptom Profile**

   a) the immediate acute phase reaction (several hours to several weeks) is marked by shock, disbelief, somatic reactions. The long-term reactions may be evident in terms of persistent fears of rape-related stimuli, nightmares, diffuse anxiety, difficulty concentrating.

   b) distress peaks in severity by approximately 3 weeks post assault, continues at a high level for the next month, and then begins to improve by 2 to 3 months post assault. After 3 months problems may persist in terms of fear, anxiety, depression, self-esteem problems and sexual dysfunction. These effects may persist for up to 18 months or longer (Koss, 1993).

   c) After the first year, 80% of rape victims report restriction of daily life. 80% of rape survivors still complained of intrusive fears at the one year mark. Trauma specific fears, sexual problems and restrictions of daily life activities are common at 1-2 years after the assault.

   d) 2-3 year -- 50% report restriction; 4-6 years -- 75% recover and 25% felt they had not recovered (Burgess & Homstrom, 1979). Only 1/3 report that it took less than 1 year to recover.

---

[1] Yehuda and McFarlane (1994) report a study of the emergency room response of women who had been raped. Women with a prior history of rape and assault had lower cortisol levels in response to the trauma of rape within hours of the rape than did women without a propr assault history who showed a normative cortisol level. The former group were more likely to develop PTSD over a 3 month period.

e) PTSD symptoms: 99%--after 1 week; 94%--2 weeks; 65%--1 month; 53%--2 months; 47%--3 months; 47%--9 months; 16%--11 to 17 years later.[1] Dahl (1993) found that the severity of PTSD syndrome during the first weeks and months after the traumatic event did <u>not</u> predict PTSD 1 year after the exposure. She found that several factors such as "the use of a weapon by the rapist, a history of previous psychological instability in the victim, and blaming of the victim from her close social network defined a risk of 90% of developing PTSD within the first year after the rape" (Weisaeth, 1994). We will consider these factors and others below.

f) **3 month adjustment is predictive of future adjustment.** Rothbaum et al. (1992) report that women who did <u>not</u> meet criteria for PTSD 3 months post assault show steady improvement over time. Thus, among rape victims a 3 month time frame should be kept in mind when evaluating stress levels.

g) PTSD symptoms (with the exception of fear and anxiety) decline within 3 months.

h) approximately 25% of women continue to experience negative effects even several years beyond the rape (e.g., depression, alcohol abuse and dependence, drug use, generalized anxiety, obsessive compulsive disorder , PTSD symptoms, difficulties with intimacy, sex, and trust). Many rape victims remain fearful of stigma, blame and public disclosure years after the assault.

i) Frank & Stewart (1983) reported that the absence of physical beating during rape, absence of previous suicidal thoughts and attempts, and the victim's perception that the assailant was under the influence of drugs or alcohol was associated with <u>lower</u> depression after treatment.

j) Not all rape victims require treatment since **1/2 recover spontaneously.** (Rothbaum et al., 1992).

4. As general anxiety symptoms decrease in rape victims, psychosomatic symptoms increase. Women who have been raped report more symptoms of illness and more negative health behaviors including smoking and alcohol use, failure to use seat belts, twice as many visits to a physician than non-victimized women. Victims are more likely to have chronic pelvic pain, GI disorders, headaches, pain, and premenstrual symptoms. High levels of fear and phobic avoidance may persist well past the resolution of initial depressive symptoms. Rape victims rate their level of sexual satisfaction significantly lower than controls. 46% of women who had experienced one rape and 80% of women who had experienced two rapes met criteria for major depressive disorder at some time in their lives. Rape victims also have a higher incidence of addictive behaviors (e.g., alcohol and hard drugs) (Falsetti & Resnick, 1994).

5. Half of the rape victims meet criteria of PTSD 3 months after the incident and the incidence does not change after 3 months. If the individual experiences PTSD 6-8 months after the incident it is likely to become chronic and not subside naturally (without intervention). The loss of a sense of trust and control in relationships may persist long after the initial symptoms of PTSD subside.

---

[1] By comparison, Rothbaum et al. (1992) reported followup of non sexual criminal assault (including robbery), finding 65% exhibiting PTSD at 1 week, 37% at 1 month, 25% at 2 months, and 12% at 6 months, and **0% at 9 months.**

6. **Rape is more likely to induce PTSD than other serious crimes** because of its unpredictable, vulnerable and personally violating features. For example, there is a small percentage of homicide attempt victims who develop PTSD. Rape victims are more symptomatic and have longer recovery times than any other form of victims.

7. It is also important to keep in mind that in many instances as a weapon of war, rape constitutes a political act that is designed to "despoil" the women and culture (e.g., in Kuwait, Bosnia, etc.). There is often a societal stigma attached to those who have been raped that results in "secondary victimization".

C. Factors that Affect Impact

1. The use of physical force, brutality, the display of a weapon, and injury to the rape victim are associated with an increased risk of PTSD. **The fear of death (life threat) and injury are predictors of PTSD symptoms** -- about twice as high as when neither are present (Resnick et al., 1993).

2. Resick and Schnicke (1992) observe that when a rape experience conflicts with prior beliefs, then the victim is less able to reconcile this victimizing event, thus recovery is more difficult. For example, women who believe themselves to be "uniquely invulnerable to crime" have more difficulty recovering than women who believe they were vulnerable like other women. Women who were raped in situations that they had believed to be "safe" were more likely to experience more severe acute and chronic reactions than women who suspected their situations were dangerous. Lebowitz and Roth (1994) describe how cultural beliefs or constructions about women and sexuality influence how women survivors of rape make sense of their traumatic experience.

3. Those assaulted at a younger age are more distressed than those who were raped in adulthood. 61% of rapes occur before age 18, translating into a five fold higher rape risk for children (Finkelhor & Dziuba-Leatherman, 1994). 75% of rapes occur between the ages of 13 and 26 (Herman, 1992). When cultural shame accompanies the rape, victims have more difficulty adjusting.

4. Women victimized in childhood are 2.4 times more likely than non-victims to be assaulted as adults. Prior victimization is associated with more depression and longer recovery.

5. The majority of rapes are committed by someone known to the victim. Acquaintance rapes can be just as devastating as stranger rapes. Victims who know their offenders are much less likely to report rape to police or seek victim assistance services. Rape victims are less likely than other crime victims to disclose victimization.

6. Unsupportive behavior by significant others predicts poorer social adjustment and proceeding with prosecution prolongs the length of recovery.

7. History of prior psychiatric disturbance and/or substance abuse history predicts poorer adjustment. Women with prior rape experience have more severe reactions to subsequent rape than first time rape victims (Dutton, 1992).

8. For the 1/2 victims who do not recover spontaneously, effective **brief** treatments have been developed (e.g., Resick et al., 1988; Veronen & Kilpatrick, 1983, Foa et al., 1991). (*We will consider these treatment approaches in Section VI.*)

D. Treatment Options

1. Muran and DiGiuseppe (1993) highlight the importance of establishing a therapeutic alliance with the client. The therapist needs to convey sensitivity, understanding, support, validating the client's "story", and conveying a positive outlook toward recovery. The therapist should allow the client control in telling his/her "story". The therapist should ask the client how he/she feels about proceeding with his/her "story". Muran and DiGiuseppe (1994, p.165) convey to clients:

   "Some women who have gone through similar experiences find they are too upset to talk about what happened to them. Does that sound like you?" If affirmative, the therapist continues: "Some women feel too much shame. They believe others will think badly of them for what happened. Others believe that it is just too hard to discuss these things. After all, the trauma was painful enough. Reliving it will just be more painful. Have you had such thoughts?" The therapist can then explore these reactions that may act as a barrier to self-disclosure.

2. Falsetti and Resnick (1994) in discussing ways to help victims of violent crime propose addressing several areas: "medical attention, legal matters and police contacts, notification of family and friends, current practical concerns, clarification of factual information, emotional responses and psychiatric consultation" (p.19). But, few rape victims seek formal mental health treatment in the immediate aftermath of rape, and usually they only seek help if persistent symptoms do not diminish with time, or if there is an impending trial, or if they have difficulty with sexual and interpersonal relationships. (See videotape "If I can survive this" produced in 1985 by the Boston Area Rape Crises Center for a discussion of these issues).

3. Kilpatrick and Calhoun (1981) and Kilpatrick and Veronen (1983) also observe that "rape crisis intervention is usually not enough" to meet the clinical needs of rape victims. They caution, however, that rape victims may not profit from formal treatment immediately following the trauma until their initial condition stabilizes.

4. Many diverse **treatment approaches** have been employed including short-term dynamic group therapy, desensitization, prolonged (direct therapy) exposure, cognitive therapy, cognitive processing therapy, treatment of sexual dysfunction, each of which may be conducted on an individual, couples or a group basis. Foa et al., (1993) observe that sometimes a composite form of treatment is used as in the case of stress inoculation training. In most instances, treatment outcome research with rape victims have focused on symptom relief following brief treatment introduced relatively early post-rape (Harvey & Herman, 1992). *(We will consider the use of direct exposure therapy and stress inoculation training in Section VI.)*

   Koss (1993) notes that common to the various treatments of rape victims are the following features:

   a) therapist provides a supportive non-stigmatizing, non-judgmental relationship that helps rape victims validate their feelings, share grief, and confirm their experiences. Highlight that the rape does not undo all the positive aspects of one's life;

   b) therapy helps to counteract the victim's blame and help the victims view rape as a criminal act; question popular myths such as "rape is primarily about sex", "most rapists are strangers", etc.[1] Address beliefs that go along with shame and guilt. Can provide written handouts;

   c) therapist provides information about trauma reactions, as well as expectation that symptoms will improve;

   d) treatment helps the clients to overcome behavioral and cognitive avoidance and isolation, addressing distorted perceptions of inadequacy, incompetence and helplessness;

   e) treatment promotes self-esteem and provides opportunities for safe attachment and ways to empower the rape victims.

5. Consistent with the narrative reconstructive perspective to be offered in Section II, Roth and Newman (1991) propose that the best way for victims to cope with rape is to gradually dose themselves by handling only manageable amounts of emotional material, and thus, coming to an understanding of its meaning. Such "dosing" allows victims to assimilate such traumatic events. Lebowitz and Roth (1994) propose that as part of the recovery process survivors should be given the opportunity, both within and outside of therapy, to consider the sociocultural context of how women are treated. Such actions can help legitimatize anger and help de-shame and de-pathologize the victim's experience. The critical role that family and friends can play in recovery should be examined. Remind the client that rape can be a very isolating experience, but the client is not alone. It is now, more than ever, that the client needs support from family and friends.

6. Intervention needs to be multifaceted by having the mental health worker also work with medical, legal, and judicial agencies so the likelihood of "secondary victimization" is reduced. There is a need to provide clients with factual information concerning the procedures necessary in reporting a sexual assault, as well as possible outcomes. It has also been reported that rape victims have been supported by helping them to organize self-help support groups (Wali, 1992). Follow-up treatment should be built into the intervention program.

7. It is worth highlighting Burt and Katz's (1987) finding that 50% of rape victims reported that they had changed in a **positive direction**, becoming less passive, more self-directed and improved their self-concept since the rape incident. Silver et al. (1983) reported that 20% of their raped victims perceived positive outcomes of such traumatic events.

8. There is a need to be culturally sensitive in providing treatment. For instance, Vesti and Kastrup (1994) note that in some societies (e.g., Middle Eastern), females are often reluctant to talk about such an ordeal. "In such cases, it may be better to allow the emotions relating to sexual abuse to surface either symbolically in the form of art therapy or through massage or physiotherapy" (Vesti & Kastrup, 1994, p.3).

9. The need not to prejudge the appropriateness of a given coping strategy is underscored by Fine (1985) who provided a case study of a woman who was raped. While her coping efforts may have been evaluated as passive, helpless and dependent (a form of "learned helplessness"), from her perspective the lack of taking action was highly adaptive. It is

---

[1] Burt (1980) enumerates other myths concerning rape including "Women want to be raped", "Women falsely accuse men of rape", "Women provoke rape by their physical appearance and dress", "Women secretly enjoy being raped", "Women ask for it by being in certain places, by drinking, and the like." See Lonsway and Fitzgerald (1994) for a critique of measures of rape myths.

critical for the therapist to explore with the client her rationale and perspective in adapting to rape and its aftermath.

10.   For a discussion of the alternative legal ways to conceptualize rape see Renner and Yurchesyn (1994). They examine whether rape should be viewed as a form of sexual assault or sexual robbery.

WHAT SHOULD YOU TAKE AWAY FROM THIS EPIDEMIOLOGICAL DATA ON RAPE?

1.   The event of completed rape poses a **greater risk** for the development of PTSD than other crime events. Of those raped, the presence of **life threat** and **physical injury** put one at specific risk (almost 80% develop PTSD). (Resnick et al., 1993)

2.   Many rape victims fail to disclose their trauma history without being specifically asked. Thus, when assessing for sexual assault (and other forms of victimization) there is a need to use well defined behaviorally specific screening questions and not global terms. Asking clients if they have been "raped" elicits much lower prevalence rates than if behaviorally specific prescriptive questions are asked. *(How this can be conducted is described in Section III.)* (Also see Jacobson & Richardson, 1987)

3.   Assess for multiple developmental and concurrent victimizations.

4.   Use repeated assessments and track rape victims over time, noting the changing symptom profile. A critical juncture point is 3 months post-rape incident.

5.   Assess for comorbidity (e.g., depression, suicidal ideation, anxiety, addictive behaviors).

6.   Use multifaceted interventions, involving significant others where feasible. Be proactive in helping prevent "secondary victimization". Work with agencies that interact with rape victims and other related agencies. For example, Datillio and Freeman (1994) report that there are more than 900 victim assistance rape crisis and child sexual abuse intervention programs, as well as 1250 battered women shelters and hotlines in the U.S. This does not include the thousands of crisis services available through community hospital emergency rooms.

7.   Assess for both negative and possible positive changes that follow from such traumatic events.

VICTIMS OF DOMESTIC VIOLENCE (Spouse Abuse)
(See Dutton, 1992, Hamberger & Holtzworth-Munroe, 1994; Hansen & Harway, 1993; McKay, 1994, and Walker, 1979, 1984 and 1991)

I was invited to consult for the U.S. military on developing a cognitive-behavioral assessment and intervention program for the victims and perpertrators of spouse abuse. While space does not permit me to describe this extensive program, it underscored for me how devastating domestic violence can be. The following brief account indicates the toll spouse abuse can take on victims:

1. Another cause of PTSD is **domestic violence.** Domestic violence has been described as occurring in up to **16% of all marriages every year** and in **50% to 60% of all marriages** over their course. It is estimated that 1.8 million wives in the U.S. are severely assaulted each year (McKay, 1994). More than 1 million of these women seek medical assistance for injuries caused by violence at the hands of a male partner. Partner violence often begins early in a relationship. Moreover, if a partner is violent at one point in the relationship, there is a 46% to 72% probability that he/she will be violent subsequently. The risk of violence tends to escalate in frequency and severity over time (O'Leary et al., 1989).

2. 1 in 5 women who visit a hospital emergency department seek treatment for injuries sustained at the hand of her male intimate. 52% of women murdered in US were victims of partner homicide.

3. **21% to 34% of all women will be physically assaulted by an intimate male during adulthood.** High rates of spouse alcohol consumption is associated with marital violence. When violence occurs it tends to be repeated and to be accompanied with verbal abuse, psychological degradation, denial of social supports and finances, and exposure to male-dominated interactions. Threats of serious harm, death or threats against others can prove very intimidating. Fear associated with inconsistent and unpredictable outbursts, capricious enforcement of petty rules are additional forms of victimization. As Herman (1992) observes, the goal of the perpertrator is not only to instill fear, but also to destroy the victim's sense of autonomy. The victim lives in a "state of siege", with few perceived alternatives.

4. 154 of every 1000 pregnant women were assaulted by partners during the first 4 months of pregnancy and 170 per 1000 were assaulted during 5 and 9 months.

5. Such violence is not limited to heterosexual couples. Physical aggression occurs in up to 40% of lesbian relationships (Browne, 1993).

6. 32% to 59% of women who have been battered have also been victims of sexual abuse (Dutton et al. 1994).

7. Spouse abuse and child abuse are clearly linked within families. McKay (1994) reports that child abuse is **15 times** more likely to occur in families where domestic violence is present. 45% to 70% of battered women in shelters report the presence of some form of child abuse. 2/3 of abused children are being parented by battered women. Of the abused children, they are three times more likely to have been abused by their fathers. The severity of the wife

beating is predictive of the severity of the child abuse. DePanfilis & Brooks, (1989) and McKay (1994) describe specific indicators that can be used of mothers and children having been a victim of abuse.[1]

8. Survivors of physical assault by male partners evidence high levels of depression, suicidal ideation and suicidal attempts, abuse substances, and experience PTSD symptoms (emotional numbing, chronic anxiety, extreme passivity, helplessness, intrusive memories or flashbacks, intense startle response, disturbed sleeping and eating patterns, anticipatory terror, low self-esteem, as well as somatic complaints). They also experience an overwhelming sense of danger, become dependent and suggestible and find it difficult to make decisions or carry out long-range planning. These symptoms are most evident when there are cumulative prolonged traumas such as physical and sexual aggression. This leads to relationship disturbance in terms of trust and intimacy in nonabusive relationships.

9. It is important, however, not to let this clinical picture color the clinician's impression (nor the victims view of herself) as being "passive" and "helpless". As Tutty et al., (1993) observe, there is a need to tap in the clinical interview what the "victim" of domestic violence has done to survive, to reduce the violence for herself and her children. Review with the client the variety of strategies she has used to survive.

10. **Treatment** of PTSD sufferers of domestic violence should address the tendency of women to internalize the derogatory attributions (self-blame)[2] and justifications of the violence against them. From a narrative perspective the women must begin to construct their own stories and not "live" the stories of others who have victimized them (Dutton, 1992). Re-empowerment and control are critical issues (e.g, see Courtois & Sprei, 1988). In the same mode, Walker (1991) suggests that "one particularly effective way to help battered women perceive control is for the therapist to explain why certain things are done or why certain questions are being asked" (p. 26). Stark and Filcraft (1988) describe the unique features of providing treatment for battered women (viz., need for ongoing protection, economic insecurity, erosion of self-esteem). See Dutton (1992) for a comprehensive and sensitive description of assessment and treatment issues with battered victims. She describes the important role of therapist's nonjudgmental acceptance, the need for the therapist to provide immediate support and advocate for safety, the willingness to help the client experience recounting of the trauma and its sequelae, educate the client about violence and abuse, help transform trauma, and use adjunctive interventions for comorbidity. She emphasizes three primary treatment goals: (a) safety first,[3] (b) empowerment through choice making, and (c) healing the psychological trauma by achieving meaning out of the victimization and rebuilding a life. Finally, Dutton highlights the value of helping battered women **develop a life-long plan for healing and self-nurturance.** The victims of domestic violence are encouraged to find some meaningful and authentic activity, a "mission" (e.g., join a social support group, volunteer in battering program, engage in political activity, etc.) that helps them to transform the trauma. The call for a "life-long healing activity" fits well with the **constructive narrative perspective** that will be discussed in Section II. Finally, Dutton

---

[1] Among suggested indicators of mothers being abused include a) mother's inconsistent or evasive explanations of injuries, accidents; b) history of accidents, hospital visits; c) delay in seeking medical help; d) symptom pattern of mother -- depressed, suicidal, physical and behavioral complaints; e) anxiety and fear in presence of partner. Also taken as evidence of possible abuse is the child being overprotective or afraid to leave the mother, child being abusive to mother. For a more complete description obtain Curriculum Guide to Domestic Violence: Its Relationship to Child Abuse and Maltreatment: Developed in 1987 by Victim Services Agency, 2 Lafayette St., New York, New York 10007.

[2] Dutton (1992) observes that while self-blame may be viewed as serving an adaptive function for other victim groups (e.g., rape victims; thus conveying a sense of control). This does not apply in domestic violence.

[3] See Hart and Stuehling (1992) for a description of a personal safety plan book.

(1992) provides a **cautionary note** on the use of **reexperiencing procedures** such as flooding with victims of domestic violence. The use of such exposure procedures have the potential of retraumatizing the battered women. Such therapeutic reexposure will likely occur within the context of the victim/survivor retelling her story.

11. A major feature of treatment must address the issue of **safety** since women are at most risk when they are in the midst of trying to extricate themselves from a violent relationship (Walker, 1991). Women should engage in safety planning and know of community resources. See Walker's (1994) recent book on survivor therapy with abused women for a more detailed account.

12. Rosen and Stith (1993) have described a comprehensive and thoughtful intervention program for treating women in violent dating relationships. They note that 4 out of 10 women report experiencing violence at some point in their dating careers. Between 41% and 53% of victims in violent dating relationships maintain those relationships, despite experiencing physical abuse. As one client noted, she would "blame herself" and constantly feel like she was "walking on eggshells, trying to fix it." Their program outlines a series of strategies on

    (1) how to help the client keep herself safe,
    (2) how to help her gain perspective, and
    (3) how to empower the client in order to develop appropriate boundaries.

    They describe how the therapist needs to refuse to minimize the violence and how the therapist can help combat the client's "tunnel vision" by using questioning artfully. The need for preventative interventions is underscored by the longitudinal research by O'Leary and his colleagues (1989) who have traced the consistency and escalation of dating verbal and physical violence in being predictive of post-marriage spouse abuse. The need for preventive intervention is self-evident.

13. Tutty et al (1993, p. 329) highlight that the treatment of women who have been battered should include **support groups** that last 10 - 12 weeks[1] , 2 to 3 hours each, and that cover:

    a) the members' current and future safety;
    b) recognition of violence for what it is, without denial or minimization;
    c) reduction of self-blame and learned helplessness, and enhancement of self-esteem;
    d) an understanding of why battering occurs, including an exploration of sexism and the woman's own belief about male-female roles;
    e) opportunities for the ventilation of anger around being victimized and to express mourning and loss should the relationship end;
    f) developing supportive networks which reduce isolation.

14. Cameron (1989) and Sullivan et al. (1992) have proposed a community-based intervention program of providing each woman who leaves the shelter **with an advocate**. The advocates were trained in listening skills, facts about spouse abuse, and strategies for generating, mobilizing and assessing community resources. As we will consider in the treatment of a variety of target groups (e.g., clients with addictive behaviors, borderline personality), a case manager advocacy intervention is warranted and it facilitates both generalization and maintenance of treatment effects. Jordan and Walker (1994) provide a comprehensive set of guidelines for handling domestic violence cases in community mental health centers. They underscore the need for multi-agency involvement and the need for multi-agency comprehensive services for victims and victims' children, as well as treatment

---

[1] Obviously, in many instances more long-term intervention will be required as in the case of a shelter program.

for perpertrators. Also see <u>Intervening with assaulted women</u>, edited by B. Pressman et al. (Erlbaum, 1989), and <u>Treating men who batter</u>, edited by Caesar & Hamberger (Springer, 1989) for descriptions of intervention programs.

WHAT SHOULD YOU TAKE AWAY FROM THE EPIDEMIOLOGICAL DATA ON VICTIMS OF DOMESTIC VIOLENCE?

1. In 1989 the Worldwatch Institute declared that the **most common crime** worldwide was **violence against women**. This violence takes place not only in the streets and workplace, but also in homes, as documented in the recent book <u>No safe haven</u>[1] written by Koss, Goodman, et al. (1994). They note that **4 million women** experience severe or life-threatening assaults from a male partner each year in the US and **1 in 3** will experience at least **one physical assault** by an **intimate partner** during adulthood. There is a higher rate of partner aggression in cohabitatin couples than in married couples. Minority women and women living in poverty are especially vulnerable to all forms of violence.

2. Given the remarkable high incidence of such victimization, there is a clear need to **conduct systematic assessment** of such assaults. The need to conduct such systematic assessments was highlighted by Saunders et al. (1980) who found in a study of mental health intake procedures, twice the number of clients disclosed abuse in response to a structured interview that included questions about victimization than in response to a standard intake interview. (*We will consider possible assessment measures in Section III.*)

3. The need to assess for other developmental and concurrent victimization experiences. There is a high likelihood of a **link** between domestic violence and ongoing child abuse, and between being a victim of domestic violence and having been a victim of childhood sexual abuse.

4. The need to be sensitive to both the time course and comorbidity of symptomatology.

5. The need to establish a nonjudgmental supportive therapeutic alliance. Avoid blaming the victim.

6. The critical need to address **safety issues** and other practical needs of the victim (e.g., shelter, income, escape plan, self-care) of the victim and her family.

7. The need for multifaceted preventative and treatment interventions. The role of group interventions and advocacy programs.

---

[1] <u>No safe haven</u> can be ordered from the American Psychological Association (202-336-5370) order number 4316421.

VICTIMS OF CHILD SEXUAL ABUSE (CSA)

(See Beitchman et al., 1992; Briere & Runtz, 1993; Burgess et al., 1978; Cole and Putnam 1992; Cameron, 1994; Courtois, 1988; Deblinger & Heflin, 1994; Finkelhor, 1990; Finkelhor & Dziuba-Leatherman, 1994; Goodwin, 1988; Green, 1980; Herman, 1981; Kempe & Kempe, 1984; Kendall-Tackett et al., 1993; Kilpatrick, 1992; Kirschner, Kirschner & Rappaport, 1993; Lundberg-Love 1990; Lynch & Roberts, 1982; Meiselman, 1978; Rowan & Fay, 1993; Rush, 1980; Russell, 1983, 1986; Salter, 1992; Sgroi, 1982; Spaccarelli, 1994; Stuart & Greer, 1984; Wolfe et al., 1989; for comprehensive reviews)[1]

A Cautionary Note

Before we consider the epidemiological statistics for child sexual abuse (CSA) it is worth repeating the caution offered by Carol Tavris (1993) in her critique of the "incest-survivor machine". While she readily acknowledges (and I totally concur) the distressingly high incidence of various forms of abuse, she also offers a warning. She observes that the authors of various "popular books" on victimization tend to cite each other's statistics as supporting evidence, without going back to critique the primary source. To quote Tavris:

"If one of the authors comes up with a concocted statistic - such as more than half of all women are survivors of childhood sexual trauma - the numbers are traded like baseball cards, reprinted in every book and eventually enshrined as facts. Thus, the cycle of misinformation; faulty statistics and unvalidated assertions maintains itself" (1993, p. 17)

In citing the epidemiological findings on CSA (as well as other epidemiological data), I should note that I did <u>not</u> go back to review all of the original studies. This omission should be kept in mind when citing the figures presented in this **Handbook**.

On the other hand, a somewhat different cautionary note is needed concerning **the widespread incidence of child sexual abuse throughout the world**. In most instances in this **Handbook**, I have cited epidemiological data from the US. As a result, the reader may get a false impression that these vicitimzation experiences are delimited to only the US. This is not the case. Finkelhor (1994) recently reported on an **international epidemiology study of child sexual abuse**. After reviewing the data on CSA from 20 countries, he identified a marked degree of comparability rates in CSA, namely,

"7% to 36% for women and 3% to 29% for men. Most studies found females to be abused 1 1/2 to 3 times the rate of men ... **The results clearly confirm sexual abuse to be an international problem.**" (p. 409)

How Widespread is CSA?

1. Definition of CSA -- any sexual experience between a child less than 16 and someone at least 5 years older.

2. a) 150,000-200,000 new cases of CSA are reported in North America per year. In 1988, 16.3 children per 1000 were physically abused or neglected (McKay, 1994). Russell (1983) reported that only 2% of the intrafamilial victims and 6% of extrafamilial victims indicated that they reported abuse to an authority figure.

---

[1] A number of moving and instructive autobiographical accounts of CSA have also been written, for example, Angelou, 1970, Bass & Thornton, 1983, Brady, 1979, Evert, 1987, Friday, 1973, Morris, 1982.

b) Approximately 1 in 4 females (10% to 33%) and 1 in 6 males have experienced sexual abuse before age 18 (16% within the family, 4.5% of girls abused by biological or stepfather; average age 11 for girls, 12 for boys). Girls are more likely to be abused by stepfathers than by biological fathers. Retrospective self-reports indicate that 64% of sexual abuse victimization occurs before age 12. Most boys, unlike girls, are sexually abused outside of the family. Uncle-niece incest is the most common form of familial molestation. Stepfathers abuse daughters at significantly higher rates than do biological fathers. 13% of victims report sibling sexual experiences (Kirschner et al., 1993).

3. Average duration of abuse is 4 years. Girls are 2 to 3 times more likely to be sexually abused. Girls are more likely to experience intrafamilial sexual abuse. Boys and girls are equally likely to experience physical abuse. Preschoolers are disproportionately more likely to be abused and more likely to have their cases come to trial.

4. Russell (1986) reported that 11% of females were abused before age 5, 41% report abuse between ages 10-13, 24% between 14 and 17. 70% of survivors report having been abused during latency age. The average age of abuse is 5.4 (Cameron, 1994).

5. 5% of the sexual abuse of girls and 20% of the sexual abuse of boys involves female perpertrators. Women who engage in such sexual abuse tend to have been victimized themselves, lack resources and suffer alcohol addiction (Kirschner et al., 1993). In fact, alcoholism, sex addiction, history of physical/sexual abuse as children, and opposite sex abuse is the common pattern for both female and male perpertrators. 30% to 50% of male offenders were either sexually molested or had witnessed incest behavior between fathers and sisters (Kirschner et al., 1993). It has been estimated that **upwards of 10 million children live in households with an addicted caregiver** and of this number an estimated **675,000 children per year were suspected of being abused** (Blau et al., 1994).

6. Men and boys convicted of sexual offenses are more likely to have histories of previous sexual victimization (Spaccarelli, 1994). Lisak (1994) indicates that male abuse victims evidence affective reactions of anger, fear, helplessness, loss, guilt and shame; negative self-schemas of guilt and shame; interpersonal difficulties; and an overall profile that is similar to female CSA victims.

What is the immediate impact of CSA?

In considering both the immediate and long-term impact of CSA it is worth beginning with Harvey and Herman's (1992) admonition that **"there is no one symptom profile for incest survivors"**.

1. $^2/_3$ of victimized children evidence symptoms of anxiety, fears, nightmares, sleep disturbance, intrusive thoughts, compulsive repetitions, both internalizing and externalizing behavior problems (crying, irritability, withdrawal, depression, diminished interest in activities, disturbed expressions of anger, aggressive behaviors), sexualized behaviors, poor self-esteem, constriction of affect, regression in behavior, especially before age 7. However, Deblinger and Heflin (1993) provide an important caveat about the impact of CSA. They note that such behavioral difficulties

> "are also exhibited by children who have suffered other childhood traumas and/or family difficulties. In fact, studies comparing sexually abused children to other

psychiatrically disturbed nonabused children **demonstrates few differences"** (p.182).

Nevertheless, child victims of CSA do seem to evidence more unusual and persistent fears in response to reminders of sexual abuse (e.g., bathing, undressing, displays of physical affection). They may also behave inappropriately sexually with peers, or wear multiple layers of underwear.

2.   Abused children often reenact their abuse in play and they often provoke physical attacks and engage in self-destructive behavior, and lose their sense of invulnerability (Goodwin, 1988).

3.   20%-50% of CSA victims evidence no symptoms. They are more likely to have been abused for a shorter period of time without force or penetration by someone who is not a father figure and to have received full support of a well-functioning family (Finkelhor, 1990). Spaccarelli (1994) observes that **"the trauma of abuse often results from the meaning of the act as much as from physical danger"** (p. 341).

4. $1/2$ to $2/3$ of victimized children show recovery during the first 12 to 18 months; 10-24% get worse.

5.   Short-term effects of CSA occurring within 2 years of the abuse have included fear, anger/hostility, increased aggression, defiance, guilt/shame, low self-esteem/poor self-image, depression, physical and somatic complaints, eating and sleep disturbance, sexual behavior disturbances, poor social and academic functioning, running away from home, truancy or dropping out of school, and early marriage. (Beitchman et al., 1992).

6.   CSA victims' symptoms vary with age (see Kendall-Tackett, Williams, Finkelhor, 1993). Rate of re-abuse is 6% to 19%.

7.   For some CSA victims, the effects may peak during adolescence or young adulthood with various "developmental triggers" (Downs, 1993). Traumatic sexualization can increase the salience of sexual issues, resulting in confusion about sexual norms or identity, and account for outcomes such as sexual precocity, compulsive sexuality, and sexual aversion or dysfunction (Spaccarelli, 1994).

What is the long range impact of CSA?

1.   Adult consequences of childhood sexual abuse:

   a)   Sexually victimized children appear to be at a nearly **four fold increased lifetime risk for any psychiatric disorder and at a three fold risk for substance abuse. Approximately 8% of all psychiatric cases can be attributed to CSA** (Finkelhor & Dziuba-Leatherman, 1994).

   b)   Briere & Runtz (1993) have noted that adults who were sexually abused as children evidence **altered emotionality** most common in the form of depression, elevated anxiety as reflected in hypervigilance to threat and danger, preoccupation with issues of control; **disturbed relatedness** as evident in poor social adjustment, fear and distrust of others, difficulty forming and sustaining intimate relationship, difficulty with sexual intimacy; **avoidance and dissociation** due in part to fears of vulnerability and revictimization and a strong desire to disengage from a distressing affect; **dependence** upon and over idolization of those with whom they form close relationships like the therapist. (Note, women with CSA are most vulnerable to be sexually victimized by male psychotherapists, Armsworth, 1989);[1] **tension reducing activities** as evident in substance abuse (a type of chemically induced dissociation), indiscriminate sexual activity, binging or chronic overeating, and self-mutilation; **impaired self-reference** as evident in low self-esteem, self-denigration, ("not feel worthy" of a relationship), self-blame and guilt. Jehu (1989) reports that many women who were sexually abused in childhood have problems with assertion and intimacy as adults, as well as experience sexual problems. These patterns may also show up in dreams where the themes of helplessness, hopelessness and victimization are repetitively replayed.

c) Gelinas (1983) and Kinsza et al. (1988) offered a similar symptomatic profile. They reported that one half of CSA victims experience depression, hypervigilance, nightmares, anxiety, anger, fearfulness, phobias, social isolation, resignation, low self-esteem and shame. They feel guilt and self-blame, manifest alcohol and drug abuse, engage in prostitution, dissociation, somatization, depersonalization, spending sprees, eating disorder,[1] have relationship, intimacy and sexual difficulties and an **increased risk of subsequent victimization**. CSA is also related to adult partner re-victimization. (Gelinas, 1983; Rimsza et al., 1988). The risk of rape, sexual harassment and domestic battering and exploitation in pornography and prostitution is **approximately double** for survivors of CSA (Herman, 1992). Luntz and Widom (1994) report on high prebvalence of childhood history of abuse in adults with **antisoual personality disorder**.

d) In mental health settings, the chief complaints of many abused women include feeling depressed, feeling suicidal, having panic attacks, sexual dysfunction, sleep disorders, eating disorders[2] and/or substance abuse in a self-medicating fashion (Bolen, 1993). Self-mutilation, which is rarely seen after a single acute trauma, is a common sequel of protracted CSA (Herman, 1992). **Symptoms of suicidality, substance abuse and revictimization are common among victims of CSA.** Cameron (1994) proposes that they seek to "avoid the truth" of what happened through alcohol and drugs, keeping busy or somaticizing. They are often "unmercifully hard on themselves".

e) While for many victims of CSA the tenacity of PTSD symptoms is evident, it is also worth noting that for **one half of CSA victims evidence remarkable strength and resilience as evident in increased sensitivity and self-reliance** (See Festinger, 1991). For example, abuse has little negative effects when it occurred only 1 or 2 times, where abuse was not forceful, where the child was believed and supported upon disclosure, with little or no family disruption (Ruma, 1993).

f) Approximately 70% of patients diagnosed with borderline personality disorder (BPD) have experienced sexual abuse. *(See Section VI for a discussion of BPD.)*

---

[1] Pogrebin et al (1992) indicate that national self-report surveys indicate that **approximately 10% of psychotherapists** admit having had **at least one sexual encounter with a client.** This is most likely an **underestimate** of the extent of the actual sexual involvement of psychotherapists with their clients. Such transgressions lead clients to often experience feelings of betrayal, and anguish at having been "victimized" by the very person who had been entrusted to help them. Such sexual exploitation can lead to PTSD and DES symptoms. In order to appreciate the variety of inappropriate sexual behaviors that can occur in psychotherapy see the thought provoking book by Pope et al. (1993).

[2] CSA has been found to be a risk factor for psychiatric disorders in general such as depression and anxiety and is not a specific factor for bulimia nervosa (Welch et al. 1994), although treatment resistant bulimic patients tend to have a history of CSA (Gleaves and Eberenz, 1993).

2. "Although only a minority of survivors of chronic childhood abuse become psychiatric patients, a large proportion (40-70%) of adult psychiatric patients are survivors of abuse." (Herman, 1993, p. 215).

3. The long-term effects of CSA are illustrated by the findings of Silver et al. (1983) who studied a nonclinical sample of 77 adult female survivors. They found that 80% reported that they were still "searching for meaning" many years after its occurrence. Fewer than 10% reported that they were not presently searching to make sense of their experience. The ability to find meaning in one's victimization appears to facilitate effective coping as evident in less psychological distress, better adjustment, and higher levels of self-esteem. The phenomenological and clinical expression of the impact of CSA is illustrated in the following narrative accounts. Downs (1993) describes how victims of CSA feel **defiled, stigmatized, damaged** and **irreparably branded**. The victims see themselves as:

    "trash", "dirty", "contaminated", "violated", "disgusted", a "bad person", "ugly", "ashamed", "guilty", "helpless", "sinful", "soiled goods", "illegitimate", "unloveable", "a slut", "whore", "good for nothing", "creepy", "been used", a "pawn", "useless", "good for nothing", "having never been a virgin" and "a person not worth taking care of", "alien", "crazy", "a spoiled identity", "victim of a series of betrayals."

    CSA had a significant impact on these victims' self-concept and on their peer relationships. Which, in turn, had progressive accumulative, debilitating effects. "My life is a failure and there is nothing I can do about it". Imagine the impact of someone continually telling herself, and others, that "I am soiled goods, a pawn". This is further illustrated in a description by a CSA client reported by Harvey et al. (1992, p. 111). She said:

    "The incest is the single most powerful factor that has influenced my life. I **lost** my childhood and adolescence. I was fearful of dating as a teenager. I have been **stuck** emotionally since the incest and have **sabatoged** my work and personal relationships because of being **emotionally immature. I** want people in my most intimate relationships to **parent** me." *(Emphasis added to highlight the key words in the client's narrative).*

    Spaccarelli (1994) has noted that **self-attributions of blame and higher perceived threat are related to higher symptomatology.**

4. Finkelhor and Browne (1986) have identified four general reactions to abuse:[1] (a) sexualization, (b) betrayal, (c) powerlessness, and (d) stigma. Porter, Blick, and Sgroi (1982) have identified 10 impact issues common to victims of sexual abuse, regardless of their age or sex. These include issues of (1) feeling as if "damaged goods", (2) guilt, (3) fear, (4) depression, (5) low self-esteem, (6) repressed anger and hostility, (7) impaired ability to trust, (8) blurred role boundaries and role confusion, (9) pseudo-maturity and failure to accomplish developmental tasks, and (10) problems of self-mastery and control.

5. $1/3$ of CSA victims grow up to continue a pattern of seriously inept, neglectful or abusive rearing as parents. $1/3$ do not evidence adult dysfunction as parents. $1/3$ remain vulnerable to

---

[1] See Trickett and Putnam (1993) for a discussion of possible psychobiological changes. See Cameron (1994) for a comparison of victims of CSA and veterans of Vietnam who have PTSD. She notes "that women were younger than veterans at the time of trauma, they were alone rather than in a group, and they were abused by caretakers. The abuse also lasted longer and was more likely to be "repressed". Therapy also began much later in life for CSA survivors and required more time for recovery." (p. 130).

the effects of social stress which can increase the likelihood of their becoming abusive parents (Oliver, 1993). As Widom (1989) has observed, CSA victims are not necessarily prone to repeat their own form of victimization. Similarly, Kaufman and Zigler (1987) report an **intergenerational transmission rate** of incestous and abusive behavior of approximately **30%. Over 2/3 do not have ongoing incest in families.** When incest recurs there are likely to be striking repetitive patterns in terms of age of abusive relationship, relationship patterns that correspond to the original abuse. *(See assessment Section III for a description of measures to tap Child Abuse Potential, especially for parents who are having difficulty with their children and who have few social supports viz., insulated parents.)*

What factors influence the impact of CSA?

1. A consistent profile is evident in a report by Downs (1993) who has identified several abue, abuse-related, and disclosure-related factors that influence the outcome of CSA. These factors include:

    a) aspects of the abusive relationship itself (e.g., single versus multiple perpertrators, duration and frequency of abuse, type of relationship with the abuser (father or step-father as opposed to others results in poorer adjustment);

    b) aspects of the specific sexual act (amount of force used or threat of force, duration, frequency, severity in the form of invasive or more intimate sexual contact are linked to degree of traumatic reactions);

    c) timing of the abuse in the course of the victims' psychosocial development;

    d) level of support by nonoffending parent following disclosure (e.g., whether this reaction is supportive, punitive, disbelieving, or stigmatizing) and family level of cohesion;

    e) familial context of CSA victim, (e.g., childhood maltreatment, parental alcoholism, family neglect and violence, maternal level of symptom distress);

    f) victim's attributional style and methods of coping with the abuse.

2. It is not clear how age effects the impact of abuse of the child. Some researchers report that younger children are more distressed than older children, others do not report such findings. For example, Black et al., 1994, found that sexually abused preschoolers displayed fewer behavioral problems than do older children and the preschoolers were less susceptible to feeling guilty.

3. When these factors are combined the following picture emerges. The severity of the abuse (duration and frequency, more intrusive sexual act, use and threat of force, perpertrator being a father, mother, or parent figure), abuse by multiple perpertrators, the unavailability of social support (parent's and institutional reactions to abuse), and victim's self-blame attributional style, are each factors that are associated with poorer adjustment. How the family reacts to the disclosure of abuse is also an important factor, as is the child's prior level of functioning. In summary, **more long-term PTSD symptoms are evident when the perpertrator is a primary caretaker, particularly father or stepfather, high frequency of sexual contact, long duration, use of violent force, penetration, lack of maternal support (Hazzard et al, 1993).**

4.   Certain family characteristics are significant predictors for increased psychiatric risk as a result of child sexual abuse. These include absence of biological parent, maternal unavailability, marital conflict and violence, child's poor relationship with the parents and presence of a stepfather, (Alexander, 1992). Note that **child sexual abuse is often accompanied by other forms of familial distress such as parental psychopathology, alcohol and substance abuse, lack of supervision, marital discord, and recent unemployment.** Mullen et al, (1993) report that CSA, in most cases, is **"only one element in a matrix of adverse family, social and interpersonal experiences which increase an individual's vulnerability to psychiatric disorders"** (p. 730). In other words, one can look upon incest as being a **family affair,** reflecting a breakdown in familial structures.

5.   The effects of social and family conflict and social disadvantage are difficult to disentangle from the effects of CSA (e.g., family disruption, conflict, decreased cohesion, reduced family support). "The severity of the abuse may <u>not</u> be **as important as the climate in which the abuse occurs."** (Gold et al., 1994, p. 24)

6.   How the police and courts treat CSA victims can also influence the victim's level of adjustment (e.g., testify on multiple occasions; confront the perpetrator; open-court appearance can lead to more PTSD symptoms than closed-court appearance or videotaped testimony). With victims there is also the need to address the belief that it could happen again.

7. $1/2$ of all incest victims made an attempt at disclosure at the time of the incest, but most of these disclosures were unfavorably received. The "victim's" accounts were often discounted and the victim was told that she was "imagining things", "was crazy". "X never did that, he loves her", and the victim is "misperceiving the situation or overture", "not really occur" and the like. Other family members often suppressed or denied the reality, extent, and effects of the abuse (Courtois, 1988).

8.   Parent/teacher and child reports of child distress often disagree. As noted previously, **adults usually <u>underestimate</u> the degree of child distress.** Thus, there is a need to use multiple sources of input, especially the child's report. General measures of child maladjustment (behavioral checklist) often do <u>not</u> pick up PTSD symptoms. Need to include specific child PTSD measures. (*See Section III on assessment and Section IV on the "dangers" of assessing for CSA*).

What can be done to help individuals with CSA?

1.   Like other PTSD populations, the treatment of incest victims is in its "infancy" in terms of good comparative outcome studies. We will consider in Section V the state of the art and specific individual and group intervention programs by Brandt, Courtois, Dolan, Jehu, Kirschner's, Neimeyer, and others. Many of these forms of intervention are conducted most effectively **on a group basis.** It is also worth noting that there is a good deal of controversy concerning what treatment emphasis should be placed on the process of recalling and retelling in detail the nature of the abusive events. Some therapists insist on a process of recall, resolution and mastery of the experience of abuse. While others view the CSA as one part of a matrix of developmental disadvantage and difficulties that should be addressed, of which sexual abuse is only one element. **For some victims the abuse has been consigned to the past and "memory work" interventions may prove counter-productive (Mullen et al., 1993).**

"Keep in mind that many CSA victims do **not** show long-term impairment in their mental health and not all psychiatric problems in those who have been abused are attributable to that abuse" (Mullen et al., p. 730).

2. The controversy about whether treatment of victims of CSA should employ so-called "memory recovery techniques" and focus on "trauma work" is illustrated in the August, 1994 issue of Applied Cognitive Psychology. On the one hand, a number of clinicians (Beutler and Hill, 1992; Ganaway, 1989; Haaken and Schlaps, 1991), as well as cognitive psychologists (Ceci and Loftus, 1994; Lindsay and Read, 1994) have cautioned that focusing treatment of recovering memories of incest may lead therapists to pay inadequate attention to other sources of psychological difficulties. Instead, a broad and flexible treatment approach is required that examines important life events, current relationship issues, and interpersonal difficulties, and not just focus treatment on trauma recovery and memory work. As Beutler and Hill (1992) observe, there is no evidence that therapeutic techniques that focus on the recoveries of histories of CSA are effective, or more effective, than interventions that primarily focus on "here and now" treatment approaches. *(See Section IV for the additional problem of possible "false memories").*

3. When interventions do attend to past trauma events, they are conducted in a collaborative fashion. For example, interventions with adult victims of CSA (e.g., Lebowitz et al. 1993; Roth and Newman 1993) help clients understand the feelings that surround the traumatic experience, but the client's self-disclosure is conducted in such a manner whereby they can control the degree to which they report CSA. *(See description of treatment of incest survivors in Section V.)*

4. It is important to recognize the range of treatment options for adult victims of CSA, most of which has little empirical support. For example, consider the following alternatives.

    A) An illustrative treatment approach toward adult incest survivors has been offered by Kirschner, Kirschner and Rappaport (1993). They highlight the need to help "normalize" and "depathologize" the client's symptoms, to provide symptom relief, to stabilize the client's situation, to uncover the history of incest, to educate the client about the importance of memory retrieval, and to help clients make sense of current mood and behavior in light of their history of victimization. It is important **not** to minimize the abuse and ensure that the responsibility is placed on the perpertrator. In therapy, it is highlighted that, "incest is a form of rape" that exploits children and takes advantage of trust and lack of power. CSA is a "family affair" that reflects a "taboo of secrecy", and a dysfunctional marital relationship between the incest victims parents. They also propose the inclusion of the victim's spouse in treatment as early as possible, as well in some instances the inclusion of the survivor's children. Any decision to involve significant others in treatment must be made **collaboratively** with the client. Such factors as the spouse's knowledge of the incest, response to disclosure and assessment of the potential impact of this disclosure on the marriage, will influence the decision about involving the spouse. Another suggested component of treatment is the proposed need for the adult survivor to confront his or her family of origin. They suggest that the survivor "cannot be fully herself without facing the perpertrator and nonperpertrating family members" (p. 150). In preparation for this confrontation the survivor is asked to keep a journal that includes an account of the details of the incestuous event, a statement of what was lost, the effects that incest has had on her life, and a list of meaningful reparations she would find to be healing. The client practices reading, role-playing and behaviorally rehearsing how the client can present this information to her family in 2 or 3 two hour family sessions. The client is encouraged to tell the family what she needs in order to heal from the "wounds of the past." The therapist conveys to the client that the "act of forgiveness" is a "gift" for all, including the survivor. Following the family session the client may write a letter indicating what was unsaid at the sessions, what new role the survivor will play in the family, as well as indicate what future reparations are needed. Kirschner et al. (1993) also indicate what factors **contraindicate** the involvement of family sessions, such as ongoing substance abuse, potential dangerousness, and a history of manipulation. (*In Section IV we will consider the controversial nature of doing "memory work" and confronting family of origin.*)

B)   Examples of a more **"here and now" focused intervention** with victims of sexually traumatic incidents have been offered by the McCarthy's (McCarthy 1986, 1990; McCarthy & McCarthy 1993a). They provide a variety of treatment suggestions and interpersonal exercises to help CSA "victims", take pride in being a "survivor". The therapy focus is on the **present and the future**. A major feature is nurturing the set of client beliefs that (a) places responsibility for the abuse with the perpertrator, (b) views sexual activity as a pleasurable voluntary activity and <u>not</u> an abusive performance-oriented activity, (c) highlights veto power over uncomfortable sexual activity, (d) recognizes and highlights that **"living well is the best revenge"**. A workbook for couples (McCarthy & McCarthy 1993b) provides examples of specific activities to develop a more comfortable, accepting and supportive interpersonal style.

There is a critical need to evaluate treatment programs that focus on the "present and future" **versus** those that also put emphasis on "coming to terms with the past" by confronting the family of origin (e.g., McCarthy's approach <u>versus</u> Kirschner's, although there is some overlap among them).

Gunderson and Chu (1993) propose that "direct contact with abusive families should occur **only when** the patient has recovered and understood the implications of the bulk of memories of abuse" (p. 78). With less malevolent forms of abuse conjoint family therapy may be employed (Schatzow & Herman, 1989).

5.   While this **Handbook/Manual** focuses on PTSD with adults it is worth noting that interventions with children who have been abused may be administered on an individual, group, or family basis (often involving a parent educational component). (See treatment suggestions on guided play therapy and cognitive-behavioral interventions for children who experienced CSA by Berliner and Wheeler, 1987; Deblinger et al., 1990; Friedrich, 1991; Galdston, 1971; Giaretto, 1981; Gillis, 1993; James & Nasjleti, 1983; Orenchuk-Tomiuk et al., 1990; James & Nasjleti, 1983; Ruma, 1993; Sgroi, 1982; Terr, 1989). Terr (1981) in her study of the Chowchilla children noted the need for active interpretation and intervention in the traumatic play of brutalized children. The endless repetition of the children's traumatic play alone provided no relief (Goodwin, 1988). For a description of a comprehensive treatment approach for child abuse in households of substance abusers see Blau et al. (1994).

6.   Providing support to non-offending parents and siblings is an important protective factor for child victims (Spaccarelli, 1994).

WHAT SHOULD YOU TAKE FROM THE LITERATURE ON CSA?

1.   An appreciation of the widespread incidence of CSA victimization and the potential long-term consequences. But it is important to keep in mind that CSA does <u>not</u> appear to predispose to any one diagnosis and that a significant number of victims are asymptomatic (see Kendall-Tacket et al., 1993).

2. There is a need to explicitly and systematically assess[1] for CSA. Courtois (1988) has proposed that **questions about sexual abuse be a routine part of all initial clinical interviews**. For example, requiring intake clinicians to ask routinely about a history of childhood sexual abuse resulted in a greater than ten-fold increase in the rate of reported abuse among females evaluated in a psychiatric emergency room setting (Briere & Zaidi, 1989). In a child psychiatric outpatient clinic, children who were asked directly about sexual molestation were four and half times as likely to report CSA (Lanktree et al, 1991). Illustrative assessment measures of CSA are offered by Courtois (1988), Martin et al. (1993), Trepper & Barrett (1993), each of which ask about childhood experiences in the context of taking a family history. *(The assessment of CSA is considered in Section III and IV.)*

3. The need to assess child victims directly and not depend upon the reports of adults (parents and teachers). The presence of sexualized fears, behaviors and depictions indicate the need for a fuller assessment of possible CSA. Great care is required when conducting such assessments (e.g., see Ceci and Loftus, 1994; Lindsay and Read, 1994). Children who have been victimized may remain silent out of fear, embarrassment, shame, or concern that no one will believe them. Deblinger and Heflin (1994) report data that 22% of victimized children recanted their allegations. The vast majority of the children who recanted later reaffirmed their original disclosures. Thus, the children's **disclosure** should be viewed as being **dynamic** and changing over time.

4. When intervening with children, great care should be taken to use age-appropriate interventions. There is also a need to **help the nonoffending parent** deal with the emotional aftermath and difficulties that interfere with her being therapeutic and supportive of the child. Also, keep in mind, that the mothers of children who have been sexually abused, may themselves, be victims of ongoing domestic violence, marital distress, and perhaps, childhood victimization experiences. The therapist should highlight to the parent how she can serve as a model for her child. The intervention needs to address the issue of parental feelings of guilt.

5. There is a need to recognize the **resilience** that many "victims" of CSA evidence; while other victims of CSA who are continually distressed can benefit from psychotherapy, most often conducted on a group basis. *(See Section V for a discussion of such group treatments with incest victims.)*

6. There is no evidence that therapy should or should not focus on retrieving the details of the abuse or on so-called "trauma memory work". Focusing on the abuse may result in the client and the therapist paying inadequate attention to current sources of difficulties.

7. The data on child sexual abuse, rape, domestic violence, and sexual harassment, when combined indicate that **a sizeable percentage of women in today's society have been "victimized"**. **Moreover, various forms of victimization often occur together**, seemingly creating a vulnerability for one another (Dutton 1992). For example, in terms of raw numbers, Hanson et al. (in press) report that "it is estimated that more than **34 million women** (in the US) have experienced some type of **crime during their**

---

[1] Great caution is required in conducting such assessments. For example, Kirschner et al. (1993) review a number of symptomatic and behavioral (in therapy and out of therapy) cues of supposedly incestual backgrounds. While many of these indicators have a good deal of face validity there is **little evidence** to document that these cues are indeed valid signs of childhood sexual abuse (e.g., the type of dress, presentation style, recurrent nightmares). I know of no studies that have examined the "false negative" and the "false positive" rates of these predictive signs, individually and or when combined, in a heterogeneous clinical population of documented and nondocumented cases of childhood sexual abuse. (Also see Lindsay and Read, 1994.)

lifetime, with more than **12 million** experiencing a **completed rape**, and nearly **10 million experiencing serious physical assault.** Importantly, over half of all crime victims (51.8%) had either experienced more than one type of crime or more than one crime of the same type" (pp. 9-10).

8.   Given the high risk of women being "victimized" in North American society, there is a clear need for preventative/educational interventions. Russell (in press) has convincingly proposed that CSA should be viewed in society as a form of "torture", and thus should receive the increased social opprobrium that comes with this label.

CRIME VICTIMS (In United States)[1]

"The very magnitude of the (crime) problem implies first that clinical psychologists should receive more training in the area of victimization and trauma than traditionally has been provided" (Norris and Kaniasty, 1994, p. 121)

By the time you, the reader, have worked your way through the data on war, rape, domestic violence, and child sexual abuse, you may be developing some symptoms of PTSD. But, most mental health workers may not have personally experienced any of these traumatic events. The same cannot be said about the likelihood about being a victim of crime. While I will enumerate a number of specific statistics about the scope and impact of crime, the most impressive presentation of this data were offered in two recent epidemiological studies on civilian trauma. The first comes from a prevalence study on a representative sample of U.S. adult women (N = 4.008) reported by Resnick and her colleagues (1993). She found that 36% of adult women samples reported exposure to rape, sexual assault, aggravated assault, or the homicide death of someone close to them. The second study is a review of multiple epidemiological studies on victimization of children as reported by Finkelhor and Dziuba-Leatherman (1994). **Since children are more prone to victimization than are adults,** I have included this latter data, as well. Tables 1, 2, and 3 capture the scope and impact of the problem.

Table 1

Prevalence of Crime and Other Criterion A Events according to DSM-III-R:
National Population Estimates for Adult Women (Resnick et al., 1993)

Event type	% sample	Estimated population*
Completed rape	12.65	12,151,084
Other sexual assault	14.32	13,755,219
Physical assault	10.28	9,874,577
Homicide of family member[2]	13.37	12,842,687
Any crime victimization	35.58	34,176,724
Noncrime disaster only	33.31	31,996,253
Any trauma	68.89	66,172,978

* Based on U.S. Bureau of the Census 1989 Estimate of the Population of **U.S. Adult Women** (age 18 or older) of 96,056,000.

To put these 1993 numbers in historical perspective consider that in 1984, 37 million Americans were victims of crime, 6 million victims of violent crimes compared to the present figures presented in Table 1.

---

[1] See PTSD Research Quarterly, Summer, 1994, Vol. 5 for abstract summaries on research on crime-related PTSD, and Davis and Breslau (1994) for a comprehensive view. Also see A. Reiss & J. Roth (1993) Understanding and preventing violence. Washington, DC: National Academy Press.

[2] In the US the homicide rate is five times higher than the average for developed countries, and three times higher than even the next highest developed country (Finkelhor, 1994). (7.9 per 100,000 US vs. 1.5 European countries.) In 1990, 23,000 people in US were homicide victims and 6 million were victims of violent crimes (Hanson et al., in press).

Table 2

Prevalence Lifetime and Current PTSD Associated With Exposure History
(Resnick et al., 1993)

Event type	Lifetime PTSD (%)	Current PTSD (%)
Completed rape	32.0	12.4
Other sexual assault	30.8	13.0
Physical assault	38.5	17.8
Homicide of family or close friend	22.1	8.9
Any crime victimization	25.8	9.7
Noncrime trauma only (disaster/accident/other)	9.4	3.4
Any trauma	17.9	6.7
Total sample	12.3	4.6

Tables 1 and 2 from Resnick et al.'s study underscore the widespread incidence and impact of criminal activity. Now consider the fact that "the rates of assault, rape, and robbery against those **12-19 years are two to three times higher** than that for the adult population as a whole" (Finkelhor & Dziuba-Leatherman, 1994, p. 173).

Table 3

Crime Victimization Rate per 1000: Adolescents vs. Adults
(Finkelhor & Dziuba-Leatherman, 1994)

Crime	Age in years	
	12-19	20+
Assault	58.45	17.85
Robbery	11.53	4.73
Rape (ages 10 to 19)	1.6	0.5
Homicide	0.9	0.1

When these rates are translated into actual numbers as offered in the recent Children's Defense Fund report "State of American's Children", the scope and seriousness of the problem become immense. Just consider:

a) murder is the third leading cause of death among children ages 5 to 14

b) nearly 50,000 children were killed by guns in the U.S. from 1979 to 1991 (almost the same number as Americans killed in Vietnam)

c) a U.S. child dies of gun shot every two hours

d) a U.S. child is 15 times as likely to be killed by a gun as a child in Northern Ireland, where there is sectarian fighting.

e) 2.9 million children were reported abused or neglected in 1992

f) 3 million children annually witness violence in homes.

g) adolescents have a substantially higher rate of assault than do young adults.

It is children such as these and their families to whom I consult in urban residential centers. For a moving account of what their life-style is like see Alex Kotlowitz's (1991) book, There are no children here (Doubleday), as well as the treatise on community violence by Garbarino et al. (1992).

Given the high incidence of violence that children living in urban ghettos experience, Parson (1994) has proposed a new diagnostic label **Urban Violence Traumatic Stress Response Syndrome** to describe the children's response. In support of his proposal Parson cites the following findings:

a) "Virtually all" of the inner city ethnic minority children in South Central Los Angeles witnessed a homicide or a shooting of a person by age 5

b) 10-20% of the 2000 homicides in Los Angeles were witnessed by dependent children; more specifically 1/2 of the homicide cases were witnessed by 136 children 18 years and under.

c) 44% of murder victims were found in African-American communities and 84% of elementary school children had seen someone physically assaulted (Parson, 1994, p. 154).

He also notes that children who witness injury and hear cries for help appear to be especially vulnerable.

Incidence of crime *(In considering the following figures, keep in mind that less than half of violent crimes are reported to police, Hanson et al., in press)*

1. 83% of the U.S. population will experience a violent crime at some point in their lives and that virtually all persons (99%) will experience personal theft. (See Norris & Kaniasty, 1994 for a list of specific questions that can be used to assess for crime victimization experiences).

2. A violent crime is committed in the U.S. almost every 20 minutes. 5% of households had at least one member who was a victim of a violent crime against persons (e.g., rape, robbery, assault).

3. A murder occurs every 25 minutes in the U.S.. Murder is the leading cause of death in African-American males between the ages of 15 and 44, as well as for African-American females between the ages of 15 and 24. For instance, the lifetime probability of being a homicide victim in the U.S. varies by sex and race. For a white female it is 1 in 496, while for an African-American male it is 1 in 29. See the July Issue of the APA Monitor (p. 54) for a description of Axsom's research on African-American mothers who had a son or daughter murdered, 2/3 of the mothers had PTSD. As Amick-McMillan et al. (1989a,b) report, family survivors of homicide victims often develop PTSD.

4. A rape occurs every 6 minutes. **As noted, rape victims develop PTSD more commonly** than victims of any other violent crimes, even when the degree of violence is the same (Kilpatrick et al., 1989). The perception of extreme threat for serious injury or death increases the risk for developing PTSD.

5.   An assault occurs every 33 seconds (Bard & Sangrey, 1986). Hanson et al. (in press) note
      that women can experience various types of assault including partner assaults,
      acquaintainship assaults and stranger assaults.

6.   **30% of sexual assault victims and almost 40% of the physical assault victims
      meet criteria for lifetime PTSD.** Assault victims are twice as likely as non-victims to
      have PTSD. Such assaults can have lifestyle and social adjustment consequences (e.g.,
      change in residence, decreased productivity, decrease participation in social activities, and an
      increased fear of crimes (Hanson et al., in press).

Impact of crime

1.   **The effects of crime are both pervasive and persistent.** In a longitudinal study of
      some 12,000 households living in Kentucky, Norris and Kaniasty (1994) found that at 3
      months crime victims evidenced depression, anxiety, somatization, hostility and fear.
      Victims of violent crimes were most severely distressed. The symptom levels declined over
      the next 6 months, but soon leveled off. After 9 months there was little evidence that crime
      victims would continue to improve. By 15 months violent crime victims were still more
      symptomatic than were property crime victims, who, in turn were still more symptomatic
      than non victims. **A critical feature of this Norris and Kaniasty (1994) study is
      that they provide much needed normative data of victim's reactions.**

2.   Rape victims are more symptomatic (or have longer recovery times) than assault victims, that
      assault victims (sexual or physical) are more symptomatic than robbery victims, and that
      violent crime victims (assault or robbery) are more symptomatic than property crime victims
      (Norris & Kaniasty, 1994).

3.   PTSD symptoms are strongly related to the severity of the crime. Kilpatrick et al., 1983,
      reports that 1/3 of sexually assaulted or mugged victims become depressed and 10% of them
      suicidal. In contrast, the incidence of depression and suicidal behaviors for burglary victims
      are 15% and 5%, respectively.

4.   PTSD is more likely to develop if the homicide victim is a child or if the incident involves
      multiple deaths.

5.   If captivity is involved in the criminal act, the longer the captivity the more symptomatic is the
      victim and the slower the recovery. Over a period of 6 to 9 years, general anxiety symptoms
      tend to diminish and psychosomatic symptoms increase. 1/3 of victims still have intrusive
      symptoms at the 6 and 9 year followups.

6.   Those who are mugged, sexually assaulted, or who experience multiple victimization are at
      greatest risk for depression. Those who are mugged are at greatest risk of suicidal ideation
      and suicidal attempts (Sorenson & Golding, 1990).

7.   The victims' reactions to the crime depends upon:

      (1) the type of crime;
      (2) the personal meaning attributed to the crime;
      (3) the history of repeated victimization;
      (4) mental health history
      (5) substance abuse history
      (6) degree of community disorganization

Prior victimization is the best predictor of subsequent victimization, (Norris & Kaniasty, 1994). For example, if two or more criminal victimizations have occurred in the previous 6 months, almost 30% of the victims become depressed versus a 13% rate of depression for a single victimization experience (Sorenson & Golding, 1990). The biggest risk factor for sexual assault as an adult was a history of child sexual assault (Hanson et al., in press).

8. A number of studies have shown that fear of crime may be the most frequent and lasting consequence of criminal victimization. Accompanying these fears are feelings of hostility, anger, and rage. Fear of crime was assessed by means of asking questions such as: "When you leave your house or apartment, how often do you think about being robbed or physically assaulted?" "How often does fear of crime prevent you from doing things you would like to do?" (Never, Rarely, Sometimes, Often) (Kaniasty & Norris, 1992). In their 1994 study Norris and Kaniasty found that **fear of crime was a very consistent predictor of subsequent crime.** Those individuals who were most worried about becoming crime victims were, in fact, most likely to become crime victims. Thus, their fear appears rational given their circumstance. Interestingly, victims of crime were neither more, nor less, cautious than others.

9. **"A small proportion of crime victims receive professional help"** (Norris & Kaniasty, 1994, p. 121). (See Getzel and Masters, 1983 for an example of such services). Usually, some form of **crisis intervention** is provided to crime victims. Crisis intervention highlights the value of addressing the specific needs of victims of traumatic events, e.g., replace resources that have been lost, provide education about the criminal justice system, arrange transportation, arrange time off work, and make needed doctor appointments (Falsetti & Resnick, 1994). In some instances, more extensive interventions may be warranted.

10. The National Organization for Victim Assistance can also be accessed as an advocacy agency for crime victims. *(See Section VIII for a list of possible support organizations.)* There is a clear need for clinicians to hook up with other agencies that provide services to crime victims.

11. In conclusion, I will quote Hanson et al. (in press)

    "Many mental health professionals are already treating victims of rape and other types of violence without knowing it because they do not screen their clients for histories of violent assault." (p. 38).

The need to systematically assess for crime victimization should be obvious, by now.

Cautionary Note About Models that Propose STAGES/PHASES of Emotional Reactions

In considering reactions to criminal activities, or for that matter almost any victimization experience (bereavement, rape, military deployment), researchers are prone to describe the victim's reactions as progressing through "stages". For example, one can find in the writings of Bowlby, Horowitz, Kubler-Ross, and others, the suggestion that the emotional reactions of victims go through various distinct phases. For example, Kubler-Ross (1969) included five stages, sequenced as denial, anger, bargaining, depression and acceptance on learning of impending death. Horowitz et al., (1993) has proposed a model that included such stages as "outcry, denial, oscillation between denial or numbing, working through, and completion". Horowitz proposes that these phases are variable in duration, and progression through these phases is often incomplete. He also proposes that symptoms can wax and wane over time, depending upon a number of factors. Miller et al. (1993) have proposed a trauma accommodation syndrome consisting of various stages. Similarly, Bard and Sangrey (1986) in their Crime Victim's Book describe the victim's reactions as consisting of "shock, recoil or impact, attribution/resolution, and recovery." Burgess and Holmstrom (1979) and Forman (1980) propose stages of reactions and recovery by rape victims. For example, Forman's (1980) stages include initial reactions, denial, symptom formation, anger and resolution. Similarly, Meyers (1994) have proposed a "stage" model to describe the reactions of survivors of disasters. She states that "it will be counter-productive to probe for feelings in the "Honeymoon" phase when shock and denial may shield the survivor from intense emotions'. During the "Inventory" phase, people seek out facts about the disaster, trying to piece reality together and cognitively frame what happened. They may have more need to discuss their thoughts than talk about their feelings. In the "Disillusionment phase people are likely to express feelings" (p.4). Thus, not only does Meyers propose phases of reactions, but she also conveys that each phase warrants different forms of interventions.

Another area where a theory of stages has been proposed is that of peacetime deployment/reentry for soldiers returning from Operation Desert/Shelled. Peebles-Kleiger and Kleiger (1994), in the tradition of Kubler-Ross's (1966) stage model, have proposed four emotional stages of adjustment to describe the deployment/reentry process. The 4 stages include: Anger/Protest; Sadness/Despair; Coping/Detachment; Return/Reunion. Each stage purportedly has its own emotionally-laden task. For example, initial call-ups bring on tension, protest, anger and preparation for separation. The final days of departure bring on Detachment/Withdrawal with fears of impending loss. As Peebles-Kleiger and Kleiger observe, "As buses are pulling out", emotional disorganization or sadness/despair set in. At about the sixth week the phase of recovery/stabilization, coping/detachment, begin. About 6 weeks before deployment ends "anticipation of homecoming" begins, and finally, reunion with the reestablishment of intimacy, familiarity and connectedness. About 6 to 12 weeks after reunion, reintegration/stabilization set in. While this model has some face validity and can be used for educational purposes, just envision the research design that would be required to actually demonstrate this profile of emotional reactions, especially with the precision of prediction that is offered. Similarly, one might ask what research has given rise to these various proposed stage theories.

The Stage Model has also been extended to explaining how groups respond to disasters (see Herlofsen, 1994). In other words, the desire to impose order on events and reactions has led many researchers and therapists to propose a stage model, but as we will consider there are **dangers in imposing such order** based only on clinical impressions.

Why get concerned about astute clinicians providing a **Stage Model** to describe people's reactions to impending death and dying and disasters, in response to crime, in soldiers and their families responding to deployment and reentry? The best answer is offered by the scholarly critique offered by Silver and Wortman (1980). **EVERY TIME YOU SEE OR HEAR SOMEONE PROPOSE A "STAGE" MODEL YOU SHOULD ASK THEM WHAT IS THEIR REACTIONS TO THE FOLLOWING SILVER AND WORTMAN CRITIQUE**[1]

Silver and Wortman (1980) note that individuals:

a) do <u>not</u> experience all of the stages,

b) do <u>not</u> necessarily progress through the stages in the same order, bounce back and forth between reactions, often demonstrating concurrent emotional reactions that do <u>not</u> occur in a linear fashion;

c) may skip entire emotional experiences;

d) may also have positive emotional experiences that are <u>not</u> usually represented in these stage theories; and

e) a sizeable minority of "victims" do <u>not</u> achieve the recovery stage.

Moreover, Silver and Wortman note that health care providers can inadvertently create more stress for individuals if they feel that "victimized" clients should experience certain emotions, for example, anger expression. Mental health workers have the potential of making clients worse.[2] Out of a desire to simplify and bring order to the complex reactions of victims, stage theories have been offered. **CAUTION IS REQUIRED IN USING SUCH STAGE THEORIES**

WHAT SHALL YOU TAKE FROM THE DATA ON CRIME VICTIMS?

1. Lock your doors! Be vigilant and street smart!

2. Note, how the pattern of victim reactions vary depending upon the crime, (rape versus other crimial acts; violent versus nonviolent), the characteristics of the victim, especially prior victimization, and the meaning ascribed to the crime. There is a need to assess for risk of future victimization.

3. The effects of crime are both pervasive and persistent. Crime victims are often in need of clinical help.

4. There is a need to work with agencies that deal with crime victims in order to reduce "secondary victimization" and to bolster "victim's" coping abilities. As will be discussed in Section VII on post-crises interventions, preventative efforts can be used to reduce the likelihood of PTSD.

---

[1] Note, that similar criticisms of Stage Models have been offered in developmental psychology to Piaget's stages of cognitive development and to Kohlberg's stages of moral development and Prochoska and DiClimente's model of readiness for change. The need for orderliness and explanation is "seductive" in all areas of psychological theorizing. **The consumer should beware!**

[2] This is not only true of mental health work. Juries in rape cases may find the victim's account less convincing if she does not evidence what they consider the so-called appropriate emotional reactions for that "stage" of recovery. Such stage theories can provide powerful expectations that there is a "right" way to respond.

5.   Be cautious about accepting "stage" theories. The data and client experience are always much more complicated than these proposed theories suggest. Adhering to or conveying such theories to clients has the potential of making them worse.

TESTING YOUR EXPERTISE[1]

Section I - Epidemiology/Diagnosis

1. Describe the variety of diverse clients who fall under the rubric of PTSD. What are the implications for how you conduct assessment and provide treatment with each client group?

2. Describe the exposure rates to traumatic events in North America. What is the exposure rates for your country (if other than the US)? What are the implications for how you conduct your clinical practice and for the development of preventative actions? Provide the argument you would use to convince your colleagues of the need to screen all treatment seeking individuals for the presence of traumatic event exposure. *(See Section III for how you can screen for victimization.)*

3. Compare the impact of natural versus technological (especially "silent") disasters. What are the implications for post-disaster interventions?

4. What gender differences emerge in response to trauma? What are the implications for assessment and treatment?

5. PTSD can take various forms (acute, intermittent, chronic, delayed) and express itself in many different domains. Describe what biological, psychological, and interpersonal changes you should expect in "traumatized" individuals. Be sure to consider potential "positive" benefits, as well. *(See Section III for further discussion of positive benefits.)*

6. Trace the history of the concept of PTSD and include a description of the specific diagnostic criteria included in DSM-IV. How exactly do the diagnoses of Acute Stress Disorder, PTSD, Partial PTSD, and Complex PTSD (or Disorders of Extreme Stress) differ? (For example, see Chemtob and Harriott's 1994, discussion of the PTSD sequela of Guillain-Barre syndrome?) Their case report suggests that a severe medical illness can fulfill the criterion for a PTSD diagnosis. Given the widespread incidence of chronic medical and psychiatric illnesses, what would be the implications of including them under criterion A of PTSD? What about the affects of "silent" technological cisasters, state terrorism, torture, racism, where ongoing stressors are evident? Should these qualify under Criterion A? What should the boundary conditions be for Criterion A? Recall Scott and Stradling's (1993) proposal *(reviewed in Section I under types of patients)* of developing a new diagnostic category called Prolonged Duress.

7. a) Critically evaluate the criteria used in formulating the DSM-IV diagnosis of PTSD. For example, what do you think of the definition of Criterion A -- the stressor? (If you want to compare your answer to other people's critiques, see McFarlane, in press; March, 1993; Simpon, in press). These authors raise serious concerns about the definition of what should and should not be included under the category of a "stressor", and also comment on the definition of the criteria "outside the range of usual human experience". For instance, can someone develop PTSD in response to the need to cope with a chronic medical or psychiatric illness? For example, see Chemtob and Harrott's, 1994, discussion of the PTSD sequela of Guillain-Barre syndrom?) Their case report suggests that a severe medical illness can fulfill the A criterion for a PTSD diagnosis. Given the widespread incidence of chronic medical

---

[1] This **Handbook/Manual** will be used in various training programs. The questions and exercises included in these "TESTS" will be used to assess the participants' knowledge, skills, and general level of expertise. Clearly, some questions go beyond the material covered in this **Handbook** and are designed to stimulate discussion and critical thinking. Find two colleagues or two fellow students and work your way through this **Handbook** as a team. I have included a number of 3 person role-plays and exercises. Doing so, will increase all of your expertise.

and psychiatric illnesses, what would be the implications of including them under Criterion A of PTSD? What about including under Criterion A, the exposure to "silent" technological disasters, state terrorism, torture, racism, and other ongoing stressors? Should these qualify under Criterion A? What should the boundary conditions be for Criterion A? Recall, Scott and Stradling's (1993) proposal *(reviewed in Section I under Types of patients)* of developing a new diagnostic category called **Prolonged Duress**. Stress Disorder (PTSD), where patients meet the criterion of "caseness" in terms of PTSD smptoms (criterion B, C, D), but they do <u>not</u> meet Criterion A (stressor). Do you think the diagnostic category PDSD is a good idea?

b) Now that you have critiqued Criterion A, turn your attention to Criteria B, C, D, E, and F, in DSM IV. What problems emerge in defining each of these criteria? How well have the authors of DSM-IV addressed issues of cultural specificity in formulating the definition of PTSD? (For example, see Kleber et al., in press, and Loo, in press). Surely one would think that the criterion of "caseness", or the number of symptoms required for criteria B, C, D would have been developed from carefully controlled field studies (see Foa and Davidson, 1993). For a controversial critique of this research process, see Kirk and Kutchins (1992) <u>The selling of DSM: The rhetoric of science in psychiatry,</u> and Simpson (in press).

c) In collaboration with your study group, formulate your own diagnostic definition of PTSD. What do you think the DSM-V diagnostic criteria of PTSD should look like? Do you think it should include a PTSD plus DES (Disorders of Extreme Stress) category? Do you think it should include measurable signs of physiological reactivity *(see Section III)* or symptoms of anger *(see Section VI)*? While your at it, you may wish to consider in your critique, the international Classification Disorder (ICD) system. With all of the critiques about personality disorder *(see Section III)*, what do you think about their "enduring alterations in including personality" as a criteria in the diagnostic definition?

8.   What is the evidence of comorbidity and PTSD? What are the implications for assessment and treatment?

9.   Select a specific "traumatized" population that you are most likely to work with (.e.g, combat veterans, rape or crime victims, victims of a disaster, child sexual abuse victims, or victims of domestic violence). Describe briefly the incidence, changing symptom profile, factors that influence outcome, and the general treatment plan you would follow with this population.

10.   You attend a conference, or read an article on PTSD, in which the presenter/author proposes a "stage theory" of reactions to traumatic events. What critical questions can you ask the presenter in order to have him/her justify the use of a "stage" theory? What are the dangers of you conveying a "stage" theory to your clients?

SECTION II
TOWARD A CONCEPTUALIZATION OF PTSD:
A CONSTRUCTIVE NARRATIVE PERSPECTIVE

It should be apparent from Section I that traumatic events occur frequently and impact large numbers of people and that the exposure to traumatic events can substantially increase the risk of several serious mental health problems, but not for all individuals. A research challenge is to understand what distinguishes those who do and do not evidence short and long-term disabilities, as well as identify those who may even become "strengthened" by exposure to traumatic events.

Two general approaches, one **empirical** and the other **theoretical**, have been offered to explain these individual differences. The first approach is empirically descriptive. The researcher attempts to identify pre-disaster (premorbid "risk" factors), disaster (characteristics of the disaster; what has been described in Section I as "dose" effects), and post-disaster characteristics ("recovery environment" factors), and then relate them, individually, or in some combination, to short-term and long-term levels of adjustment. For example, in Section I on epidemiology I summarized the research on disaster "dose" effects; in Section III on Assessment, I summarized the research on premorbid factors; and in Section VII on Post-disaster Interventions I collated a comprehensive Table of some 58 factors that have been related to adjustment. **These different compilations are essentially "atheoretical" in nature.** They merely reflect the results of empirical studies.

The **field of "traumatology"**, as it has come to be called, has not suffered from a lack of theoretical speculation. It is one thing to enumerate some 58 variables (see Table 1 in Section VII) that have been implicated in trauma research; it is another to consider how these multiple variables can be integrated into a theoretical framework to explain individual differences. Investigators have not shied away from this task. One can find in the literature on traumatology many diverse theoretical models that have been offered to explain the occurrence of PTSD and related disorders. Given both the diversity and complexity of individual's reactions to traumatic events, it is not surprising that theorists with very diverse orientations would emphasize different factors in their explanations. Some theorists have emphasized the **biological sequelae**[1] of having been exposed to traumatic events (van der Kolk, 1984, 1994), while others have proposed a **behavioral conditioning** framework (Keane, 1989a, Keane et al., 1985). Yet others adopt a **psychodynamic**[2] perspective (Horowitz, 1986; Marmar, 1991; Weiss, 1993), an **informational and emotional processing**[3] perspective (Creamer, in press; Creamer et al., 1992; Foa & Kozak, 1986; Foa et al., 1989; Rachman, 1980; Thrasher et al., 1994); a **schema-**

---

[1] Basic biological models consider a range of possible etiological mechanisms including depletion of neurotransmitters due to inescapable situations, responsiveness to endogenous opiates, and functional changes in the limbic system *(See Section I.)*

[2] For example, Weiss (1993) from a **psychodynamic perspective** of master control theory proposes that a person suffers from maladaptive or **"pathogenic"** beliefs that he/she develops in childhood by inference from traumatic experiences with parents and siblings, or that he/she learns directly from parental teachings. Such pathogenic beliefs impede the client's functioning. The therapist's task is to help the client exert control over his/her **unconscious mental life** and disprove his/her pathogenic beliefs by testing them in relation to the therapist in the form of trial actions.

[3] The **information processing** perspective proposes that people suffering from PTSD develop **fear structures** that contain images and memories of threatening events, as well as information regarding emotions and plans for action. These fear structures comprise **threat schemas** that are ready to be activated at all times in people with PTSD, especially in response to stimuli that remind them of the original trauma. Thus, for someone with PTSD, many events that are not objectively dangerous may be interpreted as potentially dangerous (false alarm reactions). In this context, PTSD is seen primarily as an anxiety disorder that results from the development of a "fear memory" and from a fear network, ala the theory of Lang (1979).

based[1] model (Epstein, 1991; Janoff-Bulman, 1992; McCann & Pearlman, 1990b), and a **contructivist narrative** perspective (Harvey et al., 1990, 1991, 1992; Meichenbaum & Fitzpatrick, 1993; Meichenbaum & Fong, 1993). Space does <u>not</u> permit a detailed description and critique of these various theoretical perspectives. The interested reader should see Goodman et al. (1993a, b). **The theoretical approach I have adopted is that of a constructive narrative perspective.**

WHAT IS A CONSTRUCTIVE NARRATIVE PERSPECTIVE ("CNP")

A "CNP" focuses on the "accounts", or "stories", that individuals offer themselves and others about the important events in their lives. Harvey et al. (1990) define "account making" as people's story-like constructions of events that include descriptions of behavioral and affective reactions, explanations and predictions. Individuals routinely develop "accounts" or "stories" of significant life events that entail change and losses in their lives in an effort to infuse these occurrences with some coherence and meaning (Harvey et al., 1990,. 1992; Sarbin, 1986). As Mair (1990) observed, "We live through stories". Similarly, McAdams (1993) proposes that people in general need to make sense out of the world and their place in it and they do this by telling ("inventing") stories. People make meaning of their lives by organizing key events into stories which they incorporate into a larger life narrative.

The CNP has a long tradition. A number of philosophical and psychological theorists have proposed that humans actively construct their personal realities and create their own representational models of the world. The paradigms, assumptive worlds, and schemas that individuals actively create, can determine, and in some instances, constrain how they perceive reality. This constructive perspective finds roots in the philosophical writings of Immanuel Kant, Ernst Cassirer, Jean-Paul Satre and Nelson Goodman, and in the psychological writings of Wilhelm Wundt, Alfred Adler, George Kelly, Jean Piaget, Viktor Frankl, Jerome Frank, and Paul Watzlawick. More recently, the constructivist perspective has been advocated by Epstein and Erskine (1983), Mahoney and Lyddon (1988), McCann and Pearlman (1990), Neimeyer and Feixas (1990) and Meichenbaum and Fitzpatrick (1992). Common to each of these proponents is the tenet that the human mind is a product of the personal meanings that individuals create. Individuals do <u>not</u> merely respond to events in and of themselves, but they respond to their interpretation of events and to their assigned perceived implications of these events. This was illustrated in the research findings on combat soldiers and sexual assault victims, where the meaning ascribed to the "victimization" experience was more predictive of adjustment outcomes, than was the "objective" characteristics of the traumatic event.

Bruner (1986, 1990), Howard (1989, 1991), Mair (1989), McAdams (1985, 1993), Polkinghorne (1988), Sarbin (1986), Shafer (1981), and Spence (1982) have each proposed the narrative as a root metaphor for psychology and for the understanding of how individuals make sense out of, and find meaning in, traumatic events. The following quotes taken from diverse sources further capture the spirit of "CNP".

"We are the stories we tell." (McCabe and Peterson, 1991, p.36).

---

[1] The **schema-based perspective** highlights that traumatic events can result in permanent change in one's frame of reference or enduring ways of understanding oneself and the world. Trauma disrupts and fragments the sense of self and **"shatters" basic assumptions.** The experience of traumatic events can lead to a new view of life and the world that include core beliefs about the world. This view of life may include that life-events are random, unpredictable and uncontrollable, that people are basically malevolent and selfish, and a loss in the belief in a larger purpose or meaning to life. Traumatic events challenge people's generally unquestioned beliefs about themselves, others, and life in general. The challenge in therapy is to help clients "integrate" (assimilate and accommodate, ala Piaget) the traumatic experience within their new schema.

"Stories are habitations. We live in and through stories. They
conjure up worlds. We do not know the world other than a
story world. Stories inform life. They hold us together and
keep us apart." (Mair, 1988, p.127).

"A man is always a teller of stories, he lives surrounded by his own
stories and those of other people. He sees everything that
happens to him in terms of these stories and he tries to live his
life as if he were recounting it." (Satre, 1964, p.22).

"To provide a plausible story for a set of facts is enormously
reassuring, particularly when the story changes a random set
of happenings into a neatly packaged account with a
beginning, middle and ends." (Spence, 1987, p.29)[1] .

"We are lived by the stories we tell. To paraphrase Shakespeare:
Beware of the stories you tell yourself, for you will surely be
be lived by them." (Howard, 1991, p.190).

"People who have been traumatized work through their experiences
by developing new realities about the causes and
circumstances of the traumatic; they build a 'healing theory'
that fully accounts for what, why, and how it happened and
why they acted as they did. The objective is to build a new
more optimistic perspective." (Figley, 1989, p.64-65).

But Figley's treatment objective of helping clients to develop a "healing theory" has been
stated in many other terms. For example, consider the following list of therapeutic objectives of
how individuals can cope with traumatic events:

Construct	Therapist
Assimilate and liquidate traumatic experience	Janet
Metabolized psychologically	Wilson
Fabricate a new meaning	McCann & Pearlman
Develop a healing theory	Figley
Reauthor or restory a life	Epston and White
Restructure and conclude the trauma story	Herman
Engage in narrative repair[2]	Shafer

---

[1] Perhaps, Spence had the various stage theorists whom I cited at the end of Section I in mind when he offered this observation.

[2] Shafer (1992, p.2) has proposed that a life is reauthored as it is co-authored. Shafer describes this reauthoring process as "narrative repair". However, I have some reservations about the use of the metaphor "narrative repair". The metaphor "narrative repair" implies that the client's story is "broken" and the task of therapy is to "fix", "repair", the client's "defective" story to its pre-damaged state. In fact, the therapy process should embrace the goal of helping clients to go beyond, rather than merely repair, to the point of constructing new more adaptive stories than those the client had prior to the trauma.

Come to terms with or resolve	Thompson
Rebuild shattered assumptions	Janoff-Bulman, Epstein
Develop a new mental schema and seek completion	Horowitz
Co-construct a better and healthier life story	Spence
Orient into a new life narrative, contruct new selves	Goncalves

Common to each of these proposals is that **psychotherapy** should be viewed as a form of **"literary method"**, where the **client** becomes the **narrator**. The one way to accomplish this objective is to help the client change his/her understanding of the past. As Watzlawick, Weakland and Fisch (1974) observed:

> The significance of the past becomes a matter not of "truth" and "reality", but of looking at it here and now in one way rather than another. Consequently, there is no compelling reason to assign to the past primacy or causality in relation to the present, and this means that the reinterpretation of the past is simply one of the many ways of possibly influencing present behavior.

Perhaps, the simplest rendering of the CNP is that offered in the Buddhist observation:

> "We are what we think. All that we are arises with our thoughts. With our thoughts ("stories") we make the world (Dhammapada).

But what are the "stories" our clients construct to cope with traumatic events? How do they transform and reframe their "problem-saturated" trauma stories from one of shame and humiliation, guilt and fear, into "solution-focused" stories of dignity and survival? Table 1 provides some examples of such reframed "narrative accounts".

Table 1
Examples of Cognitive Reframing

"A terrible thing befell me. Not only have I survived it, but I have **incorporated** it into me. I may hurt more, but I am wiser and stronger. I have **overcome the darkness** and the pain. I can move forward in my life. I can laugh and love and work. I overcame the trauma; it did not overcome me." (Schwarz & Prout, 1991, p. 370)

"For example, one battered woman came to believe that her experience of physical, sexual, and psychological victimization by an intimate partner resulted in her becoming aware of what she termed the 'realities' of the world -- experiences about which she had previously had little awareness. She further believed that she must learn to accept a **'dark' side of herself**, the part that felt anger and hate. This new view **provided a purpose** that had been gained from her tortuous experiences." (Dutton, 1992, p. 92)

"Fifty years after surviving the Bataan Death March and a subsequent 42-month internment at slave labor in Japanese POW camps, a 70-year-old veteran was interviewed. He stated that he would not repeat his experiences for a million dollars,

but recalled them as the most <u>enriching, ennobling experience of his entire life</u>."
(Sipprelle, 1992, p. 36, emphasis added)

"This accident was one of the best things that happened to me. I was living life in the
fast lane. I was losing my family ... Since the accident and the paralysis I've learned
an awful lot about myself and other people. The accident made me more aware of
how other victims feel ... God was testing my faith. I now know God ... It could
have been worse ... Without the accident I would have been lost the rest of my life."
(Meichenbaum, 1983, p. 36)

What is common to these various narrative accounts that distinguishes them from the
accounts of those who do <u>not</u> "cope" following traumatic events? While at this point we do <u>not</u>
know the exact answer to this important question, we can, nevertheless, begin to glean from the
research literature several suggestive answers. The research on narrative accounts and cognitive
and affective processes following exposure to traumatic events have implicated a number of critical
processes. Investigators have considered the importance of:

    a)   sharing one's trauma with others;

    b)   the nature of social comparison processes;

    c)   the nature and incidence of ruminations;

    d)   the amount and content of efforts at cognitively "undoing" traumatic events;

    e)   the absence of being able to find closure and the tendency to continue the search for
        meaning;

    f)   the degree to which the individual sees oneself as blameworthy and lacking in
        personal control;

    g)   the nature of the metaphorical thinking one engages in.

A brief consideration of each of these factors will help us become better listeners to the
"stories" our clients tell us and more sensitive to how their stories change over time, and over the
course of therapy. It should be noted that we do <u>not</u> know if the changes in the survivors'
narrative accounts act as causative agents in contributing to change, or if the changes in adjustment
levels contribute to narrative reconstructions, or whether some third source of variables (e.g.,
recovery of loss of resources) mediate the changes. It is likely that the clients' narratives are
dynamically interactive and interdependently connected with changes in adjustment, and with
objective and subjective replenishment of resources. But of this complex pattern, let us now focus
on the narratives that "traumatized" individuals construct.

In Section VI, I review the literature on the benefits that accrue when victimized individuals
share, in a trusting relationship, either orally or in writing, their stories of what they have
experienced. Putting one's account into words and sharing with others imposes a coherence and
completion that is <u>not</u> otherwise readily achievable. Pennebaker (1990) and his colleagues have
demonstrated the beneficial effects that result from "opening up".

But "opening up" or "sharing" does <u>not</u>, in itself seem to be sufficient for change.
Meichenbaum and Fitzpatrick (1993) have noted that as individuals began to "script" and "rescript"
their reactions to traumatic events they tend to recast their roles. Like good story tellers, survivors
redefine, embellish, alter their accounts, as they reconstrue what they expect or want from a given
situation. The narrator may adopt a stance of resigned acceptance or engage in favorable **social**

comparison processes. For example, Taylor (1990) and Taylor et al. (1983) have identified five cognitive mechanisms or narrative processes that people report using to cope with distressing situations. These include:

i) comparing oneself with those who are less fortunate;

ii) selectively focusing on positive attributes of oneself in order to feel advantaged;

iii) imagining a potentially worse situation;

iv) construing benefits that might derive from the victimizing experience; and

v) manufacturing normative standards that makes one's adjustment seem "normal"

Contrast using these forms of constructing one's narrative with the following narrative features that have been gleaned from the literature by Meichenbaum and Fitzpatrick (1993). The following features are evident in the narratives of **individuals who do not cope as well, and who evidence continuing distress**. The more distressed individuals tend to:

i) have difficulty retrieving specific "positive" memories and evidence an "overgeneral autobiographical memory" (see McNally et al., 1994);

ii) continue to search for meaning and fail to find satisfactory resolution (e.g., see Silver et al., 1983);

iii) continue to evidence intrusive ideation and are unable to resolve their "stories" and fail to "integrate" their traumas (Baum et al., 1990);

iv) make unfavorable comparisons between life as it is, as compared to what it might have been had the traumatic events not occurred (as evident in "What if", "Only if", "If only I had", and "Why me" thinking patterns) (Davis et al., in press);

v) engage in continual comparisons between aspects of life after the stressful events versus how it was before the traumatic events, continually "pining" for what was lost (Wortman & Silver, 1987);

vi) see themselves as blameworthy for their predicament (Janoff-Bulman & Lang-Gunn, 1988);

vii) see themselves as "victims" and "at risk" with little expectation or hope that things will improve or change, thus remaining hypervigilant (Foa et al., 1989).

Illustrative of this research on the narrative accounts that traumatized individuals evidence is the work on **"undoing"**, or what has been called **counterfactual thinking**. Whereas, "ruminations" reflect the survivors mentally reliving traumatic memories, "undoing" thoughts focus on how a negative event could have been avoided. We know from the PTSD literature that the frequency of ruminations and accompanying distress is one of the best predictors of future adjustment difficulties, especially if the individual continues to ruminate long after the actual traumatic events (Baum et al., 1993). If the individual's story is "stuck" on the traumatic event, if the individual continues to try to answer "why" questions for which there are no acceptable answers, then that individual will evidence continuing difficulties.

But what about "undoing" thoughts? What happens when the individual's account reflects continuous efforts to explore "what might have been?", "If only I had", or "I ought to have", simulating the event as it could (or should) have happened? Davis et al. (in press), in studying traumatized individuals (e.g., parents of sudden infant death syndrome children and surviving family members of automobile deaths of loved ones), found that distressed individuals tended to engage in more "undoing" behaviors that perpetuated their distress. The "undoing" cognitions and the stories they replayed over and over, again and again, tended to nearly always focus on their own behaviors. Such undoing was particularly problematic when future control was not obtainable, and when the individual believed that the negative events were potentially avoidable. Thus, the combination of perceived avoidance, personal responsibility, and resultant guilt, blame, and shame made for a story that perpetuated their distress. The story line of "why" did the negative events happen, and how might such negative events not have happened, can contribute to the intra- and interpersonal symptoms that were described in Section I.

In summary, it is being proposed that how individuals who have been exposed to traumatic victimizing events "tell" or "construct" their accounts can determine and influence how they cope. We will consider in the subsequent sections how assessment and treatment procedures have been used to help alter, not only the behavioral patterns of PTSD and DES (Disorders of Extreme Stress) clients, but also the nature of their narratives.

Perhaps, I can take the liberty of sharing an account to illustrate, at a personal level, what may or may not contribute to the development of PTSD. I too have a "story" to tell, an "account" to share about my involvement in the topic of PTSD. For the last several years, I have presented two- and five-day workshops on PTSD, consulted with mental health workers who conduct Critical Incident Stress Debriefing, and worked with clinicians who are responsible for the treatment of traumatized clients with PTSD and PTSD + DES. These activities have taken me around the world. In the course of conducting these presentations, I have developed a "condition", or a "set of symptoms" called "ideas of reference", namely, the belief that an individual can cause, or be responsible for, important events occurring.

Consider the following list of experiences I have encountered. For example, when I presented on PTSD in Cape Cod, Massachusetts, Hurricane Bob arrived; in Clearwater, Florida, the largest flood in recent history occurred; in Los Angeles on two occasions there were major earthquakes during my consultation, and on my latest visit to LA there was a major fire and mud slides. When I visited Milwaukee, the city's water supply went bad. When I visited Hong Kong the talks between China and England broke off. When I visited Israel a few years ago, the Lebanon war broke out, and when I was in Valencia, Spain, a coup occurred and a rebel general and his troops commandeered the city. Moreover, while driving home from a consultation at a center for individuals with traumatic brain-injuries in Toronto, Ontario, on two separate occasions, in the exact same spot on the major highway, my car was involved in two life-threatening accidents. On one occasion a passing truck dropped a metal drum through my windshield, and more recently, at the exact same spot on the highway, my brand new car was struck by lightening.[1]

Are these events mere "illusory correlations" between my presence and the occurrence of disastrous things happening? As my wife observed, perhaps I should switch research topics or stay home! One of the critical questions confronting the field of mental health is why don't these multiple stressful events cause me to experience symptomatic distress, let alone PTSD? Why is it that some individuals who are exposed to traumatic events demonstrate lingering symptoms, such as persistent intrusive memories, while others merely incorporate such events into their biographical accounts, and "move on" (perhaps, ever so carefully). These events each had all of

---

[1] If you would like, I will share with you my travel schedule so you can prepare for when I will be in your area.

the elements of what could develop into PTSD. Why do only some who are exposed to traumatic events develop PTSD, while others do not?

Perhaps another part of the answer lies in the ways in which individuals tell their stories, especially the **metaphors** they use when offering their accounts. If you ask me what it was like to have your car hit by lightening, or have a metal drum go through your windshield when you are driving 65 miles an hour on an expressway, words would prove inadequate to describe what it felt like, or what it feels like to write about it now. I, like other "traumatized" individuals, would have to depend upon metaphors to tell my story.

ILLUSTRATIVE METAPHORS OFFERED BY "TRAUMATIZED" CLIENTS

When something "bad" happens to people, like being exposed to a traumatic event or having been victimized, **words seem inadequate** to describe to someone else[1] (such as a therapist) the impact of these events and the "emotional toll" that they have taken. In order to describe what has transpired and the lingering impact, **individuals usually use metaphors, or "like-a" or "as if"**, statements -- "This feels 'like' X"; "My thoughts act 'as if' Y". As they repeat their accounts and embellish their narratives, as they attempt to make sense and find meaning in, as they try to impose coherence and develop an understanding of what has happened and how they reacted, they eventually drop the "like-a" and the "as if" parts of their metaphoric narratives. They no longer feel "like a rag doll", "a prisoner of the past"; instead, they become or act "as if" they are the "rag doll", the "prisoner of the past", a "ticking time bomb", and the other metaphors described below. They no longer believe that their thoughts act "as if" they are intrusive ideation, but their thoughts come to have a life of their own, namely, "These thoughts visit me"; "I am a time machine that can't stop"; "The depression (rage) just overcomes me".

In short, **our clients become "poets", who use the language and the tools of literature (metaphors, similes, analogies, and the like) to describe their experiences and reactions**. I would propose that our clients, as well as you the reader, cannot describe intense emotional experiences to others without using metaphors. *(What metaphors do you use to describe your intense emotional reactions?)*. But such metaphorical accounts are not mere figures of speech. It is being proposed that they have important intra- and interpersonal consequences. The language we use, the metaphors we employ, have important implications for how we appraise events and construct realities. Metaphors can act as useful "windows" into the system that individuals use to interpret their world. As Lakoff and Johnson (1980) observes:

> We define our reality in terms of metaphors and then proceed to act
> on the basis of the metaphors. We draw inferences, set goals, make
> commitments, and execute plans, all on the basis of how we in part

---

[1] It should be noted that in my analysis of the written transcripts that "traumatized" individuals **write for themselves** over repeated days (as in the research studies by Pennebaker), the subjects rarely used metaphors to describe to themselves their level of emotional distress. Since the subjects seem to "know" how much they are "upset" and "hurting", and the "emotional pain" that they have experienced, they describe the impact of such events directly, omitting metaphorical statements. They speak of having been a "victim" (rape, incest, robbery) in direct emotional terms -- "I was outraged"; "I am deeply sorrowed"; "I am hopeless". However, when individuals are called upon to **describe their experiences to others**, they are more prone to employ **metaphors**, as described in the research by John Harvey and his colleagues on interpersonal accounts. This clinical observation needs systematic study using an ipsative (within subject) longitudinal research approach in order to determine how their accounts change over time and how these changes relate to adjustment measures. Are "metaphoric" narrative changes mere **"epiphenomena"**, or are they **mediating** or **moderating** variables? Do metaphoric narrative changes follow behavioral changes, and, in turn, contribute to further changes. Moreover, do metaphors or the style of narrative construction vary across victimized groups, cultures and with what consequences?

structure our experience, consciously or unconsciously, by means
of metaphors (p.158).

Lakoff and Johnson (1980) have proposed three major groups of metaphors that characterize
our narrative constructions. These include:

a) **structural metaphors** -- in which one concept is metaphorically structured in terms of
   another (e.g., conceptualizing intimate relationships as "wars")

b) **orientation metaphors** -- in which a set of concepts is organized in a spatial
   relationship to one another (e.g., "Happy is up and sad is down", or feeling as if
   one is in a "bottomless pit")

c) **physical metaphors** -- where one's understanding of experience is in terms of
   physical objects and substances (e.g., feel like a "revved-up motor", a
   "jackhammer")

Listed below are the metaphors clients use to describe their reactions to traumatic events.
*(In Section VI, I include metaphors clients and therapists use in addressing problems with
addiction.)* It is an interesting task to categorize these metaphors into Lakoff and Johnson's three
metaphorical categories of structure, orientation, and physical. Moreoever, we can wonder what
are the phenomenological, behavioral, and interpersonal consequences of clients using certain
metaphors to tell their stories.

What do you think is the impact of the client describing herself as being "a prisoner of the
past", or as a "zombie", a "whore", a "victim of my feelings", and the like? One task for the
therapist is to help clients appreciate **how they construct reality**, how they **"live the stories
they tell"**, and how they can begin to change their "stories", and their behaviors. For example, if
the client reports in therapy that "there is a gate between me and my feelings and between me and
people", the therapist can employ the client's metaphor and ask, "Where is the gate keeper?' *(If
there is a "gate", there should be a "gatekeeper".)* The "gatekeeper" can decide when to open and
close the gate; what and whom to allow through; and the like. In short, the "gatekeeper" has to
"notice", "catch", "interrupt", "plan", "make choices", and engage in the many other executive
self-regulatory activities that are at the heart of cognitive behavioral interventions.

But clients do <u>not</u> delimit their metaphorical accounts to only "negative" features. They also
often include in their narrative accounts "positive" hopeful metaphors, as described under Item VII
below. Our clients may also convey their desires to "write a new chapter", "rejoin life", "be on the
road of recovery", etc. The therapist can use the clients' "hopeful" metaphors in therapy and
indicate to his/her clients that, "if this is their goal, for example, of "writing a new chapter", then
they have come to the "right place", because this is what "I" (the therapist) do, namely, "I help
people begin to write a new personal chapter and rescript their lives; no longer living the script that
was written for them by someone else" (e.g., the perpetrator). Moreover, the therapist can also
indicate that, "the client has already begun this rewriting process by coming to therapy, by
beginning to tell your story, by being "in touch" with your feelings, by allowing yourself or giving
yourself permission to experience emotional reactions. Let us take a moment to determine what
you have done already to begin to "restory" your life and what <u>we</u> can do <u>together</u> to further this
process". *(At this point the therapist can help the client enumerate other "signs of recovery". See
Section VI under Letter writing for many other examples of how therapists can use metaphors.)*

One object of therapy is to help clients consider and recognize a world of possibilities. As
Markus and Nurius (1986) observe, individuals need to develop images of themselves as they
would like to be. As Goncalves (1994) stresses, one goal of cognitive narrative psychotherapy is

to help clients develop "a set of new meaning lens with which to explore and make sense of reality" and "to venture into the unknown, the world of possiblity" (p. 119-120).

In summary, psychotherapy is **viewed as a means of helping clients construct a "new narrative"**. As we will see, Treatment Sections V, VI and VII are replete with many creative ways to help clients to construct a new narrative, as well as change their behaviors. Also included are multiple examples of how therapists can relate their own metaphors to clients to describe their interventions. Therapists do <u>not</u> only treat clients, they embed their interventions in metaphorical accounts. Psychotherapists (researchers) have their own "stories" to tell. Sometimes, therapists use the language of "conditioning", or the language of "information processing", or the language of "object relations", and so forth, to explain to clients (and colleagues) what they are doing and why. But keep in mind these accounts are just the therapists' metaphors.[1]

Let us consider the metaphors offered by our clients who have been "traumatized" and "victimized". The following **list of metaphors** have been collected from a content analysis that I have conducted of many hours of audiotaped psychotherapy sessions with "traumatized" clients and from reading all of the clinical transcripts that I could find in the literature. In almost all instances, the metaphors offered were initiated by the client and less frequently suggested by the therapist. I have clustered these metaphors in terms of the prominent cardinal symptoms and experiences that traumatized clients report.

Parenthetically, I should note that I have <u>never had a client</u> enter an assessment or treatment session and say:

> "I have experienced horrific traumatic events and as a consequence
> I am hypervigilant, hypersensitive, avoidant, and experience "bad"
> thoughts and pictures that I can't get out of my mind. In addition,
> as I reflect on my distressful experiences I become depressed, and
> on several occasions drink heavily to reduce how upset I am. I
> believe these "victimizing" experiences have also affected how I
> get along with others".

My clients do not usually talk to me, nor to themselves, in this behavioral prescriptive fashion. Only mental health workers who write diagnostic classification systems (like DSM IV) tend to talk to each other in such a fashion. The following list describes how clients usually talk to therapists about their experience. As you become more aware of the metaphors that your clients use to construct their narratives, **please send me additional examples of client metaphors.** *(I recognize that any request I make will only be complied with by approximately 25% of the readers -- see Meichenbaum and Turk, 1987. Thank you for a being a member of that 25% group.)* Now to our clients' metaphors. In turn, we will consider how clients use metaphors to describe their:

---

[1] **Great caution** is required when the therapist offers or imposes his/her metaphors on clients, rather than helps clients to "unpack" and explore the implications of their own metaphors. There is a danger of an **iatrogenic impact** on clients of therapists emphasizing their metaphors. For instance, consider the popular counselor John Bradshaw who had a series of programs on public television in the US (a highly credible station). Bradshaw proposed to his audience that they "speak to an **inner child**" or to the "vulnerable person" within themselves. The audience was also encouraged to comfort the "inner child" by giving the "inner child" a name, to defend the "inner child", if necessary, and to interact with the "inner child". The metaphor of the "inner child" is reified and the audience is <u>not</u> educated about the ways and the impact of how they go about constructing metaphorical stories, of which the "inner child" is only one such story. *(I should note that after watching the Bradshaw series I wrote Public Broadcasting Television and asked for my donation back. I expect more from this Broadcasting Network.)*

I.   Affective state (hypersensitivity)

II.   Feelings of being blocked and trapped (psychic numbing)

III.   Intrusive ideation

IV.   Sense of personal loss

V.   Sense of themselves and their situation

VI.   Past abusive events (often untold secrets)

VII.   Expressions of hopes and desire for "healing"

I.   Metaphoric descriptions of affective state (hypersensitivity)

1.   I am a time bomb ticking, ready to explode. A volcano ready to go off at any time.
2.   Heat-seeking missile. Tightly coiled spring.
3.   Short fuse. Low boiling point. On hyperdrive.
4.   I'm at my breaking point.
5.   Engulfed by anguish. Constantly putting out bush fires.
6.   I walk a thin red line. Walk on egg shells. I'm ready to snap.
7.   I am an emotional yo-yo. A pendulum gone mad, swinging wildly.
8.   I am in an emotional state of siege. Coming apart at the seams.
9.   I am out of control, hot and cold, nothing in between.
10.   Over the edge, emotional overload, emotional meltdown.
11.   Emotional jack-in-the-box. Emotional roller-coaster.
12.   Overcome by creepy sensations. Emotional fault-line.
13.   I feel like I am caught up in a tornado.
14.   Emotionally blind-sided, emotional quagmire.
15.   Like a jackhammer is outside my window all the time.
16.   I'm in war mode all the time.
17.   React to every stimuli as if it were new, fight or flight.

II.   Describe feelings of being blocked and trapped (psychic numbing)

1.   I live in a frozen watchfulness. Emotionally shutdown. Emotional anesthesia.
2.   I am a rabbit stuck in the glare of headlights who can't move.
3.   I feel enclosed in a steel ball, little boxes. Boxed in. Traps all over the place.
4.   I feel a gate (wall, trap) has hemmed me in. My feelings are walled off.
5.   I carry the burden of conscience.
6.   There is a stimulus barrier between me and others. .
7.   I am a spectator to life. I run on automatic pilot, no feelings. An automaton. Spaced out.
8.   My heart and mind have been severed. My mind is dead, fragmented.
9.   My emotions have been castrated.
10.   I am a time machine that can't stop.
11.   Rag doll with no feelings. Emotionally dead. Stranger in a strange land.
12.   I live in partial anesthesia. Running in circles. A dislocated person. A beseiged self.
13.   Emotionally neutered. Zombie-like. My feelings are frozen.
14.   Go through life sleep walking. A void. Sit on sidelines.
15.   Robot, with no feelings. Protective shield.
16.   Empty vase. End of my rope.

17. I am out of touch. Emotional circuit-breaker. Split off.
18. Trapped in Dante's inferno, in a living purgatory.
19. It's like receiving orders from your commander and he doesn't know his ass from his elbow and I'm stuck carrying out the orders. I'm stuck.
20. A veteran of an intensely private war.

III. View of thoughts (intrusive ideation)

1. My thoughts visit me, show up. Cognitive baggage I carry.
2. I am a passive observer to these private demons.
3. Like a gusher of ideation. Stop me in my tracks.
4. A methodical onslaught.
5. My mind has run amok.
6. Daunting memories of the past. Memory fragments bombard me.
7. My thoughts have a life of their own.
8. Like a rerun of a movie that won't stop. Like a book chapter that I just keep reading over and over again. Fixated on the trauma.
9. Not get it out of my head. A nightmare that cannot be stopped.
10. Indelible images. Crystallized experience. Engraved. An imprint of death.
11. My mind was scarred. Psychic trauma is a wound to one's mind.
12. The reminders never stop. I just want them to stop. I drink to obliterate them.
13. I want to vomit this out. Detoxify my memories.
14. Traumatic payload I carry with me. Traumatic fallout.
15. I am played on by my thoughts. It is a psychic legacy.
16. Flashbulb memory. Malignant memories.
17. I want the slate wiped clean.
18. I'm able to put it out of my mind for a little while, then **they return**.
19. I was deeply brainwashed and I have to be deprogrammed.

IV. Sense of loss

1. Hole in myself, not complete, a loser. Life is a shambles. A bottomless pit.
2. Invisible disability. Disabled life.
3. Live in no man's land between a past and no future. Time slide.
4. Robbed my soul (dignity, childhood, identity, trust, intimacy, ability to relate).
5. Hate has sewn my lips closed.
6. Part of me died. Not the same person. Lost my heart. Killed my soul. Immolation of myself. A black hole inside me.
7. Wear different lenses. Tunnel vision.
8. Make life a living hell. A doomed life mission.
9. Raped my unconscious. Emotional blackmail.
10. I fell through the safety net.
11. My life was stalled by the abuse. My life is in a holding pattern.
12. Stole my childhood. Cheated me out of my childhood.
13. I feel like I'm in a cave and can't get out ... In a pit climbing to get out and there are no footholds to help me get out.
14. Trauma sits like a psychic organizer.
15. Spiritually purged, spiritually bankrupt, a soul death.
16. Interpersonal shutdown, live around the edges. Keep the world at bay.
17. A meaning vacuum. A void. Sounds of emptiness. Sounds of a soul hurt.
18. I developed amnesia for the good things in my life.

V. Characteristics of self (identity) and their situation

1. Prisoner of the past and occasionally on parole.
2. Murderer, sinner, bad seed, damaged goods, bad penny, sick martyr.
3. Crippled, phoney, dirty, chameleon, Zelig-like character. I carry the mark of Cain.
4. Love addict, emotional mush, emotional cripple, gone to pieces. Surrender to tears.
5. Untouchable, abandoned, skin crawl.
6. Lifetime of grief. I want to turn the clock back.
7. Deadened -- no guideposts. Just a vulnerable object. Drowning in a sea of chaos.
8. Door mat, garbage pail.
9. Counterfeit world, open Pandora's box, uphill struggle. A Catch-22.
10. Stuck in trauma, in a rut, dead end. Paralysis of will.
11. Like driving a car and never trust that the oncoming driver won't suddenly cross the double yellow line (always vigilant).
12. Lot of teenager in me (refer to different parts of self -- young girl, inner child, etc.).
13. Action-junkie. Addicted to trauma. An adrenaline rush.
14. An Odyssey on which I am a passive observer.
15. An abuser within me.
16. Feel like a child.
17. A bruise that won't heal.
18. Scarred, special, different, unique.
19. Like a piece of glass in my knee that won't come out.
20. Home is like a pressure cooker, ready to explode.
21. I organize my life around avoidance. This trauma was a turning point. It split my life into two.
22. I'm in a unwinnable war with myself.
23. I always feel out of place, like wearing tennis shoes at a formal dance.
24. I entered a marriage of despair, convenience.
25. I work to "best" my parents.
26. I act like judge and jury, prosecutor and defense, and I never have an opportunity for appeal.

VI. Description of past abusive events (secrets)

1. Can of worms.
2. Skeletons in my closet.
3. Memories are not digestible. Malignant (toxic) memories.
4. Disorder of reminiscence.
5. Vacuum in my history. Gaping hole to fill in.
6. Banish all memories of the events. Seal over my memories.
7. Baggage I carry with me.
8. Engraved in stone.
9. Unfinished business.
10. It is like remaining fragments of a bullet in me and things and memories reopen the wound.
11. Part of me cannot remember. A black hole in my childhood.
12. Ghosts of old terrors come back to haunt me.
13. These memories are always lurking in the corner of my mind.
14. My story of abuse was buried, swept under the rug.
15. Unravel my secret. Peel back the layers.
16. Conspiracy of silence surrounded these events.
17. The day of the "black water" (dam collapsed), it was that day that became the reference point for me. Everything could be measured by what happened before and what happened after the "black water" day.

NOW CONSIDER SOME OF THE "HEALING" METAPHORS
THAT CLIENTS ALSO OFFER

VII. <u>Expressions of treatment goals (hopes for change)</u> -- These metaphors usually convey the client's desire to find "closure," "resolution," "peace of mind," and "self-forgiveness," as well as to "make peace or come to terms with the past," "reach the point of acceptance," "fill in the gaps," "exert control," "salvage the past," "work through feelings," "find meaning", "move on" and "begin again." They also convey metaphors to describe efforts at "rebuilding a life".

1.   Resolve the hurt. Accept the scars. Move beyond the legacy of my past.
2.   Heal the inner child. Feel like a whole person.
3.   Doing this for the little girl/boy I used to be.
4.   I want the little girl/boy in me to feel protected.
5.   I want to repair the many hurts and losses.
6.   I want this trauma to lose its gripping quality. I know the memory won't go away, but I want to someday become bored with its re-telling.
7.   I want the trauma not to be the most important, not even the most interesting part of my life story; when the trauma and its aftermath will no longer command the central place in my life.
8.   One door closes and another opens.
9.   In the same way I don't trust everything I read in the newspapers, I want to learn not to trust everything I believe or say to myself.
10. I want to believe in order and purpose. As Einstein said, "God doesn't play dice with the world."
11. Tame my mind. Defuse the situation. Emotionally ventilate. Find a sounding board.
12. I want to talk directly to my unconscious and heal it.
13. I want to be the person before all this happened.
14. I want to put away my memories like orderly shelves/cupboards. I want to "digest, assimilate, metabolize, resolve, integrate, find meaning in" this trauma.
15. I won't let him rob me of my future like he robbed me of my past (childhood, innocence, trust, youth).
16. Peel off the layers and get to the stinking part of me and make it so it doesn't stink anymore.
17. Reprogram myself. Reclaim a version of myself as a healthy human being.
18. Make peace with the past. Prevent this from happening to others.
19. I want to coexist better with my unforgettable traumatic experience.
20. Reborn again. I want to reclaim my past and stake-out my future.
21. Move from victim to survivor. Move beyond the impasse.
22. Write a new chapter. I want to be the author of my recovery.
23. I want to be the author of my own stories.
24. I want to be the director of the movie, not merely a walk-on. I want to rewrite my own script.
25. Join the world, join life. Turn the corner. Find a new path.
26. Get back on the horse, on the right track, back in the saddle again.
27. Bear witness. Raise public awareness. Find a mission, a purpose to life.
28. Find a life-line, a second chance in life, reach a turning point.
29. Get back in the driver's seat. Get on track.
30. Take charge of my life. Reclaim territory taken by these events. Reclaim my history.
31. I want to influence the legacies I leave.
32. I want to learn to roll with the punches.
33. I want to be a gardener, not just the florist. I want to steer a vessel of my own making.
34. Break free. I want to focus on where I go from here.
35. Put a new coin in my juke box and play a new tune.

36. I want to work on my unfinished business.
37. Recharge my batteries.
38. I want to get on with the business of life.
39. I want to move out of whirlpools and into still waters.
40. I want to join the circles of belonging.
41. I want to get back my true self, get back what was taken away from me.
42. I want to keep on track and get on with life.
43. I want to find a safe haven, a container for my feelings.
44 Be prepared--I want to reduce the risk for further victimization.
45. I want to salvage something positive.
46. I want to be on the road to recovery. I made a pilgrimage; I undertook a personal journey of healing.
47. I want to prove "them" wrong ("them" may refer to anyone such as a family member, perpetrator, or health care worker who conveyed that the client would not "make it"). It is the obstinate little bitch in me that won't give up.
48. Don't try to normalize my reactions. Don't tell me that I am like anyone else. Don't tell me that I have to live with this forever. I am just tired of fighting. I want this to end. I am unique.
49. A client may offer a metaphor of different "parts of me." For example, a client may convey that there is a part of him/her that will always feel "a loss" but another part that reflects "resilience and courage". The therapist solicits evidence for these different parts and helps the client live with such ambivalence, so the ambivalence does not get in the way of his/her current goals.
50. I am a Phoenix rising from the camps.
51. I want to give myself permission to mourn and to let go; to put it behind me.
52. Not allow PTSD to become a metaphor for my life.
53. Trauma can be a catalyst for change.
54. I now recognize that memory does not fade, it grows. My memory is malleable and not like a videotape. I've learned that I can manage my memory and thoughts and not have them manage me.
55. I learned that when a person has a "why" to their lives they can put up with any "how" and "what" questions in life.
56. I have shifted from I HAD TO LIVE to I WANT TO LIVE! I asked myself what was lost and what was not lost and learning to be my own therapist helped.
57. I collect memories, my own and other peoples' memories of what happened. Recapturing my memory gives me some control. I can do the reconstructive work.
58. The traumatic experience became the center around which I reorganized a previous disorganized life.

Besides becoming a more **exquisite listener** to the language your clients use to describe their reactions and situation, what other assessment tools and strategies should the clinician use? We now turn our attention to the variety of alternative assessment procedures and strategies. But before doing so, determine your level of expertise concerning Section II. As you contemplate these questions, keep in mind that many survivors of trauma have sought to fulfill the need to "tell their stories". See the following moving autobiographical and biographical accounts and take special note of how they go about constructing a new narrative. These authors include Angelou, 1970; Barath et al., 1993; Bass & Thornton, 1983; Brady, 1979; Breznitz, 1993; Butler, 1978; Cleland, 1980; Coles, 1989; Danica, 1988; Des Pres, 1980; Downs, 1984; Evert, 1987; Fly, 1973; Frankl, 1982; Fraser, 1987; Fred, 1990; Friday, 1973; Grubman-Black, 1990; Kuenning, 1991; Langer 1991; Levi, 1987; Lew, 1988; Lifton, 1967, 1973, 1979; Marshall, 1944; Mason, 1986; Morris, 1982; Moskovitz, 1993; Noel & Watterson, 1993; Norman, 1990; O'Brien, 1990, 1994; Palmer, 1987; Puller, 1980; Royce, 1964; Rymer, 1993; Satre, 1964, Scherer, 1992; Timerman, 1988; Viorst, 1986; Weisel, 1960, 1965.

TESTING YOUR EXPERTISE

Section II - Alternative Conceptions of PTSD

1. Many different theoretical models of PTSD have been offered to explain peoples' reactions to traumatic events. Compare and contrast the different perspectives including biological, conditioning, information processing, schema-based, constructive narrative? What are the strengths and weaknesses of each perspective?

2. What is a constructive narrative perspective? Critically evaluate whether it has anything to offer to our understanding of PTSD. What are the assessment and treatment implications of adopting a constructive narrative perspective of PTSD?

3. Listen carefully to how your clients "tell their stories" about their reactions to traumatic events. After the session, write down all of the metaphors they have used.

    a) How do they use metaphors to describe their PTSD symptoms?
    b) Do they include any specific "hopeful" metaphors that you can use in treatment?
    c) Which client metaphors can be considered as basic, or as "root" metaphors?

4. Now that you have solicited and recorded your client's metaphors, help the client to elaborate and describe their metaphors. Can you "pluck" the client's metaphor (e.g., "I am prisoner of the past", or "I stuff feelings") and reflect it back to the client in the form of a question: "Prisoner of the past? -- tell me about that?". Experiment by choosing a central metaphor that the client uses and help "unpack" the metaphor exploring its impact on how the client sees him/herself, the world and the future. What is the "impact", the "toll", the "price", he/she "pays" for seeing the world in this fashion? How have you explored these questions with the client?

5. Select a "positive" metaphor that your client has offered. How did you use it to convey hope and facilitate change? How does your client's use of metaphors, as well as their narrative features, change over the course of treatment?

6. Now that you have focused on the clients' metaphors, it is time to keep track of the metaphors, you, the therpaist, introduce into treatment. What are all the ways you use metaphors in your treatment? How do the metaphors you use help you achieve your treatment objectives? How do you know if the client has benefitted from your metaphor? What indices do you use to assess change?

7. For those of you who like challenges, go through the 7 categories of metaphors I list and categorize the client metaphors into Lakoff and Johnson's 3 metaphorical categories of structure, orientation and physical. What does this tell you about how people construct narratives?

8. Finally, what aspects of a person's narrative correlate with poor adjustment? If something "bad", "traumatic" happened to you, or to a family member, what would you have to tell yourself (or the "story" you would have to construct narratively) in order to develop PTSD, and PTSD and DES?

9. As a result of engaging in these exercises, how has your notetaking about each client changed? How has this keen sensitivity to how clients' use language to tell their stories affected your assessment and treatment approaches?

SECTION III
ASSESSMENT OF PTSD AND RELATED FEATURES

Goals of Section III

As part of my work on PTSD, I have been called upon to conduct assessments for litigation cases, to review assessment strategies for labor unions who are concerned with workmen compensation issues, as well as provide consultation for psychiatric facilities who treat a wide array of clinical cases; many of whom have histories, or "alleged" histories, of abuse and victimization. The goals of Section III are five-fold:

1. to outline general assessment strategies;

2. to consider the critical role of the clinical interview as part of both the assessment and therapeutic processes;

3. to review the variety of diverse, self-report, behavioral and psychophysiological measures designed to assess both PTSD and measures of comorbidity (e.g., anxiety, dissociation, depression, suicidal tendencies, alcohol and personality problems, somatization, and the like);

4. to highlight the need to assess both positive, as well as negative effects of having experienced traumatic events;

5. to describe how clinicians can engage clients in a collaborative form of self-monitoring as a means of further assessing PTSD symptoms and related difficulties.

Before we consider the specific measures, two additional comments should be offered. First, from a cognitive-behavioral perspective the distinction between assessment and treatment is intentionally blurred. Assessment is viewed as inherently a change-generating process. The types of questions we ask clients, the types of tests we administer, the involvement of significant others, each promote a personal and familial reconstructive process. For example, the clinical interview can help clients not only tell their stories, but also help them begin to construct new more "adaptive" stories. The most useful skill the clinician has is the art of Socratic questioning that guides client's discovery. The emphasis on the importance of the clinical interview does not diminish the importance of standardized diagnostic instruments. The two approaches can complement each other.

The second major observation is that the field of PTSD is progressing to the point of developing population specific PTSD measures. Thus, researchers have validated measures that can be used with rape victims, crime victims, combat veterans, victims of natural disasters, and the like. *(Note, the assessment of the impact of natural disasters is presented in more detail in Section VII.)*

These target specific measures are designed to supplement the more general PTSD symptom report measures. There is also a need to consider the role that **premorbid** factors and **recovery factors** play in influencing the individual's and group's adjustment to traumatic events. Moreover, there is a need to consider how these diverse classes of variables can be combined to predict who does and who does not develop PTSD and PTSD + DES. The most thoughtful presentation of alternative causative and predictive models to address these questions that I came across is that offered by Kazdin and Kagan (1994). Although their article focuses primarily on models of dysfunction in developmental psychopathology, their arguments readily apply to the PTSD domain. They question the assumption of single pathways of dysfunction (e.g., dose of traumatic exposure and severity of symptoms), the focus on linear relationships, the value of categorical clustering, and the like. Their proposals represent important guidelines for how researchers and clinicians should conceptualize the role of causative factors.

As a result of working through Section I of this **Handbook/Manual**, the clinicians should have an appreciation of the multifaceted nature of PTSD and the need to tap the client's functioning in various areas. The purpose of this ASSESSMENT Section is to highlight possible measures that can be used for both clinical and research purposes. Obviously, the ways in which clinicians sample from this comprehensive list of measures will be influenced by the purpose of the assessment. In considering these PTSD and comorbidity measures it is worth repeating some warnings offered by Allen (1994). He comments on the care required in selecting measures of PTSD.

1. "Care should be taken that the instrument selected for use in assessing PTSD was developed in a population with a PTSD prevalence rate comparable to that in which it is being used clinically. When used in low base rate populations, PTSD measure yield a disproportionate number of false positive results." (p. 329)

2. Often **age-appropriate norms are absent** for the PTSD measures that are employed. For example, measures developed on combat veterans are employed with aged combat veterans.

3. Scores on one instrument alone are not sufficient to make the diagnosis of PTSD.

4. Use **multiple assessments** including information from **multiple sources**, collected through **multiple methods** over **multiple contacts**.

Finally, I recognize that in some circles assessment is <u>not</u> deemed as a very useful exercise, since insurance companies do <u>not</u> wish to reimburse for the administration of lengthy assessment batteries. Perhaps their concerns are justified when clinicians employ omnibus tests that have limited reliability and validity and that do <u>not</u> lead to differential treatment decisions, nor are included on an ongoing basis to evaluate treatment progress. The field of assessment, especially in the area of PTSD, has gone well beyond that point. There are now very specific useful measures that can address diagnostic, prognostic and comorbidity issues. The assessment battery must also focus on what are the client's strengths and resources, environmental "buffers", and possible "rescue" factors, as well as on the client's adjustment difficulties. **Reviewing the test results with the client can prove to be a very therapeutic process.** For example, Dr. Lawrence Kolb (1994) in a review of the recent VA study of psychophysiology of Vietnam veterans with PTSD, speaks of the beneficial effects of reviewing the autonomic arousal data with the veterans. Such assessment information helped the veteran, his/her family, and the compensation boards to better understand the nature of PTSD. It is mandatory that clinicians be familiar with the array of instruments (interviews, self-report, performance, psychophysiological) that are available in the area of PTSD.

This Section is designed to provide information in a succinct fashion on the assessment strategies and measures available. In my academic obsessive fashion I have tried to provide a complete list of possible measures. I am sure I have omitted some key questions that can be raised, as well as some key measures. Please send me information on any omissions to be included in the next update of this **Handbook/Manual**.

Overview of Section III
Assessment of PTSD

1. Assessment Strategies for PTSD Clients

2. What questions can the clinician use with PTSD clients? The initial interviews

    a)   for clients who enter with reports of exposure to traumatic events

    b)   for clients who do not report spontaneously any experience with traumatic events (Such reports of victimization may emerge over the course of assessment or treatment.)

3. Adult PTSD assessment measures

4. Assessment measures of comorbidity

    a)   General psychopathology

    b)   Suicidal ideation and suicidal behavior

    c)   Substance abuse

5. Family assessment

6. Assessment of premorbid risk factors for PTSD

7. Need to assess positive adjustment following trauma

8. Comments on self-monitoring

Finally, as one reviews this Section on Assessment of PTSD, keep in mind that "no universally accepted gold standard PTSD criterion has emerged" (Watson et al., 1994, p. 81). As noted, there is a need for a **multi-method, multidimensional assessment approach** since there is disagreement as to what the best measures of PTSD might be. These measures may include client interviews, interviews with significant others, psychological, and physiological assessments. Moreover, repeated assessments over time in order to monitor clients and to evaluate treatment progress are useful.

ASSESSMENT STRATEGIES FOR PTSD CLIENTS:
There is a need to assess both the <u>negative</u> and <u>positive</u> adjustment of traumatized individuals.

A. **The assessment of PTSD must consider both the assessment of symptoms and experiences related to PTSD and the assessment of possible co-existing psychological disorders.** Multiple approaches should be employed in the assessment. (For example, see the <u>Psychological Assessment</u> Journal (1991), Best (1994), and Keane et al. (1992) for a discussion of multiple ways to assess PTSD.) Most frequently, the assessment approaches include the use of:

1. open-ended interview of trauma history and history of prior exposure to traumatic events

2. structured clinical interview (clinician may use rating scales and reports of significant others and available files/records)

3. standardized PTSD questionnaires

4. specific PTSD standardized measures selected for specific trauma events/history (e.g., combat, rape, disaster, crime, abuse)

5. standardized assessment of comorbidity (e.g., depression, anxiety, addictive behaviors)

6. assessment premorbid and recovery environments (e.g., prior history, social supports, community factors)

7. where feasible, assessment of psychophysiological reactivity to trauma-related stimuli

8. assessment of possible "positive" benefits that may have occurred as a result of exposure.

The assessment may be in one lengthy or two or more shorter sessions.[1] Progress should be monitored over time. Several investigators have noted the "therapeutic" benefits of repeated assessment (e.g., Foa et al., 1993).

B. **The assessment strategy obviously varies depending upon:**

1. the referral conditions (e.g., individual enters therapy having experienced traumatic stressor or whether the client's reports of traumatic events emerge over the course of treatment).

2. the purpose of the assessment (reasons for the referral) and time available.

3. possible roles of premorbid and comorbidity (multiple diagnoses).

Note: PTSD is not usually evident on general measures of psychopathology. Thus, there is a need to assess explicitly for PTSD symptomatology.

---

[1] Hoyt (1994) highlights that the assessment period should go beyond the standard 1 hour session to be extended to 1 1/2 to 2 hours with breaks interspersed.

C. The following <u>sequential decisional</u> format may prove helpful in assessing clients to determine the presence and the level of PTSD, as well as helping in the case formulation. Format I provides a comprehensive overview to be applied if time permits. Format II is a proposed <u>short</u> version. The general assessment strategy is to use a **MULTIPLE GATING APPROACH**. This **gating approach** assesses components of the targeted areas and screens as to whether increasing discrimination and more extensive assessments are warranted. *(The specific measures are enumerated later in this Section.)* Whichever assessment strategy one uses, it is important to tailor the specific assessment procedures to the needs of the individual client.

<u>Format I</u>

1. Initial interview and trauma questionnaires.

   a) elicit the client's narrative account of trauma--follow general clinical interview format.
   b) assess for emotional-behavioral aftermath (assess for PTSD <u>and</u> DES symptoms).
   c) use standardized clinical interviews (DSM-III-R based interview and semi-structured interviews tailored to specific target population).
   d) tap trauma history (Potential Stressful Events Interview).

2. Use clinical rating scales based on the interview (e.g., CAPS-I, computerized version).

3. Assess directly for PTSD symptoms (e.g., Modified PTSD Symptom Scale, Impact Events Scale, and other symptom checklists such as SCL-R-90).

4. Use PTSD measures that have been developed for specific population (e.g., rape, combat, crime victimization, resources lost for natural disaster victims).

5. Assess global adjustment (e.g., Quality of Life Inventory, Social Functioning Scale, Areas of Change Questionnaire).

6. Assess cognitive skills and possible neuropsychological involvement.

7. Assess schema changes, social support, coping responses, and secondary sequelae (involve significant others in the assessment).

8. Assess "signs of healing"/strengths and signs of positive adjustment (e.g., Solution Focused Recovery Scale, Appraisal of Positive Benefits).

9. Ask the client to self-monitor symptoms (Weekly Symptom Checklist, as well as "Signs of Healing").

10. Assess premorbid history factors and post recovery environment factors.

11. Assess for comorbidity (e.g., alcoholism and other addictive behaviors, depression, suicidal ideation/suicidal behavior, anxiety, personality disorders, marital satisfaction/conflict, sexual adjustment, anger control problems, parental stress difficulties, etc.). Individually select from this array of alternatives.

12. If feasible, assess psychophysiological and performance-based measures related to PTSD.

13. Use goal attainment scaling.

Format II -- shorter version, when time is limited

1. Conduct open-ended clinical interview -- supplement with questions for target population. (Include Trauma Assessment for Adults)

2. Administer self-report scale (modified PTSD Symptom Scale, Impact Events Scale and SCL-R-90 short form, and checklist for DES symptoms).

3. Select target specific victimization measures (e.g., for rape victims, combat victims, incest history, natural disaster).

4. Select comorbidity assessment measures as indicated (alcohol, depression, etc.).

5. Assess for strengths (signs of recovery, social support). Use goal attainment scaling.

D. **Review measures collaboratively with the client and significant others.** Note, these measures can also be repeated to assess the impact and benefits of treatment. See Miller and Rollnick (1991, p. 96-99) and Sanders and Lawton (1993) for discussions of how information can be given to clients. In the context of providing feedback to the client, the therapist can further engage the client in the specification of treatment goals and treatment planning.

E. **Conduct ongoing assessments during and following treatment. Include follow-up assessments.**

WHAT QUESTIONS CAN THE CLINICIAN USE WITH PTSD CLIENTS?

The Initial Interviews

> *Over time, we have learned that asking the right question often has more impact on the client and the process of change than having the correct answer (Miller, 1994, p.93)*

As noted, the clinical interview and the accompanying "art of Socratic questioning[1]" are considered the most critical elements of assessment and intervention. The questions that can be incorporated into the initial sessions, as well as in later therapy sessions, serve several functions, including helping the client to:

a) tell his or her story and to feel understood, accepted, supported, and not isolated; convey to the client that his or her experience is important and that **the client is in charge or in control of telling his or her story;**

b) establish a collaborative working relationship and therapeutic alliance with the therapist;

c) assess current and past levels of functioning;

d) reframe and transform his/her symptoms and find "meaning" in distress (since finding meaning in misfortune is associated with more effective adjustment);

e) establish and achieve treatment goals;

f) bolster a sense of personal control and self-efficacy by attending to signs of recovery.

A number of astute clinicians have offered general guidelines and suggested specific questions that can be used to achieve these treatment objectives. They include de Shazer, Dolan, Epston, Falsetti & Resnick, Figley, Foa, Harvey, Herman, Kfir, Matsakis, Miller & Rollnick, Neimeyer, O'Hanlon, Padesky, Peterson, Scurfield, Scott & Stradling, Thompson, Tomm, and White. The following list includes samples of questions from the writings of these and other authors. (See Meichenbaum & Turk, 1987 for a fuller list of possible questions and resources.) Three specific references were particularly helpful in putting together this Section and they are strongly recommended (Dolan, 1991, Miller & Rollnick, 1991, and Scott & Stradling, 1992).

It is important that the suggested questions not be used with clients as a form of cross-examination, nor in a prosecutorial fashion. Instead, they should be viewed as directions for thinking. As Padesky (1993) has noted **Socratic questions are designed to guide client's discovery and not change their minds nor correct their thinking.** The questions are designed to guide and coach clients to **discover** and **invent solutions** to problems. Questions also provide a framework for inviting people to examine their experience in new ways--ways that can trigger change. Inherent in these questions are presuppositions that help clients focus on aspects of their stories of which they may not have attended. As Walter and Peller (1992, p. 46) observe, **"Questions with different presuppositions invite different classes of answers,"** as the client usually accepts the premise of the questions. This list of possible questions is offered in the spirit of providing **a list from which the sensitive**

---

[1] Socratic questioning involves the therapist (teacher) asking the client (student) questions that lead the client (student) to use his or her knowledge and skills in discussing and employing new concepts or procedures. Socratic questions nurture a "discovery process", not merely call for the retrieval of specific "facts".

clinician could sample. This list of questions is <u>not</u> designed to overwhelm the clinician, but rather to provide a framework of **"collaborative inquiry"** to pursue with the client and his/her family.

Finally, I should note that I have a "fetish". I collect good questions that clinicians use. The present list reflects only a small portion of my collection. If you, the reader, have additional questions, suggestions, or reactions to this list, please send them along to me. Please feed my fetish!

We will consider interview questions that fall into <u>8 different categories</u>:

1. Questions that allow the client to <u>tell his/her "story"</u> about the trauma and its initial impact (at his/her own pace).

2. Questions designed to assess the <u>lingering impact</u> of the traumatic event and how the client views the trauma at this point (assess level of functioning).

3. Questions designed to help the client <u>reframe</u> both the stressor and his/her reactions.

4. Questions designed to help the client attend to his/her <u>strengths, coping abilities,</u> and <u>possible signs of recovery</u>. In short, what is the client doing that is working, even to some degree?

5. Questions designed to help the client generate <u>possible coping efforts/solutions</u>.

6. Questions designed to help the client establish <u>treatment goals</u>.

7. Questions designed to help the client to develop a <u>different perspective</u>.

8. Questions that can be <u>raised with significant others</u> when being seen conjointly with the client.

The **initial list of questions** that we will cover are designed for those **individuals/clients who report having "knowingly" experienced a traumatic event.** The **second set of questions** that we will consider are designed for those **clients who enter treatment for "ostensibly" some other clinical problem** (psychological or physical **pain/distress), and only subsequently does the report of abuse or victimization emerge.** Clearly, the clinician can **sample from both lists of questions.** There is some overlap, but the major difference is the emphasis placed in the initial list on the client telling his/her story of "victimization" and the aftermath that are the primary reasons for referral. There is also a need to **assess for trauma history** for events other than the one for which the client is seeking treatment. A history of these other events might effect the length, complexity and course of treatment (Best, 1994).

Finally, before we consider possible specific questions, let us examine the general therapeutic strategy that underlies many of these questions.

Note: Obviously, there are more questions listed than any client should be asked. The present comprehensive list provides a "rich" menu from which to sample strategically. I believe **the "art of questioning" is the most critical skill for therapists to develop.** These are the best questions I have been able to find. I suggest that you tape record a therapy session and write out the questions you ask the client. Then compare your questions to those included in this Section. What new questions are you likely to add to your repertoire? **How can you become more expert in asking Socratic questions?**

It should be noted that for some clinicians the long list of potential questions may appear to be too formidable, and perhaps, even intimidating, or too demanding to cover within a time-limited interview. A solution, in part, has been offered by Stuart and Lieberman (1986) who in their Fifteen Minute Hour have proposed 5 simple questions that they mnemonically characterize as **BATHE** which cover the following areas:

Background   --What is going on in your life?

Affect   --How do you feel about what is going on?
                        What is your mood like these days?

Trouble   --What about the situation troubles you the most?

Handling   --How are you handling that?

Empathy   --That must have been very difficult for you?

With this as prologue, we can now consider the general format of the questions that will be offered.

General Strategy of Questions Asked

1.   Almost all the questions are of a "what" or "how" variety. Rarely, are "why" questions being asked. "Why" questions tend to be unanswerable and lead to self-doubt, further self-preoccupation, intrusive ideation and poorer adjustment (Baum, 1993). Instead of "why" questions, clinicians can focus on **"what"** and **"how"** questions.[1]

What Questions

What would be ...
What difference would ...
What is different about...
What do you think ...
What did you learn from ...
What are the signs that ...
What would X notice ...
What would you be doing differently to be "on track"?
What will you be doing instead of ...
What actions do you want to take?

---

[1] This does not mean that the clinician won't explore "why" questions, if the client wishes to do so. Following the client's lead in exploring "why" questions may prove instructive in explicating the client's implicit theories of causation, but it should be recognized that there are no ostensible answers to "why" questions; just plausible hypotheses or "co-created stories" that clients and therapists construct. If a "why" question is to be asked, it may take the following form, **"What answers, if any, have you given yourself up to this point to the "why" questions that you keep asking yourself?"** (For a discussion of the issues of "narrative truths" versus "historical truths" see Spence, 1987).

How Questions

> How is this the same/different ...
> How do you think ...
> How would you know that ...
> How would you ...
> How <u>will</u> you know that ...
> How will you know when...
> How will you <u>specifically</u> be doing ...
> How will knowing that make a difference?
> How will you (notice, catch, interrupt, plan, handle, cope with, pat yourself on the back, take credit for, let someone else know that, begin healing from, comfort, soothe) X? The therapist can sample from this list and he/she can also use the client's metaphor such as "join life", "rewrite my script", etc. in formulating such questions. Asking such questions "pull for" specific behavioral activities.

2.   In order to focus the discussion further on the client's strengths, the interview questions highlight **when** and **how** clients have **coped** in the past with other stressors.   Another way to accomplish this is for the therapist to use examples with the word "**instead**", "How will you be doing X <u>instead</u> of Y?" This question focuses the client's attention on possible coping efforts.

3.   There is a need to help the client put his/her story of victimization into some perspective. Dolan (1991) suggests that it is useful to have the client put his/her victimization incident(s) on a "**time line**" that indicates positive, as well as victimization, events. In this way the client can indicate to the therapist, to the therapy group, to significant others, as well as to oneself, his/her "positive" life events (e.g., graduations, births, job promotions, friendships, etc.). On the time line the client can include beginnings, high and low points, turning points, episodes and patterns. The client can also be encouraged to generate and visualize a "**future time line**", considering future goals he/she would like to see happen (can include a question mark at the end of the line). The therapist conveys to the client that he/she would like to hear the "whole", or the "rest of the story", (to quote the radio commentator, Paul Harvey). The "victimization" story is only part of the story; "one chapter in the client's autobiography". The life-time chart should include both "negative" and "positive" events.

4.   The object of both the interview questions and of the subsequent interventions is to provide the opportunity and encouragement for the <u>client to come up with ideas of what should be done next</u>.

IT IS PROPOSED THAT THE THERAPIST IS AT HIS/HER <u>THERAPEUTIC BEST WHEN THE CLIENT IS ONE STEP AHEAD OF THE THERAPIST,</u> OFFERING SUGGESTIONS OF WHAT SHOULD OCCUR NEXT AND WHAT HE/SHE CAN DO TO COPE MORE EFFECTIVELY.

The "name of the game" is to arrange clinical probes so that they <u>empower and enable</u> the client and encourage the client to take <u>ownership</u> and credit for behavioral change. The questions should allow ample time for the client to reflect in order to come up with and verbalize coping strategies. **There is a greater likelihood of clients following through and evidencing more commitment if they offer the suggestion of what can be done, than if such suggestions are just offered to them by others** (see Meichenbaum & Turk, 1987). Miller and Rollnick (1991) review several lines of studies that indicate that if individuals come up with suggestions themselves, make changes, and attribute those changes to themselves, the changes will be more long lasting. **The more responsibility the client takes in deciding how much of a problem there is and what needs to be done, the greater the amount and persistence of change.** Giving clients specific advice is less effective than focusing the clients' attention on their own resources. Help the client become aware of their own abilities and encourage them to exercise options. In short, **individuals are more likely to integrate and accept that which is reached by their own reasoning processes. "People are often more persuaded by what they hear themselves say than by what other people say"** (Miller & Rollnick, 1992, p.57). This is especially true when people can choose a course of action from among alternatives that they or the therapist present. Giving clients choices increases the likelihood of adherence and follow-through (see Meichenbaum & Turk, 1987).

If the client does <u>not</u> come up with a suggestion then the therapist has a variety of ways to introduce these suggestions, either directly or indirectly.

Style of Questioning

Before we consider the list of possible questions that can be raised with clients, a word should be offered about the style and manner in which such questions are asked. In my workshops I use videotape interviews to demonstrate that it is critical that the interview not turn into a cross-examination. The goal is to have the client talk in self-initiated paragraphs instead of waiting for the therapist to solicit information by means of questions. My style of questioning is to "pluck" (highlight and reflect) key words or phrases from the client's "story". The key words may be "metaphors" or words reflecting feelings. These are said back to the client with the same affect ("mirrored") that the client says them. For example: "Stuffed you feelings?"; "Want to write a new chapter?"; "Join life?"; "Felt proud?".

As the interview unfolds a second strategy is to use a **sentence completion procedure**, instead of full sentences. Thus, as the interview relationship is developing I tend to use half sentences, allowing the client to fill in the remainder. "So you ..."; "Then you..."; or "Help me understand what...". An economy of speech by the therapist permits the client to offer his or her "account" in an unimpeded personalized fashion.

With this as prologue, we can now consider the specific questions the therapist may raise with CLIENTS WHO "KNOWINGLY" HAVE EXPERIENCED TRAUMATIC EVENTS.

1. QUESTIONS THAT ARE DESIGNED TO HELP THE CLIENT **TELL HIS/HER STORY** *(Also see Section VII on "Critical Incident Stress Debriefing" for other possible questions.)* (Suggestions for many of these questions in this section come from Scott and Stradling, 1992.) During the course of the interview be sure to give clients **choices** and convey a **sense of control** to the client. For example, in the interview there is a need to convey control and empowerment to the "survivor". The interviewer should ask permission to interview the survivor. For example, ask the client, "Is this a good time to talk with you?" "Do you mind if I ask you some questions?"

With regard to the role of emotional expression of the traumatic experience, Turnbull (1994) advises that the "traumatic experience must never be embellished by the therapist's viewpoint. The trauma has to be expressed just as the survivors experienced it, taking their perspective...It is very important during this phase to **avoid uncontrolled catharsis** which would produce a maelstorm of information without structure...Such a stormy overspill would also jeopardize the fragile, emergent sense of being back in control" (p.8).

With these observations as guidelines the following statements may be conveyed to the client by the clinician.

Giving Clients Control

Tell me everything that you feel I need to know in order for you to know that I understand what happened.

Do not share anything you wish to keep private at this time.

At any time you would like, we can take a break for a moment. We can return to it later if you choose to do so. We can take as many breaks as you feel you need. (Note, it is very important to be respectful of the client, to give the client choices, and to empower the client to discuss or not discuss issues, to start and stop the interview.)

As Lebowitz et al. (1993) describe, the therapist should convey that he/she is a **"witness, ally, and expert educator"** and someone who is concerned foremost about the client's safety and well-being. With this as the communicative set, questions may be sampled from the following lists. It is critical to pace questions and follow the client's lead in how much he/she wishes to self-disclose.

If the trauma is known to have occurred, then the therapist should direct his or her questions about the trauma, present activities, and related issues. The interview should focus on what happened just prior to, during, and after the trauma exposure in terms of Type I stressors and the overall picture for Type II stressors; how have they been affected; and how are things different for them since the trauma. Such questions convey to survivors that it is "okay" to talk about such events and that the interviewer is interested in understanding the circumstances that led to their being seen. The following list provide examples of the type of questions that can be asked. This list of questions is not in any particular order and the clinician can sample as needed.

Where do you think we need to start?

Can you tell me what happened to you? When did X happen?

Can you tell me what you have been through? Can you tell me as exactly as possible, what happened? What did you go through?

How (or what) did you do to survive?

Has X brought many changes (e.g., X is the rape, robbery, accident, combat experience)?

What has X stopped you from doing?

What gets to you most about X?

Did you think you were going to die or be seriously injured?[1]

---

[1] Note that perception of life threat is a predictor of PTSD in rape, combat and accident victims. *(See Section VII for a discussion of other predictive variables.)*

Did anyone close to you die?

Were you injured?

How do you feel you coped at the time?

Sometimes people feel that they let themselves or others down; did you feel anything like that?

What got to you most about the whole thing?

What was the worst aspect of the situation?

Can you tell me how things were before X (specify the trauma)? How have things changed?

Do you see yourself as having any particular problems since the trauma?

What you have been describing is a situation of "crisis". In what way is it different from other stressors that you have undergone in your life?

Have you ever been in a situation that has any similarity to this one? "Have you ever been in similar circumstances before? What did you do? How did that turn out? What do you know now that you didn't know then? What would you advise a friend who told you something similar?" (Padesky, 1993).

You described that in this instance (be specific) you remember feeling "helpless" (use the client's words such as "out of control", "near death", "like a child"). At any time in your life, do you remember having had similar feelings of X (e.g., helplessness, terror, etc.)?

Can you allow your feelings to surface? If not, what gets in the way?

How do you explain this entire experience to yourself?

Have you made any sense or found any meaning in X (list trauma)?

Have you shared your feelings with anyone else? Who? How did that go? What was helpful about it? What was not helpful about it?

If your emotional pain could speak what would it say?...Your head seems to be saying one thing, but your heart (gut) is saying something else; what is that?

Do you feel you have enough information about your situation and what is (has been) happening to you? What information do you feel you still need?

Are there any areas you feel we were not able to cover adequately?

What are we not talking about now that you feel we should be talking about?

Do you feel you need help for any problems that have arisen?

What do you want to accomplish as a result of being in therapy?

What do you want to change?

What are your goals?

How do you want to behave differently?

Is this the first time that you have gone for help? (If "no", discuss previous experiences.)
    Have you been in therapy before? (If "yes", discuss previous experiences. What was
    helpful? What was not helpful?)

Do you have any previous experience or views about counseling?

How do you feel about being offered counseling help or therapy?

How do you expect counselling (therapy) to help you?

How long do you expect the therapy to take to help you achieve these goals?

For additional possible questions that can be asked about the traumatic events see Section VII
on debriefing and the list of questions in Scott & Stradling (1992, pp. 10-12).

In addition to these general questions that "pull for" the client telling his/her story a number
of specific questions and areas need to be covered when the therapist is interviewing clients with a
specific victimization experience (e.g., having been raped or having experienced child sexual
abuse, having been a victim of domestic violence, having been in combat). In other words, there
is a need to tailor the questions asked to the client's specific traumatic events. Consider the
following examples that provide guidelines for such clinical probes that may be followed. Once
again, there is a need to explore this material in a very sensitive, non-judgmental, non-prosecutorial
fashion. This is not a court of law. It is therapy! In fact, the clinician may use these questions as
a "template" from which to become a more sensitive listener to the client's story. The questions
derive from research that indicates that certain features of the traumatic events correlate with long-
term adjustment (e.g., the relationship between the perpetrator and the victim, the nature of the
abusive acts, and the like). With this in mind, let us consider some of the specific material that can
be covered with **rape victims** (1A) and with victims of **child sexual abuse** (1B), victims of
domestic violence (1C), and a general introduction that facilitates the **assessment of sexual
assault history** (1D).

1.A. MATERIAL TO COVER WHEN SOLICITING AN ACCOUNT OF TRAUMATIC EXPERIENCE: Rape History

Harvey et al. (1991), Matsakis (1992) and Resick and Schnicke (1993) illustrate the value of helping rape victims tell their stories by asking key questions.

Warning: As noted, do <u>not</u> turn these questions into a cross-examination, but rather help the client formulate an account of what happened at his or her own pace. These questions provide a set of guidelines that should be followed in a sensitive fashion. Before beginning the interview, obtain the client's permission to ask these questions and explain why going over this material is important. Remind the client she can stop the interview at any point or choose not to answer any questions. The therapist should convey his/her willingness to cover this material at the client's own pace.

Harvey et al. (1991) suggest that the following items should be covered:

"1.   relationship of the perpetrator(s) to the assault victim;

2.   an account of the assault, including information on who perpetrated the assault and where, with what force, and the respondent's thoughts and feelings at the time of the assault;

3.   whether or not the respondents had confided in any other persons about the assault, and if so, in whom they had confided and when, their relationship with the confidant, and the reactions of the confidant to their story;

4.   ways they had tried to cope with the assault over time;

5.   their sense of how the assault had affected them, including how it had influenced their close, personal relationships;

6.   how they now feel emotionally in regard to the assault; and

7.   any other types of comments or input they wished to make about the assault." (p. 523)

Matsakis (1992) suggests that the rape victim be encouraged to cover the following material:

"What did the rapist look like, smell like?
What did he say?
What did he do?
What did you say?
What happened first?
What did you think then?
What did you feel then?
What happened next?
What do you think and feel now?
Were any weapons or objects involved?" (p. 225)

As we will see in Section VI his material can be used in the direct therapy exposure interventions.

Resick and Schnicke (1993) add to the list the suggestion that the rape victim be asked specific questions about the nature of the act of perpetration and questions about pre-rape experience. They suggest that the rape victim should be asked:

"What did the perpetrator say to the client before, during and after the incident?" (Such comments often stay with the client and also reflect and lead into a discussion of the perceived threat.)

With regard to pre-rape experience Resick and Schnicke (1993) suggest asking:

"Prior to the rape, how did you feel about your own judgment? Did you trust other people? How did your prior life experiences affect your feelings of trust? How did the rape affect your feelings of trust in yourself and in others?"

Dutton et al., (1994, p. 244) suggest that the clinician assess for prior victimization experiences of unwanted and threatening sexual activity. The client can be asked,

"Were you ever touched sexually, sexually abused, molested, or raped between the ages of 0-17 years (or prior to the present episode) by an adult, including parent or someone more than 5 years older than you?" "Were you ever sexually touched against your will by an acquaintance or stranger; raped, or sexually abused?"

As a result of this initial phase of questions the therapist should not only have a "feel" for what the client has been through, but also the therapist should be able to answer the following 3 questions.

1.   Why has the client sought therapy now?

2.   What are the collaboratively generated goals of treatment?

3.   What skills and resources does the client have that can be used therapeutically?

1.B. MATERIAL TO COVER WITH SURVIVORS OF CHILDHOOD SEXUAL ABUSE: Incest History (Brandt, 1993; Courtois, 1988; Herman, 1981; Kirschner, Kirschner & Rappaport, 1993)

Once again, solicit the client's permission before covering this material.

"Would it be okay if I asked you some questions about what you have been through? In order for me, for the both of us, to better understand the trauma and its aftermath I would like to have you tell me, in your own words, what you have been through. At certain points, if it is okay with you, I will ask some questions of clarification or detail. Feel free not to answer any questions if you don't want to. You are in charge! Do you have any questions of what we are to do and why it is important? Shall we begin?"

At this point the client can be asked to tell her/his story and the following questions of detail can be raised in a timely and sensitive fashion about abuse components and abuse-related events.

Abuse Components

1. Age of onset and age of the abuse and of the last encounter.

2. Number of encounters and duration of the abuse (degree of sexual exposure).

3. Nature or type of the abuse (type of contact--exposure, touching, oral sex, intercourse).

4. Degree of threat or force (violence involved) used by the perpetrator (psychological coercion, verbal prohibition, verbal threats, physical coercion, and denegrating messages).

5. Nature of the threats if the "secret" of the abuse was violated by the victim.

6. Relationship of the abuser to the "victim" (trust violations).

7. Did the client tell an adult at the time? What was the reaction? Did the victim receive any support from others in ending the abusive situation or in dealing with it's effects?

8. Has the client told anyone about the abuse since the incident? Whom? When? For example, ask, "When you were a child did you try confiding in anyone what was happening?"

9. What stopped you from telling others about what was happening to you?

10. What made people afraid to speak the truth?

11. How was the incest finally stopped?

Abuse-related events

1. What is the nature of the family dysfunction at the time of the abuse and since then?

2. Were others in the family sexually abused?

3. Was the abuser or any other family member sexually abused?

4. What happened as a result of the abuse? (parental separation/divorce, out of home placement)?

5.   What was the nature of the support of disclosure?

6.   Was public disclosure involved (e.g., insensitive repeated interviewing, stressful testimony)?

Long-term Impact

1.   Were the client's own children ever abused? Does the client fear own children may be abused?

2.   What was (and is) the meaning the victim attached to the event, to herself and to others? What does the client feel has been the long-range impact of the abuse?

3.   What has the client done to handle the impact so far? What has worked? What has not worked?

4.   What does the client feel could be tried in the future?

5.   What is missing or unavailable in the client's life?

Kearney-Cooke and Striegel-Moore (1994) also suggest that the therapist explore the client's reactions to having told about the abuse, "making clear that the therapist will offer continued support, and beginning to examine what the client has done to cope with the trauma" (p.310).

1.C. HISTORY OF DOMESTIC VIOLENCE

Hamberger and Holtzworth-Munroe (1994) highlight the need to systematically probe for victimization of domestic violence when there is evidence of marital distress or when other forms of victimization are evident (e.g., child sexual abuse). Such queries of the spouse should be done individually in order <u>not</u> to put the client at risk for possible retribution from the spouse. The probes can begin with general questions and then move to more specific probes about physical abuse. Hamberger and Holtzworth-Munroe (1994, p.307) suggest the following questions:

> When you and your partner argue, how does he act when he becomes angry?

> Does he ever call you names?

> During arguments, are you ever afraid for your safety?

> Sometimes, when men get angry with their partner, they become physical and may push or shove. Has that ever happened to you?

> What other types of physical aggression has your partner used when he has been angry or otherwise upset?

> Have you ever been injured by your partner's aggression? What happened?

They note that when probing the **male offender**, the perpetrator is more likely to admit having engaged in specific aggressive actions rather than respond to general probes about abuse. For example, Hamberger and Holtzworth-Munroe (1994, p.311) suggest the following queries.

> Have you ever pushed your wife?

> Have you ever slapped your wife?

These questions are more effective than asking the offender, "Have you been violent?", "Have you ever abused your wife?".

The interview with both the victim and the offender can be supplemented with the administration of specific self-report measures, as described later in this section.

1.D. SEXUAL ABUSE HISTORY

While some clients enter treatment because they were abused (raped, child sexual abuse) other clients enter because of other traumatic events (e.g., domestic violence, crime, difficulty handling the aftermath of a natural or technological disaster). Since prior victimization is a high probability event there is a need to conduct a history of possible prior victimization. As Falsetti and Resnick (1994, p.9) observe:

> "Practitioners may feel uncomfortable conducting specific assessment of trauma history, particularly in reference to sexual assault incidents. It is important to recognize that the potential impact of such events on the victim should outweigh any awkwardness experienced by the professional. Avoidance of such information can send the client a negative message."

They provide an example of what clients can be told prior to conducting a sexual assault history. Following a general acknowledgment that some incidents that the client will be asked about may be difficult to talk about, but that it is important to do so, the following introduction may be offered. This introductory statement used by Saunders et al. (1989, p.224) in their research with both men and women can be tailored to the specific client. The important point is for the clinician not to "shy away" from conducting a sexual abuse history.

> "One type of event that happens to men as well as women, and boys as well as girls, is sexual mistreatment or sexual assault. Men are assaulted under the same kinds of situations as women, but it may be even more difficult for a man to report an assault because he may be ashamed or fear that others will ridicule or not believe him. When asked about sexual abuse or mistreatment, many people tend to think about incidents in which they were attacked or mistreated by a total stranger. As you answer these questions, please remember that we need to know about all incidents of sexual abuse or mistreatment, not just those involving a stranger. Thus, please don't forget to tell us about incidents that might have happened when you were a child or those in which the person who tried to abuse or mistreat you was someone you knew, such as a friend, boyfriend or girlfriend, or even a spouse or family member. Now, here are some questions about some of these experiences you might have had."

2. QUESTIONS THAT ARE DESIGNED TO ASSESS THE LINGERING IMPACT OF TRAUMATIC EVENTS AND LEVELS OF CURRENT AND PAST FUNCTIONING

Lingering impact

Could you take a few moments and describe the situation you are in now?...How are things now? How have things gone since the last time we talked?

Could you give me a description of what has been happening to you in recent weeks?

What is the "trauma" (be specific) preventing you from doing with your life now?

How is the "trauma" (be specific) preventing you from having the life you want today and tomorrow?

What was the most significant event or result of X (e.g., the flood)?

Many (some) people feel they will never recover from the effects of X (the flood). Do you feel this way?

When the X occurred (e.g., the flood hit), many people felt they did not know where to turn. Do you still feel this way?

On a scale of 0 to 5, how recovered would you say you are in terms of your emotional well-being?

The following questions can be used to tap symptomatic responses (See Scott & Stradling, 1992, for a more complete list).

Ruminations [1]

In the past week (month), have memories, thoughts, or mental pictures of what happened (e.g., death of spouse/child, accident, destruction of home) come into your mind? Can you tell me about these?

Do you ever find yourself reviewing in your mind the events that led up to X (e.g., accident)? And if so, what thoughts, in particular, did you have?

Do you ever find yourself thinking, "If only I had done something differently X would not have happened, (e.g., I would not have been raped, my spouse/buddy would be alive)? If "yes", could you describe your thoughts? How often in the last month (week) did you have the thought "if only" (Never (1) to All the Time (5). *(Taps Undoing)*

Do you blame anyone or anything for what happened? Can you tell me who (what) you blamed?

Even though we don't know what caused X, do you have a hunch or theory about what caused X?

Intrusions

---

[1] These questions have been adapted from Davis et al., in press.

As a result of X (be specific) can you tell me what, if any, worries you may have?

Are you having any particular dreams related to X?

Has this event reminded you or reawakened for you any earlier painful memories?

Do you have recurring memories that interfere with your enjoyment of life?

Do your memories trigger other pain?

Could you tell me how X, or the memory of X, (e.g., rape, robbery, accident, combat experience) is still influencing you?

Have you repeatedly had upsetting thoughts (nightmares) of X?

Do you sometimes feel as though you were actually reliving X?

Do you get very upset when you are exposed to anything that reminds you of X?

What is the X, or the memory of X (robbery, rape, etc.), preventing you from doing in your life now?

How often is that picture in your mind?

Do thoughts of what happened to you sometimes pop into your head when you don't want them to?

Are there specific aspects of X, or the memory of X, that have lingering effects on you ... on others in your life ... on your relationships? Are there any other memories which are causing problems?

When you are awake are your thoughts and pictures of the trauma:
   a) so bad that you cannot think of anything else?
   b) always at the back of your mind, but you can usually get on with things?
   c) there occasionally, but they do not usually bother you?
   (Scott & Stradling, 1992, p.11).

Avoidance

Because of X, are there any situations you now avoid?

Do you try to avoid certain thoughts, images, or pictures and feelings that are related to the X? If yes, how?

Do you try to avoid certain memories?

Can you tell me as specifically as possible, what you have been avoiding?

Have you been trying to avoid situations or places that remind you of the X?

Have you had trouble recalling any important aspects of the X?

Do you feel detached or cut off from others?

Do you feel numb emotionally?

Are there times when you deliberately choose not to show your feelings or let others know how you are reacting?[1]

At times when you felt emotional, how much did you hold back or not show your emotional reactions? What emotions did you not express?

Did you find yourself holding back more positive emotions, like happiness, negative emotions, like sadness, or did you hold back all emotions equally?

Physical Symptoms

Have you felt irritable?

Have you had bursts of anger?

Do you feel jumpy or get startled easily?

When you become tense, where do you feel this in your body? Is there any place in your body that feels tense now?

Have you had physical reactions when you are exposed to or experience anything that reminds you of X?

Tell me how your health has changed since X.

Questions that tap difficulty sleeping *(See section below on ways to measure objectively sleep behaviors.)* Sleep and dream disturbances have been called the "hallmark" of PTSD (Falk et al., 1994).

Let me ask you how you have been sleeping since X occurred. Has your sleep pattern changed in any ways? How? ... Do you have sleep disturbances?

How are you sleeping the last few days? What makes it difficult to sleep?

How long does it take for you to fall asleep?

Do you usually sleep soundly through the night or do you awake during the night? Do you wake at a certain point?

When you awake, how long does it usually take to get back to sleep?

Do you remember dreaming? What are your dreams like? Do you have disturbing dreams or nightmares? Can you describe them to me? Is it the same dream,?

When you awake in the morning how do you usually feel?

Do you have a fear of sleeping?

---

[1] Suggested by Blake, 1994.

Have you noticed, or has anyone mentioned to you, how you are sleeping? Do you find yourself grinding your teeth or wandering (night walking)? Any changes?

What impact do you think your sleep pattern has on your daytime functioning?

Do you have dreams or nightmares about X? How often? What happens in the dream?

Do you think the amount of your daytime distress (amount of rumination) affects your sleep patterns?

Questions that tap changes in attention and memory

Have you noted any changes in your ability to concentrate? In what ways?

Are you able to read a newspaper, magazine, book? How has this changed?

Are you able to watch television?

Do you find yourself to be more watchful or wary of others?

Do you find it difficult remembering things? How has this changed?

Is your train of thought interrupted often? Can you give me an example?

Current level of functioning

Could you give me a description of what has been happening to you in recent weeks?

How are you getting along?

Do you find yourself crying for seemingly no reason?

Are you frequently anxious or depressed?

Do you have unrealistic fears?

Are you often so angry you lose control?

Do you ever find yourself feeling real upset and not knowing why?

Could you tell me how this X (e.g., rape) is still influencing you? What would you like to feel about this now?

Could you share with me what X, "threat to one's life", "loss of one's loved ones", "loss of one's possessions" (choose one) does to a person?...What lingers on for you?

In what ways do you think you were different before X? How are you different after X?

How do you feel about those changes? What is going on for you that you want to be different?

What do you now make of the world? Make of other people?

How are you getting along with people around you?

Do you find it difficult being close with other people or trusting others?

Is it possible to have other interests, engage in other activities, apart from living one day to the next?

Are there things you used to enjoy doing with others that you don't enjoy any more or don't do? Tell me about what has changed? (Query about changes in interest and activities.)

Everybody has "good days" and "bad days". Can you tell me what a "good day" looks like? What would I see you doing?...How does that differ from what you would call a "bad day"? How would I be able to tell the difference between the two types of days?

When a person is X (depressed, anxious) or when a person has experienced X he/she often has (or is often overrun with) "negative thoughts". Have you had such negative thoughts?...Can we discuss them and the impact they have?

When a person has had such a traumatic experience it often challenges the ways he/she sees his/her world and himself/herself. Has that been the case in your situation?...In what ways?

Have your plans for the future changed in any ways? How?

Do you use alcohol[1] or drugs to help you cope with your distress? How does it help?

Do you feel alcohol or drug abuse is a problem for you?

Do others who are important to you say your alcohol or drug taking is a problem for you?

Do you suffer from serious psychological problems?

Have you lately been seen by a professional "helper" (e.g., a psychologist, psychiatrist, social worker, etc.)? Have you been seeing someone else in the role of a helper (e.g., clergyman, rabbi, AA member)?

Past level of functioning--(Also see section on **Premorbid Assessment** later this Section)

How were things going for you before this event occurred?...Fill me in on how you were feeling about yourself?...How you were getting along with others?...How were things going in the family?

Before this (traumatic) series of events in your life did you ever undergo a severe crisis?

At any time in your past do you remember feeling helpless (hopeless)? When was that? What happened?

How satisfied were you with life in the X months before the trauma?

Has the trauma made worse any difficulties you were experiencing previously? In what ways?

---

[1] A comprehensive assessment of alcohol intake is presented later in this section.

3. **QUESTIONS THAT ARE DESIGNED TO HELP THE CLIENT <u>REFRAME</u> THE TRAUMATIC EVENTS** *(See Section VI on "Educating the Client about PTSD" for other specific ways to help clients reframe their symptoms and coping efforts.)* (See Thompson, 1985, for a discussion of these questions.) The answers to each of these questions are discussed with the client.

> Although X is a terrible thing, can you think of anything positive, even a small thing, that has come out of this experience for you?

> Compared to others who have had this experience, do you feel you are in a better or worse situation? In what ways?

> Has anything that has happened made you feel particularly lucky or fortunate? In what ways?

> Was the stressful experience as bad as it could have been or could it have been worse?

> Is this experience as negative as you would have imagined before going through it?

> Are there things that you are more aware of because of this experience?

4. **QUESTIONS THAT ARE DESIGNED TO HELP THE CLIENT ATTEND TO HIS/HER COPING STRENGTHS** These questions are designed to tap the coping skills already in the client's repertoire. (See Dolan, 1991; White & Epston, 1990, 1991 for other examples.)

The examination of the client's coping efforts usually begins with a discussion of how he/she has tried to handle the situation thus far. This is followed by an examination of the particular strengths that the client may possess. The goal of this set of questions is to help clients focus their attention on aspects of their "stories" that they would be prone <u>not</u> to attend to. The initial probes focus on what Scott and Stradling (1992) call **Coping Since:**

> How do you feel you have **coped since** the trauma?

> How do you feel you have coped with unpleasant memories?

> Are some situations now more difficult to handle than they were before the trauma? How have you handled them?

> If I had to go through what you have gone through, I probably would <u>not</u> have made it. How did you survive? Where did you find the strength?

Before we consider the questions that focus on the client's strengths an important warning should be offered.

An important caveat: It is suggested that the clinician should <u>not</u> focus on tapping the client's strengths or on finding solutions too early in the therapeutic contacts. There is a need to first hear the client's "story of woe", emotional pain, and its aftermath, before focusing on possible solutions and coping efforts. If the questions in this section are raised too soon, then the client is likely to feel that you, the therapist, do <u>not</u> understand the level of his/her distress. Another reason to listen attentively to the client's story of distress is to examine collaboratively what the client has done to "survive" and "cope" with the distress. By listening to the client's "story" the clinician can help the client appreciate the variety of self-protective actions he/she has employed. Finally, in the context of telling his/her story the client will offer specific "metaphors" that can be used ("unpacked" and "explored") in therapy.

In working with clients, it is important to listen to their stories of "victimization" and also to take note of their accomplishments. The therapist can then reflect that **in spite of** your having experienced X, Y and Z events (cite specific traumatic examples), you were **able to achieve** A, B, C (cite specific examples). (For instance, **in spite of** being abandoned as a child, date raped, incested, you were able to go to college, earn a degree, get a job, get married, etc.) **How did you accomplish that?** Help me to understand what accounts for how you were able to achieve these objectives. What contributed to your ability to "survive", and even "thrive"?

In a recent case, the therapist commented to the client that it sounded like the client "had a strong fiber", to which she responded that she was "stubborn". Over the course of treatment this was reframed that the client was "tenacious". In fact, with the collaborative input of the therapist, the client developed a "game plan" to demonstrate her "tenacity". As the client continued to improve, the therapist commented that he would <u>not</u> have predicted that the client would have demonstrated such tenacity. The client asked the therapist why wouldn't he have predicted her degree of improvement. To which the therapist responded, "I apologize. I underestimated the depth of you tenacity and the degree of your desire to get better". To which, the client responded forgivingly to the therapist, "That is okay". The therapist then noted he looked forward to seeing what furture possible improvements were yet in store.

Listening to the client's story and juxtaposing the client's "strength" against the client's "victimization" experiences, provides an excellent way to help client's construct a new narrative. Another means to achieve this objective is to use the "artful" questioning offered by solution-focused therapists, **but only after having first listened to the client's story of "emotional pain".**

In order to tap the client's strengths the therapist can select from the following questions. A number of solution focused therapists (de Shazer, 1988, 1991; de Shazer & Molnar, 1984; Dolan, 1991; Walter & Peller, 1992) have suggested variations of what they have characterized as the **"instead" question** or **"look for exceptions"** questions. Consider the following algorithmic question that I extracted from their work:

Can you	recall/	an occasion/	when you were/	but <u>instead</u> you	rallied/
	think of/	a time/	nearly overtaken/		warded off/
	recognize/	an episode/	when you almost		did not give into/
	identify/		gave into a problem/		managed to cope/
					freed self from/
					escaped grip of/
					interrupted/
					didn't give into
					the problem?

I want to know what you think you are doing right? I want to learn what kind of things you want to see happen more often?

Another format that de Shazer (1985) uses is to instruct the client:

"Between now and when we meet, I would like you to notice the things that happen to you that you would like to keep happening in the future. This will help us find out more about your goals and what you're up to."

What sort of <u>solutions</u> have you come up with for dealing with X?

If you could do anything at all when you are feeling X (sad, mad, overwhelmed), to <u>not</u> feel that way, what could you do?

What could you do (have tried) to improve your mood?...control your X?...improve your relationships??

What have you done to cope with X? What did you do? What worked? What hasn't worked? Where did you learn to X? Tell me how you learned to X?

Are there times when you have been able to (cite specific example of coping effort -- e.g., calm yourself down, "combat" the flashback, etc.)? ... What did you do? ... Have you been able to do this in other situations? How did you manage that change? (Note: the use of **What?, How?** and **When?** questions.)

Do you think that becoming more aware of when you are doing Y will provide us with more information so you can use this at another time? How would your doing that be helpful?

Can we use any of the information to change the way you are handling the situation?

Are you doing some of those things now? (Ask for examples.)

And <u>what difference</u> would doing that make?

What would you need to support yourself?

If you were to boil down your thoughts and images, what do you think your basic belief about the situation would be? Does that belief make sense, given what you have been through?

<u>What difference</u> will <u>continuing</u> to do Y (cite specific examples) make <u>in the future</u>?

The past X, or the memory of X, seems to be getting in your way. How would you know that you had handled it better, even a little bit?

What would help you recognize little (or beginning) signs of recovery?

Can you take care of yourself when X occurs? How can you do that?

What is it that you could possibly do to change your situation?

What advice would you have for someone else who has these problems?

What can you do to help yourself?

Even if others do not know about X, what would they notice about you that was different if you started to handle things differently?

How would others know you feel this way?

What would you be telling yourself when you are feeling that way?

What do you need to remember to tell yourself in order to feel okay?... in order to cope better?

What will you be (doing, saying, feeling, thinking) that will be a sign that you are healing?

What will others be noticing about you that are signs of healing?

How will your healing efforts affect your relationship(s)?

Imagine that these healing signs continue and expand. What would things be like for you now? ... sometime in the future? How can you make these part of your life now?

What else needs to happen for you to feel safe (protected, trusted, accepted, wanted)? ... for you to have that really "alive" feeling?

You said you worked it through? How did you work it through? How did you come to the decision to X? **Note, "how to" questions when asked about positive coping efforts "pull for" action verbs and bolster self-esteem.**

Additional questions that tap the client's coping strengths include asking questions such as:

What things do you do that make you feel good about yourself?

What experience shows your determination not to give into your problem?

What examples illustrate your desire to do well (excel) at work?... in your relationship in spite of X?

At which times in your life would you have been most confident that you could have accomplished Y?...have handled X?

What experiences were most important in supporting the belief in yourself?

What does that experience tell you about yourself?...about your ability to handle X?...about your ability to achieve your goals?

What can you do for yourself for enjoyment?

When were you last happy? Tell me about that? Can you get in touch with that feeling now?

Another strategy to help clients to recognize their strengths is to use *"How and "What" questions*. When the client reports an instance of coping effectively the therapist asks: **"How did you do that? How did you accomplish that? What did you do to achieve X?"** The client's answer to such questions are likely to "pull for" self-regulatory and self-reflexive descriptions that focus on transitive (executive metacognitive) verbs such as, I "noticed", "decided", "interrupted", "planned", "sought help", etc. A detailed description of these activities provides an opportunity to determine if the client can engage in any of these activities in dealing with the remaining symptoms and difficulties. **"How" and "What" questions can be used to elicit such "strengths".**

5. QUESTIONS THAT ARE DESIGNED TO HELP THE CLIENT GENERATE POSSIBLE COPING EFFORTS/SOLUTIONS AND DEVISE OWN PLANS FOR WHAT TO DO NEXT. The object is for the therapist not to become a **"surrogate frontal lobe"** or **"metacognitive prosthetic device"** for clients, doing their thinking for them. Rather the therapeutic object is to empower and enable clients to take charge of their lives.

A. **Use Imaginary Significant Other.** One interview strategy is to have the client enumerate possible coping efforts by asking the client about his/her relationship with a "significant other". The following is a strategy I have used regularly with victimized clients. If one frames the questions artfully, then clients can come up with suggestions about how to cope differently. The following uses the strategy of a "special person" (e.g., a beloved grandmother who died). (I am impressed with how often the advice this grandmother would offer the client reflects good cognitive-behavioral suggestions. This is impressive since the grandmother never took a workshop with me.) In short, the goal is to encourage clients to come up with the advice you, the therapist, would otherwise offer. Arrange the conditions for clients to become their own therapist.

1. If the client speaks about a "special person" (for example, someone who has died in a disaster or in combat), or someone alive with whom the client has a "special" relationship, then this can be used to help the client generate coping techniques. Ask the client to tell you about this relationship. (If the client does not bring up a specific relationship, then the therapist can raise the question about a special relationship with anyone).

2. The therapist asks the client to indicate what he/she liked (finds "special") in this person. Ask the client, "What did you see in this person that made him/her so special?"

3. The therapist then asks the client, "What did this person see in you?" Encourage the client to be as specific as possible. Do you see yourself the way he portrayed you? In what ways? Would you like to change his/her account of you? In what ways? How could you go about doing that?

4. Now ask the client, "If X was here now, what advice would this "special" person have for you in your present situation? What would he/she say about getting on with life?" Help the client enumerate a number of specific suggestions that this "special person" might offer if he/she were here right now. (Clients often can come up with a series of specific coping suggestions.)

5. Convey to the client that this sounds like "good advice". No wonder the client found this relationship, this friendship, this person, so "special."

6. Discuss with the client ways that he/she could implement such "worthwhile" advice. Where could he/she begin? What obstacles/barriers might get in the way? What can be done to anticipate (mitigate, avoid, eliminate) these barriers?

7. Convey to the client that it sounds like he/she has begun to figure out what needs to be done.

8. If the client continues to express despair, and even contemplates suicide, ask the client what would be the best legacy to leave your friend (grandmother, spouse, daughter, etc.)? The answer should be developed collaboratively. One possible answer is to not let this person's (cite name) memory die.

9. Ask the client, "What would be the best revenge to those who have victimized (abused, tortured) you?" The answer that should emerge collaboratively is, "The best revenge is to live life well!" Help the client specify what it means to live life well...What story

would you like your X (children, husband, etc.) to tell about you?...What do you want to be remembered for?...How can you bring that story to be?

10. Discuss with the client the need <u>not</u> to allow the perpetrator/victimizer to still "rob you", "torture you", "abuse you", "abuse your offspring", "to continue to steal from the future like he/she has stolen from the past." "Enough is enough!"

11. Explore why it is important not to live someone else's story, not to take their voice with them, but to develop a voice of your own, to write your own story.

12. The therapist may even use the Gestalt "empty chair" or psychodrama procedures in order to have the client express, with affect and conviction, the need to have the abuse end. (This can be done effectively on a group basis where public commitment statements are verbalized, as are shared experiences).

13. There is a need to translate these general client pronouncements into behaviorally proscriptive, operationally definable, short-term, achievable treatment goals. In short, there is a need to have a specific "game plan" of how the clients will follow-through in these steps, turning them into personal experiments that will yield results that can "unfreeze" the beliefs that they hold about themselves and the world.

14. After listening to the client give advice, the therapist can say, "That is sensible advice. Can I have your permission to share this advice with others, without mentioning your name? I think others can benefit from your suggestions."

B. Another mode of inquiry is to employ **questions that explicitly "pull" for problem-solving activities.** The structure of these questions is to explore collaboratively with the client: "How are things now?", "How would you like them to be?", "How can <u>we</u> help you achieve these goals?", <u>or</u> " Where one is?", "Where one wants to be?", "How can <u>we</u> work together to close that gap?". These questions start with concrete examples and subsequently focus on more abstract issues (e.g., commonalty that cuts across several specific examples). *(In Section VI we will explore problem-solving interventions in more detail.)*

What do you see as your major problem?

How is that a problem?

What do you mean when you say, "I'm useless"? What makes you say X (e.g., "I'm useless") Has something happened that leads you this conclusion? How does all the information about Y fit with your idea that your are "useless"?

Are you saying, "You are a mess" or are you saying, "You are <u>in a mess</u>"?

According to you, the disadvantages are X, while the advantages are Y? Let's look at each.

Can I summarize what I think you have said so far and you can tell me whether I got it right?

What frightens you most about X?

What could you say to yourself that would counter X?

What do you think you could say to yourself or do when you really get going?

What could you be telling yourself when you are X?

How did you handle X feelings?

Is that the way you wanted to handle them?

What things would you do differently if you were less X (e.g., depressed, bothered by these thoughts)?

Are there things you could do even when you are X?

What could you do differently?...Let's explore your options (choices).

What could you do now?

How might you take better care of yourself?

Is there any way that trying to rehearse that ahead of time would help?

What will get in the way of your doing that?

It almost sounds as if your bottom line is X? Is that the way you see it?

Is the way things are going for you now really working for you? Does it get you what you want? ... Then what can we begin to do about that?

How will you know (evaluate) whether or not these changes are working for you?

Who can you teach this to?

C. Another mode of nurturing problem-solving is to **ask questions that are future-oriented** (see O'Hanlon & Weiner-Davis, 1989). These questions are designed to encourage the client to gain perspective by looking beyond his/her current situation and present relationships and to consider new options.

How will you know when (X occurs)...(when you have had enough)?

What is different between X and Y?

X years from now, will it still be okay if Y?

How will your life be different when you realize that X?

What will convince you that you (can, cannot) control X?

How will you know that it is time to X (move on, get out, change directions)?

What would be the last straw for you?

Rosen and Stith (1993) describe how the therapist can help the client gain perspective by asking the client to **pretend** or **act "as if"** the situation is <u>not hopeless</u> or that it can be changed. (*The therapist chooses phrases from the following.*) "For the moment...for the sake of argument...let's pretend...let's act as if...you could X...or you became convinced of Y. How would you go about X? What would you do first? What would happen next?"

Another strategy Rosen and Stith (1993) suggest to help clients gain perspective and engage in more problem-solving coping efforts is to **ask questions that plant seeds of doubt.** They offer the following example:

"Often young women like you , who (do, feel X), **experience two opposing parts of themselves**; one part feels X and wants Y no matter how hurtful. The other part has doubts that doing X is the right thing to do. Usually the second part is experienced, at first, as a 'little' voice somewhere inside or in the back of one's mind...Is there a part of you that wants to X? Tell me a bit about that part of you?" (p. 431).

Note: My inclusion of this line of questioning by Rose and Stith should <u>not</u> imply that there are different parts to a person, nor an "inner child", nor another side to oneself. Rather, the phrase "part of you" is a useful metaphor, a tool for constructing a new narrative, a way to help clients to "rewrite their stories", and engage in more adaptive behaviors. As Laird (1989, p. 444) observed, the therapist can help clients "to examine the ways their lives are storied and mythologized, and to interpret their own stories and make choices about the ways they wish to story their futures." For individuals who have been victimized and who feel powerless and helpless, the metaphor of constructing new stories can be quite empowering and motivational.

6. QUESTIONS THAT ARE DESIGNED TO HELP THE CLIENT ESTABLISH TREATMENT GOALS

Following the suggestion of de Shazer (1988), Dolan (1991) proposes the use of a "miracle" question:

If a miracle happened in the middle of the night and you had overcome the effects of X (childhood abuse, rape, robbery, accident, disaster, war experience, etc.) to the extent that you no longer needed help (therapy), and you felt quite satisfied with your daily life, what would be different?...Tell me if a miracle happened and you woke up in the morning and everything was the way you wanted it to be, what would things look like? What would X be doing? What would be happening? (de Shazer, 1988).

Caution: Some clients have responded negatively to the premise of this "miracle" question, namely, they reject the implication that there is a "miracle" or "quick fix" to their distress. Clients can sometimes misinterpret the therapist's questions as suggesting that the therapist has not understood the depth of the client's emotional pain. If the therapist implies (although not intentionally) that there is a "miracle" solution that could have been employed, then the client may wonder why he or she has not used such a procedure in the past, rather than suffer all of these years. Thus, if the "miracle" question is employed by the therapist, there is a need to ensure that it is interpreted by the client in the constructive "spirit" in which it has been raised by the therapist.

What advice would you have for someone else in this situation, who has experienced a similar X, or who is having difficulty with the memory of X?

If someone came to you and told you X, how would you explain that?...Do you think any of these things would be going on in your situation?

What do you feel you need to do to protect yourself from ...? to take more responsibility for...? to take more control of your life?

What are your worst fears?...Who is going to run your life, you or your fears?

Have you ever asked yourself what are the risks if you don't change? Just how serious are things? How would you like to change them?

Suppose you learned to tolerate the discomfort of X, how would your life be different?

What goals do you think you should be working on in treatment/training?

What do you think I (the clinic) can do to help?

How will you know when your goals have been achieved?

What would it take in order for you to do Y ...?

Given your new knowledge and what you have learned about yourself, what are some of the things you can do to start taking more charge of your life ... shaping your future ... writing or reauthoring your story? The therapist should choose one phrase or use the client's healing metaphor (e.g., "get back on the horse", "write a new chapter", "join life").

What difference will doing this make to your next steps of healing?

What does this tell you about yourself that is important for you to know?

Another means to help clients establish treatment goals is to have them also **focus on non-trauma aspects of their lives**.

What are some things you most like doing?

What would you eventually like to do when...?

What do you see yourself doing in the long run?

What did you want to do with your life years ago?...What did you want to be when you were X years old, or when you were Y years old?

If you could do anything you wanted to do in your (life, work, career, relationship) what would you do?

Where do you see the relationship with X heading?

As noted, the therapist can also use a time line procedure to help clients put the traumatic events into some perspective and to help clients identify future possible treatment goals.

Also see Meichenbaum and Turk (1987), Facilitating treatment adherence (New York: Plenum Press) for a description of specific guidelines to follow when collaboratively establishing treatment goals with clients.

7.   **QUESTIONS THAT ARE DESIGNED TO HELP THE CLIENT TAKE A DIFFERENT PERSPECTIVE** (As Dolan, 1991, observes many of these questions can be raised in conjoint sessions with the client and significant others.)

Tell me more specifically how you will X more? What will you be doing differently?

How will X (use name of significant other) know that you are beginning the healing process? ... are healing? ... are progressing?

What signs could he/she look for?

What will X notice specifically that will tell him/her that you are Y (coping, "not stuffing feelings" etc.), instead of not Y?

What do you think X would say to you (or do) if he/she noticed your first small signs of healing? ... and then your next signs of healing?

What is X doing that is helpful?

What would you like X to do more of? ... less of?

What behaviors on the part of (name significant other) would you like to have occur more often?

What things is X doing/saying that you would like him/her to continue? ... to increase?

What would be a sign to you that you were in a good relationship?

What difference would it make for you to be in a good relationship?

Do you know of any other people who have had a similar experience (or people who are in a similar situation)? Who? How did he/she (they) handle it?

Another way to help clients generate coping efforts is to probe about the self-blame and dysphoric feelings that accompanies the traumatic event. Such questions "pull for" the cognitive errors such as dichotomous thinking that individuals may experience. Once these thinking patterns become evident, they can be subjected to various **cognitive restructuring procedures** that are described in Section VI, such as the **downward arrow** technique. The **downward arrow technique** is a cognitive therapy procedure that helps clients in understanding the logic and sequencing of their reasoning (e.g., clients are asked, "If that were true, why would it be so upsetting? What would it mean to you?"). We will consider in Section VI how the downward arrow technique is employed with PTSD clients

For example, to tap the clients sense of self-blame the therapist can ask:

Are you saying because you have been abused (victimized) that your are "useless", "dirty", "worthless"? (use client's words or metaphors) What is the "data" or "evidence" that would indicate that you are "worthless" because you have been abused? Are there any examples that don't fit your conclusion that you are X?

How could you have know that this time things were going to be different?

You have described yourself today as a X (use client's metaphor). It would be interesting to find out more about what this implies for you ... What would be the contrast or opposite of X, in your view? What would be the advantages of viewing yourself that way? What would that mean to you personally?

8. **QUESTIONS THAT ARE DIRECTED AT SIGNIFICANT OTHERS WHEN SEEN CONJOINTLY WITH THE CLIENT** (Dolan suggests that the therapist attempt to have the pair work collaboratively as a team. Consider the following questions that are designed to achieve this objective.)

Discuss some of the background of the relationship:

How did the two of you meet?

What attracted you to each other?

Could you each tell me what you see in each other?

What challenges have you been through?

What stressors have you met and overcome together and as a family?

Discuss concerns that spouse has:

What things do you see in your spouse that worry you the most?

How has X affected the situation at home?

Has anything changed to cause you to be more concerned about X?

What concerns do you have that make you think its time for a change?

What things give you hope that your spouse can change?

What do you think will happen if your spouse does not change?

How would you like for things to turn out?

In what ways could you help your spouse to make a change?

What do you think is the next step?

Discuss questions that focus on victimization:

What has the relationship been like, apart from the issue of the past recall of abuse? In these areas, what are the things that each of you want to have continue?

What would you have done differently if you had been aware of the abuse that the client (use name) experienced?

What difference would that have made?

How will you know that (the client's name) is healing from the memory of X? ... or continuing to heal?

What will (the client's name) be (doing, feeling, thinking) that will be a sign that he/she is healing?

What are you noticing in his/her behavior?

What will he/she be saying/doing?

To the client -- What has X done already that has facilitated the healing process? ... What is X doing now? ... What would you like to see X do more of?

What can you (significant other) do to facilitate this healing process?

How can the two of you go about bringing that about?

How will the two of you know that you are healing from the memory of X?

How will your mutual healing affect your relationships with each other and with other important people in your life?

The therapist can say to the couple, "Between now and next time we meet, I would like you to observe, so you can describe next time, what happened in your relationship that you want to continue to have happen" (de Shazer & Molnar, 1984, p.298). In this way the therapist and the couple can examine what the client and significant other want. What is working and then consider how they can do more of it or try something different.

It is also worthwhile conducting an interview separately with significant others such as wives. For example, Watson (1993) has reported that wives are often more able to give a better history of disabilities then the male PTSD client, especially about the client's "nervous" condition. In addition, Solomon et al. (1992) have reported that the spouse and children of PTSD soldiers are often experiencing a good deal of distress. The advantages of conducting interviews with the client, the spouse, children, couples, and the family need to be underscored.

WHAT QUESTIONS CAN THE CLINICIAN USE WITH CLIENTS WHO ENTER TREATMENT WHO DO NOT RAISE THE ISSUE OF VICTIMIZATION?

The clinical interview that we have just reviewed is most appropriate for individuals who enter treatment with a statement that he/she has been "victimized", or exposed to a Type I or Type II stressor. Another important clinical population is represented by individuals whose reports of "victimization" emerge over the course of assessment and treatment. We now consider the sample of questions that interviewers may use with this population. These questions are gleaned from Meichenbaum & Turk (1987), Miller & Rollnick (1992), Peterson (1968), and Yates (1992). The intent of these questions and interview formats is to enlist clients as collaborators in defining their problems and empowering them to collaboratively generate, implement, and evaluate possible alternatives. As Miller and Rollnick (1992, p. 117) observe, "Clients are not told what they have to do, but rather are asked what they want to do." The questions are designed to "get the client thinking and talking about change."

QUESTIONS THAT CAN BE RAISED IN INITIAL PHASE OF THERAPY

Note: It is not being suggested that all of these questions be addressed, but rather this is a set of questions that the **therapist can sample** from over the course of therapy. While many of these questions may be addressed during the initial phase of therapy, they can be employed again and again over the course of treatment. It is critical that the sessions not take on the atmosphere of a cross examination. The questions have been clustered by primary objectives. In Section VI we will consider in more detail the nature of the questions that can be raised within **problem-solving** and **cognitive restructuring** frameworks.

Problem Identification and Definition

I'd like to understand how you see things, can we begin with why you are here?...What brings you here?

As you see it what problem or problems bring you here?...What do you think is(are) the problem(s)?

What seems to be the problem?...How do you know you have a problem?

How serious a problem is this as far as you are concerned?

Can you tell me how you see your problem(s) right now?

I understand you have some concerns about X. Could you tell me about them?...Why don't you start from the beginning and bring me up to date?...What changes have you noticed?

What worries (concerns) you about X?...What has concerned other people about X?

What led you to seek help at this time?

What would you like to change about yourself?...change about you relationships?

Help me understand why you are wanting to work on this now?

What is the biggest problem you are facing right now?

What things make you think that this is a problem?

Who is most bothered by your problem?

Was it your idea to come here in the first place?
> If the answer is "NO", who suggested you come?
> How do you feel about coming here?

Do you feel you have been pushed by others into seeking help?

Have you been in therapy before? Tell me about what was helpful/unhelpful about that experience?

(*Commend client for being there.*) I appreciate how hard it must have been for you to decide to come here. You took a big step.

How can I be of help?

(*Interject affirming statements.*) You are certainly a resourceful person to have been able to live with the problem this long and not fall completely apart...It must be difficult for you to accept a day-to-day life so full of stress. I must say, if I were in your position, I would also find it difficult. I guess that is why you are here because you don't want to accept that kind of stress any more.

(*Explore past history with the problem.*) Were you having trouble with X before or is this the first time?...Have you had difficulties in the past with X?...Tell me about what happened?...In what ways is the present situation like (the same as) the one(s) in the past?...In what ways is the present situation different from those in the past?

(*Include general questions that tap the possibility of prior traumatic experience.*) What is the biggest problem you are facing with yourself? Have you ever had a very bad experience?...What happened?

Do you sometimes feel as if this experience is about to happen again?

(See Assessment Section below **On Specific Measures for Additional Questions That Can Be Raised About Past History and About Problems of Comorbidity**)

Problem Analysis

Could you take a few moments and describe the situation you are in now?

Can you give me a description of what has been happening to you in recent weeks?

How does this problem express itself on a daily basis? Can you give me an example?

How does it interfere with or prevent you from doing some things you would like to do?

What else have you noticed or wondered about X? What other concerns...? What are some other reasons...? What else...?

Let's take a moment and see if we can both better understand the problem(s) in a bit more detail. Think back to the last time X occurred. Could we go into more detail about the problem you are having with X?

Where is this kind of problem most likely to occur?

When did it occur last?

Who was present?

What was going on at the time?

How did you feel? What is upsetting you most about X?

What were you thinking?

How did you handle the situation?

How would you have liked to have handled the situation?

What thoughts have you had about what you might do in the future in order to handle X better?...to overcome this problem?

What is it about X which is most difficult?

What are your current issues as you see them? How do they express themselves? How do they show up?...How could you find out...?

What is different when you are not experiencing X?

(*Perform a situational analysis.*) Have you had similar feelings (give example) and similar thoughts (give example) in other situations?...In what ways, if any, are the situations similar?...What do you make of these similarities?

(*Attend to anticipatory cues.*) Can you recognize when such feelings, thoughts (be specific) are about to come on?

What are some of the things you feel?...think?...do?...If you could do anything at all when you are feeling X, to not feel that way, what would you do?

Can you tell when you are going to be in a high risk situation?...For example, what sort of things seem to make the problem(s) worse?

(*Important to assess when the problem does not occur.*) Can we explore, in as much detail as possible, when this problem with X does not happen?...Who are you with?...What are you doing?...When is it?...Where are you?...What do you think you can do to continue doing more of that?...When the problem does not occur how does that make you feel?...if you could do anything at all when you are feeling X to keep feeling that way what would you do?

Goal Statement

What is(are) your goal(s) in coming here?

How would you like for things to be different?

What is that you want to change?

If you were completely successful in accomplishing what you want now, what would be changed?

Let's take things one step at a time. What do you think is the first step we should work on?

How would your life be different if you followed this idea and did X?...or did not do Y?

So that's your goal. Let us take a moment to discuss what might go wrong with this plan and what you can do about it?

If you succeeded in achieving this goal, what else do you think might happen?

How would you like to be feeling when therapy is over? How can we help to bring that feeling to be?

How would life be different if your X (pain, distress, etc.) could be relieved?

What would therapy need to provide in order for our work together to be considered successful?

At a minimum what would you hope to happen as a result of coming to treatment/training?

What do you think will happen if you don't make any changes?...What is your worst fears about what might happen if you don't make a change?...What do you suppose are the worst things that might happen if you keep on the way you have been going?...Is that the way you want things to be?

How would you know when you do not have to come here anymore?

How will you know when that goal has been achieved?

What would have to happen at home to show you that X has been completed or that your goals have been achieved?...What would you need to do next?

On what would the outcome of treatment (training) depend?

What problems do you anticipate? How can we work together on this problem?

What encourages you that you can change, if you want to?

What do you think would work for you, if you decided to change?

What makes you think that if you did decide to make a change you could do it?

If everything goes the way you want to in therapy, what will be different for you when you are done?

If you could X, for just a little while, then how would you feel?

What do you wish your life was like?...How can we begin the first steps to achieve this?

Can you envisage a time in the future when this problem(s) is resolved?...What would that be like?

In what ways would you like things to be different?

What would happen to you if you weren't X?...What would that mean to you?

Is there any evidence to suggest that perhaps you will get better?...What is that evidence?...Anything else?...In what way?

Is it possible that you could look at this as a project you are taking on?...How could you go about doing that?

Those clinicians who have proposed a **solution-focused approach** have provided a useful strategy to help clients tap their strengths. Consider the potential impact of the following therapeutic comments.

What is different when you are not experiencing X?

Our exploring the occasions or exceptions when this does not occur, the exceptions may lead us to a solution. We want to learn what you are doing right.

If you were to wake up tomorrow with complete confidence in your abilities to handle X, what would you be able to do (to achieve)?

Since you found out what works for you, I can only suggest that you continue doing what you did this past week.

I need you to observe the kinds of things you want to see happen more.

In the same spirit Combs and Friedman (1990) suggest the following questions to help clients create a new narrative:

At what time in your life would you have been most confident that you could have accomplished this?
What experience is most important in supporting the belief in yourself?
What does that experience tell you about yourself?
Who in the family is most hopeful that you will succeed?...Who next in the family?
What do you think they see in you that you might not recognize in yourself that makes them hopeful about your success?
What experiences have you had with them that lets you know that they see you in this way?
Who will be the first to notice when you have made the changes you are seeking?...How will they be able to tell?

Analysis of Coping Efforts

What sorts of things have you tried to reduce your X (stress, depression, anxiety, flashbacks, pain, headaches)?
Is there anything you try to do to forestall X (avoid the onset of X) (e.g., feelings of anger, depression, irritability, use client's metaphor "stuffing your feelings")?
What are some ways you have attempted to reduce your discomfort?
How long have you been attempting to handle or resolve this problem(s)?
(*Important to tap social supports.*) Is there anyone with whom you can discuss your personal problems?...Who is that?...Have you found it helpful in the past if you shared things that were troubling you?...that were worrying you about X?...Do you think X would mind if you talked about this problem with him/her?
Are there any professional people (doctor, clergy) who you have been able to discuss your problems with?
How have other people in your life tried to help you with this problem?...Are their efforts helpful?...In what ways?
(*Help the client reframe the problem.*) Let me ask you a somewhat different question. What accounts for you not being more X (e.g., depressed, anxious, upset, etc.)?
(*Examine possible barriers to the use of coping efforts.*) What is your notion (theory) about the cause of your problem?...cause of the thoughts coming and going...cause of you "stuffing feelings" (use client's metaphor)?...How does this keep you from changing?
Have you known anyone in a similar situation? How did it turn out for that person?
What advice would you have for someone else who has this problem?...What advice would you give yourself?...If you wanted to know X, who do you think you might ask?
Have you had any thoughts about what might be done here in therapy to help you?
What else do you think I should find out about you and your situation to help you with this problem?
What would you like me to do to help?

Putting Present Problem(s) in Some Context--Creating a time-line[1]. (This is comparable to the time-line approach described earlier and consistent with what Miller and Rollnick (1992) call **looking back** and **looking forward.**

---

[1] Recall that Dolan (1991) has the client generate explicit **time lines** on which he/she can note past accomplishments and future hopes, as well as victimization experiences.

Looking Back

Can you recall a time when things were going well for you?...When was that?...Tell me a bit about
    that time?...What has changed?
What were things like before your present distress?
What are the differences between you X years ago and now?
Have you ever had a very bad experience?
Do you sometimes feel as if this experience is about to happen again?

Looking Forward

If you do decide to make a change, what are your hopes for the future?
How would you like things to turn out for you?
I can see you're feeling X right now? How would you like things to be different?
What are the options for you now?...What have you tried?...What could you do differently?
What would be the best results you could imagine if X did not occur?...if you could make a
    change?

Eliciting Self-Motivational Statements *(Motivational Interviewing is discussed in detail in Section VI on the treatment of clients with addictive behaviors.)*

    Miller (1983) and Miller and Rollnick (1992) have highlighted the value of conducting what
they call **motivational interviewing** that helps the client take on more responsibility for change.
Marlatt et al. (1993) describe how **motivational interviewing** can be used with clients who
have addictive behaviors. They note that:

> "Motivational interviewing is a technique designed to minimize resistance of those
> experiencing alcohol and drug related problems. Confrontational communications,
> such as "you have a problem and you are in denial" are thought to create a defensive
> response. In contrast, simply placing the available evidence in front of the client
> and sidestepping arguments is thought to better allow the client to evaluate his or
> her situation and become ready to change behavior." (p. 491).

    Such motivational interviewing techniques are not only useful with clients who have
problems with addictions, but they are useful with all clinical problems. By employing the "art of
questioning", the therapist can engage the client in a collaborative process to explore his/her desire
to change. For example, clients can be asked to generate reasons for change, to use decisional
balance sheets examining the pros and cons of both short-term and long-term changes. Clients
then can be challenged with paradoxical statements[1] (e.g., "I don't know if this would be too
difficult for you"..."Maybe this is asking too much of you"..."A program like this one requires a
lot of motivation and effort, I'm not sure you are up to the challenge"..."Of the things we have
discussed, which for you are the most important reasons for change?"..."How are you going to do
that?")

---

[1] The metaphor "verbal akido" has been offered to describe how cognitive-behavior therapists can **reframe** any client
behavior as a sign that the client is "buying" into treatment or as a favorable prognostic sign. If the client feels
"indignant", angry", or "doesn't wish to attend treatment", the therapist can commend the client for being in touch
with such feelings and judicious about seeking help. "You are in the process of taking charge of your life. Your
are taking control so you can feel in charge of your own life. Perhaps we can work together in helping you
achieve that goal."

Other examples of motivational interviewing questions include:

Are you telling me, are you saying to yourself, that in spite of X, you will be able to do
   Y?...Is that what you are saying?...How will you go about doing that?
What is the worse thing that can happen if you don't make a decision to change?
If you are not ready yet, then I don't want you to make a commitment. This is too important
   to decide now.
Are you suggesting that this is as good as it is going to get?
I respect your right not to X, but I want your decision to do that to be an informed one. Let's
   take a moment to discuss how you came to the decision to Y.

Closely aligned with the motivational interviewing format is the treatment goal of having
clients adopt a problem-solving orientation toward their situation and reactions. We now turn our
attention to how a problem-solving questioning format can be used with clients.

MOVING CLIENTS TOWARD A PROBLEM-SOLVING MODE

Another source of initial questions that the clinician can use is the thoughtful clinical behavioral analytic interview offered by D. Peterson (1968) in his book, The clinical study of social behavior. New York: Appleton-Century & Crofts. The main objective of these questions is to help clients see their situation in problem-solving terms (i.e., problem-to-be-solved and not as a series of provocations and personal threats). Once clients see their situation and emotions in problem-solving terms they are "open to" a number of interventions (problem and situational analysis, generating, implementing, and evaluating response alternative, relapse prevention, and the like).

I. Definition of problem behavior

A. Nature of the problem as defined by client

   1. "As I understand it, you came here because ..." Discuss reasons for contact as stated by referral agency or other source of information. "I would like you to tell me more about this. What is the problem as you see it?" Probe as needed to determine the client's view of the problem behavior (i.e., what he or she is doing, or failing to do, that the client or somebody else defines as a problem).

B. Severity of the problem

   1. "How serious a problem is this as far as you are concerned?" Probe to determine the client's view of the problem behavior (i.e., what he or she is doing, or failing to do, or somebody else defines as a problem).
   2. "How often do you exhibit the problem behavior (if a disorder of commission), or have occasion to exhibit desired behavior (if a problem of omission)?" The goal is to obtain information regarding frequency of response.

C. Generality of the problem

   1. Duration -- "How long has this been going on?"
   2. Extent -- "Where does the problem usually come up?" Probe to determine situations in which problem behavior occurs (e.g., "Do you feel that way at work? How about at home?").
   3. Could you tell me more about when it occurs? How often does it occur? When does it occur? Who does it bother most? How do you feel when it occurs?

II. Determinants of problem behavior

A. Conditions that intensify the problem behavior
   "Now I want you to think about the times when (the problem) is worst. What sorts of things are going on then?"

B. Conditions that alleviate problem behavior
   "What about the times when (the problem) gets better? What sorts of things are going on then?"

C. Perceived origins
   "What do you think is causing (the problem)?"

D. Specific antecedents
   "Think back to the last time (the problem) occurred. What was going on at that time?"

E.   As needed:

1.   Social consequences -- "What did (significant others identified above) do?" "How do you think this makes X feel?"
2.   Personal consequences -- "How did that make you feel?"

F.   Suggested changes
"You have thought a lot about (the problem). What do you think might be done to improve the situation?" "What would you like to have happen?"

G.   Suggested leads for further inquiry
"What else do you think I should find out about to help you with this problem?""

Imagery reconstruction as means of nurturing a problem-solving approach

An **imagery recall procedure** is a useful technique to help clients become aware of the **transactional** nature of his or her behavior. By helping clients track his/her behavior in "slow motion" clients can come to appreciate that how he/she behaves, appraises situations, thinks, and feels, may inadvertently, unwittingly, and perhaps even unknowingly, contribute to the client's problems. Clients can come to appreciate how they can make things worse. Clients often enter treatment feeling helpless, hopeless, and "victimized" by circumstance, their relationships, feelings, and thoughts. They may say, "This depression just comes on." The present approach is designed to help clients appreciate that "depression doesn't just come on," nor "visit," but how clients appraise situations and their ability to handle them is critical to how they feel. This approach does not downplay the possibility that clients are exposed to "real" stressors, especially if they have been victimized by Type I and II stressors. Rather what clients "say to themselves" about their situation is judged as being critical to their exacerbating and maintaining their distress. The imagery recall procedure is designed to help the client **collect data** so he/she can convince himself/herself that he/she is not "a poor victim" of feelings, thoughts, and circumstances. Once such data has been collaboratively collected the therapist can ask the client: **"Are you suggesting that how you reacted in that situation (give examples), what you thought (give examples), might have affected how you felt? In what ways?...Are you suggesting that you lit your own fuse even before you got into that situation?"** In turn, the therapist can ask, **"Are you saying that how you felt influenced how you reacted? Are you suggesting that how X reacted to you at times, can make things worse? In what ways does this occur?** Let us both go over this in some detail, perhaps slow motion, so we can understand what happens to you and how X comes about. **Does that make sense?"**

In addition to these interview questions, the therapist can ask the client to pick out a specific example or instance of when the "problem" is worst. The client can be invited to sit back in the chair and close his/her eyes and **replay the incident in his/her "mind's eye", in slow motion.** This time the client is asked to share any thoughts, images, and feelings that preceded, accompanied, and that followed the incident. In this manner, the client can be encouraged to attend to factors (thoughts, feelings) that indicate that the way the client sees things, thinks, appraises both events and his/her ability to handle them, may play a role in his/her stress reactions.

The therapist can say to the client, "Let's try to understand that situation in more detail by asking you to recreate the experience by using a focused imagery procedure. Sit back in the chair and relax yourself as best you can...Good...I want you to recall the last time X occurred. Please describe it in as much detail as possible sharing the sequence of what happened before, during, and after. Include in your telling not only what happened, but also the thoughts and feelings you had that preceded, accompanied, and followed the incident...Any questions about what I am asking you to do or why?"

Another way to make the request of the client is to say: "Do you remember where you were and what you were doing when you felt X (use client's metaphor... like a "bomb ticking")? What I would like you to do is close your eyes and see if you can recall what you were doing right before you experienced the initial signs of X (use client's symptoms). Cast your mind back to that stressful time. Try and put yourself back into that situation, as if it were happening again right now for the first time. Describe to me and to yourself what you were doing, feeling, and thinking."

The imagery recall can help the client become aware of the **low intensity prodromal cues** that **signal the onset of stress**. Moreover, the therapist can help the client conduct a **situational analysis** in order to determine in what other situations the client has had similar thoughts and feelings, similar reactions. In this way, the client and the therapist can search for commonalties (current concerns, issues) that cut across situations.

When these intense emotions are pursued clients often describe them in **metaphorical terms**. The client might note that he/she "stuffs feelings", "builds walls", etc. The therapist can reflect, "Stuff feelings?", tell me about that. Together, they then examine specific examples of such behaviors and the intra- and interpersonal consequences:

The therapist asks, in turn:

a)   "What is the **impact** of your 'stuffing feelings'?..."
b)   "What is the **cost** of doing X?..."
c)   "What is the **price you pay** for doing X?..."

These questions are <u>not</u> answered in the abstract. Rather, the therapist helps the client experience, in the session, the emotional consequences of such behaviors, the consequences of such a coping style. Moreover, the therapist helps the client appreciate that coping in this fashion makes sense given what the client has been through, given the client's experience. In short, the therapist **commends the client** for the ways he/she has handled feelings, done things to survive. The therapist may say:

"Given what you have been through, your 'stuffing feelings' (building walls') makes sense. It was a way of protecting yourself, of your surviving. Do you see yourself still doing that today?...When?...What is the impact?...But, one of the byproducts of that way of coping is that you tend to continue to do the same thing when it is no longer necessary. You fall into the same way of behaving, even when you have choices to do something different...Does that make sense?"

*Thus , the therapist conveys to the client that the problem is <u>not</u> one of the client being "sick" or "defective", but rather what is happening is a "normal", "natural", problem of "transfer", "over-generalization", or "stuckiness". One goal of treatment is to help the client become **"unstuck"**.*

The therapist then asks the client, "If indeed, the consequences of 'stuffing feelings' ('building walls') are X (the therapist reflects specific client examples), then what can you (the client) do about this?"

It is <u>not</u> a big step for the client to then say, "Perhaps, I should not 'stuff feelings' (not 'build walls')." At this point, the therapist responds, "That is interesting. What did you have in mind when you said, 'not stuff feelings'?" Thus, the client, once again, is given the opportunity to come up with and "own" the idea of what should be done next. In this way a problem-solving mode is nurtured.

Helping Clients Translate Metaphors into Behaviorally Prescriptive Steps-- Decomposing Vagueness

As noted, clients often use metaphors to describe their behavior and situation. Clients often describe their presenting problems in global metaphorical terms. Consider the following examples:

Example I

At the <u>beginning</u> of the session the client says the following in response to the therapist's probe:

A.   <u>Therapist</u>:   Can you tell me how you see your problems right now?

     <u>Client</u>:   Well, my life is like one big glob of misery. My whole life has been a complete personal tragedy.

At the <u>end</u> of this assistance episode the client says:

B.   <u>Client</u>:   I guess I can work on one problem at a time. There is nothing really to lose. I guess I could try it.

Consider the sequence of steps, or clinical maneuvers, (questions, statements) that you, the therapist can use to move the client from point A to B. What specifically could the therapist ask or say to move the client into a more positive problem-solving mode from the client's initial vague open-ended metaphorical description of his/her presenting problems? There is a need to move clients from metaphorical, vague, hypothetical descriptions of their problems or situation to concrete description first. In formulating your answer keep in mind that there is a need to hear the client's account and acknowledge his/her perceptions (emotional pain, barriers to change, evidence for negative thoughts) before trying to initiate change. If the therapist does not first listen to the client's "story" then each suggestion for change may elicit the infamous "yes but" response or a "you don't understand" reaction.

On the next page is a description of some possible strategies the clinician can use in moving clients from point A to point B in Example I.

Possible Therapist Comments - Example I

1. <u>Therapist</u>:   "It sounds like things look awfully black (bleak, overwhelming, hopeless) to you right now. Can you tell me what you mean when you say your life is like a 'glob of misery and a complete personal tragedy'? *(Use question, pluck and reflect key phrase. Attempt to see the world through the client's eyes.)*...In what way is that a concern for you?...How else does it affect you?...What concerns you the most?"

2. <u>Therapist</u>:   "I can see this must be very emotionally painful (upsetting, distressing) for you. (Pause) I can see how you have felt completely overwhelmed by the situation. You feel <u>everything</u> is wrong, a 'glob of misery'...So you are seeing both the world and yourself in an <u>altogether</u> negative light?" *(Convey empathy. Pause for acknowledgment. Reflect feeling and use a slight blow-up technique by using the expressions "everything" and "altogether".)*

3. <u>Therapist</u>:   "You sound pretty overwhelmed. Such feelings are not unusual for someone who has been through what you have been through. It is understandable that until you find a way to deal with X and get your stress level down, you would feel overwhelmed, as if your life is a 'complete personal tragedy'. At times you sound frightened that in spite of everything you are doing, things are getting worse, more out of control...Is that the way you see it?...I'm impressed given all that you have been through that you have been very strong to deal with all of this as well as you have." *(Provide some comparative norms, but continue to convey empathy about how the client perceives his/her ability to handle events.)*

4. <u>Therapist</u>:   "Given what you have been through (therapist cites specific examples), if at times you were not depressed then I would be more concerned. (pause) If you were not depressed <u>at times</u> then I think you would really have a problem. At least you are in touch with your feelings." *(Normalize reactions. Reframe symptoms as a strength.)*

5. <u>Therapist</u>:   "It does sound like you have a number of problems facing you. You also seem to be seeing them as a whole, a 'glob' like you said. When you think of them that way, they must seem <u>completely unmanageable</u>." *(Move toward problem-solving perspective once again by using a blow-up technique.)*

6. <u>Therapist</u>:   "Do you have any notions of how <u>we</u> can move from viewing your problems in global terms, "glob of misery", "personal tragedy", and view them as smaller more manageable problems?" *(Give the client the opportunity to come up with the suggestion for problem-solving. If the client does <u>not</u> come up with this, the therapist can say the following:)*

   "Well, one of the first things we can do in therapy is to look at your problems individually. Sometimes when people can separate larger problems into a series of smaller problems, it is helpful. We can work together, collaborate on developing and examining possible solutions to try for each problem. (Pause) Would you be willing to give that approach a try?"

   Now that I have outlined how a therapist can help the client adopt a more problem-solving stance, test yourself. See if you can summarize the strategies that were used to help this client decompose her vagueness. How did I try to get her to move to a more specific behavioral approach? Compare your answer with that offered on the next page.

Summary of Strategies

1.   Empathize and then pluck and reflect "key" phrases that are often metaphorical in nature. Solicit examples and then ask questions that "pull for" more concrete examples.

2.   Empathize and validate the client's feelings. Offer a summary statement that both acknowledges the complexity of the client's situation and its impact and begins to reframe it in problem solving terms. Use a "blow-up" procedure (slightly exaggerating the level of distress). Clients, in response may indicate that things are not quite as bad, to which the therapist can say, "Not as bad?", "What gives you hope?".

3.   Provide comparative norms and normalize reaction. Commend the client for his/her "symptoms". Reframe them as a strength and as a positive prognostic indicator.

4.   Acknowledge the client's perception. Move the client toward problem-solving and toward constructive steps.

5.   Enlist collaboration in problem-solving. Cite normative attempts by others in formulating solutions.

In order to test your mastery and expertise of these steps, how would you handle Example II?

Example II

At the beginning of the session, in response to the therapist, the client says:

A.   Therapist: Hello, my name is Dr. Meichenbaum.

Client: Hello ... I am depressed. My will is paralyzed. The depression just comes and goes, and there is not much I can do about it.

At the end of the session the client says:

B.   Client: I guess I can work on one problem at a time. I think I can try that.

How would you move the client from A to B?

Another means of fostering a problem-solving set in clients is to **establish a good working therapeutic collaborative alliance**. This is especially important in clients who have been victimized and who have trouble with issues of trust and interpersonal intimacy. But this concern is not unique to PTSD clients, since the quality of the relationship between the client and the therapist by the third session is one of the best predictors of therapy outcome (Meichenbaum & Turk, 1987). Miller and Rollnick (1992) have also noted that about 2/3 of the variance in 6-month drinking outcome study could be predicted from the degree of empathy shown by therapists during treatment. A critical feature in developing a good working therapeutic relationship is the **degree of respect** and **collaboration** between the client and therapist. A useful "metaphor" in conveying the style of this relationship is the popular television character, **Detective Columbo** played by Peter Falk. At my workshops, I encourage participants to emulate Columbo's inquiring style and use his "befuddlement" and "bemusement", as a way to put the client into a more collaborative problem-solving mode. I suggest that therapists (at times without giving up their placebo value) "play dumb". For some therapists, this is not a difficult nor challenging role to play. The following list of therapist statements illustrate the ways that collaboration, reflection, and respect of the client can be incorporated into the social discourse of therapy.

The Therapist Should Use Intermediate and Concluding Summaries

A way to nurture a **collaborative problem-solving approach** is for the therapist to provide the client with intermittent and concluding summaries, as suggested by Miller and Rollnick (1992).

Intermediate Summaries

So thus far you have said that you are worried about...You are concerned about...and it interferes with...? Anything else?

It sounds like you are torn between X and Y. On the one hand...and on the other hand...This must be puzzling for you.

Correct me if I am wrong, but it seems that on the one hand...and at the same time...Is that the way you see it?

You seem to be saying that...Does that sound like a reasonable summary of what you have told me so far?

You seem to be having a problem with X. Is that the way you see it?...Have you thought about how you are going to find a way out?

Concluding Summaries

Our hour is coming to an end, and I'd like to pull together what you've said so far, so we can see where we are and where we are going. Let me know if I miss anything important that we have covered. You came in because...I admire you for that. I asked you about problems in your life like...Your mentioned...We talked about...Your were worried about...At the same time...Your are not sure how you can...Is that a fair summary? What have I left out?

Let me see if I can summarize where we are. You are thinking that...You considered different options such as...and decided...Is that the way you see it?

We have been talking for a while. How would you summarize what we have been talking about? What will you take away from today's session?...Good, I think that's pretty much what we talked about today.

Ask Client for Clarification

Can you tell me more about X?
Would you be willing to...?
On the one hand I hear you saying X, and on the other hand I hear you saying Y. I wonder how these things go together?
What is difficult about these times when the situations are really upsetting versus those times when these situations are not so troubling? Let's take a moment to explore that. If we can figure out the similarities and differences then, perhaps, this will inform us about what you might do differently.
This sounds reminiscent of...like...Do you see a similarity, as well?
How are X and Y alike (different)?

How do you think X felt when...?

Do you see how X doesn't leave room for Y?

It seems that one of your problems is X. Now, what do you think we can do about that?

You seem to be having a problem with X. Have you thought about how you're going to find a way out?

As I have come to understand your situation it seems to me, and correct me if I am wrong, you seem to have a problem with X (give examples) in situation Y and it makes you feel Z. Is that the way you see it? I wonder where you think we should begin in understanding (analyzing) further what is going on here.

Check Client's Perceptions of How The Therapist Sees Things

What you seem to be saying is X. Does that sound right?

Am I on the right track when I say...?

What I hear you saying is...

Correct me if I am wrong, but what I hear your saying is...

Let me see if I have understood what you said. Did I understand you correctly when I said...?

Is that how you see it?

Does your problem seem to be...?

Does that make sense so far?

How do you feel about what I just said?

You seem to be telling me X. Am I correct in assuming that...?

I get the feeling that...Is that the way you see it?

Do you think it makes sense that...?

Nurturing Collaboration

Maybe we can discover that together. What do you think?

I am not sure I quite understand, can we go over that together (one more time, in "slow motion")?

Is the material we discussed clear to you?

You're not sure what to do next. I'm not sure either. We have several options. Let us consider how we might find out together.

How would you go about X?

Would you be willing to X?

What would you learn if you try X? What would you learn if you don't try X?

What do out think and how do you feel about what we have discussed so far?

Tell me what we have agreed to do (to work on)?

(*Put client in a helper role by the therapist saying the following to the client*.) I have been struggling to know how to best help clients with X. So of all the clients that I am seeing, I was wondering which one really has a handle on X, whom I could approach for some advice. Given your experience with X, I thought I would approach you, if that is okay?...Without violating the privacy of any clients that have been struggling with X, I would like to hear what thoughts, if any, you might have on how I might be of most help with clients who have a problem with X ("stuffing feelings", handling flashbacks, etc.)? (*The therapist explores with the client how he/she came up with this advice. Has he/she ever tried that? How did it turn out? Is this something the client could use? Obviously, the target problem selected is similar to that experienced by the client.*)

Statements that Collaboratively Establish an Agenda in Subsequent Sessions

What do you want to work on today?

What do you want to accomplish today?

What do you have on top for the agenda today?

Where do you want to pick up today?

I am wondering what specific problems you would like to work on?

Before we get going to far along, it might be helpful for us to establish an agenda?

It sounds like we should discuss what is going on with X? The reason I suggest this is Y.
Does that make sense to you?

Before we go into X, do you want to spend the majority of this session on that?

Let's see where we have been and where we are going? And why? How will our talking
about this (working on this) make a difference (help you reach your goals)?

I want to encourage you to take an active role in your therapy by asking questions. No one
knows more about your problem and possible solutions than you do.

What sort of things have you been thinking (doing) since last session?

What has happened since the last time I saw you?

What has bothered you most since I saw you last?

Of the various problems, where do you think we should begin?

Tell me what you are most proud of since the last session?

What surprised you most about how things have gone since the last session?

What is the best thing that has happened since I saw you last?

Let me suggest that we spend some time talking about X. Let me explain why I think that is
important, and then I want to get your reactions.

Transactional Statements that Nurture Both a Therapeutic Alliance and Elaborative Problem-Solving

Are you suggesting...?

It seems to me that...Is that the way you see it?

It looks like...It seems. like...I get the impressions that...Is it possible that you are...?

From what you tell me it sounds like...

You are someone who seems to have devoted the part of herself to X. Is that the way you
see it?...But now you are working hard to get unstuck from Y...Is that the way
you see it?

I would not be surprised if you...

Do you have any more ideas about...?

How do you know...?

When have you done something like this before?

Does it seem to you that...?

Can you think of another time when you X?

That is a very powerful notion, where did that idea come from?

What do you attribute your improvement to?

How did you pull that off?

Can you tell me how you did X?

What would happen if...?

What makes you feel that...?

What about ...makes you feel X?

What does feeling X feel like?

Is there anything else you want to talk about?

Anything you may have been reluctant to bring up initially that you want to bring up now?

Is there any way you can surprise yourself by...?

What question(s) do you think the therapist would ask or what might the therapist say in that
situation?

"Going public with the data"--Addressing "Transference" Issues

Many "victimized" clients who have problems with issues of trust and intimacy evidence therapy-interfering behaviors, or what have been characterized as transference issues. From the present perspective such client behaviors and the reciprocal therapist behaviors (countertransference) are handled by having the therapist "go public with the data," and then having him or her check it out with the client. This usually takes the form of the therapist saying something like the following to the client: **"I noticed something and I wonder if you noticed it as well?"** At this point the therapist conveys the specific behaviors or pattern of client behaviors and then asks if the client has noticed it as well. In this way, the therapist is teaching the client how to self-monitor and appraise behaviors. For example:

I noticed that when you begin to become upset (angry, sad) in therapy, even toward me, you tend to withdraw (hunch over, lower your voice, lower your eyes to the ground). Have you noticed that as well?

At times I feel like I'm involved in a struggle with you and I'm not sure what is going on. Does this connect with your experience? (Safran et al., 1990)

The therapist checks out these observations and conveys to the client the impact of such behavior on the therapist and on their interpersonal communication pattern. Is the client aware of this impact? Is this the impact that the client wanted to achieve? Does the client behave in a similar fashion with others? If he/she does behave in such a fashion, then the question arises as to what is the "impact, cost, price", he/she pays? What is the impact on the relationship?

In short, the focus of the session may shift to the client's **in-therapy behavior**. Finally, in my supervision of therapists, they often describe to me difficulties they are having with their clients to which I often respond, "Don't just tell _me_ about it? **Is there a way you (the therapist) can share this information with your client in a supportive and nurturing fashion?**" Thus, the client can learn that one can receive (and later give) constructive feedback without violating the relationship. Going public with the data nurtures the problem-solving set and fosters a therapeutic collaborative alliance.

Closing of the Session Nurtures Collaboration and Solicits Client Feedback

This feels like a good place to stop. What do you think?
We are just about out of time. I would like to hear what you think were the main points of our session today.
How would you summarize what we have been talking about (working on)?
We have covered a lot of territory today. Is there anything that I said or did that was confusing, troubling, or that bothered you?...What is it that I missed?
We have discussed quite a bit of material. I wonder if there is anything you would like to ask me or anything you have been wondering about?
What do you think was most helpful, if anything, about today's session?
What are two things you will take away from today's session that will make a difference for you this week?
Can you tell me how you see your problem(s) with X now?

IT SHOULD BE APPARENT THAT THIS SECTION ON OPEN-ENDED QUESTIONS REPRESENTS NOT ONLY A USEFUL MEANS TO HELP THE CLIENT TELL HIS/HER STORY, BUT A POWERFUL MEANS TO RESCRIPT HIS/HER NARRATIVE AND TO UNDERTAKE NEW BEHAVIORS. WE NOW TURN OUR ATTENTION TO MORE FORMAL STANDARDIZED MEANS OF ASSESSING FOR PTSD AND RELATED DIFFICULTIES.

ASSESSMENT MEASURES -- PTSD

ADULT PTSD MEASURES (See Allen, 1994; Freedy et al., 1993; Keane et al., 1992; Lating et al., 1994; Litz et al., 1992; Raphael et al., 1989; Watson, 1990; and Wolfe et al., 1987, and the Journal of Consulting and Clinical Psychology, 1991, Volume 3.for a general review of PTSD assessment instruments.) **Since PTSD is a multifaceted disorder there is a need for a multimethod assessment approach** As Davidson and Baum (1994) observe, different aspects of the stress response change at different rates.

In this Section we will examine a number of measures designed to assess PTSD and related reactions in adults. In turn, we will consider:

1. Structured Clinical Interview Measures

2. Clinical Rating Scales

3. Self-Report Measures -- General PTSD Measures
   a) Stress inventories
   b) Symptom checklists (e.g., Distress and Alexithymia Scales)

4. Combat-related Self-report Scales

5. Combat-related Interviews

6. Sexual and Physical Assault Victim Measures

7. Domestic Violence Measures
   a) Victimization Screening Questions (noncrime events, homicide, rape, sexual molestation, sexual and physical assault)

8. Child Abuse Measures

9. Crime-Related PTSD Scale

10. Natural Disaster Assessment Measures

11. Schema-related Measures

12. Social Support Measures

13. Assessment of Community Factors

14. Marital Distress Measures

15. Coping Measures

16. General Adjustment Measures

17. Goal Attainment Scaling

18. Psychophysiological Measures

19. Psychoendocrine Assessment

20. Performance Measures

21. Assessment of associated behaviors and symptoms
    a) Sexual functioning
    b) Parenting stress measures

22. Assessment of Ethnic Identification

23. Assessment of PTSD Children and Adolescents

24. Challenge of Differential Diagnoses

ASSESSMENT MEASURES -- PTSD

Blake (1993) prefaces his discussion of the psychological assessment of PTSD with a series of admonitions that are worth repeating. These include:

1. The assessment process should be for the client in helping him/her better understand the nature of what he/she has been through and to collaboratively formulate a treatment plan.

2. The assessment should be administered in a distraction-free relaxed setting so the assessment process is perceived by the client as pleasant.

3. Timely "testing breaks" should be offered.

4. I would add clients should be told only to answer those tests or items that he/she feels comfortable in answering. Put the client in charge.

5. There is a need to provide feedback and review the measures with the client.

6. Measures can be used to assess both therapy process and outcome.

7. The assessment usually begins with the client sharing information about the trauma (e.g., victim, perpetrator, bystander, rescuer), and the extent of "moral conflict" engenetered by the events.

8. More specifically Blake (1993, p. 18) suggests the following items be covered. Note, the similarity of this list with the questions already reviewed and with the factors enumerated in Section VII on post-disaster interventions. Blake's list includes:

Clinical questions that can be addressed in PTSD Psychological Assessments

A. Extent and nature of trauma exposure *(See other factors enumerated in Section VII)*
    How much exposure to death, dying, and destruction?
    How much life threat, loss, and bereavement?
    What are the parameters of the traumatic event? (e.g., speed of trauma onset, its duration and predictability)
    What was the role of patient in the trauma and extent of moral conflict engendered?

B. Presence and severity of PTSD symptoms
    Has the patient been traumatized?
    How well is the patient adjusting?
    What aspects of the trauma are being reexperienced?
    What sensory modalities are involved (e.g., visual, auditory, tactile, olfactory memories)?
    What are the other, associated features?

C. Specific form or manifestations of PTSD
    What types of problems does the patient have?
    What should be the target(s) of treatment?
    What is the best treatment-patient match, including adjunctive treatments?

D. History of prior traumatization, especially during childhood
    Personal and/or family history of psychiatric illness
    Negative life events shortly before exposure to the trauma

E. Course of the patient's PTSD and changes that occur across treatment (process of change).
    Nature of social supports and other resources (lost and gained)

F. Changes resulting from treatment (outcome).

ASSESSMENT MEASURES -- PTSD

1. Structured Clinical Interview Measures

PTSD Questions from Diagnostic Interview Schedule (DIS) -- likely underestimates the prevalence of PTSD. Performed poorly in Vietnam veteran study.

Green, 1993; Kinzie et al., 1986; Robins et al., 1981, 1982; Robins & Helzer, 1985

PTSD Interview (PTSD-I) -- 20 items patient rated on a 1 to 7 scale. Begins with a listing of catastrophic experiences which are evaluated for severity and frequency. Yields both dichotomous and continuous scores.

Watson et al., 1991

Structured Clinical Interview for DSM-III-R (PTSD Module; Patient Edition, SCID-P) -- used more with clinical and nonpatient populations. Administered by clinicians, completed in 1-2 hours. This measure is limited because it yields only dichotomous information about each symptom. As a result disorder severity and changes in symptom level cannot be easily detected (Keane et al., 1992).

Spitzer & Williams, 1985, 1986, 1987; Spitzer, Williams, Gibbon, & First, 1986, 1990. A Dutch version is available (Hovens et al. 1992)

Diagnostic Interview Schedule -- Disaster Supplement (DIS-DS) It elicits information about the disaster experience and perceptions of events, use of social supports, reactions and various DSM III-R diagnoses. Takes 90 to 120 minutes. DIS-DS is used more in community studies. A highly structured interview that can be administered by trained lay persons. The DIS generates information about the incidence, intensity and duration of psychiatric symptoms. The majority of questions can be answered "yes" or "no". Symptoms of both lifetime and current PTSD are assessed. Green (1991) **questions its validity** and low sensitivity in identifying PTSD cases and Solomon and Canino (1990) indicates that it underreports the presence of arousal symptoms. The DIS also has problems in correctly identifying subjects who are pathological in a general population sample (Falk et al., 1994)

Robins et al., 1981; Robins & Smith, 1983; See Eaton & Kissler, 1985 for a discussioin of training procedures.

Traumatic Antecedents Questionnaire -- 100 item structured clinical interview includes a comprehensive history providing detailed assessment of separations, family alcoholism, neglect, discipline, violence and sexual abuse.

Van der Kolk et al., 1991.

ASSESSMENT MEASURES -- PTSD

Structured Interview for Disorders of Extreme Stress (DES)   Pelcovitz et al., 1993, in press;
-- based on the interview the clinician uses a rating scale   van der Kolk et al., in press
that assesses emotional, cognitive, somatic and
characterological sequelae of developmental trauma. It
includes 27 item DES subcategories in six major areas,
namely, Alteration in:
i)   Affect and impulse
ii) Attention and consciousness
iii) Somatization
iv) Self-perception
v)   Relation with others
vi) Systems of meaning
(See Table 6 in Section I for an enumeration of the
specific behavioral categories)

Jackson Structured Interview for PTSD -- Reviews current   Keane et al., 1985
functioning, background information, demographics,
vocational and social adaptation, antecedent events,
precipitatory factors and symptom severity, frequency
and duration.

Structured Interview for PTSD (SI-PTSD) -- 13-item scale of   Davidson et al., 1989
DSM III items that interviewer rates on a O (absent) to 4
(extremely severe) scale. Yields both continuous and
dichotomous symptom ratings. Each symptom can be
rated for present state and for "worst ever" experience.
Total score is viewed as a measure of symptom severity.

High Magnitude Stressor Events Structured Interview --   Kilpatrick et al., 1991
assesses for lifetime history of high magnitude events --
completed rape, other sexual assault, serious physical
assault and abuse, other violent crimes, homicide death of
family members or close friends, witness someone being
injured or killed, serious accidents, fear of being killed or
seriously injured, natural or intentional human design
disasters, exposure to health threatening chemicals and
military combat. The events are summarized
chronologically. Yield an Objective Event Characteristics
Interview and Subjective Emotional Responses Scale.

Low Magnitude Stressor Interview -- assesses for the   Kilpatrick et al., 1991
presence of 11 potentially stressful events that are
excluded from DSM-III-R PTSD Criterion A. For
example, these events include job loss, financial
difficulties, marital difficulties, serious chronic illness,
nonviolent death of someone in household or friend.
Individuals asked to pick worst or most serious event for
the past year and to indicate if this is a single event or a
progression of events. Rate this event on objective and
subjective dimensions.

ASSESSMENT MEASURES -- PTSD

Potential Stressful Events Interview (PSEI)[1] -- combines the low end magnitude stressor interviews into one measure in order to obtain a detailed trauma history. On average this detailed interview can take anywhere from 1/2 hour to 2 hours depending upon extensive trauma history. The PSEI consists of five parts:

a) demographic information - 10 items
b) low magnitude stressors which occurred in the past year -- 11 items
c) high magnitude stressors that are explicitly defined in behaviorally specific terms.
d) objective characteristics -- injury self and others, suddenness, expectedness, and warning received.
e) subjective characteristics -- assess 15 different emotional responses and 10 different symptoms that are recalled from the time of the event.
    The latter section assess both the objective and subjective characteristics of the first, worst, or most recent of high magnitude stressors.

Falsetti et al., 1994; Resnick et al 1993 have developed a briefer version of the PSEI. (Greene is developing a self-report instrument based on the PSEI called the **Trauma History Questionnaire**

Trauma Assessment for Adults (TAA) -- a shorter version that was developed from the PSEI. Assesses trauma history for events other than the one for which the client is seeking treatment.

Resnick et al., 1993; Best, 1994.

General Trauma Stress Questions --
    The following questions attempt to cover a variety of areas:
i) Have you had any unusual illnesses or injuries?
ii) Have you had any near death experiences?
iii) How were you disciplined as a child?
iv) Were you ever raped or sexually molested/assaulted?

Ford et al., 1993

Multimodal Life History
    Inventory [2] -- this self-report inventory solicits general information, personal and social history, description of presenting problems and related features, as well as significant childhood experiences and memories.

Lazarus & Lazarus, 1991

2. Clinician's Rating Scales (See Streiner, 1993 for guidelines to evaluate rating scales)

Clinician's Stress Response Rating Scale

Weiss et al., 1984

Contextual Interview - independent raters define contextual threat of a particular experience.

Brown and Harris, 1978

---

[1] Available from Crime Victims Research and Treatment Center, Dept. Psychiatry and Behavioral Sciences, Medical University of South Carolina, 171 Ashley Ave., Charleston, SC 29425, (803-792-7945, Phone; 803-792-3388, FAX)
[2] Available from Research Press, 2612 North Mattis Ave., Champaign, Illinois 61821

ASSESSMENT MEASURES -- PTSD

Clinician Administered PTSD Rating Scale (CAPS-1)[1] -- based on a structured interview a 30 item and 13-item rating scale that assesses both the severity and frequency of the 17 core PTSD symptoms, 8 associated features, and extent of social and vocational impairment. It has a separate frequency and intensity 5 point rating scale for each symptom. It ascertains current and lifetime prevalence of PTSD symptoms, its associated features, symptom severity measures, indices of impairment in social and occupational functioning and validity assessment of the patient's responses. The associated features include survivor guilt, feelings of hopelessness, feeling of being overwhelmed, disillusionment with authority figures. Takes approximately **1 hour** to deliver and requires training, Neal et. al. (1993) have developed a computerized version of the CAPS that takes only **15 minutes**. Two forms of CAPs are available (current and lifetime diagnostic versions). Assesses symptoms over a 1 month period. CAPS-2 measures symptoms over the past week. (1 week status version) It yields both continuous and dichotomous scores and includes separate frequency and intensity rating scales for each symptom. CAPS-2 is primarily for use in repeated assessments over relatively brief assessment intervals.

Blake et al., 1990a, 1990b, 1993 (See PTSD Research Quarterly, Spring, 1994 Vol. 5, No. 2 for a discussion of the decision rules for the CAPS).

PTSD Rating Scale

Foa et al., 1994

3. Self-Report Measures - General PTSD

PTSD Symptom Scale (PSS) -- 17 item semistructured interview and 17 item self-report scale that corresponds to DSM-III-R criteria. It assesses the severity of symptoms over the last two weeks. The self-report scale is somewhat more conservative than the interview version. Takes about 10 minutes to administer. Interviewer can be trained within 2-3 hours. This measure does not assess frequency and intensity of symptoms.

Rothbaum et al., 1990; Foa et al., 1993

Penn Inventory of PTSD -- 26 items of scaled sentences with 3 options per statement as in BDI. Yields a score from 0 to 78. A cutoff score of 35 is used to identify PTSD with a 95% probability of PTSD. Test completed within 10 minutes. Measures the severity of traumatic event.

Hammarberg, 1992

---

[1] Copies of CAPS-1, 2 and Instruction Manual are available from Dr. Dudley Blake, Psychology Service (116B), Boise VAMC, 500 W. Fort Street, Boise, Idaho 83702-7011.

ASSESSMENT MEASURES -- PTSD

Modified PTSD Symptom Scale -- Self Report (MPSS-SR)   Falsetti et al., 1993
  -- developed from Foa et al. It consists of 17 items
  which correspond to DSM-III-R symptom crtiteria for
  PTSD. Whereas, Foa it al.'s scale assesses only the
  frequency of symptoms, the MPSS-SR assesses both
  frequency and intensity. Frequency assesed 0=not at all
  to 3=5 or more times per week/very much/almost always.
  Severity is assessed on a 5 point scale (not at all to
  extremely distressing). Assesses the PTSD symptoms
  for a 2 week period prior to the time of administration.
  Takes 10 to 15 minutes. PTSD diagnosis assigned if at
  least 1 reexperiencing, 3 avoidance symptoms, and 2
  arousal symptoms are endorsed. Range of scores 0-51
  frequency, 0-68 severity, 0-119 total. Proposed cut-off
  scores are available.

Davidson Traumatic Stress Scale (DTSS) -- self-rating scale   Vargas & Davidson, 1993
  covers three PTSD symptom clusters, in terms of both
  frequency and severity of symptoms, as well as proposed
  DSM-IV criteria.

Trauma Assessment for Adults (TAA) -- screening   Resnick et al., 1994
  instrument for assessment of traumatic events. (Both in
  self-report and interview formats)

Posttraumatic Stress Disorder Reaction Index   Pynoos et al., 1987

Cinncinnati Stress Response Schedule (CSRS) -- an 80-item   Green, 1993
  symptom checklist that covers such areas as core
  symptoms, sleep disturbance, phobic avoidance,
  obsessive-compulsive, paranoid, somatic and borderline
  symptoms. Derived in part from SCL-90 items.

Retrospective Assessment of Traumatic Experience (RATE)   Gallagher et al., 1992
  -- 45 to 70 minute semi-structured interview

Traumagram Questionnaire   Figley, 1987

Purdue Posttraumatic Stress Disorder Scale -- 15 item self-   Figley, 1989; Hendrix et al.
  report of PTSD symptoms. Yielding 3 factors labeled   1994.
  arousal, avoidance and global perception of distress.
  Useful in assessing long-term impact of a traumatic
  event. (Note, it was based on DSM-III items and items
  need to be updated)

Weekly Symptom Checklist of PTSD Symptoms -- client   Resnick & Newton, 1992
  self-report measure

Symptom Impact Checklist   Conte & Schuerman, 1987

Stress Inventory   Everly & Sobelman, 1987

ASSESSMENT MEASURES -- PTSD

PTSD Subscale of MMPI -- 49 items (does not reflect DSM-III-R criteria) The F, K, Depression, and Schizophrenic scales often demonstrate a PTSD pattern (8-2 elevation and K lower characteristic of PTSD clients (e.g., F $\geq$ 66, Depression (2) $\geq$ 78; Schizophrenia (8) $\geq$ 79; Keane et al, 1984). Subject to overreporting of symptoms and high false positive rates. A wide range of cut-off scores have been suggested in the literature ranging from 8.5 to 30 depending upon the population. It now appears as a supplemental scale in MMPI-2 as a 48 item scale with T-scores derived from combat veteran samples. Dutton (1992) reports scores for battered women.

Keane et al., 1984; Watson et al., 1986. (See McCaffery et al, 1989 and Hovens et al., 1993 for critiques.) See Schlenger & Kulka, 1989, for MMPI-2 PTSD Scale. See Fairbanks et al (1985) for discussion of various cut-off points for identifying fabricators, (e.g., F scale, T score above 88; FK index raw score of 7). See Allen (1994) for a discussion of MMPI-2 and PTSD.

Trauma Scale

Allodi & Cowgill, 1982

Harvard Trauma Questionnaire -- designed for cross-cultural comparisons. Validated on Indo-Chinese refugees.

Mollica et al., 1992

Impact Event Scale (IES)[1] -- 15 item self-report of trauma-related symptoms that measures subjective distress to specific event. It focuses on intrusive ideation (7 items) and avoidance (8 items). Subjects score symptom intensity over the preceding 7 days on a 4 point scale. Some subjects have been asked to fill out the IES for the "most difficult period of adjustment", rather than for the previous 7 days.(For use of IES with combat veterans -- see Schwarzwald et al., 1987). The scale does not reflect all DSM-III-R/DSM-IV items. (A revised form is available.) Green (1991) observed that different scoring methods have been used, making comparisons across studies difficult. Females score higher than males. The IES has been administered **to children** and **adolescents**. With children the items are administered in the form of an interview. With the death of a close friend, the questionnaire taps grief as well as PTSD. This scale has been used widely and it is sensitive to posttreatment changes in disaster survivors, rape victims and combat veterans. One can ask clients to fill out the IES for different periods of time. For example, in studies of POWs, they were asked to fill out IES for (1) the year following release, (2) the last 12 months, and (3) the worst time since imprisonment (see Falk et al., 1994).

Horowitz et al., 1979; Zilberg et al., 1982 (Note, Joseph et al., 1993, report that the IES could be improved or needs to be supplemented in order to measure such clinical features as sleep disturbance and emotional numbing). It can be used to monitor PTSD throughout the course of treatment.

---

[1] "Perhaps the single most widely used instrument for assessing the psychological consequences of exposure to traumatic events" (Keane et al., 1992, p. 3).

ASSESSMENT MEASURES -- PTSD

National Womens Study (NWS) PTSD module -- used by
    trained non-clinical interviewers. Subjects are asked
    "People experience a variety of moods and feelings from
    time to time. In your case, has there been a period of a
    month or more during which ... " (followed by
    statements specifically phrased to assess symptoms
    presence).
        Kilpatrick et al., 1989;
        Resnick et al., 1993.

Checklist of Stressful and Traumatic Events -- 51 item self-
    report instrument assessing a broad range of traumatic
    events
        Bremner et al., 1993

Post Traumatic Inventory -- 23 item Yes/No questionnaire
    about traumatic experiences specifically tailored to SE
    Asian refugees.
        Carlson & Rosser-Hogan,
        1994

Brecksville PTSD Inventory
        Smith, 1985

Life Events Survey
        Sarason et al., 1978

Civilian Mississippi Scale for PTSD -- 34 item self-report
    questionnaire which measures PTSD symptomatology
    using a 5 point scale
        Keane 1989; Thrasher et al.,
        1994

Symptom Checklist measures number and severity of a wide
    range of psychological symptoms. Consists of 43 items,
    21 of which tap PTSD symptoms. Rate Symptoms 0 =
    not a problem to 4 = an extreme problem.
        Foy et al., 1984

PTSD Symptom Checklist
        Reaves et al., 1993

Trauma Symptom Checklist - 40 (TSD-40) -- revision of an
    earlier 33-item version. Now includes a subscale on
    sexual dysfunction as well as other PTSD symptoms.
        Elliot & Briere, 1992

PTSD Syndrome and Dissociation Scale
        Coons et al., 1990

Perceived Stress Scale
        Cohen et al., 1983

Brief Symptom Inventory (BSI) -- a shorter version of the
    SCL-90-R, 53 items of "problems and complaints that
    people sometimes have" rated on a 5-point scale
        Derogatis & Spencer, 1982;
        Derogatis, 1983

Trauma Symptom Inventory -- selection of SCL-90 items-29
    items
        Derogatis,1977; Brom et al.,
        1989; Briere, 1991

Traumatic Stress Schedule
        Norris, 1990

Psychological Distress Scale - 9 item scale scored on 3 point
    scale (0 = not al all, 1 = a little bit, 2 = quite a bit). Items
    include intrusive and frightening thoughts, irritability,
    depressed affect, sleep difficulty, hopelessness,
    tachycardia, temper outbursts, worrying, and feeling
    critical of others.
        Freedy et al., 1994

ASSESSMENT MEASURES -- PTSD

Personal Stress Symptom Assessment (PSSA)   Numeroff, 1983

Toronto Alexithymia Scale -- alexithmia is the difficulty to   Taylor et al., 1985, 1990;
recognize and verbalize feelings (26-item scale).   Zeitlen et al., 1993
Alexithymia is an important construct to consider since
Pennebaker and Watson (1991) propose that the act of
not disclosing a traumatic event may have more damaging
consequences than the event itself and can lead to a loss
in affective modulation.

4. Combat-Related Self-Report Scales

Wolfe et al. (1993) notes that as the nature of combat   For a review see Friedman et
changes, the content of these scales need to change. For   al., 1986; Keane et al. 1987;
example, the Persian Gulf war involved the threat of   Lyons et al., 1988; Watson et
biological weapons, large scale civilian involvement. The   al., 1989, 1994
combat exposure scales from Vietnam war highlighted
direct threat to life during enemy attack, exposure to
artillery, participation in dangerous patrols, witness or
participation in abusive wartime violence.

Mississippi Scale for Combat-Related PTSD (M-PTSD) -- 35   Keane et al., 1986, 1988,
items using a 5-point Likert scale yielding scores of 35 to   1989; Kulka et al., 1988; Litz,
175, cutoff score 107, is used to classify individuals as   1991 (The Mississippi Scale
PTSD. Measures levels of distress resulting from   is available in both **combat**
symptoms directly associated with PTSD such as   and **civilian** versions). See
intrusive memories, interpersonal adjustment, affect   Lyons et al., 1994, for
lability, memory disturbance, ruminative features, and   research on faking on this
sleep difficulties. Perconte and Wilson (1994) report that   scale.
the Mississippi Scale is moderately related to general non-
PTSD psychological distress, "warranting some caution
in its utilization as a specific measure of PTSD severity,"
p. 133). The Mississippi Scale has been revised and
tailored to specific war experience, e.g., U.N. peace
keeping troops.

Abbreviated Mississippi Scale for Combat-Related PTSD --   Wolfe et al., 1993; Fontana &
  11-item version of the full Mississippi Scale. A different Rosenheck, 1994
  short-form 11-item version was developed by Fontana &
  Rosenheck. The latter scale was found to be more
  sensitive to change.

Mississippi Scale for Desert Storm War Zone Personnel   Litz, 1991; Engel et al., 1993
  38-item scale altered for Operation Desert Storm.   (See Sutter, et al., 1993, for
                                                               discussion of cutoff scores)

Combat Exposure Scales -- (CES) -- 7-item scale quantifies   Friedman et al., 1986; Foy et
  extent of combat experience; Laufer Combat Scale-   al., 1986; Lund et al., 1984;
  Revised; Combat Exposure Duration Scale. For   Keane et al., 1989; Laufer et
  example, the Laufer scale is a 10 item true-false scale that al., 1981; Buydens-Branchey
  assesses war zone military experiences.   et al., 1990

Combat Experience Questionnaire   Figley, 1977

ASSESSMENT MEASURES -- PTSD

Combat Activity Scale	Reaves et al., 1993
Vietnam Era Stress Inventory	Wilson & Kraus, 1985
ODS War Zone Stress Exposure Scale (ODS-SE)	Wolfe, 1990; Sutker et al., 1993
Dutch PTSD Scale -- 28 items	Hovens et al., 1993
PTSD Inventory -- 17-item scale that corresponds to the 17 PTSD symptoms listed in DSM-III-R. Individuals are asked if they suffered the symptom during "the last month" and "in the past."	Solomon, 1993; Solomon et al., 1993
PTSD Checklist - Military version (PCL-M)	Weathers et al., 1991
Military Stress Scale -- consists of 6 items that reflect the quantity of combat experienced, the seriousness of the wounds incurred by the veteran and his comrades, involvement in atrocities, hand to hand combat, and being taken prisoner.	Watson et al., 1989, 1993
Personal Change Questionnaire -- ask individual to indicate how he/she has changed since the critical event (e.g., captivity). Subjects are asked to respond to 53 traits such as "optimism" as view self before and after having been taken prisoner of war.	Sledge et al, 1980; Solomon et al, 1993
Captivity Questionnaire and Perception of Social Environment Following Repatriation	Solomon et al., 1993
Interactive Combat Traumatic Measure (ICTM) -- whereas, most combat exposure measures cover "objective" traumatic experiences (combat exposure, witness abusive violence, participate in abusive violence), the ICTM involved clinician's rating client's response to 11 traumatic events that cover target, observer, agent, failure to prevent a killing, The measure is designed to assess the client's perceived responsibility.	Fontana et al., 1992
Trauma Query Questionnaire	Bollinger, 1992
Veteran's Adjustment Scale	Boudewyns & Hyer, 1990
Women's War Time Exposure Scale (WWES) -- 27 items that cover exposure to horrific, environmental, andworking conditions, discriminating experiences, quality of care porvided and end-of-life events.	Wolfe et al., 1989
Women's Background Questionnaire -- Self-report questionnaire covering premilitary, military, and post-military information.	Wolfe et al., 1989

ASSESSMENT MEASURES -- PTSD

PTSD Diagnostic Scale   Gallers et al., 1988

Finally, there is a need to also assess the potential "positive" effects of exposure to traumatic events such as combat.

For example, consider the **Scale To Assess Appraisals**   Aldwin et al., 1994;
of War Experience -- 28 item scale that asses both   Elder & Clipp, 1989
desireable and **undesireable** aspects of war on a 4
point rating scale. For example, "learned to cope with
adversity", "self-discipline", "broaden perspective"
<u>versus</u> "separation from loved ones", "combat anxiety",
"loss of friends". Research indicates that perceiving
positive benefits from stressful combat experience can
mitigate negative effects.

5. Combat-Related Interviews

Premilitary Adjustment Index   Gallers et al., 1988

Military History Interview -- among other questions ask   Scurfield & Blank, 1985;
whether the patient was ever evacuated from war zone, as   Scurfield & Tice, 1991
well as range and severity of stressors during the entire
evacuation process.

Semi-Structured Initial Intervew for Desert Storm War-Zone   Litz et al., 1991
Personnel

War Stress Interview - Operation Desert Storm (WSI-ODS)   Litz et al., 1991; Rosenheck,
The interview is composed of several instruments and   1990; Rosenheck & Fontana,
addresses both environmental and psychological   1991
traumatic experiences. For example, it taps whether the
soldier was "target", "observer", "agent", or seeing
oneself as a "failure" at preventing death/injury.

Open-ended interview - ask veterans to describe "single most   Wolfe et al., 1993
distressing incident." (See the variety of stressors offered by
veterans of Operation Desert Storm).

6. Sexual and Physical Assault Victim Measures

(See Brassard et al., (1993), Briere (1992), Koss (1993),
Martin et al. (1993), Rodenburg & Fanuzzo, 1993, Resnick,
Kilpatrick & Lipovsky, 1991, Russell (1986), Wyatt &
Peters (1986), for a discussion of how to assess for the
effects of rape and child sexual abuse). (See Dutton (1992)
for a discussion on how to assess the impact of **domestic
violence**). Resnick et al. (1993) report on the need to ask
explicitly for the presence of specific victimization
experiences. **Table 1** is an enumeration of the questions
Resnick et al suggest should be included.

Sexual experience Questionnnaire-II (SEQ) -- assesses   Wagner & Linehan, 1994
occurrence, severity, age, and perpetrator of abuse

ASSESSMENT MEASURES -- PTSD

7. Domestic Violence Measures   Hendrix & Schumm, 1990
Abusive Violence Scale

Appraisal of violence - measures perception of the severity of   Dutton, 1992
    violence and expectations of severity and lethality of
    violence toward victim

Attribution of Violence -- measures attributions about the   Dutton, 1992
    cause of violence by intimate partner yielding scores
    about internal, stable and global attributions

Abusive Behavior Observation Checklist (ABOC) -- includes   Dutton, 1992
    psychological, sexual, as well as physical abuse. It also
    includes a list of possible injuries and questions about
    medical intervention. This is a modified version of the
    Conflict Tactics Scale (Straus, 1979; 1989) which is an
    inventory of specific violent behaviors.

Also ask client for a description of the "most recent abusive
    incident", "one of the worst", and the first abusive
    incident." Note, changes in violence over time.

Psychological Maltreatment of Women Inventory -- 58 item   Tolman, 1989
    inventory using a 5 point scale from "never" to "very
    frequently". Includes items that cover isolation, removal
    of resources, demands for subservience. Rigid
    observance of traditional sex roles and emotional verbal
    abuse. (Note, there is a high likelihood of women who
    are maltreated and/or abused to have been "victimized"
    previously. Need to check for prior history).

ASSESSMENT MEASURES -- PTSD

TABLE 1

Victimization Screening Questions as Suggested by Resnick et al., 1993, p. 985-986

<u>Screen for Noncrime Events</u>

1. Have you experienced any situation in which you feared you might be killed or seriously injured?

2. Have you experienced any situation in which you were seriously injured or suffered physical injury?

3. Have you ever seen someone who was seriously injured or violently killed?

4. For example, have you ever experienced

   a) a serious accident at work, car, or somewhere else
   b) a natural disaster such as a tornado, hurricane, flood, major earthquake, or similar natural disaster

<u>Screen for homicide</u>

The loss of a family member can be a very stressful experience. Has a close friend or family member of yours ever been deliberately killed or murdered by another person or killed by a drunk driver?

<u>Screen for rape</u>

Another type of stressful event that many women have experienced is unwanted sexual advances. Women do not always report such experiences to the police or discuss them with family or friends. The person making the advances isn't always a stranger but can be a friend, boyfriend, or even a family member. Such experiences can occur anytime in a woman's life, even as a child. Regardless of how long ago it happened or who made the advances,

Has a man or boy ever made you have sex by using force or threatening to harm you or someone close to you? Just so there is no mistake, by sex we mean putting a penis in your vagina.

Has anyone ever made you have oral sex by force or threat of harm? Just so there is no mistake, by oral sex we mean that a man or boy put his penis in your mouth or someone penetrated your vagina or anus with their mouth or tongue.

Has anyone ever made you have anal sex by force or threat of harm?

Has anyone ever put fingers or objects in your vagina or anus against your will by using force or threats?

ASSESSMENT MEASURES -- PTSD

(Table 1 Cont'd. Resnick et al. 1993)

Screen for contact sexual molestation

Not counting the incidents you have already told me about, has anybody ever touched your breasts or pubic area or made you touch his penis by using force or threat of force?

Screen for contact/attempted sexual assault

Other than the incidents that we've already discussed, have there been any other situations that did not involve actual sexual contact between you and another person but did involve an attempt by someone to force you to have any kind of unwanted sexual contact?

Screen for physical assault

Another type of stressful event women sometimes experience is being **physically** attacked by another person. Not counting any incidents already described to me, has anyone - including family members or friends - ever attacked you with a gun, knife, or some other weapon, regardless of when it happened or whether you ever reported it or not?

Has anyone - including family members and friends - ever attacked you without a weapon but with the intent to kill or seriously injure you?

In addition, subjects/clients are asked:

a) **how many** such incidents of assault types they have experienced in their lifetime and the **age** at the time of the first incident of each given type.

b) rape victims were queried about the first, most recent and worst episode, while information about other forms of assault were limited to only one incident, namely the self-defined "worst" incident of that type.

(Resnick et al. note that the presence of **fear of death,** and **serious physical injury** are particularly significant predictors of subsequent poor adjustment).

----

8. Child Abuse Measures   Finkelhor, 1979; Pihlgren et
Child Sex Abuse Questionnaire--8 item questionnaire   al., 1993

Childhood Trauma Events Scale -- 6 item self-report   Barsky et al., 1994;
  questionnaire that covers various traumatic events (death of   Pennebaker & Susman, 1988.
  a friend or family member, upheaval between parents,
  sexual abuse, physical abuse or assault, extreme illness or
  injury, or any other major upheaval) before age 17. Also
  record how traumatic each event and whether confide in
  others about the event.

Sexual Abuse Exposure Questionnaire (SAEQ) -- identify 10   Rowan et al. 1994.
  categories of increasingly invasive sexual events.

ASSESSMENT MEASURES -- PTSD

Trauma Symptom Checklist (TSC) consists of 33 items
  (there is also an experimental 40 item version) that
  measures depression, anxiety, dissociation, Sexual Abuse
  Trauma Index (SATI), sexual problems and sleep
  disturbance. Subjects also rate how often (0 = never to 4 =
  very often) they experienced some 40 symptoms in the last
  2 months.

Briere & Runtz, 1987, 1989;
Gold et al., 1994.

Childhood Sexual Experiences scale -- uses yes/no, multiple
  choice and short/answer questions to describe up to "three
  sexual experiences they had with someone 5 years older
  than themselves that occurred." Detailed questions
  concerning the nature and impact of the sexual assault are
  also addressed.

Gold et al., 1994.

There is also an adult version that assess **Unwanted
Adult Sexual Experiences.**

Assessing Environments III Questionnaire -- measures
  specific childhood punishment experiences. It consists of
  10 demographic questions and 155 True-False items that
  assess aspects of the individual's childhood history and
  family variables such as social isolation, marital discord,
  etc. For example, "When I was bad my parents used to
  lock me in a closet". "I required medical attention (at least
  once) for injuries caused by my parents." A similar scale in
  the area of sexual abuse experiences is being developed,
  (Zaido & Foy, 1994).

Berger et al., 1988

Incest History Questionnaire

Courtois, 1988, 1992

Response to Childhood Incest

Donaldson, 1983

Childhood Trauma Questionnaire -- surveys the history of
  various traumas including physical and sexual abuse

Sheikh et al., 1990

Sexual Abuse Exposure Questionnaire - an exposure scale for
  incest victims fashioned after the combat exposure scale. It
  assesses the overall level of exposure including frequency
  and duration of abuse, age of onset, use of force, perceived
  life threat, and occurrence of penetration.

Rowan et al., 1994

Sexual Experiences Survey--10 item self-report measure that
  assesses types of coercion or force, as well as types of
  molestation or sexual assault.

Koss & Oros, 1982; Koss &
Gidycz, 1985

Sexual Symptom Checklist - 20 item scale measuring sexual
  feelings and attitudes and sexual dysfunctions.

Hazzard et al., 1993

Sexual Victim Trauma Assessment

Hindman, 1989

Sexual Abuse Inventory

Russell, 1986

Questionnaire of sexual experiences in the past

Lange, 1990

ASSESSMENT MEASURES -- PTSD

Rape Aftermath Symptom Test (RAST) -- a 70-item self-report inventory of psychiatric symptoms and reactions to potentially fear-producing stimuli (scores range from 0 to 280). Contains items from the SCL-90-R and the Modified Fear Survey (Seidner & Kilpatrick, 1988)

Kilpatrick, 1988; Resnick et al., 1991

Derogatis Sexual Functioning Scale (DSFI)

Derogatis & Melisaratos, 1979

Genogram - identify intergenerational patterns of violence and forms of dysfunction within families of origin

McGoldrick & Gerson, 1985.

Solution Focused Recovery Scale[1] -- assesses the client's **signs of healing** (e.g., from sexual abuse). Includes 38 items that are rated from not at all to very much. Illustrative items include "able to think/talk about trauma," "sleep ok," "accept praise well." Client then asked to notice/monitor such "healing signs" (rather than just signs of trauma) and to offer other signs of healing.

Dolan, 1991

9. Crime-Related PTSD Scale

Saunders et al., 1990

Derived 28 item PTSD scale from SCL-90R -- the SCL-PTSD scale should be administered only as part of the whole SCL-90-R. Best (1994) indicates that "it is not a stand alone instrument" and should be used as a screening measure

Saunders et al., 1989

Brief Screening Questionnaire - 10 item scale to detect a history of crime victimization, including rape

10. Natural Disaster Assessment Measures -- (*Also see Section VII on Post-disaster intervention for ways to assess community factors*)

Conservation of Resources Questionnaire -- a 74 item inventory that asks participants to rate the extent of loss of each resource. Resources assessed cover four categories: objects, conditions, personal characteristics and energies (e.g., loss items include control over life, sense of optimism, time for adequate sleep, etc.).

Freedy et al., 1992

An objective measure of a disaster is the **Impact Ratio** which is the number of homes that were damaged or destroyed relative to the population size of that county.

Norris et al., 1994

---

[1] It is worth noting that administering this scale serves both as an assessment, as well as a therapeutic tool, since the therapist can review these items with the client and his/her family members. Inherent in the review process is not only an opportunity to help clients attend to positive signs of recovery, but inherent in the list of items are a variety of suggestions of additional behaviors the client could engage in (e.g., "Adapt to new situations"; "Engage in new recreational activities", etc.). The items on the Dolan Recovery Scale are tailored to survivors of sexual abuse. It would be valuable if similar scales with relevant items were developed for other target populations such as veterans, rape, domestic violence, and crime victims, victims of natural disasters. Note, the Dolan Recovery Scale items have not been empirically-derived, but represent a selection based on face validity. The Recovery Scale assessment is a "good idea" in need of psychometric development.

ASSESSMENT MEASURES -- PTSD

Resource Loss Questionnaire - 19 item scale rates the extent
of loss of each resource on 3 point scale (0 = no loss to 3
= quite a bit of loss). For example, "feeling that you
have control over your life, a sense of optimism, feeling
independent, a daily routine, time with loved ones,
closeness with at least one friend, companionship, time
for adequate sleep".   Freedy et al., 1994

Stanford Acute Stress Reaction Questionnaire -- assesses
acute status (e.g., dissociative reactions and numbing
which may have prognostic significance *(See Sections VI
and VII)*   Spiegel, 1993; Classen et al.,
                                                                  1993

Post Traumatic Symptom Scale (PTSS) -- a screening
measure that taps the degree of traumatic anxiety, sleep
disturbance, nightmares, startle reaction, trauma phobias,
irritability, depression, guilt, emotional lability, and
social withdrawal. The PTSS is a 10 item scale that is
especially effective when screening disaster populations
for psychiatric risk.   Weisaeth, 1985; Malt &
                                                                  Weisaeth, 1989

11. Schema-Related Measures (How trauma affects belief systems)

Trauma Constellation Identification Scale -- assesses
maladjustive cognitive schemas and negative affects   Dansky et al., 1990

Traumatic Stress Institute Belief Scale - Version D.
(Developed by Stamm & Bieber, unpublished).
Measures disruption in cognitive schemas in the areas of
safety, trust, intimacy and self-esteem.   Dutton et al., 1994

Belief in a Just World Questionnaire   Rubin & Peplau, 1975

Attribution for Responsibility for Positive and Negative
Outcomes   Brewin & Shapiro, 1984

Domain Specific and Generalized Self-Efficacy and Optimism   Bandura, 1994; Solomon,
Scales   1993; Scheier & Carver, 1985

Generalized Self-Efficacy Measure - 10 item self-efficacy
scale including such items as "I always manage to solve
difficult problems if I try hard enough", "I remain calm
when facing difficulties because I can rely on my coping
abilities."   Jerusalem & Schwarzer, 1992

World Assumptions Scale -- 32-item scale measure. Views
of self and world   Janoff-Bulman, 1988

Belief Inventory - measure self-blame and self-denigrating
cognitions in adults sexually abused as children.   Jehu, 1989

Trauma Belief Inventory   Scott & Stradling, 1992

ASSESSMENT MEASURES -- PTSD

Meaning Resolution Scale - 15 item, 5 point scale that   Silver et al., 1991
assesses how often subjects find themselves asking
"Why me?", or "Searching for some meaning?"

12. Social Support[1] Measures In general (with the   Clarke, 1993; Silver et al.,
exceptions noted below), the social support literature   1983
indicates that the more supports (family, friends, neighbors,
community "gate keepers") that a traumatized individual can
rely on in the aftermath of a trauma, the better the person's
prognosis following the event (Cohen & Willis, 1985;
Solomon, 1986). Solomon and Smith (1994) note that it
may "not be the lack of social support, but rather the **loss of
social support** that causes so much psychological distress
following disaster" (p.191). See Lehman et al. (1986) for a
discussion of what "victims" report finding most
unhelpful, namely, the discouragement of open discussion
and emotional expression.

Before we consider specific social support measures, a
caveat concerning the complexity of the role of social
support is warranted. Green (1994b, p.23) in reviewing the
literature on social support observed that women who had
high support availability did most poorly in coping with
traumatic event. "Women with excellent spouse relationship
had worse outcomes following disaster than those with
weaker spouse ties. For men, outcomes were positively
related to the strength of the spouse relationship". As
Solomon and Smith (1994, p.188) observe, "for females , in
particular, too much involvement has its costs." Thus,
strong family ties may be more burdensome than supportive
(especially for women) in times of extreme stress. Belle
(1982) in her work on low-income women has also described
the "contagion of stress" that women with high social
supports may experience. **Social supports are complex
and multidimensional -- more is not always better!**
Social involvement **can be a mixed blessing!** (Green &
Solomon, 1994)

Social Support Questionnaire (SSQ) -- 27 items describing   Sarason et al., 1983; Sarason
situations in which social support may be important   et al., 1987
Yields an availability and satsifaction score. A 6 - item
short form is also available. Freedy & Hobfoll (1994)
have reduced this to 10 items.

---

[1] Keep in mind that **social support** is a complex process that includes perceived and received social support, its
subjective evaluation, size of social network, and the qualitative character of social relationships. Of these various
indicators of social support, it is the **perception of social support** that is most closely related to adjustment
and health outcomes (Sarason, 1994). Social support is most effective when provided by similar others and when
it allows for open expression of feelings. (Lehman et al., 1986). These conditions nurture a **sense of
acceptance** and care for us and they accept us for what we are, including our best and worst points. Such
acceptance is the converse of interpersonal conflict that can exacerbate post-trauma symptomatology. Social
support can promote self-confidence and personal effectiveness that can enhance an individual's coping repertoire
(Sarason, 1994). Wortman and her colleagues have reported that others may fail to provide useful support because
they (a) may hold misconceptions concerning how the victim should be reacting, (b) may dismiss or trivialize the
victim's problems, (c) may have trouble dealing with their own reactions towards the victim.

ASSESSMENT MEASURES -- PTSD

Interpersonal Support Evaluation List -- meausres four types of intrapersonal support: appraisal, belonging, tangible and self-esteem.	Cohen et al., 1985
Social Support Questionnaire	Cutrona & Russell, 1987
Quality of Relationships Inventory -- assesses support perceived to be present in particular relationships.	Pierce et al., 1991
UCLA Loneliness Scale -- 20 item scale designed to measure social support network and degree or social integration.	Russell et al., 1978
Inventory of Sociably Supportive Behaviors -- 40 item scale.	Barrera et al., 1981
Unit Cohesion Index -- 20-item, 5-point Likert Scale.	Mangelsdorff, 1991
Purdue Social Support Scale	Burge & Figley, 1987
Crisis Support Scale -- 12 items that assess the availability of others, contact with other survivors, confiding in others, emotional support, practical support, and negative response. The client also rates various family members and friends on a 1 to 7 scale (never to always) on degree of support. Ask client to fill out scale retrospectively for right after the disaster and at present time.	Joseph et al., 1992
Parental Support Scale -- 22 item Scale that assesses parental supportiveness	Fromuth, 1986
Family Adaptability and Cohesion Evaluation Scale (FACES; now in a FACES II Form)	Olson et al., 1983
Family Environment Scale	Moos & Moos, 1986

13. <u>Assessment of Community Factors</u> -- social supports can also be measured at the level of the community. For example, Ayalon reported that 3 community variables mediated child and family responses to terrorist and war-induced stressors.

Ayalon, 1983

a) historical and cultural characteristics of the community
b) previous experience, accompanying anticipation and preparation for such stressors
c) leadership, community cohesion and communication patterns.

(There is a need to develop further indices of such community factors.)

ASSESSMENT MEASURES -- PTSD

14. Marital Distress Measures

Dyadic Adjustment Scale -- 32 items assesses the quality of the respondents' marital or cohabitation adjustment.   Spanier, 1976

Personal Assessment of Intimacy in Relationships (PAIR) -- 36 items   Schaeffer & Olson, 1981

Marital Satisfaction Measure -- Use Global Satisfaction Rating from the Locke-Wallace Adjustment Scale -- 7 point rating scale of "marital satisfaction" ranging from "Highly Disatisfied" to "Highly Satisfied".   Snyder, 1985; see original Locke & Wallace measure, 1959

Conflict Tactics Scale   Strauss, 1979

Response to Conflict Scale -- 24 item self-report scale   Birchler et al., 1994

15. Coping Measures (See Schwarzer & Schwarzer, 1993, for a listing of additional coping measures and for a critical survey of the various coping measures.)

Ways of Coping Questionnaire (Parkes, 1984, has developed a shorter 44-item version of the Ways of Coping Scale.)   Folkman & Lazarus, 1980; Folkman et al., 1986; Parkes, 1984; Vitaliano et al., 1985, 1987

Dimensions of Stress Scale (DSS) -- uses a 4 point Likert-type rating scale to ask respondents to record a major stressor event in his/her life and then to indicate his/her assessment of the event on 24 items. The 6 scales of 4 items each cover control, novelty, duration, causality, predictability, salience or importance. The DSS is an improvement over previous coping measures because it includes multiple items for each dimension.   Vitaliano et al., 1993

Coping Strategies Inventory (CSI) -- a 40 item scale that assesses coping thoughts and behaviors in response to a specific stressor. The specific subscales measure such strategies as problem-solving, cognitive restructuring, social support, express emotion, problem avoidance, wishful thinking, social withdrawal and self-criticism.   Tobin et al., 1984; Tobin et al., 1989.

Approach-Avoidance Scale -- 15-item approach and avoidance coping strategies   Cohen & Roth, 1986

Coping Inventory -- 33 coping strategies   Horowitz & Wilner, 1981

Miller Behavioral Style Scale -- 32 items to measure monitoring and blunting   Miller, 1979

Stress Appraisal Measure   Peacock & Wong, 1990

ASSESSMENT MEASURES -- PTSD

Social Adjustment Scale   Weissman & Bothwell, 1976

Coping Resources for Stress (CRIS)   Curlette et al., 1989

Coping Inventory for Stressful Situations   Endler & Parker, 1990

Social Problem-Solving Inventory   D'Zurilla, C. Nezu, 1990

Problem-Solving Inventory -- 35 item self report scale   Heppner & Peterson, 1982
    measures how individual perceives his/her general
    problem solving ability.

Coping Resources Inventory -- 60 items that measure coping   Hammer, 1980; Hammer &
    resources in 5 domains: cognitve, social, emotional,   Marting. 1985
    spiritual/philosophical, and physical. Uses a 4 point
    scale that indicates how often a person engages in each
    behavior over the past 6 months.

COPE Scale   Carver et al., 1989; Carver &
                                                                   Scheier, 1994

Cybernetic Coping Scale -- 40 item scale assessing how   Edwards & Baglioni, 1993
    individuals change, accommodate, devalue, avoid
    situations and reduce symptoms.

Chronic Stress Measure -- a 7-dimensional measure of 27   Norris & Uhl, 1993
    items that are scored on a 5 point scale. The dimensions
    covered include marital, parental, filial, financial,
    occupational, ecological and physical stress. This is an
    important measure to consider including since it was
    found that chronic stress mediates the long-term effects of
    acute disaster stress.

Coding of coping responses as evident in transcriptions from   Roth & Newman, 1993
individual and group psychotherapy sessions with adult
incest survivors and rape victims.

16. General Adjustment Measures

Psychiatric Evaluation form (PEF) -- a clinical rating scale   Endicott & Sptizer, 1972

Social Adjustment Scale -- semi-structured interview that   Weissman & Paykel, 1974;
    assesses functioning in eight areas (work, social/leisure   Weissman & Bothwell, 1976
    activities, family, sexual activity, intimate relationships --
    How do you get along at work with boss, coworkers,
    friends, spouse, children, social groups)

Social Readjustment Scale -- consists of 43 stressful events   Watson et al., 1993
    judged for severity. Patient can be asked to identify
    experiences prior to stressor such as military experience.

Global Adjustment Scale   Endicott et al., 1976

ASSESSMENT MEASURES -- PTSD

General Health Questionnaire (GHQ) -- 28 items yield an overall score and 4 subscale scores of somatic symptoms, anxiety and insomnia, social dysfunction, and depression in the recent past.   Goldberg & Hillier, 1979

Cornell Medical Index-Health Questionnaire (CMI) -- 195 items   Broadman et al., 1949

Hopkins Symptom Checklist 90 - Revised Form (SCL-90-R); Global Severity Index of the Symptom Checklist 90 - Revised. For a shortened 5 item version see Tambs & Moum, 1993. The items include: Derogatis, 1977, 1983; Derogatis et al., 1973, McIntosh et al., 1993. (See Mollica et al. 1987 for a version that has been adopted for SE Asian refugees)

"...during the last 14 days, was not bothered or distressed at all, was a little bit, quite much, or very much bothered..." (Values from 1 to 4).
1. "Feeling fearful"
2. "Nervousness or shakiness inside"
3. "Feeling hopeless about the future"
4. "Feeling blue"
5. "Worrying too much about things"

The longer SCL-90R scales yield multiple measures beside a Global Severity Index (e.g., a Positive Symptom Index, Positive Symptom Distress Index (32 items) and Separate Symptom Scales of somatization, anxiety, hostility. The Global Symptom Index is the best single indicator of current level of depth of disorder" (Derogatis, 1977). It assesses levels of psychological symptoms within one week of administration.

Health Symptom Checklist -- 20 item measure assesses aspects of physical health and well-being.   Bartone et al., 1989

Physical Reactions Scale   Falsetti & Resnick, 1992

Areas of Change Questionnaire   Weiss et al., 1973

Social Functioning-Revising Axis V for DSM-IV   Goldman et al., 1992

Inventory of Interpersonal Problems (IIP)   Horowitz et al., 1988

Problems and Targets Rating Scale   Marks, 1986; Richards et al., 1994

Vietnam-Era Veterans Adjustment Survey (VEVAS)   Stretch & Figley, 1984

VETS Adjustment Scale -- measures anxiety/depression, alienation, vigor, and confidence in skills   Boudewyns et al., 1990; Ellsworth et al., 1979

American Lake PTSTP-Constructed Symptom and Followup Questionnaire. Also see the VA Physician's guide for disability evaluation and examination.   Scurfield et al., 1990

ASSESSMENT MEASURES -- PTSD

Quality of Life Inventory (QOLI) -- consists of 17 items reflecting the areas of life deemed relevant to overall life satisfaction (e.g., health, standard of living, recreation, friendship, love relationships, home, etc.). Respondents are asked to rate each area in terms of their **importance** and **satisfaction**. This yields a comprehensive profile that can be used as a measure of pre and posttreatment assessment. The therapist can involve the client in collaboratively generating solutions that hinder his or her satisfaction in valued areas of life. There is now a version of this inventory that has been written at a 6th grade reading level. (Available from National Computer Center 1-800-627-7271)

Frisch, 1992; Frisch et al., 1992

Measure of role overload -- 4 item assess, 1) did not have enough time, 2) had too much work to do, 3) worked too many hours, 4) others expect too much of you.

Pearlin and Schooler, 1978

Self-esteem Scale - 10 item scale that measures positive and negative attitude toward oneself.

Rosenberg, 1989

Psychological Well-being -- such as the Bradburn's Affects Balance Scale -- 9 items that measure overall outlook on life   A longer version has been developed that includes either 20 or 40 items assessing well-being. Subjects are asked to rate on a 5 point scale how often a particular emotion occurred in the past week.

Bradburn, 1969; Derogatis, 1975; McIntosh et al., 1993

Subjective Well-being Measure - 2 item short-form, "At the present time, how well do you feel that you are getting along emotionally and psychologically?" and "At the present time, how upset or distressed have you been feeling?"

Howard et al., 1993

General Well-being Scale -- 18 items

Ware et al., 1979

Since PTSD can follow various forms of accidents and since bodily injury is a high risk factor for developing psychological distress, there is a need to assess the degree of injury.

Abbreviated Injury Scale -- yields an Injury Severity Score. Malt (1994) notes, however, that among the 20% of the most severely injured patients only 25% will develop long-term psychiatric consequences.

Greenspan et al., 1985

Late Effect of Accidental Injury Questionnaire (LEAIQ)

Malt et al., 1989

ASSESSMENT MEASURES -- PTSD

17. Goal Attainment Scaling (GAS) -- another means of assessing the effectiveness of interventions is to use the individually tailored measure of GAS. This approach entails:

Kiresuk & Sherman, 1968 (Community Mental Health, 4, 443-453; Jensen, 1994)

a) a collaborative consultative selection of goal areas (usually 3 to 5);

b) formulate specific indicators of various levels of attainment within a goal area. Proceed by scaling levels from least to most favorable outcomes, usually includes 5 mutually exclusive scale points ("most unfavorable," "less than expected," "expected," "more than expected," and "best anticipated success"); goals stated in behavioral terms (e.g., goal to increase nightly sleep) (-2 "most unfavorable" continue to get 2 hours less sleep than want, all the way to +2 "most favorable outcome" of "getting 2 extra hours of sleep per night");

c) indicate "most probable" outcome;

d) evaluate client's progress in terms of GAS. *Note: a good deal of therapeutic benefit accrues just from putting together the GAS.*
More generally, the therapist should explore with clients "How well do they feel they have achieved their treatment goals?"; "How do they feel they are progressing in achieving short-term, intermediate and long-term goals?"; "How satisfied are the patients with treatment?"

18. Psychophysiological Measures

Psychophysiological assessments have been used in three different ways. These include assessing the individual's physiological reactions to various challenge and tasks. These tasks measure physiological responses while the subject is being exposed to trauma related cues. For example,

Blanchard et al., 1982, 1991; Dobbs & Wilson, 1960; Gerardi et al., 1989; Pallmeyer et al., 1986; Pitman et al., 1987, Pitman & Orr, 1993; Pynoos, 1990; Shalev & Roger-Fuchs, 1993. Ornitz and Pynoos (1989) used psychophysiological assessment with children to demonstrate a failure to inhibit startle response.

(i) stimuli that are reminiscent of the trauma (e.g., audio visual reminders, combat sounds, smells such as diesel fuels);

(ii) tape recorded script-driven mental imagery (usually 30 seconds in duration) of the trauma; and of combat-related words;

(iii) intense, but neutral stimulation, designed to assess auditory startle responses (ASR).

For instance, psychophysiological assessments with combat veterans have used imagery or cue-related audio-visual trauma-related scenes (e.g., audiotape of combat sounds or a visual excerpt of the movie Platoon, or an individualized traumatically-based memory that may be induced by imagery recall or other cues (such as olfactory stimuli.) See Shalev et al., 1993, for use of psychophysiological assessment with a civilan PTSD population.

Note: Most of the research on psychophysiological measures have been conducted with combat veterans and the generalizability of these results to other trauma populations need to be determined. For example, see Shalev's work with a civilan population and Resnick's work with rape victims.

ASSESSMENT MEASURES -- PTSD

Shalev and Roger-Fuchs (1993) who have reviewed the psychophysiological research on PTSD note that such assessment procedures can be used, not only for differential diagnostic purposes, but also as a measure of treatment outcome. For instance, they note that individuals who suffer from PTSD "suffer from a defect in their capacity to effectively appraise intensive, but redundant stimuli, and to adequately regulate their arousal response" (p. 429). In particular, the PTSD client experiences an Acoustic Startle Response (ASR) or an autonomic hypersensitivity to sudden intense stimuli. This may also take the form of heightened physiological reactivity in response to cues that are reminiscent of the traumatic event. Similarly, Blanchard et al. (1994) studied PTSD victims of motor vehicle accidents (MVA). He found that their **heart rate responses** to idiosyncratic audiotapes of their accidents was most discriminatory from MVA without PTSD, and from non-MVA controls, across several psychophysiological challenges. Finally, the Veterans Administration in the U.S. has recently conducted a major study of the psychophysiology of PTSD. They studied some 1100 Vietnam veterans across 15 sites and found significant differences between PTSD and non PTSD veterans. The veterans with PTSD evidenced greater reactivity to stress-related stimuli. See the 1994 APA audio tapes (APA 94-260) by Kaloupek et al. (Order from Sound Images 303-693-5571). Illustrative of these findings are the following results:

Men with chronic combat-induced PTSD versus controls evidence:

i) significantly increased systolic blood pressure and heart rate, during exposure to combat sounds. Skin conductance and frontalis EMG have proved less reliable. Only heart rate differences were evident with a civilian PTSD population. Reduction in heart rate magnitude accompany changes resulting from treatment.

ii) a heightened startle response with accompanying increase in circulating plasma norepinephrine (which is distinguishable psychophysiologically from simulators). Findings on tonic autonomic measures are inconclusive.

iii) use differences in heart rate between stress (oral script and imagery of combat scene) and nontraumatic stimuli (mental arithmetic or neutral imagery) to discriminate PTSD and non-PTSD in veterans.

iv) research underway on event-related potentials (ERPs).

Lating & Everly, 1994; Kolb, 1993; Shalev et al., 1993. See Orr 1994 for a review of selected abstracts.

ASSESSMENT MEASURES -- PTSD

Some critical questions:

(1) Allen (1994) has noted that while psychophysiological monitoring of heart rate and skin conductions has shown good specificity, it has limited sensitivity, failing to identify approximately 1/3 of true PTSD cases, while minimizing false positives. "Additionally, some individuals do not show phasic changes from baseline when exposed to trauma stimuli because of tonic physiological arousal or arousal in response to being in an evaluative setting" (p. 342).

(2) A second concern is the commitment of those who do research on psychophysiological assessment to a "conditioning" framework. For example, Shalev, Kolb, Pitman, van der Kolk, and others, who examine the relationship between psychophysiological processes and PTSD tend to use a "conditioned emotional response" model, or an associative network model to explain the pattern of reactions in PTSD clients. But, one wonders about the need for an alternative explanatory model, especially when we keep in mind the critiques of "conditioning" theory. For instance, consider the message of Brewer's (1974) paper entitled "There is no convincing evidence for operant or classical conditioning in adult humans", or Mckeachie's (1974) article "The decline and fall of the laws of learning". It would appear that how individuals with PTSD appraise stimuli play a critical role in understanding the psychophysiological results. Should one equate such appraisal or "meaning" processes with so-called conditioned stimuli and conditional responses?[1]

19. Psychoendocrine Assessment

Much research is underway designed to assess neuroendocrine changes that accompany exposure to traumatic events (e.g., hormone and sleep assessments). These include examinations of ratios of noradrenaline to cortisol, thyroid metabolism, dexamethasone suppression test and provocation flashback tests due to the infusion of lactic acid and Yohmbine. These varied approaches are still in the early experimental stage.

Baum et al., 1983; Davidson & Baum, 1994; Giller, 1990; Kolb, 1993; Kudler & Davidson, 1994; Mason et al., 1990

---

[1] I am also continually impressed with researchers' commitment to the "catechism of conditioning" in describing their complex interventions (e.g., see Deblinger et al. 1990 or Hackman and Ziegler, 1994 who developed complex multifaceted interventions for PTSD clients, and then resort to a "conditioning" framework to explain their treatment.) Am I the only one who believes that something gets lost in the translation? (Recall Breger and McGaugh's, 1995 arguments about the inadequacy of a "conditioning" framework.)

ASSESSMENT MEASURES -- PTSD

Measure of **Sleep Disturbance** -- Disturbed sleep has been called the "hallmark of PTSD". A key question that clients are often asked is, "How are you sleeping?" Sleep disturbance in the form of difficulty falling asleep, mid-sleep awakenings and fear of sleep, frequent nightmares (more than once a month), waking up from sleep terrified without any external cause, awaken in morning with scared feelings often accompany PTSD. See the **Sleep Quality Index**[1]

Buysee et al., 1989: (Glaubman et al., 1990 report that in PTSD subjects their sleep was less efficient, completely lacking stage 4 sleep, increased awakenings and longer REM latency). PTSD clients are "less efficient sleepers", namely, of the time spent in bed, a lower percentage of it is spent actually sleeping (Engdahl, 1993).

A behavioral measure of sleep difficulties has been developed, namely, **Actigraphic Monitoring**. This monitoring device involves a self-contained microcomputer in a small case which is worn strapped to the wrist of the nondominant hand. It measures wrist movements which reflect wakefulness. One can discern discrepancies between sleep problem as reflected in self-reports versus actual behavioral indicators of sleep problems.

20. Performance-Based Measures

(i) Stroop Color Word Test employing stress-related words; where subjects are asked to name colors on which the words are printed while ignoring the meaning of the words -- delays in color naming are seen as an indicator of preoccupation. The Stroop has been used successfully with combat, rape and accident disaster subjects. For example, Thrasher et al. (1994) have used a modified Stroop procedure to assess the cognitive bias and selective processing of threat-material by ferry boat disaster survivors. Foa et al (1991) has reported Stroop interference for rape-related words; McNally et al. (1990) demonstrated that Vietnam veterans with PTSD exhibit Stroop interference.

McNally et al., 1990, 1993; Thrasher et al., 1994; Uddo et al., 1993; Wolfe & Charney, 1991; Zimering et al., 1993. See McNally et al. Cognition and Emotion (1994, 8, 351-367) for evidence of overgeneral memory (i.e., difficulty in retrieving specific "positive" memories) in PTSD and in depressed patients.

(ii) Cognitive and neuropsychological performance measures designed to tap impaired short-term memory functioning and concentration difficulties.) See Bremner et al. (1993) for a discussion of possible deficits in acquisition and

---

[1] There is research underway to determine if the incidence of sleep apnea distinguishes PTSD and non PTSD combat veterans.

ASSESSMENT MEASURES -- PTSD

retention/retrieval processes as a result of being exposed to extreme traumatic events.

(iii) Baum et al. (1983) have used a proofreading task as a behavioral indicator of concentration problems. Subjects are asked to read a 7-page passage and circle any errors they find. Subjects are typically given 5 minutes to work on this task (Davidson & Baum, 1994).

(iv) Rorschach inkblot test using Exner's scoring system has been used to assess PTSD.   Allen, 1994, for a review

21. ASSESSMENT OF ASSOCIATED BEHAVIORS AND SYMPTOMS --
Depression, suicidal ideation and suicidal behaviors, alienation, anxiety, (fearfulness -- situations avoid), emotional labiality, somatization, addictive behaviors, marital distress, problems with anger control, rage, irritability and impulsivity, eating disorder, changes in significant relationships. *(See description below of possible measures of comorbidity.)*

OTHER POSSIBLE AREAS FOR ASSESSMENT NOT FULLY COVERED IN THIS THERAPIST MANUAL

1. Sexual functioning scales (e.g., Purdue Sex History Form which asks about sexual likes and dislikes and if there is a history of physical or sexual abuse as a child)   Derogatis & Melisaratos, 1979; Hazzard et al., 1993; Trepper & Barrett, 1991.

2. Parenting stress measures (e.g., Parenting Stress Index, Parenting Alliance Inventory, Child Abuse Potential Inventory (CAPI). For example, the CAPI is a 160 item self-report questionnaire that are answered in a forced-choice agree-disagree format. The CAPI contains a physical child abuse scale and 6 descriptive factors (distress, rigidity, unhappiness, problems with child, self, family and others).   Abidin, 1992; Milner, 1986: (See Sanders & Lawton, 1993, on how to give parents feedback andWebster-Stratton & Herbert, 1993, on how to run parent groups).

CAUTION ABOUT CROSS-CULTURAL, RACIAL AND ETHNIC
COMPARISONS: It is also worth noting that not only can culture affect individuals, but individuals (e.g., Holocaust survivors) can influence cultures (see Lomranz, 1994).

ASSESSMENT MEASURES -- PTSD

22. **ASSESSMENT OF ETHNIC IDENTIFICATION SCALES** (Individuals from non-Western cultural traditions often fail to present classical symptoms of PTSD disorders. DSM-III-R criteria for PTSD may <u>not</u> be appropriate for subjects from non-Western countries). Assessment of ethnic identity has been conducted by means of behavior checklists, attitude questionnaires, self-nomination scales and cultural comparison profile techniques (see Marsella et al., 1990 Rumbaut, 1985, who has developed a 13 item Cultural Adaptation Scale[1]). It is critical <u>not</u> to impose an ethnocentric Western perspective on the issues discussed in this **Handbook**. Remember that **non-Western countries contain more than 2/3 of the world's population.**

Carlson & Rosser-Hogan, 1994; Good & Kleinman, 1985; Kinzie, 1989; Lee & Lu, 1989; Marsella et al, 1991, in press; Nagata, 1990; Nikelly, 1992. (See Marsella et al (1992) and Tanaka-Matsumi & Higginbotham (1994) who highlight the need to be sensitive to ethnocultural differences. These ethnic differences can readily influence symptom expression, prognosis and differential response to treatment.

Consideration of racial differences.

For instance, consider the implications of an Africentric world view for African American women who are at most high risk for victimization and who experience on-going high levels of stress.

Jackson & Sears, 1992; for example see Watts-Jones, 1990 African-American Women's Stress Scale.

---

[1] See T. Owan (Ed.) (1985). <u>Southeast Asian mental health</u>, Rochville, MD: NIMH.

ASSESSMENT MEASURES -- PTSD

23. ASSESSMENT OF POSTTRAUMATIC STRESS DISORDER IN CHILDREN AND ADOLESCENTS *(See Additional References in Section VIII)*

A review of PTSD in children and adolescents is beyond the scope of the present manual. See McNally (1991) -- Journal of Consulting and Clinical Psychology, 3, 531-537 for a review and Vogel and Vernberg (1993) -- Journal of Clinical Child Psychology, 22, 464-484, and Garmezy and Rutter (1985). One of the most widely used measures of PTSD with children is the **Child PTSD-Reaction Index** (see Pynoos et al., 1987 and Nader et al., 1993 for a discussion of cut-off scores). It is a 20-item scale that uses a 5-point Likert rating scale ranging from none (0) to most of the time (4). The semistructured and structured format when administered to school age children and adolescents provide a way to rate the frequency of symptoms (12-24 mild PTSD, 25-39 moderate, 40-59 severe, and 60+ very severe reactions). Finally, it is worth noting (Pynoos et al. 1994) which symptoms were found to be most discriminatory of the various levels of distress. **Extreme stress** was evident in avoidance of reminders, loss of interest in significant activities; **very extreme stress** levels were evident in estrangement from others, sleep disturbance, bad dreams, somatic complaints, and problems with impulse control. Pynoos et al. (1994) also suggest the need to systematically assess children and adolescents about possible depression, guilt responses, as well as the risk for reckless behaviors in adolescents (substance abuse, thrill seeking, and aggressive behaviors). Guilt responses may derive from being unable to provide aid, being safe while others were harmed, and taking actions that endangered others. A controversial issue in the assessment of PTSD in children who have been sexually abused concerns the use of anatomical dolls. See Everson & Boat (1994) for a discussion of these issues. Another useful resource is the North Carolina Child Trauma Resource Library, Dept. Psychiatry, CB 7160, University of North Carolina Hospitals, Chapel Hill, N.C. 27599-7160; (919) 966-7983 and (919) 966-7160.

24. CHALLENGE OF DIFFERENTIAL DIAGNOSIS

Meek (1990) has examined PTSD from an assessment, differential diagnosis, and forensic evaluation perspective. The marked overlap between comorbidity features in PTSD and other disorders presents the clinician/diagnostician with particular challenges. For instance, since depression occurs so regularly with PTSD the question arises when is it part of the same disorder or a separate condition? Moreover, when is depression an adaptive coping mechanism? Blank (1994) examines similar questions of comorbility and differential diagnosis; especially when the diagnosis PTSD and DES is considered. Wolfe et al. (1994) highlights that female trauma patients tend to receive diganosis of personality disorders and not PTSD, when the latter is justified diagnostically.

As mentioned at the outset, I consult at a center for traumatic brain injury and the overlap with PTSD is a continual diagnostic concern. Since PTSD can result from various forms of accidents, it is worth noting that there is an **overlap in symptomatology between post-concussive head injury and PTSD**. As Davidoff et al. (1988) observe, these symptoms include memory problems, attention difficulties, emotional lability, disinhibition, avoidance and loss of interest. As Scotti et al. (1994) observe, however, the time course of the two conditions differ with the post-concussive head injury being of a relatively brief duration (several days to several months), while PTSD symptoms are considered chronic after 3 months. The distinction is more difficult with severe head injury. **"It is strongly advised that the clinician screen for post-concussion syndrome whenever a case of accidental injury involves physical trauma to the head"** (Scotti et al., 1994, p.29).

The task of differential diagnoses is even more formidable when the client population is women who have head injury due to domestic violence and who have a history of early victimization. Moreover, since there is a high likelihood of continued threat from the abusive husband, the clinical picture of anxiety and depression further complicate the condition of the head injured client.

ASSESSMENT MEASURES FOR COMORBIDITY

After exposure to traumatic events there is a need to look beyond PTSD symptomatology to other forms of psychopathology and distress (see Keane and Wolfe, 1990, North et al. 1994, and Solomon et al, 1991 and Clinical Psychology, Summer, 1994 for general discussions of co-morbidity or dual diagnoses and PTSD). In this Section we will consider possible measures that can be used. In turn, we will consider:

1. General Psychopathology Measures

    a)   Interview and Clinical Rating Measures

2. Anxiety Measures

    a)   Self-monitoring

    b)   Self-report Questionnaires

3. Dissociation/Depersonalization Measures

4. Depression Measures

5. Measures of Physical Examination

6. Measures of Somatization

7. Assessment of Personality Disorder

8. Assessment of Cynical Hostility and Aggressive Behavior

9. Assessment Eating disorder

10. Assessment of Suicidal Ideation and Suicidal Behaviors

    a)   Indicators of suicidal risk

    b)   Comparison of parasuicidal and suicidal patients

    c)   Measures to assess suicidal potential

    d)   Preventative and treatment approaches with suicidal patients

11. Assessment of Substance Abuse

    a)   Interview measures

    b)   Self-report measures

    c)   Measures of psychosocial and developmental factors

12. Family Assessment

13. Assessment of Premorbid Risk Factors For PTSD

14. Assessment of Positive Adjustment Following Trauma

15. Assessment by Means of Client Self-monitoring.

ASSESSMENT MEASURES FOR COMORBIDITY
1. INTERVIEW AND CLINICAL RATING MEASURES -- GENERAL PSYCHOPATHOLOGY

Diagnostic Interview Schedule (DIS) (There is a Supplement for the Homeless) — Robins et al., 1981; North et al. 1994

Anxiety Disorders, Interview Schedule, Revised ADIS-R — Blanchard, 1986; DiNardo & Barlow, 1988

Structured Clinical Interview for DSM-III-R (SCID I and II) (Panic Disorder Module) — Spitzer et al., 1987, 1989

Present State Examination — Wing et al., 1974

Psychiatric Evaluation Form -- can be used to assess overall impairment along 19 dimensions of psychological functioning, as well as for "worst time". — Endicott & Spitzer, 1972

Schedule for Affective Disorders and Schizophrenia (SADS) — Endicott & Spitzer, 1978

SADS Change Interview (SADS-C) — Spitzer & Endicott, 1972

Target Complaints Assessment — Battle et al., 1966

Diagnostic Criteria — Feighner et al., 1972; Spitzer et al., 1978

2. ANXIETY MEASURES

(See Shear and Moser, Archives Gen. Psychiat, 51, 346-354.)

Self-Monitoring Measures

Panic Log — Clark, 1988

Daily Record of Dysfunctional Thoughts — Beck et al., 1979

Rate anxiety three times a day on a daily form using 1-100 point scale — Costello & Borkovec, 1992

Daily mood monitor -- rate each day average mood with 1 being very sad and 9 being very happy. Include illustrative examples. — Gantz et al., 1992

Self-Report Questionnaires

Body Sensations Questionnaire (BSQ) -- is a 17-item scale concerning the degree to which patients fear the somatic symptoms commonly associated with panic — Chambless et al., 1984

Agoraphobic Cognitions Questionnaire (ACD) -- lists 14 common beliefs or thoughts which are reported by panic disorder patients when they are anxious — Chambless et al., 1984

ASSESSMENT MEASURES FOR COMORBIDITY

Anxiety Sensitivity Index (ASI) -- is a 15-item questionnaire which identifies fear of a number of sensations associated with anxiety

Reiss et al., 1986; Peterson & Heilbronner, 1987

Modified Fear Survey

Veronen & Kilpatrick, 1980

Fear Questionnaire (FQ) -- is a 24-item questionnaire that assesses the presence of agoraphobic avoidance and panic severity. Mavisskalian (1986) proposed that a severe agoraphobic could be identified from a cut-off score of 30 on the Agoraphobic Scale of Fear Questionnaire. The subscale contains 5 items which are rated on degree of avoidance ranging from 0 to 8. Three of the items refer to being in situations alone away from home.

Marks & Mathews, 1979; Mavisskalian, 1986

Mobility Inventory for Agoraphobic measures the degree of agoraphobic features

Chambless et al., 1985

STAI -- State and trait anxiety inventory

Spielberger, Gorsuch, & Lushene, 1970

Beck Anxiety Inventory

Beck et al., 1988; Osman et al., 1993

Hamilton Anxiety Rating Scale

Hamilton, 1959

Zung Anxiety Rating Scale

Zung, 1975

Hospital Anxiety and Depression Scale (HAD) -- assess severity of these disorders

Snaith & Zigmond, 1983

Penn State Worry Questionnaire

Meyer, et al., 1990 (Also see Tallis et al., 1992)

Performance Anxiety Self-statement Scale

Kendrick et al., 1982

Report of Confidence as a Performer Scale

Craske & Craig, 1984

Fear of Negative Evaluation and Social Avoidance and Distress Scale (FNE, SAD)

Watson & Friend, 1969

Personal Report of Confidence as a Speaker (PRCS)

Paul, 1966

Subjective Units of Distress (SUDS) Scale (0% to 100%)

Wolpe, 1973

ASSESSMENT MEASURES FOR COMORBIDITY

3. ASSESSMENT OF DISSOCIATION / DEPERSONALIZATION -- see Allen and Smith (1993) and Gleaves (1994) for a general summary of measures including self-report scales, structured interviews, and clinician checklists.

Self-report and interview measures (e.g., the Structured Clinical Interview for DSM-IV Dissociative Disorders (SCID-D) measures amnesia, depersonalizaiton, derealization, identity confusion, and identity alteration). Steinberg et al., 1990, 1992) have developed a shortened version of the SCID-D.

Bernstein & Putnam, 1986; Boon & Draijer, 1993; Bremner et al., 1993; Ross et al., 1989; Steinberg et al., 1990; Steinberg, 1993; Vanderlinden et al., 1992 (see Kihlstrom et al., 1994 for discussion of problems with cutoff scores).

Dissociative Disorders Interview Schedule

Ross, 1989

Depersonalization Questionnaire -- 11-item scale

Shilany & Grossman, 1993

Dissociative Experiences Scale -- 28 item self-report scale; recent form uses on a 11 point scale. Taps disturbance of awareness, memory and identity including depersonalization and derealization.

Bernstein & Putnam, 1986; Carlson et al., 1993; Frischolz et al., 1990; Putnam, 1989. (Note, Putnam et al., 1993, have developed a Dissociation Scale for Children)

Perception Alterations Scale

Sanders, 1986

Dissociation Questionnaire

Vanderlinder et al, 1991

Hypnotic susceptibility -- Hypnotic Induction Profile (Some suggestion that patients suffering from PTSD have higher levels of hypnotizability)

Spiegel & Cardena, 1990 Spiegel & Spiegel, 1978 (Also see Kihlstrom et al, 1994).

Before using Dissociation measures -- see Frankl (1990) (Am. J. Psychiat., 147, 823-829; Piper (1994) (Brit. J. Psychiat., 164, 600-612, Weiner (1992), (Amer. J. Psychiat., 149, 143-144). These authors raise very important validity issues on the various dissociation scales.

ASSESSMENT MEASURES FOR COMORBIDITY

4. DEPRESSION MEASURES

Several studies have reported that depression is a key response to stressful life events like natural disasters. Many PTSD patients have a concurrent diagnosis of depression or a past history of depression. Note that such diagnostic items as loss of interest, concentration impairment, and sleep disturbance are shared by both major depression and PTSD. Major depression may complicate treatment and result in poorer outcome especially if it is unrecognized (North et al, 1994).

Another important feature when assessing depression is not only the presence of depression, but also when did the depression occur. For example, since depression and marital discord are so highly correlated, the sequence of these events is important. For example, Beach (1994, APA presentation) reported that when marital distress preceded depression, the couple responded better to marital therapy; when depression preceded marital discord cognitive therapy was more effective. Thus, the sequence of distress had significant implications for treatment outcome. Moreover, when depression was evident in both members of a maritally distressed couple, treatment was much more challenging.

Structured Interview that covers such areas as: a) cognitive functioning - subjective appraisal of memory functioning, decision making ability, frequency of negative cognitions; b) coping behavior (number of productive and wasted hours, amount of procrastination); c) personal activity (e.g., home duties, hobby involvement); d) social functioning (frequency of various social activities); e) somatic indicators (hours of sleep per night, ratings of fatigue and relaxation); f) general life satisfaction (job marital, housekeeping); g) mood, frequency of crying, enjoyment.	McLean & Hakstian, 1979; McLean & Taylor, 1992
There is a proliferation of instruments for the evaluation of depressive symptomatology including self-report inventories and interview rating scales. The self-report scales can detect and evaluate depressive symptoms, but not diagnose major depressive disorder.	Lambert et al., 1986; Polaino & Senra, 1991

Most widely used **self-report scales:**

ASSESSMENT MEASURES FOR COMORBIDITY

Beck Depression Inventory (BDI) -- measures severity of 21 depressive symptoms and attidudes within the past week. Each of 21 items composed of four alternative statements rating the severity of symptom from 0 to 3. (Versions available in several foreign languages) Items emphasize pessimism, failure, self-punitive wishes, with less weight to somatic features. Total scores between 0 and 10 are associated with no or minimal depression; between 11 and 17, mild to moderate depression; 18 to 24, moderate depression; and 30 to 63, severe depression. When clients score 15 to 22 (mild to moderate depression) it is possible to begin to work on cognitive triad, namely, negative views about themselves, their personal world and the future. When clients score 22 and higher (more severe forms of depression) it is often important to begin with behavioral assignments such as designing a daily activity schedule with the client performing and monitoring day-to-day tasks (e.g., get out of bed when not sleeping, tending to essential hygiene, and attempting to be more active overall).

Beck et al., 1961, 1979, 1988; Beck, 1972

Zung Self-Rating Depression Scale (SDS) -- comprised of 20 items scores 1-4 according to symptom frequency. Give more weight to symptoms involving physiological dysfunction. Reflecting general severity of depression. Spanish version available.

Zung, 1975

Hamilton Rating Scale for Depression (HRSD) -- quantify results of clinical interviews of patients with affective disorder. Consist of 17 items rated on 3 or 5 point scale.
Use standardized Structural Interview Guide for the HRSD. A score of 14 usually marks clinical depression. Elkin et al. (1989) used a score of 20+ to mark more severe depression.

Hamilton, 1960, 1967; Williams, 1988

Hopkins Symptom Checklist (HSCL) -- 11 self-report items concerning depressive behavior during the past week.

Derogatis et al., 1974

Center for Epidemiogical Studies Depression Scale (CES-D)

Radloff, 1975

Hopelessness Scale[1] consists of 21 items of a True/False variety. Items measure global attitudes toward the future (e.g., "My future seems dark to me." "There is no use trying to get something I want because I won't probably get it") Hoplessness score is a better predictor of suicide than is the level of depression.

Beck et al., 1974

---

[1] Reinecke (1994) suggests that a cutoff score of 9 or above on the Hopelessness Scale, in combination with a score of 23 or above on the Beck Depression Inventory (HS and BDI), yield the best prediction of suicidal potential. Obviously, the higher the score (17+) on the HS scale, the more accurate the prediction of suicidal potential.

ASSESSMENT MEASURES FOR COMORBIDITY

Depressive Adjective Checklist (DACL) -- consists of 34 adjectives (22 depressive). Multiple Affect Adjective Checklist (MAACL)

Lubin, 1967
Zuckerman et al., 1964

Automatic Thoughts Questionnaire (ATQ)

Hollon & Kendall, 1980

Dysfunctional Attitude Scale (DAS)

Weissman & Beck, 1978; Merluzzi & Boltwood, 1989

Self-Help Inventory (SHI) -- a 45 item inventory that assesses how people cope when they are feeling depressed.

Burns et al., 1987; Burns & Holen-Hoeksema, 1991

Newcastle Diagnostic Index (NDI) -- index separating endogenous from nonendogenous depression.

Carney et al., 1965, 1972; Kiloh et al., 1972

Additional measures include the Depression subscale of the MMPI, the Anxiety and Depression subscale of the SCL-90-R, the depression section of the SADS, the anxiety and depression disorder section of the NIMH DIS, the Anxiety and Depression section of the Trauma Symptom Inventory and Trauma Symptom Checklist; the latter two measures were developed by Briere. Also, see measures on dependency and self-criticism by Blatt et al., 1982.

ASSESSMENT MEASURES FOR COMORBIDITY

5. PHYSICAL EXAMINATION

Have patient receive a complete physical examination to rule   Raj & Sheehan, 1987
out the possibility of medical conditions that could
simulate anxiety and depressive disorder symptoms.
(See Raj, A., & Sheehan, M.C. (1987). Medical
evaluation of panic attacks. Journal of Clinical
Psychiatry, 48, 309-313.)

General Health Questionnaire   Goldberg, 1972

6. SOMATIZATION DISORDER -- *Somatization is important to assess since some classes
of PTSD patients (e.g., rape and Holocaust victims) tend to increase somatization complaints over
time as other PTSD symptoms decrease.*

Screening questionnaire and self-report measures.   Kirmayer et al., 1994;
For instance, individuals are asked, "Over the last several   Rasmussen & Avant, 1989;
years, have you been concerned with more than one medical   Smith & Brown, 1990;
problem for which your doctor has not been able to find a   Swartz et al., 1986. (See
physical explanation?" (see Pribor et al., 1993). Also   Escobar, 1986 for discussion
somatization is assessed using Millon Personality Scale and   of cross-cultural factors).
Somatic Amplification Scale (Barsky et al. 1990)

Measures of hypochondriasis   Barsky et al., 1994;
                                                                     Pilowsky, 1967

Physical Symptom Checklist   Bartone et al., 1989
 - 20 item scale that taps psychosomatic complaints

7. ASSESSMENT OF PERSONALITY
   DISORDERS

See Zimmerman (1994) for a recent review of the
methodological problems in diagnosing personality
disorders. He highlights that studies comparing
instruments of personality disorders have found poor
diagnostic concordance and that patients and informants
differ in their descriptions of patient's usual personality.
These measures are also biased by the patient's acute
state.

Structured Interview to Diagnose Personality Disorder   Pfohl et al. 1983

ASSESSMENT MEASURES FOR COMORBIDITY

NEO-PI-R (measure of Five Factor Inventory covering Extroversion, Agreeableness, Neuroticism, Conscientiousness, and Openness to Experience and six facets of each domain) -- consists of 240 items that are rated from strongly disagree to strongly agree. A shortened form of NEO-FFI has been developed -- see Yeung et al., 1993)

Costa & McCrae, 1992; Costa & Widiger, 1993; Caprara et al., 1993

Personality Disorder Examination (PDE)

Loranger, 1988

Personality Diagnostic Questionnaire

Hyler et al., 1982

Diagnostic Interview for Borderlines (DIB)

Gunderson & Zanarini, 1983; Kolb & Gunderson, 1980; Zanarini et al., 1989

Millon Personality Scale

Millon, 1987

Multiple Personality Measures

Putnam, 1989; Ross, 1989

8. ASSESSMENT OF CYNICAL HOSTILITY AND AGGRESSIVE BEHAVIOR *(Anger is emerging as an important discriminant of PTSD -- see Section VI)*

Anger Reaction Index -- Two question interview:

Abe et al., 1994

a) "Since the traumatic experiences, have you ever had periods of time when you felt rage toward anyone who might be blamed for the trauma or towards persons associated with the trauma?"

b) After these disturbing events, have you ever had a period of time when you would become so angry that you would physically attack some object or person?

Buss-Durkee Hostility Inventory

Buss & Durkee, 1975

Cook-Medley cynical hostility scale (an MMPI subscale) -- measures proneness to anger, resentment, cynicism, and mistrust of other people.

Cook & Medley, 1954; Kubany et al., 1994

Active Expression of Hostility Scale

Egendorf et al., 1981

Novaco Anger Control Scales

Novaco, 1991

ASSESSMENT MEASURES FOR COMORBIDITY

State-Trait Anger Expression Inventory (STAX-I)   Spielberger, 1980, 1988

Multidimensional Anger Inventory   Siegel, 1985

Self-report inventory of anger and a structured interview for   DiGuiseppe et al., 1994.
anger[1]   Also see Biaggio et al. (1981)
          for a review of anger scales.

Irritability Scale   Snaith et al., 1978

Conflict Tactics Scale   Strauss, 1979

9.   Assessment Eating Disorder

Eating Disorder Inventory   Garner et al., 1983; (Also see
          Vitousek & Manke, 1994)

Diagnostic Survey of Eating Disorders - Revised (DSED) -   Johnson, 1985
multi-item survey that focuses on various aspects of
anorexia and bulemia.

---

[1] These measures are available from Dr. Ray DiGiuseppe, Dept. Psychology, St. Johns University, 8000 Utopia Parkway, Jamaica, New York 11439 and from Eckhardt (1994).

10. ASSESSMENT FOR COMORBIDITY -- SUICIDE[1]
Assessment of Suicidal Ideation and Suicidal Behaviors
(See additional reference list in Section VIII.)

A major concern in working with clinical populations, especially those who have been victimized and who are diagnosed as having PTSD, is the possibility of suicidal behavior. (A similar concern about possible self-injurious behavior is also evident with clients who are depressed, suffering from panic attacks, or diagnosed schizophrenic.) For example, Briere and Zaidi (1989) and Anderson et al. (1993) report that among abused women 49% to 66% have a history of suicide attempts. This is complicated further when there are schizophrenic features. Westermeyer (1991) reports a high rate of suicide (9%) in the early stages of schizophrenia. Given the high incidence of depression and PTSD, depression represents a high risk marker for suicidal behavior. Reinecke (1994) reviews data which indicates that better than 80% of persons who commit suicide are depressed at the time of their attempt.

On a personal note, in my clinical career I have had two patients with whom I was working commit suicide. In reflecting on these experiences I have tried to evaluate how thorough was my assessment and my screening efforts. What, if anything, could I have done differently? The following represents my attempt to learn from these experiences. In turn, I will consider:

(1)   What are some of the indicators of suicidal risk? (Comparison of parasuicidal and suicidal patients.)

(2)   What questions should be addressed with the patient to assess suicidal potential?

(3)   What self-report measures of suicide potential can be administered?

(4)   What are the characteristics of suicidal thought?

(5)   What can be done on a preventative and treatment basis with suicidal patients?

Surely, this topic can be extended to an entire **Handbook**. For those working with clients who have been brutally traumatized, suicide is always a possibility. See the separate reference list in Section VIII on comorbidity for additional references.

---

[1] I am indebted to Dr. Bruce Bongar and his students (Ted Lunliffe, Peggy Goodall, Maureen Grace) for their helpful input.

As noted, **a central feature of many traumatized individuals is clinical forms of depression.** This takes on specific significance when we consider that approximately 15% of depressed patients ultimately commit suicide. Moreover, 80% of persons who commit suicide give warning signs about their intent. But, there is no one single predictor of whether someone will evidence parasuicidal or suicidal behaviors. Rather one needs to consider a constellation of such factors (Leigh and Reiser, 1992) including demographic, stressful life events, psychiatric history, and potential "rescue" factors. An examination of the literature reveals a number of such presuicidal indicators. In fact, the likelihood of making a successful suicide attempt is particularly high during the first year after an initial suicidal attempt. Of these many indicators "the single most significant known risk factor for suicide is a previous incident of parasuicide.[1] But, only 1% of parasuicidals will go on to kill themselves in the following year (MacLeod, 1992).

The following represents a list of high risk factors that I have gleaned from the literature. They are not in order of importance.

Suicidal Intent
1. Expression of suicidal thoughts
2. Giving away prized possessions
3. Suicidal plan
4. Availability of a weapon
5. Preoccupation with death and dying

Psychiatric History
6. Prior suicidal attempts
7. Marked personality change (clinical diagnosis of personality disorder)
8. Abuse of alcohol or drugs
9. Being anxiety prone (e.g., suffering from panic disorders)
10. Previous psychiatric treatment
11. Axis I disorders

Psychosocial Features
12. Single, middle-age who lives alone and is unemployed
13. Young female from working class background who recently has had an interpersonal difficulty -- likely to be parasuicidal
14. Experience of social exclusion (e.g., romantic breakup, loss of employment and isolation)
15. Suicidal history in family members
16. High frequency of recent stressful life events
17. Single/widowed or divorced
18. Criminal record (violence perpetrated or received in the past 5 years)

Thought Processes
19. Sense of time limited to the present
20. Preoccupation with self - suicidal notes have extremely high proportion of first person references and pronouns (high self-awareness)
21. Thinking becomes extremely concrete and rigid, dichotomous black and white thinking
22. Thought processes become inflexible, one-sided, cognitively rigid
23. Creative problem-solving capabilities curtailed, perceived insoluability of problems (view suicide as only or best solution to problem)
24. Goals become extremely short term
25. Impulsive behavior, lack of anticipated consequences

---

[1] Walsh and Rosen (1988, p.40) suggest the term "self-mutilation" be used instead of parasuicide. Differences have been drawn between the self-mutilating population and suicide attempters.

26. Passivity, tendency to deny responsibility for one's actions (evident in both suicidal notes and actions)
27. Identify with role of the victim

Depressive Symptoms
28. Depression over broken relationships
29. Despair over a chronic illness or personal problems
30. Change in eating or sleeping habits
31. Especially, a sense of hopelessness (hopeless view of one's personal future and a reduced expectancy of success)

Self-Concept
32. Feelings of guilt and self-blame
33. Shame over personal failure
34. Insecurity about one's capabilities
35. Feelings of worthlessness, drop in self-esteem
36. Depressed mood (viewing self in negative terms)

Unrealistic Expectations
37. High expectations followed by a failure to live up to those expectations
    e.g., 1) become financially poor after being well off
          2) students who usually do above average work suddenly perform below average
          3) become single after being married
          4) after holidays (holiday didn't live up to expectations)
          5) teenagers unable to live up to parent's expectations
          6) physicians unable to live up to society's expectations

38. Leigh and Reiser (1992, p. 131) have summarized these suicide risk factors as follows:
    a) Presence of a depressive syndrome, including suicidal thoughts; especially has the patient planned how he would do it?
    b) Demographic risk factors: religion (high in non-Catholics), marital status (higher in single, divorced, and separated persons), older age, male sex
    c) Presence of a painful condition or other medical disorder
    d) Living conditions -- living alone increases risk
    e) Alcohol use -- heavy use increases risk
    f) Behavioral warnings of suicide -- seeking help (including medical), talking about suicide, giving away possessions, putting personal affairs in order, hoarding drugs, buying weapons, and other similar acts
    g) Apparent lifting of depression -- suicide occurs more often following this
    h) Ready availability of the means of suicide, for example, large quantities of prescribed medication or a rifle hanging in the den
    i) Previous suicide attempt, history of depression, family history of suicide

39. Zarb (1992, p. 193) has examined suicidal risk factors for **adolescents** and concludes that the most high risk groups are:
    a) loners with poor social skills and poor communication abilities
    b) "acting out" adolescents, especially drug and alcohol abusers
    c) psychotic adolescents who experience delusions and hallucinations
    d) boys programmed early for a particular role and pushed beyond their endurance
    e) intense, gifted, rigid, compulsive, overachieving adolescents
    f) victims of sexual abuse

40. A provocative conceptual model of suicidal behavior has been offered by Baumeister (1991) who has proposed that suicidal individuals are people who are struggling to "shut

down" their emotional systems and attempting to escape from high levels of aversive self-awareness (e.g., adolescents, alcoholics, depressives, panic disorder patients, those who come from individualistic cultures). To this list we can add traumatized individuals who are **seeking to escape** the impact of intrusive memories and feelings. ("I just want the emotional pain to stop." "I don't know any other way to stop the thoughts.")

41. Young et al. (1994) have commented on the need to consider the **interaction of various suicide factors.** For example, they found that while hopelessness is an important risk factor, its significance depends on a history of drug and alcohol abuse. Hopelessness may not predict suicide in individuals who have a history of addictive behaviors. Thus, how the various factors interact is complex and warrants further investigation.

Finally, a caveat in predicting suicide: "Even with a high risk group such as 1000 parasuicides, only 10 will go on to kill themselves over the next year. A model with 80% efficient prediction rate will correctly identify 8 of those 10, but almost 200 individuals will have been falsely identified as at risk." (MacLeod et al., 1992, p. 208)

Comparison of Parasuicidal and Suicidal Patients

MacLeod et al. (1992) observe that:

Parasuicidal behavior appears to be more related to anger, hostility and irritability, whereas suicidal patients evidence more apathy and indifference or an absence of anger expression. The interpersonal relationships of parasuicides are characterized by hostility, demandingness and conflict, evidence "anger dysregulation". Parasuicidal patients are more likely to be diagnosed Borderline Personality Disorder.

Suicide most likely associated with bipolar affective disorders (10%-30%). Associated most with depressed symptomatology, sometimes related to some improvement.

Assessment of Self Mutilation (Parasuicide)

Linehan (1993) suggests that the following information be gathered on previous attempts:
1. Obtain detailed and descriptive information
2. Assess exact nature of self injurious behavior (where and how deep were the cuts, what and how much chemicals were ingested)
3. Environmental context (alone or with someone)
4. Physical effects of the attempt
5. Medical attention needed
6. Presence of suicidal ideation
7. Conscious intent of the attempt

Epidemiological Factors and Suicide

Higher rate for men than for women.

Rates higher in divorced, single, widowed, with lowest rate among married.

Higher rate in lower social classes.

Higher rates among unemployed and increased rates in times of high unemployment, especially in men unemployed for over one year.

Increased incidence of negative life events precede suicidal episode (often interpersonal problem).

Weak social supports.

Epidemiological Factors in Parasuicides

More females than males (1.5-2.5:1).

Highest rates in young females, 15-19 age group.

Higher rates in lower socioeconomic groups.

Often occurs in context of ongoing difficulty (e.g., conflictual marriage).

Measures to assess suicidal potential (See Bongar, 1991, Davis & Sandoval, 1991, Hawton & Catalan, 1982, Maris et al., 1993, Osman et al., 1994, Reinecke, 1994, for a more comprehensive listing and review of suicide prediction scales and Freeman & Reinecke, 1993, Stone, 1993 for possible interventions.) As Reinecke (1994) observes these scales are best used as a guide. The results need to be integrated with the results of a clinical interview and an analysis of the client's history.

Adult Suicidal Ideation Questionnaire (Reynolds, 1991)

Suicide Probability Scale (Cull & Gill, 1982)

Suicide Ideation Questionnaire (Reynolds, 1987) -- used widely to assess risk factors including suicide ideation, hopelessness, hostility, and negative self-evaluation

Suicide Intent Scale (Beck et al. 1974) -- 15 item assesses the intensity of an attempters wish to die. This information should be supplemented with information about availability of means, presence of deterrence or rescue factors, and knowledge of lethality.

Scale for Suicidal Ideation (Beck et al., 1979; Beck, Steer & Rantieri, 1988; Schotte, 1982; also see shortened (18-item) Modified Scale for Suicidal Ideation, Miller et al., 1986)

Hopelessness Scale (Beck et al., 1974) (Note that the level of hopelessness is a better predictor of suicidal potential than is the current level of depression.)

Reasons for Living Inventory (Linehan et al., 1983; Osman et al., 1991, 1994) -- assesses positive reasons for living if suicide is contemplated (no cut-off scores have been reported on the Reasons for Living Scale). (The answers to this scale provide the counselor with the client's reasons for inhibiting suicidal behavior. These can be used as part of the counselling process.) Ivanoff et al. (1994) have reduced the original 48-item Reasons for Living Inventory into a brief 12-item scale. The areas covered (2 items each) include survival and coping beliefs, responsibility to family, child-related concerns, fear of suicide, fear of social disapproval, and moral objections.

Plutchik Suicide Risk Scale (Koslowsky et al., 1991)

Suicidal Behaviors Questionnaire (Linehan & Nielsen, 1981)

Parasuicide History Interview (PHI) (Linehan, 1989; Linehan et al. 1991) -- is a semi-structured
45-item interview that measures various aspects of parasuicidal behavior including intent,
medical severity, impulsivity, social context, precipitating and concurrent events, and
outcomes. A full PHI is completed for each parasuicide episode (see Wagner & Linehan for a
discussion of what constitutes an episode, cluster and act). The PHI yields four subscale
scores covering suicide intent, medical risk, impulsivity and instrumental intent. (A very useful
measure)

Self-rating Depression Scale (Zung, 1965)

Depression Inventory (Beck et al., 1961)

Self-monitoring suicide ideation (Clum & Curtin, 1993)

Future Autobiography Tasks -- designed to assess how someone thinks about the future.

a)   Pick a year in the future and answer questions about that year including goals, wishes
      and desires (Yufit et al., 1970);
b)   Asked to generate things in the future that they were either looking forward to or not
      looking forward to (MacLeod et al., 1992);
c)   Picture an occasion in the future where you feel enthusiastic about something, or
      picture a situation in the future where you feel successful (MacLeod et al., 1992).

Those who are at high risk for suicide evidence "disengagement" from the future
(Baumeister, 1990) and a deficit in "positive anticipation" of both immediate (next day or
week) and long term future (year and ten years) plans and goals (MacLeod et al., 1992).
Have less to look forward to and one's life situation becomes aversive. Less likely to think
about the future and less aware of possibilities for happiness. They are also less proactive
(anticipate, plan, organize).

The following items has been used to predict subsequent suicidal attempt:

1.   problems in use of alcohol;
2.   previous diagnosis of "sociopathy";
3.   previous inpatient psychiatric treatment;
4.   previous outpatient psychiatric treatment;
5.   not living with relatives;
6.   previous parasuicide (Burglass & Horton, 1974).
(None or 1 item -- 5% risk repeat after 1 year; 5 or 6 items -- 48% risk repeat 1 year).
Repeaters also have a higher level of hostility after treatment than do nonrepeaters (McLeod et
al., 1992).

The Assessment of Elevated Suicidal Risk

"Because the suicidology literature is voluminous, diverse, and sometimes contradictory, clinicians
may have difficulty determining the relative importance of various factors when assessing an
individual" (Bongar, 1991, p.61). Even when the most effective screening instruments are used,
"the low base rate of suicide makes it very difficult for screening instruments to predict accurately
the degree of suicidal risk for any specific individual. Therefore, the reasonable and prudent
psychologist must understand the necessity of treating each patient's risk profile and management
as a unique set of variables to be addressed comprehensively in their clinical assessment and case
management" (Bongar, 1991, p.31).

Clinical Inquiry and Observation

"Motto (1989) noted that the most straightforward way to determine the probability of suicide is to ask the patient directly. This approach emphasizes matter-of-factness, clarity, and freedom from implied criticism" (Bongar, 1991, p.99). Additionally, "Schneidman (1989) found that a communication of intent is present in 80% of completed suicides. Other questions that can be raised by the clinician in assessing suicidal risk include the following.

QUESTIONS DESIGNED TO ASSESS SUICIDAL RISK

The therapist should explore the client's thoughts about death, suicide, self-harm. If positive, followup questions should cover:

1. History of suicidal behavior (previous attempts, impulses, and ideation)
2. Current suicidal plans, impulses, available methods, ideas and behaviors
3. History of alcohol and drug use or abuse
4. Feelings of hopelessness and/or helplessness
5. Recent loss or lack of social supports
6. History of depression and other psychiatric illness (Bongar, 1991, p.84)

More specifically, Hollon (1984, pages 140, 141) proposes that the following questions concerning suicidal history and present suicidal ideation should be covered:

Suicide History

1. Whether and how often the client had previously experienced suicide ideation.

2. Whether previous suicide ideation led to suicide attempts.

3. If an attempt was made,

   a)   was it made in a planned, deliberate manner?
   b)   how potentially lethal were the means?
   c)   how likely was it that the attempt would be interrupted before it resulted in death?
   d)   what have been the practical and psychological consequences of that/those attempt(s)?

4. What factors existed to deter suicide attempts?

5. What plans did the client or others make to prevent suicide?

6. History of suicide attempts in family members.

Present Suicide Ideation

1. How frequent and intense is the suicide ideation?

2. How hopeful/hopeless is the client about her/his future?

3. Does the client have a plan and, if so,

   a)   how lethal is the planned method?
   b)   how available are the means?

    c)   how likely is the attempt to be interrupted before it results in death (how likely is it that the client will be found by someone else in time to save her/his life)?

4.   How socially isolated is the client?

5.   What deterrents to suicide exist (e.g., family, friends, religious beliefs)?

6.   What precautions should be taken by the client and/or therapist to prevent suicide attempts, and is the client willing to take them?

An Example of a Suicide Intention Scale

The seriousness of an attempt can be rated on the following fifteen scales devised by Beck, Schuyler and Herman (1974). The scales are subdivided according to 1) the circumstances of the attempt and 2) the attempter's view of the act.

I.   Circumstances

1.   Degree of isolation - whether or not people were nearby -- *"How isolated was the person at the time?"*

2.   Timing - whether intervention was likely or not -- *"Was it timed so that intervention was likely or unlikely?"*

3.   Precautions against discovery - whether attempter took precautions such as locking doors -- *"Were there any precautions taken against discovery?"*

4.   Sought help during the attempt - whether or not made contact to inform others and seek help -- *"Did the patient do anything to gain help during or after the attempt?"*

5.   Final acts - person made arrangements for demise -- *"Did they make any final act anticipating they would die?"*

6.   Degree of planning - amount of effort

7.   Suicide note - present or absent -- *"Did they write a suicide note?"*

8.   Communication of intention - whether others informed in advance

9.   Purpose of act - whether to influence others or to remove self from the picture

II.   Personal Views

10.   Expectations regarding fatality risk - feelings that the act was final -- *"Did they believe what they did would kill them?"*

11.   Conceptions about the lethality, the choice of method - ideas about the risk in the particular method

12.   Seriousness of attempt - how clearly the person knew their own mind about living or dying

13.   Ambivalence toward life - how clearly the person knew their own mind about living or dying -- *"Do they say they wanted to die?"*

14.   Degree of premeditation - how well planned was the act -- *"How premeditated was the act?"* (The longer the idea of suicide in mind, the greater the suicide intent.)

15.   Ideas of reversibility - whether person thought he or she would live if given medical treatment -- *"Is the patient glad (or sorry) to have recovered?"*

This inventory also provides non-scored questions concerning the person's current reactions to the past attempt, their views about death, their estimate of previous attempts, their use of alcohol or drugs at the time of the attempt.

What are some of the characteristics of the suicidal patient?

As Ellis (1986) has summarized, the suicidal patient:

(1) feels hopeless (in fact, the level of hopelessness is the best predictor of suicide, more so, that the patient's current level of depression);

(2) manifests constricted "tunnel vision" and an inability to see alternative courses of action -- seeing his/her life situation in black-white polar terms reflecting dichotomous thinking and not think beyond obtaining immediate relief;

(3) evidences rigid thinking and an inability to generate alternatives;

(4) evidences poor problem solving skills, not thinking through the implications and ramifications of one's thoughts and actions, especially in solving interpersonal problems;

(5) overestimates the insolubility of one's problems;

(6) evidences a low sense of personal control and a low self-esteem (low self-efficacy);

(7) feels current stress will never end;

(8) is preoccupied with the present;

(9) view suicide as most desirable (or only) solution. ("Situation is overwhelming." "I don't know what else to do." "I want to escape from an impossible situation." "I need to get relief from a terrible state of mind.")

As MacLeod et al. (1992) observe, the suicidal and parasuicidal patients:

(1) demonstrate a bias in recalling negative personal experiences, remembering things or autobiographical memories in an unfocused and summarized overgeneral way. For example, when presented with cue word "happy", respond with "When I am out with my friends" as compared to reporting a specific memory of a specific incident.

(2) less oriented to the future.

What can be done on a preventative and treatment basis with suicidal patients?

(1)   Freeman and Reinecke (1993) propose that the therapist adopt a phenomenological

perspective in an attempt to understand and address the client's concerns. The therapist

should convey empathy with the client's despair, explore the client's motives for considering

suicide (e.g., desire to escape emotional pain vs. desire to communicate their concerns to

others), acknowledge their belief that there is no other alternative. In order to nurture the

client's sense of being understood and accepted the therapist can convey:

> I need us to focus on the problem or problems that are making you feel like
>
> there is no other answer but to take your life.

The therapist needs to convey that while suicide always remains an option, it is not the

client's only option, nor the best option. The **therapist** should also convey his/her

availability and explicitly indicate that he/she does not want the client to commit suicide.

See the client as often as needed. Give the client an emergency telephone number where help

can be obtained 24 hours a day. The therapist can verbally contract with the client that he/she

will call the therapist or the emergency center for help before engaging in any self-destructive

behaviors.

(2)   In collaboration with the patient develop and implement a plan to remove weapons and take

appropriate safety precautions. This may involve contacting significant others, psychiatric

consultation, or hospitalization, intensive outpatient treatment, medication, and develop a

supportive and secure environment.

(3)   Probe the patient's level of hopelessness (use Hopelessness Scale) and ask, "What, if

anything, prevents you (the patient) from taking your life?" This question will provide

opening to explore reasons for living and move toward problem-solving (use Reasons for

Living Scale). The objective is to help the client expand on his/her reasons for living (viz.,

"What has kept the client from suicide so far?"). Linehan's (1985) findings indicated that the absence of strong positive reasons to live are most indicative of suicidal behavior. Address the client's sense of hopelessness, demoralization and fatalism.

(4)   Help "normalize" depression -- therapist might comment: "Given your (the patient's) life circumstance I can understand that you might be depressed. (Cite specific examples.) Depression and disappointment should be viewed as a normal part of life rather than believing that such feelings should not exist. That does not make the emotional pain any less, but I can understand what might lead you to be so depressed. Moreover, convey that it is understandable and natural that someone might consider suicide when he/she sees no other way to fulfill his/her desires. If someone felt that there is no other way to handle "the emotional pain", or if someone feels that "the emotional pain will never end", then suicide may seem to be the only or best solution.

(5)   Reframe suicide as a possible solution to problems. For example: "Your feeling hopeless does not mean that your situation is hopeless. It simply means that you are depressed." Describe the effects of depression -- possibly, use metaphors such as, "depression acts as a prism (lens) that you see the world through", or use the metaphor of, "A horse who wears blinders (like depression) and as a result has its vision restricted." "A person who only tunes into one channel." Indicate that the client experiences the world through blinders of which he/she has no awareness. Have the client collaborate in citing specific examples from the client's experience (supporting data) for the applicability of each metaphor. Ask the client for his/her reaction -- Does this "ring true" with your experience? Convey to the patient that: "He/She is plain wrong in his/her belief that suicide is the only (emphasize only) solution, or for that matter the best (emphasize best) solution, to your problem(s). If you believe that suicide is the only or best solution to your problems, then that is 'depression speaking'." Convey that you would hate to see the client use a "permanent solution" for what may turn out to be a temporary problem. "Why don't we see how you feel in a few weeks. Let's take

one day at a time and see if we can't find a better way to deal with this situation." Discuss

with the client how he/she can anticipate possible problems.

(6)   Help the client engage in problem-solving by tracing how he/she came to the solution that

suicide was the only or the best solution. Trace thinking process. Help the patient generate

alternatives. Use imagery of various possible alternative solutions. Help the suicidal client

create the perception of options and nurture the hope for change. Time projection can be

used to encourage the suicidal client to adopt the notion that life could get better. (See the

Future Autobiography task described under the assessment measures.) Focus on the

advantages and disadvantages of suicide and point out the advantages and disadvantages of

other solutions to their problems. Help the client break what appear to be numerous and

overwhelming problems into smaller, behaviorally prescriptive units that can be addressed

individually. Help the client develop more adaptive ways of coping instead of using alcohol,

drugs, avoidance strategies. Since drugs and alcohol exacerbate an individual's suicidal

intentions and render clients less likely to be receptive to help, the addictive behaviors need to

be addressed directly.

(7)   The therapist can help the "victimized" client reframe suicide as a way of giving away

"power" and "control" to the perpetrator, instead of taking her own power back.

(8)   Help the client to look for "gray areas" instead of employing black or white thinking. As one

suicidal client concluded, "Gray can be a beautiful color." Cognitive restructuring

procedures *(to be discussed in Section VI)* can be used to help the client to question the

conclusions that he/she is "worthless" or a "failure" and that "life is futile", and the future

"hopeless".

(9)   Beebe (1975) suggests having the client image his/her completed suicide and then confront

"illogical justifications" such as:

"My family will be better off without me."

"They will be sorry."

"My family's pain will stop."

"I will remove the burden from my family and friends."

Discuss with the client the advantages and disadvantages of solving the immediate problem by means of suicide versus the long term effects on others such as family members (children when they grow up).

Ask what "legacy" the patient wants to leave his/her children? What does he or she want to be remembered for?

(10) Beck (1994) has offered additional clinical suggestions on how suicidal clients can be helped. He indicated that he assesses the client's level of hopelessness each session, since hopelessness is one of the best predicators of suicide. He will assess the client's level of hopelessness at the beginning of the session and then explore with the client what options exist beside suicide. Following this discussion, toward the end of the session the therapist would once again assess the client's level of hopelessness. Such assessments may be conducted by means of open-ended interview questions, or assessed by means of asking the client to provide a rating on a 0% to 100% or 1 to 10 point scale of the degree of hopelessness, or assessed by the Beck Hopelessness Scale. The change in the level of hopelessness from the beginning to the end of the session reveals the client's suicidal potential. But changes in a positive direction that are offered in therapy are not sufficient. As Beck observes, he is sensitive to the fact that the suicidal client may have a "relapse" during the coming week. In anticipation of this possibility he comments[1] to the client:

> "I can see that you seem more hopeful and feel better now than at the beginning of this session. But when you are home, it is possible that your feelings of hopelessness may return. Can you see that possibly occurring? ... Should your feelings of hopelessness return, I am wondering what you might do at that time? ... I also want you to know that your re-experiencing such feelings of hopelessness and thoughts of suicide are not all bad. At that moment it means that all your problems are present; that is, the time when you are having what we call "hot

---

[1] This quotation reflects a paraphrase of the essential clinical suggestions offered by Beck (1994).

cognitions". **It is critical to catch your cognitions when they are hot!** At that very moment, you can call me on the phone if you need to or if you wish you can write down your thoughts and feelings, as well as what is happening. On the phone, or when you come to our next session, we can go over them." (Note: Beck indicates that his clients have not abused the phone call privilege.)

In short, Beck is proposing that the clinician help the suicidal client reframe his/her suicidal thoughts and feelings as a "learning opportunity" to be collaboratively explored with the therapist. Consistent with Beck's views that therapy is a "journey of exploration", he challenges his clients to adopt an attitude of "curiosity" and "inquiry". For example, if the suicidal client conveys a negative self-image the therapist may wonder aloud, 'Where did all of these feelings of helplessness, hopelessness, and thoughts of suicide come from?' The therapist may convey that therapy is **like a jigsaw puzzle**, a puzzle to be solved with its many pieces. If the client highlights developmental and familial factors that contributed to his/her distress, the therapist can encourage an inquisitive attitude by asking the client if he/she has any brothers or sisters. "Is there any way that the client could obtain information from his/her siblings that might help explain what was different about how they reacted versus how the client reacted? ... Would this help provide useful information, another piece to the puzzle?"

Clearly, there are many additional variations on the clinical suggestions offered by Beck and the others included in this list. The important point is that the therapist is active in suggesting to the client ways that he/she can become his/her own therapist, viewing his/her thoughts and feelings as occasions to engage in self-reflection, as occasions for learning, as opportunities to collect data where one's thoughts are viewed as "hypothesis worthy of testing". The ways in which the therapist goes about accomplishing these objectives will surely vary depending upon the client. **A critical objective of the therapeutic process is to nurture hope and to ask clients to put into their own words,** "What prevents them from committing suicide?"; "How can they find meaning given what has happened?"; "How can they not only move on, but find ways to help themselves and others?"; "How does one find hope?" (Note, the use of "How" and "What" questions as a means of having the client **take ownership** and **responsibility for behavioral change** and for **staying alive**).

(11) Parenthetically, it is worth noting that suicide prevention centres do <u>not</u> reduce the suicide rate (Jennings et al., 1978; MacLeod et al., 1992). Thus, a more active intervention is required (e.g., see Freeman & Reinecke, 1993). Berchich and Wright (1992) recommend a "focus on symptom relief". Even minor relief can help to build hope in the patient (p.85).

(12) The procedures and clinical maneuvers described in this Section represent short-term immediate therapist interventions. For some traumatized clients who are suicidal, more long-term interventions are required. This is especially true of individuals who are diagnosed **borderline personality disorders**, as described in Section VI.

A major concern with clients who are diagnosed with borderline personality disorders is the possibility of **self-mutilation**. There is a need to carefully consider each specific incident of self-mutilation. An important first step is to better understand the client's motivation for self-mutilation. As Fleming and Pretzer (1990) observe, there is a need to:

(a) Examine with the client the specifics about those occasions in which they have self-mutilated and occasions when they have been tempted to self-mutilate. Then to consider the commonalities evident across these situations. The following questions can be used to cover this information.

(b) Consider <u>precipitants</u>.

What led up to your wanting to hurt yourself?

When did you start feeling like hurting yourself? What was going on before that?

How were you feeling beforehand?

What other feelings did you have?

What was your immediate reactions when (the precipitating event) happened?

What thoughts ran through your head?

Consider goals

What did you hope to accomplish?

How did you expect to feel afterwards?

How did you expect others (be specific) to react? How would you like them to react?

Suppose you had not done (self-mutilation), what do you think would have happened? How would things have been different? How would you have felt then?

We will consider the treatment of such clients in Section VI. At that time we will also consider the important innovative work by Marsha Linehan (1993) on cognitive-behavioral interventions with borderline patients in reducing parasuicidal and self-mutilation behaviors.

11.   ASSESSMENT FOR COMORBIDITY--SUBSTANCE ABUSE:
Alcoholism Assessment -- Determine the Nature and Severity of the Problem

(See Allen & Litten, 1993, Galanter, 1988, Hickey, 1994, Jacobson, 1989, and Popkin et al., 1980, for critical reviews of Alcoholism Measures. The National Center for PTSD Clinical Newsletter, 1993, 3, Issue 3/4 was devoted to Dual diagnosis: PTSD and Alcohol Abuse)
(Also see additional reference list in Section VIII.)

The epidemiological data on comorbidity presented in **Section I** highlighted **the high incidence of substance abuse in PTSD clients.** In several studies, 23% to 76% of PTSD patient have been found to have concurrent diagnoses of alcohol abuse and PTSD (Everly & Lating, 1994). Comorbid rates for PTSD and lifetime prevalence of alcohol abuse and dependence range from 68% to 82% (Hyer et al., 1993). On average alcohol abuse occurs in approximately 30% of those with PTSD, and thus, should always be assessed (McFarlane, 1994). Horvath (1994) highlights the comorbidity of addictive behaviors and a variety of mental disorders, besides PTSD. **About 20% of patients in treatment for mental disorders also have a current addictive behavior disorder, and more than 50% of patients in addictive behavior treatment programs also have a current mental disorder.**

These epidemiological data are illustrated in findings reported by Joseph et al. (1993), who in reviewing the literature on increased substance abuse report that distressed Israeli combat veterans and survivors of a variety of civilian disasters (Brisbane floods, Hurricane Hugo, Buffalo Creek), as well as a transportation accident, evidence an **increase use of both alcohol and smoking.** They also report that after some natural disasters a **decrease** in the use of drugs and alcohol was reported (Quarantelli, 1985). **Thus, there is a need to assess for changes (increase and decrease) in addictive behaviors of both prescribed and nonprescribed substances following exposure to traumatic events.** At first addictive substances may have been used as a form of self-medication by individuals with PTSD, but in time this coping mechanism may come to represent an additional problem. The severity of addiction is predictive of responsiveness to treatment, so assessment for dual diagnosis takes on specific significance.

With this data in mind, I was asked to present at a Veterans Administration and at a psychiatric hospital that treated **dual diagnosis clients** (PTSD and substance abuse). One of my tasks was to review the variety of measures that can be used to assess substance abuse (especially alcohol abuse) in this population. The following list reflects the handout I distributed. In perusing this extensive list, note that the clinician initially can use brief self-report measures and then standardized interview measures. These can be followed with more detailed measures that assess abuse, as well as measures of related psychosocial constructs.

In considering these measures it is also worthwhile recalling the Lee Robins longitudinal data on Vietnam Veterans reported in **Section I.** She highlighted the need to address the changing pattern of Veterans' substance abuse behavior. **There is a need to assess addictive behaviors over time.** Other PTSD clients such as rape and disaster victims also evidence an increased use of substances as a way to cope.

In **Section VI** we will consider the challenge of treating the client with PTSD and alcohol problems. For now, let us consider how one assesses the degree of alcohol addictive behavior and associated psychosocial factors. In conducting such assessments it is important to keep in mind Penk's (1993) admonition that "substance abuse successfully masks or controls PTSD symptoms".

Alcohol Assessment Measures -- assess for alcohol abuse (problem drinking) and alcohol dependence (e.g., tolerance/withdrawal and psychological dependence -- salience or importance of drinking in one's life, craving and inability to abstain). A number of diverse measures are available to assess alcoholism and comorbidity (see ARF, 1985; Miller & Marlatt, 1984; Schuckkut, 1984; Sher & Trull, 1994). The Brief Drinker Profile (BDP; Miller & Marlatt, 1984), the Rutger Alcohol Problem Inventory (RAPI; White & Labouvie, 1989), the Family Tree Questionnaire (Mann et al., 1985); and direct questioning about the amount of consumption may be used, (e.g., "self-reporting of at least 5 or 6 drinks on one occasion in the past month and alcohol-related problems such as accidents, arrests, missed work due to alcohol at least three times in the past three years", see, Marlatt et al., 1993).

A **sequential gating assessment** strategy can be used that begins the assessment with a brief open-ended interview such as the SAAST or MAST, or even something as general as the rating scale used by Joseph et al. (1993). For example, respondents are asked to indicate whether they are using various substances (e.g., alcohol, cigarettes, sleeping tablets, prescribed medications) **more than** they usually did in 6 months immediately preceding the disaster, and in the 6 months following the disaster. Such open-ended assessments can be supplemented with detailed self-report measures that assess Addiction Severity and Level of Care Index (see list below). When treatment planning is being considered the therapist can select from the list of psychologically-based measures (e.g., expectation, efficacy, high risk, family history measures). From this test protocol, the therapist should be able to provide the client with feedback concerning typical drinking behavior (frequency and quantity), alcohol related life problems, family history, other psychopathology, as well as "strengths". The results of all testing should be reviewed with the client. Marlatt et al. (1993) provide clients with graphic feedback depicting patterns of alcohol use over time.

Of the various psychological measures listed below special mention should be made about the role of **alcohol expectancy in predicting alcohol abuse**. Goldman (1994) has reported that alcohol expectancy measured in a variety of different ways, predict relatively large amounts of variance in drinking outcome 45% to 68%. These expectancies may be organized along both the **positive-negative dimension** and the **arousal-sedation dimension**. It is the arousal-sedation dimension that appear to most distinguish heavy from light drinkers. **Heavy drinkers**, when exposed to alcohol cues, most anticipate **arousing effects** of alcohol such as becoming more energetic, courageous, sociable and funny when they drink. In contrast, **light drinkers'** expectations reflect that booze will have a **sedating effect**. Thus, it would be valuable to assess the individual's expectations about alcohol intake. *(In Section VI we will consider the treatment implications of research on alcohol expectancy.)* As you review the list of possible measures below keep in mind that expectancy measures represent just one of several useful sources of information. Both interview, self-report, report by significant others, and behavioral observation measures have been used to assess addictive behavior. We being with interview measures.

Interview measures

It is important to appreciate that there is no "gold standard" when it comes to assessing alcohol consumption (Room, 1990). Research on measuring alcohol consumption has indicated general overlap across measures, but also some important differences, especially in assessing heavy drinkers. In fact, this may be due to methodological differences including the wording and order of the questions. Some research has suggested better coverage rates when **beverage specific questions** are asked as opposed to global estimates (Russell et al., 1991). Individuals who provide inconsistent information across assessment measures tend to be heavier drinkers. Room (1990) suggests that two questions be used to describe general drinking behavior, namely, **usual frequency and frequency of 5 or more drinks per occasion in the last year**.

Horvath (1994) suggests that clinicians incorporate general questions about addictive behaviors in their interviews and also use follow-up questions when clients mention their drinking behaviors. These assessment questions can be followed by a cost-benefits analysis that is discussed in Section VI on the treatment of addictive behaviors. For example, the clinician can ask:

> "Do you have any habits that it would be good to change, or that others want you to change?"

When clients spontaneously indicate that they drink alcohol, the interviewer can follow this up by using the following measures.

Comprehensive Drinker Profile Self-administered Alcoholism Screening Test (SAAST) -- a 35-item test with yes/no format. Key items include:

Colligan et al., 1988; Hurt et al., 1980; Miller & Marlatt, 1984

2.   Do you feel you are a normal drinker? (No)
4B. Do close relatives every worry or complain about your
      drinking? (Yes)
8.   Are you always able to stop drinking when you want to?
      (No)
11. Has your drinking ever created problems between you
      and your wife, husband, parent or other near relative?
      (Yes)
17. Do you ever drink in the morning? (Yes)
18. Have you ever felt the need to cut down on your
      drinking? (Yes)
25. Have you ever been told by a doctor to stop drinking?
      (Yes)
27. Have you ever been a patient in a psychiatric hospital or
      on a psychiatric ward because of problems related to
      drinking? (Yes)
31. Have you ever been arrested, even for a few hours,
      because of driving while intoxicated? (Yes)

Diagnostic Interview Schedule (DIS, Version III) and the SCID include assessment of substance use and can be used to diagnose substance abuse disorders.

Robins et al., 1981, 1982; See Lucas et al., 1977, for a computerized assessment of alcohol-related illness

Composite International Diagnostic Interview

Eaton et al., 1994; Rounsaville et al., 1993; WHO, 1990

Time-line (TL) Drinking Behavior Interview -- provides a retrospective report of drinking for a selected period of time (e.g., last 1, 6, 12 months). It is designed to assess daily drinking behavior and whether the time was spent in jail or in hospital for alcohol-related reasons. As a validity check husband and wife are interviewed separately and discrepancies between reports are resolved at a joint meeting of spouses.

O'Farrell et al., 1993

Another important approach to interviewing clients with alcohol problems is what Miller calls **motivational interviewing**. The "artfulness" of this questioning approach is worthy of careful study by clinicians. (For an extensive bibliography on motivational interviewing by W.R. Miller and colleagues write: Dee Ann Quintana, Project Coordinator, Research Division - CASAA, Dept. of Psychology, University of New Mexico, Albuquerque, NM, 87131-1161.) Penk (1993) in the same tradition highlights the need to establish a therapeutic alliance with clients by having both the client and clinician seek to obtain information about the client's physical health and ways to improve physical health.

Amodeo & Kurtz, 1990; Horn et al., 1987; Meichenbaum & Turk, 1987; Miller, 1983; Miller & Marlatt, 1984

Self-report measures (see Room, 1990 and Wyllie et al., 1994 for comparison of different consumption measures)

Brief Drinker Profile (BDP) — Miller & Marlatt, 1984

Drinker's Check-up — Miller & Sovereign, 1989

Self-Administered Alcoholism Screening Test (SAAST) (variant of MAST) — Swenson & Morse, 1975 (See Allen & Litten, 1993 critique)

MacAndrew Alcoholism (use MMPI scales and new MMPI-2 scales) — McAndrew, 1965; also see Penk, 1993

Addiction Severity Index (ASI) — McLellan et al., 1983

Alcohol Use Disorders Identification Test (AUDIT) -- 10-item test taps frequency of drinking, dependency symptoms, and signs of harmful consumption — Claussen & Aasland, 1993

Quantity-Frequency Index (e.g., number of drinks per day) — Armor & Polich, 1982

Addiction Severity Index -- evaluates the total number of years an individual has abused alcohol (viz., drinking to the point of intoxication, consuming three or more drinks per day, drinking on a regular basis, drinking on three or more days per week) — McClellan et al., 1985

Self-Report Scale (See their critique on reliability and validity of self-report scales and their Appendix for the most critical questions to include.) — Embree & Whitehead, 1993

CAGE screening items — Ewing, 1984

Alcohol Use Inventory (AUI) — Horn et al., 1986; Wanberg et al., 1977

Khavari Alcohol Test — Khavari & Farber, 1978

Alcohol Withdrawal Assessment - Rating Scale — Ende, 1991

Clinical Institute Withdrawal Assessment (CIWA)	Allen & Litten, 1993
Alcohol Dependency Scale -- provides a continuous measure of the extent and severity of the alcoholic's physical and psychological dependence on alcohol and total number of alcohol-related hospitalizations, arrests and job losses.	Leonard & Blane, 1992; Skinner & Horn, 1984 (See critique by Allen & Litten, 1993)
Severity of Alcohol Dependence Questionnaire (SADQ) -- a 20-item questionnaire	Stockwell et al., 1979; Woody et al., 1993
Lifetime Drinking History -- important to tap age of onset of alcoholism	Skinner, 1979
DSM-IV Questionnaire (See detailed questions to measure abuse and dependence.)	Grant, 1992
Daily Drinking Questionnaire	Collins et al., 1985
Addiction Severity Index (now in fifth edition) (Adolescent versions exist.)	McLellan et al., 1981 (See critique by Allen & Litten, 1993)
Self-Report Quantity Drinking Questionnaire	Greenfield, 1986
Substance Abuse Problem Checklist	Carroll, 1983; Sullivan et al., 1992; Weick et al., 1989
Rutgers Alcohol Problem Inventory	White & Labouvie, 1989
Alcohol Problems Questionnaire	Drummond, 1990
Level of Care Index -- measures addictive behaviors and complications, treatment motivation, relapse potential, and recovery environment.	Mee-Lee, 1988

Measures of psychosocial and developmental factors related to drinking behavior

Situational Confidence Questionnaire	Annis, 1982; (See critique by Allen & Litten, 1993)
Drinking Expectancy Questionnaire	Young & Knight, 1989
Alcohol Expectancy Questionnaire (Also an adolescent version.)	Brown et al., 1980, 1987; Goldman et al., 1991; (See critique by Allen & Litten, 1993 and Goldman, 1994 for a list of other expectancy measures)
Drinking Self-Efficacy Questionnaire	Young et al., 1991

Readiness to Change Questionnaire -- Stages of Change Readiness and Treatment Eagerness Scale (SOCRATES) and URICA Scale. This model considers five stages (Horvath, 1994);	DiClemente & Hughes, 1990; Montgomery et al., 1990; Rollnick et al., 1992

(1) precontemplation ("I am not interested in changing")
(2) contemplation ("Maybe I should cut back or stop this")
(3) preparation ("I'm taking small steps now, and plan major action soon")
(4) action ("I am abstaining/moderating [for 1 to 180 days]")
(5) maintenance ("I have accomplished my goal [for over 180 days], but need to make sure I don't relapse")

Reasons for Limiting Drinking Scale (RLD)	Guydish & Greenfield, 1990
Alcohol Denial Scale	Newsome & Ditzler, 1993
Assess life style -- balance or ratio of "shoulds" and "wants" (include pleasurable activities)	Marlatt & Gordon, 1985
Temptation and Restraint Inventory (TRI)	Collins & Lapp, 1992
Assess **high risk situations** (self-monitor, examine fantasies, description of past lapse episodes). Assess nature of **social support**, particularly the number of contacts with alcohol and drug-using friends and the degree to which a new social network of non-substance abusing acquaintances have developed and been maintained.	Marlatt & Gordon, 1985; Penk, 1993
Alcohol cue reactivity -- use imagery reactivity assessment	Stark, 1992
Family Tree Questionnaire	Mann et al., 1985
Parent's alcohol-related problems as assessed by Research Diagnostic Criteria (RDC)	Andreason et al., 1977
Children of Alcoholics Life Events Schedule (COALES)	Roosa et al., 1988
Adolescent Alcohol Involvement Scale (AAIS)	Mayer & Filstead, 1979
Obtain medical tests, neuropsychological tests, information about sequalae (arrest records, reports from significant others), biochemical markers	Allen & Litten, 1993

**Behavioral measure of heavy drinker of alcohol   Schmidt & Cooney, 1992
consumption** is above one of the following criteria:

a) 350 grams ethanol/week (28 standard .5 oz ethanol drinks)
b) 300 gms/week if patient said she/he wanted to cut down on
drinking
c) 100 gms per occasion (8 standard drinks) twice a month or
100 gms per occasion once a month if patient said he/she
wanted to cut down (standard drink calculated to have 12.5
gms ethanol, equivalent to one can of beer, one glass of wine,
single shot of spirits)

Note that when asking clients how much they drink or how
many glasses a day they drink, also ask them to indicate the
height and width of the glass they use (personal
communication, suggested by Kathleen Mooney).

Patient Perception of Services Interview -- patients   Thom et al., 1992
are asked to answer each question using a 10-point rating scale

1. How big a problem is your drinking in your opinion? (Not
    a problem at all --- Extremely severe problem)
2. How important is it to you to stop drinking? (Not at all
    important --- Of greatest possible importance)
3. How confident do you feel that you could stop drinking if
    advised to do so? Also ask, how confident are you that
    you will be able to follow the advice given to you about
    your drinking) (Not at all confident --- Of greatest possible
    confidence)
4. How helpful do you expect AA (the alcoholic clinic, your
    SP) to be in dealing with your drink problems? (Not at all
    helpful --- Extremely helpful)
5. How well do you feel you got on with the alcohol
    counselor you saw? (Very badly --- Extremely well)
6. Also ask the patient whether there was anything he/she
    would have liked to talk about, but did not.
7. Also ask the patient if there was anything which the patient
    had found upsetting or annoying about the consultation.

Combination of measures -- investigators have examined   Yates et al., 1993
how various measures can be combined to predict relapse. For
example, Yates et al. (1993) reported that the combination of
chronicity or duration of heavy drinking, daily alcohol
consumption or the number of daily standard drinks, and
treatment history or the number of previous alcoholism
inpatient treatments, was the best predictor of alcoholism
relapse.

12. FAMILY ASSESSMENT

The major focus of the measures just reviewed has been on the individual. Since PTSD can affect the entire family there is a need to include family assessment measures. As noted, in Section I, **vicarious traumatization** has been found to affect the wives and children of Vietnam and Israeli veterans with PTSD. Veteran's PTSD was found to contribute to impaired social relations among their wives in a variety of settings, from inner feelings of loneliness, through impaired marital and familial relations, and extending into wider social networks (Solomon, 1994). This interpersonal impact is not limited to combat veterans. For example, Green and Solomon (1994) note that traumatized families evidence high rates of "irritability distress" (irritability among family members, fighting, not enjoying activities together). The value of assessing families during highly stressful situations was also illustrated by Ben-David and Lavee (1992) and Lavee and Ben-David (1993). They studied how Israeli families behaved while in a sealed room during SCUD attacks. Based on reports of the emotional atmosphere, the allocation of roles to family members and interpersonal interactions they placed families into one of four mutually exclusive categories: secure, indifferent, cautious, and anxious and related these styles to the level of adjustment. This research highlights the potential value of assessing and diagnosing family units, and not focus on only individuals. It would be fascinating if this typology (or some variation) applies to families in other traumatic settings and across cultures.

The potential of considering family coping style in the assessment process was highlighted by Gerrity and Steinglass (1924, p.230) who describe functional family coping with natural disasters. They describe **functional family coping** to include:

a) reordering of priorities, especially the redefining of material possessions as having less meaning than in the past (i.e., changed outlook on what was now important);

b) personal and fairly constant immersion into recovery activities, directed toward safeguarding what could be saved, and letting go of what could not;

c) the development of a new understanding of the meaning or purpose of life (e.g., a new relationship with God, or a realignment with one's family or social world).

In contrast, **dysfunctional family coping** consisted of:

a) displacement of emotion about the disaster toward other people or things;

b) avoidance of family resulting in a sense of isolation;

c) family conflict expressed as anger and unresolved daily arguments.

The assessment process can help family members validate and legitimize each other's trauma-related experiences. During the course of assessment and the treatment that follows family members can also be educated about post-traumatic reactions and the recovery process. The therapist can correct misconceptions and false expectations. The interview questions can also help family members develop: (1) a more open communication process; (2) a flexible plan of readjustment; (3) address episodes of renewed anxiety (e.g., deal with "reminders" and new adversities); as well as, (4) manage behavioral alterations (e.g., develop a flexible plan to restore sleeping arrangements). Recall that from a cognitive-behavioral perspective assessment and treatment are interwoven processes. This is illustrated in the checklist of questions offered by Figley.

Figley (1989) suggests that the therapist ask him or herself the following questions when seeing a family where PTSD has been implicated:

1. Do the family members have a clear understanding and acceptance of the sources of the stress affecting them?

2. Do the family members see the difficulties that they face to be family-centered, or do they blame one or two members?

3. Do family members appear to be solution-oriented or blame-oriented?

4. What are the general levels of tolerance for one another in this family?

5. How committed are family members to one another?

6. How much affection is there in this family?

7. What are the quality and quantity of communication among members in this family?

8. How cohesive is this family as a group? (Do family members like to be with each other as much as they would if they were not in the same family?)

9. How flexible are family roles?

10. Do family members tend to utilize or avoid resources outside of the family? (Examine family's history of resource utilization.)

11. Do family members serve as a resource to others as well? (Have they been in a helper role for others?)

12. Is there evidence of a history of familial psychopathology (e.g., depression and anxiety disorders, alcoholism, intergenerational violence).

13. Is there current evidence of family violence?

14. Is there current evidence of substance abuse in the family? (In general, addiction problems should be dealt with first.)

The therapist can use various self-report scales to obtain this information such as the Family Relationship Index (cohesion, expressiveness and conflict) which are measured by three subscales of the Family Environment Scale (e.g., Holahan & Moos, 1983; Moos & Moos, 1986); FACES measure (Olson et al., 1983); the Family Functioning Scale (Bloom, 1985; Bloom & Lipetz, 1989); Family APGAR score which provides a 5 item assessment of perception of supportiveness, closeness, dependability (Smilkstein, 1980); Family Assessment Device and the McMaster Model Clinical Rating Scale that assess problem-solving, communication, roles, affective, responsiveness and involvement, and behavior control (Miller et al., 1994). In addition, the therapist can use **"mapping"** procedures that permit family members to provide a genogram of which family members live in and outside of the home, their gender and relationship to the client. Carroll et al. (1992) have provided a review of possible family assessment measures. *Later in the treatment Section VI we will consider possible Family-Based Interventions.*

In addition, a number of clinicians have highlighted the powerful role of **circular questions** in explicating the nature of the relationship between family members (see Neimeyer, 1993; Penn, 1982, 1985; Tomm, 1985). Circular questions are designed to reveal relationships and differences among relationships in families. Some authors have characterized these efforts as a form of "gossiping in the presence of others" (Neimeyer, 1993). Illustrative examples of circular questions include the therapist asking family members to each answer such questions as:

1. What he/she hopes to get (have happen) by being here?

2. What would happen in this family if this identified problem were to disappear?

3. *(Assess the transactional nature as well as the who? ... what? ... when? ... where? ... how? ... how much? ... of the situation.)* What makes you say that she is X (e.g., obstinate)? ... What was she doing that you would describe as X? ... What did you make of that situation? ... How do you react when he does X? ... Just how do you react? ... And when you get X what does he do? ... And then what happens? ... When X occurs what do you usually do? ... When he does X, what do you think it means? How does that make you feel? ... What else could you have done? ... If you had a chance what would you do differently? ... If you decided X, how would things change? If instead of X, you ...

4. *(Use hypothetical questions.)* If instead of your father leaving (walking out, X), your mother would leave. What do you think would happen? ... If this were to continue, then what do you expect will become of the relationship in X years from now? ... How would the way the family gets along change if X was not present? ... What ideas and thoughts need to die (change)? ... Why? ... What difference would that make?

5. *(Fostering change.)* If you wanted to convince X of Y, how would you go about it? What would you do? Do you think that would work? ... If instead you did Y what do you think would happen? For instance, there seems to have been a fair amount of X (misunderstanding, criticism, problems communicating) within the family. Perhaps, substituting Y (curiosity, asking questions for criticism, etc.) may make it easier? What do you think?

6. *(Future oriented questions.)* What would be reasonable for next week (month, year)? ... Are there any goals that you all agree on, and see yourself working toward together, right now? ... How do you plan to help him (or each other) reach these goals? ... How will you each know if that goal has been achieved? ... What would he/she (the family) have to do to show that X had been completed? ... Would you be surprised if some day X? ... Can you imagine ...? Let us imagine ... How (What) do you think about X? ... Who will be the first to notice X? ... What kind of things are you most grateful for? ... What sort of things about X make you laugh?

Some families are so preoccupied with present difficulties or with past injustices/grievances that they have little or no sense of a future. By asking a series of questions about the family's future, the therapist can help the family create a future for themselves.

Another aspect of the initial assessment of families is to have them appreciate their strengths and the familial crises they have survived and overcome. This discussion is designed to help families appreciate how they need to work together. In the context of assessment family members (adults and children) need to be educated about PTSD, so they can better understand the nature, cause, and pattern of the client's behavior. It is critical that family members avoid blame, criticism and misinterpretations of the client's behaviors. For example, the client's social withdrawal does not mean that he/she doesn't love the family, but rather may be a way of handling discomforting emotions and ruminations. Moreover, the therapist raises with the family and client as to how family members can be enlisted as "allies" in the healing process (e.g., What should the spouse do when first noticing that the client is going to have a "time-slide" and ruminate? How can family members be given a role in helping the client take medications, keep appointments, etc.?). Note, it is critical that the specific suggestion that family members can play should come from the client. As a result of addressing the questions in this Section family members and the client can engage in a co-constructive narrative process.

In short, the therapist can help families create a more "benign story" of events, a more charitable account. For example, in one family where a family member committed suicide, the family came to view his act as a result of the fact that he was a much "too sensitive" individual. On the one hand, this sensitivity led to his caring for others (he was a psychiatrist), but on the other hand, his sensitivity also contributed to his taking his life. Note, this implicit theory was therapeutic in limiting the postmortem search for other contributing factors to the suicide (e.g., marital distress). **What is critical is <u>not</u> the "validity" of the stories the family tells, but their viability, plausibility, coherence and adaptiveness.** Therapists are in the business of helping individuals and families co-create stories. The "art of questioning" is the most useful tool in this reconstructive process.

13. ASSESSMENT OF PREMORBID RISK FACTORS FOR PTSD

While the disorder of PTSD can develop in individuals without any predisposing conditions, particularly if the stressor is especially extreme (depending upon severity, duration and proximity of exposure), a number of predisposing factors have been implicated as increasing the risk or vulnerability. The authors of DSM IV highlight "social supports, family history, childhood experience, personality variables and preexisting mental disorders" (p.426). The following list considers such predisposing factors in more detail.

PTSD is a multifaceted disorder that can be influenced by:

a)   pre-event factors   (e.g., genetic and psychological vulnerability, developmental history, personality)

b)   event factors   (e.g., proximity, exposure, meaning of the stressor)

c)   post-event factors   (e.g., social supports, cultural acceptability, "secondary victimization").

There is a need to not only assess current symptomatology and post-trauma environment, but also the individual's or group's premorbid adjustment. For example, it is important to remember that epidemiological studies indicate that **20% to 30%** of the general population at any point in time will be **suffering** from one or more **psychiatric disorders**. Such disorders may interact with trauma exposure characteristics. Such "vulnerable" groups may require interventions that are different in form and duration than non-previously disturbed individuals. *(In Section VII an extensive Table of 58 factors that have been related to adjustment at the level of the individual, family, group and community is offered.)*

In general, premorbid risk factors become less important as the intensity of the stressor experience increases. Nevertheless, PTSD is more likely to occur in individuals who have had previous exposure to traumatic stressors, or who have had pretrauma adjustment problems, or who evidence ineffective coping skills. (See Breslau & Davis, 1992; Gunderson & Sabo, 1993; Solomon, 1993; Watson et al., 1990). Some of the premorbid factors that have been identified in the literature include:

1.   Pretrauma experience, exposure to **severe adverse life events** (like combat)[1] prior to the trauma can predispose individuals to PTSD. Prior disaster exposure or previous exposure to other traumatic events (Freedy et al., 1994).

2.   Prior victimization such as childhood sexual and physical abuse acted as a premorbid factor for soldier's exposed to battle (Bremner et al., 1993; Engel et al., 1993; Zaidi & Foy, 1994). Elder and Clipp (1989) note that those soldiers who had the poorest adjustment premilitary, tended to have the highest combat exposure, supporting an interactional model of premilitary, combat, and post-military experiences cumulatively putting soldiers at risk.

3.   Depression and anxiety onset prior to trauma such as criminal victimization are predisposing factors to the development of PTSD. But the relationship between precrime depression and PTSD may occur only under high crime stress exposure (Green, 1994). Preexisting

---

[1] Note that some traumatic pre-stress experiences may not generate PTSD symptoms, nor increase their severity. For example, Solomon et al. (1987) report that soldiers surviving previous battles without psychological sequelae decrease their risk for stress reactions after a second combat experience. However, a history of combat stress reactions increases the likelihood of PTSD in the future. Moreover, the level of acute stress disorder often predicts subsequent PTSD.

psychopathology has been linked with the likelihood of the development of PTSD in combat veterans and in civilian survivors of disasters, especially alcohol abuse in men and depression in women. Note, some 20% of men have a predisaster lifetime diagnosis of alcohol abuse (North et al., 1994). The need to assess for prior history of clinical disorders is reflected in the research on depression which indicates that persons with a single episode of major depression have a 50% risk of recurrence; the risk climbs to 70% for those patients who have had two episodes, and peaks at 90% for those patients who have had three or more episodes (Munoz et al., 1994). Whether this risk is due to biochemical "kindling" effects and/or changes in psychological factors (attributional, social support) is not known. **Vulnerability factors need to be considered in identifying high risk groups.**

4. Developmental and familial instability. (Family history of psychiatric disorder, growing up in a family with economic problems, multiple childhood separations). For example, Boulanger (1986) reports that an abusive father figure for Vietnam veterans seems to have acted as a vulnerability or predisposing factor for the impact of the trauma. If the father was traumatized in combat this was also a risk factor.

5. Family history of antisocial behavior and anxiety.

6. Early substance abuse (drunkenness, experience with drugs, especially the greater the variety of drugs used).

7. Repeated trouble with authority (stealing, lying, vandalism, running away from home, early sexual experience, school suspension, academic underachievement, delinquency). Early conduct problems (fighting, truanting, school expulsion, arrests) are predisposing factors.

8. History of prior psychiatric disturbance (namely, depression and anxiety disorders). Prior history of anxiety and related behavioral difficulties; high trait anxiety and worry behavior in children (see Lonigan et al., 1991).[1]

9. Absence of social supports and presence of familial distress.

10. Timing of onset of PTSD or age differences -- the **age** at which the traumatic events were experienced can play a significant role.

    a) Although age effects in children are not completely consistent (Green, 1994), younger children (5-10) appear more vulnerable than older children (11 and older) to the same traumatic events (Garbarino, 1993).

    b) The developmental stage that an individual is at can also influence his/her response to stressful events. For example, soldiers who were less than 20 and who served in Vietnam were more vulnerable than their older colleagues. For this "vulnerable" group the war experience overlapped with the "ego-identity" stage discussed by Erikson. See Williams-Keeler and Jones (1993) who observed that "war represented a riveting experience of an altered reality for which there was little forewarning, but which has the power to change them for the rest of their lives" (p. 8). Whereas, the average age of combat soldiers in Vietnam was 19.5, those who served in WWII averaged 26.

    c) In contrast to the Vietnam Experience, Elder et al. (1994) reported that for veterans of WWII, that late service entry (closer to age 30) as compared to early service entry (closer to age 18), resulted in greater risk of negative trajectories on physical health. This is in

---

[1] Note, the measure of trait anxiety was collected after the disaster at the same time as the PTSD measure. In interpreting such temperament measures caution is thus warranted.

part due to work-life disadvantages due to social disruptions. There is a clear need to adopt a life-span perspective in considering the impact of traumatic events. How does exposure to the trauma interfere with the developmental tasks at that age period?

    d) Green (1994) reports that individuals who are middle-aged have most difficulty adjusting to natural disasters given the "burden of additional age-related stressors".

    e) Schnurr (1994) notes that in older individuals stressful events associated with aging such as retirement, medical disability and bereavement may exacerbate the course of PTSD.

11. Sex differences -- while men had a slightly higher likelihood of experiencing traumatic events than women, women more often develop PTSD after trauma; women have a higher prevalence of PTSD and with more increased chronicity. There is a higher rate of postdisaster psychopathology and risk for PTSD in women or girls than in men (North et al., 1994; Solomon, 1994). For example, Breslau and Davis (1992) reported that after exposure to traumatic events women in a community sample were **four times** more likely to manifest chronic PTSD symptomatology than were men.

12. Gender differences in children -- boys are more susceptible to stressors such as divorce than are girls. By age 10, girls admit to more internalizing symptoms than do boys after disasters. For example, studies of children after the Armenian earthquake revealed that girls had higher PTSD scores than boys, especially in the form of ongoing anticipatory fears.

13. Minority status renders individuals at greater risk for PTSD for repetitive traumas and poorer outcomes, as does lower socioeconomic status.

14. Genetic susceptibility to PTSD -- True et al. (1993) have conducted a study of 4042 twin pairs of Vietnam victims. Identical twins were much more similar than fraternal twins in their response to trauma, as evident in reexperiencing, avoidance and arousal symptoms. The True et al. data suggest that there may be an inherited personality disposition that plays a role in determining the level of exposure and responsiveness to traumatic events.

15. Temperament variables have been implicated as predisposing factors to stressful events. However, it is not the temperament per se, but rather the "goodness of fit" between the temperamental style and the supportiveness of the environment that may predispose individuals to stressful reactions. This was highlighted in the classic developmental research by Thomas and Chess and in the longitudinal study of the children of Kuaui by Emmy Werner. Strelau (1994) has discussed the role of "emotionality", "sensation seeking", "adaptability" in the adjustment patterns of adults in response to traumatic events.

16. Hiley-Young et al. (1993) suggest that the clinician consider the following questions when addressing an individual's prior adjustment to traumatic events:

    a) "What other significant events or previous loses have occurred in the survivor's life prior to the traumatic event?

    b) How did the survivor adapt to these events?

    c) What current life stressors was the survivor experiencing at the time of the traumatic event?

    d) How much social support does the survivor have? Is the survivor accessing social support?

e)   What does the event mean to the survivor?

f)   How has the event affected the survivor's social life, job, health?

g)   What coping strategies does the survivor use? How flexible is the coping repertoire? *(See the discussion under positive adjustment for a description of the relative benefits of different coping efforts.)*

h)   Does the survivor have a history of substance abuse?"

17. Ayalon (1983) has highlighted the importance of assessing not only individual factors, but also group and community factors. She analyzed how communities in Israel responded to terrorist attacks. Such factors as group identity and cohesiveness, degree of preparedness, definition of prescribed roles, group support during trauma episodes, communication patterns, were predictive of both recovery and the reduction of "secondary victimization" (i.e., blaming the victim). Similarly, those who have studied PTSD in the military have noted that the quality of leadership and the degree of combat group morale (level of unit cohesion) were also predictive of the incidence and severity of PTSD (Gal & Mangelsdorf, 1991).

14. NEED TO ASSESS POSITIVE ADJUSTMENT FOLLOWING TRAUMA

After reading the plethora of "bad" or traumatic events that individuals experience, it is quite easy to become distressed or to vicariously become traumatized. As noted earlier, the story of how people handle traumatic events is a **remarkable tale of resilience and courage**, and a testimonial to the indomitable human spirit. In part, this story has been documented in the research efforts of those investigators who have had the foresight to explore and assess the "positive" effects that follow from exposure to disasters, either natural or of intentional human design.

A number of investigators have explored the patterns of positive readjustment in those who have been exposed to traumatic events including rape, natural disasters, prisoner of war (e.g., Aldwin et al., 1994; Antonovsky, 1979; Antonovsky & Bernstein, 1986; Burt & Katz, 1987; Elder & Clipp, 1989; Fairbank et al., 1991; Festinger, 1991; Garmezy, 1993; Gillespie, 1942; Lyons, 1991; Sledge et al., 1980; Stokes, 1945; Ursano et al., 1986; Wolfe et al., 1993; Yarom, 1983). Their research indicates that how individuals appraise and cope with stress play a significant role in determining readjustment. Another important factor is the nature of the social supports available. As Flannery (1990) observed, sometimes shared catastrophic experiences can strengthen marriages, families, and communities. These studies indicate the necessity of assessing for the potential "positive" consequences that may follow from exposure to traumatic events.

The value of attending to both the "positive" and "negative" efforts of being exposed to traumatic events is underscored by Elder and Clipp (1989) who studied combat veterans later in life. They reported that

> "heavy combat veterans believe that their experience engendered valuable coping skills, self-discipline and an increased appreciation of life. The down side of this legacy involves searing memories of personal loss and immobilizing fear. Combat anxieties and nightmares often extend into later years ... **but these memories of combat experience are independent of adjustment patterns**" (p. 336).

Such coping techniques as positive reappraisal,[1] reanalysis, and active coping were most often associated with enhanced well-being. In contrast, such coping techniques as externalization, wishful thinking, self-pity, personal neglect, passivity, withdrawal and avoidance were significantly more closely associated with symptomatic functioning (Solomon et al., 1993). Wolfe et al. (1993) note that while overall adjustment may be favorable, this does not preclude the possibility that clients may have difficulties with specific trauma-related experiences. But these difficulties do not have to get in the way of overall adjustment. See Aldwin (1993) for a discussion of coping with traumatic stress.

Another central feature of those who cope most effectively is their ability to find meaning and purpose in their suffering (Frankl, 1963). This may take the form of reordering priorities, developing greater self-knowledge, rebuilding shattered assumptions (Joseph et al., 1993). This ability to reframe events was illustrated in two studies on prisoners of war. Surely, captivity by an enemy during war would seem to constitute a very traumatic event. In this light, consider the findings on 164 ex-POW Israeli soldiers versus matched controls who were not captured. Solomon et al. (1993) examined both the positive and negative consequences of captivity. They found that many trauma captured victims were able to **compartmentalize** their reactions and reframe the events. These results are consistent with Sledge et al. (1980) who assessed the impact of war captivity four years after release of ex-US airforce officers held in Vietnam. Sledge et al.

---

[1] There is some suggestion that more adaptive functioning requires a balance of around three positive thoughts to two negative ones, since typically greater subject weight or importance is given to negative thoughts (Kanouse & Hanson, 1971; Schwartz & Garamoni, 1986, 1989).

(1980) found that approximately one-third of US Air Force Vietnam POWs reported having benefited from their POW experience. A number felt they benefited from their captivity. I know of two videotapes of Vietnam veterans talking about the "positive" experiences of their captivity. They demonstrate the human ability to cognitively reframe events. (See the videotape of Halyburton and Cherry at the 1989 Mountain Empire Conference. They describe their experience as POWs at the "Hanoi Hilton" during the Vietnam war. Order from Dr. Bert Allen, office 615-929-0116. Another film describing Vietnam captivity is offered by J. Charles Plumb, 805-683-1969.)

Gordon Turnbull (1994) who has extensive experience in working with "survivors" of various traumatic events including the Lockerbie airplane disaster and the debriefing of British hostages from Lebanon and British POWs after the Gulf War concludes "that individuals who experience good outcomes following treatment for their PTSD often express their belief that the experience of trauma has eventually proved to be a positive event in their lives which has increased personal insight and helped them to "grow"" (p.4). The trauma event becomes a "watershed" event and recurrent flashbacks and nightmares provide an opportunity to "review the traumatic event, extract its meaning, integrate it and move on into the future".

After reviewing the literature on positive adjustment to traumatic events, Wolfe et al. (1993) concluded that, "the individuals most likely to show long-term positive adjustment may be those who are able to re-experience their trauma with a relatively high degree of voluntary control either on their own, with the aid of therapy, and who are willing to endure the discomfort of doing so" (p. 98).

15. COMMENTS ON SELF-MONITORING
How can we increase the likelihood of clients doing "homework"?[1]

A central feature of intervention is helping the client become more aware of the habitual transactional nature of his/her behavior and to change that pattern ("deautomatize" his/her behavior) and, in turn, learn more adaptive behavior. The crux of treatment is seen as helping the client engage in more adaptive behaviors between sessions so he/she can collect "data" (the results of "personal experiments") that can be taken as "evidence" to "unfreeze" his/her beliefs about self, others and the world. Thus, what happens between sessions is viewed as where the learning process can occur most effectively. The therapist is thus a "catalyst", a "coach", a "collaborator" in this process. Central to the therapy process is having clients perform activities in vivo between sessions. As a critical first step (a "foot-in-the-door" technique), the clients are asked to engage in some form of self-monitoring as a way of collecting data. Asking clients to engage in self-monitoring, or "behavioral prescriptions", or "homework", may seem straightforward, but it **involves a good deal of clinical skill and psychotherapeutic preparation.** There is a critical need to lay the groundwork for the acceptance of the idea of performing the self-monitoring and personal experiments. This Section describes, in some detail, the clinical steps that can be employed when asking clients to self-monitor or to perform some other activity outside of treatment.

Following these guidelines will increase the likelihood that clients will "self-monitor", perform "homework assignments", undertake "personal experiments", between sessions. Let me suggest that the next time you ask a client to self-monitor or "do homework" you audiotape the session and then compare how you went about making this request with this checklist of proposed guidelines. Are there any changes you could implement in how you make such requests? Are there other things that you do that "work" that I have not included? Please pass these along.

Another form of assessment is to ask clients to self-monitor (keep track) of a variety of behaviors (e.g., PTSD symptoms, thoughts, signs of recovery, etc.) Just asking clients to self-monitor is often insufficient to achieve client adherence. The following detailed outline provides a guideline on how to solicit client collaboration. This is especially important because, "homework", or having clients **engage in personal assignments between sessions, plays a critical role in the interventions** of direct therapy exposure, cognitive restructuring, problem-solving training, and stress inoculation training. The "homework" or assignments may take various forms including:

a) having clients monitor and record different aspects of their behaviors (e.g., automatic thoughts and accompanying feelings, PTSD symptoms, interpersonal behaviors, and the like -- each assignment is tailored to the specific client)

b) scheduling and implementing more productive behavioral and cognitive activities ("uplift times", self-care behaviors)

c) undertaking bibliotherapy and journaling

d) listening to a taped version of the session (e.g., audiotapes of direct therapy exposure sessions).

e) performing both interpersonal and personal experiments such as being more assertive, relaxing, using coping techniques, or undertaking an "as if" experiment. The **"as if" experiments** have been suggested by George Kelly and by Paul Watzlawick. Kelly

---

[1] Below I will discuss why the word "homework" is **not** used with the client.

suggested that clients be asked to behave "as if" they had certain characteristics/attributes that were different from their traditional mode of behaving. Watzlawick has asked clients to behave "as if" the people they interact with have specific needs that will interrupt the client's usual response pattern. For example, an assertive/aggressive individual may be asked to view those he/she has most difficulty with as needing to receive nurturance, support and reassurance. Both of these "as if" experiments are designed to help clients break the negative transactional interpersonal cycle, by having the client perform a "personal experiment". The client's sense of curiosity and inquiry are challenged to see what would happen if? The client is asked, "Would you be willing to do X?" The results of such personal experiments are examined in treatment in order to determine the results ("data") that are incompatible with the client's prior expectations and beliefs. The discussion has a flavor of what did the client discover, what surprised him/her, what did he/she learn about self, others, and the like.

Research indicates that the clients' noncompliance with "homework" is predictive of poor improvement in cognitive therapy (Burns & Auerbach, 1992; Neimeyer et al., 1985; Persons et al., 1988; Primakoff et al., 1986). For example, Persons et al., 1988 report that clients who did homework improved three times as much as those who did not. Neimeyer and Feixas (1990) found that subjects who engaged in cognitive therapy with homework improved more than did subjects assigned to a condition that received cognitive therapy without homework.

It is easy to "blame" the client when he or she does not do "homework", but the therapist must take some responsibility for client noncompliance. Here are a series of steps that the therapist may go through when requesting "homework". Note, these suggestions take some time to implement, so the therapist should allow ample time in the session in order to cover these points. A basic premise behind these guidelines is the research finding that **individuals become more committed to positions that they offer and that they verbalize.** Not only does this collaborative approach empower and enable clients, it is also more effective in enhancing adherence/compliance (see Meichenbaum & Turk, 1990).

1.   Be sure to review why the client is in therapy, work out a statement of goals for treatment, and whenever "homework" is given relate the specific assignment to these treatment goals.[1]

2.   Nurture the client's commitment to change by using some form of "contract" (See Meichenbaum and Turk (1987) for a discussion of the various ways such a contract can be used). These contracts do not have to be formal, nor written. The key element is the need to make explicit the responsibilities of both the client and the therapist. An example of such a procedure is offered by Burns (1989) who sends his clients a contract/memo called "The Concept of Self-Help" in which he highlights the client's responsibilities and need for self-help assignments. The therapist is not there to "fix" or "remove" PTSD and other symptoms of depression, anxiety, etc. The therapist does not have a "cure" for what the client has been through, but rather is willing and committed to "work together" to help the client "cope better", "move on", "get unstuck", "resolve the hurt", as framed in the client's own words. *(See Section VI on Letter Writing for other descriptive statements that can nurture a collaborative relationship of mutual commitments.)*

      Caution is required, however, in using such contractual arrangements with clients who have been "victimized". It is critical that the PTSD clients not view such efforts as yet

---

[1] Sherman and Anderson (1987) found that outpatients at a psychiatric clinic were much less likely to terminate treatment if they imagined staying in therapy and described why they stayed. These findings are consistent with the emphasis of the present **Handbook** that encourages therapists to **elicit reasons** for various therapeutic activities from the clients.

another means to coerce them, nor "revictimize" them. There is a need to follow the client's lead. Nevertheless, such contractual procedures, especially as therapy unfolds, can prove helpful in motivating clients to engage in self-monitoring and other therapeutic tasks, especially in the case of clients with borderline personality disorder and clients with addictive disorders.

3.   The therapist can convey from the outset of treatment that improvement in therapy requires the client to be active, to take on responsibility, to work, to practice and to engage in active problem-solving behaviors, to do "homework" between sessions in order to benefit from treatment. The therapist can also use examples that the client has shared to convey that the client has skills and potential strengths in his or her repertoire to undertake various personal assignments.

4.   Underscore the importance of doing work between sessions, "the other 23 hours", when the "real" therapy is done. Underscore that doing homework is a "vital aspect" of treatment. Convey the expectation that the amount of benefit from therapy depends on the amount of effort the client invests in "homework" and practice between sessions. For example, the therapist can compare therapy to the acquisition of other skills (e.g., playing a sport like learning tennis or learning to play an instrument). In order to learn and change there is a need to practice, rehearse, work on these activities between sessions. Just coming for the lesson or to the therapy session would prove insufficient and a waste of time and money. **We can work together as a team to find out how things are, how you would like them to be, and what we can do to help you achieve those goals.**

5.   Whenever possible, give the client an opportunity to generate the suggestion for the specific homework assignment. As noted, remember that the therapist is at his/her therapeutic best when the client is one step ahead, offering the suggestions that the therapist would otherwise offer. For example, the therapist can use the "art of questioning" to point out that the client's behavior (problems) vary across time and over situations. The therapist, in his or her best Peter Falk "Columbo"-like style, can wonder aloud, "What is different among those times when the PTSD symptoms, depression, and anxiety are worse and the times when things are not so bad?" The therapist may ask the client, "How can we find out what the differences are?" If a series of such questions are asked it is not a big step for the client to come up with the suggestion that perhaps he or she could "keep track". To which the therapist responds, "Keep track? That's interesting. What did you have in mind?" If the client does not come up with the idea of self-monitoring, the therapist can always introduce this idea directly or by means of conveying that other clients have found that "keeping track" has proven helpful. **The general guideline is to always allow and encourage the client to come up with the idea first.**

6.   Provide a rationale for each component of the homework assignment. Generate a list collaboratively with the client of what is to be done for the next week and why. Explore how doing this assignment will relate to the client's treatment goals and how it can make a difference. Connect homework assignment to the original reasons for the client seeking help and to the goals to be achieved. For example, if you were going to ask the client to read something that had been **carefully selected for their reading level**, the therapist might introduce it by offering a rationale:

> They say that seeing a picture is worth a thousand words, then perhaps reading a chapter may be worth a dozen therapy sessions. I am giving you this to read because of your sense of curiosity and desire to learn more. I would like you to look it over and then we can discuss what does, and what does not apply, in your situation. Does that make sense to you? Is this something you think you would find useful?

7. **Caution: With clients do _not_ use the term "homework".** Instead, consider such terms as "assignments, tasks, practice, rehearsal". For many clients the word "homework" holds surplus meaning that may interfere with adherence. If you use the word "homework", then put quotation marks around it with you fingers and say, what some people may call "homework". For many the connotation of "homework" is drudgery, being badgered by others to do homework, "busy work", etc.

8. Describe homework in simple terms. **Keep it simple (easy to do, easy to remember, and meaningful)**

    a) Match the format for recording to the client's abilities and resources.

    b) Give the client a choice -- collaborate. "Would you rather do X or Y? (e.g., record in a diary fashion or use a tape recorder?)" Note that the choice _not_ to do the homework is not offered.

    c) Encourage the client to observe and record as soon as possible after the act.

    d) Record actual thoughts (e.g., "I am a terrible parent", rather than, "I was thinking I was a terrible parent").

    e) Build in incremental tasks, starting with small steps and then building upon these. For example, in treating depression clients are often asked to fill in a double column technique[1] (see Beck et al., 1987). At first, use just two columns and subsequently add the additional two columns. (Use a "foot in the door" approach gradually increasing the request.)

9. Perform a comprehension check after each assignment has been given. Conduct an illustrative example of the homework in the session with the client (and significant other, if indicated). One way to assess the client's comprehension is to use role-reversal. Ask the client to imagine for the moment that the therapist is a new client and the client is the therapist, who is to explain the "homework" and why he/she should do it.

10. On some occasions the therapist can use an "imaginary other" client to convey points. "I can recall another client who ..." In this way the therapist can help clients anticipate possible problems/obstacles, so if they do occur they are issues that have been discussed previously in therapy. They become a "deja vu" experience with an accompanying consideration of how to handle them.

11. Ensure that the skills to do the "homework" are within the client's repertoire. Begin "homework" assignments with success, however small. Break the task into smaller-sized steps.

12. Anticipate and subsume the reasons for nonadherence (e.g., use imagery, role playing, imaginary other). Some therapists ask the client to call if he/she is having difficulties and/or to call in after completing an assignment.

13. Insure that the client has the beliefs and confidence in conducting the "homework". For instance, does the client believe that doing the task is worthwhile? Does the client believe that he/she has the ability to perform the task? Discuss with the client what he can do this coming

---

[1] The double column technique entails asking the client to record the distressing situation, feeling, automatic thought, and later incompatible thoughts and behaviors.

week (or between sessions). For instance, say, "We have discussed a number of issues, or explored your feelings about X (summarize what has been the focus of the sessions). I am wondering if we can now examine what you can do this week that can make things better for you, that can help you achieve your goal of X?"

14. Problem-solve with clients about possible difficulties in implementing the "assignment". Webster-Stratton and Herbert (1993) suggest that the therapist use the "art of questioning" as a way to help client's put into words the reasons, possible obstacles, and procedures by which the client can conduct the agreed upon assignment. The therapist can sample from the following questions:

"Have you dealt with (or overcome) this problem in the past?"

"What advice would you offer someone else who has this problem?"

"What might make it hard for you to do this assignment?"

"What kind of things could distract you from your goals to achieve X?"..."How will you deal with that?"

"What do you think you can do at home, perhaps as a form of practice, that would be most helpful? ... that would prove to you that X?"

"What can you do to make it easier for you to complete this assignment this week?"

"How will you remember that?"

"Do you think there is another assignment that might be more useful for you?"

"What thoughts come to mind when you think about this assignment?"

"Does this assignment to (be specific) seem relevant to your treatment goals? ... to your situation? ... to your life?"

"How could we make this assignment more helpful?"

"Do you think you will have any problems doing X? What problems do you anticipate?"

"Can you think of any way to accomplish this?"

"How on earth are you going to do that?"

"Is there any way you could be more creative about X in order to achieve your goal of Y?"

"What will you have to do to keep your plan working?"

"One thing that others do when they are confronted with this problem is that they X. Does that strategy sound like it might work for you?"

If therapy is conducted on a group or family basis ask, "Can anyone else (in the group) think of a way that might help X try this assignment?"

(In subsequent sessions explore) "What difficulties did you find in doing this assignment?"

"What seems to get in the way of your doing X (e.g., self-monitoring PTSD symptoms, noticing triggers, practicing coping techniques, listening to the audiotape)?"

15. Check on self-monitoring in subsequent session. Near the beginning of the session review the assignment from the previous week before moving onto new material. Most importantly, explore the client's reasons for noncompliance in a nonjudgmental tactful fashion. Perform a fine-grain analysis of the factors (both internal and external) that may have gotten in the way of performing the task. Ask near the beginning of the session:

"Were you able to attempt the activity of doing X?"

"What is that you have done this week that is different? What have you done that makes things better for yourself?"

"How do you feel about that?"

"What did you discover about yourself (about your situation, about others) as a result of undertaking this experiment (activity, self-monitoring)?"

"How far did you get?"

"If not, what happened to prevent you from trying it?" (Note, the client may not comply with the request for many different reasons including that he/she perceived it as being irrelevant, too time consuming, too threatening, badly administered, or because of possible secondary gains for maintaining present behavioral pattern (See Lazarus, 1994, Meichenbaum & Turk, 1986, Meichenbaum & Fong, 1994 for a discussion of possible reasons for noncompliance). The reasons for client nonadherence with the agreed-upon assignment should be explored with the client. Often noncompliance occasions can be highly instructive (see Number 18 below).

16. Set up the assignment so it is a "no-lose" situation.

   a)   Instruct the client not to change any specific behaviors at this point, just "keep track". (If the client is going to be noncompliant, let him/her be noncompliant with the suggestion not to change.)

   b)   If the client does not follow through completely, indicate that "nobody quite accomplishes all that he or she plans". Use the metaphor of learning a skill to explore what is needed (e.g., learning to drive a car, ski, choose a skill that is familiar to the client). Ask the client, what does it take to become more expert, or what did he/she do when teaching someone else?

   c)   Comment that the client should not expect immediate relief from undertaking the assignment.

   d)   Reinforce the client for having tried, not for the outcome.

   e)   Use the client's expression "It doesn't work" as an occasion to enhance adherence. When the client says, "It doesn't work", referring to the homework assignment, the therapist can reflect the phrase, "It doesn't work?"; initially highlighting the word "it". The purpose of this reflection is for the therapist and the client to ascertain what did the client "do" that "did not work". Be specific in examining exactly which aspects of the homework task the client did not undertake. In turn, the therapist can then reflect the phrase, "doesn't work?", in an inquisitive fashion. Thus, there is an attempt to ascertain with the client what is the operational criteria by which he/she judges that his/her behavior did <u>not</u> meet his/her prior expectations. "Doesn't work?" What exactly did the client expect?

The therapist can then ask the client, (1) "How would you know if "it" (homework) did work?", (2) "Are you (the client) suggesting that it would never work, that it is no use, that absolutely nothing can be done?"

By the therapist "blowing-up", or slightly exaggerating, the client's conclusion, the client is likely to say, "Well, it is not all that bad." At which point the therapist can say, "Not all that bad? Tell me about that." Once again, there is an attempt to involve the client in a collaborative problem-solving process.

In discussing the diary process with the client the therapist can also use the Carl Rogers' expression that even though there may be ups and downs in therapy, what the client is going through will prove to be, "Just irreversible!" The client will never be the same again. "Even if lapses and set-backs (symptoms) reoccur in the future, the client can never unlearn what he/she has learned in therapy. The processes of change are just irreversible!"

f)   **Use paradoxical procedures.**
After having reviewed all of the previous steps, if the client persists in not doing the homework, in the spirit of Milton Erickson, the therapist can compliment the client for his/her noncompliance. The therapist can comment, "What a relief!", and then highlight that the client's decision to choose not to do the homework, and moreover, to tell the therapist, "is one of the best (prognostic) signs that the client is well-suited for treatment". Commend the client for being so discerning on deciding what works best for him/herself. Convey that the client just doesn't go along with whatever is asked of him/her. It is such independence of judgment that is a promising sign. Explore with the client what would "make sense" at this point in helping him/her achieve the treatment goals. In short, the therapist can set things up so that anything that the client does indicates that he/she is "buying into" treatment.

Arnold Lazarus (1994)[1] has suggested another form of paradoxical approach. In response to his client's non-compliance, Lazarus tells his client:

> "I owe you an apology. I am sorry for having made such a mistake. I overestimated the things you can do. It is entirely my fault to ask you to do something that you are not ready to do. You must forgive me."

Lazarus notes that clients often respond by indicating that they do have the ability and they will demonstrate so in the coming week.

g)   The sense of collaboration can also be conveyed by **establishing a joint assignment for both the client and the therapist.** Lazarus (1994) offers the example of exploring with the client how he/she can bring his/her family into therapy. As a result of a discussion, the therapist indicates that **both** the client and the therapist will spend time this coming week thinking through and writing out how this treatment goal could be achieved. Thus, the therapist brings into the subsequent session "homework", as well.

---

[1] Lazarus presentation at the Evolution of Psychotherapy Conference in Hamburg, Germany.

17. Yost et al. (1986) suggest a number of probes that can be used to foster a collaborative caring approach to performing assignments.

   a)   "What thoughts come to mind when you think about doing this assignment?

   b)   Does this seem relevant to your life? To your treatment goals?

   c)   How would doing this be helpful to you?

   d)   Would it be more helpful for us to spend time on X or on Y?

   e)   In what ways, if any, did this homework help you to feel less distressed this week?

   f)   How can you see these concepts (activities) being of help to you?

   g)   Is what is happening here being helpful to you?

   h)   How could we make this more helpful?"

18. At the beginning of each session (after initial opening) **carefully review** the homework. If homework was <u>not</u> completed, reinforce some aspect of the client's efforts, but then examine in a sympathetic, but firm fashion, the reasons for noncompliance (e.g., pessimistic attitude, feelings of helplessness) and then use problem-solving techniques to examine and remove barriers. In discussing the client's difficulties in complying with the assignment:

   a)   identify with the client's frustration. "I can hear that it is frustrating when you try to do X and Y occurs."

   b)   find some element of the client's effort to reinforce. "Now at least you are more aware of what you are/are not doing." "Now you can recognize something after you have done it. That is a good starting place." "You seem to be able to better analyze the situation and think about what you want to have happen." "You seem to be able to catch yourself in the middle and sometimes even before you start."

   c)   help the client become less self-critical and more tolerant of imperfections. Normalize possible failures. "Indeed things don't sound as "happy", as "well-controlled", as "much like you want them to be". Most people seem to set too high standards for themselves. Is that a problem for you? ... Remember, no one is perfect."

   Also, use homework as an occasion to have the client engage in metacognitive reflective behaviors of how he or she "noticed", "stopped yourself", "interrupted", "implemented a game plan", "thought about your goals", and the like. As the sessions unfold, ask the client **how he or she handled the situation this time as compared to how he or she handled it in the past. "What's different?"** Ask **process questions** as to how the client "pulled it off". **(Note the use of "What" and "How" questions.)**

   "What did you do to bring about this change?"

   "How did you do that?"

   "How did you come to the decision to do that?"

   "How did you get yourself mobilized to ... ?"

"What do you find helps you keep control of your (anger, depression, intrusive thoughts)?"

"How did you handle the situation differently from how you have handled this situation in the past?"

"Where else were you able to do this (be specific)?"

"How did this make you feel?"

"Do you think anyone else who is important to you noticed this change?"

"How would they notice?"

"How would you replay the situation another time if it happens?"

"How would you like to respond in the future if this occurs again?"

"What are the lessons you learned from this episode?"

"What does this mean for how you see yourself as a person?"

"What have you learned from doing this assignment?"

"What have you discovered about yourself from doing X?"

"Tell me more about that. How did you feel about that?"

Remember it is not enough for people to change, they have to take ownership for their changes. Make sure clients take credit for their efforts and the changes they have brought about. The therapist can reflect, "Hold on, are you telling me, are you saying to yourself, that you were able to do X, and this differed from how you behaved in the past (be specific)? Now you were able to "notice", "catch", "interrupt" (use metacognitive verbs with specific examples). And you didn't just do it in situation A, but also in situations B and C, and as a result you felt (reflect feelings). Then what does this mean about you as a person?"

This self-attributional process should not be left to chance. The therapist should build self-attributions into treatment and help the client **explore opportunities for generalization** and **transfer.** For example, consider the potential value of asking the following questions.

"For what other problems could you apply this strategy ... these coping techniques?"

"Are there any situations where this wouldn't work?"

"Do you ever find yourself asking yourself questions that we ask each other here in therapy? When do you do that? What impact does it have on how you feel and behave?"

"How are you going to keep doing these things when our therapy sessions are finished?"

"Can you anticipate any barriers or obstacles that might get in the way of your continuing to do X? How will you notice these? What can you do to anticipate and handle them?"

"I have another client who has a problem that is like yours. Would you mind if I shared with her your plan and described how you did this? I would share this anonymously, not mentioning your name". "Do I have your permission to share how you handled this with others who have similar problems?"

TESTING YOUR EXPERTISE

Section III - Assessment Strategies and Procedures

1.   You have been approached to evaluate a client for PTSD for workers' compensation or litigation purposes. A thorough assessment is requested. Indicate the assessment strategy and specific measures you would use, and why? (Remember you may have to justify your decision in court.)

2.   A client enters treatment with you reporting a history of victimization. Time is limited. What assessment strategy and specific measures would you use and why?

3.   What psychometric tests (if any), what standardized interviews (if any), have you used over the last 6 months with your PTSD clients? What assessment measures do you intend to add to your clinical practice? Why did you choose these measures?

4.   How does your clinic (hospital, colleagues) use psychometric measures to assess PTSD? What suggestions do you have to offer them? What arguments are you likely to encounter in response to your suggestions for systematic assessments? How will you handle these objections to the role of assessment?

5.   How thoroughly do you and your colleagues assess for your clients' "victimization" experiences? Indicate what specific information you would cover with a client who was:

        a) raped
        b) a victim of child sexual abuse
        c) domestic violence
        d) crime victim
        e) natural disaster victim

    Why did you include these items?

6.   How expert are you in asking Socratic questions? Tape record treatment sessions (initial and middle sessions) and write down the specific questions you used. Compare your list of questions to those included in this Section. How many "what" and "how" questions did you use? Which questions from this Assessment Section do you think you should add, or try, in your therapy session? ... How did these questions work?

7.   Listen to a tape recorded session and note the number of times you act like a **"surrogate frontal lobe"** for your clients. In what ways are you doing the thinking for your clients? How could you use the "art of questioning" to help clients come up with the suggestion themselves? How do you, over the course of treatment, change the way you relinquish control and "ownership" to the client and nurture collaboration?

8.   Give an example of how you were able to have clients come up with the therapeutic suggestion you would otherwise have offered. Be specific in indicating the strategy and sequence of questions you used.

9.   Describe how you can use a "significant other" who is not physically present in therapy as a means to help the client generate coping strategies. Team up with a fellow student and role play the exercise of using an imaginary significant other. Invite a third student to watch this interaction and provide a constructive critique afterwards. Now switch roles so you have three attempts in using this procedure. Now try it with a client.

10.   Role play with two other students (one playing the role of a client, the other a commentator/critic, as you play the role of the therpaist), the scenario of moving the client from a hopeless state where he/she describes his/her problem in vague metaphorical terms into behaviorally proscriptive solution-focused terms. Listen to the audiotape/videotape of the role play and analyze how successful you were in helping the client to:

a) identify, define and analyze the situation in problem-solving terms
b) conduct a situational and a developmental analysis
c) generate and implement solutions

11.   Use the imagery reconstructive procedure in your role play scenario or with a client in order to facilitate the problem-solving process. How were you able to help your client to develop a "transactional" view of his/her behavior? Does the client now recognize how he/she inadvertently, can create reactions in others that confirm his/her views of self and the world? Does the client recognize the role of appraisal processes?

12.   What is "motivational interviewing" and how can you incorporate this into your clinical interviews? What questions and comments can you include in your sessions to enhance your therapeutic alliance? How can you use client in-therapy behaviors to facilitate the therapeutic alliance and to foster change? *(See Section VI for more detailed examples of motivational interviewing.)*

13.   How expert are you when it comes to specific assessment objective? What are the specific steps and questions you can use to:

a) screen for victimization
b) assess for suicide potential (what are the high risk factors)
c) assess for addictive behaviors
d) conduct a differential diagnoses
e) assess for comorbidity -- depression, dissociation, anxiety, somatization, etc.
f) conduct family assessments

How many of the tests listed in this section do you have in your possession that you could use? List which interviews and tests, if any, you use as part of your clinical practice.

14.   How would you handle a suicidal patient? Spell out the specific "game plan" you would use. Role play a scene where one person is suicidal and you, as a therapist, have to assess suicidal potential and treat the suicidal client. Invite a third student to take notes on the role play and offer a constructive critique. Now switch roles and do this two more times so everyone has a chance to play each role.

15.   a) Use the same role play procedures to practice how to give clients "homework".
b) Tape record a session in which you ask a client to self-monitor his/her behavior. Now compare the steps you incorporated into your request against the checklist of items included in this section. How many of the suggested procedural steps did you include? Now try to give "homework" to another client. Have you changed your approach in any way? How? What difference, if any, did it make?

16.   The next time a client indicates to you in therapy that he/she noticed some personal change, note how you respond. What is the subroutine of questions and statements you can use in order to insure that the client "takes credit" for the reported changes. Compare how you responded to the suggestions included in the Section on "self-monitoring". You can practice these techniques in a role playing scenario with two fellow students.

SECTION IV
CAUTIONS IN THE ASSESSMENT OF CLIENTS
WHO REPORT "VICTIMIZATION" EXPERIENCES[1]
Examining The Nature of "Traumatic Memories" And The Need to Help The Helpers
(See additional reference list in Section VIII.)

In the last section we examined the extensive interviews and varied assessment measures that could be used with clients suffering with PTSD and associated clinical problems. In this Section we will consider some of the "dangers" and cautionary actions that should be observed in the assessment of clients who report being "victimized". **The danger resides in the potential iatrogenic (therapist-initiated) influences on the assessment and therapeutic processes.** Therapists may inadvertently, unwittingly and, perhaps, even unknowingly, contribute to, or even explicitly help to "co-create" with clients "false memories", maladaptive behaviors, and even psychiatric conditions. The concern about iatrogenically-generated memories received heightened visibility when Steven Cook (age 34) of Philadelphia filed a $10 million law suit in Ohio accusing Cardinal Joseph Bernadine, Archbishop of Chicago and another priest of sexually abusing him between 1975 and 1977 when he was a teenage seminary student in Cincinnati. Mr. Cook said he first recalled memories of sexual abuse while in therapy when hypnosis was used. This case obviously created a sensation concerning the validity of client's memory recall. Mr. Cook eventually dropped his charges against the Cardinal and the priest, saying his memory of abuse was "unreliable". In response, the Illinois legislation is debating whether an age limitation should be implemented so that people over 30 would <u>not</u> be allowed to accuse victims of abuse that occurred when they were children. This legal question is clearly tied to the issues of "repressed memories" and the so-called "false memory syndrome" to which we now turn our attention. (Based on the literature, what advice would you offer to the Illinois legislature?) Equally publicized was the recent accusations of child sexual abuse by the television comedienne Roseanne Arnold, as documented on a television documentary, 60 Minutes (April 17, 1994). This issue has captured both the media's attention, as well as that of professionals.

The relevance for clinicians is highlighted by the recent court case in Napa, California, where Gary Ramona was successful in bringing a law suit against his daughter's psychiatrist, family counselor and the Medical Centre in which she was treated. She had reported flashbacks of childhood sexual abuse while being treated for bulimia and depression. Ramona claimed his daughter's allegation cost him his family, job, and reputation. Ramona was awarded $500,000.[2]

Few issues have so inflamed the public and mental health communities as the controversy over allegations of childhood sexual abuse (CSA). Some have proposed that "overzealous therapists" may sometimes unintentionally insinuate in the minds of their clients' memories of abuse that never happened (see articles by Calop, Wyke and Yapko, 1993). Since the report of past memories (often from the distant past) play such a critical role in the diagnosis and treatment of PTSD, the client's autobiographical accounts take on special significance. Moreover, the accompanying legal implications of such accounts further highlight concerns about the "authenticity", "validity", and "accuracy" of the client's reports of victimization. But, as Ross

---

[1] I am particularly grateful to my colleagues Ken Bowers and Michael Ross for their helpful input and stimulating discussions about these issues.

[2] For details of the Ramona case see Ewing's (1994) description in the <u>APA Monitor</u>, (July issue, p. 22) or *Ramona Isabella*, California Superior Court, Napa, CA, C61898. This case is important because it highlights that if psychotherapeutic treatment harms a close relative of a client (e.g., due to false accusations), then the psychotherapist may be held legally liable for financial damages.

(1993) has observed, "Assessing the validity of memories is devishly tricky" (p. 18), and I might add, "fraught with dangers".[1]

In this section we will consider these and related issues. More specifically, we will examine:

(1)   how often do clients fail to report memories of early childhood sexual abuse (CSA) when there is independent corroborating evidence that it has occurred, evidencing what has been characterized as "memory deficits", "restricted reports", and "repressed memories";

(2)   how do clinicians go about making judgments about the "authenticity" of their client's memories;

(3)   how clinicians may contribute iatrogenically to their client's difficulties;

(4)   how clinicians can proceed in conducting therapy without knowing if the reported memories are "valid" or not.

These issues are not idle academic concerns but, rather, reflect a dilemma that therapists who work with PTSD clients may confront on an ongoing basis. The issue of "recovered memories" was highlighted in a recent meeting of the False Memory Syndrome Foundation (see FMS, 1993) that was held in Valley Forge, Pennsylvania, on April 16-18, 1993. At this meeting some 600 people attended, including 34 members of the press and 5 individuals, who, like Steven Cook, had retracted their accusations. The FMS society now has 7,500 members and a distinguished scientific board. But in a fascinating article in the January 1994 issue of Philadelphia Magazine[2], Stephen Fried has traced the history of the FMS Foundation, noting that it is **not an impartial scientific body**. He provides a detailed expose of the family who began the FMS Foundation and the various "players" in the scientific community who have become embroiled in the controversy over "repressed memories". Fried estimates that 6% of parents in the FMS Foundation are being sued by their children accusing them of child sexual abuse; 18% of the parents have been threatened by such suits; and 33% are concerned about legal issues[3]. Even though most accusations have not led to actual legal suits, the threat of such claims have had a negative impact on clients, their parents, and their therapists. (Interestingly, a comparable meeting of some 280 families was held in the Toronto area.) At these meetings there were a number of scholarly presentations on the challenge of ascertaining the reliability and verifiability of client's memories of abuse, but there were also discussions of how the accused parents could **sue their daughter's or son's therapist**. In fact, one prominent presenter admonished attending lawyers, "treat therapists as the real perpetrators at sexual abuse trials", and he encouraged them to "cross examine therapists vigorously as any key witness in a murder case". The pursuit of legal action against therapists is, indeed, being followed, as illustrated in recent estimates that the number of false accusation cases in North America has risen **substantially** in the last few years. In most instances, the treated clients were female (some 90%), between the ages of 30 and 40, and the alleged perpetrator was usually the daughter's father or stepfather. The families were usually in the middle to upper-middle class. The alleged abuse occurred some 15 to 30 years ago.

---

[1] The American Psychiatric Association has released the Fact Sheet on Memories of Sexual Abuse (FSS 007 $1 each) which seeks to clarify the issues surrounding memories of sexual abuse and provide guidelines for therapists. For copies contact APA Division of Public Affairs, 1400 K St. N.W., Washington, DC. 20005 (202) 682-6220.

[2] The Philadelphia Magazine article by Stephen Fried entitled "War of remembrance: The most dysfunctional family in America" can be obtained by calling 212-564-7700 for $2.95.

[3] Lindsay and Read (1994) report that the FMS foundation has received some 13,000 contacts from parents who claim that they have been falsely accused; only approximately 7% led to litigation.

As we will consider, it is very stressful for therapists to work with traumatized clients, leading to what McCann and Pearlman (1990) characterize as "vicarious victimization", or what Figley (1993) has described as "compassion fatigue", or Maslach (1990) has called "burnout". Now, the possibility of inadvertently contributing to iatrogenically-generated memories and the threat of being sued by your client or your clients' parents compounds the therapist's stress levels. For a discussion of these legal issues see Sales et al. (1994), Slovenko (1993) and Wakefield and Underwager (1992).

Before I consider these thorny issues, it may be instructive to share my personal clinical involvement with the "recovered memory" controversy. Four specific consulting and research activities have thrust this issue upon me.

1.   I supervise a number of clinicians (psychiatrists, psychologists, social workers) who have asked me to listen to their taped therapy sessions. Many of their clients report "victimization" experiences due to child sexual abuse (CSA) or due to Satanic ritual abuse (SRA). These clinical accounts are not unique to the clinicians I supervise as evident in reports by Ganaway (1989), Greaves (1992), McHugh (1992), van Benschoten (1990) and Young (1991). In fact, an entire special issue of the journal Psychology and Theology (Rogers, 1992) was devoted to SRA. Also see the accounts by Ofshe (1992) and Wright (1993).

        As a group of clinicians, we have struggled with how best to view our client's reports and react to their accounts. We do not wish to "revictimize" clients by doubting their stories. The issue of recovered memory has been further complicated by the fact that some clinicians were called upon to testify in court as to the "authenticity" of their clients' autobiographical accounts, without having any independent corroborating evidence.

2.   While recognizing the widespread incidence[1] of childhood sexual abuse, I wondered how do clinicians make such weighty decisions about the "authenticity" of their clients' reports of victimization. In an attempt to identify the nature of the clinician's decision tree, I conducted a "quasi experiment" at several of my recent workshops on PTSD. I presented the clinicians (N=700) with a videotape of myself interviewing a 31-year-old male client who reports having been sexually abused as a child. The audience of clinicians was asked to indicate if they believed the client's report of victimization and to indicate with what degree of confidence. Moreover, they were asked to enumerate the factors they used in formulating their decision. An examination of these results described in this Section will prove instructive.

3.   A third reason I have spent time pondering these issues is that some of my recent clients have requested at the outset of therapy that I help them determine if they had been abused as children. They asked me to help them do "memory work". We will consider how the clinician may respond to such client requests.

4.   Finally, I have consulted at several residential settings where children and adolescents have been interviewed repeatedly by Child Protection Service and clinical personnel about alleged sexual abuse. How should such interviews be conducted? Space will not permit me to examine this latter question with children. The interested reader should see Brewin et al. (1993), Bruhn (1990), Ceci and Bruck (1993a,b), Gardner (1992), and Jones (1992).

---

[1] Prevalence rates range from 27%-51% for narrowly defined childhood sexual abuse to 31%-67% when noncontact experiences are included (Loftus et al., 1994). For example, in 1985 there were 1.7 million cases of CSA reported. (See Section I on the epidemiology of CSA.)

With this as prologue, we are now ready to consider generally the nature of the problem of iatrogenically-generated memories, and more specifically examine:

1.   What problems arise concerning memories of traumatic events: Issues of "repressed memory"[1]

2.   How do clinicians make decisions about the "authenticity" of their clients' autobiographical accounts?

3.   How can clinicians best handle their clients' requests for undertaking "memory work"?

4.   How can one help the helpers who work with clients who have been "traumatized"?

Finally, I should note that as this volume was going to press, two publications appeared. I will review these in the next annual PTSD **Handbook/Manual** update. The two references include:

(1)   Norbert Schwarz and Seymour Sudman (Eds.), (1994). <u>Autobiographical memory and the validity of retrospective reports.</u> New York: Springer-Verlag.

(2)   Hypnosis and delayed recall: Part I. <u>International Journal of Clinical and Experimental Hypnosis</u>, October, 1994, Vol. 42. Part II will appear in the April issue.

In addition, the August, 1994 issue (Vol. 8, No. 4) of <u>Applied Cognitive Psychology</u>, edited by Michael Pressley and Lisa Grossman on "Recovery memories of childhood sexual abuse", includes a scholarly article by Lindsay and Read and six commentaries. This journal issue is worthy of a careful read!

---

[1] We all know that forgetting occurs. The question is whether it occurs at a different rate for traumatic events such as childhood sexual abuse and whether such forgetting is "intentional" and "motivated". In contrast to forgetting is the interesting phenomenon called **"flashbulb memory"** where one cannot get a memory (e.g., of the Kennedy assassination) out of one's mind. These "flashbulb memories" raise questions about the nature of the memory for traumatic events. This phenomenon was first labeled by Brown and Kulik (1977) (see Cognition, <u>5</u>, 73-99) and more recently examined in an edited volume by Winograd and Neisser (1992) <u>Affect and accuracy in recall</u> (Cambridge University Press). Also, see Zilberg's book review in <u>Imagination, cognition and personality, 13</u>, 367-370 and Black's (1994) APA presentation on "distorted" memories. Black notes that studies of children's memories for events (e.g., Chowchilla kidnapping) reflect accurate recall for the "gist" of the events, but distortions in terms of details such as the sequence of events, misrepresentation of details, or the inclusion of details that had been suggested in the post event inquiry. Moreover, there is likely to be less **distortion** and misrepresentation for **single, dramatic, traumatic events** than for more prolonged traumas such as in the case of child sexual abuse. The APA presentation by Black (1994) on "True memory of childhood trauma" can be ordered from Sound Images 303-693-5571, Tape 94-222).

The Nature of the Problem of Memories of Traumatic Events

Ever since Bartlett's (1932) classic studies on remembering, researchers have convincingly demonstrated that **recall can be an act of creative construction.** Bartlett's initial research, and those who have followed, as summarized by Brewin, Andrews and Gottlib (1993), Loftus (1993) and Ross (1993), indicate that the accounts and details of recalled events may be supplemented, changed, and omitted as the rememberer constructs his/her memories, "or stories", in terms of his/her current interpretation of past events. The research indicates that memory involves reconstructive elements and is strongly influenced by current beliefs and moods. As Spanos (1994) observes, people typically organize their recall of past events in a way that makes sense of their present situation and is congruent with their current expectations.

Johnson and her colleagues (1993) have developed a theory called "source monitoring" to describe the processes by which individuals make judgments about the origins and nature of their memories and beliefs. Rememberers not only have memories, but they also have implicit theories or offer inferential explanations about their memories. Source monitoring theory provides a useful framework to understand how clients may incorporate "suggestions" and "fictions", and offer them as "facts". In recall, imagined events are sometimes difficult to disentangle from real events, as individuals make such judgments based on contextual information (time, place), sensory information, and semantic detail. The discussion that follows on the possibility of iatrogenically-generated memories in our clients should be viewed within this historical perspective and within the framework of source monitoring theory. But what does Bartlett's research on relatively benign memory material have to do with the emotionally-laden memories that client's report of traumatic "victimization" experience?

In a thoughtful article entitled, "The reality of the repressed"[1] , Loftus (1993) raises the challenging question of whether individuals can have "bad things" happen to them for a prolonged period of time, as in the case of child sexual abuse, and fail to remember it for several years, only to retrieve the memory of the victimizing events years later, often with, but sometimes without, the help of a psychotherapist. She is especially concerned about the class of memories that emerge in adulthood after so-called "memory work". The "memory work" may involve the therapist having the client use cue-recalled memory retrieval procedures such as looking at family picutre albums, watching scary horror films, free associative and meditative procedures, engage in age regression, body work interpretation, guided imagery, dream interpretation, hypnotic procedures[2] , sodium amytal interviews, bibliotherapy, journalling, and group procedures with other incest survivors. Direct client exposure to any of these procedures may color the way client's retrieve memories and the nature of the client's narrative reconstruction and may contribute to "illusory memories" (Lindsay and Read, 1994). After reviewing the literature Loftus (1993) concluded (also citing Kihlstrom, 1993) that **"the evidence for the delayed recovery of valid repressed memories is rather thin"**.

On the other hand, clinical researchers who have examined the question of dissociation and repression in response to CSA have argued that various "coping efforts" or "defense mechanisms" can lead to "repressed memories". They highlight that "victims" of CSA have often had their accounts and credibility challenged, and may even themselves try to conceal or forget ("disavow and disown") the fact that the abuse may have occurred. Such patterns of coping could perhaps lead to "repressed memories" (Berliner and Williams, 1994, Herman and Schatzow, 1987). In contrast, researchers who operate within a general laboratory framework using very different experimental paradigms, with entirely different classes of memories, have

---

[1] See the replies to Loftus' article in the <u>American Psychologist</u>, May 1994, <u>49</u>, pp. 439-445.

[2] See Peter Bloom (1994) article on "Clinical guidelines in using hypnosis in uncovering memories of sexual abuse". <u>Intl. J. Clinical Exp. Hypnosis</u>, <u>42</u>, 173-178.

challenged the concept of repression (e.g., see Holmes, 1990, and Loftus, 1993). They suggest that what clinicians point to as "repression" may be reluctance to report memories given the "demand characteristics" or context of the situation. They also go on to imply that in some (not all) instances, the recall of memories of victimization, such as child sexual abuse, reflect the "unintended influence of inquiring therapists".

Where does the "truth" lie between these two camps? Could both be correct in some instances? Moreover, if we (as therapist) cannot decide on the "authenticity" or "validity" of our client's memories or "stories" without independent corroborating evidence, then how should clients and therapists proceed in this limbo state of uncertainty?

Before we consider the practical implications of this debate, let us consider briefly the data that clinicians offer to support their arguments for "repressed" memories.

Among others, three clinical studies have been offered as evidence for memory impairment or "repressed memories". First, Herman and Schatzow (1987) reported that among 53 treatment-seeking incest clients,[1] **26% reported severe memory impairment,** or being amnesic for victimization experiences, or manifested absence of recall of sexual abuse. Severe memory problems were most likely to be reported in cases of abuse that began early in childhood and ended before adolescence.

Similarly, Briere and Conte (1993) reported that **59%** of adult clinical clients who had reported sexual abuse histories **had forgotten,** or failed to report, the sexual abuse that they had suffered in childhood prior to age 18.[2] In both of these studies, those clients who initially had no recall experience of victimization were more likely to be from the group of patients who were at the youngest ages at the time of the abuse and who received the most violent forms of abuse.

Those who question the "repression" model challenge these studies in terms of their dependence on retrospective reporting and the limited documentation of independent corroborative data of abuse. Further, the clients were in therapy and the therapists could have influenced the reports.

There is a need for clearly documented cases of child sexual abuse and then systematic assessment of subsequent lapses in recall of these victimization events. A set of important studies by Linda Meyer Williams has shed new light on these issues. Williams and her colleagues (Williams, 1992, Spiegel et al., 1993)[3] report the first study of documented child sexual abuse cases. She tracked down a group of 129 (out of a possible sample of 206) women who had been sexually abused as children from infancy (10 months) to age 12. These cases had been independently documented at the emergency department of a major urban hospital where the children had been taken for treatment between the years of 1973 and 1975. In 1990 to 1991, some 17 years later, she interviewed these women, who now ranged in age from 18 to 31. The sexual abuse they had experienced as children ranged from sexual intercourse (36% of the cases) to touching and fondling (about $1/3$ of the cases). Some form of physical force was used in 62% of the cases. All the perpetrators had been men, 34% of whom were immediate relatives of the victim. The majority of the female victims (86%) interviewed were African Americans. In a

---

[1] 70% of 48 women were able to obtain corroborating evidence for their abuse; 30% did not find such corroborating information; 5 women chose not to search for such information.

[2] Subjects were asked, "During the period of time between when the first forced sexual experience happened and your 18th birthday **was there ever a time when you could not remember** the forced sexual experience?" The main result obtained in this largely female (93'%), largely Caucasian (90%) sample, was that 59% of 450 said "yes" (see Loftus et al., 1994; Lindsay and Read, 1994 for critiques).

[3] Williams study is now in press, Journal of Consulting and Clinical Psychology.

comprehensive two to three hour interview that was conducted under the guise of looking at the lives and health of women who had received medical care at the City Hospital, subjects were asked questions about life experiences and current life satisfaction.

The results indicated that **38% of the women were amnesic for the abuse or chose not to report the sexual abuse that they had experienced in childhood.** When the sample was restricted to women who had been at least 7 years of age when the known abuse occurred, 28% failed to report the incident during the interview. Out of the total sample, **12% denied ever having been sexually abused during childhood, while 62% of the wormen did report the abusive incident in the interview, and 88% reported some sort of childhood sexual abuse".** In support of her contention that many abuse survivors report periods of not remembering, 47% of the William's sample who now recall their abuse, reported there was a time in the past when they did not recall it.

As evidence for the "amnesic" or "memory impairment" hypothesis, Williams also reports that 53% of the women who had been "amnesic" for sexual abuse, reported other childhood sexual victimization experiences. Thus, the women were not reluctant to report or self-disclose childhood victimization experiences in general, but rather, they failed to offer reports (even when probed explicitly) about the prior documented instances of child sexual abuse.[1]   While the Williams studies are as yet unpublished and more detail (including possible control groups) would be helpful, the initial findings are quite provocative, but should be interpreted with caution in light of findings by Femina et al. (1990). Femina et al. (1990) studied people who were abused as children and who had denied the abuse when interviewed years later. They found that when these adults were interviewed a second time they invariably acknowledged remembering the abuse and described their earlier denial as due to factors such as embarrassment about what had occurred rather than as being due to memory loss. (See Spanos, 1994 for a more complete discussion of these issues.)

The studies by Herman and Schatzow, Briere and Conte, and Williams and her colleagues, each raise the theoretical possibility that some form of amnesia may occur. While each study has its methodological flaws, they should give pause to those who would readily dismiss the model of amnesia of traumatic memories. As Lindsay and Read (1994, p. 314) observe, the findings of the Williams and related studies indicate that **"total forgetting of a history of childhood sexual abuse is possible, but is far from normative".**

Additional reflection comes from the speculations of Terr (1994) who compared the memory recall capacity of individuals who have been exposed to what she has called Type I stressors (sudden, unexpected "blows") and Type II stressors ("prolonged anticipated, repeated traumatic events like child sexual abuse"). Type I stressors engender memories that are clear, full, detailed experiences and which individuals ruminate about. They are often "pictures" that people who have been traumatized cannot get out of their minds. In contrast, those victims who have been exposed to long-standing repeated traumatic events, as in the case of sexual abuse, are likely to use "defenses" or "coping efforts" such as dissociation, denial, avoidance, self-hypnosis, emotional distancing and attempts to remove themselves in any way possible from the trauma

---

[1] Loftus et al. (1994) note that for some victims in the Williams study the abuse would have happened so early in life that one would not expect them to remember the experience. **Before age 5 one can expect a major fall-off in normal retention** (Brewin et al., 1993).   Studies of recall of early memories have usually indicated that people are unable to recall events that occurred before 3 years of age (Spanos, 1994).   As a sign of the fallibility of memory, Loftus et al. (1994) report that research indicates that 25% of subjects fail to recall having been in a hospital the previous year and 14% fail to remember they were in a car accident the previous year.

experience. "Through the practice of dissociation, voluntary thought suppression[2], minimization and sometimes outright denial, they learn to alter an unbearable reality." (Herman, 1992, p. 381). The accompanying rage and anger that may be turned against oneself, the accompanying anxiety and depression, and the inability to share their "story" with others over many years could lead to self-imposed forgetting, discounting and distortion. Moreover, Courtois (1992) has reported that one-half of incest victims indicate that when they attempted to report incest to significant others as a child it was denied, or rejected, and the veracity of their reports were challenged. When we consider the debate about the possibility of amnestic memories, there is a need to keep in mind this social and developmental context, where not telling, not remembering, disavowing, disowning, dissociating, may represent "survival" skills. Under these conditions could amnesia, intentional forgetting and "repression" occur?

Some possible answers come from the recent study by Loftus et al. (1994). They studied 105 women who were in outpatient treatment for substance abuse. "54% of the 105 women reported a history of childhood sexual abuse. Of these, the majority (81%) remembered all or part of the abuse their whole lives; **19% reported they forgot** the abuse for a period of time, and later the memory returned. Women who remembered the abuse their whole lives reported a clearer memory, with a more detailed picture. They also reported greater intensity of feelings at the time the abuse happened." (p. 67). It is interesting to consider the variety of questions that Loftus et al. recommend for assessing such accounts. The questions include:

"People differ in terms of how they remember their abuse. Which of the following experiences best characterizes your memory?

1.   Some people have always remembered their abuse throughout their lives, even if they never talked about it.

2.   Some people have remembered parts of the abuse their whole lives, while not remembering all of it.

3.   Some people forget the abuse for a period of time, and only later have the memory return.

They also suggest adding additional items.

4.   There was a time when I would not have been able to remember the abuse, even if I had been directly asked about it.

5.   There was a time when I would not have been able to report the abuse because I had no idea that it had even happened to me."

They then ask clients, "When you think about your memory for your abuse, how would you describe the memories?" The answer to such questions are scored for clarity, detail, coherence (makes sense), confusion, feelings at the time and feelings today. As Loftus et al. (1994) observe, no matter how sensitive the questions, no matter how reliable the

---

[2] An interesting finding about the potential adaptiveness of "forgetfulness" was reported by McFarlane (1994). He reports on a 1-year follow-up study that compared firefighters who, as a result of their stressful jobs, developed PTSD versus those who did not develop PTSD. Those without PTSD failed to report that they had been injured in over 50% of the cases. In contrast, the PTSD group were able to recall in more accurate detail the nature of their prior injury. In short, the firefighters who were coping more effectively had a "muted account of the trauma", whereas those firefighters who manifested difficulties were more readily "stuck" on the details of the trauma experience. In terms of when individuals can first recall memories, Black (1994) notes the **lack of recall of events by children before 24 to 36 months.** She ties this to the development of the hippocampal tract.

rating system, **the difficulty lies in asking individuals about a memory for forgetting a memory.** As Spaccarrelli (1994) observes, "the difficulty lies in the need to not only verify that sexual abuse has occurred, but also to verify that the victim actually has no memory of it until the apparent moment of recovery" (p. 355).

Gold et al. (1994) have proposed that clients be assessed for **various degrees of repression** of sexual abuse memories. They use the following question when probing their client's memories.

"Was there ever a period of time when for at least **one full year** you were **unable** to remember any or all of the abuse?"

In a study of 105 female clients they report:

a)   9% report a vague sense or suspicion, but no definite memory;

b)   14% had partial memory (flashbacks, remember some aspects);

c)   16% remember at least one episode of abuse in its entirety, but not all of them;

d)   30% always retained a fairly complete memory of all or most episodes of abuse;

e)   29% completely blocked out any recollection of the abuse.

They go on to indicate that the major focus of their treatment is on **enhancing present functioning rather than on uncovering of abuse memories.** They avoid the use of hypnosis as a means of establishing the existence of repressed memories of sexual abuse. Rather, they allow clients to approach memories of sexual abuse at their own pace in as uncontaminated a fashion as possible.

The concerns about iatrogenic (therapist-generated) influences are shared by Frankel (1993) who has recently critically examined the literature on the adult reports of childhood abuse. He searched the literature on personality disorders (e.g., borderline personality, multiple personality) to ascertain the extent of evidence for independent corroboration. He concluded that there is **limited evidence of such corroboration** in the literature of adult reports of childhood abuse. He is not doubting that childhood sexual abuse occurs, nor does he wish to "revictimize" clients by doubting their reports, but rather he is waving a warning sign for clinicians to be cautious in how they query and interpret their client's reports of abuse. Frankel notes that memories brought forth by the variety of inquiry methods or recall procedures such as hypnosis, dream analysis, visualization or guided imagery work, age regression, meditation, and the like, **are undependable** and subject to distortion, alteration, elaboration and fabrication. Along the same lines, see Pettinati (1988) for a discussion of why hypnotically-based memories are not permitted in a court of law. **Hypnosis does not improve the accuracy of reports per se, but rather increases one's confidence in the reports that are offered.** Calof (1993) reports that when he uses hypnosis with his client's he tells them at the outset that they will lose their rights to use the therapeutic information against a perpetrator in a court of law because hypnosis was employed in its retrieval.

The concerns about potentially iatrogenic influences are further heightened when we examine the way the popular media (television talk shows, movies, books[1] , and the like) have

---

[1] Other popular books include Davis (1990) Courage to heal workbook, Fredrickson (1992) Repressed memories, Blume (1990) Secret survivors. These books usually convey that 1/3 of women are survivors of abuse; 1/2 the

discussed the sexual abuse phenomenon. Consider what the very popular book, Courage to heal by Bass and Davis (1988), has to say about helping individuals discover memories of abuse. As you read this quote, keep in mind that this book has sold some 700,000 copies and for some in the field it has become "the Bible" of the recovery movement. Bass and Davis advise readers:

> "If you are unable to remember any specific memories ... but still have a feeling that something abusive happened to you, it probably did ... If you think you were abused and your life shows the symptoms then you were."

But concerns about possible iatrogenic influences do not derive only from popular books. Even in texts by well-regarded clinicians one can find directives that warrant caution. Consider the following quotes from Kirschner, Kirschner and Rapaport (1993):

> "If the therapist believes that incest material is present, it is critical that he or she strategically move to help the client bring the material to the surface." (p. 94)

> "The essential message we convey to our clients is: The truth can, will, and must come to the surface and we will both show courage in facing it. And, in this way, healing will take place." (p. 27)

In order to "unearth memories", Kirschner et al., 1993, propose a number of creative assessment measures that include asking the client to draw a picture of her home or apartment indicating the layout of the rooms, activities in each, and so on. Guided imagery is used to help the client revisit the various rooms at various age periods to help recreate memories of what happened. Other assessment procedures include the use of family pictures with possible perpetrators, role playing at the age of possible abuse, and keeping journals of autobiographical memories. As Kirschner et al. describe (1993), the "clinician serves as **a midwife** in the process of disclosure" (p.26). But **do such assessment procedures permit the client and therapist to "discover" historical truths, or "co-construct" narrative truths?** This is the dilemma that confronts the clinician. It is a dilemma that calls for a great deal of caution.

This dilemma is further complicated when we learn that sexually abused children frequently make incomplete or tentative disclosures (79%), or recant their previous disclosures (22%) (Sorenson and Snow, 1991). Thus, however we conceptualize "repression", it should not be viewed as an all-or-nothing phenomenon. Recall of traumatic events can change over time and across circumstance.

When considering the client's memory of past events it is important to keep in mind Holloway and Ursano's (1984) observation that "remembering is an active reconstruction process that uses past experience to describe a present state". It is necessary to consider the meaning, metaphorical and symbolic value of the recalled experience. "History is a record of present beliefs and wishes, not a replica of the past" (p.105).

But the concerns about iatrogenic influences are not limited to the phenomenon of recovered memories. Another very controversial area where victimization and psychiatric diagnosis emerge is in the area of **multiple personality**. I have been called upon to consult for inpatient psychiatric facilities where they have treatment centers for clients with multiple personality disorder (MPD). McHugh (1992) has noted that the diagnostic incidence of MPD has taken on "epidemic" proportions, particularly in certain treatment centers that specialize in this disorder. He notes that while MPD was reported less than 200 times for a good part of the late 19th and early 20th century, in the last decade in the U.S. 20,000 people have been

---

survivors cannot remember the abuse; "healing" is contingent upon recovering the repressed material. (See Read and Lindsay, 1994).

diagnosed with MPD, largely attributed to sexual abuse.[1] What is going on here, especially when clients report having dozens and dozens of so-called different personalities? But such concerns are not new; the historical buff can read Weissberg's (1993) article on the potential iatrogenic influences in the classic case of Anna O, as well as Powell and Boer (1994). *(See the discussion in Section VI on treating flashbacks for further discussion of MPD).*

But where does all this controversy leave the practicing clinician? How do clinicians who do not have independent corroborating data like Linda Meyer Williams operate? How does the clinician provide a supportive therapeutic environment, but reduce the likelihood of iatrogenic influences? How can the clinician remain responsible to his/her clients, but reduce the likelihood of "insinuating memories", with the risk of clients eventually "retracting" their accounts and possibly bringing law suits against their therapist? These are thorny questions. In order to understand how clinicians operate in this state of uncertainty, I performed a small quasi-experiment at my two-day workshops on PTSD. I wanted to understand how clinicians make decisions about their client's reports about childhood sexual abuse, especially when we are reminded that the recall of childhood events may be biased and inaccurate (see Yarrow et al., 1970).

How do Clinicians Formulate a Judgment about the "Validity" or "Authenticity" of their Client's Reports of Child Sexual Abuse (CSA)? Some Preliminary Answers from a Quasi-Experiment

In an attempt to better understand how clinicians make a decision about the "validity" and "authenticity" of their client's reports of child sexual abuse I have performed a series of "quasi-experiments" at my workshops on PTSD. In collaboration with Sandra McKenzie, a graduate student at the University of Waterloo, we have analyzed the decisional responses of some 700 clinicians who watched a videotaped consultative interview between myself and a young male client (31 years of age) who reports having been a victim of two years of child sexual abuse between ages 4 to 6 by a couple who ran a babysitting and after-school program. During the course of the interview the client reports that he had no recollection of the abuse until he began therapy. In this case I was not the client's primary therapist, but rather was asked to see the client as an outside consultant in order to help the client and the client's therapist consider the present clinical picture and to formulate a further treatment plan. During the interview we explored the nature of the child sexual abuse. The conditions under which the client's memory of the abuse emerged, his level of functioning both now and in the past, the impact of the abuse, and the client's explanation or "theory" of how such "bad things" could have occurred for two years and not been recalled for some 25 years, and only then, with the help of the therapist. No form of hypnosis or other specific retrieval procedure was used by the therapist. Interestingly, the client reports detailed memories for other events during the period of ages 4 to 6, but had a "blank", a "gap" about the abuse. He refers to his memory loss as a type of "Swiss cheese memory".

At various workshops I have shown this one-hour interview and I have asked the audience who are made up of various occupational groups (psychologists, psychiatrists, social workers, psychiatric nurses, marriage and family counselors, etc.) to make a judgment as to whether the client's report of child sexual abuse "actually took place or not". They were asked to indicate: Yes, No, Can't Tell. In addition, if they answered "Yes" or "No", to indicate their degree of confidence in their judgment on a 0% to 100% scale, where 100% is "absolutely sure" and 0% is "completely unsure". Moreover, these 700 clinicians were asked to indicate in an open-ended fashion the factors that influenced their decision. It is recognized that clinicians would not be expected to make such a judgment on the basis of one interview, but rather would

---

[1] See Gleaves (1994) for a discussion of the prevalence and incidence of multiple personality disorder.

use a pattern that emerges over several interviews to draw such conclusions. Nevertheless, the analysis of this one session is instructive in elucidating how clinicians formulate such decisions.

In considering the following data, keep in mind that all 700 clinicians are watching and evaluating the exact same videotaped interview. I have interviewed this client on two occasions one year apart. In my own mind, I feel "I can't tell" whether the abuse did or did not occur. While the client's account is conveyed in a most convincing and emotional manner, there are internal inconsistencies and no evidence of independent corroboration. In a moment we will consider how the clinician and the client can operate in this "limbo of uncertainty" about the validity of the client's report of victimization. For now let us consider how the 700 clinicians responded to the request to make a judgment about this client's report of child sexual abuse. In the workshop I asked the audience, after they had watched the videotape interview and filled out the questionnaire, to predict what percentage of clinicians, like themselves, would vote "Can't Tell", "Yes", "No". While clinicians are not very consistent in predicting how other clinicians responded, they are quite consistent in how they responded. The answers offered by clinicians were remarkably reliable across the country. Only 15% of clinicians indicate "I Can't Tell", 36% say "Yes" indicating a judgment in the validity/authenticity of the client's report of child sexual abuse, and 49% indicate "No", or disbelief in the client's reports of child sexual abuse. Perhaps, these results are not unexpected given the contradictory and ambiguous features of this specific interview.[1]

The second aspect worth reporting from this study concerns **the confidence rating** offered by the clinicians in formulating their judgments. Interestingly, not only are most clinicians willing to take a stand indicating a "Yes" or a "No", but they do so with a good deal of confidence. (The N is 587 because the unsures did not offer confidence ratings.) Figure 1 illustrates the clinician's confidence in their judgment "Yes" or "No", along a continuum of 0% to 100% confidence (with 100% being "absolutely sure"). An examination indicates that most clinicians (50% to 54%) are willing to make such judgments about authenticity with a good deal of confidence, namely 76% confidence or more. Not only are they willing to offer such a decision about authenticity, but generally they feel quite confident in offering that judgment. Note, that both the groups who offered a "Yes" and a "No" response are equally confident, showing remarkably similar profiles across the confidence range.

---

[1] The difficulty in discerning the **"truthfulness"** of an individual's statements is not unique to the case of CSA. For example, Ekman and O'Sullivan (1989) report on the unfounded confidence that professional "lie-catchers" have in their ability to discern the truthfulness of individual's statements. The average accuracy of these investigators in detecting deceit is rarely above 60%, with chance being 50%.

Figure 1

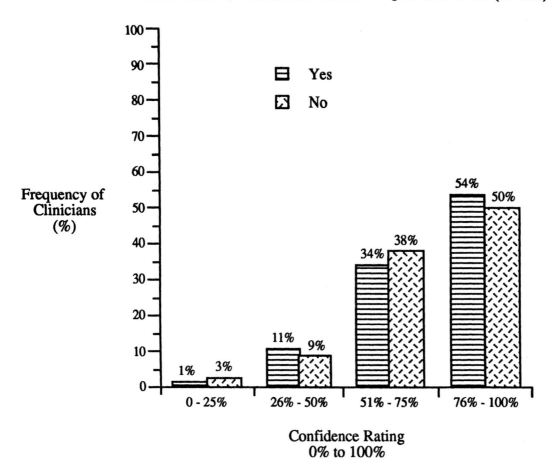

CLINICIANS' CONFIDENCE IN   JUDGMENTS (N=587)

I recognize that this request of clinicians is somewhat unrealistic. As noted, clinicians would not usually be asked to make such a "weighty" decision based on only one interview and in the absence of other test or interview data. Also, the demands of both the workshop and the specific features of this particular interview may have influenced the obtained results. Nevertheless, an analysis of how clinicians made such a decision is, indeed, instructive. What factors do clinicians report as being important in deciding on the validity/authenticity of the client's report of early victimization? Parenthetically, it is worth noting that the obtained results did not differ by sex -- male versus female therapists, by professional group, nor by years of overall clinical experience, or by years of experience working with victims of child sexual abuse.

An Analysis of the Factors Clinicians Report in Influencing their Judgment of the "Validity" and "Authenticity" of the Client's Report of Child Sexual Abuse (CSA)

From our analyses of these 700 reports by clinicians we have identified the following factors that can be summarized as a series of questions that clinicians ask themselves as the client tells his "story" of CSA. These questions are not offered in any specific order of importance. It was impossible at this phase of our research to explicate the importance and/or order of the clinician's decision tree. This summary is offered as a checklist or template against which you could compare how you might assess "authenticity" of a client's report of CSA. Consider how you would proceed if you were a subject in our study, or when you hear a report of CSA in your office, or for that matter, when such reports of alleged CSA appear in the media. What factors guide your decision making process? Consider the factors reported by some 700 clinicians. Note that the assessment of the authenticity of a client's report would not be determined by the presence or absence of a single factor, but rather clinicians reported that they used a complex configural model of emerging patterns of multiple factors. The following list of factors are not meant to imply that we know which factors are valid discriminators. Rather, this list represents what 700 clinicians have reported using in formulating their decisions. Also see Yapko (1994) who has reported on the results of a survey of clinician's views about the nature of memories and the role of hypnosis. He developed a Memory Attitude Questionnaire and a Hypnosis Attitude Questionnaire. It would be interesting to see how clinicians' responses to the Yapko Questionnaires relate to their reactions and judgment to the videotaped interview.

Finally, before examining the factors that emerged from our research on clinician's judgement, it is worth juxtaposing these factors with the findings that emerge from research on memory, as summarized by Lindsay and Read (1994) and Berliner and Williams (1994). For instance, Lindsay and Read (1994, p. 326) observe that the following factors increase the likelihood of subjects/clients developing "false memories".

a) "long delays between the to-be-remembered event and the attempt to remember;
b) suggestions that particular events occurred;
c) the perceived authority of the source of the suggestions;
d) the perceived plausibility of suggestions;
e) repetition of suggestions
f) lax memory-judging criteria (guessing, giving free rein to one's imagination, etc.)
g) mental rehearsal of imagined events; and
h) hypnosis and guided imagery:"

To be added to this list of possible iatrogenic factors, Berliner and Williams (1994) propose the following:

a) presence of an influential interviewer who is seeking to confirm a preconceived idea
b) repeated interviews
c) individual differences in suggestibility
d) therapists' beliefs that most psychological symptoms can be attributed to sexual abuse history
e) beliefs that many survivors "repress" their memories of abuse
f) beliefs that remembering the victimization experiences is a central task of therapy
g) therapists who use recovery memory techniques

Table 1
Factors Clinicians Use in Assessing the "Authenticity" of Client's Memories

1. <u>Does the client mention any credible corroborating evidence for the therapist to follow up on</u>?

    As the client tells his/her "story" is there any independent corroborating data that the account or "facts" being reported are indeed "true"? For example, is there any corroborating information from a "credible" significant other, or from medical or legal documentation, or any other information (e.g., school records) that would confirm the client's account?

2. <u>What were the conditions under which the recall of the childhood sexual abuse (CSA) was solicited</u>?

    Did the memories of child sexual abuse (CSA) emerge for the first time during therapy? Were repeated interviews and assessments used to determine CSA? Is it possible that the notion of CSA may have inadvertently, unwittingly, unknowingly, or perhaps even explicitly, been <u>suggested</u> to the client by someone else such as a therapist, a family member, participants in a "survivor's" group, or from book authors on abuse, or from a movie or TV program? Did such suggestions occur in the absence of any explicit memory that the client was abused?

    Could the client's report of victimization have been influenced by the therapist's assessment procedures? Were procedures such as hypnosis, age regression, visualization, guided imagery, dream work, body image interpretation, meditation, sodium pentothal interview, used to solicit the memory of CSA? Was the client in therapy when the initial memory of CSA first occurred? Was the client exposed to others who reported CSA as in group therapy?

3. <u>What is the client's current level of reported adjustment and what was the level of functioning over the course of his/her development</u>?

    Clinicians listen for reports or solicit evidence about the level of functioning at various times of the client's life in order to determine if a pattern of symptoms/signs of comorbidity/level of adjustment fit the clinician's "picture" or theory of childhood sexual abuse. The clinician ascertains the client's level of distress and adjustment at the time:

    1) prior to the reported incidence of CSA;
    2) at the time of the abuse and immediately thereafter;
    3) between the time of the abuse and the time of the initial flashback;
    4) between the initial flashback and the present point of adjustment;
    5) present time, in terms of the speed of recovery, evidence of current distress and signs of comorbidity.

    In short, clinicians tend to consider the emerging pattern of the client's adjustment (e.g., phobias, sexual difficulties, depression) as a "clue" to the "validity" of his or her account of CSA.

4. <u>What was the nature of the client's family and their response to the CSA</u>?

    Closely aligned with a consideration of the client's life-span adjustment pattern, clinicians often consider the characteristics and dynamics concerning the client's family, both at the time of the reported abuse and thereafter. Did the client attempt to report the CSA to others and how did they respond? Were significant others aware of the abuse? Does such abuse tend to run in the family?

5.   <u>What is the client's presentation style when relating his/her account of CSA?</u>

Clinicians are sensitive to the style and manner with which the client provides his/her account of CSA. Clinicians are attentive to both the <u>presence</u> and <u>absence</u> of verbal and nonverbal features of the client's account of CSA. For example,

(1)   What is the client's affect (emotionality, body language) when relating his/her account of CSA?

(2)   What is the <u>language</u> that the client uses to describe his/her account of CSA? Is the account filled with psychological jargon that may imply that the incident may have been suggested by others?

(3)   Given the details or parts of the client's overall account of CSA, is the client's story plausible, consistent, coherent and convincing?

(4)   What is the client's level of overall suggestibility?

6.   <u>What are the characteristics of the client's memories/flashbacks of CSA?</u>

Clinicians also report attending to the characteristics of the client's recall/memories/ flashbacks (both initial and subsequent reexperiences).

For example, clinicians are attentive to:

a)   how specific, vivid and selective the reported remembrances are;
b)   was it an isolated event or a series of traumatic events;
c)   the client's emotional and behavioral reactions to the flashback "time-slides" (i.e., how distressed was the client to both the initial and subsequent flashbacks);
d)   the level of implicit distress about the "reality" of memories;
e)   the client's account (or implicit theory) of why he/she "forgot" or "chose not to remember" the incident of CSA (client's theory for "Swiss cheese" memory where there are blank periods of recall for certain memories and not others), the client's theory of repression.

7.   <u>Are there any "secondary gains" that the client has received or may receive as a result of reporting CSA? Is the retrieval of the memory of abuse self-serving?</u>

Clinicians are also attentive to what are the consequences ("secondary gains") that may follow from the client's report of CSA. For example, do such reports of CSA:

a)   lead to legal, financial, social benefits (e.g., avoidance of certain responsibilities, increased attention, need to be listened to);
b)   provide a needed explanation for behavior (e.g., "excuse");
c)   affect the client's social relationships?

8.   <u>Closely related is a judgment as to whether the therapist or the clinical setting has a private or research agenda or "stake" ("secondary gain") in the validity of the client's memory.</u>

Clinicians are sensitive to the benefits that accrue to the therapist who is involved in the memory retrieval of abuse.

As noted, this list reflects the factors that clinicians report as guiding and influencing their decision making. There is an important **caveat** that must be taken into consideration when considering these decisional factors. **Although these 8 general factors are offered by clinicians, there are no studies that I know of which indicate that they are, indeed, valid signs of authenticity.** I know of no studies that compare confabulated versus well-documented accounts of CSA and that have cross-validated the discriminating factors. In spite of the absence of validated signs clinicians who offered both "Yes" and "No" responses with a good deal of confidence (75% or more) **often report using the same indicators!** For instance, while most clinicians agreed that repeated probing by a therapist may implant "false memories", there was more disagreement among clinicians when other factors were attended to. In the case of the amount of detail in the client's account, clinicians disagreed on its significance. Those who voted "Yes" (memory valid) noted the vivid and detailed nature of the client's memory, while those who voted "No", reflecting their disbelief in the authenticity, suggested that the amount of detail in the reported memory was "too detailed" to be believable. Some reported that the client's body language and accompanying affect indicated the validity of the memory, while other clinicians pointed to the same index as evidence for invalidity. A similar pattern of disagreement was evident when the issue of the consistency or inconsistency of the client's account was considered. Some pointed to the inconsistency as evidence of questionable memories, while others pointed to the same inconsistency as evidence for "validity". We are in the midst of analyzing this data further. At this point, it is important to appreciate that clinicians are prone to make decisions (take a stand with a fair degree of confidence), but in doing so they often employ cues for which we have little or no independent validation. This obviously contributes to the marked disagreements we found.

What shall we take from the findings of this quasi-experiment?

(1)   Most clinicians (85%) are willing to offer a decision about the "authenticity" of a client's account of CSA, and 50% of them do so with a good deal of confidence (76% - 100%).

(2)   In formulating this decision of "authenticity" clinicians have an implicit framework of self-interrogative questions and markers that they employ.

(3)   These indicators are held with a good deal of confidence, even though there is no independent validity for such markers in discriminating between "authentic" and "inauthentic" reports of CSA.

(4)   The issue of validity of these markers is vital, particularly when we learn that both the "Yes" and "No" groups often use the exact same indicators to support their positions.

(5)   Clearly, there is a need to replicate these results with clinicians in other settings than in a workshop, with other clients and interviewers, and with more sophisticated rating scales of decision making, so weighting factors and configural models of clinical judgment can be tested. There is a need to study how clinicians, and for that matter, how clients judge the validity of their autobiographical memories.

Guidelines For How Therapists and Clients Can Handle Autobiographical
Reports of Childhood Sexual Abuse and Other Reports of Victimization

What do you do when a client comes in and asks you to help her find out if she was abused as a child? What do you do when a client who is being seen for some other problem (e.g., depression, eating disorder) spontaneously reports that she believes that she may have been abused as a child? What do you do if you, the clinician, have a hunch that the client may have been abused as a child, but is not reporting any recollection of such events? How do you proceed without iatrogenically (inadvertently, unwittingly, and perhaps even unknowingly) co-constructing or "insinuating" such memories of victimization in your clients? Moreover, how do you proceed so you do not revictimize your clients by doubting their reports?

These are very difficult questions that need to be debated in the clinical literature. I am sure that I do not have the answers to these tough questions. I can report, however, the guidelines I use when confronted by these clinical challenges. (I would welcome receiving your answers to these questions.)

1. I remind myself that my job is that of a therapist and not that of a judge or jury. It is not my job to determine the "authenticity" or "veridicality" of my client's reports. I **embrace the notion that I can help clients without knowing the "truth"**. Given the discussion offered in Section II, it is the "narrative" truthfulness, and not the so-called "objective" truthfulness, that is the focus of therapy. I must deal with what the client presents and then help him/her to "move on" or "go on" with his/her life, taking charge and responsibility for the present and future, and "not getting stuck in the past". With this as prologue, I explore collaboratively with the client what has led him/her to raise concerns about victimization at this time? What decisions has he/she made? What is his/her notion about what he/she wants to happen in therapy, especially as a result of so-called "memory work"? How do they feel this will help?

2. I show respect for the client's report of victimization and do not challenge the "authenticity" or "validity" of the memory, even if the particular circumstances sound somewhat far-fetched, or even if there are contradictions in the account. As Gunderson and Chu observe, there is a need to "ally with the patient's sense of having been victimized". Gunderson and Chu (1993) also indicate that in the early stages of therapy "acknowledgment of past trauma is valuable, but extensive exploration is not". As a therapist, I convey empathy and attempt to validate the client's account by listening in a supportive nonjudgmental fashion. But, I also convey at a later time that without independent corroborating input, both the client and I cannot be sure each aspect of the account is accurate. Thus, as a therapist, I feel I am walking a "tightrope", having the client learn something about the nature of autobiographical accounts on the one hand, without "revictimizing" the client by doubting their story, on the other hand. If the client wishes or insists I will explore with the client his/her desire to collect "corroborating" information. I will discuss how the client might go about collecting such information. Who does the client feel he/she can check with; what will the client do or say? The ways the client might inadvertently bias the corroborator's report is also considered.

3. I discuss, in a non-didactic fashion, with the client the nature of autobiographical memories and how susceptible such memories are to various factors such as assessment. In a nontechnical fashion, I explore with the client his/her notions about memories and the experiences he/she has had that influence his/her memory. I indicate that memory is not stored like a VCR videotape and retrieval procedures like hypnosis are not a remote control switch that can simply allow clients to play back their lives. Moreover, I highlight how that mood and concerns can color the nature

of the memories that are retrieved. "Moods can act like a channel selector on a television set." "Human memories are <u>not</u> like fixed images in a family photo album". Memories can be shaped by factors that occur later in life (see American Psychiatric Association, Fact Sheet, 1994). For instance, someone's mood can act like a flashlight that seeks out memories that are consistent with one's current mood and disregard or discount memories that are incompatible. I also note that without independent corroborating information there is no way for the two of us of to know whether the exact description of what is reported actually took place. It is clear that something "upsetting" occurred and I don't doubt that this is still distressing the client. But if we used any procedures to retrieve memories (like hypnosis or dream analysis or imagery procedures), it is possible that we may fill in gaps, alter memories, and perhaps, even co-create new memories that may not have occurred. The object of this discussion is to indicate to the client that I will <u>not</u> use assessment procedures that may lead to the emergence of unreliable data. At the same time great care is taken to <u>not</u> reject the client's search to better understand, work through, and resolve the impact of his/her past on present behavior. Thus, I commend the client for asking such questions, but caution him/her about becoming "stuck" in the past. There is a need to examine this material in some detail with the client so he/she does <u>not</u> see my concerns about "memory work" as a personal rejection. I attempt to maintain an empathic, non-judgmental stance toward the client's reports of autobiographical memories.

As a result of this discussion, the client should come away with the following understanding:

1. Remembering is a reconstructive process and not a mere retrieval of records of past experience. Memory is not perfect, with more forgotten than remembered.

2. Various assessment and retrival procedures can influence and lead to distortions and errors in people's recollections of past events. Memories can be influenced and distorted.

3. Reconstructive memory procedures can lead to "illusory memories", rather than assure that everything that they remember is true.

4. People can be very confident in their memories and beliefs, but at the same time, be very wrong. People can strongly believe in inaccurate memories.

5. "Healing" and "improvement" do <u>not</u> depend on the recovery of memories.

4. The focus of our **discussion is** more on the **present and future**. We also consider how such past experiences and the emotional impact they have had on the client "takes a toll", "has an impact", on the client and significant others. We consider the "price" the client continues to pay for such distressing experiences. We explore how his/her past gets in the way of achieving his/her current and future goals. In the Sections on treatment (Sections V and VI) we will consider further how therapists can address the client's distress that results from "victimization" and **feelings of guilt and shame** , as well as the variety of clinical techniques that have been used to help clients "take charge of their lives".

5. One focus of the discussion is on the issue of **responsibility**. Many patients may have feelings of having been responsible for having been victimized. It is important to put the responsibility on the perpetrator. The patient was not responsible for what

went on at that time, but the patient can take responsibility for caring for themselves **in the present** and **in the future.**

6. Finally, consistent with the constructive narrative perspective that provides the motif for this **Handbook,** Gunderson and Chu (1993) propose that the recovery of past trauma helps victimized patients "to have a sense of personal history, to understand how they have experienced and reacted in their lives, and to change their sense of identity and self-worth." It is this **reframing and understanding** of the role of trauma in their lives "that helps traumatized people to move on."

The discussion of traumatic memory underscores the observation that the assessment and treatment of PTSD clients present unique and particularly stressful reactions for therapists. These stressful reactions can cause **"vicarious traumatization"** and **"compassion fatigue"** in therapists, a topic to which we now turn our attention.

HELPING THE HELPERS

"I love my work but lately I find it contaminating my personal life. I have nightmares about the horrible things I hear about from clients, my sex life has deteriorated, I'm irritable and distractible, I'm afraid for my kids and tend to over-protect them, and I don't trust anybody anymore. I don't know what is happening to me." A therapist (as cited by Courtois, 1993, p.8)

Working with clients who are "in crisis", who have been traumatized, who have experienced human-induced victimization (e.g., family violence, war, torture, criminal assault, sexual violation), as well as horrific natural disasters, can have a "traumatizing" impact on "helpers". The emotional and personal demands, as well as the technical challenges of this work can lead to what have been called "burnout" (Maslach's, Pines), "compassion fatigue" (Figley)[1] and "vicarious traumatization" (McCann & Pearlman). A number of authors (Chu, 1990; Courtois, 1993; Danieli, 1988; Haley, 1974; Wilson & Lindy, 1994; Yassen, 1993) have discussed the impact on the therapist of working with "traumatized" clients. Agger and Jensen (1994) have described distressed therapists as "wounded healers". (See the National Center for PTSD <u>Clinical Newsletter</u>, Spring, 1993 issue for a discussion, as well). Straker and Moosa (1994) have discussed the stress on psychotherapists of working with traumatized clients in a country with continuing conflict and political repression.

Wilson and Lindy (1994) have described two major types of emotional strain experienced by therapists who work with traumatized clients. Under the heading of "countertransference", they describe two types of therapist tendencies: Type I they characterize as the therapist's tendency to **avoid** and engage in **empathetic withdrawal**. Type II is the therapist's tendency to **overidentify** and engage in **empathetic enmeshment**.

The recognition of the potential negative impact of working with traumatized individuals is not limited to psychotherapists. It has long been recognized by those who work with emergency workers, firefighters, police personnel, and body handlers, (e.g., see McCann et al., 1988; Medeiros & Prochaska, 1988; Mitchell, 1985; Raphael et al., 1983, 1984; Talbot, 1990; Talbot et al., 1992). For example, Raphael and Wilson (1994) review the literature that indicates between 20% to 80% of rescue workers have shown symptoms of prolonged stress response. They provide an analysis of the major themes common to rescue work. These themes that contribute to such stress reactions include:

1)   force and destruction involved

2)   confrontation with death (massive, gruesome and mutilating death)

3)   feelings of hopelessness ("helplessness of humanity")

4)   feelings of anger (anger that more was not done, as well as sometimes being the recipient of anger from survivors)

5)   significant loss and accompanying grief ("identification sympathy")

---

[1] Figley (1994) has developed a questionnaire to assess "Compassion fatigue" (Florida State University). Also see forthcoming edited book on <u>Compassion Fatigue</u> by Figley (1995, Brunner/Mazel).

6)   attachment and relationships ("strong bonds") that develop among rescue team members

7)   elation or "feelings of triumph" among some rescue workers

8)   survivor guilt ("not do more")

9)   voyeurism.

We will consider the use of debriefing procedures with such emergency workers in Section VII. At this point the focus will be on psychotherapists and counselors who work with "victimized" clients or the "survivors" of traumatic events.

What can "helpers" do to protect themselves from the stress that "comes with the territory" of working with such challenging clinical populations? A number of suggestions have been offered in the literature and from the group of diverse therapists with whom I have had the privilege of working with.

1. Recognize that "vicarious traumatization", as well as potential "secondary victimization" are highly likely in working with PTSD population. As Pearlman (1994) has noted "vicarious traumatization" can result from the cumulative impact of trauma work and be evident in the form of "depression, despair, cynicism, alienation, psychological and physical symptoms, withdrawal, and a heightened sense of vulnerability". Listening to descriptions of "horrific tales" can take a toll. The "secondary victimization" that many health care providers experience compounds this situation. There is the "danger" that counselors who work with "traumatized" clients may come to feel isolated, distinct and rejected from other health care providers. For example, questions may be raised by others, either surreptitiously or explicitly, as to whether the therapist may be inadvertently, unwittingly, and unknowingly, iatrogenically suggesting to his/her clients that they may have been victimized or abused. Such insinuations are especially stressful and threatening to therapists since there is the possibility of legal suits against therapists by clients and their family members who may retract their stories of abuse and charge their therapist as the "cause" of their accounts of abuse. As noted, at the meeting of the False Memory Syndrome Foundation, workshops were offered to clients, family members and lawyers on how to represent "retractors" in court and how to sue therapists.

2. In order to cope with such distress therapists need to engage in personal, professional, and organizational activities. (See Pearlman, 1994; Raphael et al., 1983-1984 for a more complete account of possible activities), and Daneli (1994) for a series of exercises that therapists can engage in to deal with vicarious traumatization. At this point I will enumerate a number of specific suggestions.

Personal Interventions

A.   Therapist should recognize emotional, cognitive and physical signs of incipient stress reactions in self and in colleagues (increased self-awareness).

B.   Therapist should not delimit clinical practice to only PTSD clients; balance victim and non-victims case loads.

C.   Limit overall case loads. Monitor case loads in terms of size and number of trauma cases.

D. Engage in self-care behaviors (e.g., relaxation activities of leaving work at work, vacations, exercise, "soothing" activities like a massage).

E. Recognize not alone in facing the stress of working with traumatized clients ("normalize" your reactions).

F. Engage in "healing activities" and in activities that renew meaning of life, both in therapy and out of therapy settings. Some therapists report bringing into their offices "signs of life and hope" such as plants and pictures that remind them of beauty and rebirth. Ensure physical and mental well being (nutrition, sleep, relaxation, activity, creative expression, humor). Replenish!

G. Adopt a philosophical or religious outlook and remind oneself that he/she cannot take responsibility for the client's "healing", but rather should act as a "midwife on the client's journey toward healing". Recognize limitations! Remind self of the "healthy" parts of the client's story. [1]

H. Share reactions with the client. As one astute clinician noted, "Sometimes I tell my clients that there is a **part of me** that does not want to hear such horrific things, but there is another part of me that says we must continue because it is important, and doing so, is part of the healing process. But I would not be honest with you (the client), if I did not comment that no one should have suffered, nor endured, what you have experienced. I am heartened by your willingness and ability, your courage to share your story, as part of the healing process". Such statements to clients can often foster a stronger therapeutic alliance, highlighting the therapist's empathy and humanity. Such statements also convey to the client that his/her reactions are not unique, nor are those of the therapist.

Professional Interventions

A. Maintain collegial on the job support, thus limiting the sense of isolation. Use case consultation and supervision. Establish a "buddy system". Ensure that you have an opportunity to share your reactions with understanding and supportive others and obtain peer supervision. Use a team for support, join a study group, attend conferences. I have had an opportunity over the last year to listen to audiotapes of a group of clinicians (family physician, psychiatrists, social workers) who each work with traumatized clients. These monthly meetings have proven both supportive and instructive for the participants. As an invited consultant I have provided feedback on their reactions. This supervisory model has worked well.

---

[1] I recall having been asked to review a text on cognitive-behavior therapy for a journal. In the book, someone observed that what impressed her most about cognitive-behavior therapy was that the therapist never seemed to "give up". With this observation in mind, I have often wondered why it is that various forms of cognitive therapy seem to work so well with depressed clients (see Munoz et al., 1994). My tongue-in-cheek answer is that cognitive-behavioral interventions "work", in part, because they **help to prevent depression in psychotherapists**. No matter what the client tells the therapist, from a cognitive-behavioral perspective, the therapist recognizes that the client's narrative account is only "part" of the story that is colored by mood, current appraisal and social context. Another way to cope with the accounts of "victimized" clients is to view such descriptions as a set of coping techniques that were at one time adaptive and functional, but are currently being overused or no longer needed. The current treatment need is to help the client feel safe enough and resilient in order to become "unstuck", and discontinue what was needed in the past, but that is no longer needed at the present time, and to employ "healthier" ways to achieve his/her goals.

B. Where indicated the counselors can undergo debriefing. Talbot (1990) suggests that counselors discuss together the cases that were seen; what each counselor did; how did they perceive their clients; what was the experience like for them; do they "identify" with the traumatic events that their clients experienced or with their clients? Sometimes, outside professional services are useful in helping conduct these group meetings. Such sessions may cover such topics as, What is it like working with "traumatized" clients? What is most difficult or challenging? What is most rewarding? What do you need now? How can we be of help?

C. Jassen (1993) has described how a time-limited group approach can be used with clinicians who have a history of trauma. The group can help therapists deal with self-doubts, ways to manage their own memories and feelings that are elicited in treatment. The need for such preparatory groups is underscored by the observation that often peer counselors are used. For instance, in the Veterans Centres, 60% of the counselors in the Readjustment Services program are combat veterans, having served in Vietnam. Catherall and Lane (1992) consider the potential advantages and disadvantages of using patient therapists.

D. Become knowledgeable about PTSD. Seek professional training. Obviously, your reading this **Clinical Handbook** shows good judgment, and hopefully, it will prove helpful.

Organizational Interventions

A. Some therapists, like their clients, find a "mission" in trying to find meaning. They work actively to change the circumstances that lead to "victimization" or they work on alleviating the distress of survivors. This may be done at a local, national or organizational level. Legislative reform, social action.

B. Encourage your local, state and national organization to educate professionals and nonprofessionals about PTSD. Engage in preventative activities.

C. Join a network of others who work with a PTSD population.

Finally, please share with me what else you do to cope with the stress of working with clients who have been exposed to traumatic events. I will summarize these for a future edition of this **Handbook**.

TESTING YOUR EXPERTISE

Section IV - Assessment Issues Concerning Autobiographical Memories and Helping the Helper

1.   Discuss the controversy concerning "false memory syndrome". What are the critical issues? What is the evidence for "repressed memories"?

2.   a) Have you used "memory recovery techniques" with your clients? Which techniques have you used? What "memory recovery techniques" are being used in your mental health setting? What are the pros and cons of using each technique?

      b) What precautions are being followed not to co-create "illusory memories" in your clients?

3.   You have been asked to offer a presentation to your colleagues on the dangers of generating iatrogenically "illusory memories" in clients. What specific "warning signs" should your colleagues look out for in working with clients concerning autobiographical memories of victimization? Why might they not take your advice? What can you do to anticipate their couterarguments?

4.   Search the book shelves of your hosptial and mental health center that are available to clients. What do the books say about "recovery of memories" What are the pros and cons of making such books available to your client population?

5.   Once again, set up a role play with you and two fellow students. This time have one person play the role of a client who comes to treatment in order to determine if he/she has been sexually abused. One person should play the role of the therapist indicating how he/she would handle the situation. The third person should act as the constructive commentator. Then switch roles.

      a) How do you educate the client about the nature of memory without being judgmental and rejecting?

      b) What do you say about the client's desire to seek corroboration?

      c) How do you help the client to live with "uncertainty" when corroboating evidence is not forthcoming?

      d) How do you handle the client's report of CSA or the client's report of combat experience?

6.   a)   Piper (1994, p. 606) concludes that:

            "Therapists do not uncover objective facts and details of a life story, or **historical truths**. Rather, therapists aid in producing **narrative truth**, which is both a reevaluation of the past in the light of present-day experience, as well as a product of the communication between therapist and patient."

            What are your reactions to Piper's conclusion? Given your answer, what are the implications for your clinical practice (assessment and treatment).

b)   How does the debate about the "authenticity" of clients' autobiographical memories impact on your clinical practice? How has this controversy affected your assessment and treatment procedures?

7.   How can therapists inadvertently, unwittingly, and perhaps, even unknowingly, iatrogenically influence their client's memories? How can the assessment procedures, hypnosis, group work, and assigned bibliotherapy influence the client's recall?

8.   A colleague asks you to help him/her determine if the client's accounts of childhood sexual abuse, solicited over a series of clinical interviews reflect "valid" memories. He/she does not have independent corroborating evidence concerning the client's autobiographical account. What factors are you likely to use in formulating your judgments as you listen to the client tapes? As you listen to this client's, (to Stephen Cook, to Roseanne Arnold, to Ramona's daughter's) account of CSA, what factors do you use in formulating a decision about the individual's autobiographical recollections? Compare your list of factors to that reported by 700 clinicians included in this Section.

9.   a)   Discuss the emotional reactions you have had in treating clients who have experienced traumatic events.

b)   What are the "warning signs" that you use to indicate that you are distressed as a result of your clinical work?

c)   What steps, if any, have you taken to reduce your stress?

d)   Compare your list of coping efforts with thos enumerated in this section.

e)   What further steps can you take to reduce the likelihood of "vicarious traumatization" and "compassion fatigue"?

f)   What are all the "reasons" why you won't do any of the things you know would help? How can you address these "obstacles" and "barriers" to engage in "self-help" and in helping your colleagues?

g)   Approach a trusted colleague and ask him/her about the stress he/she has experienced in working with "traumatized" clients. Engage in a discussion of how each of you "cope" with such distress. What do you do during the session? What do you do before and after the session? What do you do when you are not at work to handle "compassion fatigue" and reduce the likelihood of "vicarious traumatization"? Write out a list of these activities and share it with a colleague or with your fellow students.

h)   What does your clinic, your local professional organization, do, if anything, to help the helpers? What do you think they should be doing?

SECTION V
TREATMENT ALTERNATIVES

Goals of Section V

Thus far, we have considered the epidemiological, description, diagnosis, and assessment of clients who have experienced various forms of traumatic events. We now turn our attention to the variety of diverse treatment procedures that have been employed with PTSD clients. Two predominant characteristics emerge from this literature review. First, clinicians have been remarkably creative in employing almost any type of intervention with PTSD clients. You name it, and it seems to have been tried with PTSD clients (as noted in Table 1). This enumeration of the psychologically-based treatment options (the references for which are included in the back of this **Handbook/Manual**) is followed by a consideration of pharmacologically-based interventions. Given the neurophysiological impact of traumatic events, the potential role of medication for redressing PTSD symptoms and accompanying signs of comorbidity is reviewed. In anticipation of the discussion on medication, we can consider the observation offered by Shalev (1993). He concluded that, "Psychotropic drugs can alleviate PTSD symptoms, but they do not cure PTSD" (p. 104).

The second characteristic of this treatment literature is the remarkable **limitations of good outcome data** for both psychological and pharmacological intervention studies. Surely, the field of treatment of PTSD in is its "infancy". The high standards that have been employed in the cognitive behavioral treatment of patients with panic attacks and unipolar depressed outpatients have not yet been in evidence in the area of PTSD. Whenever there is some promise available in the treatment of PTSD clients, as in the case of exposure-based treatment and in some forms of group intervention, these are highlighted. For example, Blake (1993) reports on 8 studies that have compared different treatments for adults with PTSD. Most of these treatment studies have been with Vietnam combat veterans, rape victims, and occasionally with crime and vehicle accident survivors. The various treatments compared include a wide array of interventions including Transcendental Mediation, cognitive and cognitive processing therapy, systematic desensitization with and without biofeedback, assertion training, stress inoculation training, imaginal flooding and exposure-based methods (e.g., Saigh's work with war traumatized children), supportive and psychodynamic psychotherapies, and hypnotherapy. Blake (1993), p.16) concludes that the treatment literature appears

> "to be fairly uniform in reducing at least part of the complex of symptoms known as PTSD. Treatment effects are typically seen in reduced 'positive' symptoms, i.e., psychophysiological arousal and startle, intrusive thoughts, nightmares, and anger. On the other hand, it is not clear whether these treatments also reduce 'negative' symptoms of PTSD, i.e., numbing alienation, and restricted affect."

But this conclusion should be tempered by Green's (1994) observation that:

> "While studies have generally found treatment to be effective, about half of those treated may still meet full criteria for PTSD at termination suggesting that this disorder may be refractory to short-term treatment" (p.353).

It should also be noted, however, that at this time **there is not sufficient evidence to suggest the superiority of one form of treatment over any other, nor an appreciation of how the various treatment components can be combined most effectively.** After reviewing some 255 reports of treatment studies of PTSD and the few randomized controlled clinical trials (e.g., only 5 double-blind pharmacotherapy studies[1] and 6 studies of behavioral techniques with PTSD clients), Solomon et al. (1992) concluded that:

> "Drug studies show a modest but clinically meaningful effect on PTSD. Stronger effects were found for behavioral techniques involving direct therapeutic exposure, particularly in terms of reducing PTSD intrusive symptoms. However, severe complications have also been reported from the use of these techniques in patients suffering from other psychiatric disorders. Studies of cognitive therapy, psychodynamic therapy and hypnosis suggest that these approaches may also hold promise. However, further research is needed before any of these approaches can be pronounced effective as lasting treatment of PTSD (p. 633). ... As with pharmacotherapy, practically every form of existing psychotherapy has been tried on those suffering from PTSD. Although almost all of these have been reported as efficacious in **case reports, few have been subjected to systematic tests**"[2] (p. 636). (*Table 1 in this Section indicates the broad range of treatments that have been used with PTSD clients.*)

Finally, Yehuda and McFarlane (1994) provide an important caveat when considering treatment outcome studies. They highlight that the longitudinal data of PTSD patients indicates a changing course. As a result, different treatments may be more efficacious at different points of the disorder. Moreover, given that exposure to a traumatic stressor is insufficient to cause PTSD, interventions may need to be more multi-faceted than just focusing on the trauma.

In addition to the enumeration of various treatments of PTSD three additional items are addressed in this Section:

(1)   An evaluative consideration of some generic forms of intervention, namely, pharmacological interventions, exposure-based interventions, group interventions, ceremonial rituals, and the treatment of torture victims.

(2)   A critical eye is also cast on some popular forms of intervention with PTSD clients, for example, the popular procedure of **eye movement desensitization and reprocessing (EMD/R)** as developed by Francine Shapiro. According to the EMD/R Institute over 8,000 clinicians have taken its training course. What is the basis for this enthusiastic interest and what **cautions** are required?

(3)   An outline of **treatment guidelines** that are common to many forms of treatment of clients with PTSD are considered.

(4)   A consideration of the general treatment factors that should be considered in determining the possible **length of the treatment** of clients with PTSD.

---

[1] Only 134 patients with PTSD (mainly combat veterans) have been studied in double-blind placebo controlled studies. The treatment effects have been quite modest (van der Kolk et al., 1994).

[2] In evaluating the relative efficacy of different psychotherapeutic procedures there is a need to consider possible methodological pitfalls. For example, Dar et al. (1994) highlight the possible misuse of statistical tests in psychotherapy research. These pitfalls include: (1) the neglect of reporting effect size -- that is, reporting that one treatment is statistically significant from another is not sufficient; (2) reckless "data mining"; (3) inappropriate use of null hypothesis testing; (4) the atheoretical nature of interventions. They cite Kukla (1989) who observed that **"when theory does not play a selective role, our data gathering activities belong to the realm of journalism rather than science"**. We should keep Kukla's quote in mind when considering the treatment outcome studies with PTSD clients. To be added to Dar et al.'s list of pitfalls are the failure to consider the limited generalizability of the clinical sample used in treatment studies and the failure to consider the attrition rates (v.z., how many of those client-subjects who were originally interested in treatment actually entered and completed treatment and the post treatment and followup assessments?).

Overview of Section V

1. What are the Diverse Treatment Approaches That Have Been Employed With PTSD Clients?

    Table 1 - An Enumeration of Alternative Treatments

2. Pharmacological Interventions for PTSD

    Table 2 - Summary of Treatment Guidelines

3. General Evaluative Comments on the Treatment of Clients With PTSD

    a) Pharmacological Interventions

    b) Exposure-based Interventions

    c) Eye Movement Desensitization and Reprocessing (EMD/R)

4. Ceremonial Rituals for Returning Combat Veterans

5. Treatment of Torture Victims: Testimony and Other Methods

6. The Potential Advantages of Group Treatment of PTSD

    a) Examples of Group Treatment with Incest Victims

7. General Treatment Guidelines: What Can Be Done To Help Clients With PTSD And DES?

8. How Long Should Treatment Take with Clients With PTSD and PTSD + DES?

WHAT ARE THE DIVERSE TREATMENT APPROACHES
THAT HAVE BEEN EMPLOYED WITH PTSD CLIENTS?[1]

Table 1

An Enumeration of Alternative Treatments

Pharmacological interventions -- there is little evidence to suggest that the use of medication interferes with the psychotherapeutic process (McFarlane, 1994) and there is some suggestion that it can enhance psychotherapeutic interventions (Kudler & Davidson, 1994). As discussed below, medication is rarely sufficient in the treatment of PTSD. *(See evaluative comments below.)*	Davidson; Friedman; Friedman & Charney; Kudler & Davidson; Schwartz; Shay; van der Kolk
Crisis intervention (see Lindeman, 1944, who was a forerunner of later interventions)	Burgess & Baldwin; Burgess et al.
Individual and group psychodynamic psychotherapy	Briere; Brom et al.; Dietz; Horowitz; Kearney-Cooke & Striegel-Moore; Lindy; Marmar & Freeman
Individual therapies (supportive psychotherapy)	Brende & Parson; Courtois & Sprei; Ochberg; Roth & Batson
Time-limited dynamic psychotherapy -- individual and group. For example, Weiss and Marmar (1993) proposed a 12-session treatment protocol for **well-functioning** individuals who suffer **single traumatic events**. Those individuals who have a prior history of trauma require more intensive treatment. The treatment focuses on transference relationship and interpretation of defenses.	Deitz; Kollers et al.; Weiss & Marmar
Time-limited trauma therapy -- a 6 session treatment begins with "abreaction" trauma work where the client interview is videotaped and then the client is given an opportunity to watch the tape from the perspective of a dispassionate imaginary outsider. The review session is tape recorded and is the focus of a subsequent recursive review. This is repeated in the session and at home. The treatment is completed with the client drawing a graphic of the traumatic experience.	Tinnin

---

[1] See Hyer et al. (1993) for a description and annotated bibliography of psychotherapy of chronic PTSD clients.

Individual behavior therapy, implosion, imaginal and in vivo exposure, direct therapeutic exposure, traumatic incident reduction, relaxation, and assertion training. *(See comments below on exposure-based interventions.)*	Boudewyns et al.; Boudewyns & Hyer; Brom et al.; Brooks & Scarcano; Cooper & Clum; Fairbank et al.; Foa & Rothbaum; Foy et al.; Keane et al.; Keane & Kaloupek; Levis; Litz et al.; Lyons & Keane; Moore; Richards et al.; Rychtarik et al.; Saigh
Systematic desensitization and EMG biofeedback assisted densensitization; in vivo desensitization; trauma desensitization	Brom et al.; Blanchard & Abel; Kipper; Peniston; Saigh; Tang; Wolff
Eye-movement desensitization and reprocessing, EMD/R. *(See evaluative comments of EMD/R below.)*	Boudewyns et al.; Hassard; Herbert & Mueser; Jensen; Lohr et al.; Marquis; McCann; Metter & Michelson; Shapiro
Guided imagery-based interventions -- this covers an array of diverse procedures including direct therapy exposure, hypnosis, image habituation training and various ways to alter the traumatic memory, *as described in Section VI.*	Foa & Rothbaum, Goulding, Muus, Spiegel, Vaughan & Tarrier.
Individual and group cognitive-behavioral stress inoculation training	Ayalon; Foa & Rothbaum; Meichenbaum; Resick et al.; Solomon; Veronen & Kilpatrick
Dialetical behavior therapy and problem-solving	Linehan; D'Zurilla
Marathon therapy group--weekend session (e.g., with female Vietnam veterans who are scattered across the country)	Buechler
Cognitive restructuring or cognitive processing therapy	Beck; Frank et al.; Jehu et al.; McCann et al.; Resick & Schnicke

Inpatient treatment program -- individual treatment programs within a general milieu. Within the VA system a number of programs have been developed in such varied sites as Augusta, Ga, American Lake, Honolulu, Miami, Pittsburgh, Battle Creek, Michigan, Coatesville, Pa. These programs vary widely in their structure and their treatment components. For example, the Coatesville program has a 90-day extended inpatient program that uses multiple treatment modalities including a therapeutic community, group treatment 3 times a week, patient education that focuses on PTSD and war experiences including combat film footage 5 times a week, relaxation training, peer group work without the therapist present 2 times a week, 1 or 2 times a week individual treatment and in some instances family involvement, AA and Narcotics Anonymous meetings, and biofeedback treatment. Every 6 weeks the unit visited the Vietnam memorial. Clients monitor their progress daily and weekly. Other treatments include imaginal flooding, behavior and cognitive therapy, and medication. Other VA programs are somewhat less ambitious and more focused on specific treatments. For example, American Lake is a 12-week inpatient program, Battle Creek is a 5-week program, Augusta, Ga program focuses on direct therapy exposure (viz., 10-12 50-minutes within a 20-week program). The evaluative data of these programs is in a very preliminary stage (see references).

Boudewyns et al., 1990; Hammarberg & Silver, 1994; Harmond et al., 1987; Munley et al., 1994; Perconte, 1989; Scurfield, 1990. See Seidel, Gusman and Abueg, 1994, (Psychotherapy, 31, 67-78) for the most comprehensive and thoughtful inpatient (3-4 month) treatment program for PTSD-alcohol Vietnam veterans.

Eclectic inpatient program -- with male abuse patients. Combines psychoeducational, cognitive-behavioral, and art therapy techniques *(See description below on treatment of incest survivors.)*

Zaidi, 1994

"Sanctuary" milieu treatment program -- an interdisciplinary approach that employs, art and movement therapy, psychodrama and group interventions within a highly managed and supportive inpatient environment.

Bloom

Multifaceted outpatient intervention -- Koach[1] program with Israeli soldiers

Solomon et al.

---

[1] Chronic PTSD veterans of the 1982 Lebanon war who had not responded to treatment received the Koach Treatment program. While both participants and therapists were generally positive about the effectiveness of the Koach program on subjective measures, objective psychometric assessments indicated both short-term and long-term negative effects. There is a need to include both subjective and objective assessments in the evaluation of any treatment intervention.

Second Generation Inpatient Program -- this VA   Johnson et al., 1994
inpatient program also works with Vietnam veterans but it
focuses on reintegrating the veterans into ongoing life
experience and does not focus on the war-related experience
(i.e., first generation programs). The first generation
programs take as a central premise the need to "purge" an
emotional load that was tied to war experiences. The second
generation programs work to integrate PTSD clients with
clients with other diagnoses, involve families, focus on "here
and now" reintegrating skills (problem-solving, coping skills
training). Johnson et al. (1994) highlight the importance of
helping Vietnam veterans to redefine their PTSD symptoms
into the language of current life challenges rather than being
"stuck" in the "language of war". For example, the symptoms
of sleep disturbance such as nightmares are viewed as events
that disturb marital relations, avoidance can be viewed as a
hindrance to family life, anxiety can trigger abuse of
symptoms. **The focus is on current life problems
rather than on the roots of the war experience.**
Illustrative of this approach is a 90-day inpatient program for
PTSD Vietnam veterans offered by Hackman and Ziegler
(1994). The multi-faceted treatment program adopted a "here
and now" psychoeducational and cognitive-behavioral
orientation. The treatment did not focus on trauma, nor did it
use direct exposure procedures.

Readjustment Counseling Services -- conducted in 196   Blank
Veteran centers across the US. These are mainly outreach
programs, establishing a presence where the need is. Since its
inception 12 years ago 750,000 veterans and over 250,000
family members have been seen. The majority of counselors
are peer counselors.

Partial Hospitalization and day treatment programs   Lipton; Kooyman
-- attend daily hospital milieu treatment program. Kooyman
(1994) describes a day treatment program for traumatized
refugees that recently opened in the Netherlands. (For further
information contact Kooyman at tel. 31-1719-46090; Fax 31-
1719-47080). The main focus is on helping the refugees learn
to cope with cultural differences, practical problems and an
uncertain future.

Outpatient group program for women veterans --   Wolfe, Mori & Krygeris
Wolfe et al. (1994, Psychotherapy, 31, 87-93) describe how
the treatment needs to be adapted to female patients This
innovative pilot project is sensitive to the gender differences in
terms of combat experience, noncombat victimization
experiences, and the tendency of participants to not seek help.

Gestalt techniques -- A variety of Gestalt therapy procedures have been used, especially the **empty chair procedure** whereby the client is asked to imagine her "younger self" seated in the empty chair next to her (as in the case of a victimized child of child sexual abuse). The client is asked to talk to the child and help the child develop a different perspective. Ask the child what is happening? How is she feeling? What does she need? How would she like things to change? What is she doing to survive, to cope? This exercise provides the basis for discussion of how the client can use this information in dealing with her current stressors. There are many variations on who is put in the **empty chair** by the client. Therapists have asked clients to dialogue with the other part of herself, with the protective self, with the perpetrator, even in front of her family indicating what she still wants and needs. The empty chair may be supplemented with role playing, psychodrama as in the instance of dialoguing with a parent who was not there when she was needed.

Scurfield; Serok

Marital and family therapy; multi-family therapy

Figley; Imber-Black et al.; Goenjian

Hypnosis and hypnotherapy

Brende; Brom et al.; Dolan; Eisen; Frankel; Hammond; O'Hanlon; Putnam & Loewenstein; Silon; Spiegel; Spiegel & Cardena

Solution-focused and strategic therapy

de Shazer; Dolan; Kingsbury

Reauthoring therapy

Epston; Gergen; O'Hanlon; White

Transcendal Meditation

Brooks & Scarano

Abreactive treatments -- use narcosynthesis with clients who have complete or partial amnesia or who have recurrent violent episodes that are triggered by trauma-related stimuli, especially if the patient had been drinking beforehand. A videotape is made of the entire session and later reviewed and processed by the patient and therapist.

Kolb

Posttraumatic therapy

Ochberg

Reintegration therapy

Meiselman

General skills multimodal training -- An example of such a skills-oriented treatment program was offered by Flannery et al. (1993), called **Project SMART**. This structured psychoeducational stress-reduction group approach consists of 8-10 sessions, 90 minutes each, of 8-10 clients. The treatment approach adopts a holistic model designed to help traumatized clients control their symptoms (use coping skills of telling their "stories", relaxation) fosters self-care (exercise, diet), bolsters self-efficacy (use stress-inoculation skills, address unexpressed anger), and encourages the use of social supports. The clients receive handouts and workbooks that include descriptions of the physiology of stress, information about PTSD, descriptions of coping behaviors). The treatment ends with the group members reviewing their progress (nurture self-attributional statements), a reassessment of pretests, and a small farewell party. Comparative outcome data of Project SMART, especially relative to other treatments, or relative to a matched credible control group is limited or absent. (But this is true of almost all the treatment procedures enumerated in this Table.)

Draucker; Flannery; Loo; Schwarz & Prout; Scott & Stradling; Walker

Group psychotherapy, rap, self-help groups, Outward Bound activities. (See Egendorf, 1975, Lifton, 1973, and Shatan, 1973 for a description of rap groups. See comments below on the potential benefits of group interventions and general discussion of group procedures by Rose, 1989, and Yalom, 1985.)

Brandt; Brende; Caul; Cole; Goodwin & Talwar; Herman & Shatzow; Mann et al.; Mennen & Meadow; Motta; Pearlman & Charney; Scrignar; Singer; Smith; Tsai & Wagner;

Community-wide and school-based interventions

van der Kolk de Jong; Klingman; Joyner & Swenson (Hurricane Hugo Outreach Support Project) APA-Red Cross Intervention; Pynoos; Weisaeth; Wenckstern & Leenaars; WHO

Outpatient clinic established to treat refugees and victims of state terrorism. For example, Kinzie (1994) describes the University of Oregon's psychiatric clinic that was established to treat Southeast Asian refugees. They found that 70% of the clinic clientele were suffering from PTSD.

Agger & Jensen, Kinzie

Family-based interventions (outreach programs, multiservice casework approach including direct advocacy, parent and sibling support groups, family therapy)

Getzel & Masters; Masters et al.

Family support centers (Families may endure more stress than troops and homecoming may be more stressful than departure)

Figley

Ritualistic approaches -- testimony rituals, sweat lodge, memorials, revisit the scene, talk to other survivors, read survivor literature, survivor mission (e.g., Mothers Against Drunk Driving MADD), make amends, Holocaust museum. Novac et al. (1994) have noted the variety of self-help groups and social activities that Holocaust survivors and their off-spring engage in that serve a "healing function" (e.g., providing help to Jewish Family Service, doing research on the Holocaust, teaching children about the Holocaust, and participating in leaderless groups).

Agger & Jensen; Cienfugas; Oberchain & Silver; Silver & Wilson (See description below of ceremonial ritual for soldiers and testimony ritual for political refugees who were victimized.)

Art and movement therapies (write story, poetry, draw, paint, dance, journaling) (See Section VII on how art has been used with children who are victims of war, fires, etc.) Johnson et al. (1994) in describing work with Vietnam veterans, highlight the need for public presentation of the veteran's art products. Such public presentations are ways to become reengaged. Kathriner (1991) describes how he has Vietnam combat veterans bring their art work (e.g., drawings) to group so they can use their works of art as a way "to speak of the terror they have experienced." But the use of art is not only a means of emotionally sharing, but also away to "reconstruct." For example, he encourages the veterans to draw **a bridge** in their picture which symbolized the veteran's hopes, goals, and progress in the program. If the clients are hesitant to engage in such drawings, characterizing it as "child's play", Kathriner suggests that this be reframed as a way for the clients to go back to their childhood (perhaps when the past was more supportive). "There are no mistakes, no art expression is wrong or inadequate." *(See the discussion of the use of art work in Section VII on post-disaster interventions.)*

Barath; Golub; Johnson; Kathriner; Landecker; Lerner; Matsakis; Spring; Yates & Pawley; Zelmut & Metrick

Relapse prevention programs -- simultaneous treatment of substance abuse

Aboytes; Bollerud; Jellinck & Williams, Kofoed et al.; Ruzek et al.; Schnitt & Nocks

Sexual Dysfunction Therapy

Becker & Skinner; Kirschners

Cross-cultural counseling

Kinzie; Westermeyer

Brief Inpatient Programs (e.g., 28 day cognitive-behavioral program to 3 to 6 month programs)

Alford et al.; Lipton; Scurfield et al.

Multifaceted residential treatment program that combine a milieu, self-help and network therapy. This 1 month program (called Project Koach) is described in detail in the April 1992 issue of Journal of Traumatic Stress (Volume 5, No. 2 and Volume 7, No. 1). The treatment took place 4 years after the end of the Lebanon war.

Solomon and colleagues

Integrative Biopsychosocial Approach	Schwartz; Marmor et al.
Integrative Bodywork (Massage) Therapy and Psychotherapy	Timms & Connors
Pastoral Care and 12-Step Programs	Fly, Parlatz; Sinclair; Brende & McDonald; Sorenson
Self-help books for "victims", family members, parents of children who report sexual abuse, and the like. Some books use a workbook format; others inform about PTSD and the possible aftermath of mutual hurt, mistrust, stigmitization and the value of designing "healing rituals"	Bass & Davis; Catherall; Flannery; Grubman-Black; Lees; Lew; Matsakis (See the book review section of the <u>Journal of Traumatic Stress</u> for reviews of these and other books, e.g., January 1994 issue)
Self-help audiotapes -- musical depiction of how a young woman copes with the victimization of sexual abuse as told over several songs	Wheatley, 1993; audiotape "Break the chain"
Outward bound programs	Rheault
Other intervention possibilities include **political action, community development, general education and crisis counseling**	Norris and Thompson

PHARMACOLOGICAL INTERVENTIONS FOR PTSD

The literature on pharmacological interventions for clients with PTSD is quite extensive and complex. The literature recognizes that **different medications appear to affect specific symptom clusters in PTSD**. With this in mind the most practical and thoughtful discussion that I could find is by Kudler and Davidson (1994). They present a decision-tree that clinicians can use in prescribing medication and how these decisions have to be individually tailored for clients with PTSD. Their proposed first line of intervention is the use of antidepressants (e.g., Amitriptyline) which they propose should be used for at least 8 weeks before moving onto another class of antidepressants. They note that while depressed patients usually respond to antidepressant medication within 2 to 4 weeks, PTSD clients may take a longer period. They describe how the clinician needs to collaborate with the patient and his/her family in the monitoring of medication effects (sleep, startle, intrusive ideation, avoidant behaviors), and how pharmacological interventions need to be integrated with other forms of psychosocial intervention.

In determining both the types (combinations) dosage and timing of pharmacological interventions they propose some basic questions that the clinician should ask:

1)   What is most bothersome to the patient?

2)   Is there a reason not to prescribe this particular medication (namely, any contraindications, costs--financial and side-effects)?

3)   Is the patient better than he/she was before taking the medication?

See Kudler and Davidson (1994) for a description of the answers to these questions for different classes of medication (e.g., different classes of Antidepressants--tricyclics, selective serotonin reuptake inhibitors, MAOIs), anxiolytics, sleep aids, ways to decrease autonomic arousal, mood stabilizers, and antipsychotics). Their discussion highlights the complex sequential strategy that is being followed in the pharmacological treatment of PTSD and the need to provide continual monitoring. Two observations are worth highlighting. One is their discussion of the search for predictors of response to treatment (e.g., avoidant behaviors are indicators of poor prognosis) and the need for caution in the use of medication to treat acute stress reactions.

With the discussion of Kudler and Davidson (1994) as prologue, we can now consider the variety of specific medications that have been used with PTSD clients. In considering the following list it is worth repeating the conclusions drawn by Solomon and Shalev (1994). They highlight the preliminary and often contradictory outcome results of pharmacotherapy with PTSD. They note that such **inconsistencies** may be due in part to the fact that the pharmacological treatment of PTSD may take a long period of time and the various clinical trials have not been sufficiently long. Given the current state of the art, they conclude:

"Overall, the effect of pharmacological agents on PTSD is **at best palliative**. Pharmacotherapy alone is rarely sufficient for complete remission" (p.16)

This conclusion is consistent with that offered by Vargas and Davidson (1993) who observed:

"Pharmacotherapy alone is rarely sufficient to provide complete remission of PTSD. Once the illness has become chronic, it is likely that drug therapy will need to be long-term (at least one year's duration)." (p. 744). In considering discontinuation of medication, the therapist considers the "degree of symptom remission, consequences of relapse, progress made in psychotherapy, freedom from ongoing stresses, and drug side-effects."

Davidson and Baum (1994) similarly conclude:

> "Many drug protocols have been tested and have provided patients some relief, but **long-term drug treatment for PTSD seems unlikely at this time**" (p.366).

When medication is used, Sutherland and Davidson (1994) observed that:

> "drugs that have serotoninergic action are more likely to achieve positive effects and that there is a tendency for efficacy to emerge with longer treatment periods (at least 5 to 8 weeks) and higher doses of medication" (p. 413).

They also note that the response to pharmacotherapy of PTSD is relatively slow. It may take **8 weeks or longer for beneficial effects** of drug treatment to become evident with chronic PTSD. In some instances of chronic PTSD the prolonged use of medication may be warranted.

Table 2

Summary of Treatment Guidelines

Pharmacological treatments are designed to control:	See Solomon et al., 1992; Sutherland & Davidson, 1994; See Lipton, 1994, pages 193-201 for a discussion of what the physician might relate to the patient.
a) insomnia, exaggerated startle response, difficulty concentrating, reexperiencing symptoms	
b) physiological hyperreactivity and avoidance of stimuli that resemble original traumatic event	
c) tonic hyperreactivity of the sympathetic nervous system	
d) reduce explosiveness and elevate mood (e.g., see Shay, 1992, who successfully used Fluoxetine[1] with Vietnam veterans.)	
Consider the following guidelines for the use of medication which often consists of **multi-drug therapy**	Saporta & Case, 1993; Solomon et al., 1992; Vargas & Davidson, 1993 (See Davidson, 1993, American Journal of Psychiatry, 150, 1024-1029 for a discussion of predictors to response.)

---

[1] van der Kolk and his colleagues (1994), in a recent unpublished study, reported on the therapeutic benefits of the anti-depressant **Fluoxetine** with PTSD clients. Fluoxetine, as noted, is a serotonin re-uptake blocker that reduced overall PTSD symptomatology, especially arousal and numbing symptoms and associated features in both male and female, veteran (VA outpatient clinic) and nonveteran (hospital trauma clinic) clients, relative to a double-blind placebo control group. The therapeutic benefits of Fluoxetine were most evident in the **Trauma Clinic sample** within 5 weeks of treatment. They evidenced "substantial improvement in both numbing and depression", while the VA sample only became less depressed, but there was no meaningful change in numbing symptoms. Overall, the trauma clinic population responded more favorably to the treatment. van der Kolk et al. highlight the need to consider the nature of the traumatic stressor, the length of prior treatment, the chronicity and severity of the presenting symptoms, and the confounding effects of receiving disability benefits, when evaluating the outcomes of any treament intervention.

Frank et al., 1990

Specific medications:[1]

i) Tricyclic antidepressants (TCAs) (imipramine) -- reduce specific PTSD symptoms such as hyperarousal, intrusive recollections, flashbacks and traumatic nightmares, but **less effect on avoidant symptoms and emotional numbing** (avoidance, memory disturbance, impulse control). Note that maximum benefits from medication is not likely to be acheived in less than 3 weeks and medication should be taken continually for at least 8 weeks. Medication may be required for 8 to 10 weeks before improvement is seen.

ii) MAO Inhibitors (Phenelzine) -- reduce intrusive rather than avoidant symptoms and reduction in general hyperarousal anxiety and depressive symptoms. Requires dietary restrictions, alcohol and medication abstention. Note, Phenelzine is the most intensely studied drug for treatment of PTSD.

iii) Serotonergic drugs such as Fluoxetine and Amitriptyline which are useful in improvement of avoidance symptoms.

iv) Propranolol -- acts centrally and peripherally at beta-receptors, an adrenergic beta-blocker -- diminish sympathetic nervous system arousal and is an effective treatment for anxiety and panic disorder.

v) Other drugs used include Clonidine, Naltrexone, Carbamazepine, Lithium, Alprazolam. Clonidine (Catapres) which acts centrally on the brain is an adrenergic agonist or adrenergic blocking agent. It has been found to be useful in treating traumatized adult war veterans and Cambodian war refugees (Terr, 1989). Carbamazepine and Lithium may be effective in managing poor regulation of impulses. Alprazolam carries with it the risk of addiction and chemical dependence and "its short half-life increases the risk for rebound anxiety and serious withdrawal symptoms" (Solomon et al., 1992, p. 634). Naltrexone, a long-lasting opioid antagonist should be used with caution with persons with a history of trauma (Ibarra et al., 1994).

vi) While other anxiety disorders such as panic disorder and agoraphobia show significant response to placebo in drug trials, patients with PTSD are much less responsive to placebo medication reflecting the refractory nature of PTSD.

vii) Medication is often used to treat various forms of comorbidity -- anxiety, depression, guilt, rage

---

[1] See Gadow (1991) and Roth (1988) for a discussion of psychopharmacology with children and adolescents.

SUGGESTED MEDICATIONS FOR THE TREATMENT OF THE EARLY
SYMPTOM COMPLEX FOR POSTTRAUMATIC STRESS RELATED SYMPTOMS *

Target Symptom	Medication	Dosage
Acute		
Hyperarousal	Clonidine	0.1 - 0.4 mg/day
Anxiety/Panic	Propranolol	40 - 160 mg/day
	Clonazepam	1 - 8 mg/day
Insomnia	Flurazepam	30 mg/hs
	Temazepam	30 mg/hs
Agitation	Lorazepam	1 - 8 mg/day
	Haloperidol	2 - 20 mg/day
Chronic		
Re-experiencing	TCAs (tricyclic antidepressants)	50 - 250 mg/day
	phenelzine	30 - 90 mg/day
Avoidance, Explosiveness	Fluoxetine**	20 - 80 mg/day
Depression	TCA	150 - 250 mg/day
	TCA + Lithium	
	TCA + thyroid	

* From Friedman & Charney, 1991

** van der Kolk reports that while Tricyclic antidepressants (imipramine) were effective on intrusive PTSD symptoms and amitryptiline on numbing PTSD symptoms, **fluoxetine proved to be most effective for the whole spectrum of PTSD symptoms.** Often a stepwise strategy of pharmacotherapy is used with most effects on symptoms of reexperiencing and hyperarousal and less of an effect on avoidance behaviors.

See Meichenbaum & Turk (1987) Facilitating Treatment Adherence for a discussion of what the prescribing physician and the adjunct counselors need to do to increase the likelihood that the client will indeed take the prescribed medication. See the specific guidelines on what clients have to be told in order to insure that they will take the medication as prescribed.

GENERAL EVALUATIVE COMMENTS ON THE TREATMENT
OF CLIENTS WITH PTSD

Pharmacological Interventions

In Section I we examined the biological impact of traumatic events as reviewed by van der Kolk (1993) and others. PTSD has been characterized as a psychophysiological disturbance as evident by increased arousal, hypersensitivity, pervasive outbursts, numbing responses and reexperiencing (Silver et al., 1990). As a psychobiological event it can produce potentially long-term neurobiological changes. These findings have given rise to the promise of pharmacological interventions as a means of providing symptomatic relief to clients who have PTSD and PTSD + DES. In the same way that we should maintain a critical stance when evaluating various forms of psychotherapy (e.g., see my critique of Eye Movement Desensitization), we should also not be swayed uncritically by more biological interventions. There is clearly a place for medication in the clinical armamentarium, but the treatment decision to use medication with clients with PTSD should be fully informed by the literature. Consider the following set of observations.

1.   At the time of a review by Solomon et al. (1992) there were only 5 double-blind, placebo-controlled clinical trials of pharmacotherapies for PTSD. Four of these studies have been of antidepressants (tricyclics, phenelzine sulfate and monoamine oxidase inhibitor). Only 134 people with PTSD have been enrolled in published double-blind studies, most of them being Vietnam combat veterans (van der Kolk, in press). More recently Sutherland and Davidson (1994) reported 6 placebo-controlled studies (5 used antidepressants and 1 benzodiazepine).

2.   Few pharmacological studies actually assess the adequacy of the double-blind, and those studies that have typically have found that it was not maintained (Munoz et al., 1994).

3.   In pharmacological studies of depression when investigators have used an active pill-placebo to better mimic the kind of side effects produced by active medications, the evidence for the effectiveness of medication relative to the active placebo is reduced (Munoz et al., 1994). We do not know whether these findings would also apply in the treatment of PTSD.

4.   Ethnicity, gender and developmental stage all influence the effectiveness of psychotropic medications and it is not clear how these differences impact pharmacological treatment of PTSD (see Munoz et al., 1994).

5.   Meichenbaum and Turk (1987) review a line of studies by Buckalew and his colleagues that indicate that it is not only the pharmacological features of medication that is critical to its effectiveness, but also its "visible properties". **Medication**, like all forms of treatment, **can have meaning ascribed to them**. Consider that research indicates that when pharmacologically equivalent medication is altered in terms of its visible properties, differential patient responses are evident. For example, while holding the pharmacological features constant, investigators have manipulated the **size, form** (pills or tablets), and even the **color** of psychotropic medication, each of which affected treatment outcome. For example, it has been found that symptoms of anxiety show most improvement when green tablets are used, whereas depressive symptoms respond best to yellow tablets; blue tablets are associated with a depressant tranquilizer effect and red and yellow are best suited for stimulant, anti-depressant effects. White tablets prove to be least effective. Moreover, capsules are viewed as being significantly "stronger" than pills. In short, **medications may have more than pharmacological effects**.

6. There is more to pharmacotherapy than choosing an appropriate medication and dosage level. The quality of the doctor-patient relationship is critical to the effectiveness of the medication (see Fawcett et al., 1987; Lipton, 1994; Meichenbaum & Turk, 1987; Rickels, 1968). For example, Lipton (1994) highlights the value of providing adherence counseling when prescribing medication. He tells patients with PTSD that "the medication will <u>not</u> change the way they think, nor solve their problems. The medication is designed **"to help you feel better, sleep better, calm you down in order to deal more effectively with problems, and make you more amenable to psychotherapy. When you are excited and agitated it is difficult to think clearly and be objective."** See Meichenbaum and Turk (1987) for a more detailed description of how physicians can talk to patients whenever they prescribe medication. There is a critical need for non-medical personnel (e.g., psychotherapists) to undertake **adherence counseling** with their patients.

7. <u>How to Increase the Likelihood of Patient Compliance and Treatment Adherence</u>

    At a minimum, patients who are taking psychotropic medication should know the following: (Provide this information not only orally, but in written form.)

    a) The medication's name.

    b) The purpose of taking the medication (what treatment goals will be achieved by taking the medication).

    c) A brief description of how the medication works (in nontechnical terms).

    d) Educate the client about the time delay before benefits are evident (several weeks). In some clients it is important to educate the client about the need for long-term therapy and the general slow response to medication.

    e) Selecting the correct type and dosage of medication should be a **collaborative process** between client, family, and the doctor. (When the client is on an inpatient program, the mental health staff should be enlisted as collaborators in providing feedback about medication effects.)

    f) How often to take the dose and at what times of the day to take it.

    g) How long to take the medication and whether a refill is required or optional.

    h) Warnings about foods, drugs and activities to avoid when taking the medication.

    i) *What to do if the patient misses taking a dose or misses taking medication for a* day or more.

    j) Most likely side-effects and what can be done to address these.

    k) Telephone number of his/her doctor to call if want more information about effects of medication.

8. Assess for history of adherence in taking medication. Since previous noncompliance predicts future noncompliance, there is a need to conduct a compliance/adherence history. This is especially critical when we learn that 80% of physicians overestimate their patient's level of adherence. There is a need to systematically assess for patient

compliance. For example, Morisky et al. (1986) suggest the following 4 questions be asked:

a)   Do you ever forget to take your medicine?

b)   Are you careless at times about taking your medicine?

c)   When you feel better, do you sometimes stop taking your medicine?

d)   Sometimes if you feel worse when you take the medicine do you stop taking it?

9.   The following list of references discuss the issues of compliance/adherence in more detail.

a)   Haynes, R.B. et al. (1987). A critical review of interventions to improve compliance with prescribed medications. Patient Education and Counseling, 10, 155-166.

b)   Meichenbaum, D., & Turk, D. (1987). Facilitating treatment adherence: A practitioner's guidebook. New York: Plenum Press.

c)   Morisky, D.E. et al. (1986). Concurrent and predictive validity of a self-reported measure of medication adherence. Medical Care, 24, 67-74.

d)   Morrow, D. et al. (1988). Adherence and medication instructions: Review and recommendations. Journal of American Geriatric Society, 36, 1147-1160.

GENERAL EVALUATIVE COMMENTS
Exposure-Based Interventions

A central premise behind exposure-based interventions is that PTSD encompasses not only fear of trauma-relevant stimuli, but perhaps more importantly, **a fear of the memory of the trauma** (Rothbaum & Foa, 1992). Thus, treatments that expose clients to fearful memories, either imaginally or in vivo, will facilitate change. Indeed, exposure-based interventions have demonstrated reductions in PTSD clients' levels of distress, intrusive memories, and physiological arousal. The **effectiveness** of exposure therapies have been primarily with **combat veterans, rape victims and children living in a war zone,**[1] while their effectiveness with other populations such as accident victims and adult survivors of child abuse have <u>not</u> yet been demonstrated (see Blake, 1993 for a review). These interventions have been primarily effective in reducing so-called "positive" symptoms of PTSD (namely, psychophysiological arousal and startle response, intrusive thoughts, nightmares and anger). Changes in "negative" symptoms of PTSD are less evident (namely, psychic numbing, alienation, and restricted affect). Green et al. (1980) have observed that "positive" and "negative" symptoms of PTSD may have different determinants and different courses and this may contribute to their differential response to treatment.

Solomon et al. (1992) have noted that direct therapy exposure may be **contraindicated** for patients who have a history of psychiatric disorders. A survey of therapists expert with DTE by Litz et al. (1990) indicated the following client characteristics as possible **"warning signs"** against the use of DTE. They included:

i)   current substance abuse and history of impulsivity
ii)   ongoing life crises (e.g., suicidality)
iii)   failed previous treatment with DTE
iv)   a history of noncompliance
v)   a recent claim for compensation
vi)   difficulty using imagery
vii)   absence of reexperiencing symptoms
viii)   inability to tolerate intense arousal
ix)   as well as a history or presence of a co-existing psychiatric disorder

Allen and Bloom (1994) noted that exposure techniques are contraindicated by "marked psychological dysfunction, personality disorder, suicidality, impulsiveness, substance abuse, or treatment resistance) (p. 428).

Similar concerns have been raised by Pitman et al. (1991), who reported that 6 of 20 combat-related PTSD patients treated with flooding experienced serious complications including retraumatization, increased anxiety and panic symptoms, alcohol abuse, and obsessional thinking. As a result of such findings, much care is required in selecting candidates for direct therapeutic exposure. For example, Litz et al. (1990) proposed that

> "The ideal exposure candidate can provide a concise description of the traumatic event(s), had no debilitating concurrent diagnosis (psychiatric, Axis I or II; or medical, e.g., heart desease), possesses adequate motivation for change, and has demonstrable psychophysiological reactivity to specific, re-experienced traumatic memories." (p. 91)

---

[1] See Saigh 1987a,b, 1989b.

Note that these are stringent criteria that may not readily include the diverse clinical population found in many VA hospitals and vet centers.

Thus in some cases exposure-based interventions may make clients worse. For instance, when repeated reexposure results in intolerable arousal, increased shame and guilt (see Davidson et al., 1993; Pitman et al., 1991). Also see Kilpatrick and Best (1984) for cautionary observations on treating sexual abuse victims with exposure-based interventions. Dutton (1992) has also cautioned about the use of exposure-based interventions with victims of domestic violence. *(In Section VI, I will review the specific treatment procedures of Direct Therapy Exposure.)*

An important point to keep in mind when considering exposure-based interventions (or for that matter any interventions) is the need to insure that the **client is a collaborator** throughout treatment. As we will consider in Section VII, some clients may be reluctant to mentally "relive" and "reexperience" the trauma-related events in the course of treatment. Clients may resist doing so-called "memory work" of traumatic events. There is a danger of the therapist "pushing" his/her agenda of the way to conduct treatment without "spelling out" the options for the client, and without preparing clients for such interventions. **For example, there is a need to insure that clients have stabilized their symptoms and their situation, have engaged in "self-care" work, bolstered their self-esteem, before undertaking exposure-based interventions.** Clearly, as we shall see, there is some value in helping clients reexperience and reintegrate traumatic events in their narrative, but this therapeutic process needs to be collaborative, with the clients being "informed" and "in charge" throughout. At this point we do not know how best to combine exposure-based interventions with other forms of treatment.

The **need for such collaboration is underscored** even in a simple treatment example offered by Flannery et al. (1993). They observed that when conducting **relaxation training** with victimized clients of sexual abuse, the therapist used the word "relax" as a cue for engaging in the progressive muscular and deep breathing relaxation exercises. For some clients, the word "relax" had been used by the perpetrator of the assault, and thus, had the opposite effect in treatment. Thus, there is a need to explain to the client exactly what is going to happen and why, and solicit reactions and suggestions. When in vivo exposure is used it is important to insure that clients are not put into dangerous situations.

GENERAL EVALUATIVE COMMENTS

Eye Movement Desensitization and Reprocessing (EMD/R): Some Cautionary Observations

The clinician is confronted with a dilemma and challenge when it comes to treating clients with PTSD. While the client's needs are self-evident, specific treatment guidelines based on well-controlled comparative outcome studies are limited, if not absent (see Blake, 1993). Moreover, therapists of diverse theoretical persuasions have each promoted their specific forms of intervention. Perhaps, no treatment approach has generated more heated debate than that of Dr. Francine Shapiro's **Eye Movement Desensitization and Reprocessing (EMD/R).** Since its introduction in 1987, some 8000 clinicians in America, Israel and Australia have been trained in EMD/R. On the one hand there are remarkable testimonials attesting to "undeniable miracles of EMD/R" as a means of rapidly resolving traumas (sometimes within a single one-hour treatment session) that have ruled people's lives for 20 years (Butler, 1993). While "EMD/R seems to work best with healthy adults who have suffered a single trauma -- a car accident, a mugging, a hurricane", it has been extended to a wide array of other populations who have experienced Type II stressors and such diverse clinical problems as agoraphobia and depression (Butler, 1993, p. 20; Marquis, 1991). In fact, Steketee and Goldstein (1994) report its applicability to clients with panic symptoms and Kleinknecht (1993) with phobic clients.[1]

In contrast, to such enthusiastic endorsements, (see Shapiro, 1994b, Puk, 1994) those who have examined the basis of such claims have **proposed caution.** They have noted that **the enthusiasm far outreaches the data in the case of EMD/R.** Before we consider their concerns and the basis for their call for clinicians to proceed judiciously, we will pause briefly to describe Shapiro's EMD/R. What is the nature of the treatment procedure that has led some 8000 clinicians to pay over $200 each for both introductory and advanced EMD/R training? What form of treatment can in one, or in a few sessions, so reverse years of emotional pain and maladjusted functioning due to exposure to traumatic events?

EMD/R is a variant of exposure-based interventions. It combines having clients envision traumatic scenes, focus on sensations of anxiety, cognitive restructuring and engage in directed saccadic ege movements. More specifically, according to Shapiro (1989) and Page and Crino (1993) EMD/R requires patients to focus on a traumatic memory and generate a statement summarizing their thoughts about the trauma (e.g., "I should have done X.", "I'm powerless.", "I am out of control."). Patients are then instructed to visualize the traumatic scene, briefly rehearse the belief statement that best summarizes their memories, concentrate on the associated physical sensations, and visually track the therapist's index finger. The finger is moved rapidly and rhythmically back and forth across the person's line of vision from extreme left to extreme right at a distance of 30-35 cm from the patient's face and at a rate of two back and forth movements per second. This is repeated 12-24 times after which the patient is requested to blank the picture out and take a deep breath. At the same time, the client is asked to focus on the bodily experience associated with the image, as well as on an incompatible belief statement (e.g., "I did the best I could.", "It's in the past.", "I learned from what happened.", "I'm in control."). The therapist then records the level of patients' discomfort on a Subjective Units of Distress (SUDs) scale, and, if it has not decreased, checks that the scene has not changed. If it has changed the procedure is repeated with the new scene before returning to the old one. (See Shapiro, 1989, for more detailed procedural guidelines. For example, she notes that besides eye movements, other rhythmic motor responses such as tapping alternate hands on a chair rest or broadcasting alternating tones in a client's ear can be used or using alternating lights.)

---

[1] See a recent (August, 1994) newsletter published by the EMD/R Institute enumerating other applications.

As part of the reprocessing, the client may be asked to remember the most distressing picture associated with the traumatic event such as a rape, to identify the bodily and affectively charged feelings and cognitions associated with the incident (e.g., "I'm helpless."; "I am going to die."; "It's my fault."). Then, during the reprocessing phase, the client chooses an incompatible positive thought to focus on such as, "It's past; I survived"; "I have control"; "I'm going to live." Patients are asked to recall the image and descriptive statements as well as any residual affect and provide a new SUD rating. The procedure is repeated until SUDs ratings are reduced to 1 or 2 on a 0 to 10 point scale. In addition, ratings of validity in the beliefs are obtained. Jensen (1994) describes how Vietnam veterans treated with EMD/R focused on such belief statements as "I was inadequate," "I will never forgive myself." In lieu of these belief statements clients come to associate the traumatic picture with statements such as "I did what I could to save my buddy."

The rationale offered clients in explaining these procedures is that "traumatic events may become **locked** in the traumatized individual's nervous system, and that visually tracking the therapist's fingers may be a means of 'unlocking' the event, ultimately causing the individual to recall the event in a different, less traumatic way" (Shapiro, 1990a) (as reported by Jensen, 1994). (*Note: that this rationale is incompatible with what we know about how memory works from a constructive perspective. It is not as if events, even traumatic events, get "engraved" or "locked" in one's nervous system*). Shapiro (1994a) highlights that EMD/R contains many components besides the eye-movements (e.g., "attention to negative and positive self-attributions, somatic manifestations, issues of self-control/self-esteem, and much more").

As noted, improvement has been reported after brief one session interventions lasting only 45 to 90 minutes with individuals who have experienced single trauma events. It is claimed that when treating patients who have experienced a single traumatic experience only 1 to 4 sessions with EMD/R are generally necessary. With Type II stressors, more long-term intervention is employed or as Shapiro (1994a) has noted recently, "no prolonged molestation victim or traumatized Vietnam veteran can be fully treated in this manner" (p.154).

Before adopting this form of treatment the critically-minded clinician should consider the following findings and conclusions offered by authors who have reviewed the literature on EMD/R, and in turn, Shapiro's response (1993).

Boudewyns et al. (1993) and Jensen (1994) have systematically assessed EMD/R with Vietnam combat veterans and found that while it is effective in reducing subject's subjective distress in the clinic/laboratory, **neither psychological (standardized measures assessing PTSD), nor psychophysiological outcome measures, supported the effectiveness of EMD/R.**

Acierno et al. (1994), in a recent comprehensive review of EMD/R, concluded:

"In contrast to results obtained from case studies, controlled experiments utilizing objective and subjective dependent measures have **failed to support the efficacy** of the EMD/R technique beyond that its imaginal exposure component (p.287) ... Despite these scientific weaknesses, widespread adoption and distribution of EMD/R persists (p.297)."

Moreover, they go on to highlight that unbiased replication of EMD/R "is impeded by Shapiro's practice of prohibiting individuals not associated with her EMD/R Institute from training others in the technique". **They caution against the marketing of EMD/R as a prescriptive technique for the treatment of PTSD or any other trauma-related anxiety.**

These general conclusions have been echoed by many other reviewers. For example:

"Overall then, broad claims for EMD/R efficacy are premature" (Steketee & Goldstein, 1994, p. 156).

"While the interest and enthusiasm which eye movement desensitization has generated is substantial, the **amount of empirical research evaluating the procedure is small.** In addition, the quality of the research to assess its **validity is meager** both in terms of assessment variables and the control of extraneous factors inherent in the clinical procedure." (Lohr et al., 1993, p. 166)

"Until the results of more methodologically sound studies are available, we recommend that clinicians approach the use of eye movement desensitization with due reserve." (Herbert & Mueser, 1992, p. 174)

"We urge therapists to be cautious in uncritically accepting strong claims about the efficacy of eye movement desensitization, especially in the light of the availability of other empirically demonstrated treatments for PTSD and related conditions (e.g., Cooper & Clum, 1989; Keane et al., 1989; Foa et al., 1991)." (Mueser & Herbert, in press, p. 2)

Page and Crino (1993) note that EMD/R workshops are being conducted and "certified" practitioners are using EMD/R with all types of clients. But they caution that, "the speed with which the technique is being assimilated into clinical practice in the **absence of firm evidence of efficacy** is both surprising and disturbing." (p. 291)

"In summary, we recommend extreme caution in embracing, using, or endorsing EMD/R." (Metter & Michelson, 1993, p. 415)

After concluding, **"to date there are no good controlled outcome studies that establish EMD/R as an effective intervention"**, Marafiote (1993) takes Shapiro to task for promoting and training therapists on an unproven procedure. Others have taken Shapiro to task for the manner in which she provides training to professionals.[1] For example, see Rosen (1992) who also observed that Shapiro's claim that EMD/R is different from a form of hypnosis is **"unsubstantiated"**, "yet this and other claims have promoted an **almost cultist enthusiasm for the new movement**" (p. 216).

In addition to these cautionary statements, it is worth noting that a series of recent dismantling studies by Richard Spates and his colleagues at Western Michigan University have indicated that the eye movements are not essential to treatment outcome. A similar conclusion derives a comparative study by Pittman et al., 1993. Metter and Michelson (1993) report the results of a study that indicated that EMD/R was not different from controls, and possibly less efficacious than having subjects "stare at a dot on the wall". Similarly, Boudewyns et al. (1993) compared EMD/R with an imaginal exposure control group who were matched with the EMD/R group, but they did not receive saccadic eye movements. They found that on neither psychological test measures nor on the psychophysiological measures were there differences. Acierno et al. (1994) reviewed several studies that found that **the importance of eye movement was not supported.** For example, in one study eye-focus desensitization where the client focused on the therapist's finger **as it was held stationary**, rather than moving from side to side, was equally effective as EMD/R. Clearly, the role that the eye movement component plays in EMD/R needs to be reconsidered.

---

[1] Part of the controversy derives from Shapiro's training policy where therapists who wish to learn EMD/R must attend designated workshops and the participants must sign a statement promising not to train others in EMD/R.

The EMD/R is a complex treatment package and there may be clinical features that are worth keeping or exploring in more detail. For instance, Steketee and Goldstein (1994) note that EMD/R is a rapid way to access client's fear-related memories. Moreover, patients receiving EMD/R are asked to image the traumatic scene and to report the "negative" cognitions associated with the image. Patients are asked, "What words about yourself or the incident best go with the picture?" The patients are asked for their feelings associated with the image and their accompanying beliefs. For example: "I'm a horrible person."; "I can't feel safe."; and "I am out of control." The therapist also elicits the alternative belief statements that patients may try on, such as: "It was beyond my control."; "I did the best I could."; "I survived and can exercise control."; "I was not helpless. I was able to do something." Shapiro notes that initially these "positive" cognitions may not be perceived as plausible or valid by patients but with repeated exposure and control of their images the patients are more likely to accept, assimilate, reframe, and reintegrate the traumatic event.

This critique of EMD/R is designed to provide a **general warning** to investigate treatment procedures before they are broadly promoted. As Steketee and Goldstein (1994, p. 157) observe there is a **"tendency within mental health to adopt new therapies wholesale with little or no scientific evidence for their efficacy"** This Section is designed to provide a needed warning against such "wholesale" adoption.[1] Are the criticisms of EMD/R by Acierno et al., Lohr, Herbert, Mueser, Page, Crino, Metter, Michelson, Spates, Steketee and Goldstein, Jensen, Boudewyns et al., Rosen, Marafiote, and others, merely reactionary comments or are they consistent with Butler's concerns about EMD/R as being **"too good to be true"? As Doctor (1994) observes, we should "let EMD/R stand, or fall, on the empirical and clinical results" (P. 202).**

---

[1] In search of a control group for EMD/R. I have wondered what would constitute a "credible" control group to run against Shapiro's EMD/R group. Consider a therapist saying the following to a PTSD client. "I realize you have tried many diverse treatments with regard to your reactions to your traumatic event (accident, rape, etc.). I would like us to try something new that has been developed by Dr. Francine Shapiro. It is called EMD/R and I don't know if it will work in your case, but it is clearly worth our trying. It has been used successfully with many clients like yourself who have experienced traumatic events.

Dr. Shapiro observed that people who have experienced traumatic events often have difficulty sleeping. They often have bad dreams, nightmares, a fear of falling asleep, multiple awakenings, and difficulty falling back to sleep. One of the things we know is that during sleep people engage in what is called rapid eye movement or REM sleep where their eyes move in a rapid fashion from left to right and from right to left. Have you heard of REM sleep? One day when Dr. Shapiro was daydreaming she discovered that if she could just keep her eyes "relatively still", so that they don't flirt from right to left, and from left to right, a sense of calm and ease overcame her. Moreover, she realized that if she thought about some of the stressful things that had happened to her at the time she was exerting this eye control, the strong emotions tied to her bad memories changed. It was as if these memories lost their devastating charge. The bad memories became like a book or a movie that she had read in the past. The bad events seem to shrink in both size and impact, as if she were watching the distressing events on a small television screen where she could control the volume and change channels if she chose.

While no one quite understands why exerting such eye control in this fashion works, it is clear that for many folks it helps. There is speculation about the connectives in the brain, corpus callosum, posterior and anterior commissures and the changes to the biochemistry of the brain, but I won't bother you with all that.

Thus, in treatment I am going to ask you to think about the "worst" scene tied to your traumatic events, your feelings and thoughts surrounding this event, and then we will work together to see if you can learn to just keep your eyes still as you image them. I will raise my finger from above your head toward your nose and then from down below toward your nose. With each pass you are to keep your eyes from engaging in the type of rapid eye movement from left to right and back again that accompanies your distressing dreams and intrusive thoughts. Later on you will learn to take over this approach so you can come to use your own finger. Moreover, given what you have been through and the "victimization" you have experienced, you can choose which finger you want to use. Some of our clients in an expression of defiance have chosen to use their middle finger. In their own way they see this as a personal statement of who is in charge of their lives, their bodies. If you can learn to control your reactions (eye movements here) what does this mean for the "rest of your life"? "

ONE OBJECTIVE OF THIS HANDBOOK/MANUAL IS TO NURTURE A CRITICAL QUESTIONING ATTITUDE TOWARD HOW WE PROCEED. WITHOUT RESEARCH WE SHOULD BE CAUTIOUS IN PROMOTING OR ENDORSING ASSESSMENT AND TREATMENT APPROACHES. IN OUR DESIRE TO BE OF HELP TO OUR CLIENTS LET US NOT LOSE TOUCH WITH OUR CRITICAL STANCE AND OUR ABILITY TO GAIN DISTANCE FROM (AND EVEN LAUGH AT) WHAT WE DO!

Ceremonial Rituals for Returning Combat Veterans[1]
(See Obenchain & Silver, 1992; Perez, 1991; Silver & Wilson, 1988)

Perez (1991) observes that "ritual refers to the ways in which individuals seek to normalize their worlds." Through ritual behavior predictability, continuity and control are sought. "Rituals (and the resultant routines) help us ground and anchor ourselves." (p. 224). Perez notes how various spiritual and social ceremonial activities help individuals maintain internal order and balance. Many different forms of rituals exist including healing, purification, reconciliation, mourning/bereavement. A number of therapists, following the suggestions of Native American Indians, have used various forms of rituals as instruments to help PTSD clients reestablish stability and control. Such rituals or ceremonials interventions may include:

a) sweat lodge ceremonies that convey an appreciation of the individual's sacrifice for others
b) confirmation of membership in the community
c) experiences viewed positively as reflecting knowledge and wisdom, not readily available to others ("lessons of survivorship that are worth salvaging")
d) ceremonies that convey valued uniqueness

Obenchain and Silver (1992) discuss the advantages of having a woman lead such as sweat lodge ceremonies with combat soldiers. A somewhat different ceremonial procedure used with combat veterans followed the model of the 12-step program.

Sorenson (1985) and Brende and McDonald (1989) have developed a 12-theme and 12-step program for combat veterans with PTSD. Using the Alcoholic Anonymous approach as a model, on an inpatient basis Brende and MacDonald conducted psychoeducational groups three times a week. Each week the theme changed (e.g., surrendering to a "higher power", seeking meaning in survival, understanding in turn such emotions as anger, rage, fear, guilt, grief, as well as finding a purpose, love and meaningful relationships). They used religious metaphors such as "surrendering one's self-destructive and self-centered life-style to God" so individuals could "gain freedom from the bondage of victimization". PTSD was viewed as an "addictive" behavior with its accompanying destructive life-style. A similar 12-step program has been developed for survivors of noncombat traumatic events. The organizers have even created a group called Trauma Survivors Anonymous. The group meetings are designed to break the "victimization cycle". The steps to be taken include:

1. Acknowledge symptoms
2. Seek help
3. Surrendering to God, as individually understood (e.g., "surrendering one's baggage")
4. Taking action
5. Daily prayer and meditation

They have also adapted the AA serenity prayer for PTSD to state:

"God, help me to accept that I have little or no power over symptoms of victimization and destructive behaviors. Help me to recognize which of these I can begin to change. Grant me the wisdom to know the difference."

They also provide individuals with daily prayers that combine surrender, acceptance, and ways of taking action. **Obviously, this mode of intervention can apply only with individuals whose personal beliefs match the tenets of a 12-step AA religious format.** (*Also see critique of AA model in Section VI*)

---

[1] Other examples of rituals and religion will be considered in Section VIII.

Treatment of Torture Victims: Testimony and Other Methods

> *"Rejected by mankind, the condemned do not go so far as to reject it in turn. Their faith in history remains unshaken, and one may well wonder why. They do not despair the proof: they persist in surviving -- not only to survive, but to testify. The victims elect to become witnesses."* (Weisel, 1965)

Systematic torture of human beings occurs in more than 60 countries throughout the world (Chester & Jaranson, 1994). It has been estimated that some 5% to 15% of the world's 14 million refugees have been sibjected to torture (Basoglu, 1992). Torture is one of the most damaging events that people can experience (see Allodi, 1994; Basoglu, 1992; Engdahl & Eberly, 1992; Page, 1992; Turner, 1989; Turner & Garst-Unsworth, 1990; van der Veer et al., 1992; Vesti & Kastrup, 1994), with as high as 70% of torture victims experiencing PTSD (flashbacks, dissociative episodes, avoidance behaviors, hypervigilance). (Pope & Garcia-Peltoniemi, 1991). Torture can have somatic and psychological impact (e.g., major depression). Vesti and Kastrup (1994) report a dose-response relationship for torture victims. The more force, injury, threat, and the longer the duration of the torture, the greater the disability. Like other traumatic events the absence of imposed meaning, and the absence of support from family and peers, also intensifies the reaction. While a few individuals undergo torture with little or no subsequent dysfunction, most show both short-term and long-term difficulties[1] . These reactions may take various forms as described by Becker (in press), and Kornfeld (in press) with torture victims from Chile, Guiao (in press) with victims from the Phillipines, and Simpson (in press) with victims from South Africa. Simpson highlights that those who sought help usually came to centers that were labeled, "Human Rights Organizations", and not Mental Health centers. Simpson also discusses the disquieting duplicity of mental health workers in torture exercises. This chilling account needs to be read widely given that Amnesty International cites 144 countries as being guilty of human rights violations.

After reviewing 46 studies, Somnier et al. (1993) describe the most characteristic psychological reactions[2] to torture as "sleep disturbance, recurrent nightmares, anxiety, depression, chronic fatigue, memory defects, loss of concentration, and changes in identity". Added to the stress of torture is also the stress of exile which has been described as a "form of torture where we each come apart; our **internal world is in pieces**. We lived **psychologically mutilated**" (as reported by Chester and Jaranson, 1994 -- note the powerful metaphors to describe horrific events).

Certain treatment centers (the Kovler Center[3] in Chicago, the Center for Victims in Minneapolis, the pioneering (1984) Centre in Copenhagen Denmark, the Centre in Toronto, London, and Amsterdam and in Argentina, Zimbabwe, Turkey, Pakistan, and Philippines) have specialized in the care of

---

[1] Allodi (1994) reports that **9 years after** a hostage-taking incident in Holland 1/2 of the victims **and** their families had symptoms of PTSD. Interestingly, nearly half of the other Dutch hostages and their families could see "positive" value deriving from the hostage-taking incident. Lenore Terr (1993) in her moving account <u>Too scared to cry</u> describes the long-term effects of kidnapping of children in the famous Chowchilla incident.

[2] Basoglu et al. (1994) have reported that despite the severity of the torture experience, the survivors had only moderate levels of psychopathology. A number of factors appear to have a protective value against PTSD in survivors of torture. These factors include prior knowledge of and preparedness for torture, strong commitment to a cause, and strong social supports.

[3] The Kovler Center in Chicago (4750 N. Sheridan Rd., Chicago, IL, 60640) puts out a newsletter on work with torture victims.

refugee victims of torture. There are now more than 60 treatment centers for torture survivors worldwide (Vesti & Kastrup, 1994).

Vesti and Kastrup (1994) highlight that torture affects all aspects of human life, and thus, a multifaceted treatment approach is required covering psychological, social and somatic treatments, as well as legal advice and spiritual guidance. They also provide some treatment guidelines for working with torture victims. These include:

1. Any procedure that may remind the survivor of the ordeal should be avoided, if possible.

2. Treatment should be both physical and psychological and the two should run parallel (e.g., medical care given to address the physical injuries, rest, physiotherapy, relaxation exercises).

3. Recognize that the symptoms may worsen when the trauma is addressed. This possibility should be anticipated and discussed with the client ahead of time.

4. Involve significant others, offering help (assessment, treatment) to spouse and children of the torture victim.

5. Address practical problems (e.g., housing, education, financial concerns, family problems). For example, while most torture victims remain in their country of origin, many find asylum in another country. With exile comes many problems that need to be addressed as illustrated by the increased divorce rate among torture victims in asylum (Vesti & Kastrup, 1994). Since many torture victims are also refugees, there is a need to also address the experience of being uprooted. Abe et al. (1994) highlighted the value of community-based interventions that foster cultural identity, social supports, information exchange, and helping survivors look for missing family members. The importance of these steps were highlighted by their finding that maintaining cultural traditions and ties were found to act as "buffers" to PTSD.

6. Treatment may be long-term, starting initially once or twice a week. Treatment focuses initially on building a trusting relationship, followed by cognitive and emotional phases that respectively, consider a detailed account of what happened followed often by affective ("abreactive") reactions. Such emotionally-laden sessions should include ample time in order to insure that the client is able to regain composure and reorient to the reality of the present, before leaving the session. Allodi (1994) proposes that "a detailed history or abreaction should not be stimulated, but if there exists already an environment of safety and a relationship of trust, the patient may wish to self-disclose, and a catharsis may follow. The patient's story should be accepted and the patient reassured that it is normal and appropriate to have such a posttraumatic reaction" (p. 283). The interview is not an interrogation, but an opportunity for the client to permit his/her "story" to unfold.

7. There is an attempt to help clients find "meaning" in the events (see Montgomery, 1992), and the description of the **testimony procedure** described below. As a result some form of "reintegration" is sought. As one treated client described to Vesti and Hastrup (1994, p.18)

> "My memories of the torture are not overwhelming me the whole time any longer; I have put them **in a drawer** that I sometimes open to look at, but it is a drawer that I can close

again. Yet, I must admit that sometimes the drawer still
springs open by itself."

*(Once again note that the client is able to use a metaphor, "the drawer", to describe
ways of coping. The literature with trauma clients is replete with examples of clients
who have improved, each providing "healing metaphors". Are such metaphors mere
epiphenomena or is the revised "story" critical to the healing process?)*

8. Herman (1992) describes how the testimony procedure has been used in a **group
    setting**, where group members are asked to narrate one another's written experiences.
    This provides an opportunity for the participants to gain a new perspective and an
    opportunity to exert some control over their emotional reactions as they listen to their
    poignant accounts being read by someone else.

9. There is a need to address issues of guilt, shame, and self-blame that may be
    experienced. Torture victims may have been forced to sign confessions, provide names
    of others, and the like. In the course of treatment clients need to recognize that they had
    "no real choice" and that everybody has a "breaking point". *(See Section VI for a
    discussion of how to treat issues of guilt.)*

10. Ex-torturers (who in turn may have been tortured) should be treated in a different
    setting and should undergo societal punishment, before treatment is provided (See
    work by Haritos-Fatouras, 1988, for a discussion of the behavior of torturers).

11. Interpreters are sometimes required. Select interpreters carefully. Do not use family
    members or relatives, nor someone who has been a torture victim him/herself. The
    interpreter will need training, supervision, and debriefing. Consistent with the goal of
    collaboration, the client is given the option to reject this specific interpreter. See van
    der Veer (in press) who, based on his experience with the Social Psychiatric Services
    for Refugees in Amsterdam, highlights a number of practical cross-cultural factors
    besides the issue of interpreters (e.g., cultural biases evident in language, symptom
    presentation, role of gifts, and the like).

12. Moreover, there is a need to be sensitive to cultural differences (use focus groups or
    advisory groups as consultants in order to understand the nature of the client's
    background. This suggestion is not only useful from a cross-cultural counseling
    perspective, but Camille Wortman describes how she **uses an advisory group** in
    her research project on parents of Sudden Infant Death Syndrome (SIDS). This
    advisory group reviews her assessment instruments, research design and objectives,
    and may even act as a go between to help solicit subjects (i.e., a "snowball sampling"
    procedure). In the case of conducting cross-cultural counseling there is a critical need
    to invite a member(s) of the particular ethnic group to observe and comment on the
    treatment sessions from their specific cultural perspective. *(In Section VII there is a
    description of such "focus groups" being used in disaster relief efforts.)*

13. Group therapy or mass commemorative meetings may be used to help victims of torture
    and their families.

Engdahl and Eberly (1992) observe that the treatment of victims of torture present particular
clinical challenges and therapists need to:

1)   insure that a trusting relationship is established and that confidentiality is insured;

2)   assess for survivor's "trauma story" and the impact of the victimization experience, especially in the possible form of somatic complaints;

3)   be sensitive to cultural differences since some victimized groups may not have words for concepts such as "stress" and "anxiety" (e.g., spouse may not know that victim was raped);

4)   help clients appreciate that their reactions (e.g., "breakdowns", "confessions") under torture are not signs of weakness, but rather are predictable and should not cause shame nor guilt;

5)   as noted, sensitize the client to the possibility that discussing torture experience may trigger increased distress, sleep disturbance, but these are usually temporary;

6)   as noted, involve family members in the treatment process.

To be added to this list of treatment guidelines, Chester and Jaranson (1994) propose:

1)   the need for "retelling, reframing, reworking, and bearing witness to the client's story";

2)   effective re-telling has to occur within a contextual framework (e.g., description of political and social events);

3)   the need for survivors to reconnect through whatever means possible, including rituals and symbols (as described below in terms of the testimony method);

4)   when a community of individuals have been tortured and victimized the intervention may need to focus on the entire community (see Teter and Arcellona, 1994).

In the U.S., Mollica[1] and his colleagues in Boston (Mollica & Lavelle, 1988) and Kinzie and his colleagues in Portland (Kinzie & Fleck, 1987) have provided specific interventions to refugee survivors from South-East Asia. In a recent article Morris et al. (1993) have noted the need for clinicians to be **sensitive to the cultural differences in treating different refugee groups**. For example, those who have provided treatment to **S.E. Asian refugees** have placed less emphasis on eliciting the refugee's story of torture, allowing it to emerge gradually. Instead, emphasis is placed on current life resettlement issues (e.g., housing, employment, welfare). Mollica and Kinzie highlight the dangers of focusing on the past at the risk of overlooking important current life problems.

In contrast, those clinicians who worked with refugees from **South America** (Chile, Argentina) have emphasized the need to explore memories of their torture experiences. One procedure that has been used to help these South American refugees to tell their stories is to use a **testimony procedure** as introduced by Cienfugos and Monelli (1983). This procedure encourages the individual to recall and work through the trauma story and put the torture experience in perspective. It helps the individual appreciate the lack of his/her freedom under torture. The testimony procedure helps the individual to reassert his/her rights. It is also important to work with the victim's spouse or family, often using different combinations of treatment.

---

[1] For example, Mollica found that 50% of his refugee patients suffered from PTSD and on average these refugee patients had experienced 10 traumatic events.

Agger and Jensen (1990, p. 120) have provided a detailed outline of how such a **personal testimony** procedure might be conducted over the course of 12-20 weekly sessions.

1. Preparation -- if a language interpreter is needed
    If possible the interpreter is introduced to the method verbally and by hand-out material (an example of a testimony or an article about the method) before the start of therapy.

2. Contact, working alliance, and reframing
    The client approves of the therapist and the interpreter and on the basis of respect and trust a forum is created for mutual exchange and for the client to provide a detailed, extensive, chronological account of the client's traumatic experiences. The therapy sessions are recorded and a verbatim script of the client's account is prepared. The client and therapist revise the document together. In this way fragmented recollections can be reframed into a coherent story. In later sessions a final written testimony is read aloud by the client. This may be followed by a "delivery ritual" where the testimony is signed by the client, the therapist, and other members.

3. The giving of the testimony
    The interpreter's translation of the client's words are either recorded on a dictating machine and written out between sessions by a secretary, or -- if these resources are not available -- are written out in hand by the therapist during sessions (if the client is very eloquent the therapist can agree with the client on a more condensed version). Each session starts with a recapitulation of the last sentences from the former session. The therapist interrupts by asking questions about emotional reactions now and then, or about situations which need clarification. Typically, a testimony will contain the following elements:

    (a) Background: Age, country of origin, social data, important political, cultural and/or religious aspects.

    (b) The situation that led up to the traumatic event.

    (c) The trauma story in details: Dates, hours, places. Description of torture methods and the reaction to them. Examples of daily life in the prison. This can be complemented with drawings of places and situations.

    (d) The flight: Why and how did the client escape.

    (e) Life in exile.

    (f) Dreams and hopes for the future and realistic possibilities.

    (g) A final statement where the client declares that this is a true account.

4. Collaboration on editing and revising the testimony
    Errors are corrected, situations are described more precisely. More therapeutic work on the emotional level may be done. The final document is written out.

5. The delivery ritual
    The document is signed by the client (is he/she does not want to be anonymous), with the interpreter and the therapist as witnesses. The document is read aloud either by the client (if language capabilities allow it) or by the interpreter. The document is handed over to the client. It is now in the possession of him or her and he/she can decide what use to make of it.

6. The private pain has become political dignity

The client can use the document for private purposes: as evidence in an asylum case or for example, as a highly motivating text in language school. He/she can also use it for political purposes: send it to international organizations of exile groups as documentation, or allow it to be used in professional contexts as informative material. When used for the latter, the client and the therapist might decide to eliminate some parts of the testimony in order to reduce the risk of further private pain through recognition.

7.   The testimony revisited
      After termination of therapy, the document can be used if the client wants to return for therapy at a later time.

      Pope and Garcia-Peltoniemi (1991) have thoughtfully discussed the important role of trust, cultural factors, medical needs, treatment interventions, and the challenges to clinicians of working with torture victims. They also list the many centers in the US and Canada that treat torture victims.

THE POTENTIAL ADVANTAGES OF GROUP TREATMENT OF PTSD

(See Allen & Bloom, 1994; Brandt, 1989; Brende, 1981; Catherall, 1986; Courchaine & Dowd, 1994; Courtois, 1988; Gold-Steinberg & Buttenheim, 1993; Koller et al., 1992; Mennen & Meadow, 1992; Roth & Newman, 1993; Scurfield, 1985; Solomon, 1992; van der Kolk, 1987; Yalom, 1985)

A major mode of intervention with individuals who have experienced traumatic events is **group therapy** that may be used alone or in conjunction with other forms of treatment such as individual treatment. Many different forms of group treatment have been used (e.g., crisis intervention, rap groups, survivor groups, couples, spouse and family groups, etc.). The groups may be open-ended, focusing on psychoeducation, or on reexperiencing past traumas (a "there and then" orientation), or be highly structured, task-oriented, with a "here-and-now" interpersonal process and coping skills focus. Sometimes, these various features (goals and procedures) are combined. Allen and Bloom (1994) have enumerated the diverse group interventions that have been used with PTSD clients. They include "Yalom-style process groups, cognitive-behavioral, psychoeducational, psychoanalytic, self-help, Jungian dream work, art, movement and psychodrama groups. They review the outcome research with group interventions that are usually combined with other forms of intervention. While they note several demonstration studies where group interventions have led to symptomatic improvement (e.g., work by Scurfield, Solomon, Marmar, Roth), they conclude that

"the most characteristic of the outcome research on group and family therapies is **how little data is available**" (p. 434).

Whatever the group format, the group process can serve a number of therapeutic purposes. The group process helps to combat the sense of isolation and uniqueness, stigmatization feelings of shame, guilt, and self-blame that many PTSD clients experience. The resolution of traumatic experience is facilitated by **the presence of survivors with the same, or a similar, set of traumatic events** (Courchaine & Dowd, 1994; Roth & Newman, 1993; Roth et al., 1988; Scurfield, 1985; Smith, 1985). Clients working together with people who have had similar experience provides a common bond, "normalizes" experiences, reduces a sense of alienation, fosters identification of common issues, provides an opportunity to share common coping techniques. In summary, **the group process can serve a variety of purposes.** More specifically these include:

a)   shared reliving of the trauma and exchange of useful constructive information in a safe place, (but note that the therapist should **not push for details too early**, but rather follow the client's lead)

b)   reduction of the sense of isolation and provision of sense of legitimacy, validation, cohesion, common purpose, comfort, and support; foster a sense of acceptance in a nonblaming supportive environment

c)   work together with others who have had similar experiences which provides a common bond -- that conveys a sense of universality

d)   reduction of feelings of stigmatization, isolation, alienation -- not feel "peculiar" or "unique"; confirm the reality of trauma experience and assign meaning to events

e)   increase social supports and shared expression of emotions and learn from others

f)   identification of common issues, share coping methods and gain insight into features of own trauma that needs resolution; process "unfinished business" in a supportive atmosphere

g) seeing others share and survive periods of intense affect is encouraging and empowering; encourages members' readiness to assume responsibility for change and decrease dependency

h) act in a helper role offering support, reassurance, suggestions and insight; restore self-pride; and develop a sense of group caring by sharing similar problems with one another (vicarious learning); combat the client's sense that he/she has "nothing to offer others"; help clients think about lives of other group members, and thus, lessen focus on negative self-ruminative thoughts and feelings of isolation

i) diminish guilt and shame and enhance a sense of trust; share grief and loss *(See discussion of guilt reactions in Section VI)*

j) resolve issues of secrecy. Herman highlights the need to have victimized clients (e.g., incest survivors) self-disclose to people besides the therapist; this underscores the further value of the group.

k) generate feelings of hope by providing participants a chance to witness individuals arrayed along a continuum of recovery; gain feelings of optimism about progress and/or potential for progress in rebalancing relationships (i.e., a safe environment to develop new attachments)

l) generate group ideology, language, slogans that enable participants to define and understand stress in a new and more optimistic fashion

m) commitment to a plan can be enhanced by clients formulating it in public (the value of conveying decision to others)

n) undertake responsibility to fulfill role of sharing in the "here and now" group discussions

o) provide opportunities for self-attributions about the changes each member has made. For example, many groups use the last few sessions to have the participants review (process) the changes they have made.

  i)   "How has each member changed from the beginning sessions to now?";

  ii) "What has each participant done to contribute to such changes?"; (highlight how members have contributed to the change of their peers);

  iii) "What have they given each other?";

  iv) "What ways can they use and treasure these gifts in the future?"; "What are their expectations about how they can use what they learned in groups in the future?";

  v)   "What has each member learned (taken away) from this group experience?";

  vi) "Who in their lives could they share and teach what they have learned from this group experience?" The therapist attempts to help the group members translate "endings" into a form of "new beginnings". The end of the group is a form of a "healthy goodbye", although informally participants may be encouraged to stay in touch with each other and provide social support when it is needed.

Treatment guidelines. A number of clinicians have provided guidelines for conducting group sessions (e.g., see Courchaine & Dowd, 1994; Lipton, 1994; Yalom, 1985). Some of the specific suggestions for working with PTSD clients will be highlighted.

1.   The sessions are usually weekly and last 90 minutes. The last few sessions may be spaced out, with possible booster sessions over the course of the year. Courchaine & David (1994) suggest that in crisis intervention groups that sessions be conducted twice a week (1 1/2 - 2 hours) for 8 to 10 sessions and that followup telephone calls with departed group members by the therapist be conducted once a week for the first month, twice a month for the second month followup and once a month the third month.

2.   The group composition is usually homogeneous in terms of target populations (e.g., combat veterans, rape victims, etc.). Such homogeneity permits greater sharing and common understanding of what clients have experienced. Homogeneous groups become cohesive more quickly, offer more immediate support to group members and provide more immediate relief. Courchaine and Dowd (1994) also propose that gender consistent groups be conducted when sexual issues of victimization are involved. Homogeneous groups are also usually established when there is a clearly defined recent stressor (e.g., raped victims, bereaved widows, cancer patients). There may be some advantages of forming heterogeneous groups in order not to reinforce a "victim" identification, thus conveying the universality of distress. Yalom (1985) proposes that group members be "homogeneous for ego strength". He notes that therapists tend to deselect or exclude potential group participants as not fitting, rather than select clients on specific criteria. The therapist attempts to identify clients "who won't work" based on how they would relate to others in the group.

3.   The size of the group varies, but usually consists of no less than 7 or 8 members, otherwise absence or attrition may delimit the group's effectiveness. Over 12 members can prove unwieldy and thus, 8 to 10 is usually the recommended number of participants. The groups are usually open with new members being added as needed. This is in contrast to a closed group where the composition of the group is set for the entire treatment. The advantages of the open group are several fold. First, since the immediacy of treatment is desireable, preferably within 5 to 8 weeks after a crisis, the use of open groups insures that participants will not have to wait for a new group to start. An open group also allows new members to see older members who have progressed toward resolution. Such older members provide "hope" to new members and convey, by means of being a coping model, the need to take responsibility for change. Also Courchaine and Dowd (1994) highlight, since most crises involve some form of loss, an open group allows for an ongoing exploration of the client's reactions to individuals leaving the group. The advantage of a closed, time-limited group is that it builds a sense of intimacy that can be helpful. The closed group format is usually employed with an inpatient population, while the open group format is usually employed with outpatients.

4.   Allen and Bloom (1994) note that some traumatized clients may require group introduction to group psychotherapy, and would benefit from individual psychotherapy first where the issues of safety and trust can be addressed. Clients can be introduced to group gradually as noted in the following steps.

5.   The clients are each seen individually before the group meetings in order to discuss the format, purpose, and any reservations that the client may have. The client is provided with information about what the group therapy process entails, expectations and responsibilities in terms of attendance and confidentiality, group goals and objectives. There is a need to address the potential participant's concerns about being overwhelmed by the other group members self-disclosure. In short, it is important to prepare participants before the start of the group. For example, discuss the dangers of subgrouping (which is a

natural process), as a possible way of contributing to what Yalom describes as the development of a "conspiracy of silence" -- (keeping secrets) that may get in the way of one of the group goals to conduct interpersonal learning. Reluctant clients are encouraged to attend several group meetings (anywhere from 1 to 10 have been suggested in the literature) in order to determine if the group process is suited for him/her. The client is not obliged to talk at these initial 1 to 2 meetings. The client is encouraged to attend these sessions before making a decision not to attend group meetings.

6.   The client may be offered the opportunity to meet with individuals who have been in the group for a while. (This is to be used when an open-ended groups format is employed.)

7.   The client is told that he/she will get **"most help in the process of helping others"**. As clients share experiences they usually feel more relaxed in the presence of others who have been through similar experiences, who have had similar feelings, thoughts, and reactions.

8.   Groups are usually client-driven as the therapist begins by asking clients to describe any specific problems that they may be experiencing. As Lipton (1994, p. 112) observes:

> "The most effective group leader does not provide answers, but helps group members work out answers on the basis of their personal knowledge and experience. ... The therapist is most effective when raising questions needing answers from the group, rather than trying to give answers. Answers and suggestions are always better accepted from peers than from staff."

In order to empower, enable and to establish collaboration, Lipton conveys to the group members:

> "I am more like a teacher or coach. When you learn more about how PTSD works and what to do, you can decide what to work on and what you want to accomplish. I don't want you to do something because I said so, but because you decided that it makes sense to you. When you get more practice in knowing how to avoid problems and how to deal with them, your ability to stay in control and accomplish what you want will gradually improve." (p. 125)

This does not mean that the therapist doesn't counsel and teach coping skills, but consistent with the tenor of this **Manual**, the effective therapist can employ a series of questions that lead the participants to come up with the treatment ideas. The participants are invited to contribute to the agenda at the beginning of each session, as well as to share their status and progress since the last session.

9.   Another way to engage clients is to use brief **videotaped** films (usually less than 10 to 15 minutes) as a catalyst for group discussion. For example, for individuals who have been to my workshops they have seen the brief videotape I show to incest and rape survivors. The incest and rape victim groups are shown a videotape[1] of an interview with the poetess Maya Angelou who describes how, as a child of 7 1/2, she was raped. She later spoke the name of the perpetrator and he died. As a result, for a lengthy period of time she was electively mute. I show this initial portion and then stop the tape and explore with the group their reactions. After this discussion, I ask them to watch the next portion of the videotape to see how Maya

---

[1] A list of videotapes are included in Section VIII.

Angelou reclaimed her "voice". At this point I show her offering a most engaging uplifting poem. It invariably elicits strong positive emotions in group members. This leads to a group discussion of how each member can find his/her own voice. Not that they will become poets, but if Maya Angelou could reclaim her voice, then how can each client engage in such "healing" activities. This discussion leads to:

a) very specific individualized plans, with short-term, intermediate, and long-term goal statements;

b) an examination of possible barriers and obstacles that might get in the way of such behavioral changes;

c) public commitment statements to the group of what, when, and how individuals will undertake change;

d) self and group monitoring of progress;

e) relapse prevention beforehand should things not work out;

f) self-attribution ("taking credit for") changes individuals have made;

g) discussion of how the clients can teach this to others.

In short, showing "inspirational tapes" to clients is _insufficient_ to bring about sustained change. The various steps just enumerated are needed to "nail down" change and to have clients take responsibility and credit for change.

10. The treatment focus is not delimited to reexperiencing or retelling the past traumatic experiences (i.e., "war stories"), but rather focuses on the present. The central message conveyed is, "Not let the past rob the present and the future. We cannot do anything to alter the past, but we can exert control over the present and the future."

11. Group is an effective setting to address issues of guilt, shame, and self-blame, as members encourage clients to become more "objective". *(See discussion of treatment of guilt reactions in Section VI.)*

12. The group setting is also a useful arena to explore "secondary gains", compensation issues that may be getting in the way of making changes.

13. Short-term spouse groups have also been run in order to educate them about PTSD, how to avoid getting angry, critical and blaming of clients, and how to communicate more effectively. Spouses and clients may meet in group sessions together.

14. Various combinations of groups have been used, namely, process-oriented, therapy ala Yalom, trauma-focussed groups, client led groups, spouse groups, client and spouse groups, family groups, client only group meetings (without therapist). The size of the groups have varied markedly. Sometimes group meetings are supplemented with individual therapy. At this point there is no data that I know of that can provide guidance to clinicians as to which combination of treatments is best for which clients and their families.

15. Zahava Solomon and her colleagues have used spouses of combat soldiers who had received treatment to "recruit" (inform and invite) other participants to join treatment.

The popularity of group treatment of PTSD clients is underscored by Motta (1993) who reports that surveys indicate that Vietnam veterans prefer to be in groups with others who have had similar combat exposure. Groups with veterans are often time-limited and address issues of anger, impulse control, guilt, depression, and relationship difficulties. The therapist can convey to clients that each member of the group is at a different point on the path to recovery *(this statement is designed to address individual differences)*.

Hazzard et al. (1993), in discussing therapy groups for victims of sexual abuse, advise that in forming groups it is important to ensure that "no member is strikingly different from the other members in terms of variables such as ethnicity, abuse history, or perhaps other variables such as sexual orientation. It is also helpful for leaders to facilitate discussion of participants' personal similarities and differences and how these affect members' feelings of acceptance and trust." (p. 466). Mennen and Meadow (1992) observe that clients who are actively psychotic, suicidal, manifesting multiple personality disorder, be excluded from group interventions. With more long-term interventions (1 to 2 years) a more heterogeneous group composition might be considered. With such longer term intervention, clients can be asked to make a briefer initial commitment to treatment (e.g., 6 weeks) that can be reexamined and renewed at that time. Another caveat about group work has been offered by Gunderson and Chu (1993). They note that with clients who have borderline personality disorders the **group process may not work**.[1] Clients who are unable to recollect their abusive experience without becoming overwhelmed may benefit little from peer support groups. Premature reexperiencing by others may trigger maladaptive reactions.

16. Herman (1992) describes the **rituals of farewells** that can be used in group treatment. For example, each participant in the group is asked to prepare in writing for the final sessions an assessment of her own accomplishments, as well as an estimate of the recovery work that lies ahead for her. Each participant is also asked to provide the same kind of assessment for every other group member, as well as provide feedback for the group leaders. Finally, each member is asked to prepare an **imaginary gift** for every member of the group (e.g., the wish of group members to share part of themselves, etc.). The "gift" may take the form of the participant making a statement, "I wish you...".

17. Finally, Yalom and his colleagues are exploring the differential benefits of having victimized clients such as incest survivors focus their treatment attention only on interpersonal issues that arise in the group versus a group format that examines past history, as well as ongoing group processes. In the interpersonal focus group treatment, the therapist "shepherds" (to use Yalom's metaphor) group members through an examination of ongoing "here and now" processes. The questions asked by the clinician are designed to have group members provide each other with feedback, and in turn, become more self-reflective (e.g., examine first impressions of group members, discuss how these initial impressions have or have not held up; who are you most upset with; who is most supportive; do you relate to others out there like you relate to group members; how can you use what you have learned here, out there?).

The following Section illustrates the ways in which group intervention have been employed with incest victims. Note the variety of diverse alternatives.

---

[1] *We will consider the treatment of patients with borderline personality disorder in Section VI.* Linehan has used group skills training with borderline patients to reduce parasuicidal behaviors. Also see Diekstra et al., 1988, Justice and Justice, 1990 and Prazoff et al., 1986 for how cognitive behavioral group therapy can be conducted in crisis intervention.

Examples of Group Treatment with Incest Victims

A variety of diverse group treatment approaches have been used (both short-term and long-term) with incest victims (see Hunt and Schatzow, 1994; Lebowitz et al., 1993; Kearney-Cooke & Striegel-Moore, 1994; Mennen & Meadow, 1992; McCann and Pearlman, 1990). Most of the groups are time-limited and structured. The amount of structure varies markedly, as does the number of sessions, criteria for membership, and characteristics of group co-leaders (mixed male-female, or both same sex).[1] Most group treatment approaches select clients who have experienced the same trauma (incest), or allow victims of a related trauma (e.g., some other form of sexual assault). Usually, the group membership are relatively homogeneous. The group structure may include: (a) an agenda of specific topics set for each meeting; (b) specific topics set for the first several meetings with the discussion topics for later sessions to be determined by group members; (c) a more leaderless group, with controls relinquished to clients from the outset. At this point, there is no comparative outcome studies to examine the different treatment formats, nor the length of treatment, nor the selection criteria.

Calhoun and Resick (1992) propose that participants be screened and those who (1) are suicidal, (2) suffer from heavy substance abuse, (3) self-mutilate or report multiple personality, or (4) have never spoken about his/her trauma should not be included in the treatment groups. As noted, sometimes clients are both in group and individual therapy concurrently, as described in Linehan's intervention with borderline patients (see Section VI).

Most of the group intervention programs with adult survivors of CSA focus initially on safety, containment and stabilization. Once safety and self-care are in place, then the other treatment tasks can be addressed. For example, Pearlman and her colleagues have developed a 12 week intervention that covers: "Knowng and caring for oneself" that focusses on affect tolerance; "Developing your relationship with yourself" that focusses on developing adaptive cognitive self-schemas; "Creating mutually satisfying relationships"; "Sharing your narrative" that focusses on trauma memories in the context of their self-identities; "Integrating spirituality and identity"; "Understandng bodily and other sensory experiences". The groups have a maximum of seven members and are run by two cotherapists.

Another illustrative **short-term** group therapy model has been offered by Brandt (1989) with adult **female survivors of childhood incest**. Features of her program include:

a)   10 weekly sessions, $1^1/_4$ to $1^1/_2$ hour in length; 6-8 members; 2 female therapists; heterogeneous age group; homogeneous problem; and screened clients.

b)   Session 1 -- Introductions -- Discuss how see self, how feel about being in group, do not talk about incest in the initial session.

---

[1] I know of no data that has systematically examined the impact of female coleaders versus mixed (male and female) coleaders with incest survivors. Some clinicians (e.g., Scott & Stradling, 1992, p. 161) report clinical impressions that a mixed led group has specific promise because it exposes the incest survivors to a model of a more accepting male working collaboratively with a female. In contrast, Mennen and Meadow (1992) argue that female incest survivor groups be co-led by two females since the female participants "will feel more comfortable with women". They also note that a male therapist conveys to participants that a male's presence is needed to legitimatize treatment. Calhoun and Resick (1993) note that male therapists tend to view a sexual assault such as rape as a sexual crime rather than as a crime of violence. As a result, male therapists tend to focus too much on the sexual aspects of the victimization experience. But there is no specific data to decide the sex composition of the leaders.

Sessions 2 and 3 -- Tell histories of incest in detail ($1/2$ of the group one week, $1/2$ the other week). Set short-term goals to be accomplished within 10 weeks. Then set long-term goals.

Sessions 4, 5, and 6 -- Open groups -- Discuss whatever topics the group members wish (e.g., family of origin material, life situation)

Sessions 7 and 8 -- Participants have been asked to write letters at home to the abuser or to anyone else (not mailed). Read the letters and discuss them in group.

Session 9 and 10 -- Termination phase, discuss progress, "unfinished business" and reassess goals.

c)   Topics covered include difficulty with trust and intimacy, repeated victimization, poor choice in relationships, sexual difficulties, current emotional distress, physical symptoms, fears concerning own children, difficulty relating to authority, cross generation occurrence of incest (See Herman, 1981, for other possible issues).

A somewhat different **long-term** group format for **incest survivors** has been offered by Gold-Steinberg and Buttenheim (1993). They emphasize the need to prepare participants for retelling and resolution, to share at their own pace and in their own way. They work with clients to "book" their days of when they intend to share their "stories" of incest. The telling begins with the client sharing her hopes, expectations, and fears of telling and to share what has been "helpful" and "hurtful" in past tellings. Group members are also encouraged to share their hopes and feelings about the "telling." Following the "telling" the survivor has an opportunity to reflect on the "telling" experience, both at the end of that session and at the beginning of the next session. Thus, a ritual surrounds the retelling.

At this point we have little data to compare the relative effectiveness of the short-term and long-term interventions with incest victims. We also do not know whether such retelling "there and then" focused groups are more effective than "here and now" groups that only focus on ongoing group interactions.

Yet other group formats for sexual assault victims have been offered by Alexander, Neimeyer and their colleagues (1989) and by Resick and Schnicke (1992). Alexander et al. (1989) use a time limited **Interpersonal Transactional (IT)** group format. In the IT group the therapist introduces a new disclosure topic each week that focuses on issues common to the experience of incest (e.g., feelings of being different, positive and negative perceptions of self, feelings of helplessness, issues of trust, family secrets, ambivalence toward parents). A supportive nonjudgmental discussion of these topics progressively becomes more intimate over sessions. The unique feature of the IT format is the use of **dyadic group composition** in exploring each topic. Upon introduction of each topic group members split into pairs to discuss the topic for approximately 4 minutes, after which they rotate to a new partner. These dyadic interventions provide the basis for subsequent whole group discussion. (See Neimeyer, 1988, for a discussion of clinical guidelines.) The structured IT approach is to be contrasted with the process group formats suggested by Courtois (1988), Sprei and Goodwin (1983) and Yalom (1975).

Another structured group format for sexual assault victims has been offered by Resick and Schnicke (1992, 1993). They developed a short-term (12 $1/2$-hour sessions) **Cognitive Processing Therapy (PT)** that includes:

a)   education about PTSD symptoms
b)   an information theory of PTSD
c)   exposure

d)   cognitive therapy

The exposure component consists of writing and reading a detailed account of the sexual abuse (e.g., rape) including sensory and emotional content and highlighting any "stuck points", or areas of incomplete processing of the conflict. These stories are eventually read to the group with accompanying affect. The cognitive therapy component included training in the identification of thoughts, feelings, and beliefs in such areas as **safety, trust, power, esteem and intimacy**; each of which McCann et al. (1988) highlighted are affected and disrupted by victimization. Roth and Newman (1993) have developed a coding system to evaluate ongoing group therapy sessions to monitor the clients' progress along these different dimensions.

The cognitive therapy component is quite didactic in educating clients to the role of maladaptive beliefs and faulty thinking styles. Worksheets and homework are given.[1] Modules discussing each of the central themes of safety, trust, power, esteem, and intimacy are given to clients in session 7. A different theme (including handout material) is given each session. The various themes provide the basis for group discussion of the participants' "stuck points".

Kearney-Cooke and Striegel-Moore (1994) provide what they call a "feminist psychodynamic" approach for the **treatment of child sexual abuse** in clients who have anorexia and bulimia nervosa. Following the general guidelines of Herman (1992) of (1) establishing safety; (2) remembrance and mourning; and (3) reconnection with real life they describe an innovative treatment approach. The therapist is seen as a "partner on a journey of recovery", "bearing witness", and helping clients "move to **writing a new story of her life and body**. This is no longer a **tale** of repeated victimization, but instead...a process that leads to more vitality and energy" (p.318). (Note, their description in terms of a constructive narrative perspective).

Following an initial assessment during which the specific details of the abuse are explored *(see Section III for a description of the questions to be asked)*, they then have clients enter individual and/or group interventions. They also note that the therapist should be sensitive to the possibility that the client may report having been sexually aroused or felt sexual pleasure during the abuse. (This may also be reported by victims of rape.) As a result the client may mistakeningly assume responsibility for the abuse. The therapist needs to help the client reframe such sexually arousing feelings as a "biological response to physical stimulation, resulting from the touching of parts of the body that are easily excitable". It is underscored that the responsibility for the abusive behaviors lies with the perpetrator. They provide a number of innovative suggestions, some of which I will summarize.

1.   Help clients develop **affect tolerance** and "soothing" techniques (e.g., listening to relaxation tapes, meditation, gardening, exercise). Provide the client with a "transitional object" such as a letter *(see Section VI)*, a relaxation tape from the therapist, a collaboratively-generated list of people to call if she feels alone or has trouble dealing with difficult times. Learn ways to distract self without using food and alcohol.

2.   Assist clients in **memory recall** - guided imagery of specific incidents or theme-centered guided imagery where a specific topic such as sexual experiences are traced developmentally. In order to facilitate recall they use a metaphor of a magic rope that

---

[1] A number of clinicians have developed self-help workbooks for incest victims, but these have <u>not</u> been critically evaluated. For example, see books by Donaldson & Green (1987), Gil (1988), Hagan (1990), Mellody & Miller (1989) and Nestinger & Lewis (1990).

can take the client safely back in time (reaching hand over hand) moving back through time, stopping at any point. "Don't censor. Trust whatever scene comes. Describe it as if it is happening in the here and now." (p.312). Afterwards the therapist and client explore what the client learned about herself and about life as a result of the memory recall. In order to insure that such memories do not get out of control in nontherapy times, clients are encouraged to keep a special box for storing memories that they can bring to sessions. In therapy the client can open the box and "work through" the memories. "When they close the box, they will be closing off the memories until the next session." (p.311).

3. **Creating concrete representations of the abuse.** Clients are asked to sculpt in clay or draw their memories or the most salient image. This process facilitates structure and integration of memories as the therapist explores with the client (or group of clients) the memory of the events. Clients are once again asked, "What did you learn about yourself and about life?" Kearney-Cooke and Striegel-Moore also suggest that after clients are assisted in memory recall with its intense accompanying affect that the therapist insure that the client is refocused on the present by allowing 10 to 15 minutes for "here and now" discussion. The therapist might say:

> "You've shared a lot today. We will spend time in the
> next few sessions working with this memory. Let's
> stop and see if we can understand what it means."
> (p.313)

4. **Reenactment of the abusive experience.** Use psychodrama, role playing, Gestalt "empty-chair" procedure (e.g., talk and comfort "shamed" child). This can be conducted on a group basis as a supplement to the individual guided imagery procedures. These reenactment procedures can be used to address and dramatize the victim's fears and intense anger toward the perpetrator. The involvement of the group helps to break down feelings of isolation. These reenactments are carefully structured, with safeguards, as other group members are called upon to play different roles and to provide support. *(See discussion of treatment of recollections in Section VI for a description of imagery-based intervention procedures.)*

5. **Deal with shame.** As noted in Section I, victims of abuse are prone to characterize themselves as being "damaged goods, insignificant, worthless", with accompanying feelings of shame and self-blame. Consider the impact of the client using the following metaphor as part of her narrative. "I think of **my body as a toy** for someone **to play with.** I feel humiliated and **dirty** most of the time". As Kearney-Cooke & Striegel-Moore (1994, p.315) observe clients need "to be encouraged to examine self-talk about shame", and in the terms of the present manual to co-construct a different narrative. They suggest (p.315) that the therapist convey to clients that the **brain can be compared to a computer.**

> "Our brain will believe what we tell it, that is, how we
> program it. For example, "I am bad" can be replaced
> with "Something bad happened to me".

Kearney-Cooke and Striegel-Moore (1994) also describe the way a **Shame Ritual** can be used. The key elements of which include:

1. Participants are asked to cover selves with black clothes in order to remember the times they felt "ashamed of their bodies".

2. Find a partner who will be a listener for the first half of the ritual and then switch roles.

3. The listener covers the speaker with a cloth, places her hands on the speaker's shoulders and walks the client backwards as a symbol of receding into the past. The listener then asks, **"Tell me about the times you have felt ashamed of your body"**. The listener encourages the client to provide multiple examples moving back through time. This request is followed by the listener asking, **"Tell me (or them if in a group) about the masks you wore to hide the shame"**. In turn, the listener asks, **"Tell me about the ways you punished your body because of the shame"**. Subsequently, the listener asks, **"Which names would you be called if you no longer felt ashamed of your body"**. Repeating the names spoken, the listener moves her partner forward and removes the cloth. The participants thank each other and then **exchange roles**.[1]

Such rituals provide group members with an opportunity "to grant each other **absolution** as nobody else can", and to contribute to a new narrative. Consider the following altered narrative offered by a client (as reported by Kearney-Cooke and Striegel-Moore, 1994, p.316).

> "Shame will no longer **pollute my body**, soul,
> emotions. It is time to **let go of shame**. Most of it
> belongs to someone else. I no longer need to use **my
> body as a battleground** where I hide, but want to
> take care of it."

(Note, the rich use of metaphors to describe the beneficial impact of going through the therapy process and the shame ritual.)

6. The last element of the treatment is the attempt to address the high risk of revictimization, in the form of physical and sexual abuse, that victims of child sexual abuse experience.

Ending the Cycle of Repeated Victimization.

In this phase of treatment clients are taught how to:

a) identify early signs of an abusive relationship,

b) examine feelings and attitudes about abuse,

c) facilitate responsible decision making about various forms of self-protection (interpersonal, sexual),

d) change clients' perceptions from perceiving themselves as a "sexual object" to being a "sexual being",

e) develop assertive, refusal and negotiation skills,

---

[1] At this point I am not endorsing, nor advocating, such procedures that may inadvertently reinforce a sense of multiple selves, but rather merely describing the Kearney-Cooke and Striegel-Moore approach.

f)   explore the client's partner's ability and willingness to relate to the client in a nonabusive way.

The reason I have provided such a detailed account of the Kearney-Cooke and Striegel-Moore intervention package is not that it has been empirically validated, but rather to highlight the creativity of clinicians. Surely, in some cultures the proposed shame ritual may not be appropriate, and different interventions will be needed. Moreover, how should the clinician who is working with adult victims of child sexual abuse decide on a treatment intervention? Should you adopt the more structured short-term program of Brandt; the long-term intervention package of Gold-Steinberg and Buttenheim; the interpersonal approach of Alexander and Neimeyer; the cognitive processing approach of Resick and Schnicke; or that offered by Kearney-Cooke and Striegel-Moore? Keep in mind this is only a limited list (see below). Perhaps, you should invent your own intervention package. But all of these treatment packages have been developed for women who are victims of child sexual abuse. What about male victims?

The application of group interventions with **men** who have been sexually abused as children is reported in the literature less frequently. Isely (1992) describes a short-term (9 session) psychoeducational model that may be of use for this underserved population. Group exercises are used in order to free-up participants to share their stories at their own pace. For example:

a)   having group members first share in groups of two

b)   generating in the group as a whole, characteristics associated with being "a real man" versus "being a male sexual abuse victim"

c)   sharing their "counterfeit identities"

d)   discussing male myths

e)   discussing a model of abuse accommodation (Summit, 1983)

f)   learning how to selectively share their secrets.

Zaidi (1994) describes a time-limited (10 session) intervention for **inpatient male victims of childhood sexual abuse (CSA)**. In a pilot demonstration project she used an eclectic treatment package to address the four major themes or "traumagenic factors" that characterize the long-term effects of CSA. These 4 factors include:

a) **stigmatization** -- impaired self-concept, feelings of shame, guilt
b) **powerlessness** -- impairment of self efficacy, especially in response to perceived authority figures
c) **betrayal** -- diminished sense of trust
d) **traumagenic sexualization** -- dysfunctional sexual behavior

The intervention package combines psychoeducational, cognitive, behavioral, and art therapy techniques. More specifically, the treatment sessions included:

Session 1 - Understanding child abuse (psychoeducational presentation that is designed to address stigmatization and mitigate self-blame). The participants completed self-drawings and drawings pictures of an opposite sex member in order to explore their self-concept, body image, and interpersonal perceptions. Participants were asked to interpret their artwork to the group.

Session 2 - Share family context. Complete genogram and present it to the group in order to tap family of origin, developmental relationships, and cross generational patterns. Also, instruction was given on coping techniques (e.g., relaxation, deep breathing, and guide imagery exercises).

Sessions 3-5 - Confronting the memories. Prior to session 3 client generates a time line of childhood experiences which facilitated disclosure of specific abusive episodes. (I should note that in Sections VI and VII are described other biographical procedures that could be included -- see time lines of landmark "positive" events and a steps and ladders approach.) Group discussion is less structured and participants consider what they experienced, felt and did to survive the abuse.

Session 6 - Reaching the abused child. Following the disclosure of abuse histories, partiticpants wrote a letter to an abused child. This exercise was completed between sessions and it was designed to "access empathetic feelings for the child within and to heighten awareness that the child victim is not culpable" (Zaidi, p. 723). The participants read their letters aloud to the group and they are discussed.

Session 7 - Expressing the anger. Prior to the session, the participants wrote a letter to the abuser and shared this with the group. The group discussion focused on how the participants' "internalized" the messages from the perpetrator and the ways in which early traumatic experiences influence views of self, world, and relationship to others (intimacy, sexual relationships, trust).

Session 8 - Exploring obstacles to intimacy. Use an art collage to explore the nature of "what it means to be male", "female".

Session 9 - Learning about effective discipline. Use information, role playing, exercises on how to communicate more effectively.

Session 10 - Looking ahead. Consider feelings related to the ending of the group, consider what was learned, issues requiring further exploration, and plans for follow-up treatment.

There is a need to evaluate this treatment program. Little has been written about treatment of male victims of sexual abuse.

In summary, we see marked variability and creativity in how clinicians have conducted group interventions with individuals who have been victimized. In some instances (Alexander et al, Resick & Schnicke) preliminary outcome data is provided, relative to limited control groups. But this data base is very much in its infancy. To be added to this collection is the group applications of direct therapy exposure and stress inoculation training to be described in a later section. Given the impact victimization has on interpersonal trust and intimacy, the group process holds much promise.

Other examples of group psychotherapy with sexual abuse survivors have been offered by Alexander et al. (1989), Cole and Barney (1987), Courtois (1988), Ganzarin and Buchek (1987), Goodman and Nowak-Scibelli (1985), Hazzard et al. (1993), Herman and Schatzow (1984) and Neimeyer et al. (1991). Hazzard et al. (1993) suggest that candidates for such sexual abuse survivor groups should be screened initially on a battery measure developed by Colrain et al. (1989) which assess for psychopathology, suicide and abuse histories, symptomatology, and demographic variables. While some of the group programs are short (e.g., 10 sessions in the Brandt program), other programs (e.g., Hazzard et al.) meet weekly for $1\frac{1}{2}$ hour sessions for a year. Group discussions focus on **"sharing the secret"**, **placing responsibility of abuse on the perpetrator, interpersonal issues, coping skills, and relapse prevention.**

In Section VI we will consider how task-oriented group training programs have been used with PTSD and DES clients (e.g., work by Linehan with borderline patients, use of stress inoculation training, and other cognitive behavioral interventions). In Section VII we will consider how group defusing and debriefing procedures have been used in post-disaster interventions.

General Treatment Guidelines: What Can Be Done to Help Clients with PTSD and DES?

Before we consider a number of specific intervention procedures it is helpful to consider some general treatment guidelines that emerge across a variety of diverse treatment approaches. In this Section, I will outline the general treatment objectives[1] and the rationale for each. In the subsequent two Sections, I provide **a detailed account** of how to implement each of the suggested therapeutic procedures. Although these clinical procedures are outlined in a sequential fashion, they may often be **implemented concurrently.** For example, while the therapist is addressing the client's presenting symptoms of hyperarousal, insomnia, anger control, depression, addictive behavior, the therapist may also spend time on helping the client "restructure" his/her "story", and also reestablish relationships. These guidelines should **not** be seen as a lock-step prescription, but rather a framework to be followed **in a flexible fashion,** depending upon the client's needs and treatment goals.

As Susan Solomon (1994, p. 20) has observed:

"PTSD is a complex disorder, highly resistant to cure by any of the treatment modalities available to date. The development of new modes of intervention is called for."

The present treatment guidelines provide an integrative cognitive-behavioral treatment approach that derives from a constructive narrative perspective. The treatment approach can be viewed as consisting of **five phases,** each with their own treatment goals.

---

[1] Herman (1992) has proposed that the treatment of traumatized clients can be viewed as consisting of (1) establishing safety, (2) restructuring the trauma story, and (3) restoring connectedness between the survivor and the community. The present analysis builds upon and elaborates on the Herman model. (For other descriptive accounts of treatment protocols for PTSD clients see Brom et al., 1989; Marmar and Horowitz, 1988; Schwarz and Prout, 1993.) No matter what the form of intervention, it appears that **the earlier the intervention the better the outcome.** Early intervention reduces the likelihood of disruptive behavioral patterns becoming entrenched.

Phase I -- <u>Introductory Phase</u>

The treatment goals are to:

1) Establish a therapeutic relationship or "alliance".[1]

2) Encourage the client to share his/her "story" at his/her own pace. Allow for the expression of feelings that should be "validated". Collaboratively establish treatment goals.

3) Ensure the client's safety and address practical needs first. Recognize the need for rest and respite in a safe environment.

4) Conduct assessments -- both psychological and medical. Assess the client's strengths.[2]

5) Educate the client about the nature of PTSD and accompanying sequelae.

6) Validate and help the client reframe his/her reactions, and engender "hope".

7) Consider the treatment options collaboratively with the client, namely individual, group, couples, family, day or inpatient treatment[3] , and examine specific treatment formats designed to address the client's problems of comorbidity.

---

[1] McFarlane (1994) observes that trust is an essential feature of the therapeutic alliance with traumatized clients. The client must feel secure and confident that the therapist is genuine, empathetic and warm, and that **the therapist can also cope with bearing witness** to the trauma and understanding its signficance" (p. 402).

[2] **Caution** is required in **assessing the client's strengths.** As one client observed: "I recently went to see a therapist and I know she means well, but she kept asking me, "What would need to happen for you to feel better?", and she also tried to "tap my strengths". On the surface these are reasonable questions. But I didn't know the answers and in the asking somehow I felt she had <u>not</u> been hearing what I had been telling her. She didn't help me find the triggers or what I could do about them". The **caution** is <u>not</u> to pursue the client's strengths brefore hearing the client's narrative account. Once again, it is not the clinical procedure, but the **timing** that proves critical.

[3] The decision to have clients participate in individual, group, couples, family, day, inpatient treatment, or some combination of these interventions, has <u>not</u> been systematically examined. In fact, we don't know which form of individual, group, or family-based intervention is best for which type of traumatized client. The severity of the client's distress (risk to self and others); the nature of the client's presenting problems (e.g., does it involve significant others as in the form of intimacy and sexual problems); does it involve comorbidity; the impact of the trauma on the family members; the nature of the social supports; and the like, each can influence the treatment decision-making process. In general, clinicians seem to operate with implicit algorithms that they use in suggesting treatment alternatives. **It is critical to examine the pros and cons of the different treatment options in a collaborative fashion with the client.**

Phase II -- <u>Address the Client's Presenting Symptoms and Signs of Comorbidity</u>

The treatment goals are to:

1) Help stabilize the client's clinical picture, reduce symptoms and provide relief.

2) Teach coping skills to address the specific symptom, for example, directly treat flashbacks, intrusive ruminations, hyperarousal, irritability, avoidance, insomnia. Assist client in affect modulation and emotional regulation so he/she does <u>not</u> fluctuate between numbing and withdrawal and hypervigilance and overarousal. Keep in mind, however, that it is possible that PTSD symptomatology can be reduced, but the client can still have a number of life adjustment problems.

3) Check to determine if psychotropic medication[1] is indicated. Provide adherence counseling for prescribed medication.

4) Address the clinical picture of comorbidity or coexisting disorders (e.g., depression, panic attacks, anger control problems, addictive behaviors, interpersonal and sexual difficulties by such procedures as panic control training, stress-inoculation training, relapse prevention training, cognitive therapy).

5) Ensure the client's safety in terms of addressing the dangers of "stigmatization", "revictimization" and "secondary victimization" (e.g., address issues that might arise from dealing with the legal and medical systems).

Phase III -- <u>Help the Client to Restructure His/Her Story and Transform Traumatic Memory, Shift from "Victim" Role to "Survivor" and "Thriver" Roles</u>

The treatment goals are to:

1) Help the client retell his/her story (reexperience, recollect the trauma in the "here and now") and "revise" the account in a way that leads to "integration" and "a sense of mastery", as well as provide an opportunity to "find" meaning. Enable the client to

---

[1] The complexity of the PTSD and DES populations underscore the need for a **bio-psycho-social** integrative treatment approach.

reexperience the trauma memories with a relatively high degree of voluntary control, evidencing a sense of mastery over intrusive recollections and the ability to tolerate discomfort.

2)   Reexpose the client to traumatic cues in a structured and supportive manner (e.g., use direct therapy exposure, various guided imagery procedures, hypnotic induction procedures, offering testimony, graded in vivo behavioral reexposure).

3)   Address the client's "shattered" beliefs and resultant intra- and interpersonal difficulties (e.g., feelings of guilt, self-blame, rage/anger, grief/sadness[1], helplessness, hopelessness, victimization) by means of cognitive restructuring procedures, problem-solving, letter writing, "journaling", and client self-selected ways of expression -- artistic, engaging in a ritual, undertaking a "mission".

4)   Examine the potential of personal growth that can emerge from traumatic events (move from "victim" to "survivor" to "thriver"). Shift time orientation from the past to the present and future. Provide opportunities for the client to regain "self-esteem" and "trust" in others and self. Foster social relationships rather than social withdrawal and detachment. Help client establish a more satisfactory lifestyle and develop and strengthen social supports.

5)   Help the client mobilize own resources such as implicit belief systems (e.g., religious and philosophical belief systems). Have clients consider whether engaging in a restorative or reparative individually or group-initiated activity (ritual) would be helpful (e.g., Native-American Indian purification sweat lodge ceremony; revisit the site of victimizaton; engage in memorial service; help others). Help the client develop a sense of being able to build upon the experience and to develop a future sense of goals.

---

[1] Scurfield (1985) observes that focusing on the client's initial reactions of rage and anger invariably uncovers the client's feelings of grief and sadness.

Note: The therapist should **not** try to provide meaning, but the

meaning should come from the client.

Phase IV -- Help the Client to Reconnect with Others and Restore Familial,

Social and Occupational Functioning

The treatment goals are to:

1) Reestablish relationship with significant others and work on client's interpersonal goals (may involve significant others in treatment or have the client participate in group sessions and group rituals and activities).

2) Address interpersonal difficulties and issues such as intimacy, trust, sexual difficulties -- may involve couples sex therapy.

3) Address the possibility of "revictimization" by employing cognitive restructuring and interpersonal problem-solving procedures.

4) Address issues of "reparation" and family of origin issues which may take the form of a "symbolic" "metaphoric" "coming to terms", rather than direct confrontation. Address the issue of the "impossibility of getting even" and the "psychic costs" of being preoccupied with "revenge". Such "reparation" work may contribute to feelings of resolution.

5) Explore with the client the value of undertaking **restorative** attempts of rewriting his/her "narrative". The form this may take should come from the client (e.g., letter writing, soldier who killed his buddy in friendly fire may decide to visit his buddy's family, may visit grave site, may "bear witness", and the like).

6) Empower and enable the client by encouraging and helping the client to arrange to **act as a "helper"** for others. Nurture "connectedness" to others by helping the client "find a mission", if he/she wants. For example, this may take the form of trying to raise public awareness, help other victims, do preventative work. Encourage reengaging activities. Provide opportunity for the client to reassess his/her priorities and life goals.

Note: The therapist should hold a broad definition of what constitutes "healing activities".

The actual time in psychotherapy should be viewed as only one part of the healing process. It is a "catalytic time" designed to help clients undertake "reparative work" and to perform "personal experiments" in vivo. The therapist reviews with the client the consequences ("results", "data") from such personal experiments and the lessons learned. Some of these personal experiments may be conducted in the therapy session in the form of examining issues that arise between the client and the therapist and in the form of behavioral rehearsal. Most personal experiments will occur in vivo in the form of the client undertaking "homework" as discussed in Section III.

Phase V -- Termination Phase

The treatment goals are to:

1) Bolster the client's self-confidence, sense of competence and self-efficacy. Ensure that the client documents and "takes credit" for accomplishments. While self-attribution processes takes place throughout treatment, it receives special attention in the termination phase.

2) Discuss the "recovery work" that lies ahead.

3) Discuss relapse prevention efforts -- client is taught ways to anticipate, accept and cope with possible lapses, setbacks and reexperiences. Discuss that PTSD symptoms may reoccur when the client is stressed or under specific conditions (e.g., anniversary date).

4) Arrange for booster-sessions, follow-through sessions, and "pulsed" sessions (provide follow-up sessions at critical junctures such as court appearance). Include follow-up assessments.

In summary, it is important to consider how any specific treatment procedure (e.g., pharmacological interventions, direct therapy exposure, stress inoculation training, hypnosis, cognitive restructuring, couples or group therapy) is **embedded in an overall treatment package.** As outlined, the initial assessment and termination phases, the extra-therapeutic activities, each constitute critical features of treatment. Thus, when clinical investigators examine the relative effectiveness of a specific treatment approach, one should keep in mind the overall therapeutic regimen in which it is situated. This is true of all therapeutic relationships, but especially is the case in working with clients who have been victimized. In fact, the quality of the client-therapist relationship by the third session has been found to be one of the best predictors of treatment outcome for all modes of psychotherapy (see Meichenbaum & Turk, 1987).

But what can the therapist do to enhance such an "alliance"? Some suggestions come from a study by Hamilton and Coates (1993) who asked abused women to describe which health care providers they found "most helpful" and those they found "least helpful". The women reported that the **helpful therapist:**

a)   listened respectfully and took me seriously;
b)   believed my "story";
c)   helped me to see if I was still in danger and explored with me how I could deal with this;
d)   let me know I am not alone;
e)   helped me see my strengths;
f)   helped me understand the impact of traumatic events on myself and on others;
g)   helped me plan for change.

In contrast, the **unhelpful therapist:**

a)   did not listen, did not have an accepting attitude;
b)   questioned my "story";
c)   dismissed, or minimized, the seriousness of my situation and the importance of the problem;
d)   gave advice that I did not wish to receive;
e)   blamed or criticized me.

In addition, as noted in Section III, there is also a need for the therapist to empower and enable **clients** so they **have choices** in terms of the material to be covered, the pace of disclosure, and the options for action.

The Value of Having Clients Tell Their Stories: With Some Cautionary Observations

Common to many forms of intervention with traumatized individuals is the practice of providing them with an opportunity to tell their stories. This may take many different forms. For example, in Section VII we will consider how Critical Incident Stress Debriefing uses self-disclosure; in Section VI we will consider the potential therapeutic value of having clients "talk" and "write" (as well as use other forms of artistic expression) in order to put their traumatic events and reactions into words and pictures. Whether it is in the form of a clinical interview (see Section III), or more explicit retelling in the context of guided imagery procedures (see Section VI), therapists have embraced the principle that "healing" is enhanced by helping clients to translate and transform their highly emotional, often fragmented, "fixated", indelible images, and, sometimes, contradictory accounts into more coherent narrative accounts. As Herman (1992, p. 179) describes in citing an incest survivor,

> "Keep encouraging people to talk, even if it's very painful to watch them. It takes a long time to believe. The more I talk about it, the more I have confidence that it happened; the more I can integrate it."

But **great caution** is required before therapists impose this therapeutic dictum to self-disclose on all traumatized clients. Some clients do not wish to "stir up" old memories. Some clients do not wish to self-disclose. Should therapists respect the client's decision in this area? Is self-disclosure a necessary condition for change? Can self-disclosure ever make things worse? For instance, in examining such questions Clark (1993, p. 48) observed,

> "In the act of conversing, individuals construe meaning. They create a framework of reactions to it, that may previously have been lacking. ... However, there are also conditions under which, far from being helpful, **conversational interaction may actually hamper coping.** ... Conversations that reinforce the idea of trying harder (problem solving) may be **less helpful** than those that suggest a reexamination of one's abilities (accepting). Once the individual accepts his/her limitations, problem solving can be used to consider new options."

Thus, it is being proposed that it is not the opportunity for self-disclosure per se, but the type of therapeutic reaction to such disclosures that may prove critical. Moreover, not all clients respond favorably to the opportunity to retell their stories as evident in the following client's

reactions. She observed:

> "I don't believe in let-it-all-hang-out, or it'll-feel-better-when-you-get-it-out
> mentality. In my experience it only makes it worse, because the session ends and
> I'm left with it. An no one's there when I relive it, or dream about it, or stay
> awake for hours thinking about it. If I have to tell my story, why not suggest I tell
> it in the third person so I can distance myself from it, while I tell it. It seems like
> it's a benefit for the therapist to have the story told. I am not so sure how much it
> does for me.'

It is also important to keep in mind the prior discussion on cultural differences *(see*

Section V on treating torture victims). As reported there, members of some cultural groups (e.g.,

from SE Asia) who had been traumatized preferred to focus on "here and now" problems, rather

than reconsider the past. Similarly, there is some suggestion in the CISD literature that some

individuals may "get worse" by participating in self-disclosure debriefing groups (see Section VII).

What is the treatment guideline that follows from this discussion? Well, like most areas of

the treatment of PTSD, there are no simple answers. For many clients, soliciting their accounts

and helping them to "transform" their "stories" will prove therapeutic. But, such self-disclosure

may also prove to be unhelpful for some. Perhaps the best advice is to explore these issues with

your clients and to allow the client to **gradually** recollect and reexperience the trauma in what

Scurfield (1985) calls, "tolerable doses of awareness".

An Emphasis Should Be Placed on the Constructive Rather Than Only on the Restorative

The treatment goal should <u>not</u> be to merely return the client to the level of functioning prior

to the traumatizing experience. As Turnbull (1994) observes, the aim of treatment "is not to ignore

the very real potential for **personal growth** afforded by the disruption of the pre-existing

schematic model of the world and the need to build a new one." (p. 7). In terms of a constructive

narrative perspective, the exposure to traumatic events provides a unique opportunity to achieve

"positive growth". *(See the discussion of the potential salutogenic consequences of exposure to*

traumatic events in Section III.) **There is a need for the therapist <u>not</u> to hold a**

pathological bias, but instead to be sensitive to the client's strengths and

resources and to actively listen to how the client changes his/her narrative in an adaptive fashion over the course of treatment. For example, consider the following "restorative" features of the client's new narrative that emerged over the course of treatment *(also see accounts offered in Sections II and VI).*

> "I'm <u>not</u> so hard on myself these days."
> "I can notice, catch myself; refocus on the present."
> "I can share with others."
> "I am starting to get bored with the story of X."
> "My memories do not go away, but they are losing their gripping quality."
> "My memories are no longer able to stop me in my tracks. I have control (authority) over them now."
> "My memories no longer make me feel undone."
> "I have choices now; I can choose to leave it if I want to."
> "I can bear the pain of what happened."
> "I can celebrate life now (join life, write a new chapter, rescript my life, take charge)."
> "I have learned to cherish laughter."
> "The pain of what happened has immunized me against the most petty hurts."
> "I focus on the present and the future and leave the past in the past."
> "I am stronger because of what happened to me."
> "I can make a gift of what happened to me to others."
> "Life has new meaning for me."

This array of client statements indicates that they can move beyond just merely coping with the aftermath of trauma to achieve a new and higher plateau of adjustment. In short, the goal of treatment is to help clients, not only improve their behavior, but to also change the "story" they tell to themselves and to others. The remaining Sections of this **Handbook** are designed to specify how these objectives can be accomplished. But how long should therapy take? We now turn to this important question.

HOW LONG SHOULD TREATMENT OF CLIENTS WITH PTSD and
PTSD + DES TAKE?
Factors that Influence the Nature and the Length of Treatment[1]

In this time of managed care[2] there is increasing emphasis for short-term, focused, goal-oriented, efficient and highly accountable forms of intervention. When I present workshops on cognitive-behavioral treatment of anxiety, depression, anger-related problems I can specify the treatment outcome results that provide guidelines for determining the duration of treatment, and moreover, how psychotherapy can be combined synergistically with pharmacotherapy and other forms of intervention. When it comes, however, to the treatment of clients suffering from PTSD and PTSD + DES, especially with Type II stressors or recurrent exposure to Type I stressors (e.g., repeated rape), there is much disagreement on how much treatment is required. As noted in the discussion of the group intervention with incest victims, treatment has varied from as brief as 12 weekly sessions to 2 years.

Lipton (1994) argues that "PTSD is too overwhelming of one's life and personality to be treated successfully by brief treatment. ... On average, I would predict treatment will last **at least two years**, but recognize that there is apt to be a huge margin of error." (p. 208). How big a margin of error is not specified. Moreover, there is no data to indicate that Lipton's conclusions about brief treatment are warranted.

The research on direct therapy exposure and stress inoculation with rape victims and combat veterans, and group therapy with incest survivors, all indicate that brief therapy (less than 20 sessions) has led to significant improvement. It is likely in the present atmosphere of financial restraints that extensive (2-year) treatment will <u>not</u> be supported by insurance companies.

In considering the issue of the length of treatment it would be helpful if any decision were informed by the literature on dose (number of sessions) and effect (outcome) relationships. Scott and Stradling (1992) observe that in studies of dose-effect relationship in psychotherapy (e.g., Howard et al., 1986), approximately 50% of clients are "markedly improved" by 8 sessions and 75% "markedly improved" by 26 sessions.[3] Counseling sessions past 26 sessions led to minimal additional improvement (less than 7% additional improvement). While similar studies with PTSD

---

[1] In considering the length of treatment it is worth keeping in mind the recent findings on who seeks psychotherapy in the U.S., as reported by Vessey and Howard (1993). Their analyses of multiple mental health surveys indicate that "about 2/3 of outpatients are female, about 50% have had at least some college education, about 50% are married, 9 out of 10 are white, and about 80% are between the ages 21 and 50. **Those who are most in need in terms of suffering from DSM disorders are least likely to ever seek nor receive services."** (p. 546). The major reason for seeking psychotherapy is depression. What we don't know is what percentage of this population have a history of "victimization" and are also suffering from PTSD and DES? The answer to these questions will influence the nature and length of treatment.

[2] Hoyt (1994) reports that more than 30 million Americans are now covered by HMO prepayment plans that delimit the number of psychotherapy sessions. He also notes that one visit, without further contact, is the modal or most common length of treatment, generally occurring in 20% to 50% of cases.

[3] More specifically, Howard et al. (1986) examined data based on over 2,400 patients covering a period of 30 years of research. They found that by 8 sessions approximately 50% of patients were measurably improved and that approximately 75% were improved by 26 sessions. Smith, Glass and Miller (1980) conducted a meta-analysis of almost 400 psychotherapy outcome studies involving more than 25,000 patients and control subjects. They found psychotherapy to be effective with the mean length of treatment being approximately 17 sessions. Given the "tenacity", "chronicity" and "retractibility" of PTSD, especially that accompanying Type II stressors, the often accompanying social stigma, the delay between the trauma and the provision of treatment, more long-term treatment may be indicated. For example, in Section VI we will consider Linehan's year-long treatment with "Borderline Patients".

clients have **not** been conducted, a similar set of treatment guidelines seem reasonable. PTSD clients without a personal or family history of prior victimization and a history of emotional disorders should be closer to **8 sessions**, while those with Disorders of Extreme Stress (DES) resulting from early, prolonged, interpersonal intentional human victimization, will require **26 sessions or longer,** as in the case of clients with Borderline Personality Disorders as discussed in Section VI. The decision about the number of sessions should be **collaboratively decided with the client.** There is no "magic" number.

In considering the issue of the length of treatment it is worth keeping in mind Fisch's (1994) admonition. He observes:

> "How long or short therapy is also depends on whether the therapist knows when to stop. It may seem trite to say, but if one has no idea of when something is done one runs the risk of going on interminably. Therapy, therefore, can be briefer if the therapist *(and I would add the client)* has some rather clear idea of what needs to occur to mark the endpoint of therapy" (p.131).

Let us consider some of the factors that should be considered in the determination of the length of treatment.

1. The type and extent of the trauma (severity, duration, intentional human design). Traumas involving brutalization, exposure to human suffering, mutilation and mass death, degree of grotesqueness can exert acute and persistent effects. Those individuals with multiple traumas may need more time to process and integrate their experiences.

2. The time that has elapsed since the trauma occurred.

3. The nature and intensity of the posttraumatic symptomatology. The number of triggers (specific, indirect, symbolic, general stress) that elicit rumination and related symptoms.

4. The nature, degree and duration of comorbidity (e.g., depression, substance abuse). Presence of physical illness, degree of physical wound, disability.

5. The amount of delay between the development of symptoms and the beginning of formal treatment.

6. The nature of the narrative that has been constructed -- sense of coherence, closure, perception of "victimization", ability to self-disclose and the nature of other's response to self-disclosure.

7. Characteristics of both the client and his/her situation.

    a) premorbid adjustment -- see enumeration of possible risk factors in Section III

    b) characteristics of the client - history of prior victimization and prior mental disorders, coping resources, ability to formulate a therapeutic alliance, especially in clients who have experience of betrayal of trust and problems with intimacy

    c) "secondary victimization" experience and post-trauma environment

8. The degree of social supports in the recovery environment. Amount of turmoil at home, interpersonal conflict, and involvement in treatment of significant others, possibility of employment and societal ostracism.

9.   Keep in mind that the traumatic events may be associated with a number of pre-existing and ensuing stressors (e.g., family split up, foster placement, etc.) and these will influence the length of treatment.

10.   As noted, there is a need to provide treatment for co-morbidity problems (e.g., addictive behaviors), address problems with sexual difficulties, teach coping strategies to manage depression, anxiety, rage/anger, as well as PTSD. There may also be a need to include family members in treatment.

11.   Allen and Bloom (1994) concluded that "longer treatment may be necessary if the traumatic experience was intense and prolonged, treatment is distant from the traumatic event, and social support is compromised" (p. 427).

Alternative Treatment Models

1.   **"Pulsed" or distributed interventions.** Another treatment model worth mentioning is that offered by Budman and Gurman (1988) where the client is seen **intermittently** and treatment is **"pulsed"**. Following brief treatment, a collaborative plan is established with the client (and perhaps with family members) for treatment to be provided at the time of critical events (e.g., transitional junctures, such as the time of an anniversary date or when judicial procedures are about to begin, and at other stressful times, as well as on "positive" occasions when the client wishes to report and review progress and signs of recovery. Pynoos et al. (1994) have described how **pulsed interventions** can be provided for children who have experienced disasters. Interventions can be provided at certain critical junctures. These may include occasions of anticipated or reported reminders of the trauma, when subsequent adversities occur, or when important life transitions or challenges occur. For instance, interventions such as group discussions may be conducted when students are about to reenter the damaged school that was rebuilt or when the class who was "victimized" (with the injury/death of some students) is about to graduate. Commemorative rituals may also be used as part of the intervention. Such interventions should be planned in collaboration with the students.

2.   **Short- versus long-term group treatment.** An example of the range of treatment alternatives is offered by Mennen and Meadow (1992) who describe group treatment of incest victims. They note that most groups are limited, short-term (4 to 18 sessions with an average of 10 sessions). They propose that for the same type of clients long-term (1 to 2 years of group treatment are required). Moreover, the format of these groups vary markedly.

What can one conclude from this list of possible factors? There are a number of factors (premorbid, trauma-related, and recovery environment) that need to be considered in formulating a decision about the duration and frequency of treatment. The items enumerated in Table 1 should be reviewed with the client so an informal decision can be made. Note, this decision can be reviewed with the client at various intervals in the course of treatment. The decision to continue in treatment should be done collaboratively. Remember keeping clients in treatment for too long of a period of time when it is no longer needed can be detrimental to the client. The goal of treatment is to help the client become his/her own therapist. The therapist must guard against nurturing overdependence and from acting as a **surrogate frontal lobe** for clients. Tomm (1987, p. 182) suggests raising the following questions with clients in order to explore the issue of the length of treatment.

a)   "Do you ever hear yourself asking yourself the kind of questions we discuss here in therapy?" (This question conveys that a goal of treatment is to have the client become his/her own therapist.) Can you give me some examples?

b)   "Do you ever wonder if continuing in therapy might actually interfere with your ability to learn how to find solutions on your own?"

c)   "If therapy did stop, who would be the most upset? Who would be most relieved?"

d)   "You have been doing well with therapy. How will you continue to do well without therapy?"

To this list of questions, I would add a number of characteristics in how clients tell their stories differently over the course of treatment. As therapy progresses the client should become more reflective, becoming an observer of his/her behavior and incorporating metacognitive (transitive) verbs such as "I can now see how I can drive myself crazy"; "I can notice when I get worked up."; "I have started to take charge of my life.", etc. Also, more metaphors that reflect hope and personal control should become part of the new client's narrative. Finally, not only do the clients offer different, more adaptive accounts, but their behavior should also change. Clients should take "ownership" and co-responsibility for changes they have brought about. In short, the therapist can review with the client his/her changes and consider together the decision to phase out gradually and eventually terminate (following relapse prevention training).

Table 1
Checklist of Factors[1] that Need to be Considered in Determining the Length of Treatment: The More "Yes" Responses, the Longer the Treatment

I.   Trauma-related Factors

1.   Has the client been exposed to a Type II versus a Type I stressor?

2.   Did the traumatic events occur early in childhood?

3.   Was it a prolonged stressor?

4.   Did the stressor involve threat to life? Personal injury? Death of a loved one? Exposure to grotesque stimuli?

5.   Was the traumatic event (e.g., incest) part of a class of stressors (e.g., marital distress, physical abuse,highly dysfunctional family, etc.)?

6.   Does the client perceive him/herself as responsible for what happened? (Feelings of self-blame, guilt, shame?) (For example, participate in atrocities or responsible for death or injury to others)

II.   Post-trauma Response

1.   Did the client evidence dissociative responses at the time of the trauma? And since then?

2.   Is the PTSD symptomatology, especially intrusive ideation, widespread? Do many events trigger intrusive ideation? Has the intrusive ideation persisted for a long time since the time of the trauma? Is the client continuing to "search for meaning", but in an unsatisfactory fashion?

3.   Does the client evidence DES symptomatology (loss of relatedness, affect regulation difficulties, problems with identity and trust)?

4.   Does the client evidence "negative" symptoms such as "anhedonia", lack of interest, an inability to maintain a sense of humor?

5.   Is there evidence of comorbidity (e.g., depression, suicidal ideation/behavior anxiety, substance abuse, somatic complaints)?

6.   Is there evidence of physical injury?

III. Premorbid or Pretrauma Factors

1.   Has the client a premorbid history of high risk factors (e.g., prior psychopathology, prior victimization, exposure to multiple traumas)? *(See Sections III and VII for an enumeration of these factors.)*

---

[1] Table 1 in Section VII on post-disaster intervention provides more detailed factors.

IV. Post-trauma Recovery Environment

    1. Does the client have an unsupportive social support environment? Experience familial rejection and societal ostracism?

    2. Is the client exposed to a high-expressed emotional (high EE) environment with criticism, blame, intrusion, and conflict?

    3. Has the traumatic events triggered a number of ensuing stressors (e.g., dislocation, loss of social supports, reopened "old wounds" and "familial conflicts")?

    4. Are there continuing stressors (e.g., possibility of reexposure, litigation, medical treatment)?

V. In Therapy Behaviors

    1. Is the client unable to establish a "therapeutic alliance"?

    2. Has the client been unable to share the nature of the traumatic events with others?

    3. Has the client's attempts to self-disclose to others led to negative reactions?

    4. Does the client have difficulty relating (trusting, self-disclosing) to others?

    5. Are there "secondary gains" that the client will receive if the client does not improve?

    6. Is the client unmotivated to receive treatment?

TESTING YOUR EXPERTISE

Section V - Treatment Alternatives

1. Critically evaluate the "state of the art" in providing treatment to clients with PTSD. Include both pharmacological and psychological interventions in your assessment.

2. Set up a role play situation where one individual plays the part of a PTSD client who is taking prescribed psychotropic medication. As the therapist, conduct an adherence counseling session. Have the third person at the role play critique how well the therapist educated, addressed, and anticipated the client's noncompliance with medication. Use the enclosed checklist. Take turns.

3. What are the contra-indications or "warning signs" in using direct therapy exposure procedures?

4. You have a colleague who is considering whether or not to sign up for a workshop on Eye Movement Desensitization and Reprocessing (EMD/R). What advice would you give him/her? What questions would you encourage him/her to raise at the workshop, if he/she decides to attend?

5. How can ceremonial rituals be used with combat veterans and torture victims? Explain the effectiveness of these procedures in terms of a constructive narrative perspective. Finally, what rituals have you used with PTSD clients to facilitate "healing"?

6. What role does cultural differences play in how you use assessment instruments and conduct treatment?

7. a) What has your experience been with group work and PTSD clients?

   b) What are the advantages of using group interventions with PTSD clients?

   c) What specific problems arise in conducting group work with PTSD clients? How can these problems be addressed?

   d) Role play how you can prepare a client for group participation.

8. Describe the specific decision rules and procedures that you would follow when conducting groups with PTSD clients. Comment on the group size, open/closed format, treatment orientation, length, screening procedures, specific treatment interventions. How do you decide, in collaboration with the client, if individual, group, couples, or family is the best treatment?

9. Describe the five phases of intervention with PTSD clients, namely

   a) Introductory
   b) Addressing presenting symptoms
   c) Restructuring memories
   d) Helping clients reconnect
   e) Termination

   What are the specific goals, tasks, and procedures of each phase? Contrast the ways you presently treat clients with PTSD with this five phase model. What critical differences appear?

10.   Describe how you presently decide on the length of treatment for PTSD clients (besides those limitations imposed by an outside agency). What factors do you take into consideration in formulating this decision? Compare your list of factors with that included in this Section. What premorbid, trauma, post-trauma response, recovery, and in-therapy behaviors do you take into consideration in determining the length of treatment.

        (Whenever a clinical PTSD case is presented use Table 1 in formulating a decision about the treatment length? Have a colleague use the same checklist, and then determine what degree of agreement exists in your judgement? Discuss your differences.

11.   How can you use the treatment guidelines suggested in this section to set up an inpatient treatment program for PTSD patients? What have you done to increase the likelihood of fostering generalization and maintenance of the treatment effects? Remember one cannot "train", or "treat", and then "hope" for transfer. What explicitly have you done to increase the likelihood that the client has "internalized", or "owns", the treatment interventions?

SECTION VI
SPECIFIC TREATMENT PROCEDURES FOR ADULTS
WITH PTSD AND RELATED PROBLEMS

Goals of Section VI

All of the previous Sections of this **Handbook** have led up to this point. The critical question is how can we best help individuals who have been "traumatized"? As discussed in the last Section there are innumerable ways to proceed. The treatment strategy adopted in this **Handbook** is to follow a constructive narrative perspective, whereby the goal is to help clients to achieve their collaboratively generated treatment goals, achieve symptom relief and change the "stories" they tell themselves and others about their traumatic events. Note that the treatment process begins with building a trusting, supportive therapeutic alliance that is very respectful of the client's needs. As noted, the treatment process begins with the initial assessment process. The questions asked in Section III and the feedback sessions of the test results provide the basis for the present therapeutic efforts. In turn, we will consider how the therapist can **collaboratively**:

1. **educate** the client about the nature of PTSD and the recovery process;

2. help the client cope more effectively with **"flashbacks"**; treatment of **"alters"** in multiple personality disorder

3. help the client cope with **"intrusive ideation"** by means of **direct therapy exposure; imaginal and in vivo exposure procedures; guided imagery procedures; hypnosis;** and **stress inoculation training procedures**

4. help the client deal with **anger and rage reactions** by means of self-control and interpersonal training

5. help the client address and alter maladaptive beliefs and dysphoric feelings such as depression and guilt (shame, self-blame) by means of **cognitive restructuring procedures** and **problem-solving procedures**; how to **structure** the therapy session

6. help the client **"rescript"** his/her story by means of **letter writing** and taping procedures; use of **"healing" metaphors**

7. help the client deal with characterological and interpersonal problems as in the case of **borderline patients**

8. help the client deal with comorbidity problems such as **alcoholism** and related **addictive behaviors**

9. help the client and family members by means of **family-based interventions**.

The primary goal of this Section is to provide enough detail so clinicians can implement ("try out") and evaluate these therapeutic procedures.

EDUCATING THE CLIENT ABOUT
THE NATURE OF PTSD AND THE RECOVERY PROCESS[1]

(See Epstein, 1992; Herman, 1992; Meichenbaum, 1993; Prout & Schwarz, 1991; Scurfield, 1985; van der Kolk, 1994)

It is important to keep in mind that the "educational" process to be employed in therapy is **not** a college lecture, but rather reflects the ongoing social discourse and Socratic dialogue that occurs over the course of therapy. An **inductive form** of counseling is used. The educational process also <u>occurs continually</u> over the entire course of therapy as the thrust of what is being communicated changes. Initially, the therapist may wish to emphasize the **"normalization"** and **"legitimization"** of the client's reactions to traumatic events. Then, after having listened to the client's story and provided the conditions where client's can relate the accompanying emotional toll, the therapist may help client's reframe their **symptoms as being "signs of recovery."** This sets the stage for the therapist to educate the client about the **bio-psycho-social model of PTSD** and the physiological impact of having experienced traumatic events. Other features of the educational process may cover:

i)   debunking popular myths;

ii)   providing information concerning possible triggering events and lingering effects;

iii)   providing information concerning specific issues such as flashbacks, "memory work", relapse prevention, and the like.

The purpose of education is **not** only to convey information, but to also instill hope, engender meaning, and help client's construct a new narrative. Remember the best form of education is when clients can <u>discover</u> the information on their own. The adage that the therapist is at his or her best when the clients are one step ahead of the therapist, offering the information that the therapist would otherwise offer, applies to the entire educational process. When clients provide the insight, "own" the information, this can be both empowering and enabling.

Parenthetically, it is worth noting that the authors of DSM-III-R and DSM-IV view how people react to traumatic events as "symptoms", illustrative of a PTSD or PTSD plus DES disorders. This is clearly one way to view how people react to traumatic events. But there is another version that is incorporated in this Educational Section. Each of the symptomatic behaviors such as intrusive ideation, denial, numbing, dissociative reactions, hyperarousal, dichotomous thinking, self-blame, and the like, can be viewed (or reframed) as "coping efforts" and "survival instincts". Surely, if the therapist wishes to obtain reimbursement from an HMO or from some other outside agency, the "story" the therapist tells the agency is that scripted by the authors of DSM-IV. But that need not be the <u>same</u> story one co-constructs with one's client. This Section considers how the therapist can help clients come to view their reactions in a more "positive" adaptive light as a means of self-protective activities. As the radio commentator Paul Harvey often admonishes, "There is a need to hear the rest of the story!" From the present constructive narrative perspective, the carefully crafted and sensitively paced collaborative educational process that takes place over the entire course of treatment, is designed to help clients develop a different "story", one that is enabling and empowering.

---

[1] See the section on letter writing and healing metaphors for additional examples as to how clients can be educated using cognitive reframing procedures.

The therapist who is a true artisan is able to weave the following points into an educational tapestry that appears seamless. Moreover, it is proposed that these points should not only occur in the course of therapy, but one should ask the critical question, "How many of these points does the client say to him/herself and believe?" If your PTSD client was asked by a neutral observer, "What have you learned in your therapy about PTSD?", how many of the points described below would he/she incorporate into his/her answer? It is important to ask our clients such questions, and then listen and learn from their answers.

Once again, keep in mind that these points should not be offered in a didactic fashion, but instead should be blended into the social discourse of counseling. The points the therapist can convey include the following.

A. "Normalizing" and "Legitimizing" the Client's Reactions

1. After listening to the client's story, acknowledge the gravity of the trauma. Traumatic events can produce symptoms in almost anyone, regardless of pre-trauma experience. Convey that the client is not alone in having these feelings, but is having a normal response to an abnormal situation.[1] The client needs to appreciate that underlying any PTSD symptom is both a hard practical reality and an attempt at resourceful accommodation. In order to avoid pathologizing the client's condition, the therapist can use the term **post traumatic reaction** and **not** **post traumatic stress disorder**.

2. Lipton (1994) takes a somewhat different, but potentially complimentary, approach in his educating clients about PTSD. He provides clients with a description of PTSD and the DSM-IV list of accompanying symptoms. The client and therapist (and family members, where indicated) review the list together. Special emphasis is placed on the initial sentences that describe Criterion A (which is highlighted), namely, "The person has experienced an event that is **outside the range of usual human experience** and that would be **markedly distressing to almost anyone**. It is noted that PTSD is "normal". It can happen to anyone who has experienced what the client has experienced. Everyone has his/her **"breaking point"**.

   It is **not unusual** for people to have strong emotions in response to traumatic events. The fear of physical and psychological injury, the fear of death are **"normal"** in such circumstances. It would not be normal if you were not frightened and upset by such events. Expecting yourself not to be frightened under such circumstances is unrealistic. Any feelings of being "different", "stigmatized", "inferior", "weak" are **understandable, but unwarranted."**

3. The therapist can use the metaphor of psychological aftermath or aftershock to describe the immediate and delayed reactions to traumatic events. These reactions may appear during, soon after, and/or much later (e.g., intrusive imagery, numbing, startle reactions, rage, grief, etc.). Convey that trauma means "wounding". In the same way that a body can be wounded, so can the "psyche" or "mind" be "wounded". "Just like a broken leg must be bandaged and allowed to heal, psychological wounds from catastrophic events need care and attention and time to heal. It is all right not to be all right! It is normal to be distressed by death."

---

[1] Scott and Stradling (1992) caution about using the phrase "it is a normal response to an abnormal situation", since this phrase does not capture the variability of response to traumatic events. As noted in Section I, PTSD is not a necessary nor determinate response to traumatic events. Clients may wonder if PTSD is so "normal", then why didn't more individuals who were exposed to traumatic events (e.g., combat, disaster, etc.) have similar reactions? Thus, caution is warranted when using the phrases about "normal reaction".

4. Indicate that it is <u>not</u> unusual that one may fear that he or she is "losing control". This does <u>not</u> mean that "you are going crazy". Rather, this is a sign that there are important features to work through about the trauma. While the client should not take responsibility for the "victimization" experience, the client can take responsibility for caring for oneself. While time alone does <u>not</u> diminish powerful emotions as we have come to expect with most other unpleasant and upsetting life experiences, there is a need to learn to **leave the past behind** and stop spending time with it, allowing one to go on, **move on with life** (Lipton, 1994).

B. <u>Providing a Bio-psycho-social Perspective of PTSD</u>

1. In a timely fashion, the therapist can educate the client about the PTSD reactions and process and about recovery by offering the following rationale[1]:

> "People who have been exposed to traumatic events are often haunted by memories of the past trauma. This reaction is understandable given what they have been through. Such past events, for some, can become an "organizing force", a "pivotal point", in their lives. Because of the emotional impact of such traumatic events individuals may exert a good deal of effort and organize their lives in such a way as to avoid the emotional distress that accompanies their memories of the trauma. When they encounter reminders of the trauma this may trigger a renewed emotional reaction. The traumatized individual acts "as if" the trauma is recurring again and again. As a result of this process, people who have been exposed to traumatic events often suffer from a generalized hyperarousal (e.g., being startled easily, being hypervigilant). Moreover, as I mentioned they tend to react to specific reminders of the trauma, as if the trauma was actually happening again *(repetition of important points is appropriate -- see next Section on educational guidelines)*. Such physiological responses can trigger either a "fight or flight" response. People who have been exposed to traumatic events are prone to go immediately from the stimulus (the trigger) to the response, without making the necessary intermediate assessment or appraisal of the meaning of what is going on, without asking themselves, "What is happening?" This automatic response makes sense given what they have been through. This automatic response reflects the "wisdom of the body" taking over, the "survival instinct" at work. This automatic response, however, can lead to an overreaction to specific reminders. Sometimes the reminders are external (give examples); sometimes the reminders are internal (give examples). If the arousal gets too intense and lasts too long, then the individual attempts to "shut down", "go numb", "turn it off" (give examples). Since traumas can overwhelm a person's sense of safety and security, the individual is vulnerable to stimuli that are dimly reminiscent of the original trauma. This can lead to intrusive recollections and ruminations.
>
> Physically and emotionally traumatic survivors (with PTSD) are alert to anything that might threaten their physical and emotional safety. They overreact to any perceived danger. They often numb themselves against the possibility of pain.
>
> When clients reexperience trauma (have flashbacks or nightmares) this can trigger the re-release of the stress hormones and the process begins once again. Once we understand how this process operates, <u>we</u> can work <u>together</u> to change it." ... This was quite a bit to cover, lets go over this together.

---

[1]The pace with which this is covered is tailored to the client. Some therapists audiotape their sessions and give their clients a copy to listen to between sessions.

Solicit the client's reactions to this description of PTSD and the implications it has for understanding their reactions and the processes for change (e.g., the need to live in the present, to "notice," "catch" and "interrupt" the cycle, to come to expect, understand and change such reactions). There is a need for us to work together to help you get control of your **alarm system**. "Not every time there is smoke, there will be fire." As a result of our working together you will be able to gain distance, and eventually, transform these reminders so you can feel safe.

2. There is a need to help clients recognize and name symptoms. This can be enhanced by having the client self-monitor[1] or fill out a daily symptom checklist, or to record "triggers". By objectifying the client's symptoms it conveys some sense of control and reduces the preoccupation that some clients have that "there must be something wrong with me for having certain reactions". Highlight for the client that his/her symptoms may include:

    a) reexperiencing the trauma (flashbacks, intrusive thoughts, nightmares that "plague" people). These are traumatic reenactments.

    b) avoiding any reminiscent cues about the trauma and reexperiencing of the "protective" emotional numbness of the initial exposure that was used for "self-protection";

    c) exaggerated or ready arousal of vigilance, agitation, anger that interfere with concentration and daily functioning.

    d) For example, discuss with the client his/her tendency to **drift into reexperiencing the trauma**. Note that while all people tend at one time or another to reflect both on the past and the future, ask the client if he/she notices that he/she is tending to do this more frequently and that the thoughts tend to linger longer and the ruminations are distressing. Does the client have feelings of not being able to control such recollections and ruminations, as if they appear "uninvited", disturbing and "out of control"? Clients may report, "It was almost like yesterday."; "My mind works so quickly. It is like snapping on an electric switch."; "The thought and pictures come from nowhere."; "The pain/stress starts to open the door to bad memories."; "I'm caught off guard."; "Why can't I go back to some of the good memories? Why is it always the worst memories?"
    The therapist can ask clients if they have feelings of "losing time", being "detached", or that things seem "strange". Ask clients if, at times, people ask them, "You didn't hear what I said. You are not here. Where are you?" The therapist can offer the example of someone driving a car on a long stretch of highway and having one's mind wander without realizing it, until you ask yourself if you had past a certain exit. Has the client had similar experiences? Note, at times, clients may not even realize that they are ruminating or having "time-slides" into the past. This discussion of ruminations will lead to an examination of how to cognitively reframe intrusive ideation and ways to control them, as described below.

    If these effects can be labeled, described and predicted then their "strangeness" is diminished. Such experiences can now be shared with significant others, rather than be concealed.

3. Comment on the temptation and dangers of using alcohol and drugs as a way to cope or "shut down," avoid and reduce the impact of PTSD symptoms, or as a means of what Baumeister calls "escaping from oneself". Also convey information about how people "shut down", withdraw, avoid, and "self-soothe" interpersonally and about the possible effects of having

---

[1] In Section III we examined how therapists can ask clients to self-monitor.

been "victimized" on such interpersonal areas as trust, intimacy, and sexual relations. Comment on the transactional nature of behavior, namely, help the client to appreciate that how he/she behaves can inadvertently produce reactions in others, that confirm the client's views of self and the world.

C. Reframing Symptoms

1. A central feature of this educational process is helping clients **reframe symptoms** as **"signs of coping"** and as **"self-protective and healing efforts"** and a **"normal part of the recovery process"**. A caveat is warranted when conducting this reframing. **It should not be undertaken too early in the therapy process.** The therapist first must hear the clients' "emotional pain", otherwise clients will not feel you appreciate the seriousness of their distress. Keeping this warning in mind, the therapist can help clients to reframe symptoms: (Note the *therapist* should sample from the following list according to the client's symptoms and not overwhelm the clients.)

    i)   intrusive ideation (flashbacks, ruminations, nightmares) as an attempt to make sense of the experience; the brain's attempt to assimilate the experience. Intrusive ideation indicates that the client is not just letting the experience go, but rather is attempting to understand it; flashbacks/nightmares are access routes to memory, aspects of dramatic memories that are unwillingly relived. Flashbacks are retrieval cues, reminders to process or work on and find meaning in the traumatic experience that has happened. Flashbacks and intrusive ideation indicate that you are actively trying to process the information, trying to make sense of what happened. Intrusions represent "time slides", often accompanied by unbridled emotions. They are the psychological residuals of catastrophic stress. The therapist can comment to the client that almost all persons who experience a traumatic stressful event such as a natural disaster or combat reexperience the event in some form (e.g., dreams, nightmares, recollections, flashbacks). Such instances of reexperiencing can serve to remind us to never forget the worth of the people and things you lost. If you didn't care about the loss, you wouldn't be having flashbacks and intrusive thoughts. Help me to understand (play "Columbo"), what of worth was lost, what heroism was evident, what efforts of survival took place. Where indicated by the developmental history, highlight that for some clients, the present trauma may reawaken memories of an earlier trauma. Indicate that intrusive symptoms are not a sign of losing one's mind or of "insanity", but rather reflect the normal content of thought in a **sensitive personality** after trauma. As I mentioned it is all right not to be all right. *(See the discussion below on flashbacks for other examples of how one can convey the "normality" of such reoccurring preoccupations.)*

    ii) denial/numbing are ways that the mind takes a "time out," as a way of "dosing" or of "pacing" oneself, so you only have to deal with so much stress at one time; a way of restricting the range of feelings you can deal with at one time; a way of withdrawing from distressing information at a time when you are incapable of confronting or assimilating the information. One can look upon denial as an adaptive response to the meaningful implications of the trauma.

         Denial allows an individual to postpone or control the pace at which you process the information and implications of what happened. Denial eases upon you, a little bit at a time, what happened so you can rebuild at your own pace, step by step, one at a time.

         Avoidance. The therapist can convey to the client that we both need to appreciate how important it is for you to keep the specifics of the event away from your awareness, but now that you feel safer and more in control you can afford to gradually feel the panic at your own pace (pain, distress, terror, etc.) that went with that moment.

Emotional numbing is often episodic (comes and goes) and it "mutes" feelings. It allows you to keep yourself in reserve. It can be viewed as the client's attempt not to lose control (e.g., control anger and rage episodes) so as not to become overwhelmed. The therapist can convey to clients that the repeated reliving of the moment of trauma or horror may be one way of breaking through the sense of "numbing" and "disconnection". Such comments convey to clients that their **symptoms serve some purpose** and are not mere random uncontrollable events. Perhaps there are alternative, more adaptive, ways to avoid or break through the emotional numbing, instead of having to use reliving traumatic memories. Such comments convey a sense of choice.

Even detachment or isolation from others can be protective, especially if the individual fears the loss of emotional control. In response to a fear of hurting others these can act as a form of protection.

iii)   dissociation at the time of the event can be viewed as a potentially useful "auto-hypnotic skill"; as a useful mechanism for "safeguarding" the integrity of one's personality; as a "defense" against trauma, fear, anxiety; as a way of keeping painful events out of awareness and memory. Dissociation reflects the ability to forget in order to "survive". Some events that are too horrific to "invite in" so you pushed them away and rejected them. Later these thoughts and feelings may return in the form of intrusive memories and feelings. In order to illustrate the processes by which traumatized individuals "watched bad things happening to them as if they were only vaguely participating", tell the patients about Bettleheim's (1943) experience of how he used "dissociation" during his time in a concentration camp, or how Frankenthal (1969) used dissociation to cope with the violence of being repeatedly raped by SS troops in a concentration camp. Dissociation may also be viewed as the mind's way to "give up". You may have tried everything and nothing worked. Then the conscious mind gives up the struggle. If not, it can become totally exhausted. The nonconscious mind takes over, but it is not quite ready to take on the horror. Instead, the mind becomes detached. Dissociation is like a patient in a surgical operation who can watch himself, forming an out of body experience. Does that make sense? Note that the use of addictive substance-like alcohol can act like a drug-induced dissociation and note how impulsive behavior can act as a flight from one's feelings and escape from oneself. Comment that the use of addictive behavior made sense to the client at the time. Later in this section we will examine ways to help the client examine the pros and cons of maintaining addictive behaviors. Even self-mutilation behaviors can be reframed as the client's attempt to exert some personal control. When abused as a child you learned not to "feel". Such attacks were random and violent. You learned to cut yourself in order to make things "right", to punish yourself, and to control your pain.

iv)   hyperarousal and hypervigilance -- you were trained (for combat) to sense and see danger before it occurred. You were taught, to the point where it was second nature, to react quickly and attack any perceived danger. You worked hard to develop an uncanny ability to sniff out danger, to sense and anticipate risks. This skill was critical to your survival and to the safety of your buddies. In civilian life, some soldiers continue to exhibit this same behavior in the form of hypervigilance. They fall back into a combat mode of functioning. Does this make sense? Can you offer any examples? The therapist can use an example of "referred pain". Emotions toward different objects can be transferred at an "unconscious" level. If medication has been prescribed, the therapist can convey that the prescribed medication that the client is taking will help "muffle" the client's arousal and false alarm-system so he/she does not react "as if" every time "there is smoke there will be fire". Ascertain if the client has used his/her own medications (e.g., alcohol, drugs) as a way to dampen down reactions.

v)   behavioral self-blame can be viewed as an attempt to control future behavior; self-blame serves as a means to maintain the belief that one is in control of one's fate and provides a means by which the individual can take responsibility for the past and maintain the belief of a sense of control in the future. Self-blame can convey a sense of justice and order, a means of making sense of traumatic events that otherwise might seem incomprehensible. The therapist can help the client cognitively reframe such attempts of blaming oneself as a means of exerting "control". It is a coping style that makes sense given the client's view (appraisal) of what happens, but it is maintained at a "high" price. Explore with the client whether this view makes sense. Collaborate with the client to generate examples. Note, Bulman (1989) in her study of rape victims has drawn a distinction between the potential adaptive value of **behavioral self-blame** (attribution to specific events such as "I drove on the wrong street."; "I wore the wrong clothes.") and the **characterological self-blame** (attribution to stable characteristics such as "I am a gullible person."). It is the behavioral self-blame that proved more adaptive since it implied something that could be done in the future. The actual validity of such behavioral self-blame is not the critical issue, but rather it provides a causative model that implies change and possible control. Dutton (1993) indicates that self-blame processes may play a different, less adaptive role in victims of domestic violence.

vi) black-white dichotomous thinking -- comment that this type of either-or thinking at one time may have been highly adaptive (e.g., when working with combat veterans as suggested by Bradshaw et al., 1993). "When you were a soldier the enemy was bad and worthy of death while your comrades were good and should be protected. Such black-white thinking was necessary and provided safety and insured survival. But now in civilian life, sometimes feelings get triggered as when you are in an argument or you sense a threat or an impending danger and you *slip back into your old combat black-white mode of thinking*. This is natural given this overlearned thinking style. Does this make sense?" At this point the therapist explores with the client examples of such thinking styles and considers what is the **impact** on oneself and on others. ... What is the **toll**? ... What is the **price** the client pays for such "slipping" back into the old combat way of thinking? Such discussion will lead to collaborative suggestions about what can be done differently to change? (Remember -- grey can be a beautiful color!) Note, this educational approach does not characterize the client's thinking as a "cognitive error", nor as a distortion, but rather views such cognitive patterns as instances of **overgeneralization**, namely, the client is continuing to do something which is no longer needed. It is a **"stuckiness" and "transfer" problem**. The client needs to learn to "notice", "catch", "interrupt" and "change" such patterns.

vii) the therapist can speak of the "wisdom of the body," e.g., "mind is taking time out from overstimulation"; "denial is one of nature's small mercies". Highlight that these "symptoms are **survival strategies**" that were used at the time of the trauma, but they are no longer needed;

viii) highlight that the client did what he/she had to do in order to survive. **"There is a wisdom in survivorship that is worth salvaging."** The victim can elect to become a "witness" and to stand up and create a new light. There is a need to respect painful memories, instead of trying to resist them. By bearing witness, by writing, drawing, reaching out, by **finding a "mission"**, the individual can remember and mourn. As Herman (1992) observes, "Psychotherapy does not get rid of the trauma. The goal of recounting the trauma story is integration, not exorcism." (p. 181). There is no "magic bullet", nor quick way of purging. Rather the object is to help individuals **transform** their trauma story.

ix)   the therapist can comment that the **desire for revenge** is the "mirror image" of the traumatic memory, with the role of the perpetrator and the victim being reversed (Herman, 1992). Forgiveness is also a gift to yourself. **What is the best revenge? To live life well!**

x)   in terms of the **interpersonal consequences** of PTSD, the therapist can help the client appreciate the **transactional** nature of his/her behavior. Convey that the "psychic trauma" is **like a stone** that is thrown into a pool of water. It creates a ripple effect, not only for the victim, but also for those who are close. Let's take a moment to see if this happened for you. In this context, highlight the transactional nature of human behavior as illustrated in the case of depression or aggression. Then have the client apply to his/her own behaviors. For example, ask the client, **"What do you think we know about someone who is depressed? ... They are depressing!** They behave in a way that tends to turn other people off. (Have the client give examples.) But, the reactions of those who are turned off merely reinforce (strengthen) the depressed individual's concerns about being rejected and abandoned. Thus, depressed individuals behave inadvertently, unwittingly, and perhaps, even unknowingly, in ways that produce the very "data" (reactions from others) that confirm their beliefs about themselves and others.

xi)   The therapist can note, "While we cannot take away the trauma, not take away the scars left by trauma, one can learn to live in spite of the wounds that will not heal." (Sinclair, 1993). Moreover, when clients embrace a "disease" model for his/her distress the therapist can draw a distinction between "disease" and "illness behavior" by observing that, "Just because someone has a disease that does not mean that he/she has to be sick." (Lipton, 1993). Whereas "victimization" can be equated with "brokenness", survivorship can be equated with "mending" and "healing". We will work to help you move from seeing yourself as a "victim" to that of a "survivor", and even to the point of being a "thriver".

Note that these reframing attempts do not reflect a particular commitment by the therapist to a specific model. For example, while I doubt the simplistic view of a conscious versus nonconscious mind, as suggested in the reframing of dissociation (point iii), the reframing provides a useful therapeutic message. **The critical features of these reframings are not their scientific validity, but their viability and plausibility for the client.** In the same way that the authors of DSM-IV have a "story" to convey (these behaviors are symptoms of a psychiatric disorder), the present constructive narrative model also has a "story" to convey. The "story" co-constructed with the client is that these behaviors were and are "survival skills", "coping devices", and "the initial signs of recovery". This approach is consistent with the suggestions offered by Frank (1987) who observed that helping clients make sense of symptoms raises their morale by combating feelings of confusion and demoralization. Symptoms are not as ominous as the client had feared. In fact, the present reframing process helps clients view their symptoms as a first step in the healing process and a favorable sign of recovery.

D.   Bolstering Client's Self-efficacy and "Hope"

1.   "Commend" the client for being distressed, depressed, or whatever the presenting symptoms. The therapist might say something like the following: "Given what you have been through, if you didn't have stressful reactions, weren't depressed, didn't have a short fuse at times, didn't dwell on what happened (use client's symptoms), then I would be really

concerned. These behaviors show me, show both of us, that you are in touch with your feelings. You are trying to make sense of what happened and in time move on. You are in the process of learning to enhance your tolerance for "bad" (or dysphoric) feelings."

2. **Discuss the nature of therapy.** Do <u>not</u> raise false expectations. Highlight that each person is **unique**, each person' situation is **different**, and that there is <u>no</u> prescription for recovery. Indicate that therapy is a **vehicle** through which each client can be helped to **discover** his/her own **singular path** to a personal healing or a **unique pathway** to the recovery after traumatic stress. Comment that there is <u>no</u> one approach that is best for everybody. What works for one person may <u>not</u> be effective for someone else. What is encouraging, however, is that there are quite a few different ways that have been shown to be promising. The questions <u>we</u> will explore is which ones will be best for you? If the one approach we choose doesn't work for you **don't be discouraged**. It might mean that it isn't the right approach for you. With so many possibilities, we are bound to find something that works for you. I'm willing to stick with you until <u>we</u> find something that works best for you. Indicate that one does not come into treatment and get "fixed". It takes time to connect to the process of recovery and move on and heal. One does not heal overnight. You recover one step at a time. I am reminded of one client who wrote,

> "A terrible thing befell me. Not only have I survived it, but I have incorporated it into me. I may hurt more, but I am wiser and stronger. I have overcome the darkness and the pain. I can move forward in my life. I can laugh and love and work. I overcame the traumas, they did not overcome me." (as cited by Peterson et al., 1991).

The therapist can ask the client, if he/she may turn out to be like this client. This is the fascinating aspect of therapy, to watch someone like this client change.

<u>**Discuss the possibility of lapses and relapses.**</u> If <u>we</u> try something and it doesn't work that may prove quite helpful and instructive. It is like a scientist who is performing an experiment. Sometimes the experiment works and that is great. But sometimes the experiment flops. Now, when does the scientist learn most? Often when the experiment flops.

It is like my teaching my young son to ride a two-wheel bike. At first I run along side holding on to his bicycle seat. After he develops some confidence, he says, "It is okay dad, let go." With some concern, I let go. Now sometimes he rides by himself, but sometimes he falls. Now, when does he learn most? Often when he falls. Did he go too fast? Did he turn the wheels too quickly? Was the ground wet and the bike slid out on him? Is he going to be **23** years old riding downtown on a three-wheel bike or a two-wheel bike with training wheels?

When will you learn most from therapy? It is often when things don't "work", don't go the way you want, or the way we expect. If everything we do works then it is possible that you are not fully challenging yourself. Convey that each lapse (relapse) is a normal part of recovery. If we never make mistakes we would not learn anything. *(The object of this discussion is to lay the groundwork for relapse prevention.)*

Convey to clients that as therapy proceeds unexpected events can often effect our lives, just like a wrong turn might affect a cross-country journey. But the quality of the whole trip is seldom changed by a single wrong turn or by a temporary setback.

3. As noted previously, in the context of lapses the therapist can come back to the issue of **"stuckiness".** **Convey** that the "survival skills" that the client once used and that were

adaptive at one time may no longer be appropriate, may no longer work. It is **not** that the client is "crazy" or "sick," but rather he/she reacts to present situations the way he/she did in the past. The issue is one of **"stuckiness"** and **"traumatic transfer"**, or **"overgeneralized response"** to things and to others. The client is using an **outworn way of dealing** with stressors, an **outmoded way of behaving**. Have the client highlight what he/she has done to "survive". For example, as noted, illustrate that the soldier who was on guard for oneself and for one's buddies developed the ability to be hypervigilant. In combat this was adaptive and needed. One of the problems is that the same soldier may still be on guard and hypervigilant when it is no longer necessary.

4. Indicate that PTSD is **definitely responsive to treatment** and that **healing** can be a **lifelong process**. While therapy may take longer than the client wishes, it will **not** go on forever. Convey hope in the human capacity to heal from the effects of trauma. "There can be life after trauma." Convey to the client that at present it may be difficult to imagine that a time will come when the trauma will no longer command the central place in his/her life.

5. Convey to the client that symptomatology may **not** go away completely, nor forever. This does **not** mean that the client is "stuck" or will have a negative outcome, but rather that there is a need to "work through" and "move on" and not allow the past to rob you of the present and the future (convey hope). Indicate that there are both "positive" and "negative" symptoms which indicate that one never completely forgets. Sometimes memories just appear, other memories are tied to, or connected to external or internal events. Together _we_ will search for these connections.

   Note, clients may have been told, "Put the trauma behind you." or, "Forget it. It is over! Move on!" Many clients find such messages "unhelpful" since these messages are viewed as negating the meaning and impact of their experience, and "short-circuiting" their attempts to integrate the traumatic experience (Roth & Lebowitz, 1988).

6. Indicate, however, that it is possible that as we discuss and work through what happened and why, as we begin to refocus on the trauma, symptoms **"may get worse before they get better"**. This is to be expected. But this is a necessary step in order to work through what happened. "I will be with you throughout the process" (Scurfield, 1985, p. 242). "We can develop a **partnership in survival** in dealing with an event that still remains toxic." "We will walk the path together, aware of a general direction and of predictable pitfalls, but ready to discover new truths at every turn." (Ochberg, 1991, p. 6). Herman (1992) compares the **recovery process with running a marathon**. Like a marathon, the recovery process is a **test of endurance**, requiring long preparation, repetitive practice, conditioning or toughening-up, and psychological determination and courage. The therapist's role is that of a coach or trainer. Note, that in drawing the analogy between the recovery process and the marathon, the **therapist should introduce the general analogy of a marathon** and then explore by means of a Socratic dialogue with the client examples of how the analogy fits or does not fit, and the implications for how therapy can proceed.

7. As a result of such efforts, post-trauma symptoms can be controlled, reduced in their severity and frequency of occurrence, and possibly even eliminated (positive expectancy conveyed). Also, convey that this process will help the client "gain an understanding of what has been happening, what is currently happening, what might happen to you, and what you can _do_ about it" (convey sense of choice and control). Highlight that while the memory of the trauma may not go away, it will lose its gripping qualities, its ability to stop you in your tracks and make you feel completely undone. It will lose its power to control you. Indicate that some symptoms may come back or recur under stress or with certain reminders.

8.   "Finally, although this may be difficult to believe right now, you may even find that there will be some positive benefits to you and your life as a result of the experiences you have had and your willingness now to face and work through what you must work through. For example, you must be very strong to have experienced what you experienced and be here, talking to me about it today" (Scurfield, 1985, p. 242). Convey that the exposure to such extreme stressful events can also have positive, salutary or health-promoting effects as it leads to new adjustive processes. Help the individual give up the view that such stressful events only lead to irreparable damage. Help the client appreciate that the trauma that arises is a developmental opportunity. Comment on the **Chinese word for crises** which also has the symbol for opportunity within it. "What we have is a human system in transition." A crisis can help us to replace an old form of knowing with new ways of knowing and experiencing. It is like someone emigrating to a new country with a new language, customs, and we have to learn anew (Herman, 1992). Exposure to such traumatic events reflects both stress, but also an opportunity for learning and challenge. Does this make sense?

E.   "Educationing" about other Related Issues

1.   Educate the client about popular "myths" that are tied to his/her traumatic events. For example, for a discussion of the myths surrounding rape see Matsakis, 1993; Roth & Lebowitz, 1988. The client may mistakenly feel that he/she is responsible for the traumatic event (e.g., instead, highlight that rape is a criminal act; sexual abuse was an abuse of power and trust). Highlight that the client did all that he/she could under the circumstance. It is difficult to accept not being in control, but the client can now concentrate on what he/she can control in terms of the healing process.

2.   Help the client (e.g., veteran) appreciate that PTSD is not just a "function" of the individual per se, but it also reflects the social organization in which he is a part (e.g., consider how the veteran or rape victim is treated). As Greening (1990) observes, there is a need to avoid defining PTSD in a too narrow fashion that "pathologizes" the victim; there is a need to examine the role of the pre- and post-trauma environments. For example, this does not deny the horrors of war, but helps to put the present adjustment into a larger context that conveys opportunities for change.

3.   Other elements of what can go into the educational process are distributed throughout this manual. For example, in the sections on flashbacks, memory work, debriefing, and in other sections educational information is included. Education, conducted in a collaborative fashion, is part of each phase of the intervention. It does not merely occur at the beginning of therapy, but occurs on an ongoing basis.

4.   The following guidelines taken from Meichenbaum and Turk (1987) provide further suggestions as to how the educational process can be conducted. **Note that the points just reviewed should not be presented in a lecture format, but over sessions these points are weaved (like a tapestry) into the social discourse with the client.** It is worth audiotaping your individual or group sessions with your clients and noting how many of these points have been covered.

GUIDELINES TO FOLLOW WHEN GIVING INFORMATION[1]
DO NOT ACT LIKE A SURROGATE FRONTAL LOBE FOR YOUR CLIENTS

Be selective in the information to be given -- the fewer the instructions given, the greater the recall. Giving too much information, as well as too little, can contribute to treatment nonadherence. Use inductive education so clients have a chance to offer suggestions.

Be specific, clear, detailed, concrete, and simple in communicating and when giving instructions. Use short words and short sentences. Limit the number of words per sentence and the number of syllables per word. Use "down to earth" nontechnical language. Use simple language without psychiatric or psychological jargon. Keep in mind that if clients do not understand what you are saying they are unlikely to tell you that they don't understand. Rather, they just don't do what you asked them to do.

Be careful about the timing of the information. Give small amounts of information at each session. Don't overwhelm or overload the client with details. Information should be dispensed in discrete quantities over time. Individually pace and tailor the program. Different clients need different kinds of information at different paces. Check for client receptivity and understanding.

Organize the material. Greater recall of information presented in the first third of communication and greater recall of the first information offered.

Whenever possible, present information about the course of action to be followed near the beginning of the session. Provide the rationale for recommendations and statement of treatment goals.

Include the rationale for the treatment regimen, the specific client behaviors required and the possible positive consequences of following the regimen. Don't ask clients to do something without sharing the rationale and relating it to their treatment goals.

Determine if the information corresponds with the client's private theories about PTSD and what should be done about it. Evaluate the client's perceptions of the treatment regimen at the time it is initiated and after it has been implemented.

Provide advance organizers of what you're about to say (e.g., "First, I am going to describe X, then I will describe the changes needed in Y. Then we will discuss why this is important. Does that make sense to you?").

Repeat important information where feasible. Reinforce essential points. Emphasized material is recalled better.

Use concrete examples, illustrations, mnemonic devices, analogies, metaphors, retrieval cues such as acronyms, anecdotes, self-disclosure. Heighten personal relevance of the material and tie it to personal experiences.

Use oral and written material, better than either alone. May supplement presentation with audiovisual material and visual graphic aids (slides, audiotapes, videotapes, films, anatomical models, educational sheets, take home booklets, newspaper or magazine articles, cartoons,

---

[1] These suggestions and the research from which they are derived have been summarized by Meichenbaum and Turk (1987).

diagrams, charts). Use memory aids. Insure that the client can comprehend the written material.

When providing clients with a course of action to be adhered to, stress how important it is.

Check the client's comprehension. Ask questions and solicit feedback. Also encourage clients to raise questions and take notes or write summaries if they wish. As therapy progresses ask the client to summarize the session -- what was important and why? What will the client take away from today's session? How will he/she apply (use) this on a daily basis?

Promote active reworking of the material (e.g., ask the client to restate in their own words the information given). Clients may need to rehearse the information mentally so that it is stored correctly and readily retrieved. The therapist can assess whether the client understands the information and can satisfactorily carry out the behaviors. For example, the therapist can ask the client to engage in a **"role reversal"**. The therapist can ask the client to imagine the therapist is a new patient who suffers from PTSD. Ask the client to explain to the therapist what PTSD is and how it affects someone. Ask the client to indicate what the new patient can look for as his/her first signs of recovery. Use role reversal when teaching other techniques. Don't just ask the clients what they need to do, but also "why". Solicit the reasons and commitment of the client to follow through.

Encourage clients to discuss the treatment regimen with the therapist and participate in planning their treatment.

Help clients set realistic goals that can be subdivided into easily attainable measurable steps.

Elements or components of the treatment regimen should be taught in a gradual, incremental fashion, rather than prescribed for implementation all at once.

Insure that the client has the requisite skills required to follow the treatment plan.

Individualize instruction, give feedback and offer praise for the client's effort. Nurture the client's self-confidence that he/she can be successful in following the treatment regimen.

Involve the client and significant others (where appropriate) in therapeutic planning and decisions.

Don't oversell the program.

Help the client remove barriers caused by the treatment.

Remember that clients tend to recall and use information that is presented as a good case study[1], or as a good story, better than information merely presented in a didactic fashion. It is not information alone that leads to change, but information that is "owned" and collaboratively generated with the client that contributes to change.

---

[1] A substantial and robust effect in attitude change research is that information conveyed in the form of case histories has greater persuasive impact on people's judgment than does more abstract or factual base rate information (Meichenbaum & Turk, 1987).

HOW CAN THE THERAPIST TREAT THE CLIENT WITH "FLASHBACKS"?

(See Dolan, 1991; Herman, 1992; Matsakis, 1992; Meichenbaum, 1993; Musicar & Josefowitz, 1992; van der Kolk & van der Vert, 1991)

Treatment Objectives

1. Client to accept and integrate experience embedded in the flashback and control ruminations.

2. Client to control when flashbacks and ruminative behaviors occur and his/her reactions to them. Reduce total time in ruminations and reduce the degree of distress they engender.

3. Client to avoid and minimize the impact of flashbacks and ruminations.

4. Influence what the client says to self about the flashback and ruminations (meaning the flashbacks hold).

5. Client to reexperience memories of own choosing without sustained distress and suffering.

Treatment Format of Own Choosing (4 possible phases)

Phase I.   Education

Phase II.   Strengthening Coping Skills

      A.   Identifying triggers

      B.   "Getting grounded"

Phase III. Changing the Memory

Phase IV. Processing and Integrating the Flashback Afterwards

Phase V.   Other Issues

      A.   Flashbacks During Sex

      B.   Treatment of "Alters" in Multiple Personality Disorder (MPD)

Treatment Guidelines

I. <u>Education</u> -- RECALL THAT THE GOAL OF THE SOCRATIC EDUCATIONAL PROCESS IS TO LAY THE GROUNDWORK SO THE <u>CLIENT COMES UP WITH THE IDEAS OF WHAT SHOULD BE DONE NEXT IN TREATMENT.</u> If the client does not come up with ideas the therapist can always offer suggestions.

    a) Help the client to better understand the nature of his/her flashbacks and ruminative behavior. Flashbacks have been characterized as "waking nightmares" and as "engraved reverberating legacies of trauma". Explore with the client the nature of his/her flashbacks, nightmares and preoccupations. Explore with the client what it feels like to experience an event with all your senses, as if it were recurring, even when one is fully awake and sober. Convey that this is a different "realm of experience" and may lead some individuals to feel that they are "losing their mind". Has the client had any of those thoughts? Help the client appreciate that such feelings are "normal". Also help the client appreciate that flashbacks are persistently reexperienced memories of often superintense recollections; memories that are "frozen in speechless terror".

Also explore with the client other related responses. As Herman (1992) observes, "traumatized people [often, sometimes] find themselves reenacting some aspect of the trauma scene in **disguised** form without realizing what they are doing" (p. 40). The therapist can explore this possibility with the client. Note that one cannot just put traumatic events "away", like an old piece of furniture in the attic. At some point the memory of the trauma may return. There may be so many triggers that it is not possible to prevent or avoid such flashbacks and ruminations. But the client can learn to control how long, how disruptive, and how disturbing such thoughts and feelings may be. The client can learn that when such thoughts begin the client can keep their impact or the "bad times" to a minimum.

b)   Highlight that flashbacks are memories, but these memories are unlike other memories because they are often accompanied by intense, painfully charged emotions such as feelings of terror and dread. Convey that a flashback means that an "old" memory has been triggered by an evocative event (sometimes an inconsequential resemblance to the past, sometimes a symbolic resemblance). The therapist can use the metaphor of "conditioned response" to an evocative stimulus to explain flashbacks, as well as research on state dependent memories.[1]

Convey to clients that extreme emotional and physiological arousal often accompanies the flashbacks. Such flashbacks may make the individual feel immobilized and he/she may become unaware of immediate surroundings. Flashbacks are a form of memory and memories are a form of acting, an action of telling a story. Trauma tends to keep the memories "frozen". They **"freeze"** the person so he/she is often unable to take any further action. **Immobilization** is a central feature of having been exposed to trauma. Convey that the client may be either barely able to shift attention from such memories or must regularly struggle to resist attending to them.

The therapist can also convey that traumatic events do not "fit" well with a person's usual view of him or herself and with his/her view of the world. The result of this "misfit" is the development of an **association** of the memory of the traumatic event with what are called **"alarm reactions"**, ideas of harm, altered states of mind, and special intense memories, a kind of **emotional flooding**. *(Check to see if these descriptions make sense to the client and explore what can be done. This discussion will lead naturally to the client, with some assistance from the therapist, suggesting that one should identify "triggers" for alarm reactions, consider ways to "unfreeze" memories, and ways to retell his/her story.)*

c)   Warn clients that flashbacks may appear in the form of dreams, nightmares, intrusive ideation, and intense discomforting feelings, as well as intrusive reexperiences.

---

[1] As Meichenbaum (1985) has noted, the critical feature of these explanatory schemes such as "conditioning" are not their scientific validity, but rather their plausibility and credibility for the client. The explanatory model should also help the client make sense of his/her symptoms and condition, imply a series of possible specific treatment interventions, and convey hope.

Explore whether the client has developed avoidance or a phobia for traumatic memories.

d)   Help the client to normalize and reframe flashbacks as an instance of the client attempting to heal from the traumatic experience so that he/she can "go forward in life". The client may have been offered advice by others or believe that "forgetting is the only way to cope"; that "time heals all wounds"; that "this will be behind you soon"; that "it is only in your head"; that "you need to move on". Explore if the client has received such advice and how this made him/her feel. Indicate that in therapy we will explore what else can be done and explore how the client can learn to develop an improved "coexistence" with the continuing intrusive symptoms.

e)   Flashbacks are the "minds attempt to make sense of a very important and significant life transition events. This is normal and adaptive." Discuss with the client other examples of where individuals are preoccupied by thoughts or current concerns. Ask the client if he/she knows anyone who gave up cigarette smoking after many years of smoking? Discuss the discomfort and preoccupations that the smoker goes through, namely, continual urges, reminders, intrusive images -- even dreams of cigarettes -- after such a major change. If the cigarette smoker is going to succeed in stopping, then he/she must deal with the initial discomfort, must accept the intrusive images rather than fight them.

Note: When using metaphors like **"the smoker"** the therapist should use **Socratic questioning** procedures so clients can discover the comparisons and apply them to his/her symptoms and situation. The objective is to "normalize" the phenomenon of intrusive ideation. Whenever there is a major life transition, as in the case of smoking or when experiencing a disaster, individuals are prone to be preoccupied with them. Scott and Stradling (1992) even use the example of what happens if someone wins a large lottery. While working or doing something else, thoughts of what to do next with the winnings will "visit" individuals. Baumeister (1993) describes an instance of an athlete who was 91 years old who still wakes at night remembering how he was beaten out for a medal by $1/10$ of a second in the mile run back in the 1912 Olympics. Another athlete recalled how in the Final Four of the NCAA basketball tournament in the final seconds of the game he missed a free throw after having made 28 in a row. Ten years later he said he still thought about that "awful game" every single day.

The intent in offering these examples is not to equate such events as giving up cigarettes or athletic disappointments with the horrendous features related to the client's trauma, but to convey that the process of intrusive ideation is a "normal" way for individuals to remember.

f)   Convey that what will be done in this phase of treatment is to consider the 3 stages of flashbacks, namely,

        i)   the "triggers"
        ii) the "surfacing" of memories
        iii) the "aftermath"

g)   Convey that you will help the client examine his or her own flashback pattern. Reassure and comfort the client that he/she will be able to learn to tolerate discomfort, not "fight" and "counteract" old traumatic memories. For example, consider the metaphor offered by Scott and Stradling (1992) to convey these points:

        "One can think of a person's mind as being very much like a railway station. You are standing on one of the station platforms. You cannot control what trains come into the station. On some days there may be, say, special trains to take people to a race track. The trains that come into the station depend upon what is going on in the outside world. But you can choose whether you get on a train or not, or ignore it or wave goodbye to the occupants of the train. ... When you try to stop your intrusive thoughts it is as if you are jumping on the railway track to try and stop the train. Maybe you should calmly greet the thoughts like you great the train and then wave them goodbye. Practice keeping your cool about the thoughts. ... Just as you can't force a physical wound to heal quickly, you can't force a psychological wound to heal quickly either. In both cases, you have to flow with the healing process, not fight it." (p. 51)

Also consider the following descriptions that can be given to clients:

"The struggle is not to forget what happened. You will never be able to do that. The goal is to cope with it, to work through it, to make adjustments."

"These memories are not like having the flu and getting over it. It is always with someone like a parent losing a child, or survivors of the Holocaust, or a plane crash, or a war. How does one keep going? How does one have a goal to keep going forward, to keep trying to get through this, no matter how hard?"

"How do you turn a new page on these private demons? How do we write a new page, turn a new leaf?" "How do you bridge the gap of living your life in a world of trauma, in a world of the traumatic past and connect that to the present and future?" "How can you accept, acknowledge and go on with your life?" ... The therapist conveys that these are some of the questions we need to explore.

Some veterans have conveyed that they live a "double existence" made up of the "traumatic past" and the "bleached present". They ask, "How can I reconcile myself with the past?" The therapist can convey that without such a "split", perhaps the client may not have been able to come back into life. *(Note, the clinical strategy is to commend the client for his dissociative symptoms and then to move on to possible ways that the client can integrate the past and the present, how the client can "use" and "tame" past horrors with current experience.)*

h)   Listen for how the client discusses his/her flashbacks, especially the metaphors that convey the absence of control (e.g., these thoughts just "visit" me, "show up", "have a life of their own", "controlled by them", etc.). Then explore the impact of these experiences. Obtain specific descriptions since these will provide a basis for identifying triggers.

i)   Convey to the client that the treatment should prove helpful in lessening the likelihood of flashbacks occurring and in minimizing their impact when they do occur, but that the treatment is not "fool proof" in preventing flashbacks. Instead of stopping such thoughts, the client can develop the skill to just practice watching a video of the traumatic scene (shrinking it to the size of a small television) for X minutes; not searching for the impossible to stop the thoughts. Give yourself permission to let go of the intrusive memory. Accept them, rather than fight them. "Is there a way to integrate the reliving experience into the client's life?"

j) Listen for the common themes, beliefs and emotions surrounding the flashbacks (e.g., belief that the flashbacks are a sign of "going crazy", "stuck forever", "being a victim"). Acknowledge and normalize such feelings and fears as understandable, normal, given the severity of the stressor and the intensity of the emotions surrounding the flashbacks.

k) Also, listen for common themes of fears of abandonment, loss of control, vulnerability that are reflected in the flashbacks and dreams. These will be used later on in the treatment as described in the Section on cognitive restructuring.

l) Educate the client about the difficulty (if not the impossibility) of actively suppressing ruminations and flashbacks. Comment on the research of Wegner (1989) who found that when one actively attempts to suppress aversive thoughts from entering consciousness, the thoughts later tend to "rebound" into one's awareness, with even greater frequency than before. Wegner has noted that intentionally suppressed thoughts occur about twice as often as thoughts the subjects were told not to suppress. The attempt to control what cannot be controlled can lead to maladaptive reactions (e.g., becoming obsessed with keeping certain thoughts out of mind). The therapist can ask the client to perform a simple experiment of "not thinking" about "white bears" or "pink elephants" for a specific period of time and discovering it has just the opposite effect of suppressing such ideation. Active suppression is not a useful solution to the problem of ruminative thoughts. Instead, developing a strategy or plan of action for addressing the source of the disturbing thoughts or cognitively reframing or reappraising the thoughts are more useful strategies, as suggested by Clark (1993). *(Below we will consider several specific strategies to accomplish these goals.)*

m) Comment that when the mind is not actively occupied it can leave a void or create a vacuum that is quickly filled by painful ruminations. A wandering mind invites ruminations. We can only concentrate on one thing at a time. This is why some people need to keep busy and why some people become "workaholics" in order to control ruminations. Comment on how some people who have been victimized by horrific events (e.g., Holocaust, prisoner of war experiences) attempted to cope by thrusting themselves into their work, without learning to "integrate" and "accept" their memories. When they retired and their life style changed, the traumatic memories came back for some, especially at "anniversary" times of the event. Just keeping busy will often not be enough.

II. Strengthening Coping Skills

A. Identifying triggers

a) Explore with the client the situations that are likely to trigger flashbacks. The following questions will help the client identify triggers.

Possible questions to ask the client about flashbacks:

i) Please, describe your flashbacks and ruminations.

ii) Do you have any idea what may have triggered these flashbacks/these feelings? What do you think started them?

iii) When have you felt this way before?

   iv)   What situation were you in the last time when you felt this way? Was there anything about the situation that was particularly troublesome or bothersome?

   v)   Is there something going on in your life right now that reminds you of how you felt during the "traumatic" time? ... during previous flashbacks?

   vi)   In what ways, if any, is the current situation and your past situation <u>similar</u>?

   vii)   How is your current situation <u>different</u> from the situation in the past in which you have had similar feelings/similar flashbacks? What is different about the settings?

   viii)   What aspects of the experience are most likely to trigger your flashbacks?

   ix)   Can you think of any events or feelings that you could have recognized sooner to know you were ruminating?

   x)   What actions, if any, did you take to feel better and to control your feelings/flashbacks?

   xi)   What actions would you like to take to feel better should these flashbacks reoccur?

   xii)   What do these images, thoughts, feelings, or sensations mean to you?

b)   Have the client identify what are triggers and different types of triggers.(e.g., anniversary reactions, current stressors, conversation and other reminders, media presentations).

c)   Have the client <u>self-monitor</u> possible triggers by means of a keeping diary or journal. The self-monitoring should address questions such as:

   i)   when the flashback occurred;
   ii)   where was the client;
   iii)   what he/she was doing;
   iv)   who was there with him/her?;
   v)   the client can write down "the trigger/reaction/traumatic memory".

d)   See guidelines in this **Manual** on how to help clients adhere to the request to self-monitor (Section III).

e)   Help the client to see any patterns to the flashbacks (e.g., anniversary effects, triggering external or internal stimuli).

f)   The processing of this information helps to nurture the client's sense of control. Convey that knowing how to limit or minimize the <u>duration</u> and <u>intensity</u> (impact) of the flashback experience when it begins to occur can be reassuring. The client will also learn ways to recover more quickly afterwards so that flashbacks do <u>not</u> interfere with his or her life.

B.   <u>Developing coping strategies to handle and avoid flashbacks.</u>

a)   Lipton (1994) has proposed a number of coping strategies clients can use to control flashbacks and ruminations. They include:

i) reduce exposure to triggers -- coach client on how to prevent and avoid triggers, some of which the client might bring on as a result of hypervigilance (engaging in so-called "war games").

ii) catch ruminations faster -- become aware of and search for low intensity prodromal cues so the client can develop a plan, a "script" to react instantly and appropriately.

iii) control the amount of time spent with thought/memory -- learn ways to apply concentration to "here and now" behaviors (may not be able to stop thinking of things, but can learn to control the time spent on thoughts); learn not to think of more than one thing at a time; learn to "switch channels" like a television set. Practice and perform experiments by increasing time reading, watching television, and other activities that require sustained attention. Gradually increase the length of time for these activities.

iv) invite significant others to help in the process of catching, interrupting, and learning to control ruminations. They can comment on when they spot the client "being somewhere else", "not here", so they can tell the client in a supportive fashion.

v) engage in a regular schedule and activities that provide enjoyment and that require concentration, as well as relaxation (e.g., exercise).

b) In a collaborative fashion help the client explore ways he/she can avoid situations that trigger flashbacks and cope with responses should they occur. Note that such avoidance constitutes a self-protective act.

c) Discuss how such strategies can be implemented -- once again follow the self-monitoring guidelines.

d) "Getting grounded" -- metaphor offered by Musicar and Josefowitz (1992)

i) Help the client maintain at least some awareness of his/her present reality and self when the flashbacks occur. There is a need to help the client keep in "present reality" and not "slip", nor become "engulfed", in "past reality" of the trauma.

ii) Teach the client deep breathing and relaxation skills -- see guidelines in Meichenbaum (1985) on ways of conducting relaxation training. Once again, follow the self-monitoring guidelines in order to enhance client adherence. Help the client appreciate that there are things the client can "choose" to do in response to flashbacks.

iii) Discuss ways the client can learn to bring oneself back to the present, staying aware of the present. Dolan suggests that the client can use an associational cue (e.g., an object, a poem) that acts as a reminder of safety and comfort. For example, see Ochberg's survivor poem that is included in Section VIII of this **Manual.**

iv) Help the client to identify the first signs of a flashback and then use coping responses such as stress inoculation self-instructional procedures. For example, "I'm having a flashback My name is _____. I am _____ years old. I am in (state place) and then employ other self-coping statements." (See Meichenbaum, 1985, for possible coping self-statements. Note, how these coping self-statements can be collaboratively generated with clients.)

v) Another option is for the client to find a "safe place" when having a flashback. Note, this "safe place" may be an external physical place such as with a friend or it could be a "safe place" within oneself. This imagery-based "safe place" is especially useful with children (see Rhue & Lynn, 1991; also described in Section VII)

vi) The client may be given an object by the therapist to use that reminds the client of the therapeutic relationship or that helps to make the client feel safe.

vii) The client can select a particular trigger to work on.

e) Dolan suggests that the therapist use the following probes to strengthen the client's coping abilities: (Note the use of **"What"** and **"How"** questions.)

i) How did you get past those feelings/flashbacks the last time you had them?

ii) What _difference_, if any, does it make when you make the connection between how you are reacting now and the feelings (memories) that are triggered of the past?

iii) What would be the first small sign that you were calming down? ... that you were able to handle the flashbacks?

iv) What do you think the next small sign might be or has it already happened?

v) How do you think that would be helpful?

vii) What difference will that make?

viii) What did you learn from what you went through that would (could) help you if you ever felt (or experienced) that again?

ix) How would you know that you were doing what you needed to do, in order that... (e.g., you can handle your flashback, can notice the onset of your flashback, etc.).

III. **Changing the Memory** _(In the next Sextion on Direct Therapy Exposure we will consider several ways therapists have helped clients alter their traumatic memories.)_

There are a variety of imagery-based procedures that have been designed to add and alter an individual's traumatic memories (e.g., imagery recall of traumatic events and working to transform the sequence and impact of the events; "uncoupling" the dysphoric affect that is tied to the recalled memory). Common to many of these procedures is the message that the client should "stay with" the flashback and not try to "combat it," or "avoid it", but rather to do just the opposite. The therapist may suggest that the client will "learn something important and valuable from the memory that he/she needed to understand all along in order to begin to integrate the memory and move beyond it " (Dolan, 1991, p.156). (The _various_ ways to help clients transform traumatic memories is described below.)

IV. **Processing and Integrating Flashback Afterwards**

a) Help the client to make sense of the flashback experience by "externalizing" it so it can be accessible to everyday consciousness.

b)   The client is encouraged to write, talk about, and even draw the experience so it shifts from a "seemingly random, senseless reliving of the past" to a more meaningful controllable portion of one's biographical narrative. Help the client to "externalize" the "emotional pain" and express feelings by talking, writing, drawing, using clay, or any other medium that the client suggests or prefers. Have the client describe what may have been lost, but also what has been saved and cannot be touched by the traumatic incident.

c)   The client and the therapist need to examine the "messages" about the client and about relationships that are encoded in the flashback. Listen for themes of culpability, responsibility, and vulnerability and then use the cognitive restructuring procedures described below.

d)   Help the client make sense of and deduce the "messages" of his/her distressing dreams.

e)   Ensure that the client "takes credit" for any changes in controlling flashbacks. The therapist asks the client to describe how he/she was able to "notice", "catch", "interrupt", "self-monitor", "control", "find meaning in" the flashbacks. *(The therapist should take note of the frequency with which the client spontaneously employs these metacognitive verbs in his/her narrative account.)*

f)   The therapist should conduct relapse prevention procedures exploring with the client what he or she will do if the flashbacks reoccur.

V.   Other Issues

A.   Flashbacks During Sexual Relationships

Dolan (1991, p.176) suggests that the therapist and client consider the following steps concerning the handling of flashbacks should they occur during sexual relationships:

a)   As soon as the client is aware of the flashback open her[1] eyes (if closed) and notice where she is. Notice differences between the partner and the perpetrator, between the current physical surroundings and those recalled in the flashback.

b)   The client should focus on her symbol for comfort and security (e.g., may engage in relaxation response or self-talk or comforting image).

c)   Stop attempting to respond sexually until the flashback is over. Let your partner know what is going on in order to enlist the partner's help.

d)   Have the partner say reassuring words or engage in reassuring activities that you have identified together as being useful in this situation.

e)   Do not resume sex until both feel comfortable. (Dolan also suggests that the client tell the "little girl inside" that it is safe now. Caution is needed when employing such metaphors as "the little girl", or "inner child", or Dolan's use of the metaphor of "talking directly to the unconscious", or "obtaining the unconscious' permission",

---

[1] In this example the female gender has been used, but these procedures could be collaboratively generated and used with males who are having flashback experiences.

especially with borderline and multiple personality disorder clients. Caution about iatrogenic terminology.

Note, the therapist needs to keep in mind that there is no "little girl inside", no "inner child". These are metaphors that are part of a constructive narrative. It is important to remind the client that it is helpful for some people to think of themselves as if there is a part of them with an "inner child" or "little girl", and if this helps the client then we can use this as part of the "healing process". Clearly, the therapist's and client's attitudes toward using such metaphors will influence their usefulness. The "as if" quality of such metaphors needs to be conveyed. For example, the therapist can say, "It is as if there is a part of you that is X."

If sexual dysfunction continues for sexual assault victims then some form of sexual dysfunction therapy ala Becker and Skinner (1983, 1984) and Kirschner, Kirschner, and Rappaport (1993) may be appropriate. (Also see Foa et al., 1993.) A major focus of these interventions is helping the client separate the past from the present and experience feelings of choice and control that she now has. The "victimized" client may avoid intimacy and sexual pleasure because it represents a loss of control, leads to guilt, rekindles the "victimization" role. These feelings need to be explored and addressed. Also explore a "trust hierarchy" that the client can employ in deciding with whom to develop intimacy and sexual relations.

B. Treatment of "Alters" in Multiple Personality Disorder (MPD)

How one treats "alters" depends on how one views the nature of MPD. There is a great deal of controversy surrounding the diagnosis of MPD with very strong opinions being held on both sides. (For example, see Saks, 1994, for a discussion of MPD from a legal perspective.) Some view MPD as a reflection of a dissociative disorder resulting from a history of victimization (due to childhood sexual abuse), while others view MPD as a form of iatrogenic (therapist-induced) disorder. Before we consider the treatment options let us briefly consider the nature of the controversy.

An important recent scholarly analysis was offered by Spanos (1994)[1] who provided a **sociocognitive perspective of MPD.** Spanos proposed that MPD patients learn to present themselves as possessing multiple selves and learn to reorganize and elaborate on their personal biography in order to make it congruent with their understanding of what it means to be a multiple. Spanos is not suggesting that patients diagnosed with MPD are faking multiplicity, but rather **they are inadvertently taught multiplicity as a byproduct of the assessment and treatment processes.** The MPD patients come to adopt a view of themselves that is consistent with the views conveyed to them by their therapist. To support his argument he cites historical, cross-cultural, experimental and clinical data.

(1) Historically, the nature of MPD has changed significantly. Spanos (1994) notes that in the 19th and 20th century MPD patients rarely displayed more than 2 or 3 alter identities. In contrast, modern MPD patients may display on the average 15 or more alters and some of these patients exhibit more than 100 alters. In my experience this is especially true at psychiatric centers that I have visited that specialize in MPD. The incidence of MPD has exploded. Between 1945 and 1980, 128 cases of MPD were reported in the literature; in the following decade, approximately 20,000 cases were diagnosed (Cote, 1994).

---

[1] I was saddened to learn that Nicholas Spanos recently died in an airplane crash. The field is in his debt for his incisive analytic scholarship.

(2) **The strong connection between child abuse and MPD is of recent origin**. Case reports in the early 20th century and before was much less likely than modern cases to be associated with reports of child abuse. (Obviously, this may be due to inadequate attempts to assess for child abuse) Nevertheless, it is important to keep in mind that while most MPD patients (some 97%) report child sexual abuse, most abused individuals do not develop MPD (see Beitchman et al., 1992; Read and Lindsay, 1994).

(3) While MPD is a rare phenomenon among the clinical population, cross cultural studies of spirit possession and experimental studies of hypnotically-induced subjects indicate that multiplicity is quite widespread. Laboratory studies indicate that multiple identities (even with amnesias) can be readily created in many normal people under socially demanding circumstances. These results highlight that MPD can be considered goal-directed enactments aimed at meeting social expectations.

(4) **MPD appears to be a culture-based syndrome**, largely restricted to North America. When MPD has been reported abroad, as in the case of Switzerland, the diagnosis of MPD has been primarily offered by a handful of psychiatrists. In fact, in one study cited by Spanos, 6 of 655 psychiatrists who were sampled offered 66% of all of the MPD diagnosis. Also interesting, whereas in North America women are three times as likely than men to receive an MPD diagnosis, in Switzerland the MPD diagnosis was given to men 51% of the time.

(5) In North America, the advocacy of MPD has taken on characteristics of a **social movement**, where therapists and patients may attend MPD workshops and conferences, subscribe to national MPD newsletters, and even use MPD patients as cotherapists to convince skeptical new patients that their MPD diagnosis is correct. One estimate reported by Spanos was that some 17% of therapists treating MPD in North America are themselves patients or former patients diagnosed with MPD or other dissociative states.

(6) **"The data suggests that the procedures used to diagnose MPD often create rather than discover multiplicity"** (Spanos, 1994, p.153).

To support this observation consider the potential biasing effects of the following clinical probes that have been used:

> "Do you ever feel as if you were not alone, as if there is someone else, or some other part watching you?"

Another highly suggestive clinical procedure **that can "teach" multiplicity is the use of leading hypnotic interviews**, where the client is asked to have his/her alter personalities "come forth" and talk to the therapist. In the context of the interview the client is asked if the

> "alter has a name; how long she has been there; the patient's age when the alter came; whether the patient knows her; whether she ever takes over the body; whether she ever directs or influences the patient when the patient has the body; her mission or function; and whether there are other people back there" (Bliss, 1986, pp.196-197).

Spanos observes that one major characteristic that **distinguishes therapists who diagnose MPD and those who do not is the use of hypnotic procedures.**[1] Such interviews "repeatedly inform the patient that he/she has other parts that can be addressed and communicated with, as if they were separate people" (Spanos, p.153; Also see Mersky, 1992). The therapist may prod MPD clients not only to reveal alters, but to also unearth memories of child sexual abuse or other forms of victimization. Therapists may use leading and suggestive questions to elicit abusive memories from their patients. When patients express doubts about such reports "their uncertainty may be represented to them by their therapists as evidence that they are unwilling to face the fact of their abuse" (Spanos, 1994, p.156). The therapist can inadvertently cue and legitimatize multiplicity. See Gleaves (1994), Putnam (1989), and Ross (1989) for a further discussion of MPD and Frankel (1993) for a critical discussion of the questionable relationship between MPD and childhood sexual abuse.

Perhaps, the most succinct critiques of MPD were offered by Piper (1994) (British J. Psychiat., 164, 600-612) Amer. J. Psychotherapy, 48, 392-400) who highlighted:

a) the vague, over inclusive, diagnostic criteria for MPD, and the questionable validity of measures of dissociation;

b) the recent sharp increase in the number of patients alleged to have MPD;

c) the questionable relationship between MPD and childhood abuse;

d) the ways clients are encouraged and reinforced for "multiplicity" (Also see Merskey, 1992, Brit. J. Psychiat., 160, 327-340.);

e) the unresponsiveness of MPD patients to treatment.

With regard to the potential iatrogenic features of MPD, consider the potential suggestive impact of the following therapeutic techniques that Piper (1994) enumerates. The therapist

a) may ask directly and repeatedly to meet an "alter"

b) may give friends and relatives of MPD patients training in "calling out" the patient's "alters"

c) may conduct extensive interviews with the MPD patient (2 1/4 to 4 hours) to reach the alters

d) may press his/her thumb against the MPD patient's forehead, citing repeatedly the name of the alter, and saying "I want to speak to you"

e) may conduct an "internal group therapy" with alters

f) may propose a "bulletin board" where alters can post messages for each other

---

[1] **Hypnotic procedures do not reliably enhance the accuracy of recall.** As Spanos (1994) observes, under some circumstances, hypnosis may lead subjects to become even more **overconfident** in their inaccurate recall. There is little or no correlation between the accuracy of recall and the confidence that people place in their recall.

g) may interview each alter, taking a history from each one and asking the alters to produce a map or diagram of how they fit together (a kind of "internal genogram")

h) may have the therapist engage in age-appropriate play behavior with each alter

Obviously, each of these techniques, alone, or in combination, especially when conducted on a group basis with other MPD patients, could encourage ideas of multiplicity and nurture MPD role enactments. I have witnessed such assessment and treatment techniques at various clinical sites at which I have consulted. I can assure you that these were very troubling visits. These concerns are further strengthened when we learn that patients who eventually receive a diagnosis of MPD receive an average 6 to 7 years of mental health care before the MPD diagnosis is offered (Read and Lindsay, 1994). But what are the alternatives to these procedures? Could one treat "MPD patients" without calling forth and working with alters? We now turn our attention to this challenging question.

Whatever one's opinion about the potential iatrogenic influences on MPD, the question emerges as to **how one should treat clients who report "alters"?** The following provides some suggestions.

1) Help the client to understand what precipitated the need for "alters" to occur. Help the client to notice the triggers for dissociative episodes or "switching" (reframe this behavior as an exaggerated form of avoidance). Hammond (1990, p. 347) has used the **metaphor of a pressure cooker** to convey to MPD clients (and other PTSD clients) ways to reappraise the "internal pressure" that they feel. The pressure cooker metaphor helps clients view their dissociative behaviors (development of alters) as only one means to release emotions, a way of coping (dissociative response) that **made sense** at the time. But now in therapy, we (therapist and client) can learn other less destructive, self-injurious, more adaptive ways to "notice" and "handle" the pressure they feel. The therapist says:

> "Have you ever seen an old-fashioned pressure cooker? My grandmother used to have one. You would latch it shut, and turn up the heat, and the bubbling water and steam inside created tremendous pressure. After a while, some of that pressure had to be released or something would burst.
> Right now you're experiencing tremendous pressure, from all the feelings inside. And it's important for us to use **a safety valve** to release that pressure, gradually, safely, in a protected and controlled way so that no one is harmed in an explosion of emotions."

The client and therapist can then use the **pressure cooker metaphor** as a means to engage in problem-solving steps. By means of a series of collaborative probes such questions as the following can be addressed:

a) How does the client notice when the "pressure" is beginning to rise? (individual profile)

b) What is common across situations (both internal and external) when the pressure is about to rise?

c) What are the different **safety valves** that the client can use to let off the pressure? What has worked in the past? What gets in the way of using these "safety" procedures?

      d)   In turn, consider with the client where, when, how, and why the client should use these "safety" procedures? What will the client do (or say to herself) when these procedures "don't work"?

2)   Reframe the use of "alters" as a former coping technique that is no longer needed *(see the Section on education of PTSD for a further discussion of dissociation)*. The client need not get "stuck" using one "safety" procedure of using alters.

3)   Exchange information about victimization, how to relive the past, and then learn how to "put it behind them" and "get on" with their lives. Help bolster other intra- and interpersonal coping skills.

4)   Silon (1992) describes how **imagery, training and hypnotherapy** has been used to treat dissociative responses. The dissociative behavior is likened to the **metaphor of a "wall"**. In order to treat the "wall of fear and denial" while under a trance, clients are asked to imagine their unique personal "wall" and to describe it in detail. The goal is <u>not</u> to knock the wall down, but to transform it. The client can choose to make the wall lower, thinner, add windows, and then decide to come out from behind the wall, knowing he/she can go back if he/she needs to. The **transformation of the wall** is used as a **metaphor** for empowering the client. These metaphors are then translated into daily action. "Alters come to be viewed as **a wall** from which one can come out from behind." The wall metaphor can be used to teach coping skills.

5)   Because of the danger of reifying the client's alters and treating them, as if, they "exist" as separate personalities, the therapist <u>should not ask different alters to appear</u>, nor refer to them by name. For example, do not ask the client, "Can I now speak to Angie?" "Don't cross examine, Angie, to see if she knows about another alter, named Beverly", and the like. The therapist should <u>not</u> use any interview, hypnotic, drug-induced, imagery-based, psychodrama, or group procedure that could inadvertently "strengthen" or "teach" the multiplicity of personality. If for some reason the therapist uses the name of an alter the therapist should qualify it by saying, "whom you (the client) call Angie."

The intent of this treatment guideline is <u>not</u> to invalidate the client, nor challenge and confront his/her use of alterns, but rather to be aware of and respectful of the social influence potential of the therapeutic relationship. If one does not treat the alters directly, then what are the alternatives?

6)   It is proposed, from a cognitive-behavioral constructive narrative perspective that the therapist:

      a)   help the client appreciate the ways she used dissociative techniques as a "coping device" and as a "survival skill" when she was "victimized" at an earlier age. For example, one client described how she would imagine that "aliens" would enter her room at night and sexually molest her, when describing her step-fathers' incestuous behaviors. Moreoever, she was distraught and felt abandoned as her mother failed to intervene. As an adult, the aliens returned in the form of voices (hallucinations), and later emerged, in the form of multiple personalities.

      b)   In therapy, she learned how when "overwhelmed", "stressed-out", when she felt "powerless", she would "time-slide" back into her old way of coping by dissociating. Thus, the central problem was that she was "stuck" using a coping procedure that worked at one time in her life, but that was only working now at a very high personal and interpersonal "price". In collaboration with her therapist she developed a "Power Book" that included a number of alternative coping techniques, besides dissociating.

c) With regard to the alters, the therapist wold comment that when the client felt "overwhelmed" and "powerless" she would act in ways to "take back" or "give up" control. **A part of her** would **act as if** she was that unprotected, victimized child, while another part would **act as if** she would want to escape, and so forth. This pattern makes sense, given what she had been through. But now she has, alternative ways to "notice", "catch", "interrupt", and "control" this pattern.

d) Note: It is <u>not</u> being suggested that there are different parts of people. There is only you. You can, however, tell stories, use metaphors, that imply that there are different "parts of you". Such metaphors can be used to help clients deal constructively with alters, instead of confronting, dismissing, pathologizing, nor inadvertently reinforcing. There is an explicit need to develop and evaluate treatment approaches that don't further "victimize" clients and iatrogenically co-create multiple personalities.

e) Chu (1994, Psychotherapy, 31, 94-100) has offered similar treatment advice when he admonishes therapists who treat patients with MPD as follows:

> "Therapists should use language consistent with the least degree of fragmentation that the patient is able to accept, e.g., "part" or "aspect" being preferable to "personality" or "person". Therapists should avoid wholesale naming of personalities who do not already have names. (p. 99)

I recognize that the present proposed guidelines for treating MPD patients are controversial and will elicit strong reactions in some therapy circles. Hopefully, it will stimulate debate and research on MPD from a constructive narrative perspective. MPD is a very interesting way to tell stories about yourself. When viewed from this perspective, new therapeutic interventions are suggested.

HOW CAN THE THERAPIST TREAT THE CLIENT WHO EXPERIENCES INTRUSIVE IDEATION? DIRECT THERAPEUTIC EXPOSURE (DTE) AND GUIDED IMAGERY-BASED PROCEDURES

(See Fairbank & Keane, 1982; Foa et al., 1993; Herman, 1992; Keane et al., 1989, 1992; Keane & Kaloupek, 1982; Scott & Stradling, 1992; Smucker et al. 1993)

Consider the following contrasting quotes:

"Each session of exposure therapy is like peeling a layer off of an onion, and after a few sessions, you get to the stinking part in the middle, and then it doesn't stink anymore." (Rothbaum & Foa, 1992, p. 222)

"After many repetitions, the moment comes when the telling of the trauma story no longer arouses quite such intense feeling. It has become a part of the survivor's experience, but only one part of it. The story is a memory like other memories, and it begins to fade as other memories do. Her grief, too, begins to lose its vividness. It occurs to the survivor that perhaps the trauma is not the most important, or even the most interesting, part of her life story." (Herman, 1992, p. 195)

VERSUS

"Relentlessly doing memory work for long periods of time can actually make some clients worse -- it forces them to bring up more of what they already feel unable to handle. Approaches that emphasize resource building rather than memory work can fare better." (Yapko, 1993, p. 37)

"Abreaction, in itself, is not necessarily or uniformly therapeutic ... Abreaction is useful primarily in the service of helping patients reframe their sense of their lives and themselves. It is this reframing and understanding of the role of trauma in their lives ... that enables many traumatized clients to move from a position of feeling chronically victimized to a sense of having successfully survived and overcome their abuse." (Gunderson & Chu, 1993, p. 80)

These four quotes set the stage for our discussion of direct therapy exposure (DTE) and various other interventions designed to help clients do "memory work". What is the right balance, the right timing, to have clients undertake "memory work" of reliving their traumas, and with which clients should such "memory work" be done? Should one follow the advice of Foa and Rothbaum and Herman or that offered by Yapko and Gunderson and Chu? While the field cannot, at this time, answer these questions, a consideration of the specific techniques involved in conducting DTE will permit clinicians to make more informed treatment decisions **in collaboration with their clients**. The therapist can work with the client in order to help him/her appreciate the value of "giving oneself permission" to "recall" his/her thoughts and accompanying feelings in a graduated "dosed" fashion, rather than attempting to "work through traumatic memories" as quickly as possible. With DTE the therapist helps the survivor to reexperience his/her trauma in tolerable doses. This may require going over the incident again and again in greater and greater detail.

In considering DTE it is important to keep in mind that despite the reported success of this procedure with traumatized clients, **the DTE procedure should be used with caution.** As Falsetti (1994) observes:

Some professionals have noted the potential of severe complications including the precipitation of panic disorder, exacerbation of depression, and relapse of alcohol abuse (Pitman et al. (1991).[1] In addition, flooding has received considerable criticism because it does not address faulty cognitions and fails to enhance the development of coping skills (Kilpatrick et al., 1982; 1985).[2]

With this controversy in mind let us consider the rationale and procedures of DTE. *(A summary procedural checklist is offered at the end of this section.)*

Rationale for DTE

A number of investigators have viewed the prolonged exposure (reexperiencing procedures) of DTE within a **conditioning** framework or from an **informational fear structure** framework ala Peter Lang (e.g., see work by Foa, Keane, Fairbanks, Saigh, Deblinger and their colleagues). They propose that PTSD results from inadequate processing of the trauma. Treatment requires activation of the fear memory in a safe environment through direct exposure techniques as victims are asked to recall the trauma (e.g., rape assault) in detail and then helped to process the memory until it no longer is intensely distressing. This imagery-based exposure may be combined or supplemented with in vivo exposure. DTE is viewed within a reevaluation, habituation and information processing perspective. It is a form of desensitization to intrusive imagery, a type of controlled reexperiencing of the trauma.

It is also worth noting that the same DTE procedures can be viewed within a somewhat different perspective, such as the present **constructive narrative** framework. This narrative perspective was well-stated by van der Kolk and van der Vert (1991). They proposed that traumatic memories are "unassimilated" and "fragmented" scraps of overwhelming experience which need to be integrated within existing mental schemes and they need to **"be transformed" into "narrative language"** (p. 447). In order for this to occur the traumatized person has to return to the memory often in order to "complete it". The traumatized individual needs to look back at what happened, to tell and retell his/her story so the events can be given a place in his/her life history, in his/her autobiography. With the telling or unfolding of the story comes relief. **The traumatic events need to be put into a story, placed in time with a beginning, middle and an end.** "Trauma stops the chronological clock and fixes the traumatic moment in memory and imagination. Such traumatic memories are not usually altered by the mere passage of time. These traumatic memories become fixed and the intense vehement emotions interfere with their natural processing. These traumatic memories are not organized on a linguistic line. But all memories are changeable by constant reworkings and reorganization. By having the client tell and retell the story, the emotions become defused and the memories begin to change."

---

[1] Pitman, R.K., Altman, B., et al. (1991). Psychiatric complications during flooding. Therapy for post-traumatic stress disorder. Journal of Clinical Psychiatry, 52, 17-20.

[2] Kilpatrick, D.G., Veronen, L.J., & Best, C.L. (19485). Factors predicting psychological distress among rape victims. In C.R. Figley (Ed.), Trauma and its wake, Vol.1. New York: Brunner/Mazel.

Kilpatrick, D.G., Veronen, L.J., & Resick, P.A. (1982). Psychological sequelae to rape. In D.M. Doleys, R.I. Meredith, & A.R. Ciminero (Eds.), Behavioral medicine: Assessment and treatment strtegies. New York: Plenum.

Length and Format of DTE Sessions
(See Lyons & Keane, 1989 for a detailed procedural description.)

1. Therapists have used anywhere from 9 to 14 sessions either biweekly or weekly outpatient sessions.[1] The sessions have varied from 60 to 90 minutes each, usually 90 minutes. There is a need to **involve the spouse or significant other** in the therapy process so he/she can understand what is happening, what is the likely impact of treatment in terms of the client's level of distress, and why this is necessary. Moreover, the client's spouse or significant other act as an "ally" in helping the client to listen to the audiotapes of the DTE sessions. However, the **decision** to involve the spouse should be **made collaboratively** with the client. All decisions about the form of treatment and duration are **made jointly** with the client. Consistent with the suggestion about empowerment, the client is told that he/she, **"Can stop reexperiencing the process at any time you want. You have complete control!"** In this way the client has control over the pacing of recall.

2. The initial sessions (1 and 2) usually focus on **gathering detailed information, offering the treatment rationale,** and **formulating a treatment plan.** The remaining sessions consist primarily of **imaginal exposure to the trauma event** (e.g., rape). Clients are asked to describe their rape in great detail in the present tense, as though it is really happening. Typically during the first two imaginal exposure sessions, clients are allowed to choose the level of detail that is tolerable to them. In the remaining exposure sessions clients are asked to describe the assault (or other trauma scene - such as combat) in as much detail as possible. The clients' levels of distress are monitored both within and across sessions by obtaining ratings on Subjective Units of Distress (SUDs ratings -- 0% to 100%, in 10% units where 0% and 100% are preestablished end points). The imaginal exposure sessions are tape recorded and given to clients to take home and listen to at least once each day in order to provide further exposure trials. The therapist and clients may listen together to a tape following an imaginal session. The clients may choose to ask a significant other to listen to the tape with them. In addition, clients are encouraged to practice gradually exposing themselves to situations that are <u>not</u> dangerous, but that they fear because of the trauma event.

    In order to help clients tell their story of the trauma events Foa and Rothbaum and Smucker et al. suggest that the following questions can be raised in a sensitive manner:

    a) When did it happen?

    b) How long did it last?

    c) Ask the client to tell his/her story from the start of the incident and ask the client to indicate when he or she is done. If the therapist uses imagery as a means of recall do <u>not</u> insist on the client closing his/her eyes.

    d) Ask the client to describe all of the things he/she is aware of. Describe the immediate surroundings.

    e) Tell me what happened. Go through the incident. Start at the beginning of the incident and then move through it to the end. Tell me when you are there.

    f) Is there an earlier incident similar in some way to this one?

---

[1] Because of the severity of symptoms, some clients may require inpatient treatment (Herman, 1992).

g)   How does the incident seem to you now?

Based on this information a hierarchical list is generated of major stimuli that are feared and avoided. In subsequent sessions, the client is asked to imagine the scenes (e.g., rape assault, combat scene) and these are relived in imagination. As noted, the client is asked to **describe these scenes aloud in the present tense.** The level of detail is left to the client for the initial two imaginal sessions, but thereafter the client is encouraged to include more and more details (e.g., what happened, what were your thoughts, feelings, physiological reactions, feared consequences). Descriptions are repeated several times each session for 60 minutes and tape recorded. As noted, clients are assigned homework to listen to the tapes, as well as engage in **vivo** tasks. Examples of such in vivo tasks for rape victims may include walking alone, dating, watching television or reading the paper for fear of encountering reminders. The tasks are collaboratively chosen and usually are selected from the hierarchy that match the level of anxiety covered in the session. Care is taken in the sessions to **ensure that the client's anxiety level is reduced before the session is terminated.** This is part of the reason that 90 minute sessions are usually used.

But before these treatment features are implemented there is a need to prepare the client for DTE. The following describes some possible ways that treatment rationales for DTE have been presented to clients.

Preparing the client for reliving the traumatic event.

3.   Courtois (1992) discusses how therapists can create a therapeutic environment that is conducive to the client remembering and working through the distressing traumatic experience, as in the case of rape victims or victims of child sexual abuse. Some clients and family members may have reservations about "reliving the traumatic events". They feel that they should leave "well enough alone". The therapist should be respectful of these views and mutually explore with clients the pros and cons of different treatment alternatives, namely, (1) working through the memories by means of direct therapy exposure; (2) employing other treatment options such as imagery reconstruction and psychodramatic techniques; (3) coming to terms with the traumatic events gradually by means of stress inoculation training; or (4) focusing treatment on the aftermath of the traumatic events (e.g., the "shattering" of the client's basic beliefs about trust, intimacy, safety, self-respect, and the like). The client should be made a "partner" in determining the best approach or combination of procedures that fit his/her particular clinical needs. Be respectful of those clients who believe that "silence in the aftermath of trauma may be constructive". Explore this view with the client before undertaking "memory work", or what Brende (1981) describes as the reexperiencing of trauma through "therapeutic revivification".

If the direct therapy exposure (DTE) approach is adopted, then clinicians spend a good deal of time preparing the client for such interventions. For instance, the therapist may share the rationale for the DTE, as illustrated by Foa et al. (1993) who told their clients the following:

"It is extremely difficult to digest painful experiences and it takes a great deal of effort to deal with such experiences. Many of your **assumptions** or expectations about men, sex, or the world in general may have been **shattered** and you have not had the opportunity to rebuild them. We're here to help you do that. Often the experience comes back to haunt you through nightmares, flashbacks, phobias, depression, etc. because it is "unfinished business"." What we are going to do is the opposite of our tendency to avoid discomfort. We'll help you to digest the experience by helping you to stay with it long enough to get more used to it. The fleeting images or thoughts about the rape that you do have, like flashbacks or nightmares, stop short of finishing the process when the intense fear or emotions make it too uncomfortable. We will help you use imagery to approximate the memory as closely as possible -- not only seeing the attack in your mind, but reliving it with all the emotions and feelings you felt at the time. The goal is to be able to have these thoughts, to talk about the rape, or even see the cues associated with the rape without experiencing the intense anxiety that is disrupting your life." (p. 264)

Another **metaphor** to describe DTE is offered by Courtois (1992) who compares the process of not directly addressing the traumatic memory as being **like building your house on top of a toxic waste deposit**. Imagine someone telling you to just not dig around, don't stir things up. Don't think about it and just go on and build a garden. Sell and don't tell anyone about the toxic site. This is not possible. One option is not dealing with the toxic impact of the abuse. Instead, Courtois suggests that the therapist convey that he/she will help the client "dig out and shape up his/her foundation in order to achieve a sense of wholeness and a continuity to his/her life experience". This will allow the client to "recapture lost parts of him/herself, and to experience him/herself more fully than previously possible". "As a result of this process clients have reported that "they could allow themselves to really feel the feelings, letting the feelings take their course without immediately trying to stop them. They could report on them without embarrassment and shame."

Hammond (1990, p. 346) uses the **metaphors** of **setting a broken bone and lancing a wound** as a useful way to prepare a victim of trauma for the painful memory work of reliving a past traumatic event. He says to the client:

> "The work that we have to do is very much like what must happen after a child breaks her leg, or an adult has a painful, infected wound that must be lanced. The physician doesn't want to cause the patient pain. But he/she knows that if he/she doesn't set the bone or lance the wound, the patient will continue to hurt for even longer, and will remain disabled and never recover properly and normally. It's hard and painful for the physician to do that procedure and create pain through setting that bone or lancing that wound. But it's an act of caring, that allows healing to take place.
>
> And this process of facing painful memories and feelings from the past will be painful for a short time, just like setting a broken bone. But then you won't have to continue hurting from what happened, and healing will finally take place."

In this way, the therapist conveys the adage of "the need for short-term pain for long-term gain".

Ochberg (1991, p. 12) has also described ways to have the client reexamine the traumatic event.

> "As I have come to know you I have the feeling that you are still **captured by your trauma history** and **fixated to the trauma**. You also feel unable to recollect without the fear of being overwhelmed by overpowering emotions. You also recollect, at times, when you do not want to recollect, especially when you are unprepared to remember. Is this the way you see it?" (Check the client's perception.)
>
> "The purpose of our hearing the details of the trauma story is for the two of us to **revisit the scene** of the trauma of the terror and horror, and in so doing **remove the grip** of terror and horror. The purpose of our doing this is more than catharsis or an emotional venting. There is a need to put the trauma in its

place so it is only **one chapter in your personal history**. Does that make sense?"

"It may prove painful to explore these memories, but we will revisit the trauma together and you can stop the process at any time. You are in charge."

Ochberg (1991, p. 12) also offers the following introductory statement to clients:

"Highly charged emotional events are filed in the brain's special filing system according to their emotional tone, their emotional meaning. These traumatic memories are not stored alphabetically or by dates (chronologically). One goal of our working on these trauma memories, by our **revisiting the trauma** is to create a new memory by the two of us **reexploring the trauma** and putting this memory right next to the original file. By putting these two memories together what do you think it will do? How do you think it will help?"

Falsetti and Resnick (1994, p.12) suggest:

It is similar to watching a scary movie over and over. At first it may be very scary, but by the 20th viewing it would not be as scary. Similarly, by replaying a frightening memory it becomes less frightening as it is recounted and replayed numerous times in a safe environment.

The "expertise" of the therapist is to choose or combine the preparatory examples that best suit the client prior to conducting the direct therapy exposure (e.g., Foa/Rothbaum, Courtois, Hammond, Ochberg, your own).

4.   Some **additional caveats** are offered when conducting DTE and undertaking such "memory work".

   a)   the specific proposed therapeutic process needs to be described to the client in detail and the client's continuing permission to employ the procedure needs to be obtained;

   b)   keep in mind the need for pacing in working through the traumatic memories;

   c)   McCann and Pearlman (1990) suggest that **"self-work" should occur before "memory work"** -- bolster the client's self-esteem by using time lines, interview questions as described in Section III, establish a "safe" therapeutic environment before undertaking recovery work.

5.   Sessions 3 to 9 are used for detailed imaginal exposure to the original trauma. A hierarchy of avoided situations is constructed to be used both imaginally, as well as for in vivo exposure homework. These seven sessions are devoted to reliving the trauma (combat, rape) scene in imagination.

6.   Some therapists **combine imaginal exposure with relaxation training** and with "homework" of **listening to audio tapes** of the recorded imaginal exposure sessions. The audiotape should include thoughts, feelings and behaviors. At first the client may listen to the tape in the counsellor's office and subsequently with a supportive friend or relative. Clients are encouraged to play the tape once a day, but not turn it off until the client feels relaxed and develops a sense of control. Scott and Stradling convey to the client that when he/she begins listening to the tape he/she might find it painful at first. Although the client

may be tempted to switch off the tape at the most distressing point, he/she should not switch it off until he/she has reached a less distressing point.

Some clients may desire expressing their feelings about the trauma by writing or other forms of expression (e.g., see Resick & Schnike, 1992). These may be supplemented with **in vivo exposure**, when feasible. For example, the client may choose to return to the traumatic scene, usually with a supportive other person. The DTE treatment format have involved the following sequence:

a) Initial 15 minutes review recent week, symptoms, moods, signs of recovery, homework assignment.

b) 10 minutes of relaxation by means of muscular relaxation or cue-controlled, slow deep breathing with accompanying self-dialogue to relax and use visualizing soothing imagery. In this way clients are taught how to manage anxiety during the exposure and develop a sense of control. Later in therapy the therapist can help the client consider how these coping procedures can be used outside of therapy.

c) 45 minutes of exposure. (The client and therapist collaborate in carefully preparing a written script, describing the traumatic event in detail. The script includes a description of **context** (where, when, who present), **fact** (what happened, what said), **emotion** (what felt, both negative and possibly any positive emotions), and **meaning** (what beliefs, thoughts, fear of consequences). If there were several traumatic events, a separate scenario is developed for each one. The scenes presented usually progress from the least to most stressful/difficult. The client "narrates" or describes the scene aloud to himself/herself and to the therapist, **in the present tense**, while the therapist encourages the client to express feelings as fully as possible. Throughout the DTE, the client is **reminded that he/she is in control**, determining the design, timing and pacing of the exposure trials.

d) 10 minutes of relaxation.

e) 10 minutes of integration of information.

f) Courtois (1992) observes that memory work should be done in the early to mid-phase of the therapeutic session with adequate time left for processing. Such sessions are more likely to be 75 to 90 minutes, rather than the usual 60 minutes.

7. The client is asked to imagine the traumatic scene (e.g., assault scene) as vividly as possible, as if it were happening right now. The client is encouraged to describe the traumatic scene in the first person and in the present tense. The client's description should proceed slowly including all exposure cues. For the first two exposure sessions, the clients are discouraged from verbalizing details that were extremely upsetting. Foa et al. (1993) suggest that with rape victims that "during the remaining sessions, they should be encouraged to describe the rape in its entirety, repeating it several times for 60 minutes per session. The clients' narratives are tape recorded and they are instructed to listen to the tapes at home at least once daily." In later sessions the dangers of avoidance behavior (avoid realistically safe situations and rape-related thoughts) may increase PTSD symptoms. Clients are encouraged to practice confronting such situations in their everyday lives. The clients are encouraged to play daily the audiotape of the trauma at a preset time for 15 minutes. In this way the client can tackle the avoidance through graded exposure to the feared stimuli.

The therapist should insure that the client relives the traumatic event, not merely describes it. The client should include external and internal cues (thoughts, feelings, physiological reactions and feared consequences). The client's description should include the time prior to the traumatic event, the event itself, and the post-event.

8.   The client should select the incident to be imagined and reported. The selected incident should eventually be one that the client has tended to have flashbacks or that was outstandingly traumatic. Whenever possible, give the client **choices** and **control** in the session.

9.   As noted, there is a need to prepare the client for the intervention. There is also a need to continually assess whether the client feels he/she can tolerate the increases in PTSD symptoms that may accompany exposure episodes.

10.   The implementation of DTE is offered in the context of a continual educational process. Thus, there is a need to provide the client with information about PTSD symptoms especially the client's attempt at avoidance behavior. The goal of DTE is to **intentionally expose** the client to the very memories that he/she has been actively avoiding. Repeat the rationale of why exposing the client to "painful" memories will prove beneficial; namely, review the need to reexperience the traumatic incident as many times as it takes to accomplish its "resolution." Also reassure the client by stating:

> "Since the client has survived the original traumatic event there is no way he/she can't survive the replay. Only by replaying it is he/she going to be able to resolve it and put it behind." (Rothbaum & Foa, 1992)

A "conditioning" or an information processing framework are often used as a rationale (e.g., Peter Lang's associational network model). Some clients ask, "Is there any way out of this distress?". Dolan reminds the client that "the only way out, is through". As noted before, Scott and Stradling compare the distress that clients feel during the first few weeks of dealing with imagery to that of an ex-cigarette smoker who is struggling with urges, reminders. With time, it becomes easier.

11.   Explain to the client what he/she is to expect as a result of treatment. Convey that the client may experience increased symptoms and that these symptoms may last several weeks before reduction. Note that this increase is only temporary and not a sign of treatment failure, nor of the client "losing control" or "going crazy". If significant others are involved with the treatment, then educate these individuals about DTE treatment and possible side-effects.

12.   **Therapeutic relationship variables are critical** in order to create a trusting alliance, which is needed to help the client throughout this frightening experience. The therapist must be sensitive, supportive and nonjudgmental when listening to the client's traumatic account. The therapist should also be aware of the impact of hearing such accounts on him/herself. There is a need to debrief therapists. Provide support for therapists. "Heal the healers." This may be especially critical for therapists who have a history of personal victimization. *(See Section III on "healing the healers")*

13.   Some therapists using DTE teach their clients progressive muscle relaxation. Client's are asked to engage in relaxation at the beginning of each imagined session, at the end of the session, and encouraged to use such relaxation in vivo between sessions.

14.   The client in DTE is asked to describe traumatic events along a hierarchy and to provide ratings of "subjective units of distress" (SUDS) on a 0% to 100% scale at various points during the imagined exposure (e.g., every 10 minutes).

15. Do <u>not</u> terminate the session if the client remains distressed. As noted, continually reassure the client that if he/she has survived the actual trauma then he/she can survive the recall. Be sure to process the client's reactions and address the client's concerns.

16. **The need for caution**. In considering the use of exposure-based interventions such as DTE there is a need to use a graduated approach with some clients, as suggested by Kilpatrick and Best (1984); Mueser and Butler (1992); and Pitman et al. (1991). See additional treatment guidelines for DTE by Litz et al. (1990). Solomon et al. (1993) notes that **DTE may be contraindicated** for clients who have a psychiatric history. Johnson et al. (1994) indicate that exploratory abreative emotionally arousing interventions may be **counterproductive** for people struggling with chronic PTSD conditions. *(See evaluative comments on DTE in Section V)*.

17. **If the client manifests extreme resistance to DTE then use a gradual approach like stress inoculation training** *(described below)*.

IMAGINAL AND IN VIVO EXPOSURE PROCEDURES

A somewhat different exposure intervention procedure was offered by Richards et al. (1994). Following from the work by Issac Marks with agoraphobic clients, these exposure procedures are designed to address the avoidant behavior of PTSD clients. Such avoidant behaviors have been most resistant to change

Richards et al. (1994) describes how imaginal and live **exposure procedures** have been used with traumatized patients.

   a) **Imaginal exposure** consists of asking patients to relive their traumatic memories. These were recorded and later listened to by the patient. In recalling his/her memories, the client used the first person and present tense including rich detail about the circumstances, their responses and feelings. "Initially, patients were asked to imagine the complete sequence of their traumatic memories. With practice more detail would emerge, enabling patients to make a hierarchical list out of the elements of their traumatic memories. Less distressing elements were relived first. At times, the therapist used a "rewind and hold" imaginal procedure, asking patients to concentrate on the worst aspects of the memory, to freeze and hold the image while repeatedly describing in detail all they could possibly remember about this part of the trauma. Patients relayed this over and over until their anxiety reduced" (Richards et al. p. 672). They asked patients to rate their levels of anxiety using a 0% to 100% Subjective Units of Distress (SUDs) rating scale. Patients conducted "homework" between sessions of listening to the audiotape, to the point where the patients SUDs were reduced by 50% to 75%.

   b) **Live exposure** involved patients re-entering trauma-related situations that they had been avoiding. Initially, the therpaist accompanied patients, encouraging the patient to remain in the situation until SUDs were reduced by 50%, or at least until 1 hour of exposure had been completed. SUDs ratings were obtained every 5 minutes. The therapist provided encouragement and support so the patient could <u>not</u> engage in avoidance behaviors. Eventually, the patient was taught how to engage in self-directed exposure homework exercises.

In order to improve the patient's overall social adjustment, there is a need to encourage the patient to engage in both imaginal and live exposure involving "current and handicapping real-life avoidances and <u>not</u> only those avoidant behaviors that are delimited to re-entering situations where the traumatic events have occured."

Richards et al. (1994) also notes that conducting exposure treatments can take a "toll" on the therapist. Thus, the therapist requires training, peer supports, and supervision, *(as noted in Section IV on "How to help the helpers").*

GUIDED IMAGERY-BASED INTERVENTIONS

Direct Therapy Exposure of having the client reexperience the traumatic events by means of imagery (supplemented by listening to the audiotape of the session and graded in vivo reexposure) is only one of several different imagery-based procedures designed to help the client "integrate" their distressing memories. Clinicians have developed a variety of other imagery-based procedures. A few that we will consider include:

1. Adult nurturing "victimized" child imagery as described by Smucker et al., Goulding's redecision therapy, and Dolan's supportive imagery techniques.

2. Hypnotically-based imagery (Spiegel et al.)

3. Traumatic Incident Reduction Imagery (Moore)

4. Imagery Rewind Imagery Procedure (Muus)

5. Cognitive Processing Therapy (Resick and Schincke) that emphasizes writing assignments.

These imagery-based procedures are sometimes supplemented by means of psychodrama, Gestalt empty-chair techniques, and cognitive-behavioural skills training (e.g., assistiveness training and cognitive restructuring procedures, as discussed below).

1. In a treatment of **survivors of childhood sexual abuse** Smucker, Dancu and Foa (1991) suggest that the client be taught how to "go back over the abusive event and **change the imagery** so that it has a different ending, one which will have the client feeling more empowered and in control" (p. 6). The imagery procedure leads the client to (1) <u>confront</u> and <u>drive away the perpetrator</u> and (2) <u>protect</u> and <u>soothe</u> the frightened child.

   The client is coached during imagery. The therapist asks questions about what is happening; what are you thinking; how reacting; what is the response of the perpetrator. Now, ask how would the client like the **image to change**. The client then describes what the child in the image is doing to change the scene.

   <u>**Use adult-nurturing child imagery**</u> (the imagery exercise continues with the adult soothing the child in the image in any way that seems natural). Adult mastery imagery -- protects the child from the perpetrator such as by driving the perpetrator away.

2. Dolan (1991) suggests that when the client is imaging the abusive scene, the therapist can use the metaphor "younger self" or "little girl", and then have the client consider several questions and procedures as to how she can comfort and help the "younger self." For example, while the client is imaging the therapist can ask:

   a) What are you experiencing right now? What are you needing there that you are not getting? Go inside and notice what difference it would make to change the scene.

    b)   What does that "younger self" need to hear right now?

    c)   What can you say to comfort her?

    d)   Tell the "younger self" the message she needs to hear. Notice what difference that makes. Now, imagine this difference as years go by? What is the difference this will make in the future? Notice all the different ways the healing message affects you?

    e)   What difference does knowing that mean for the "little girl" part of you, now and in the future?

    f)   You can continue to be aware of that difference and continue to experience it in whatever way meets your needs.

    g)   Is there anything else you need right now?

3.   van der Kolk and van der Hart (1991) also offer examples of how "victimized" individuals (Holocaust, rape, and incest survivors) were helped by asking them to alter the meaning of the traumatic event in some way. For example, a therapist had a Holocaust survivor imagine a flower growing in her assignment place in Auschwitz, or a rape victim was asked to imagine having all the power she wanted and applying it to the perpetrator. van der Kolk and van der Hart note that once **flexibility is introduced into the client's memorial image (narrative account)**, the traumatic memory starts to lose its power, its grip over current experience. "By imagining these alternative scenarios many patients are able to soften the intrusive power of the original unmitigated horror." (1991, p. 450). Imagery procedures are being used to help the client construct a different narrative as illustrated in the following example offered by Goulding.

4.   Mary Goulding, under the heading of **Redecision Therapy**, has proposed that the following guided imagery procedures be used with victimized childhood sexually abused clients. In order to put the victimization experience "behind them" she invites the client to:

    (a)   go back to the imagined scene of victimization **as a reporter**, taking the child aside and providing support and understanding, highlighting that the child is <u>not</u> responsible for what happened, nor guilty for his/her decisions and actions (e.g., for not telling anyone);

    (b)   the client (reporter) describes the feelings that the child is having and the decisions he or she is making;

    (c)   the client (reporter) can also describe what feelings the child is having later when the child has grown up, what feelings the child has learned to "bury", or chosen <u>not</u> to experience;

    (d)   the client (reporter) can also choose to speak to the abuser (in the fantasy image) and say "I am X", "I am not Y";

    (e)   the client is encouraged to take his/her "adult self" along with him/her in this imagery exercise and to change the scene in ways that the client finds helpful, to congratulate the child who survived, and to probe how he/she survived and coped.

This imagery-based exercise provides an opportunity for the client and the therapist to discuss how the client can take charge of his/her experience and "move beyond the past". The client and therapist explore how the past affects the client's life right now. How the client can give herself/himself permission to experience distress (e.g., flashbacks, ruminitions, anxiety) without "getting stuck". *(Note, as highlighted in Section II, it is not that clients have PTSD symptoms, but what they say to themselves about them that is critical. These exercises are designed to alter what the clients say to themselves, and to others, about their symptoms.)*

The discussion focuses on how the client should not allow "the abuser's face or imprint to be on the rest of the world". The client is encouraged to "go beyond", "to outgrow" the victimization experience, instead of "getting bogged down" with the personal formula of, "I can't be happy until X" (he changes, he apologizes, I get revenge, etc.). Instead, the personal formula translates into, "I can be happy even though X". The focus is on what the client is going to do with the "now", and with the "future".

Collaboratively with the therapist, the client can begin to explore and implement options. Namely, how can the client learn to trust again? How can the client express feelings like being sad, scared, angry, without being overwhelmed? How can the client leave the past in the past? Other decisions such as whether to confront the perpetrator or to forgive, and the like, are individual decisions to be made by the client. In therapy the client can explore these decisions and possible consequences with the therapist.

5.   Some therapists use **psychodrama techniques** or the Gestalt procedure of empty-chair to help clients replay and rescript the abusive episode. Such memory work may be supplemented by other forms of intervention such as social skills training.

6.   Therapists often invite the client to **write letters** to the perpetrator as a further way to foster and consolidate changes. These letters are usually not sent. The client may also be asked to keep a daily journal tracking changes and monitoring signs of recovery. *(See the Section below on letter writing.)* Another form of writing activity is illustrated in the intervention procedure called Cognitive Processing Therapy.

Cognitive Processing Therapy (CPT)[1]

CPT is a variant of DTE. Like DTE it is a short-term (12 session) structured therapy program, also based on an information processing model of PTSD (see Creamer et al., 1992; Ellis et al., 1992, Foa et al., 1989; Foa & Kozak, 1986; McCann & Pearlman, 1990; Resick & Schnicke, 1993). CPT goes beyond prolonged exposure activities by helping clients examine the beliefs and meanings attributed to the event. Following the suggestions of McCann and Pearlmann (1990), CPT focuses on issues of safety, trust, power, esteem and intimacy that are affected by trauma and victimization. As we will consider below in the section on cognitive restructuring, CPT and related procedures are designed to help individuals "identify" and "modify" their "stuck points".

CPT can be conducted in either group or individual sessions. The treatment includes a cognitive information processing explanation of traumatic event reactions and writing assignments about the event and the meaning it holds (as noted below). Resick and Schnicke (1993) suggest that writing about traumatic events are often more detailed than oral accounts and can more readily expose "stuck points". The treatment focuses on helping clients develop skills to identify, analyze and confront such "stuck points" and other maladaptive beliefs. Sessions are also devoted to five

---

[1] *Also see discussion of CPT in Section V on Group Treatment of Incest Victims.*

major beliefs surrounding issues of safety, trust, power, esteem and intimacy. Moreover, the written assignments can be viewed as an additional form of exposure and an opportunity to construct a new narrative.

In CPT, clients **write about the traumatic event** in detail including thoughts, feelings (e.g., disgust, shame, anger, depression) and sensory memories. As described by Calhoun and Resick (1993, p. 60), clients are encouraged to "write at a time and place where they can express their emotions and are instructed to read the account to themselves **daily**. During the session they read the account aloud and the therapist helps them label their feelings and **identify stuck points**. This component of the treatment lasts only 2 sessions (of the 12 sessions)."

In evaluating CPT it is worth highlighting Falsetti's (1994) observation that:

The average educational level in CPT studies have generally been **above the high school level** and many of the worksheets used in the treatment are quite complex, thus may need to be simplified to be understandable for some clients" (p.27).

Use of Hypnosis -- Hypnosis can also be used for teaching coping skills and for helping clients find "meaning", resolve, reframe traumatic events.

Classen et al. (1993), Spiegel (1988), and Spiegel and Cardena (1990) describe how hypnosis can be used to help clients access, restructure, and learn to control traumatic memories and then to "put them aside with relative ease following therapy" (Classen et al., p. 189). One hypnotic technique involves asking patients (if they are hypnotizable):

1.   to enter a trance and to maintain a pleasant sense of floating relaxation in their body.

2.   to imagine in their mind's eye an imaginary screen on which they are to picture two images (side by side, or on two sides of a movie screen). The first image is drawn from memories of the traumatic experience. They are to view some aspect of the traumatic memory and to tolerate the accompanying discomfort.

3.   to balance this image with another image that reflects/represents what they did to protect themselves, or protect the lives of someone else.

4.   "The split screen is metaphorically a way of helping patients to put the trauma into perspective by seeing it as a part, but not all of themselves." (Spiegel, 1988, p. 28)

A somewhat different mode of hypnotic work is described by Herman (1992, p. 186). She describes how hypnosis is used to **uncover memories**. *(As noted in Section IV this memorial retrieval process is fraught with dangers.)* For example, the client may be asked to imagine they are watching a portable TV which has a "safe channel". Another channel has "a tape" that covers the traumatic experience. These traumas can be recovered and replayed in slow motion. A number of other retrieval procedures (age regression, dream work, guided imagery) are described. Given what we know about the susceptibility of clients under these circumstances I would be very reluctant to use hypnosis or other related procedures to retrieve memories. **Hypnosis may be useful to facilitate integration of, and coping with, traumatic memories, but it should not be used as an "uncovering" procedure.**

Other Imagery-based Techniques to Help Clients Alter Memories

A number of imaginally-based procedures have been used to help clients alter their reactions to traumatic events. We will examine a few of these procedures.

Moore (1993) describes another direct imaginal exposure procedure called **Traumatic Incident Reduction** (TIR). Like DTE it is designed to "strip the emotional charge" from the traumatic events and to help clients "integrate and assimilate" past traumas. The treatment is usually conducted on a one-on-one basis, and according to Moore, sessions can last from as short as 20 minutes to $2^1/_2$ hours. The average session is $1^1/_2$ hours and the number of sessions is usually brief (a handful of sessions). In each session the therapist (who is called a "facilitator") helps the client (who is called a "viewer") undergo a repeated review of the traumatic event. The client is asked to review the traumatic incident as many times as it takes to accomplish "resolution" and in order to "feel good about it". The major features of TIR include (see Moore, 1993, for details):

1. the client selecting the incident to be imaginally reviewed. The selected incident usually involves that which is most "troubling" to the client;

2. as in DTE, the therapist probes about the details concerning the incident -- "When did it happen?"; "How long did it last?"; "Who was present?", etc.;

3. the client, while in a relaxed imaginal state, is invited to describe aloud the scene from start to end, telling what happened following his/her "plot-line". The facilitator (therapist) listens attentively, without comment, except for general encouragement and occasional timely probes as to whether the incident is getting "lighter" (emotionally less painful and less distressing);

4. this process is repeated as needed;

5. the selected incident may be "traumatic", reflecting a series of traumatic events as the therapist asks about an earlier incident which is similar in some way to this one. The TIR may, in turn, be applied to these other events. In order to assess the client's progress the therapist asks, "How does this incident seem to you now?"; "Did you make any decisions or come to any conclusions at the time of the incident?"

Muss (1991a,b) has offered an innovative imagery procedure that he calls the **Rewind Technique**. It consists of the following steps:

1. The client is asked to image (view) their trauma **as if** he/she was watching it unfold on a screen in a movie.

2. The "movie" begins with the peaceful moments before the trauma happened (e.g., a couple of minutes of description up to the most disturbing aspects of the traumatic episode).

3. The client is then asked to **mentally rewind** the film so that the events are seen again, but this time **in reverse order**.

4. The client is encouraged to use this **rewind procedure** when he/she experiences intrusive thoughts and images.

5. This **rewind procedure** can be applied to other traumatic images should they occur. This rewind procedure has been applied to individuals who have experienced **Type I stressors** like automobile accidents or victimization experiences. Muss offers case reports of favorable results with as little as two weeks of practice.

Image Habituation Training (IHT) is another form of exposure intervention that was reported in a series of case studies by Vaughan and Tarrier, 1992. In this procedure clients are asked to generate short narratives of the traumatic event and to record them on audiotape. Each narrative is followed by 30 seconds of silence during which the client is instructed to imagine the traumatic event as vividly as possible. The client is asked not to alter nor avoid the image while visualizing it. This reexposure procedure resulted in the improvement of PTSD, mostly for individuals who experienced crime-related traumatic events.

Trauma Desensitization as developed by Brom, Kleber and Defares (1989) is a variant of systematic desensitization. Stimuli that were previously avoided are categorized in a hierarchical fashion according to how threatening they are. The client is asked to **imagine these scenes**, thus reexperiencing the trauma, and then taught to use a variety of coping skills to exert control. Brom et. al. (1989) used trauma desensitization with a diverse group of individuals with PTSD resulting from traffic accidents, crime, and the death of someone close.

The imaginal reexposure procedures (e.g., the Goulding **Guided Imagery** procedure, the Moore **Traumatic Incident Reduction** procedure, the Muus **Rewind** procedure, the Vaughan and Jarrier **Image Habituation Training** and the other procedures such as the Dolan **Imagery Techniques**, the **Direct Therapeutic Exposures** of Foa and Rothbaum, Keane and Fairbanks, the **Hypnotic Induction Procedures** by Spiegel and Cardena, the **Eye Movement Desensitization and Reprocessing Procedure** of Shapiro described earlier) are each designed to help clients tell their "stories", share their "accounts" of traumatic events in a safe setting. Clients are encouraged to put into words what happened in a way that the events now have a "beginning, middle and end". In the Section on letter writing below, I examine the benefits of clients telling their "stories" as a means of "getting unstuck" from the most traumatizing features of the events. Moreover, in each of these imaginally-based procedures clients are asked not only to tell (and retell) their "stories", but also the therapist helps clients appreciate what they did to "survive"; what self-protective acts they engaged in. There is an attempt to help clients "reprocess", "assimilate", "make sense of", "find meaning in" the event. With retelling there is an attempt to "uncouple", "decondition", "habituate", "desensitize", "restory", "rescript" the traumatic incident and the accompanying intense affect. The specific concept used in understanding why these procedures work vary with the theoretical persuasion of the authors. At this point we do not know the relative merits of the respective imaginal procedures. We do not know which procedure is most effective with which type of PTSD client as evident on which class of presenting target symptoms. For example, research suggests that intrusive ideation with rape and combat victims is most responsive to direct therapeutic experience (DTE), but so-called "negative" symptoms (psychic numbing, avoidance, anhedonia) are less responsive to DTE (Solomon et al., 1993). Moreover, some researchers like Dutton (1993) have proposed that imaginally-based reexperiencing procedures should not be used with PTSD clients who have experienced domestic violence.

As noted, some therapists supplement imaginally-based reexperiencing procedures with **in vivo** behavioral procedures of having the victims visit the site of the trauma (e.g., Ayalon, 1985, had victims visit the site of terrorist attacks). Many "survivors" have also visited and revisited the site of traumatic events (e.g., combat soldiers who return to the battlefields of Vietnam, the Normandy coast on the 50th anniversary of D-day, and many other examples). Why should such personal journeys prove therapeutic? Let us conclude the Section on direct exposure by considering the answer offered by one soldier who described his return to Vietnam. Carefully analyze Don Ross's description (U.S.A. Today, May 26, 1994) of his experience since the Vietnam war and the therapeutic role of his return (in vivo exposure) to Vietnam. (Note, the emotionally-charged metaphors and narrative changes in his account.)

"(After the war) I was angry too. Angry at being tagged a "loser" or a "dupe" or a "baby-killer". Angry at being spat upon. Angry that, just as I had put my uniform in a closet, I also had to hide my veteran status away from public view or run the risk of being a "social leper".

Resentment, frustration, bitterness. I know them all well at one time or another. Occasionally, I succumbed to societal pressure and felt guilt about Vietnam. But in my heart I never could let go of a rock-bottom sense of certainty that I had ultimately done the right thing.

What I did let go of, eventually, were all of these other nagging emotions. At some point -- it occurred over time, not in a sudden flash of release -- I turned the corner on Vietnam and my part in it. I have come to terms with Vietnam and my part in it. Talking about it, thinking about it, reading about it, watching a film about it -- all usually evoke some still-strong emotions. Because most of my life since Vietnam has been measured in some way against my time there.

Now (after the returned visit) I have new Vietnam experiences and feelings to draw upon, a deeper understanding of a people and their culture, a broader sense of the destruction, the suffering and destruction wrought by war, and perhaps best, new friends among those who were once enemies. For that I leave here a changed man. ... And more than ever I remain very proud of having served in Vietnam."

Note the shift in his narrative account from a "loser", "dupe", "baby-killer", "social leper", "someone who has succumbed to societal pressure" and who experienced "nagging emotions" to someone who after his return visit to Vietnam has "a personal sense of vindication", has "come to terms with Vietnam", who has a "deeper understanding and greater appreciation", who is "changed, proud" and "able to make friends with former enemies". I would propose that both the imaginal and in vivo reexperiencing (retelling) provides the opportunity for survivors to produce new narrative accounts that are more adaptive. These experiences permit traumatized individuals to move from "victims" to "survivors", and even to becoming "thrivers".

The following checklist provides an outline of the procedures to conduct **Direct Therapeutic Exposure (DTE)** and related **guided imagery-based interventions**.

Table 1
Procedural Checklist for Direct Therapy Exposure
and Guided Imagery-based Interventions

1. Help the client to tell his/her "story" of traumatic events.

2. Assess for possible contra-indications for conducting Direct Therapy Exposure (DTE) and related imagery procedures (e.g., psychiatric history, suffering chronic PTSD, victim of spouse abuse).

3. Focus initial treatment on relief of PTSD symptoms ("self-care") and bolster the client's sense of self-esteem (e.g., have client highlight prior coping efforts along a "time line", "signs of recovery", and other "strengths").

4. Offer the client a rationale for DTE (e.g., "conditioning" or "information processing" perspectives). Use appropriate metaphors to describe treatment and check for client comprehension. Describe the treatment protocol both "in therapy" and "out of therapy" (e.g., listening to audiotape and undertaking graded in vivo exposure).

5. Discuss with the client the various treatment alternatives (e.g., DTE, graded exposure of stress inoculation training, guided imagery techniques). Discuss possible "side-effects".

6. Teach relaxation procedures and other coping techniques such as cognitive self-guidance.

7. Following appropriate introduction and preparation, have the client engage in imaginal repeated exposure (45 minutes).

    a) The amount of detail and affect expressed by the client during imagery recall increases over the 3 to 14 sessions.
    b) Ensure that the client describes scenes in the present tense.
    c) Ensure that the client's anxiety level is reduced before the session is terminated.
    d) Audiotape the session.

8. Encourage the client to listen to the audiotape of the session for at least 15 minutes on a daily basis, either alone or with a trusted other. Prepare the client for this request and provide reassurance.

9. With the client's permission invite significant other to a treatment session to explain the nature of treatment, possible consequences and how he/she can act as an "ally".

10. Use guided imagery procedures tailored to the specific client (e.g., DTE with rape victim or combat veterans; a guided imagery altering procedure with incest victims or use cognitive processing therapy procedures).

11. Conduct relapse prevention and self-attribution training procedures.

12. Discuss with clients how undergoing DTE procedures have helped them alter how they see themselves, their past and future, and the world. Note, changes in the clients' narratives.

A FLOW CHART OF STRESS INOCULATION TRAINING

In contrast to the exposure-based Direct Therapeutic Exposure procedure which some clients find too overwhelming, an alternative cognitive-behavioral treatment approach is to use the **more graduated stress inoculation training (SIT) approach.** A number of detailed therapist manuals of SIT are available that have been applied to both PTSD and non-PTSD populations. Meichenbaum (1993) has reviewed some 200 experimental and clinical case studies that have appeared since Meichenbaum's (1987) initial presentation of SIT. As applied to the PTSD population, Best et al. (1987), Foa et al. (1991),[1] Veronen and Kilpatrick (1983) have used SIT victims of sexual assault. SIT has also been used quite successfully in the treatment of patients with panic disorders[2] and anger control (see Meichenbaum, 1993), both of which are often clinical features of PTSD. Most SIT consist of between 8 and 14 sessions, and SIT has been administered on both an individual treatment protocols and a group basis, as well as on a preventative basis. In some instances, SIT has been applied on a briefer (several hours) psychoeducational basis to large groups (usually when applied on a preventative basis). Let us consider the general procedural guidelines of SIT before we consider some specific applications.

SIT is designed to provide clients with a sense of mastery over their stress by teaching a variety of coping skills and then providing an opportunity to practice those skills in a graduated ("inoculation") fashion, both within and outside of the clinical settings. The SIT approach is tailored to the individual problems and needs of each client.

SIT is implemented in three phases. The **first phase (conceptualization)** provides the preparation for treatment and includes an educational component from which the client can better understand the nature and origin of his/her stress and related emotions (fear, anxiety, depression), and then, collaboratively generate coping strategies.

The **second phase** focuses on **skills acquisition, consolidation, and rehearsal.** The clients are taught a variety of coping skills to address stress, anxiety, fear, and anger in terms of physiological, behavioral and cognitive-emotional areas, or via three emotional channels (ala Lang's tripartite model). Consistent with the suggestions of Lazarus and Folkman (1984) clients are taught how to change (1) the stressful situation when possible; (2) the "meaning" of the situation; (3) their emotional reactions to the situation. Put in simple terms, these translate into four main ways to handle stressful situations: (1) **leave it;** (2) **change it;** (3) **accept it as it is** and obtain support elsewhere; and (4) **reframe it** or interpret the situation differently. A variety of coping skills are taught and practiced that include direct-action and problem-focused coping and emotional-regulative palliative coping. The skills training includes a definition, rationale, practice, feedback or review of when and how the coping skills can be employed. The skills taught may include relaxation training, self-instructional or guided self-dialogue, problem-solving, attention

---

[1] The ways that SIT have been implemented have varied across clinical trials. For example, the SIT approach used by Foa et al. (1991) did not use in vivo exposure to feared situations, in contrast to Kilpatrick et al. (1982) who included such in vivo exposure. As a result, in the Foa et al. study with rape victims they found SIT to be most effective at the immediate followup period, whereas at 3.5 months followup a prolonged exposure treatment group was more effective than SIT.

[2] A detailed description of the successful application of cognitive behavioral treatment procedures with clients suffering from **panic attacks** is beyond the scope of this manual. Hollon and Beck (1993) concluded that **81% to 90%** of panic disorder adult patients who received cognitive-behavioral treatment were **panic free at a 1 to 2 year followup.** As Magraf et al. (1994) concluded, "We are no longer dealing with experiemtnal treatments that still have to prove themselves. Instead, cognitive behavioral treatments rest on firm experimental evidence that justifies their application in everyday practice." (p. 118): See Hollon and Beck, Cognitive behavioral therapies, in S. Garfield and A. Bergin (Eds.), Handbook of psychotherapy and behavior change Wiley, 1993 and Magraf et al. (1993) Psychological Treatment of Panic. Behaviour Research and Therapy, 31, 108-120.

diversion, interpersonal, and other individually tailored skills. The guided self-dialogue, and the other coping skills are taught as ways to handle four aspects of the stressful event, namely, (1) preparing for a stressor, (2) confronting or managing distress, (3) coping with feelings of being overwhelmed, and (4) reflecting on how the coping efforts went.

The **third phase** of SIT focuses on **application training**, whereby clients have an opportunity to rehearse their coping procedures in the session in the form of imagery rehearsal (coping modeling), behavioral rehearsal (role playing), as well as performing in vivo graduated exposure. Self-attribution training, relapse prevention, and follow-through (booster sessions) are built into SIT.

The following schematic outline provides an overview of the SIT treatment procedures. A more detailed presentation is offered in Meichenbaum (1987). As noted, SIT has been successfully applied to a variety of clinical problems that PTSD clients may experience including intrusive ideation, panic attacks, anger reactions, interpersonal anxiety, and general stress responses. As noted, SIT has been conducted successfully on both a preventative and treatment basis. SIT has also been implemented by training others to conduct the intervention (e.g., nurses, probation officers, policemen training other policemen, marine drill instructors).

SCHEMATIC OUTLINE OF STRESS INOCULATION TRAINING

Phase I: Conceptualization

1. In a collaborative fashion, identify the determinants of the presenting clinical problem or the individual's stress concerns by means of (1) interviews with the client and significant others; (2) the client's use of an imagery-based reconstruction and assessment of a prototypic stressful incident; (3) psychological and situational assessments; and (4) behavioral observations. (As Folkman et al., 1991, suggest, have the client address "who, what, where, and when" questions: "Who is involved?" "What kind of situations cause stress?" "Where is this kind of situation likely to occur?" "When did it occur last?" *(See interview questions in Section III.)*

2. Permit the client to tell his or her "story" (solicit narrative accounts of stress and coping, and collaboratively identify the client's coping strengths and resources). Help the client to transform his or her description from global (often metaphorical) terms into behaviorally specific terms.

3. Help the client break down the global stressors into specific stressful situations. Then help the client decompose stressful situations and reactions into specific behaviorally prescriptive problems. Have the client consider his or her present coping efforts and evaluate which are maladaptive and which are adaptive.

4. Have the client appreciate the differences between changeable and unchangeable aspects of stressful situations.

5. Have the client establish short-term, intermediate, and long-term behaviorally specifiable goals.

6. Have the client engage in self-monitoring of the commonalties of stressful situations, stress-engendering appraisals, internal dialogue, feelings, and behaviors. Help the client appreciate the transactional nature of stress, and the ways in which he or she inadvertently, unwittingly, and perhaps, unknowingly, contributes to stress reactions. Train the client to analyze

problems independently (e.g., to conduct situational analyses and to seek disconfirmatory data - "check things out").

7. Ascertain the degree to which coping difficulties arise from coping skills deficits or are the results of "performance failures" (namely, maladaptive beliefs, feelings of low self-efficacy, negative ideation, secondary gains).

8. Collaboratively formulate with the client and significant others a reconceptualization of the client's distress. Socratically educate the client and significant others about the nature and impact of stress, and the resilience and courage individuals manifest in the face of stressful life events. Using the client's own "data", offer a reconceptualization that stress is composed of different components (physiological, cognitive, affective, and behavioral) and that stress reactions go through different "phases" (viz., preparing for the stressor, confronting the stressful situation, handling feelings of being overwhelmed, and reflecting on how the coping efforts succeeded - sometimes well and sometimes not as effectively as one had hoped). The specific reconceptualization offered will vary with the target population; the plausibility of the reconceptualization is more important than its scientific validity. In the course of this process, facilitate the discovery of a sense of meaning, nurture the client's hope, and highlight the client's strengths and sense of resourcefulness.

9. **Debunk myths** concerning stress and coping, such as: (1) people go through uniform emotional stages of reaction in response to stress; (2) there is a "right" way to cope; (3) one should not expect to experience stressful reactions well after stressful life events have ended. Address myths concerning specific target problem (e.g., rape, domestic violence, child sexual abuse).

Phase II: Skills acquisition and rehearsal

1. Skills training (tailor to the specific population and to the length of training)

   a) Ascertain the client's preferred mode of coping. Explore with the client how these coping efforts can be employed in the present situation. Examine what intrapersonal or interpersonal factors are blocking such coping efforts.

   b) **Train problem-focused instrumental coping skills** that are directed at modification, avoidance, and minimization of the impact of stressors (e.g., anxiety management, cognitive restructuring, self-instructional training, communication, assertion, problem-solving, anger control, applied cue-controlled relaxation training, parenting, study skills, using social supports). Select each skill according to the needs of the specific client or group of clients. Help the client to break complex stressful problems into more manageable sub-problems that can be solved one at a time. *(See discussion below on problem-solving interventions.)*

   c) Help the client engage in problem-solving activities by identifying possibilities for change, considering and ranking alternative solutions, and practicing coping behavioral activities in the clinic and in vivo.

   d) **Train emotionally focused palliative coping skills,** especially when the client has to deal with unchangeable and uncontrollable stressors (e.g., use perspective taking; selective attention diversion procedures, as in the case of chronic pain patients; adaptive modes of affective expression such as humor, relaxation, and reframing the situation).

e)   Train clients how to use social supports effectively (i.e., how to choose, obtain, and maintain support). As Folkman et al. (1991) observe, help clients appreciate what kind of support is needed (informational, emotional, tangible), from whom to seek such support, and how to maintain support resources.

f)   Aim to help the client develop an extensive repertoire of coping responses in order to facilitate flexible responding. Nurture gradual mastery.

2.   Skills rehearsal

a)   Promote the smooth integration and execution of coping responses by means of imagery and behavioral rehearsal.

b)   Use coping[1] modeling (either live or videotape models). Engage in collaborative discussion, rehearsal, and feedback of coping skills.

c)   Use self-instructional training or guided self-dialogue to help the client develop internal mediators to self-regulate coping responses.

d)   Solicit the client's verbal commitment to employ specific coping efforts.

e)   Discuss possible barriers and obstacles to using coping behaviors.

Phase III: Application, relapse prevention and follow-through

1.   Encouraging application of coping skills

a)   Prepare the client for application by using coping imagery, together with techniques in which early stress cues act as signals to cope.

b)   Expose the client to more stressful scenes, including using prolonged imagery exposure to stressful and arousing scenes.

c)   Expose the client in the session to graded stressors via imagery, behavioral rehearsal, and role playing.

d)   Use graded exposure and other response induction aids to foster in vivo responding.

e)   Employ relapse prevention procedures: identify high-risk situations, anticipate possible stressful reactions, and rehearse coping responses.

f)   Use counter-attitudinal procedures to increase the likelihood of treatment adherence (i.e., ask and challenge the client to indicate where, how, and why he or she will use coping efforts).

g)   Bolster self-efficacy by reviewing both the client's successful and unsuccessful coping efforts. Insure that the client makes self-attributions for success or mastery experiences (provide attribution retraining so the client takes "credit" for changes he/she has made).

---

[1] A coping model is one who demonstrates initial distress, anxiety, fearfulness and then models both intra- and interpersonal coping efforts. A "coping" model is more effective than a "mastery" model who demonstrates only desireable behavior throughout (Meichenbaum, 1977).

2.   Maintenance and generalization

    a)   Gradually phase out treatment and include booster and follow-up sessions.

    b)   Involve significant others in training (e.g., parents, spouse, coaches, hospital staff, police, administrators), as well as peer and self-help groups.

    c)   Have the client coach someone with a similar problem (i.e., put client in a "helper" role).

    d)   Help the client to restructure environmental stressors and develop appropriate escape routes. Insure that the client does not view escape or avoidance, if so desired, as a sign of failure, but rather as a sign of taking personal control.

    e)   Help the client to develop coping strategies for recovering from failure and setbacks, so that lapses do not become relapses.

SIT As A Preventative Approach: Application To UN Troops

The potential of SIT as a preventative intervention was illustrated by Weisaeth (1994) who examined the unique demands placed on United Nations soldiers, in what he described as "UN Soldier's Stress Syndrome". The fear of death and injury, the exposure to grotesque stimuli and the sights of carnage and deprivation involving innocents, the uncertainty about the rules of engagement for using deadly force, the enforced passivity of peace-keeping troops when facing danger can result in "a helplessness so severe that the UN soldier's self-respect was damaged". They also experienced "a persistent fear of losing control over their anger" (p.23). The continuing suppression of anger, the exposure to danger and mass deaths, the low control and high responsibility, the time and group pressures, the lack of information, the high risk of failure or "responsibility" stress, and the continual taunts, cumulatively contributed to the UN soldiers' somatic and psychosomatic symptoms and to psychiatric signs of distress. Recent reports from UN forces in Canada[1] and Norway indicate the increasing rates of PTSD in peace-keeping troops when they return home.

What can be done to help reduce the likelihood of such debilitating consequences? This was a question I was asked to address at a meeting of mental health officers of UN forces. In my presentation, I highlighted a number of factors including the important role of leadership, group cohesion, and proactive activities such as exercise, debriefings, as well as the potential benefits of SIT as a means to better train the UN soldiers to address the complex, uncertain, and provocative situations they may find themselves in. As Weisaeth (1994) observes, the enforced passivity which is counter to the way soldiers have been trained to react, the continuing uncertainty about what they can and cannot do, and most often the absence of seeing the consequences of their efforts, can each contribute to a high level of helplessness and group demoralization.

SIT focuses on preparing soldiers for the variety of stressors they are likely to face in such situations. On a preparatory basis, before the UN soldiers are sent to combat areas, they can go through the 3 phases of SIT training. The lack of preparatory training has been found to be an important factor in predicting the development of stress reactions and PTSD. In a collaborative fashion small groups of soldiers could discuss the nature of stress and coping (e.g., "warning signs" in self and others), the nature of the possible stressors, and potential intra and interpersonal

---

[1] These factors were also found to be principle stressors in the Canadian UN Forces, as derived from a standardized Peace-keeping Interview and Survey (Eyre, 1994, personal communication).

coping efforts, as well as detailed information about their mission, the nature of the culture and the history of the specific conflict. Videotapes can be used as part of the training regimen. For instance, in preparing emergency workers for rescue missions in the Armenian earthquake, videotape footage was shown to them before they went to the disaster site. Such preparatory activities, if carefully "engineered" in terms of group preparation and debriefing afterwards, could. be employed with UN soldiers. The focus of the footage should be on coping processes and not on the mere exposure to grotesque scenes. Included in the videotapes should be footage of positive outcomes of the soldier's efforts such as a food envoy getting through, a conflagration stopped or avoided, etc.

The skills training phase of SIT would focus on the behavioral, cognitive and affective regulation skills needed to enhance individual and group coping skills. A variety of skills including physical and mental relaxation skills, problem solving, and coping with provocations could be taught and practiced. Meichenbaum and Novaco (1977) and Novaco et al. (1983) describe how SIT can be applied on a preventative basis with police officers and military recruits. Another example is offered by Weisaeth (1994) who describes how UN soldiers were taught to engage in self-dialogue in provocation situations of verbal and physical taunts such as, "You are a coward", "UN..United Nothing", "You are not a man if you can watch women and children being killed". Mothers brought bodies of their dead children to the UN troops as a means to provoke them to take sides. Under such conditions the UN soldiers were taught to ask themselves: "What are they trying to make me do?" The answer to this question is discussed among the group of soldiers as they are instructed to watch, and if necessary, restrain each other. As Weisaeth (1994) observes, "it is vital that each UN soldier have sufficient self-respect to maintain an acceptable self-image regardless of the circumstances...When facing provocations the UN soldiers may find it helpful to say to themselves, "This says nothing about me, but perhaps something about them." It takes a special kind of courage to respond with self-control when taunted." In the Meichenbaum and Novaco (1977) application phase of SIT with policemen, actors were hired to taunt and tease the officers who had previously been trained to cope with such events. The officers practiced in groups how to deal with such provocations.

Meichenbaum (1994) describes how, in the SIT training of Israeli military recruits, soldiers who had gone through the SIT training were included as trainers. Similarly, Novaco et al. (1983) had marine drill instructors act as co-leaders in their SIT training. A similar approach could be used with the UN forces.

Stress inoculation training has also been used to prepare workers for occupational traumas and rescuers to deal with the demands of their tasks (Ersland et al. 1989). In considering such training programs it is important to keep in mind that when well trained rescuers are unable to implement and perform their skills they are particularly at risk for developing PTSD. For example, Weisaeth (1994) reported that among well-trained sailors who were unable to rescue passengers during a ship's fire that resulted in 159 deaths, 50% of the crew suffered PTSD and other stress related disorders two years after the fire.

In evaluating the role of SIT training and experience, Weisaeth (1994) concludes, "if a person is given adequate education and training he is very likely to be reliable and act rationally, even when facing extreme stress" (p.89). Thus, a high level of training may be the best preventive of later PTSD. Stress inoculation of employees in high risk occupations has also been shown to increase resilience" (p.100).

But few clinicians reading this manual will have occasion to work with UN soldiers who must learn to control their reactions, anger and stressful emotions. But such clinical distress arises regularly for those dealing with clients who are experiencing PTSD, as the next Section describes.

HOW CAN THERAPISTS HELP CLIENTS HANDLE
ANGER / RAGE MORE EFFECTIVELY?
Cognitive-Behavioral Treatment of Anger Control and Conflict Resolution
(Treatment suggestions from the work of Deffenbacher, DiGiuseppe, Hamberger and Holtzworth-Munroe, Novaco, Meichenbaum, Tafrete)

Many PTSD clients have problems with cynical hostility, anger control, rage reactions, irritability, impulsive behavior, and the inability to tolerate discomforting emotions (e.g., see the discussions of PTSD, anger, and Vietnam veterans by Carroll et al. 1985, Kubany et al., 1994 and Matsakis, 1988). For example, Novaco (1994)[1] reports that in a recent study of Vietnam veterans with PTSD they scored two standard deviations higher on an anger scale than did hospitalized psychiatric patients in state hospitals. Traumatized individuals may fear losing their temper and getting angry. It may take little to "light their fuse". Out of a fear of hurting others individuals may withdraw and isolate themselves as a form of protection.

But, the role of anger is not delimited to combat soldiers. Anger has proven to be an important discriminator of PTSD among refugees from Southeast Asia (Abe et al., 1994) and among victims of technological disasters (Green et al., 1994). Because of the emergence of anger as an important diagnostic sign, see Deffenbacher (1994) has proposed a detailed description of how anger can be included in future DSM diagnostic systems.

In order to appreciate how anger, rage, depression and self-hate can become intertwined consider the following description of an incest survivor.

> "Although I sometimes feel numb and cold (unloved and unloveable), there are times when I feel I have too much feeling. I have so many strong emotions -- pain and anger mostly. I sometimes feel like these emotions are going to swamp me. I've never felt in control enough to express these emotions with someone else. No wait! Anger, I have shown, and it's scared both me and the person to whom it was directed. I'll never show anger again. I can't control it. The anger escalates to the point of mindless rage. Sometimes when things are going well, I feel resentful. How much better would I have done without having to have had the burden of memories? How much time have I wasted? I guess I have all this extra stuff to carry around with me. I mean, anyone would understand how wonderful it would feel to have had a normal childhood, with loving parents, to have been introduced to sex by someone suitable who loved me. I didn't get to experience that. I haven't been "cheated out of my childhood" so much as I've been **cheated out** of having **simple thinking**. I can't just BE. I can't just FEEL. My mind never slows down enough. I have to be constantly vigilant. I have to think about the way I should be thinking, interpreting what others are thinking, feeling or planning. It's hard work keeping the brain at that speed. I get tired and then I get angry! Sometimes I drink too much and that makes things even worse!"

For many, the use of alcohol may be a trigger for aggressive behavior.

Stress inoculation training (SIT) has been used successfully to help clients learn anger-control and conflict resolution[2] procedures. Listed below are the component steps in SIT training

---

[1] Novaco's (1994) APA presentation is available from Sound Images 303-693-5511 Tape APA 94-013. Also see Deffenbacher (1994) APA Tape 94-113.

[2] The term **conflict resolution** may be used in lieu of anger control. For some clients, they believe that their feelings of anger are justified and the focus of treatment should not be on controlling their anger. They do recognize, however, that conflicts arise and exacerbate interpersonal situations. In SIT, the focus is on what

for anger control. On the subsequent pages are examples of coping self-control strategies that clients are taught. In order to learn to use such coping strategies clients may be shown videotapes of individuals who become angry and who lose control. They are asked to generate possible coping strategies and then given an opportunity to watch the same scene with the main character now coping with anger. Following this demonstration, clients discuss, practice and try out, "in vivo", the coping techniques. The following treatment guidelines are based on the work of Deffenbacher (1988), DiGiuseppe et al., (1994), Novaco (1975) and Meichenbaum (1985). Novaco[1] (1994) has developed a 12 session SIT training manual for PTSD clients with anger control problems. The three phase intervention program includes cognitive preparation skills, acquisition and application training. In a collaborative fashion clients learn a variety of (a) arousal regulatory skills (e.g., self-monitoring, relaxation, attention diversion skills), (b) cognitive restructuring skills (e.g., modifying attentional focus, adjusting expectations of self and others, modifying appraisal of provocations, engaging in problem-solving thinking, and using self-instructions, and (c) behavioral coping skills (e.g., communication skills, assertiveness skills). These skills are practiced in imaginal and behavioral rehearsal, in exposure and/or "barbing" provocation situations. This SIT training is designed to empower clients to gain control over their anger. The SIT may be used as an adjunct to other forms of intervention.

Novaco also highlights the clinical skillfulness required to work with clients who have anger control problems. For instance, the therapist needs to maintain composure when the client relates tales of anger and aggression and acts in a provocative, confrontational, fashion in therapy. The therapist should also be familiar with self-defense and self-protective behavioral skills. Now let us consider the procedural steps in more detail.

Treatment Steps

1. Enhance the client's personal awareness (e.g., warning signs, intra and interpersonal cues that indicate that he/she is becoming angry and that his behavior is escalating toward violence. These cues are signals that he/she needs to take a "time-out" (TO). In addition, he/she should identify the source of anger and accompanying beliefs. For example, DiGiuseppe et al. (1994) highlighted the therapeutic value of having clients examine their beliefs about anger. These beliefs may include:

   a) lack of emotional responsibility for becoming angry (tendency to blame others)

   b) tendency to condemn and disparage others, viewing other people's behavior as being unreasonable

   c) feelings of self-righteousness, demandingness and entitlement, deservingness and unfairness

   d) holding a "hydraulic metaphor" cathartic discharge model of anger expression

   e) the notion that anger expression is an effective way to control others, especially when one feels as if he/she is not receiving sufficient respect

---

things "light the client's fuse", and act as "triggers", how the client can learn to interrupt the "cycle", learn to undertake a "goal, plan, do, check" approach, identify high risk interpersonal situations, and "notice, catch, interrupt dysfunctional cycles" and produce more adaptive responses. The object is to help clients gain control of the "turbulent" emotions of anger.

[1] You can obtain the SIT manual from Dr. Ray Novaco, Program of Social Ecology, University of California, Irvine, CA. Also see A. Whitehause (1994) description of anger control training with head injury clients (J. Cognitive Psychotherapy, 8, 140-160.)

A useful way to have clients enhance their awareness of anger and its impact is to conduct a careful assessment using self-report measures (DiGiuseppe, Novaco, Spielberger scales) and the Eckhardt Structured Anger Interview, as well as have the clients self-monitor. *(See Section III for a description of these measures which have a great deal of therapeutic utility)*. The feedback session with the client can facilitate a therapeutic alliance. The assessment process can be used to help the client and the therapist agree on the goals and tasks of therapy, as well as nurture a therapeutic bond, three key aspects of therapy, as noted by Bordin. In fact, it would be useful to have clients fill out relationship or therapeutic alliance scales over the course of therapy in order to monitor this "alliance" process (e.g., see Bordin, Safran and Segal scales).

The following questions suggested by Nicholas Long (1993) in their Life Space Crisis intervention approach can be used to help clients better understand the sequence of events that lead to aggressive behavior.

What happened to you?   (Stressor)

How did you feel when that happened to you?   (Feeling)

How did you show that feeling in your behavior?   (Behavior)

How did others react?   (Reaction)

Did their reactions help manage this problem or did it make   (Reciprocal Reaction)
things worse? What did you do?

Do you know when you are getting out of control or does it   (Warning Signs)
just happen?

Are you telling me, are you saying to yourself, that you go   (Assess Time Line)
from being angry to suddenly being out of control? ... Can you
remember anything you said or did between the time you got
mad and the time you lost control (had to be restrained)?

If X did not stop you when you were really angry, what might   (Possible Outcomes)
you have done? ... So by stopping you, X protected you from doing
something that would have caused you more problems?

Is there anyway you can learn to "notice", "catch" "interrupt",   (Take Ownership)
"stop" yourself? What are your choices? How can you become
your own coach, your own therapist?

2.   Educate the client about the components and functions of anger. Use the client's description of his/her anger to become more aware of the arousal, cognitive and behavioral components of anger and aggression. Highlight the adaptive and maladaptive features of anger. For example, anger reflects loss of control and can result in doing things we regret that can alienate others. It can be self-destructive and still leave the "problem" unsolved. Help the client recognize the gradations of emotions and the process of anger escalation. Help the client draw a distinction between feeling "bothered, irritated, upset, hassled, annoyed, frustrated" versus "angry, burned up, pissed off, irate, furious, boiling over, outraged". Enhance emotional awareness by having clients keep Hassle Logs and Personal Goal Logs (see Whitehouse, 1994).

3.   Learn to use of time out (TO) procedures. The TO procedures consist of:

   a)   identifying early and identifiable cues (i.e., personal profile of warning signs)

   b)   not view taking time out (TO) as "rolling over", "giving in", "running away", or "selling out"; view TO as an opportunity to exert control (use sports metaphor) and avoid becoming aggressive.

   c)   remove self for a period of time (e.g., walking away, may be short, lasting only a few minutes to 20 to 30 minutes, depends on the situation).

   d)   tell other person that he/she will take a break to "cool down" and provide an estimate of how long he/she will be away. In training, the client can rehearse such exit lines as:

      i)   "I need some time to think it over."
      ii)   "I'll get back to you tomorrow."
      iii)   "I am getting angry now and I will say things I do not mean."
      iv)   "I need some time to calm down."

   e)   handle others' possible negative reactions to time out

      i)   "Call me what you will, but I am not going to get caught up in this."
      ii)   "I need to get my act together."

   f)   give oneself permission to take time out

      i)   "I am getting pissed off. It is okay to take time out."
      ii)   "Let my feet do the talking, not my hands."

   g)   discuss and practice what to do during time out (e.g., not brood, not think about retaliation, curse, but rather use anger reduction procedures such as reevaluate the situation and engage in relaxing "cool down" activities).

   h)   once "cooled down" he/she should return to the scene and call time in (not avoid the situation)

   i)   role play and imagery rehearse the use of time out procedures

   j)   practice taking time out (discuss when it is best to take TO)

4.   Use applied relaxation and visualization coping skills to reduce arousal, especially slow deep breathing techniques. Practice over 6 to 12 sessions, use homework, address concerns about adherence, practice in nonstressful situations and with a hierarchy of imaginal coping scenes. Solicit commitment statements and reasons why the client should use TO and other coping techniques, as described below.

5.   In Deffenbacher's **Anger Management Training** clients are asked to develop a relaxation scene, as well as several anger scenes, each based upon real events. Once the client is proficient in the relaxation scene, the first anger scene is presented. Following the experience of the anger scene, the therapist guides the client back to the imaginal relaxation scene. The anger and relaxation scenes are alternated. Such imagery techniques may be supplemented with behavioral rehearsal and role playing that includes exposure to anger provoking stimuli. The exposure stimuli include those statements and behavioral cues from others that would provoke anger. Provocation via "barb" techniques can be used by the therapist as a trigger

for the client to engage in social skills training, social problem-solving, and self-control training. Tafrete (1994), as part of a recent APA symposium reported on how volunteer clients who had problems with anger were exposed to planned verbal provocations by the therapist in order to provide the client with opportunities to practice their coping skills. A major clinical concern in undertaking this phase of treatment was whether the therapist put him/herself at risk. Tafrete reported that exposing 45 subjects to over 500 provocations did <u>not</u> elicit verbal or physical attacks on the therapist, but instead elicited a strong therapeutic bond and alliance. The patients eagerly engaged in the "barb" exercise, even instructing the therapist as to how he/she could conduct the provocations more effectively. While great caution and preparation is required when conducting such skills training with provocation, it is clear that exposure techniques have a clear role in SIT. The more similar the elements of training and the real life settings, the greater the likelihood of generalization. Once clients recognize the "costs" to themselves, to their relationships, and to others of their anger and aggressive behavior, they are more likely to consider alternatives, especially if they develop some proficiency in using these skills.

6. Cognitive restructuring procedures *(see section below)*: Attend to

   a) catastrophic interpretation of events (use of dramatic terms, "awful", "can't stand it")

   b) demanding and coercive language ("shoulds, oughts, have to, need to")

   c) overgeneralizations ("always, never"), negative labels ("hopeless, stupid")

   d) categorical thinking (inflammatory labels such as "jerk, slob, asshole, SOB")

   e) misattributions (one track thinking)

   f) either-or black-white thinking

7. Teach problem-solving skills *(see Section below)*.

8. Self-instructional training. (A list of self-statements is collaboratively developed and discussed with the client.) (See Meichenbaum, 1987, 1993 for further clinical discriptions.) For example, the following coping strategies were developed by a client.

> This is going to upset me, but I know how to deal with it. ... Try not to take this too seriously. ... Time for a few deep breaths of relaxation. ... Remember to keep my sense of humor. ... Just roll with the punches; don't get bent out of shape. ... There is no point in getting mad. ... I'm not going to let him get to me. ... Look for the positives. Don't assume the worst or jump to conclusions. ... There is no need to doubt myself. What he says doesn't matter. ... I'll let him make a fool of himself. ... Let's take the issue point by point. ... My anger is a signal of what I need to do. ... Try to reason it out. ... I can't expect people to act the way I want them to. ... Try to shake it off. Don't let it interfere with my job. ... Don't take it personally.

9. Use of humor. Find appropriate ways to vent anger and to use it appropriately.

10. Skill building (listening, communicating, assertiveness, child-rearing, supervisory skills). Discuss what strategies are best to use at what phase in the de-escalation cycle. Practice in vivo.

11. Use self-attribution and relapse prevention procedures. The **self-attribution** process ensures that the client **"takes credit"** for changes he/she has implemented. The relapse prevention procedure ensures that the client has identified **high-risk situations, early warning signs,** and has a **plan and backup plans of action.**

12. Enlist peers and family members as "allies" in the treatment package.

13. Include follow through and booster sessions, where indicated.

14. Also see Shay (1992) for a discussion and demonstration of how medication can be used in the treatment of clients' explosiveness. Tafrete (1994) has conducted a meta-analysis of anger control procedures. Some 16 studies have been identified.

As part of the SIT, clients are asked to review situations in which they "lose control" and become angry/aggressive. In the course of this discussion the client's anger is viewed as going through different phases such as:

a) preparing for the stressful situation ("getting worked up");

b) having to deal with the confrontation;

c) dealing with the anger at its most severe point;

d) reflecting back on how he/she handled the situation.

The client explores the thoughts and feelings at each phase and comes to appreciate that "anger" does <u>not</u> just happen, but how the client appraises the situation, what the client says to him/herself at each phase is influential. Clients are taught to "notice", "catch" themselves, and to produce incompatible coping self-statements (see Meichenbaum, 1985 for a detailed account of how these coping self-strategies are collaboratively generated and practiced). The following pages illustrate some of the handouts that clients are given after such discussions.

It is important to recognize that the therapist does <u>not</u> give the client a list of self-statements to memorize, nor provide a bibliotherapy booklet for the client to read, without ample preparation. Rather the client and the therapist take note of when and how the client's anger/aggression varies across situations and over time and the role that the client's thoughts, feelings and behaviors play. They examine the content and impact of the client's self-statements at each phase (prepare, confront, handle, reflect). If such thoughts and images can make the situation worse then what different thoughts and images might the client engage in? The answer to this questions is considered collaboratively. Thus, in a subsequent session the therapist can say to the client.

"I have been giving some thought to what we talked about last time concerning when you became angry. We discussed how your anger varied across different situations. We also examined the kind of thoughts and feelings you had at each phase of the situations. Our discussion led us to generate a list of possible coping self-statements that you could say to yourself at each phase -- for example, when preparing for, confronting, handling and reflecting upon the situation."

I have taken the liberty of summarizing our discussion by putting together a list of the coping self-statements you offered, as well as some suggestions that have been offered by other folks like yourself that I have worked with who have had similar problems with anger control.

I would like us to go over this list together and see how they might apply in your case. **Remember each person is unique and each person's situation is different.** Thus, some of the suggestions included on this list may be useful for you in helping you handle your anger, while others may <u>not</u> work.

Once we have examined the pros and cons of this list, we can consider how you can use these strategies to control your anger, avoid and resolve conflicts."

Following an examination of the coping self-statements the client is asked to put together an anger control script that he/she can use in provocative. *(See the discussion below on how sobriety scripts are used to treat addictive behaviors).* The following 5 pages include examples of the type of material that is shared with the client.

EXAMPLES OF SELF-STATEMENTS REHEARSED IN STRESS INOCULATION TRAINING FOR CONTROLLING ANGER
(From Novaco, 1975; See Meichenbaum, 1985, for a description of how to help clients collaboratively co-create an individualized coping approach)

Preparing for provocation

This is going to upset me, but I know how to deal with it.
What is it that I have to do?
I can work out a plan to handle this.
If I find myself getting upset, I'll know what to do.
There won't be any need for an argument.
Try not to take this too seriously.
This could be a testy situation, but I believe in myself.
Time for a few deep breaths of relaxation. Feel comfortable, relaxed, and at ease.
Easy does it. Remember to keep your sense of humor.

Impact and confrontation

Stay calm. Just continue to relax.
As long as I keep my cool, I'm in control.
Just roll with the punches; don't get bent out of shape.
Think of what you want to get out of this.
You don't need to prove yourself.
There is no point in getting mad.
Don't make more out of this than you have to.
I'm not going to let him get to me.
Look for the positives. Don't assume the worst or jump to conclusions.
It's really a shame that he has to act like this.
For someone to be that irritable, he must be awfully unhappy.
If I start to get mad, I'll just be banging my head against the wall. So I might as well just relax.
There is no need to doubt myself. What he says doesn't matter.
I'm on top of this situation and it's under control.

Coping with arousal

My muscles are starting to feel tight. Time to relax and slow things down.
Getting upset won't help.
It's just not worth it to get so angry.
I'll let him make a fool of himself.
I have a right to be annoyed, but let's keep the lid on.
Time to take a deep breath.
Let's take the issue point by point.
My anger is a signal of what I need to do. Time to instruct myself.
I'm not going to get pushed around, but I'm not going haywire either.
Try to reason it out. Treat each other with respect.
Let's try a cooperative approach. Maybe we are both right.
Negatives lead to more negatives. Work constructively.
He'd probably like me to get really angry. Well I'm going to disappoint him.
I can't expect people to act the way I want them to.
Take it easy, don't get pushy.

Reflecting on the provocation

a. When conflict is unresolved

Forget about the aggravation. Thinking about it only makes you upset.
These are difficult situations, and they take time to straighten out.
Try to shake it off. Don't let it interfere with your job.
I'll get better at this as I get more practice.
Remember relaxation. It's a lot better than anger.
Can you laugh about it? It's probably not so serious.
Don't take it personally.
Take a deep breath.

b. When conflict is resolved or coping is successful

I handled that one pretty well. It worked!
That wasn't as hard as I thought.
It could have been a lot worse.
I could have gotten more upset than it was worth.
I actually got through that without getting angry.
My pride can sure get me into trouble, but when I don't take things too seriously, I'm better off.
I guess I've been getting upset for too long when it wasn't even necessary.
I'm doing better at this all the time.

SELF-THOUGHTS TO CONTROL ANGER: CLIENT HANDOUT[1]
(See Deffenbacher, 1988)

Our thoughts play a key part in our becoming angry and in increasing our anger. Below are listed several types of thoughts that can increase anger. Following each example are some helpful alternatives which can help you to manage anger more effectively and to deal more appropriately with frustrating, irritating, and disappointing situations.

A.   Catastrophizing Thoughts -- This is the tendency to make things worse than they are, i.e.,
                     "terrible, awful, devastating", etc. You then respond angrily,
                     and perhaps, attack as if these things were very bad.

   Examples:
        1.   This is the worst thing that's ever happened.
        2.   I just can't stand the way that he/she is talking to me.
        3.   This is terrible!

   Examples of helpful self-thoughts to be used instead of catastrophizing:
        1.   It's not the end of the world. It's just frustrating.
        2.   It's just not worth getting all angry about.
        3.   I'll just make the best out of this situation that I can.
        4.   Hang in there. It'll be over soon.
        5.   Getting all bent out of shape doesn't help. Then I have two problems. What I am
              dealing with and being all angry.
        6.   Hang loose and cope. Don't let it get you down. It's not worth it.
        7.   Why should I get all upset? Who will know or care in a week anyway.
        8.   Look, I'll do what I can. If it works, great. If not, well I did the best I can. No
              need to go crazy about it.
        9.   So what if I don't get what I want? Sometimes I do and sometimes I don't.
              There's no guarantee. No reason to blow up about it. Stay cool.

B.   Demanding/Coercing Thoughts -- This is the tendency to make your wants into demands for
                     yourself or the rest of the world. It is the tendency to think
                     that things "should", "ought", "need to be", "have to be",
                     "are expected to be", "must be", certain ways. When you
                     demand that people or situations be a certain way, then you
                     tend to become very angry and upset. You often feel
                     justified in your anger when the demand is not met.

   Examples:
        1.   He/she should have known that would hurt my feelings.
        2.   They should have done that.
        3.   It's not fair! (implying that it ought to be)

      "Who appointed you a god who gets to tell others how to live or be?" Actually, only you did! Frankly, there is no absolute reason why things "should" be the way that you want, other than that you want it. Stay with your wants, desires, and preferences. It is frustrating, disappointing and inconvenient when you do not get what you want. Stay with that. You can cope with that.

---

[1] This handout is based on work by Jeffrey Deffenbacher and his colleagues.

Examples of helpful self-thoughts for demanding/coercing:
1. There's no one right way; we just have a difference of opinion.
2. Look, I want it this way and I am going to stick up for what I think, but they don't have to do it my way.
3. I can't expect people to always act the way I want them to.
4. I don't like this. It's not going my way. So what am I going to do about it? Getting all righteous won't help. How am I going to handle the hassle. That's it, focus on it as a problem to be solved, not as a personal threat.
5. I don't really know why he/she did that. Maybe I need to ask him/her.
6. So I don't get what I want . So what's that big deal. Sure, it's frustrating (disappointing, hurts, is a hassle, etc.), but I can cope.
7. Sure it's not "right" from my point of view, but they have "rights" too. Who says they've got to agree with me?

C. <u>Overgeneralized Thoughts</u> -- This is the tendency to go way beyond the facts in our thinking, to make things far bigger than they really are. These thoughts take irritation or frustration and blow them out of proportion, making you more angry.

Examples:
1. That ruins the whole evening (time).
2. He/she is always inconsiderate.
3. This always happens to me when I am in a hurry.
4. I'm never going to get over this.

Rarely are things "always" or "never" a certain way, even though they may be negative in a given situation. Stay with that. You can cope with a specific situation. Big broad labels are rarely true, e.g., "worthless", "worst", "total junk", etc. Try to stay with the realistic negative feelings and cope with that, rather than blowing them out of proportion and going way beyond what is true.

Examples of helpful self-thoughts for overgeneralized thinking:
1. What's really true? So it's frustrating. Stay cool and cope with that. It's only this hassle in this situation, nothing more.
2. It's frustrating, but I don't need to make a federal case out of it.
3. This irritates me, but that's all. I don't have to let it get to me.
4. All things considered, this is pretty small.
5. This is negative, but other things are going positive.
6. Stay with the situation. I'm the one who really suffers when I get really angry and out of control.
7. No big deal. No need to make myself all upset about this.

D. <u>Categorical Thinking</u> -- This is the tendency to label situations in very extreme, angering terms. For example, labeling some one a "jerk", "slob", "bastard", "an ass", "son of a bitch", "worthless", "no good", etc. just cranks your anger up. Many of these expressions tend to be obscenities and carry with them extra anger automatically.

Examples:
1. That jerk (slob, son of a bitch, ass, etc.)...
2. God damn it.
3. That thing is just a worthless piece of crap.

These categorical labels and obscenities increase anger, but rarely are they true. Think for example of the two common meanings of the word "ass". One is a small horse-like animal and the other the buttocks. Now what has that got to do with the person or situation to which it has been applied? Try to replace these labels with realistic behavioral descriptions.

Examples of helpful self-thoughts for categorical thinking:
1. He/she is not an ass, just a person with whom I have a disagreement.
2. God damn it? No, it's just frustrating and not the way I want, but I can cope with that.
3. It's just broke, that's all.
4. There I go "helling again". It's not hell, just a hassle. Hassles I can deal with.

E.   One-Track Thinking -- This is the tendency to think of things only one way, often tending to personalize the reasons, rather than thinking about multiple reasons for why things happened the way that they did. If you hold a negative interpretation that is not true, your anger will follow at a higher level.

Examples:
1. He/she is doing that to get to me.
2. They wouldn't have done that if they were my friends.
3. It's all my (their) fault.

Sometimes your interpretation may be true. Staying with reality, this would lead to frustration, disappointment, hurt, loss, etc. However, often there are other reasons or explanations you have not thought of. Your anger may be at an inappropriate or exaggerated level if you had all the facts.

Examples of helpful self-thoughts for one-track thinking:
1. Don't jump to a conclusion. Check out the facts.
2. Maybe they didn't know. I better check it out first, before going off half-cocked.
3. I may not have all the facts.
4. Getting angry does not help me figure out what went wrong.
5. Where's my evidence that this is the only reason?
6. Maybe there just "constipated" (or some other humorous explanation).

COGNITIVE RESTRUCTURING PROCEDURES[1]

I. By Way of Introduction

The discussion thus far has highlighted that the exposure to traumatic events, either Type I or Type II stressors, can significantly influence an individual's or group's beliefs about themselves and about their world. **Traumatic events can "shatter" basic assumptions and world views and in its wake leave a belief system that is debilitating and disabling.** Individuals who have been victimized can come to believe that "no one can be trusted," "no place is safe," "I am unloveable," "I am worthless," "I am a pawn", and the like. Such beliefs cover areas such as self-esteem, safety, intimacy, and trust (McCann & Pearlman, 1990). Moreover, many traumatized individuals are depressed -- a common comorbidity condition of PTSD, especially when the PTSD is accompanied by Disorders of Extreme Stress (PTSD-DES, see Section I)[2] .

Cognitive restructuring or cognitive therapy procedures provide very useful clinical techniques to help PTSD clients become better observers ("detectives") of their thinking processes and of the tacit implicit assumptions or beliefs they hold. These cognitive therapy techniques can be employed on an individual, group, couple, or family basis. A number of books have been written on cognitive therapy procedures and these will not be reviewed here. Instead, I will summarize and describe a few of the cognitive restructuring procedures and illustrate how they can be applied to clients with PTSD.

In considering cognitive restructuring procedures it is first useful to draw a distinction between:

a) **cognitive events** -- conscious or readily retrievable automatic thoughts (AT), images or internal dialogue. Such AT are often idiosyncratic, spontaneous, and rarely questioned. AT are usually treated like "God-given" assertions, rather than being viewed as "hypotheses" worthy of testing. These AT can act as

---

[1] Subsumed under the heading of cognitive restructuring are a variety of diverse psychotherapeutic approaches covering the work of Albert Ellis, Aaron Beck, Arnold Lazarus, and others. As Meichenbaum (1994) has noted, it is critical that we do not impose a "uniformity myth" across these diverse approaches of rational-emotive therapy (RET), cognitive therapy, and cognitive restructuring. These procedures have different objectives, use different therapeutic techniques, and have different outcomes. For example, "RET can be distinguished from other cognitive behavior therapies, especially in its therapeutic goal; namely, the client's achievement of a new philosophical outlook" (Engels et al., 1993, p.1083). **One must ask how successful is RET in achieving such goals?** The answer to this question is complex. For instance, Gossette and O'Brien (1992) conclude, "behavior change is relatively insensitive to RET interventions" (p.20). Haaga and Davison (1993) observe that RET's "professional impact thus far exceeds its scientific status" (p.215). Haaga and Davison (1989) conclude that "in many areas RET either (a) is supported only by preliminary, unreplicated findings...(b) has not added anything to simpler treatments that do not strive for profound philosophical change that RET seeks" (p.494). Muran and DiGiuseppe (1994) in discussing **cognitive therapy** procedures with **rape victims** observe that characterizing the client's beliefs as being "irrational" and focussing upon such beliefs "ruptures the therapeutic alliance. Survivors perceive such an intervention as insensitive and invalidating (p. 171). These negative conclusions about RET should be juxtaposed with Engels et al. (1993) recent meta-analysis of RET which concluded "that RET on the whole succeeded in improving subjects' well-being, compared with placebo treatment or no treatment ... its effects were maintained over time" (p.1088). Given this controversy, RET procedures will not be reviewed in this therapist manual. The focus will be on cognitive therapeutic procedures that have a much more substantial empirical basis (see Hollon & Beck, 1994).

[2] Space does not permit a detailed presentation of the outcome studies of cognitive therapy with unipolar depressed clients. After critically reviewing the literature, Hollon and Beck (1993) concluded that there is an enduring effect for cognitive behavioral therapy of depressives, with only about 20% of all treatment responders relapsing or seeking additional treatment.

"self-fulfilling prophecies". Individuals often behave in ways that elicit reactions from others that confirm their views of themselves and their world.

b) **cognitive processes** -- information processes that can occur in an automatic, if not "unconscious" fashion. This describes the processes by which individuals selectively attend, retrieve and integrate information. For instance, they refer to the mental heuristics and implicit decision rules that individuals employ to process information (e.g., availability and salience mental heuristics, confirmatory bias).

c) **cognitive structures** -- represent the implicit beliefs, schemes, and readiness sets that provide the "if...then" rules by which one functions. These represent the dominant current concerns or "core organizing principles" that guide and influence both cognitive events and processes. For example, a victimized client may hold the belief that, "If I have been hurt by a male, then I cannot trust any men." *(See Meichenbaum and Gilmore, 1984, for a more complete discussion).*

The exposure to traumatic events can influence all three processes. For example, PTSD clients often have a number of **automatic thoughts** that can have a negative impact on how they feel and behave. For example, "I'm a nobody," "I can't do anything right," "I can't be close to anyone." Also, the way they feel (e.g., hopeless, guilty, shamed) can have a negative impact on how they think. Thus, feelings and thoughts are viewed as two sides of the same coin, each of which can escalate and exacerbate a debilitating depressive cycle. Moreover, the way that PTSD clients interact (e.g., distrusting, explosive, dependent) may inadvertently, unwittingly, and unknowingly come to produce the very reactions in others that help to maintain the behaviors they complain about. Thus, the automatic thoughts (cognitive events), appraisal processes (cognitive processes), and implicit beliefs (cognitive structures) become self-fulfilling prophecies. For example, the depressed PTSD client may behave in a "depressing" fashion, turning others off, but not realize the **transactional nature** of his/her behavior. Given that the depressed traumatized individual feels vulnerable and is preoccupied with feelings of loss, rejection, and abandonment, these preoccupations (or "current concerns") can color the way events are appraised and contribute to inadvertent behaviors that come to produce the very reactions in others that the client fears.

One task for the therapist is to help the client come to appreciate this transactional pattern, and moreover, help the client learn how his/her thoughts (automatic thoughts, appraisal processes, thinking errors, implicit beliefs, and tacit assumptions) can contribute to his/her difficulties; help the client appreciate how they unwittingly, and perhaps, even unknowingly can contribute to his/her own difficulties and distress. In this way their thoughts become "self-fulfilling prophecies".

In order to accomplish these objectives the clinician may use a variety of cognitive restructuring techniques (e.g., self-monitoring as discussed earlier) that help clients become more aware of the interdependence of their thoughts, feelings, behavior and resultant consequences, and in turn, learn to "notice," "catch," "interrupt," "test out," "experiment with," "try on," "refocus on," "remind themselves to attend to," different automatic thoughts, feelings, beliefs and behaviors.

Hollon and Garber (1990) have summarized these diverse cognitive restructuring procedures as consisting of essentially three general groups of questions that the therapist can raise with clients over the course of treatment. These questions are raised in a collaborative fashion.

1. **Evidence-based questions** -- therapist and client work together to help the client view his or her automatic thoughts as "hypotheses worthy of testing", rather than as "God given assertions," or as incontrovertible facts. The therapist helps the client to:

   a) review data or reconsider existing evidence at hand. For example, a client may say, "I am a nobody", and the therapist adopts an inquisitive style like the television character of the detective Columbo, conveying confusion between the client's automatic thoughts and other data that the client has offered indicating competence (as illustrated in the example below, the therapist is specific in noting these discrepancies). Also note that even the client being depressed and seeking help can be reframed as a strength (e.g., "being in touch with feelings").

   b) encourage the client to collect additional "data" by self-monitoring and by running personal behavioral experiments. Over the course of treatment the therapist helps the client take the resultant data as "evidence" to "unfreeze" his/her beliefs.

2. **Alternative-based questions** -- therapist helps the client to generate and consider alternative explanations for events, in addition to those he or she first adopted. For example, the therapist asks, "Are there any other possible explanations for how others have reacted or how the client reacted?"

3. **Implications-based questions** -- therapist helps the client to examine whether his or her initial beliefs, even if true, necessarily implies everything that, at first, they seemed to imply.

4. The following illustrates an example of the ways these different types of questions are combined. The therapist can say,

   "Hold on, I am a little bit confused. On the one hand you say 'you are a nobody.' But this is where my confusion comes in, because on the other hand, you have done X, Y, and Z. How does doing X, Y and Z go along with your being a nobody? Help me understand that?"

   Later on the therapist can ask,

   "Where did this notion of being a nobody come from?"

   The client often indicates that this was what someone else (e.g., the victimizer) often told him/her. The therapist then examines with the client,

   "What is the impact?...What is the cost?...What is the toll?...of calling yourself a nobody? Is this the impact you want?"

   Moreover, it is pointed out that the client is still living someone else's story,

"Letting the perpetrator to continue to victimize you, 'rob you', even though he is not here any longer. Do you think it is time for you (the client) to begin to write your own story?"

Another example of such reframing was offered by Resick and Schnicke (1993, pp.86 & 91) with rape victims. They tell the client:

"The rapist owned an hour (or a few hours) of your life. He did have control over that bit of time. Do you want him to continue to own the rest of your life by influencing you to behave differently, as though you are going to be raped at any moment?...The rapist owned X (e.g., three hours) of your life and we can't change that. Do you want him to own the rest of your life and to dictate what you can and cannot do?"

With this as a prologue, let us consider the goals and specific cognitive restructuring procedures.

II. Cognitive Restructuring Procedures[1]

The Cognitive Restructuring procedures are designed to achieve three major objectives:

(1) help clients become more aware of their automatic thoughts and the interdependence and transactional impact of their thoughts, feelings, behavior and the reactions of others;

(2) help clients alter their ways of processing information and behaving;

(3) help clients explore and alter basic schema by performing "personal experiments", whereby they can collect data that will "unfreeze" their beliefs about self and the world.

We will briefly consider some of the therapeutic strategies that can be used to achieve each of these treatment goals, and then **consider how one can structure the therapeutic sessions.** We begin with how to help clients become **more aware of their automatic thoughts (AT).** Then we will consider how to help clients **alter how they process information,** and **alter their basic beliefs.** We will also consider how to **treat guilt reactions.**

A. How does one help clients become more aware of the nature and impact of their automatic thoughts (AT)?

There are a number of ways a therapist can help clients become more aware of their AT:

1)   ask directly
2)   use imagery reconstruction
3)   solicit the client's advice
4)   use videotape modeling films
5)   have clients self-monitor
6)   analyze specific incidents

1) Ask directly. The therapist can **ask directly** about the clients' thoughts, images, and accompanying feelings, either those occurring prior to the session, during the session, or as part of exploring a specific incident. For instance, the therapist can ask:

[1] The present description of cognitive restructuring is limited to individual interventions, but they could readily be adapted to group, couples, and family treatments.

> What thoughts, if any, were running through your mind before you
> came in to see me?
>
> What kinds of feelings and thoughts are you having right now?
>
> I notice *(your becoming upset, your tone of voice changed, that is, the
> therapist can go "public with the data")* and I wonder what you
> were feeling as you X? What thoughts, if any, did you have when
> you Y? ... What were you thinking about when X?

Caveat concerning the probing for automatic thoughts. It is important to keep in mind that for many clients they do not view themselves as going about "talking to themselves" or having AT. In fact, most of the time their behavior is "automated" or "mindless", occurring in a "scripted" fashion, in the ways that Abelson and Schank, Langer, Thorngate, and others describe (see Meichenbaum & Gilmore, 1984). One objective of cognitive restructuring is to help clients "deautomatize" their behavior and to increase their awareness, or "mindfulness". Once they learn new coping skills, the object will be to help them automatize and "rescript" their new more adaptive behaviors.

While clients may be reluctant, initially, to discuss their automatic thoughts, they are more willing to examine their feelings. From the present perspective, every time there is a major shift in affect, it is proposed that there is an accompanying alteration in appraisal and AT. If clients come to entertain the possibility of this "going togetherness" between feelings and thoughts, then this raises the possibility of altering their behavior. The following lines of questions are designed to help clients increase their awareness of these therapeutic possibilities. The therapist can sample from the following array of questions:

> You look very (upset, hurt, angry, tense, sad, etc.) right now. Can
> you tell me what that feels like?
> I noticed you are X--*(therapist "goes public" with the data)*. Am I
> reading things right?
> What makes you feel X?
> What does that feel like?
> What were you afraid of when X occurred? At that point, what, if
> anything were you thinking?
> Can you share with me what thoughts went along with those feelings
> of X? What was going through your mind that led you to feel
> this way (be specific)?
> Do you remember what you were thinking? Do you remember
> having any other thoughts or images (pictures) go through your
> mind at the time?
> You say you had thought X. What did that thought mean to you at
> the time? ... What does it mean to you now? ... What comes to
> mind when you think that?
> When you think X, how does that make you feel?
> I wonder, if most people wouldn't feel X if they said to themselves,
> (or if they believed) Y.
> It seems natural that you would feel Y, given your belief that X.

IT IS CRITICAL NOT TO QUESTION NOR CHALLENGE THE CLIENTS' AUTOMATIC FEELINGS AND THOUGHTS AND BELIEFS. RATHER ACKNOWLEDGE THEM AND CONSIDER THE CLIENT'S BASIS FOR HIS/HER BELIEFS. AFTER THE CLIENT HAS TOLD HIS OR HER STORY THE

THERAPIST CAN QUERY THE BASIS FOR BELIEFS. IF THE THERAPIST
PROBES TOO EARLY, THEN THE CLIENT FEELS THAT THE THERAPIST
DOES NOT UNDERSTAND THE EXTENT OF THE CLIENT'S "PAIN". TIMING
IS CRITICAL! REMEMBER THE CLIENT SHOULD HAVE A SENSE OF
CONTROL. ASK THE CLIENT ABOUT HIS/HER REACTIONS TO THERAPY.

2) Use Imagery Reconstruction. The therapist can use an **imagery
reconstruction procedure** whereby clients are asked to image a specific stressful
incident and then to imaginally review it in "slow motion", reporting on any feelings and
thoughts that preceded, accompanied and that followed that specific incident. In this
way, the therapist helps clients to become more attentive to the prodromal, low intensity
cues (chain of events), and their accompanying feelings and appraisals. The therapist
helps clients to collect data so they can come to appreciate that their dysphoric feelings
(depression, anxiety, anger) do not just occur, but rather how they appraise events and
their abilities to handle them, are critical and highly interdependent.

Note that the imagery reconstruction process need not only attend to an analysis of
"negative" stressful encounters. For instance, Walter and Peller (1992) share with their
clients examples of athletes who improved their performance by studying either
videotapes or using imagery rehearsal procedures of "positive" coping efforts. For
example, Jim Frey the manager of a major league baseball team had his players improve
their hitting by watching videotapes of only when they got a hit, or the high jumper
Dick Fosbury broke the world record by imaging himself making the "perfect" jump.
Only when he could visualize this in his mind's eye, right before he jumped, would he
make a run at the bar. In both instances, the athlete is becoming his own "director". Is
there any way that this could apply in your case in your handling different situations?

3) Advice giving. If clients evidence difficulty engaging in such an imagery
procedure, then the therapist can ask the clients to envisage a specific stressful incident
and predict ("guess") what kind of thoughts and feelings someone else might have to
give him/herself in order not to handle the situation very well ("become more stressed
out", or "lose control", etc.). The therapist explores with clients how they came up with
their answers (e.g., by experience, observation, discussion with others). This leads to a
discussion of what different thoughts and feelings would this person have to engage in,
or what advice the clients might have for someone else so he/she could handle the
situation more effectively. Once again, the therapist explores with the clients how they
came up with their "advice". Finally, the therapist explores with the clients what
obstacles or barriers (internal and external) might get in the way of someone using such
coping techniques (thoughts, feelings and behaviors), and what can be done to
overcome these barriers.

4) Videotape Modeling Film. Another way to solicit the clients' AT and have
them recognize their impact is to use **videotape modeling films** of individuals who
are evidencing difficulty coping. For example, we have used short (less than 10 minute)
films of individuals who become angry in a social situation. In the videotaped film,
voice overplay is used so the audience can hear the individual's thoughts and feelings
before, during, and after the provocation situation. The client (or group of clients, since
the treatment can be conducted on a group basis) are asked their reactions to the
videotaped vignette. The therapist asks a sequence of questions:

> What is going on in the videotape? What happened? How did the
> main character in the videotape react? What is getting him so upset?
> What role did his thoughts and feelings play? How did he view the
> situation? What was the impact of what he felt, thought, did? What

toll did it take on him? on others? ... Has anything like what is portrayed on the tape ever happen to you? What happened? When? How did it turn out? How would you handle the situation differently today? What might get in the way of your doing that?

Note that the use of this initial videotape is only one part of a complex sequence of interventions. This initial videotape is followed by a group discussion and then the introduction of a **video-taped replay of the same scene,** but now the protagonist in the film is coping and handling the situation. More specifically, the intervention steps include having clients:

1. watch a think-aloud model who evidences difficulty coping (e.g., with anger, handling flashbacks, depression, addictive behaviors).

2. use the videotape for a discussion of the role of cognitive, affective and interpersonal factors, and then solicit advice on how the main character in the videotape might handle the situation more effectively.

3. watch the same scene once again, but this time the main character evidences cognitive, affect-regulation, and interpersonal coping skills. Once again, the main character thinks aloud, but now incorporating a variety of coping self-statements and behaviors (e.g., relaxation, taking time out, problem-solving).

4. discuss the coping videotape modeling film in order to note if any of the suggestions that the participants had offered before hand were used by the main character in the videotape. The therapeutic discussion focuses on how the main character in the coping videotape went about **"noticing"** when he was getting upset and how he was working himself up in this high risk situation; **"catching"** himself; **"interrupting"** the sequence; **"using his game plan"**; **"reminding"** himself of his goals in the situation; **"checking"** to see how things turned out; **"patting"** himself on the back for what he did to cope; and **"asking" himself** what he had learned from the situation. Note that the therapist "bathes" the discussion with executive metacognitive transitive verbs ("notice, catch, interrupt, plan", etc.). **Over the course of treatment the therapist monitors the degree to which the client(s) spontaneously incorporate such transitive verbs in their story-telling or narrative accounts.**

5. have group members break up into small groups of three in order to practice the suggested coping techniques. For example, one participant can act out the role of the protagonist in the videotape, one the role of the other central character, and the third party can provide an ongoing commentary of possible coping techniques. *(This process is similar to script writing described below in the Section on treating clients with addictive behaviors.)*

6. review how the role-playing and behavioral rehearsal went and then discuss where, when, and how each client can use and practice these coping skills. The therapist **solicits**

commitment statements from clients. Ask clients, "How likely are you to apply what was shown in the film?" "How useful or applicable will the techniques demonstrated in the film be in your personal life?" How confident are you in performing this activity? How confident are you that it will work? (The therapist can solicit the client's self-efficacy estimates ala Bandura.)

7. consider **relapse prevention** processes, namely, what factors (either external or internal) could get in the way of your implementing the coping skills; and what can the client(s) do if the coping procedures do <u>not</u> work? The therapist can also use **counter-attitudinal statements** with clients in order to have them generate the reasons to engage in the coping efforts. For example, the therapist can challenge the client(s) by using paradoxical statements. For example, the therapist could say:

> Are you telling me, are you saying to the group, are you saying to yourself, that when you are out there and having to face X, or handle your Y (e.g., angry feelings, depression, flashbacks, ruminations, urge to drink) you are going to do Z? How would you do that? Why would you put out the effort to react differently? How will that help?

(Note that the research on behavior change indicates that if clients can come up with the arguments for engaging in behavior change, then they have a greater likelihood of following through.)

8. check on the client implementing the coping procedures and how it went between sessions. Make sure that the client takes credit for successes. "Last week we discussed X. What happened with that? How did you do that?"

In summary, a useful way to have clients become aware (and change) their AT and behavior is to use videotape modeling films. In the future, clinicians will have a library of such videotape modeling films in their offices as a supplement to other therapeutic procedures. It is important to keep in mind that the watching of such films is embedded in a sequence of behavior change procedures. **The observation of coping films without active discussion, practice, commitment statements, relapse prevention efforts is insufficient to achieve change.**

<u>5) Self-monitoring</u>. Another way to help clients tap AT is to encourage them to record the situations in which they become distressed and to record their thoughts, feelings, situation, i.e., engage in **"thought-catching"**. *(See the discussion in Section III on how to motivate clients' to self-monitor)*. For instance, the therapist can convey to the client:

> In this session we talked about several recent incidents in which you felt stressed, upset (lost control, were "stuck", stuffed feelings, etc. -- use the client's specific metaphor and phrases). We also observed (noticed) the kinds of things that ran through your mind and the impact these thoughts had on your feelings and on your behavior,

and in turn, how your feelings affected your thoughts. (Therapist
should give specific examples and check them out with the client). In
fact, it is rare that people express stress without there being a thought
behind it. In the coming week, let's explore if this applies in your
case. How might we best go about determining the role your
thoughts play?

At this point the therapist follows the guidelines on collaborative self-
monitoring described in the Assessment Section III.

Several other procedures have been used to help clients become aware
of their automatic thoughts. These include setting up specific behavioral tests
in vivo or in therapy, use role playing and behavioral rehearsal, use the
Gestalt procedure of an "empty chair" technique, use an ABC analysis - A
(stimulus); C is how you reacted; B are the thoughts and feelings that
intercede between A and C (the ABC analysis was suggested by RET).

B. How does one help clients alter the ways they process information?

The first step is to help clients **become aware** of how they process information,
namely, the ways they selectively attend to information of the present, past and future,
the ways they generate inferences, so that the client's thoughts can become hypotheses
worthy of testing. A good beginning point in this process is to have the client engage in
a **situational analysis**, noting the variety of situations in which the client has had
similar thoughts and feelings.

"Do you have similar feelings of X (be specific), and similar thoughts
of Y in other situations? The therapist should use the client's specific
metaphors ("stuff feelings", "build walls", "dredge up worries", etc.)

By pursing the similarity across situations or by asking **"like a"** questions, the therapist
can help clients become aware of how they appraise situations and how their "mood",
"emotional state", colors their accounts. For instance, the therapist can help the client
appreciate how feeling depressed can act as prism or as a set of blinders, coloring how
the client sees things from the past, present, and the future.

Use of the Metaphor of Prejudice

The therapist can introduce the **metaphor of "prejudice"** (as suggested by Christine
Padesky, 1990) to convey to the client the nature of cognitive restructuring efforts. For
example, Padesky asks the client if he/she knows anyone who is prejudiced (e.g., racial
or gender prejudice). The therapist then explores with the client what are the
characteristics of someone who is prejudiced. They then discuss how a person who is
prejudiced tends to selectively attend to data, overgeneralize, ignore, distort, discount,
use stereotypes, and does not accept data that is incompatible with his/her prior beliefs.
Also, explore how a prejudiced person behaves such that he/she creates reactions in
others that confirm prejudicial beliefs. The therapist explores these examples with the
client without using psychological jargon.

By means of **Socratic questioning**, Padesky has the client explore the metaphor of
prejudice. The therapist says:

"Would it be OK with you if we talked for a little while about something
other than the topics we've been exploring these last few weeks?...I'd like

to talk with you about prejudice. Do you know what prejudice is? Can
you think of someone in your life who has a particular prejudice against a
person or group of people, where you can see that their prejudice is
wrong?"

The therapist then examines with the client examples of how the prejudiced person might
respond when confronted with information discrepant with his/her belief. The client
may be asked how he/she might go about trying to change the prejudiced person's mind.
After such a discussion the therapist can ask the client, "Why do you think I've been
talking with you about prejudice a week after we discussed your "core beliefs?" The
therapist can then explore with the client if his/her beliefs act like a prejudice? As
Padesky notes, "the therapist and client can then consider specific examples where the
client may have distorted, discounted, talked about the data as an exception, or didn't
notice relevant information" (p.55).

If such indirect Socratic discovery procedures do not work, then the therapist can be a
bit more directive by saying to the client, "I don't want you to take this the wrong way,
but **at times** I think you are a prejudiced person." As the client looks inquisitively, the
therapist then interjects, "You seem to be prejudiced about yourself." The therapist then
explains that the client tends to only see the negative side of him/herself. The therapist
and client then explore whether this metaphor makes any sense and whether there are
any other examples that the client can offer of selectively attending to data, discounting
or ignoring signs of strength and of recovery, of becoming "unstuck".

Together, the client and the therapist explore sequentially the impact, cost, and personal
price of being prejudiced about oneself. **"What is the impact?...What is the
toll?...What is the price?**...of such a personal prejudice?". The answers to these
questions are addressed not in the abstract, but rather by having the client offer specific
"experiential" examples. The therapist then explores what the client can do to change
this invalidation prejudicial process? Once again, the "art of questioning" is used to
nurture collaboration with the client. Encourage the client to discover and own possible
solutions. **Remember the therapist is at his/her best when the client comes
up with the suggestions of what should be done.**

Mental Contamination as a Metaphor

The therapist can introduce the metaphor of **mental contamination** to convey to the
client how their thinking processes are influenced by factors of which they are not
always readily aware. (See Wilson and Brekke, 1994, for a review of the literature on
mental contaminants such as halo, anchoring and priming effects). In order to
introduce the concept of **mental contamination**, the therapist can ask the client if
he/she has been reading, or heard anything about, various forms of contamination or
pollution (e.g., radiation, radon, pollution of natural resources). ... The reason I ask is
that some scientists have drawn an analogy between physical contamination and mental
contamination...In an analogous fashion to how our bodies may become contaminated
by viruses and bacteria, by pollutants such as radon gas of which we are not aware, it is
possible that our thinking processes might also become contaminated. What does it
mean to say that our thinking processes can be contaminated? For instance, we each
have biases, hold stereotypes and prejudices. For example, we may think that a
particular person cannot do something or is more prone to engage in a specific form of
behavior because of his/her race, religion, or gender -- whether or not there is any
substance to this belief. At this point, have the client give specific examples by asking,
"If you saw X (a member of a particular race) in situation Y, what would your automatic
response be?" Use several examples to help the client appreciate that we carry around

with us an "overlearned, nonconscious implicit filter" through which we see the world. Our upbringing, our culture, our emotional needs, can each **"clog" or "contaminate" our filter.** For instance, as soon as we see something we are prone to quickly **categorize it.** Such categories can taint how we see things, how we feel, how we behave, and influence the decisions we make. Let's see how these ideas apply in your case. (At this point the therapist encourages the client to "try on" the idea of "mental contamination").

The next step is to explore with the client when he/she is most prone to fall victim to such sources of contamination. The discussion should highlight that when an individual's cognitive capacity is being taxed due to preoccupations, fatigue, distress, dysphoric emotions (e.g., being depressed, anxious), it is difficult for individuals to expend the energy, effort, and control to combat such contaminants.

The final focus of the discussion is on what the client can do to combat such "contaminants"? How can the client exert the mindful controlled efforts to become sensitive to when he/she is being "prejudiced" about himself/herself and about others? How can the client learn to "anticipate, notice, catch, interrupt" the presence of such contaminants? What can the client do to check his/her filter and keep it clear, unclog it? Once again, by using an analogy to physical contamination, the client and therapist can generate behavioral strategies of how to monitor, avoid, control, seek support from others, and the like. **It is critical that these discussions be translated into very concrete steps that the client can use in the subsequent week.**

The metaphors of **prejudice** and **mental contamination** can be used as organizing frameworks in cognitive restructuring. It is important for the client to recognize that all individuals are prone to such processes, and in many instances they are adaptive processes. For example, when confronted by a danger we need to respond quickly, we immediately categorize the event and react. But this same process of automatic categorizing can be maladaptive. *(See Meichenbaum & Fong, 1993 for a discussion of these processes.)*

Question Asked As A Means of Changing The Client's Ways Of Processing Information

Another means of helping clients alter the ways they process information is by asking critical questions that help clients to:

a) evaluate their thoughts and beliefs
b) elicit predictions
c) explore alternatives
d) question faulty logic.

Let's consider each of these interventions briefly.

a) ### Evaluate thoughts and beliefs.

The therapist helps the client learn how to listen more attentively to how he/she talks to self and others and how he/she uses language. For example, the client may say "I am a terrible mother" to which the therapist, "plucks", the phrase "Terrible mother?". In this way the therapist helps the client consider data that is consistent and inconsistent with the label "terrible mother". In other words, helps the client to:

- define and "operationalize" his/her AT

- consider facts that do and do not fit the label (e.g., "Has this always been true?"; How does your saying, "You are a terrible mother", go along with (cite examples that don't fit)?
- encourage the client to collect information or to perform a personal experiment to "test out" his/her conclusion.

- Do you always believe what you read in the newspapers? Why not?

- Do you always believe what you tell yourself?

- In this case were your thoughts telling you all you needed to know?

- How can you know whether your thoughts are just giving you information that causes you to get out of control (get depressed, get into trouble, take away your hope)?

- Are you saying that you needed some more facts before you react (before you decide what to do, before you take your next steps)?

- Okay. How could you go about getting such information.

- Are you suggesting that the depression just doesn't come on, but how you view things, what you say to yourself, what you do and feel, and how others' react, all come into play? ... That is a powerful idea!

b) **Elicit predictions.**

In order to have the client view AT and beliefs as "hypotheses" worthy of testing, the therapist can solicit predictions of what might happen. For example,

- What do you think will happen to your feelings when your thoughts (give specific examples)?
- What do you picture happening or think will happen when X? How can we find out?
- How do you know that will indeed happen?

It is helpful to have the client write out the prediction in therapy in order to compare it with the results obtained subsequently.

c) **Explore alternatives.** *(See discussion below on problem-solving for other ways to help clients generate alternatives.)*

In order to nurture perspective taking in clients a series of questions can be asked that nurture generating alternatives.

- Are there any other explanations for what happened?
- Can you think of an example recently when you caught yourself jumping to a negative conclusion that you later found out was an incorrect prediction (conclusion), or the wrong interpretation?
- Are there other equally likely ways of looking at the situation?
- How much responsibility do you really have for X? Could there be any other reasons for X?
- How would you know that was the way he/she viewed it?

- Is it possible that there are other reasons for the way he behaved, which had nothing to do with you?
- Let's assume for the moment that the worst possible thing actually happened. What would happen then? If we analyze it further, is it possible that we might come to a different view of things?
- What would happen if X? Can you make a prediction about Y? Are you willing to test that out?
- Let me ask you to image a situation that causes you to become "anxious" (or depressed, feel guilty, hostile). Now I would like to change the image so you only become disappointed (feel regret, annoyance, irritation -- a less intense emotion). What changed? (M. Maultsby suggested this procedure as a way to teach clients to attend to the gradation of emotion and the nature of cognitive and behavioral changes).

Another way to help clients consider alternatives is to encourage them to **perspective-take**. By helping the client to view an incident from different perspectives the therapist can help the client alter the way he/she processes information. Consider the potential therapeutic impact of asking clients to address the following questions.

> How do you think X saw the situation? ... interpreted the incident?
> What leads you to that view?
> How could you check out whether that is the way he/she sees things?
> Have you discussed this with X?
> What would you like to see X do differently than he/she does now?
> Is there any chance that he/she might not react as negatively as you think? ... How could you find out?

d) Question faulty logic.

The teaching of logical errors should be conducted in **an inductive collaborative fashion** and not as a didactic lecture format. The therapist can reflect a number of client examples that reflect such errors as:

- **dichotomous thinking** - black/white thinking
- **all or none thinking** - equate one mistake with total failure
- **overgeneralization** - negative event seen as beginning of a never-ending process
- **personalization** - blame self for negative events without considering the influence of external factors.

The therapist can indicate that he/she noticed something and was wondering if the client noticed something similar. At this point the therapist "goes public with the data", reflecting the client's thinking errors, offering multiple examples. As the client provides examples, the therapist can then label the client's error in thinking.

> "This is what some call black/white thinking, or to use a fancy term, dichotomous thinking."

In order to counteract such thinking errors the client and therapist can collaboratively generate a strategy such as:

Whenever I find myself making a negative prediction or drawing
a negative conclusion about my ability to handle the situation, I
will ask myself, "Have I only had failures in this situation in the
past or have there actually been times when I did okay?"

Other self-questions that clients are encouraged to ask themselves include:

I will ask myself exactly what is at stake?
Are there alternative explanations or interpretations for how I am
    feeling?
Is there data that contradicts this conclusion?
What is the evidence for calling myself X? or labeling the
    situation Y?
Does this situation reflect a "threat" signaling potential harm, or a
    "challenge" signaling an opportunity?
What would that mean if X?
Are there other ways of looking at the situation?
There are times when I don't do as well as I would like, but at
    other times I do okay; what are the differences?
Have I only had failures in situations in the past or were there
    times I did okay?
So what if this did not work out; why is it so horrible?
So what if it happens?
What can I learn from this experience?
What answers can I give to that thought?
How does this carry over to other situations? Is that the way I
    want things to be?

Yost et al. (1986) in summarizing this self-interrogative process suggests that the
client engage in the following five basic questions:[1]

(1) How else can I view or interpret the situation, or how would others view it?
(2) Is the anticipated consequences likely to be as bad as it seems?
(3) Is there some other explanation of the situation?
(4) How likely is the anticipated consequence to occur?
(5) Is the assumption behind my belief "true" or has it ever not been "true"?

During the course of treatment the therapist can monitor the frequency and manner in
which clients spontaneously ask questions that cover the **evidence, alternative
explanations** and **implications** of their thoughts, feelings and behavior. Is the
client becoming his/her own therapist? Has the client taken the therapist's voice with
him/her? Has the client become an observer of his/her own behavior? For instance,
does the client ever say something like:

"I now know how I can drive myself crazy?; "I actually caught
myself. I interrupted what I was doing." "I used my plan and
asked myself questions." "I can see how I can be my own judge

---

[1] See Resick and Schinke (1993, p.69) for a list of questions that clients can be given in the form of a Challenging
Questions Sheet. Illustrative questions include: "What is the evidence for and against this idea?", "Am I
confusing a habit with a fact?", "Am I using words or phrases that are extreme or overexaggerated ("always,
forever, never, should")?, "Am I thinking in all-or-none terms (e.g., either-or, black-white, right-wrong, good-
bad)?, "Am I thinking in terms of certainties, instead of probabilities?"

and jury." "I can stay with the bad feelings (anger, depression, guilt) and not let them overwhelm me, as well as with the bad times (flashbacks, ruminations) and not let them stop me in my tracks." "I can get unstuck and refocus on what I have to do."

Whenever clients offer evidence of altering the ways they process information it is critical for the therapist to insure that **they make self-attributions (take credit for the change)** and that they take notice of how they are handling the situation now **differs from** how they handled it in the past. As discussed in detail below, **it is not enough to just have clients change their behavior, it is critical for them to take ownership and responsibility for the change.** Clients (like scientists) do not readily accept the data, as evidence, to unfreeze their beliefs. Doing so is an active process that needs to be nurtured and reinforced by the therapist. For example, the therapist in a timely fashion can sample from the following list and ask the client:

> Are you telling me, are you saying to yourself, that you can actually "catch yourself" and start to "counteract" your automatic thoughts? ... that you can begin to reason with yourself? ... that you can begin to talk yourself out of your depression? ... that you're not a "mere victim" of your feelings and circumstances? ... that you don't' have to let the past "rob" you of your future? ... that you could put his (perpetrator's) voice away and you can begin to write your own script?

> I am impressed, how did you do that? ... How did you handle the situation differently now than how you handled it in the past? ... Do you think that when you are so depressed (angry, anxious -- give specific examples) you are going to be able to say (or ask yourself) -- give specific example -- and that this would work? ... What might get in the way of your doing that?

> That's great! Now you are taking the first important steps in solving your problems in living (in dealing with the aftermath of the trauma; in coping with your traumatic reactions). You are beginning to identify the automatic thoughts that flash through your mind in an instant. Not only are you beginning to identify them, you are starting to do something about them ... How do you feel about that?

> Do you see how thinking of it (be specific) that way (be specific) is different from what you were thinking (saying to yourself) at first?

> You seem to be saying, and **correct me if I am wrong**, or if I have not picked up on what you mean, that you have decided to do X in order to improve (state client's goal). One way you are going to do that is to do Y. Is that right? ... Let us examine how you are going about doing that ... Are those things you can arrange to continue doing in the future? ... So you have some ideas of things you can do ... This sounds "like" X or reminiscent of when you did Y? Am I correct in making this comparison? Do you see any similarities? Is that how you see it?

Are you suggesting X? Am I correct in drawing the conclusions that Y?

IN SUMMARY, A CRITICAL WAY TO HELP CLIENTS CHANGE HOW THEY PROCESS INFORMATION IS FOR THE THERAPIST TO DEVELOP THE "ART OF QUESTIONING". IF YOU, THE READER, TAPE RECORDED YOUR THERAPY SESSIONS HOW MANY QUESTIONS DO YOU ASK <u>VERSUS</u> DIRECTIVES AND INTERPRETATIONS DO YOU OFFER? DO THE NUMBER AND NATURE OF THE QUESTIONS YOU ASK CHANGE OVER SESSIONS? DOES THE NUMBER AND NATURE OF YOUR CLIENTS' QUESTIONS CHANGE OVER SESSIONS?

C. <u>How does one help clients alter their basic beliefs, assumptions, and schemas?</u>

As noted, traumatic events can **shatter one's assumptions and beliefs** and result in clients "getting stuck" on certain issues such as trust, intimacy, self-esteem, safety, and meaningfulness. Traumatic events can challenge one's sense of invulnerability, safety, fairness, justice, with the consequence of contributing to feelings of helplessness, futility, low self-esteem, meaninglessness, and hopelessness.

Such traumatic events, especially exposure to Type II stressors, can lead individuals to draw certain conclusions about themselves and about the world. As noted, these are often expressed in the form of affect-laden cognitions, such as "I am unloveable", "I am alone", "Nobody wants me", "I will always be alone", "I am a loser", "I am a victim". Such automatic thoughts can act as schema, implicit rules, tacit assumptions, readiness sets, or what Meichenbaum and Gilmore (1984) characterized as "core organizing principles" that color the way individuals attend, perceive, process information, and behave. These implicit beliefs often take the form of **"if...then"**, **"in order to"**, and **"depends on"** statements. For instance, "If I make a mistake, then it means I am a loser", "In order to be happy, I have to X, or Y must occur", "My value as a person depends on X". These statements may reflect themes about competence, control, acceptance, equity/fairness, and the like. The first step is to help clients become more aware of such tacit assumptions and then to help clients to change them and reduce their impact.

<u>How can we help clients become more aware of their schema?</u>

1. Several procedures have already been suggested. These include using <u>Socratic questioning</u>; having clients <u>explore specific metaphors</u> such as "prejudice" and "mental contamination", as well as personally generated metaphors.

2. Another method is to ask clients to do <u>self-monitoring</u> of specific thoughts, feelings and behaviors and then to conduct a <u>situational analysis</u>. In a collaborative fashion, the client and therapist can begin to <u>explore what is common across the various situations when the client is experiencing distress such as PTSD symptoms</u>. What do these various situations have in common? Note, that the client might answer by saying, "I don't know", to which the therapist might answer, "I don't know either. How can <u>we</u> go about finding out?". *(The therapist should* <u>not</u> *come across as the "expert", or as a "surrogate frontal lobe", but instead should act as a collaborative co-investigator.)*

3. Another means to tap the client's "core beliefs" is to <u>note the themes</u> that are common to the client's <u>automatic thoughts</u>. Is a specific theme evident?

4. Listen for global words that the client uses, such as, "I'm just worthless", "I am unloveable". Ask the client to share the thoughts and feelings that go through his/her mind when you say you are "worthless", "unloveable". The therapist can reflect, "Unloveable, tell me about that. How long have you felt that way?". The therapist can also perform a developmental analysis, exploring if in the client's mind, the past manages to help create problems in the present. After listening to the client's account, the therapist can have the client reflect on the "fabric of conclusions" that the client has drawn from those developmental experiences. The therapist may even use some form of role-playing to help clients examine the nature of his/her beliefs. For instance, some therapists have asked the client to engage in an imaginary role play with his/her absent parent, conveying their feelings as a child. They are also asked to bring to the role play the information the client now has as an adult. Such exploration may help reveal the types of "stories" the client was consistently told as a child (e.g., the high level of criticism, lack of approval, etc.).

5. Another means for tapping core beliefs is to present the client with sentence completion statements to be completed. For example,

> "In order to be happy I have to..."
> "Being rejected would mean..."
> "Making a fool of myself would mean..."
> "I am afraid of becoming..."

In summary, the therapist can use a variety of diverse interview, self-monitoring, and self-report assessment devices to try and tap the client's beliefs. **Two warnings** are warranted before we consider how the therapist can help change the client's "core" beliefs.

1. It is important to appreciate that from the present perspective the therapist does not help the client to discover his/her "schema" or "core organizing principle". There is no specific "core" belief that is to be discovered. **Therapy is not an "archeological dig"**, where a truth is to be unearthed. Rather, the therapeutic effort is designed to help clients co-create a "story", an explanation that makes sense of the client's present behavior and past experience, that helps to generate some meaning and hope. **Therapy is an exercise of collaborative co-construction**, whereby the client and therapist are going to co-create a "story", a "narrative", and they are going to act "as if" the beliefs that are being examined help the client make sense of his/her experience.

   The critical feature of this effort is not the accuracy nor the veridicality of the client's explanation, but rather the coherence, adaptiveness and utility of the client's explanation. **In therapy we do not help clients to discover "truths", we help them construct "truths"**.

2. A second warning. I never characterize my client's beliefs as being "rational" or "irrational". To do so suggests that you, the therapist, have the axiomatic system of what constitutes rationality. Second, it is pejorative to characterize someone's belief as being "irrational". Moreover, it is likely to lead to reactance and the "hardening" of the client's beliefs.

How do we help clients change their beliefs?

1. <u>Increasing the client's awareness</u> is surely one step in the change process. For instance, earlier it was mentioned that when clients describe stressful, emotional reactions they are likely to **use metaphors** to describe their experiences (e.g., "build walls", "stuff feelings", etc.). The therapist can select what Pepper described as a "root metaphor" and have clients explore the impact ("toll, price") he/she pays for viewing the world in this fashion. Out of such discussions will come a series of possible suggestions as to what the client can do to alter their beliefs (e.g., "not stuff feelings"). The therapist and client can then explore and practice how this can be accomplished.

2. Another means to help clients alter their beliefs is to help them <u>perform personal experiments</u>. These experiments may be done in four arenas:

   a) The client can perform an experiment in <u>non-therapeutic settings</u> so he/she can test out his/her beliefs. Such tests may yield consequences ("data") that will provide "evidence" to unfreeze the client's beliefs.

   b) The client can <u>perform an experiment</u> using the <u>therapeutic setting</u> in the form of behavioral rehearsal.

   c) Another variation of this in-session experiment is for the <u>therapist to use the client's reactions in therapy</u> (what has traditionally been characterized as "transference" behavior). The therapist can comment that he/she noticed something about the client's behavior and wondered if the client had noticed it as well? *(The therapist goes public with the data.)* This provides an opportunity to explore the client's thoughts and feelings in the session and whether he/she has had similar thoughts and feelings "out there", with others, with what consequence for others and for him/herself?

   d) A fourth way to have the client perform an <u>experiment</u> is to do so <u>historically</u>. The client can go back and reconsider past events (including the victimization experience) from his/her present perspective and understanding. To facilitate this process the client can be asked to generate a "time line" of both stressful as well as "positive" events. *(See Sections VI and VII for examples of how such a "time line" can be used to help alter the client's narrative and beliefs, his or her view of the past)*

   e) Another means of helping clients to alter their beliefs is to encourage them to conduct what Jeff Young (1990) describes as a **scheme diary**. Following the guidelines on self-monitoring offered in Section III, the client can be asked to keep track of the following (adapted from Young):

TRIGGERS: (What set off my reactions?)

EMOTIONS: (What was I <u>feeling</u>?)

THOUGHTS: (What was I <u>thinking</u>?)

BEHAVIORS: (What did I actually <u>do</u>?)

LIFETRAPS: (Which of my "<u>buttons</u>" got pushed? What early life experiences might be related?)

COPING: Realistic Concerns   (In what ways were my reactions justified? What did I do to cause or worsen the situation? Is there anyone I can check this out with?)

OVERREACTIONS: (In what ways, if any, did I <u>exaggerate</u> or <u>misinterpret</u> the situation?)

PROBLEM-SOLVE: (In what ways could I <u>cope better</u> in the future or solve the problem?)

LEARNED: (What have I learned from this situation that I can apply in the future?)

The client and therapist can examine these diary cards in order to identify the commonalities that cuts across the various situations. In this way the client can see how situations fall along a continuum.

A useful way to help the client alter his/her tendency to engage in black-white, dichotomous, categorical thinking is to invite him/her to analyze an interpersonal problem along **a continuum**. For example, the client may be asked to consider a concept of being "trustworthy" along a continuum of 0% to 100%, by first enumerating the specific behavioral features of what it means to be "trustworthy" and "untrustworthy", and then place people the client knows, has known, as well as oneself along the continuum of "trustworthiness". The therapist then discusses with the client the basis for his/her judgements and helps the client recognize that just about every concept can be viewed in terms of degrees. Help the client appreciate that viewing things as "black and white" makes them seem more extreme. For example, the therapist can help the client consider the concept of being "trustworthy" along a continuum.

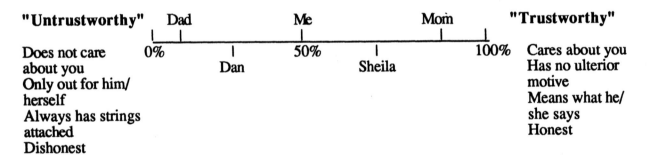

As a result of these experiments the client can <u>reevaluate his/her belief on a 0% to 100% scale</u>. The objective is to help clients <u>view</u> their beliefs in <u>probabilistic terms, instead of in absolute terms</u>. There are some events from the present and from the past that fit the client's beliefs, but there may be many instances where the data does <u>not</u> fit. For example, the client can enact personal experiments, whereby he/she can learn that instead of being an "unloveable person", "I am a person who is liked by some people in some situations, but not liked by others in other situations".

<u>Setting up tests using graded behavioral experiments</u>. Perhaps the best way to help clients alter his/her beliefs is to perform specific personal experiments as a way of doing "hypothesis testing". The guidelines to follow in having clients undertake such experiments are the same as those offered for self-monitoring. *(See Section III)* As noted, there is a need to nurture client collaboration, offer a rationale, give clients choices, solicit commitment statements, and address relapse prevention issues. The personal experiments may take on an "as if" quality, as described in Section III. Or the

client might be encouraged to collect "data"; for instance, asking the client to collect information about his/her spouse's reactions or record behavior such as supportive comments received from others. The client is asked to compare the outcome with his/her prior expectancy.

In order to nurture this inquiring stance on the part of the client, the therapist may use some of the following questions:

Is there anything to be done?

Is it as bad as it seems?

Could you try it out and see how far you get?

Could you surprise yourself and see what happens?

What do you think might surprise you most when you try X?

In the past you have had a tendency to get sidetracked with other concerns such as X. Could this happen here? What could be done to reduce the likelihood of X occurring?

Could we take a moment and consider the situations in which your "old ways of thinking", your old schemas (beliefs) might become reactivated? Let's take some time and draw a plan of action should that occur.

It sounds as if in the absence of evidence to the contrary you assume X. Is that correct?

If worst did come to worst, what would that mean?

What might be the biggest problem that you would encounter?

Perhaps the wonder is that you survived and functioned so well, for so long. Help me understand how you did that.

What leads you to the conclusion that you are X?

Do you think you are in an "impossible situation", or do you see yourself as an "impossible person"? What leads you to the conclusion that you are X (e.g., "impossible person", "worthless", "unloveable")?

The therapist can also help the client recognize that his/her beliefs at the time of the victimization experience reflect reasonable explanations. They represented "survival skills", but they may no longer be needed. The problem may be one of "stuckiness", of continuing to use what worked at one time, but is no longer needed today. The therapist can use a number of metaphors to describe this process. (*These are enumerated in Section VI.*) It is not the belief per se, but what the client says to himself/herself about his/her belief that is critical.

Yet another mode of helping clients to alter his/her beliefs is to have the client consider the advantages and disadvantages of relinquishing his/her tactic assumptions. The therapist could ask the client, "What if your worst fear came true (give an example)? Would X occur (e.g., your career end, your family disown you, etc.)?" The therapist can use a slight "blow-up" procedure in offering possible consequences.

Another procedure designed to influence the nature of and impact of client's beliefs is called the **downward arrow technique**. It has been used with victimized clients (e.g., see Neimeyer, 1993). This procedure was first introduced by Beck, Rush, Shaw, and Emery (1979). The object of the procedure is to help clients recognize the pattern of self-invalidating ideation and then to learn to critically evaluate and interrupt this self-defeating cycle. The therapist uses a **series of recursive questions** that begin with the client's "automatic thoughts" that "flash through the client's mind" when confronted with a distressing situation. By helping the client to " deconstruct", or to examine the meaning attributed to an event, the client can learn to tease out the more fundamental or "core issues." In this way clients can explore and control their overreactions to events.

The therapist and client collaborate in exploring the emotional overreactions to events, the series of inferences and implications that can contribute to tacit beliefs, dysfunctional feelings, and maladaptive behaviors. Neimeyer (1993) has described how the **downward arrow procedure** can be adapted to the group so other members can watch how such analyses may apply to their own automatic thoughts and emotional reactions. Essentially, clients are asked to "try and pick one of your thoughts and uncover the thought that is behind it until you reach what seems to be your most basic thought. It is like peeling an onion."

The downward arrow procedure involves the therapist asking a series of questions in the form, "**Suppose that were true; what would that mean to you?**" Neimeyer (1993) observes that, "this technique has the effect of eliciting associated beliefs and conclusions that are held at progressively lower levels of cognitive awareness, but that nonetheless powerfully affect the individual's mood and behavior" (p. 69). He compares this procedure to "peeling an onion", or to a "domino effect", or to searching for "lower rungs of a ladder", moving from thoughts directed toward external situations to those bearing on increasingly central issues.

Specifically, the therapist can sample sequentially from the following questions.

i)   "Suppose that indeed X did happen to you, what would get to you most about that?

ii)   And suppose that were true, why would that be so upsetting? What would that mean to you?

iii)   Well, assume that happens. Why would that be so upsetting?

iv)   And if it is true that you haven't fully done X, what does that mean to you?

v)   If so, then what?...And then what?

vi)   Perhaps, you can ask yourself such questions as, "If it were true, why would it be so upsetting to me? What would it mean to me?"

vii)   Just because of X, does that mean Y?

viii)   Even if your being A, does it mean B?

ix) So what is the worst thing that might occur? And if that occurred would this be so horrible?

x) What if you did X (over-react to what happened to you). What if X occurred, what does that mean to you?

The pattern of thoughts and beliefs that follow from such probing can be put on the blackboard using the **downward arrows**. For instance, Neimeyer (1993, p. 70) offers an example with a depressed inpatient whose initial automatic thought was, "She is talking down to me." By means of systematic probes the following chain of implicit beliefs emerged.

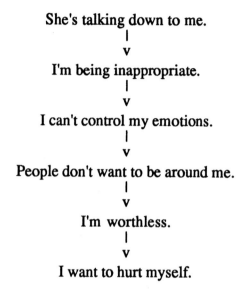

She's talking down to me.
|
v
I'm being inappropriate.
|
v
I can't control my emotions.
|
v
People don't want to be around me.
|
v
I'm worthless.
|
v
I want to hurt myself.

In the presence of the group, the therapist was able to help the client identify cognitions at each level, critique the implication links, and discover the **"If...then"** rules that characterize each step (what have been called "Personal rules of living," or "Nonconscious algorithms," or "Tacit assumptions"). In this way the client (and the group members) are able to see how the client unnecessarily magnified events and "blew up" their implications.

Cognitive behavioral therapists caution that the **downward arrow procedure should <u>not</u> be used too soon in treatment.** There is a need, first, to have clients experience their distressing emotions fully before exposing them to critical analyses. There is also a need to use the procedure in a sensitive collaborative fashion so the client does <u>not</u> feel "attacked" and can appreciate the purpose of such probes, namely, that individuals are <u>not</u> mere "victims" of their feelings. "Depression does <u>not</u> just come on." "Rage does <u>not</u> just take over." "Feelings of helplessness do <u>not</u> just appear." Rather, how individuals appraise both their situations and their ability to handle them; how individuals follow implicit beliefs-- the "as if rules"--play a critical role in influencing their emotional reactions and behavior.

Finally, it is important <u>not</u> to conduct the downward arrow procedure at the end of the session. There is a need to allow ample time for the client to process the material that has been covered, to react to the downward arrow procedure.

The goal is to help clients begin to "take ownership" of their cognitive restructuring procedures and to become their own therapist. The therapist can ask the client, **"Do** you ever find yourself out there, asking yourself questions that we ask each other here in therapy? Can you give me examples? How does that help?" Such questions convey the transfer of the ownership features of this treatment approach.

How to Help Clients Cognitive Reframe Events

Another form of reframing is to help clients recast their distressing behaviors, such as having a highly **distressing nightmare** so it becomes a "sign of coping". For instance, consider the following case of a 63 year old woman who was a victim of an earthquake, presented by Abueg et al. (1994). The client offered the following:

"I dreamt that I got raped by somebody. Then I don't know where I am and don't know how I am going to get home. I'm going up a hill, and the steps keep getting steeper and steeper. How am I going to get up? Finally, I did. I don't know how. Then I went to look for a bathroom, and all I could find was a tin can. How can I urinate in this container?" (Abueg et al., 1994, p. 248)

Now put yourself in the shoes of the therapist (Edward Kubany). What could you say to the client that could cognitively reframe this in a positive fashion?[1] Consider the following:

"The dream may be telling you that these are very difficult times; but the very fact that you "got to the top" suggests that you have the internal resources to surmount the obstacles and get through these difficult times. Yes, the tin can is no luxury, and you're going to have to live out of your suitcase for a while. And in a sense you have been raped - by Mother Nature - but you can recover from that too". (Abueg et al., 1994 p. 248)

Following the discussion of this reinterpretation, the therapist considered with the client the nature of the loss of the total destruction of her home. The therapist noted that:

"None of her treasured memories were gone. Only your house is gone. You can relive the wonderful times that were associated with every lost item any time you want to. No one can take that away from you."

In fact, the client and her husband conducted a **funeral service for their home**. Each provided a eulogy describing the happiest events associated with their home. The client was reminded that she could continue to keep all her cherished memories alive. *(In Section VII we will consider how rituals can be used as part of the "healing process".)*

In the same spirit, Abueg et al. (1994) describe a victim of an earthquake who was overwhelmed by his losses. Given his history of prior victimization he was asked to use imagery reconstruction procedures to find some meaning and hope. The client was asked to image the reconstruction efforts not as a process of starting over, but given his prior victimization, "as someone starting from a new plateau, older, but wiser." The client was, thus, better equipped than ever to help others and himself. He was someone who not only survived, but had "transcended much personal adversity".

---

[1] A variation on treating the client's distress from nightmares was offered by Hoyt (1994). Clients were asked to write down the recent nightmare, change it, and write down the modified version. The client then rehearsed the changed nightmare in imagery while in a relaxed state.

III. Problem-Solving Procedures

The therapist can also use problem-solving procedures a la the work of D'Zurilla and Goldfried, Nezu, Haley, Wasik and others. A critical aspect of the problem-solving intervention is to help "victimized" individuals achieve both intrapersonal and interpersonal goals. For example, for many "victimized" clients a primary goal is to reestablish interpersonal relationships without being revictimized. As Resick and Schnicke (1993) note, there is a need to convey to "victimized" clients that such processes as trust and intimacy fall on a continuum and that developing "trust" in another person takes time as one obtains more information about others. The therapy focuses on the specific procedures by which clients can establish, assess, and maintain trusting relationships. **The treatment objective is to help clients see interpersonal situations as "problems-to-be-solved," and "relationships-to-be-experienced," rather than as personal threats and interpersonal provocations that trigger "old baggage."**

A number of authors who have described **problem-solving therapy** have enumerated **various phases** to the intervention. Although the number of phases vary across clinical descriptions, they usually entail:

1. identifying and defining the problem

2. generating alternatives to solve the problem and weighing the benefits and costs associated with each, as well as potential obstacles

3. making a choice with accompanying detailed planning and relapse prevention

4. implementing the selected alternative, and back up plans if needed

5. evaluating the outcomes

6. making self-attributions about change (i.e., taking responsibility and ownership) and building in generalization and maintenance procedures (e.g., booster sessions, follow-through).

Of these various therapeutic objectives, **problem definition is one of the most difficult.** Once the client can come to see his/her situation, symptoms, reactions of others, and behavior as a **problem-to-be-solved**, rather than as a personal threat or interpersonal provocation, then the various solution options can be implemented and tested sequentially. As part of the definition of the problem the client is engaged in a discussion of possible specific goals (short-term, intermediate and long-term) that can be worked on. *(In the assessment section -- Section III -- I have included detailed questions and procedures that can be used to facilitate this definitional process.)* Also highlighted in Section III is the need to insure that the therapist's questions also **focus on the client's strengths.** In fact, the therapist should intentionally use words that convey "challenge" and "opportunity", and not delimit his/her terminology to the word "problems". For example, in the course of problem-solving training the therapist should be sure to include **solution-focused questions:**

> Have there been any times or siutations when the problem has been absent? How do you explain that?

> Have there been any siutations when the problem has not occurred, despite the fact that you expected it to occur? How do you explain these situations?

How did you handle that?

Where else have you been able to come up with a solution?

Tell me about one thing that you handled well or that you feel good about.

What is the best thing that happened since I saw you last?

What's going well that you would like to continue doing more of?

But such efforts at "pulling for" the client's strengths should not occur before the therapist has permitted the client to tell his/her story. **It is important to appreciate that therapeutic efforts at solution-finding and solution-implementation should not occur too soon. There is a need to hear the client's story first.** If the therapist "rushes" the process, then the client may feel that the therapist does not understand the seriousness and impact of the trauma. The following section describes the kinds of questions the therapist can **sample from** in implementing the various steps in problem-solving interventions. These questions are offered as examples:

A)   **Questions designed to help clients define their situation as-a-problem-to-be-solved** (also see Section III on Assessment).

The objective of these questions is to help the client determine **"who, what, where, when, with whom, and why"** the client is experiencing problems.

> Can you describe the problems you are now experiencing?
> When and where do these occur?
> How do others react?
> What is it about the situation that makes it a problem?
> How would you like things to be?
> What do you think is most important to work on?

B)   **Questions designed to help clients specify goals.**

As noted earlier, clients usually enter treatment with a perception of his/her problems and situation as being "troubled, helpless, hopeless", with accompanying feelings of being "victimized, powerless and ineffective". These feelings are usually expressed in global, amorphous, often metaphoric, terms. One objective of this phase of the problem-solving intervention is to help clients break (decompose) their global goals into smaller, behaviorally specifiable, prescriptive, attainable goals. Moreover, it is important to help clients draw a distinction between **potentially changeable** and **potentially unchangeable goals**. Not all problems have solutions, and thus, different modes of coping may be required in each instance. In order **to handle potentially changeable goals more direct action problem-solving efforts** may be indicated. In the case of **potentially unchangeable goals** the client may need to focus his/her efforts on handling and finding meaning in the difficult and distressing feelings by means of **using palliative emotionally-focused coping efforts**. This distinction has been discussed in some detail by Richard Lazarus and Susan Folkman (1990).

Such goal specification can also be nurtured by using the following therapist probes:

> How would you like things to be?

> Let me ask a different type of question. If you had a magic wand
>   and could change things, what would you change?
> Let's assume that life could be the way you want, what would you
>   change? Does that sound <u>completely</u> impossible?
> What would you be doing differently if you reached this goal?
> What is it that you would like to have happen?
> How would you know when you reached your goal(s)?
> How would reaching this goal make your life different?
> How would reaching this goal affect others?
> How would they feel? How would you feel about the change?
> Are you suggesting that it might be worth your effort to work to
>   achieve these goals?
> How are things now and how would you like them to be? What
>   can <u>we</u> do, working together, to achieve these goals?
> Are there any indications that you are heading in the right direction?

Throughout this discussion the client **should be encouraged to describe his or her goals in positive terms**, rather than in negative terms. What does the client want, as compared with what the client wants to eliminate, avoid, or reduce? The discussion of goals should <u>not</u> merely reflect that the specific situation is "troublesome", but rather what does the client want to change, what desired outcome would the client like to achieve. Convey to the client that setting goals will permit the two of you to determine if the client is making progress.

Often the goals that the client sets will be interpersonal in nature. As Kinney, Haapala, and Booth (1991) observe, clients can be encouraged to view interpersonal problems in terms of skills deficit, (e.g., his or her child's disruptive behavior, such as screaming or fighting, can be viewed as a lack of communication skills; spousal conflict as an absence of negotiation skills; and the like). By means of the questions that the therapist asks, the therapist can help the client view his or her interpersonal problems as consisting of **a series of component steps.** (Many of the following questions were suggested by Kinney et al., 1991).

> What do you think X means by (or when she said Y)?
> What does she do that makes you say that?
> When does she do it?
> How often?
> What happens before she does it?
> What happens after she does it?
> What does she do that makes you say that?
> How would we know when things were better?
> What is <u>one</u> change in your wife's (son's, your own) behavior, even if it were
>   a small change, that would really mean something to you?
> What change would let you know that she is (you are) really trying and that
>   things are improving?
> What would your wife (what would you) have to do, even one small thing, to
>   show that she is willing to work things out with you?
> Are you interested in trying something new to see if you can achieve your
>   goal?

Note, these questions could readily be reworded in order to have clients examine how they could prove to themselves that they are making progress. Raising these questions will help the client formulate specific, attainable, goals. Kiresuk and Sherman (1968) have described how goal attainment scaling can be used with clients. For example, clients can be asked to select a specific treatment goal and indicate what is the best anticipated success (+2), more than expected success (+1), expected level of success (0), less than expected success (-1), and most unfavorable outcome likely (-2). Specific behavioral examples of each of these points can be collaboratively established with the therapist. *(See the discussion of Goal Attainment Scaling in Section III on Assessment.)*

Once clients enumerate specific problems to be worked on, the client and the therapist need to **collaboratively** establish a flexible working agenda. Consider the following questions as a means to achieve this goal.

There are several problems that you have mentioned. Which problem would you like to work on first?

You have mentioned a number of problems you have worked on. (The therpaist enumerates the list and asks the client for feedback). "Have I forgotten any problems/issues that you need to work on? Which one of these problems has taught you the most? Is there any way you can use what you have learned in solving X?

Solving any one of your problems is likely to have a "positive" effect on other problems. Which one of your problems do you think is most likely to respond to this "positive" ripple effect?

C) Questions designed to help clients generate alternatives.

What do you think you can do about that situation? ... Is there anything you can do to change the situation? ... Have you ever tried to think of different things you could do? ... Like what? ... What might you do to cope with this problem?

That is certainly one alternative you have. I wonder if you can think of any other alternatives.

Let's think about this for a moment. Are there any other possibilities? ... How could you go about doing something like that? ... How do you think X would react if you shared that?

I wonder if we could come up with any other options?

Is there anything you are particularly good at? How could that skill be used to solve this problem?

Are there any similar problems that you have solved before? Could you think of using a similar type of solution in this case?

If you were to try something different next time the problem appears, what would you do?

Which of your solutions so far have proven the most effective?

Let's suppose that a friend of yours with a similar problem as yours came to you and asked for advice. What would you tell him/her?

What advice would you have for someone else who has this problem? ... How did you come up with that advice? ... Is there any way you could use that yourself?

How could you go about deciding if that is best?

This may be a time to consider yourself and your welfare first. If that were true, then what would you have to do? ... What advice would you give yourself? ... What would it mean to you if you did X? ... What meaning would it have for you to be a "success" as you have defined it here?

Can we generate a list together of solutions that you have tried that have not worked in your case and then analyze the list together to see what we can learn from what you have tried? ... Then we can generate a list together of what solutions, if any, have worked on some occasions ... We can then work on what is different about these two types of situations.

Do you think you can make a list of all the things you feel you have to do, but feel that can't (or won't) do? Then choose to do just one. Choose a behavior that requires the least effort, the least time, the least involvement of others. Let's discuss whether this is a feasible plan. What do you think? ... Let us begin right now, if that is okay. (At this point the client and therapist in the session begin to make a list and explore which behavior the client is likely to choose and why) ... Once the client chooses a behavior the therapist can play "devil's advocate" by mildly challenging the client to produce arguments as to <u>what</u>, <u>how</u> and <u>why</u> he/she is going to try and change this one behavior. The therapist can comment: "Are you saying to me, are you saying to yourself, to the group, that you are going to do X, even with a history of Y? ... Come on, when is the last time you did X? ... What would others think about you if you did X? ... How would you feel about yourself if you did X? ... What would this mean about you as a person?"

So you are concerned that X ... What do you plan to do about that?

So one thing you could do is X. Is there anything else you could do? Do you think it would help if you X? ... Is there a way that you could X? What is it about that option that might help you get what you want to have happen?

Have you any thoughts about other things that you could do to improve your situation with X? ... What do you do to handle this on your good days?

I can see you have mixed feelings about X. What do you see (think) are some of the disadvantages of trying this? **(Review disadvantages before advantages, so the client will be less likely to raise "yes but" reactions)**

I noticed that when you talk about options this helps you see that you have other options. For example, (Provide affirming statements with examples).

What things do you typically find difficult to do that might make you feel X? Do you think it would be helpful if you spent some time doing Y?

Let's break the problem into it's parts so we can deal with one step at a time. Does that make sense? Where should we begin?

I am wondering if it would be helpful to try writing down the pros and cons, the advantages and disadvantages, both short-term and long-term, concerning doing X. Putting together such a **Balance Sheet** *(as suggested by Janis and Mann)* may be helpful in choosing one solution over another. You could later revise your solution, if necessary, based on your experience. *(There is a need to help clients implement solutions gradually, each time checking them out.)*

D) <u>Questions designed to help clients implement an action plan</u>.

What will you learn if you try X (be specific)?

What will you learn if you don't try X (be specific)?

Now that you know this, what is the next step?

Is there anyway you can surprise yourself by doing X?

I know another person with a similar problem who did X. Do you think that something similar would be of help in your case?

What would you need to do in order to achieve this goal...in order to pull this off?

What would you need to do in order to take steps toward achieving this goal?

What can you do to support yourself in trying something different?

What do you think you can do about that situation that you have not already tried?

Can you envisage (forsee) any things that might get in the way of your doing X? What would that be? ... Let's take a moment and consider how we can address each one. Being prepared and anticipating each one and having a "game plan" can help.

What are the reasons for you to do X? ... Could there be any other reasons besides X for you to do Y?

What are the reasons for you <u>not</u> to do X? ... Why won't they keep you from proceeding?

Have you thought about X?

What are the advantages and disadvantages of doing X?

What do you want to do about your problem?

How could you go about setting it up so he/she/they can do that? ... How do you think they would react if you put it to them in that way? ... I wonder if <u>we</u> could come up with any other ways to do X?

If you could X for just a little while, then how would you feel?

Is there any evidence to suggest that perhaps you will get better? ... What would that evidence be? ... Anything else? ... What else? ... In what way?

I am not sure you are ready for this yet. It may be too soon for me to even suggest this. If I am out of order, please let me know ... but would you be willing to try X or some part of X?

E) <u>Questions designed to help reduce the likelihood of relapse. (Help the clients to see lapses and relapse as part of the recovery process)</u>

How are you going to keep yourself from falling back into the pattern of X?

If you are never making mistakes, never having setbacks, then that means that you are not challenging yourself and not learning. Am I reading the situation correctly?

Are you suggesting that progress will be gradual and take time? I guess you're right. One has to crawl before you walk and walk before you run.

Although it didn't work in that situation, as you describe it, what did you learn about yourself and about how you handled it?

It sounds like you have the "tools" to work with and now it is a matter of finding out how best to apply them.

How would you know that this session (our meeting today) was helpful? ... Of the different things we talked about, what do you think will prove most helpful?

In addition, clients may indicate that their solution efforts didn't work. **"It didn't work!"**. When I hear the client tell me this, I usually reflect back to the client, **"It didn't work?"**. In turn, I ask a series of questions:

a) **It...it...it...didn't work?** (I try to find out what was the "it". What did the client do and <u>not</u> do in the situation?)

b) **"Didn't work?"** (I am asking the client to share with me the specific data, or to operationally indicate the discrepancy between his/her prior expectations and what happened)

c) I then ask, **"How did that make you feel?"**

d) I then ask, **"How would you know if it did work?"** (What data would the client take as evidence that it would work?)

e) I might ask the client, **"Are you suggesting that it will never work...that it is of no use...that nothing could be done...that no one who has** had this problem has been able to change?" (By using a slight "blow-up" procedure, the client is likely to say, "Well, it's not that bad!...To which, I respond, "Note too bad?" Tell me about that...Where do you get the hope?")

(The social psychological research indicates that if a client has a fixed belief it is better to use a somewhat paradoxical approach, rather than a confrontative approach. If the therapist challenges, attacks, confronts, or characterizes the client's belief as being "irrational", this only tends to "freeze" the client's beliefs, see Kruglanski, 1990.)

F) **Questions designed to help clients make self-attributions or take credit for the changes they have brought about that foster personal agency**.

As noted, it is **not** enough to have clients change their behaviors. It is also critically important to increase the likelihood that they will attribute the changes to their own instrumental efforts. White and Epston (1990), who view therapy as a process of **"restorying"** and as a means of helping clients co-create a new liberating narrative, have offered several useful questions that can be employed with clients. They encourage them to see **problems as "external" of themselves** and then to **take "ownership" for change**. Consider the potential usefulness of the following questions in achieving these goals. **(Notice the use of "How to", "What", "In what way", "Where"** -- questions. This format of questions "pull for" descriptions of metacognitive, action-oriented, self-regulatory activities).

> How did you **manage** to resist the influence of the problem on this occasion?
> Where else did you do that?
> Hold on, this is a bit too fast for me. What exactly happened? What exactly did you do? ... What happened just before that? ... What happened next? ... How did he/she react? ... How did you feel about that? ... What does this tell you about your problem? About yourself? ... What does that mean to you now?
> What does your success at **resisting the problem** say about you as a person?
> What difference will this news about yourself make to your next steps?
> In what ways do you **think** these discoveries (new actions) might affect your attitude toward yourself? ... Affect your relationship with X?
> What have you done to **get yourself ready** for such a breakthrough?
> So what is the difference between you as a person now and you as a person when you first come in?
> Last week we discussed your doing X, what did you do to move toward this goal?
> How did you do that? **Share** with me the **steps** you went through to accomplish X. I would never have predicted that at this stage of therapy you would have accomplished this. How did you do that? (If in a group, ask who else had been unprepared for this news?) Where did you **get these ideas from**?
> What happened that **reinforced your notion** that you could do X?
> What did you **learn** from that experience?

If you continue to act on these ideas what difference would that
make for how you **feel** about yourself? ... for how you would
behave in the future?

What kind of person doesn't buckle under to the pressure of X? ...
doesn't fall victim to the myth that Y?

What would be some of the signs that you are making progress? ...
healing? ... Anything else (any other indicators) that you are
progressing (healing, getting unstuck, moving on)?

How did you do that?

What did you do that led you to feel that way ... that gave you
hope?

How did you arrive at this different way of seeing the situation? ...
seeing how you can handle the siutation?

In summary, the problem-solving intervention is designed to help clients
assess their situation in problem-solving terms, noticing strengths, skills and
resources they already possess and developing a "here and now" orientation,
rather than a "there and then" orientation where one is "stuck" in the past.
The enumerated questions that can be sampled from are designed to facilitate
this process. But having clients address these questions is <u>not</u> sufficient for
change. **The clients must practice in therapy and in his/her daily
lives these skills.** Some clients may **need specific skills** training with
instruction, modeling, practice, feedback, and the like. In order to see how
such skills training can be conducted see the discussion on self-monitoring
("homework") in Section III. A collaborative approach is required in helping
clients develop a flexible coping repertoire.

IV. Treatment of Guilt Reactions[1]

For many with PTSD some form of **guilt plays a critical role.** Guilt is a form of anxiety
that arises when people think they have done something wrong and they are unable to accept
failures in judgment and unable or unwilling to come up with sufficient justification for
something they have done. With guilt, repetitive self-questioning may take the form of,
"Only if?", "What if?", "I should have known better or done more", "I could have (should
have) done X to prevent Y", and so forth. It is being "stuck" in this line of narrative that can
exacerbate maladaptive behavior, and even lead to suicidal ideation and suicidal behavior
(Hendin & Haas, 1991). For example, Foa (1994) observes that Vietnam veterans with
PTSD, whose intrusive memories involved atrocities that they had inflicted on others,
experience mainly feelings of shame and guilt, rather that fear (as did sexual assault victims).
She observed that during the reliving of their trauma memories, these veterans did <u>not</u> exhibit
the "emotional habituation" that is usually observed in assault victims, and that exposure-
based interventions did <u>not</u> alleviate their feelings of shame and guilt. Thus, some other form
of intervention is required. Opp and Sampson (1989) have developed a taxonomy of
different types of guilt, each of which may require different forms of intervention. These
include survivor guilt, moral/spiritual guilt, and betrayal/abandonment guilt.

<u>Cognitive restructuring procedures</u>, as described by Kubany (1994) and Williams
(1987), have been used to help guilt-laden PTSD clients become "unstuck." They have
proposed **"deconstructing" the incident and the circumstances surrounding it.**
More specifically, they suggest the following treatment guidelines:

---

[1] For a discussion of the distinction between guilt and other emotions like shame and fear, and for a consideration of
the interpersonal functions of guilt see Baumeister et al. (1994).

1. Have the client with PTSD develop a "safe," "trusting therapeutic alliance; then have the client tell his/her story in detail, reviewing the incident, going over the events and accompanying feelings and thoughts (uncertainty, fear, distress), including the details about the trauma, the events that led up to the traumatic event(s) and the factors that contributed to the decisions that were made **at the time**. **Explore** with the client his/her **reasoning**, given the information that was available at that time. Help the client to recognize that he/she had no way of knowing that the decision, **at that time**, would have had those consequences. Help the client tolerate the sense of helplessness, lack of control and sense of vulnerability.

    Kubany (1994) notes that "Going through the event may increase the client's realization that his/her reactions and decisions reflected sound judgment **at the time**" (p.10). The therapist attempts to help the client accept the premise that he/she could <u>not</u> have known how the situation was going to turn out. Also highlight for the client exactly how much time was actually available to make a decision; how quickly the decision had to be made; and that the client probably did the best he/she could have given the circumstances. There is also a need to help the client appreciate that the unchosen alternatives may have been truly far worse choices than the selected decision.

2. Herman (1992) observes that the survivor who is struggling with issues of guilt needs a therapist (or others) who can acknowledge that the traumatic event has occurred, who can suspend preconceived judgments, who can "bear witness" to the tale. In such a context the survivor is more likely to come to a "realistic judgment of his/her conduct and construct a fairer attribution of responsibility. As noted, there is a need for a detailed account of the circumstance of what happened, and a careful exploration of the particular reasons contributing to self-blame. As the therapist observes,

    "Hindsight is a wonderful thing. We can look back and say, 'maybe, if I had only ..." "If only I had ..." "Why me and not them?" "Why not me instead of him?"...At the time of the traumatic event there seems to be some doubt you could have forseen how things would have turned out. What options did you really have? Remember hindsight is always much more accurate...When we look back at our behavior we tend to distort events in the direction of guilt and personal responsibility. Let's see if this has occurred in your case."

3. Hoyt (1994) in describing a case by Talmon illustrates how a client's guilt reactions were cognitively <u>reframed</u> to yield a different narrative. The therapist observed, "Your depression is your way of expressing to your family your regret and sorrow for causing the accident? ... Now that you have taken full responsibility for causing the accident, you seem ready to go back to your regular self ... I am sure you want to find a renewed way to show them your positive feelings." (p. 148)

4. Lipton (1993) proposes that **group therapy discussions** provide a most useful means to improve client's objectivity, to remind the client that he/she did the best he/she could at the time, to address survivor guilt, and to highlight for the client how he/she is being unfair to himself or herself. With the support of the group the client can change his/her internal dialogue to more readily approximate coping self-statements, such as, "I did the best I could at the time. What happened was not my fault." The client needs to remind himself of the facts over and over and **"not allow the past to rob the present and the future"**.

The group may have a specific beneficial impact in addressing issues of guilt because many clients convey that only those who went through what they went through, that have experienced similar events, will understand. Such **cohort identity** provides the basis of credibility that allows clients to accept the suggestion to "move on". It is <u>not</u> only the cognitive restructuring procedures, but who is offering such advice, when and how, that are critical. **The group process is often a useful medium to address guilt reactions.**

5. Another approach is for the therapist to ask the client what advice those who died would give if they were here now? Kubany also suggests the use of such **role-reversal procedures**, namely, asking the client a series of well-crafted questions that focus on the subjective interpretation of the events and that deconstructs the incident. For instance, the therapist can ask the client:

   i)   What if it had been you who had died?

   ii) Would you want your surviving buddy to suffer for the rest of his life because of your death?

   iii) Would you blame your buddy for "moving on", or for "getting on with life?"

   iv) What have you learned from this traumatic incident that you can share with others, so out of your "survivorship" can come something worth "salvaging?"

   These cognitive restructuring efforts are designed to help the client construct a different narrative, as illustrated in the following case example.

6. <u>Case Example</u>. A school teacher and mother of a 10 year old sought treatment. She was remarkably distraught, suicidal, and suffering from PTSD symptoms. What led her to seek treatment was horrific in nature. Some 6 months earlier her husband was out of town and she was home alone with her only daughter. In the middle of the night she heard a strange noise and thought that someone was breaking into her home, as happened in the previous year. This time in a state of complete panic she reached for the gun in the night table that her husband kept beside the bed. As she yelled out for the would-be assailant to stop, her bedroom door slammed open, and in a state of "mindless fear", she pulled the trigger and...accidentally shot and killed her daughter. There was no robber in the house.

   The guilt, the self-blame, the PTSD reaction with the many continual reminders, took a tremendous toll on her and on her relationship with her husband, reaching the point of her considering killing herself. She wanted to believe it was only a dream. She wanted the pictures of what happened to stop. It is bad enough when something bad happens to one's loved one, but when you are responsible for that mishap, the reactions are even more severe. How shall one proceed in treatment, what could a therapist say or do in order to be of most help?

   The treatment strategy adopted included the following steps:

   a)   listening to her story, reviewing the circumstances in details (as described above), and validating her loss. The therapist sought to understand the client's loss by asking the client to talk about her daughter. In fact, the client brought in a family picture album to review with the therapist in order to determine what was so "special" about her daughter and unique about their relationship. What did she see in her daughter? The client noted that her 10 year old daughter was, "wise beyond her years".

b) The client was then asked: What do you think your daughter saw in you? What made your relationship together so special?

c) The therapist then asked the client: "If your daughter, who was so wise beyond her years, was here now, if she was curled up in your lap, what advice, if any, would she offer to help you get through this loss, to help you deal with the grief and guilt?" With support from the therapist, the client was able to generate a variety of coping suggestions.

d) At this point the therapist commented, "I can now more readily understand what you meant when you said that your daughter was, so special and wise beyond her years. The client and therapist then explored how the client could follow through on the suggestions that her daughter would have offered. "Does the client owe it to the memory of her daughter to follow through on her suggestions? ... Where should we begin? ... What are the possible obstacles or barriers that might get in the way? ... If these obstacles should occur what could the client do to anticipate and handle them?"

e) Finally, as the client began to make progress she eventually developed a "mission" in order to educate parents about the dangers of keeping guns in their homes. In fact, she became very knowledgeable about epidemiological data on accidental deaths in the home due to guns and impassioned to develop a memorial to her daughter

This case illustrates an approach of having the client discover and generate possible coping techniques, rather than having the therapist offer suggestions. As noted earlier, there is **a greater likelihood of the client following through on coping techniques if she offers the suggestions than if they come from the therapist**.

Surely, these interventions did not take away the "pain" of that irreversible traumatic night; but from the loss of her daughter, the client felt a need that others should learn so her daughter's life was not lost in vain. In other words, the therapist helped the client construct a different, more adaptive, narrative.

V. Structuring The Therapy Session

Now that we have considered a number of specific cognitive structuring procedures we can consider how these techniques can be **blended into an overall therapeutic process**. As described, the cognitive restructuring procedures are collaborative, problem-focused, goal-oriented, designed to reduce acute distress, and to **enable** and **empower** clients to take on greater responsibility and ownership for change. It highlights the client's strengths and resources and helps them co-construct a more adaptive narrative. In order to achieve these goals in the various sessions, the therapist:

___ 1.   asks the client for a description of how things have gone since the last session. (reviews major events of past week and current status)

___ 2.   asks the client what concerns or questions he/she may have and solicits feedback regarding previous session.

___ 3.   collaboratively establishes an agenda and provides an overview of what will be covered in this session and why -- gives the client choices and solicit feedback.

____ 4.   indicates how what will be worked on in this session <u>follows from</u> previous discussions and relates to the client's treatment goals.

____ 5.   shares the rationale for why things are being covered in the session.

____ 6.   assesses the client's reactions to the proposed agenda and negotiates any differences.

____ 7.   reviews "homework" from previous session. *(See the discussion on how to employ "homework" offered in Section III)*

____ 8.   focuses on main agenda items and on related specific issues. Limits discussion of "peripheral issues" -- if in doubt, asks the client how this topic relates to the agreed upon agenda and to the client's goals.

____ 9.   asks the client for his/her reactions during the course of the session.

____ 10.   provides intermediate encapsulated summaries ("Thus far..."; "One of the things we worked on so far is X. Let us now consider Y").

____ 11.   does <u>not</u> skip from topic to topic, and if there are shifts comments on the shift.

____ 12.   develops new "homework" collaboratively with the client. (As noted in Section III, the "homework" should be clear, specific, feasible, and relevant to the client's goals. Anticipate possible problems, obstacles and barriers. Also do <u>not</u> use the word "homework".)

____ 13.   asks the client what are two things he/she will take away from today's session. Explores where, when, and how the client will carry these out and what barriers or obstacles might get in the way. Discusses how such barriers/obstacles can be anticipated and handled should they occur. Help the client identify high risk situations, early warning signs and plans of action.

____ 14.   solicits from the client "commitment" statements and the reasons why he/she will carry out these steps. *(See the discussion on motivational interviewing in Section III)*

____ 15.   provides a summary of what was covered in the session and how it relates to the client's goals. (Can also arrange to tape record the session and give a copy to the client to listen to before the next session.)

____ 16.   as therapy proceeds over several sessions, asks the client to summarize what were the main things that were covered in the session and why.

____ 17.   solicits feedback regarding current session, asks the client whether he/she has any questions or concerns about what did or did not occur during this session (For example, asks the client, "Has there been anything I said or did that you found confusing or disturbing?" ... "Can you see what we are doing and how it relates to what you hope to achieve?" ... "Can you put into your own words how what we are working on relates to your personal goals?, What would you say?"..."Is there anything we have been working on or that you have learned in therapy that would be worth sharing with others? What would that be?")

___ 18. the therapist takes notes after each session (Be sure to include in the notes the specific client metaphors so these can be used in subsequent sessions).

___ 19. therapist reads the notes before each session.

LETTER WRITING, AUDIOTAPING AND VIDEOTAPING AS THERAPEUTIC TOOLS: USE OF "HEALING" METAPHORS

Why Does Talking/Writing About Traumatic Stress Help?

"Give sorrow words: the grief that does not speak whispers the o'er-fraught heart and bids it break."
(Shakespeare's MacBeth)

"What cannot be talked about can also not be put to rest; and if it is not, the wounds continue to fester from generation to generation.
(Bettleheim, 1984, p. 166)

As Shakespeare and Bettleheim observe, having traumatized individuals put into words, either orally or in written form, their experiences is a critical feature of the "healing" process. This hypothesis was tested in a series of studies by Pennebaker and his colleagues (see Pennebaker 1990). The Pennebaker program of studies indicated that having individuals such as Holocaust survivors, adults who have been terminated from their job, and freshman college students who are adjusting to a new setting, each write about their respective experiences has resulted in improved psychological and physical well-being. More specifically, Pennebaker has reported that those subjects who had an opportunity to write or talk about upsetting events improved their long-term immune functioning, lowered their autonomic nervous system activity, reduced visits to their physician, and evidenced improvement on self-reports of adjustment (Pennebaker & Beall, 1986).[1]

Harvey et al. (1991) have described how **account-making** about severe stress (e.g., discussing sexual assault experience) facilitates coping and adjustment. As noted in Section II, accounts are people's story-like construction of events. Victims/survivors who provide well-developed accounts are more likely to develop a perspective on events, become more hopeful about the future, and develop closure regarding stressors. When people fail to talk about a traumatic experience they tend to live with it, dream about it, and ruminate about it, in an unresolved manner. This repetitive or recurrent process provokes higher arousal levels (resting autonomic levels), higher depression and illness rates. By putting these images and their accompanying emotions into language, they become more organized, understood and resolved. This is illustrated by a study of incest victims by Silver et al. (1983). Those women who were able to relate and make sense of their traumatic experience reported less psychological distress, better social adaptation, higher levels of self-esteem and greater resolution of the experience.

While it is not clear exactly what features of the writing and talking processes contributed to adjustment, a number of hypotheses have been offered to explain these changes. As noted in Section I, traumatic events can (a) provoke an increased number of intrusive, fragmented and disorganized thoughts about the upheaval as distressed individuals tend to often think about them for an inordinate amount of time (Horowitz, 1976) and (b) significantly alter or "shatter" basic core beliefs about trust, intimacy, esteem, control and safety (Janoff-Bulman, 1993; McCann & Pearlman, 1992).

Pennebaker and others have demonstrated that writing or speaking about the upheaval can clearly affect the ways people think about the events over substantial periods of time. More

---

[1] See Clark (1993) for a discussion of the relative merits of writing versus talking about distressing events and Murray and Segal (1994) for a discussion of how inviting clients to write about their traumatic events can be incorporated into the psychotherapy process (e.g., as implemented in Cognitive Processing Therapy by Calhoun & Resick, 1993).

specifically, a number of investigators (see Pennebaker & Francis, 1994, for a review) have proposed that writing and talking about distressing events can:

(1)   facilitate the expression and labeling of feelings;

(2)   make the thoughts and feelings about the event more organized (i.e., since language is both more structured and social, talking and writing forces one's thoughts to be implicitly more integrated, less fragmented, leading to a more coherent explanation and an increased likelihood of accepting unchangeable aspects of the situation);

(3)   influence the accessibility of the thoughts and feelings (i.e., not being as preoccupied as a result of putting their stories into words) and solicits feedback from others;

(4)   foster some insight and reframing about their predicament and reach some degree of acceptance about themselves and closure about their situation;

(5)   provide an opportunity to explore the meaning of events and reconsider his/her reactions; draw connections between past events and present circumstance;

(6)   foster new perspectives and creative problem-solving.

As Pennebaker and Francis (in press) conclude, "Failure to translate upsetting experiences into language [or some other form of expression] can result in psychological conflict and stress-related health problems." (p. 21). The strategy of having clients who have been traumatized put into words their experiences has been embraced by most therapists who work with PTSD clients. This is illustrated in the heavy emphasis placed on encouraging clients (1) to describe their traumatic experiences; (2) to audiotape sessions, and subsequently, to listen to them; (3) to write letters, keep journals, offer testimonies, and the like. As we will consider, such letter writing may take various forms (as described below). These descriptive accounts may be offered in individual, group and family therapy, in debriefing sessions, and in informal social support settings. Note, there are **cultural differences** in how readily acceptable it is to "share" descriptions and feelings about traumatic events with others.

If one accepts the conceptual framework that the nature of the narrative that an individual offers or "scripts", both contributes to and reflects the level of adjustment, then a promising way to influence and alter the client's "story" is to employ letter writing and audiotaping. (even though the letters may never be sent). A number of clinicians have used these "reauthoring" procedures in a creative fashion to help clients change their narrative accounts (see Brandt, 1989; Capacchione, 1979; Dolan, 1991; Epston et al., 1992; Friedman, 1992; Harvey et al., 1993; Herman, 1992; Meichenbaum & Fitzpatrick, 1993; O'Hanlon, 1992; Shaefer, 1993; White & Epston, 1990; Zaidi, 1994). The various ways that letter writing and audiotaping have been used include having the:

1.   therapist write a letter to the client sharing his/her observations;

2.   therapist write a report to the referring physician (agency) and then, review the letter with the client. Ask for the client's input and feedback. Ask the client to co-sign the report and ask the client if he/she would like a copy of the letter for his/her records. The letter should incorporate the guidelines included in this section.

3.   client write a letter to another person (relative, spouse, and so forth);

4.   client write a "rainy day" letter, namely, have the client write a letter to oneself when he/she is feeling strong and hopeful indicating strengths and "signs of recovery". The client can be asked to describe him/herself sympathetically in the third person (Kelly, 1955). The letter can be read

when the client feels the need. (Note, the notion of "rainy days" needs to be introduced carefully. Some clients do not like the notion of future "bad days". Moreover, when clients "feel down" they prefer to remind themselves that they have survived other bad days and feel they are in no mood to read about positive attributes. Once again, the therapeutic rule should be to collaborate with clients in considering which form of letter writing would be most helpful.);

5.   client write a letter "from the future", namely, write a friend or therapist "as if" several years have passed. Write the letter "as if" the positive events that the client would like to have happen (e.g., experiences in relationship, job, school, etc.) have indeed happened;

6.   client write a letter of disclosure and personal strengths to a supportive other (e.g., family member)

7.   client write a letter from a real or imaginary supportive other, specifying advice that he or she might have offered (e.g., script a letter from a wise older person, a therapist, a popular figure);

8.   client write a letter "as if" the client were someone else (a la George Kelly's fixed-role therapy) or communicate with a "future self" who is benevolent, strong and wise;

9.   clients write a letter to themselves as "an abused child" in order to combat the sense of culpability and to underscore what the child did to survive. Client reads this letter to the group (Zaidi, 1994).

10. client write a letter to the perpetrator or abuser or to anyone else the client feels would be important to talk to more openly and honestly about the traumatic events. Client reads the letter to his/her therapy group. *(See guidelines below for writing letters to perpetrators.)*

11. client write a letter (or keep a journal) of what his/her experiences were during and after the traumatic event (e.g., kidnapping). The client may also ask family members to write their experiences during and after the trauma, as well. Jay (1994) describes how some families developed a ritual; namely, each year, on the anniversary of the traumatic event, the family read their recollections together. This annual ritual permitted the victimized individual and his family members to acknowledge, both the trauma, and their survival.

12. Holocaust survivors have made video testimonials conveying their memory of events in order to leave a legacy behind. Healing through sharing (Danieli, 1994).

13. Torture victims have written "testimonies" of atrocities. In group, another member may be asked to read aloud the "survivor's" account.

Dolan (1991) provides examples of how such letters can be written. The client is asked to write a letter **"as if"** one were an "older, wiser self".

Imagine that you have grown to be a healthy, wise older (woman, man) and you are looking back on this period of your life. What do you think that this older, wiser you would suggest to you to help you get through this current phase of your life? What would she/he tell you to remember? What would she/he suggest that would be most useful in helping you heal from the past? What would she/he say to comfort you? And does she/he have any advice about how therapy could be most useful and helpful? (p. 36).

Or the client can consider writing the letter form the viewpoint of a supportive, but deceased wise relative, friend; or the client can create a supportive other. Dolan suggests that the therapist ask the client what difference this supportive person has made in the past, even if that person did not know what the client was struggling with. The client is asked to imagine what this person would say, and then write a letter or make an audiotape describing the client's strengths that would be highlighted and to indicate the advice that would be offered.

If therapy is conducted on a group basis such letters can be read to the group. Also, in therapy the client can be asked to report (1) how he/she felt at the time of the trauma (e.g., rape); (2) how he/she felt as she wrote about it, and (3) how he/she feels about it now that he/she has read it to the group. These questions "pull for" the client gaining some distance and perspective on changes in feelings since the traumatic incident.

Letters to the perpetrator (e.g., as in the case of child sexual abuse) present specific "healing" opportunities, but also possible dangers. Once again, there have been many clinical suggestions as to how such letters should be written. These letters are usually not mailed.. For example, Dolan suggests that a series of letters may be written including:

1.   an initial letter providing a detailed description of the abuse conveying feelings about the abuse, efforts at coping, and any desire for retribution;

2.   a second letter indicating what the perpetrator might write including what has been said during past confrontations, also covering the client's fears about what may occur;

3.   a third letter indicating what the client would like the perpetrator to say, including the perpetrator taking responsibility for the abuse and expressing a desire to make amends. "This is the letter the client needs, but has not received (and is unlikely to receive)."

4.   after an interval of several months (e.g., 3 months) the client in collaboration with the therapist (and perhaps, significant others) can decide if the letter should be sent. Any decision about confronting the perpetrator needs to be weighed carefully and collaboratively with the client. As noted in Section I on the discussion of incest victims, **great caution is needed when conducting such "family of origin" work.**

In this Section, I will examine the features (e.g., **structure, metaphors, empowering verbs**) that can be incorporated in the **social discourse** and **letters written by the therapist to the client**. The suggestions in this Section can also be followed in the ongoing therapeutic communications by the therapist, **directly** or **indirectly** to the client. For example, a psychologist described how he would conduct a conversation about the client's medication with the consultant psychiatrist (either in person or on the phone) in the presence of the client. With the client's permission, the therapist would describe to the psychiatrist the client's present condition and progress using many of the phrases, metaphors, and examples included in this Section. The therapist indicated the progress the client had made and what were the specific skills/efforts that helped the client achieve his/her goals. Moreover, the psychologist noted the "unfinished business" and possible treatment plan for future action. This **"overhead conversation"** is a form of **indirect suggestion** that can prove to be a powerful social influence procedure, and a useful means to help clients "reauthor" their stories and to construct more adaptive narratives.

Before examining the specific ways such discussions or letters can be written, let me suggest you try an exercise (on the next page). Select a specific client and practice writing a letter (or at least sketching the outline of such a letter; include key phrases). You can then compare your answer to that offered in the remainder of this Section.

Exercise - Letter Writing

In order to appreciate the potential of such "reauthoring" procedures consider the following exercise of composing a letter to a client. Take a few moments and imagine a client, a friend, or a relative, who experienced a <u>traumatic event</u>. The event may be the result of an acute stressor (natural or human-made), or it may be the result of long-term chronic victimization (e.g., incest, sexual abuse, torture, etc.). Now, <u>outline</u> a letter you would write this person in order to help him or her cope more effectively. Put down some key phrases you would include in your letter.

Now that you have tried formulating such a letter, compare your letter with that outlined in the next several pages. Consider the variety of ways that therapists use metaphors and "empowering verbs" to help clients alter their narrative accounts.

Note: The following material could be incorporated **in a letter**, but it could **also be incorporated into the social discourse of therapy**. Where are all the opportunities for the therapist to use such statements in his/her interactions with clients? How many of these statements do you, the reader, now employ with clients?

1.   Introductory Comments of the Letter

a)   Friedman (1992) suggests the following opening features: The therapist can begin the letter by conveying the rationale for writing a letter to the client. For example, the therapist indicates or conveys:

   i)   his/her pleasure in having met the client;

   ii)   the reason why and value in the therapist writing this letter, namely, the need to convey thoughts while they are "fresh", that the client has made such a "positive" impression that the therapist felt compelled to provide some immediate feedback; the client is invited to think about this between now and the next session; the therapist looks forward to next session;

   iii)   what impressed him/her about the client, highlighting the specific positive attributes and changes. (Use positive metaphors that the client may have offered in the first session such as the client saying, "I want to begin to write a new chapter and join life." The therapist can indicate that he/she looks forward to working with the client in helping this reauthoring process and seeing what these new chapters will look like. Convey the metaphor of a "collaborative journey" by using the client's positive metaphor in the letter.);

   iv)   empathy with the amount of distress the client has experienced, about how difficult change can be. The therapist comments on how he/she admires the strength and courage in the client for making this effort (citing specific detailed examples);

   v)   comment on how the victimization experience has resulted in a "loss of innocence", "loss of childhood and youth", "loss of dreams", "loss of trust", "loss of identity". (Choose one or more that were offered by the client -- don't overwhelm the client.)

   vi)   indicate that those who had "victimized" the client had an expected "role" in mind for you (the client) to play. A role that was scripted by others (use the name of the perpetrator). Your lines, your scenes had been sketched out. Indicate that the client is at a **choice point** to determine whether he/she is going to play the role that others have dictated and continue to direct, even though they are no longer present, **or** will the client begin to write his/her own role, create his/her own scenario. Indicate that coming to therapy and the other "signs of recovery" (be specific) show that the client has already begun to make his/her choices, to take charge of his/her life, to develop a new way of being and behaving, to write a "new chapter";

   vii)   much interest in learning how the client achieved these changes or showed strengths, indicating that perhaps the client can let him/her "in on the secret" of what and how he/she has done to survive and achieve in spite of substantial barriers;

viii) comments on the goals that the client sought (or implied as working toward) (e.g., the therapist can comment on some of the changes that the client is "already establishing" -- convey action by using the present participle in the letter);

ix) what the therapist is looking forward to hearing about, learning from, getting to know more about, the next time he/she meets with the client (the therapist can say, "When "we" meet again..."--communicating collaboration by the use of "we".).

In addition, as part of the introduction, the therapist can also:

b) convey how interesting an experience it was to meet the client and hear the client's story of both his/her protest and survival (using both terms);

c) convey that the client has furthered his/her protest by coming to tell and share his/her story (complimenting client);

d) convey client's choice by saying, "I feel privileged you chose to share your story with me.";

e) empathize with the feelings and circumstance of the client. (Comment that people who experience loss often want to "stop the storm, the struggle, and they want to make things calm again." It takes courage to be here, to undertake a personal journey of healing, that one can't stop a process of change and of potential growth-- using metaphors that convey a process.);

f) convey that traumatic memories are a "series of still snapshots or a silent movie". (Herman, 1992) (The role of therapy is to provide the words and the music that give meaning and that conveys feelings of hope, that help clients break out of being prisoners of their past stories).

For example, one therapist commented to her client:

> "Although I have talked to many people who have suffered in their lives, it is different for everyone. People are quite amazing in how they find ways to cope with really "terrible" things that have happened to them ... I admire your courage to come here and share, although I know you don't feel so courageous right now ... What you need to know is that you CAN learn ways to stop yourself from X (use the client's metaphor, for example, "falling into a pit of depression"). You don't have to be a "prisoner of the past" ... I know that you would really like to have someone just take away all of the bad feelings, but we can't change the past, although, believe me, I would, if I could. No one should have suffered as you have. What we can do is find ways to stop the past from "attacking" you *(client's metaphor)* in the present and in the future."

2. Normalizing the Client's Reactions

The therapist:

a)   anticipates that the client may have had doubts about being believed (convey empathy);

b)   **uses the clients metaphors** (e.g., "It is understandable that in spite of the strengths that others see in you [cite examples] you feel ..." [cite specific metaphors client used "trapped", "hollow", "empty", "dirty", "tired"]);

c)   conveys choice by saying, "You are entitled to your resentment (anger, painful memory);

d)   comments that after a certain degree of abuse, some abused persons often start to believe that they deserved such abuse. (Build in qualifiers, not all abused clients.) Note that the emotional aftermath of trauma is often not located in the "centre of reason", but in the "reservoir of emotion";

e)   notes that crisis and change can be "twin brothers" if allowed (e.g., "Trauma is both a wounding and a choice point. Traumatic events give us a chance to stop and take stock, look at one's life, and make choices."). Indicate that the Chinese word for "crisis" is made up of Chinese features for the word "crisis", but also Chinese characters for the word "opportunity";

f)   conveys affirmation that the client can "make it," highlighting what the client has been "doing well," and the "distance" the client has already come.

3. Metaphors that Can Be Incorporated in a Letter and in Therapy -- Whenever possible the therapist can use the client's metaphors and have the client give examples of the metaphors *(See additional possible metaphors at the end of this section.)*

The therapist can **choose** from the following list those expressions/messages that are judged most appropriate to the client and that the therapist feels most comfortable with:

a)   sharing can relieve an "emotional weight" and provide a sense of relief

b)   client has evidenced a "life force" that refused to "buckle under"; a "surviving self" that has the power to emerge and flourish; a "strong fibre"

c)   client has paid dearly for a "strong will", a "vocal nature" (use client's phrase)

d)   in spite of X... the client was able to create a very good Y... (give examples of courage and survival skills); to make a leap of faith that X

e)   client had "grit", "pride in self"

f)   client has evidenced a "survival instinct, a "spirit that never submitted"

g)   client seems to be... (use client's metaphor--e.g., "On the right track; "Opened a new chapter"; "In the process of joining life"; "Getting reengaged"; "Got on the horse again"; "Opened a door and discovered there is a lot of room to explore"; "Moved through three stages of life. Stage 1 up to age X being a victim. Then moving into Stage 2 being a survivor. Now searching for a new Stage 3 person")

h)   client has refused to be "ambushed by grief," and instead, decided where, when, and how to grieve on his/her own terms

i)   client has taken steps (indicate behavioral signs of recovery) of what he/she can do on a daily basis -- one step at a time. In this way, the client can begin to create a new person, a person he/she needs to be in order to go on. (Help the client specify why such changes are important and "how" he/she has been able to undertake such changes.)

j)   client has begun to get "unstuck" from all of the "if only", and "why me", questions

4 .   Highlighting intra- and interpersonal strengths and supports with examples

The therapist comments on how the client:

a)   refused to deny his/her "true self"

b)   ruthlessly opposed ... (use striking adjective) in the face of ..."You could have easily done ... but you didn't. What does this tell you about yourself?" (The therapist can ask questions that pull for the client drawing conclusions about his/her strengths).

c)   evidenced special wisdom as demonstrated by ... How were you able to see through ... (hypocrisy)? How were you able not to let the terror stop you?

d)   has started to see him/herself through his/her own eyes, or through the eyes of someone the client admires (name person); not through the eyes of (name perpetrator). (Use question -- **When** did you no longer accept X's definition of you as being "garbage", "door mat", "hollow", "phoney" (use the client's descriptive term)? **How** did you go about doing that?

e)   rejected the widely shared myth that ... (e.g., that women solve their problem by being rescued by men; victimized people cannot succeed; etc.). Use such enabling statements. For example, the therapist can raise a question that the client might like to entertain, "Why didn't you just accept his definition of you? Help me understand that. (Note the language is designed to invite collaboration.)

f)   impressed the therapist by ... (e.g., not caving in, not seeking sympathy, not giving up, etc.) and the capacity to transform personal pain and despair into contributions to the quality of your life and the lives of others that would otherwise never have been made (Harvey et al., 1992).

g)   impressed with the client's ability to stave off the natural tendency to focus on X ... to get bogged down, get stuck by X ... to not get caught up in the mystery of the "why" questions.

h)   the therapist comments on the client's use of social supports that work like an "echo of reality". Other people can provide assurances that one is still in touch with the "real" world (Kfir, 1989).

i)   social support works like hidden footholds in a sheer canyon wall. Once you find them they provide a step-by-step passage to safety (Kfir, 1989).

5. **Convey Comments on Collaboration, Choice, and Control to the Client (Include Healing Metaphors).** The therapist can:

a)   convey that "we will walk the path together, aware of general direction, looking out for predictable pitfalls, but ready to discover new truths at every turn" (Ochberg, 1991, p. 6).

b)   convey his/her reactions to the horrific tales of victimization. The therapist can indicate that at times part of you (the therapist) wanted to leave (explain why) and part of you wanted to stay (explain why). The therapist should indicate why it is important to continue and hear the pain, the distress, but also record the client's resilience and strength.

c)   convey empathy by responding in a direct fashion. When hearing such traumatic accounts, the therapist may comment, "That's terrible!", "What pain," instead of reflecting "That must have made you feel X.", "I can now understand how come you feel Y."

d)   comment on how the therapist looks forward to assist the client in "writing a new chapter of the events in your life, a new history that could predict a very different kind of future than your old history" (Epston et al., (1991, p. 104).

e)   help the client to remember just as much as he/she needs to remember and just as little as he/she needs to remember. Able to leave "then" time then, and able to be in the "now" time now. (O'Hanlon, 1992).

f)   convey an appreciation to the client that he/she has:

   i)   added to your stock of knowledge

   ii)   given testimony to the courage and resilience of the human spirit

   iii) renewed your faith

   iv)   encouraged you to pursue further the significance of people rewriting their stories

   v)   helped you to recognize that a major loss can force someone to think and feel along new dimensions, see the world differently

g)   ask the client if you have his/her permission to share his/her examples with others (without disclosing his/her name). In making this request, indicate to the client that you are reminded of the observation that **"story-telling" is everyone's universal gift and reflects their bedrock capacity to survive.** Is the client willing to make a gift of his/her survivorship to others?

h)   in later sessions, discuss ways in which the client can find a "mission", "engage" in some activity (e.g., share experience with others, provide help for others, undertake political or social actions) that will give meaning to the experience and help the client salvage something from survivorship (e.g., see Dutton, 1993; Herman, 1992; Johnson et al., 1994, for descriptions of how victimized clients can be encouraged to be reengaged in activities that foster connectedness and self-worth).

6. Relapse Prevention

Comment on how there may be lapses, set-backs, backsliding, reexperiences, anniversary effects. The recovery process does not follow a simple progression, but often detours and doubles back.

a)   Use relapse prevention metaphors such as falling off a bike, prevention example, glass in knee, journey not always smooth, steps backward are part of the learning process-- two steps forward, one step backwards (see Meichenbaum & Turk, 1987, for a description of relapse prevention procedures).

b)   Convey life as a process -- provide a developmental perspective.

7. Possible Additional Metaphors That Can Be Used In Therapy

a)   "One of the rewards of being a therapist is being a witness. I like to think of myself as a kind of archivist. You know the person who keeps the archives of growth, the record of personal milestones." (Dr. Price-Munn, 1993). (Give examples of the client's records and milestones", or, better yet, ask the client to suggest what are some of the things that you might have recorded in your therapy notes that document his or her resilience and courage. Therapist comments on being impressed and inspired by the client's struggles, determination, and successes (not that there won't be lapses and setbacks along the way).

b)   Compare someone who has experienced a traumatic event(s) as being like someone who emigrates to a new land and must build a new life within a new culture from the one left behind (Herman, 1992). Ask the client to see if this metaphor applies to his/her life.

c)   "Crisis means a change in the flow of life. The river flows relentlessly to the sea. When it reaches a point where it is blocked by rocks and debris, it struggles to find ways to continue its path. Would the alternative be to flow backwards? That is what a person in crisis craves, to go back in time. But life doesn't provide a reverse gear, and the struggle must go forward, like the river, with occasional pauses to tread water and check out where we are heading" (Kfir, 1989, p. 31) ... Water adapts itself to the configuration of the land. One must be flexible.

d)   "When a flood occurs, the water does not continue forever. There is a rush, but it is temporary and eventually the storm stops, the land dries up, and everything begins to return to normal. Emotions can be viewed the same way." At this point, the therapist can ask the client to recall times when he/she has experienced feelings such as sadness or anger, and what happened after she allowed herself to feel her emotions? (Resick & Schnicke, 1993, p. 55) ... Another flood metaphor was offered by Solomon (1990:

> "Traumatic experiences are like flooding a piece of land. When the water recedes, it leaves visible and massive damage. It may also leave behind invisible structural flaws that makes one more vulnerable to subsequent stressors."

e)   "When the roots of a tree hit a large stone or other obstacle, do they try to shove the stone away or crack it? No. The roots just grow around the obstacle and keep going. The stone may have interrupted or slowed the tree's growth for a while, but no stone, no matter how large, can stop the tree from growing." (Stone symbolizes obstacles to personal growth.) (Matsakis, 1992, p.133)

f) Dolan (1991, p. 74-75) uses the story of the sinking of the ship, the Titanic, as a metaphor to convey the point that not taking precautions given a warning can be life-threatening. According to Dolan, the Captain of the Titanic decided to hide the seriousness of the damage from his crew and passengers and this plan tragically backfired. No one's life would have been lost if the Captain had been willing to admit the seriousness of the situation and be less stubborn. Another metaphor Dolan (1991) uses is that of "glass in the knee" (p. 182) and what happens if the wound is not fully cleaned out. "Sometimes pieces get buried so deeply that it takes a long time to finally reach the surface where they can be released." (p. 183).

g) As reported by Kingsbury (1992), Milton Erickson compared therapy to a process where clients get by a "log jam in a river." The therapist metaphorically can kick the "right log" and help the client become unstuck so the mass of logs will move.

h) A metaphor to address the issue of **length of treatment**:

Scott and Stradling (1992, p. 51) offer the following metaphor when clients ask, "How long will treatment take?" The counselor answers, "It is difficult to say, but treatment will go quicker and be more successful if you don't get angry with yourself about X (e.g., intrusive thoughts). Just as you can't force a physical wound to heal quickly, you can't force a psychological wound to heal either. In both cases you have to flow with the healing process, not fight it."

i) A metaphor for dealing with **intrusive ideation**:

"What if a person's mind is very much like a railway station? You are standing on one of the station platforms. You cannot control what trains come into the station. On some days there may be, say, special trains to take people to a race. The trains that come into the station depend upon what is going on in the outside world. But you can choose whether you get on a train or not, or ignore it, or wave goodbye to the occupants on the train ... [When you try to stop the thoughts] ... it is as if you are jumping onto the railway track to try and stop the train. That's pretty painful. [Client asks, what can I do?] ... Maybe calmly greet the thoughts and then wave them goodbye. Practice keeping your cool about them."

Scott and Stradling (1992, p. 57) who have offered the railway station metaphor go on to suggest that the client should be encouraged to simply greet flashbacks, in the same way as a person standing on a railway platform who might wave back to some unknown person waving from a train that was passing through the station. The client "could choose to get irritated with the person waving to her and the noise of the passing train or alternatively she could choose simply to greet it calmly as it passed by. The option of saying "The train should not come" is not a viable one. At the appropriate time the client can choose to **board other trains of thought** (p. 118, 119).

j) Dutton (1992, p. 95-96) offers the following healing metaphor to **women who have been battered**. "Assume a house is being damaged by a fire that encircles it. Attempting to repair the damage to the house would not be wise until the immediate threat being presented by the fire is addressed. However, one might take certain action (e.g., douse the house with water) that could reduce the chances of the house becoming damaged even further. As with the house, beginning to repair the damage of psychological trauma incurred from abuse is difficult, if not impossible, while the battered woman is continually faced with recurrent episodes of battering or threats of it. Most of her energy is needed to stay safe. The healing process requires an opportunity to experience one's vulnerability in a safe place where there is emotional and spiritual support. The possibility of creating a safe environment -- for a period of time long enough to effectively complete the healing process -- is difficult while living in the context of ongoing battering."

k)   The therapist may tell the client, "What exposure to traumatic events does is to **"disintegrate" or "shatter" our assumptions of the world.** We each live with basic assumptions about the world, but when these are violated it can have a real impact on us. Let me give you an analogy (example)."

> "You drive a car, correct? Well, we all live with the assumption that when we drive down a two lane road, that an oncoming car is not going to cross the double yellow lines. It becomes very hard to drive if one believes it is likely that a car will cross the double yellow line at any time. As a result we become hypervigilant, continually worry when it might occur, might avoid driving, and replay in our mind past accidents and near misses. What used to be a pleasant ride in the country turns into a potential disaster around each bend. When someone has a traumatic event happen, like you, it is like driving down a narrow two lane road with double yellow lines the whole way, never knowing when the next driver will cross the double yellow lines ... Does that make sense to you?" (Analogy suggested by Schwarz and Prout, 1991).

l)   Herman (1992, p.68) describes an example of **reframing.** A 14 year old rape victim received help from a friend when the rape victim noted that "I'm not a virgin anymore". To this, the friend observed:

> "This doesn't have anything to do with being a virgin. Some day you will fall in love and you'll make love and **that** will be losing your virginity. Not the act of what happened (he didn't say rape). That doesn't have anything to do with it."

m)   Kazanis (1991) has suggested the following therapeutic messages:

> "There is a part of you that wanted (desperately) to speak and you kept searching for ways to speak and ways to be heard."

> "There was some force inside of you that sought the light of day."

> "You were able to bring your grief alive and share it in a way that gave comfort and relief, that helped you find meaning."

n)   Sinclair (1993) compares "victimization" with "injury" and "brokenness" and the need to mend and rebuild. He observes to clients:

> "We cannot take away the trauma; not take away the scars left by the trauma. But we have to learn to live in spite of the wounds that will never heal."

o)   Kfir (1989, p. 38) offers the biblical stories[1] of Job and King David as "healing" metaphors. This is especially useful with clients for whom the Bible has some psychological presence and who are struggling with "why" questions.

"Consider two biblical figures who suffered tragedies, Job and King David. Job's tragedies were monumental and included the loss of his family and fortune and his bout with leprosy. In the face of these big losses he despaired. [Why?] ... He could not go on with life unless he understood <u>why</u> those things happened to him.

King David likewise suffered greatly. Persecuted by King Saul for years, he fled into the desert. He lost his baby for his sins, lost his most beloved son, Absalom, who led the mob against him, had to give up his dream of rebuilding the Temple as a punishment for the bloodshed, and, in the end, lost his best friend, Jonathan. In spite of all that, David was never in crisis. [Why?] ... He did not ask God for explanations. He took what life dished out to him and went on with living."

Kfir also uses the biblical figures of Job and King David to consider the nature of social supports.

Job's three friends sat with him, gave information and explanations, assisted, urged, and demanded Job's recovery. Job ignored their help and pleaded to God to intervene. For Job, only the divine would be an acceptable source of answers. Nevertheless, his friends didn't leave him, nor did they feel insignificant even though their advice was not heeded.

David, throughout his life, found comfort in the assistance of Jonathan who "gave" from a distance. The Bible doesn't tell much about this assistance, but it was there, a reality in the minds of two friends.

These classic biblical stories illustrate the points that people try to cope with stressful events in very different ways with different consequences and that people need different kinds of help. There is <u>no</u> one way of giving support or providing intervention." (p. 38). Discuss these examples with the client and consider how they can be applied.

q)   In the same spirit as Kfir, Kirschner et al. (1993) report on the use of the religious metaphor of what Maslow called the **"Jonah complex"**. "In the biblical story, God called Jonah to become his prophet. Jonah responded by fleeing and sailing away on a boat, whereupon a storm arose and he ended up in the belly of a whale. There, he reconciled with his destiny and was miraculously saved. He then began his true work." Those who **flee from their own potential** or from their calling are like Jonah. "The survivor, having learned to mistrust herself, **flees and hides from her authentic self** in the shame-filled belly of the whale. In this way, she avoids pursuing her true path in life." (p. 58).

---

[1] Religious metaphors should be used if appropriate to the client and if it feels "authentic" and "genuine" to the therapist. But as Propst (1983) has described for religious clients, the Bible is replete with examples of useful metaphors. I will consider the role of religion in Section VII on post-disaster interventions.

8. **Language of "healing" -- Comment on the client's ability to cope and to demonstrate resilience and courage** (The following phrases that emphasize active verbs may be useful.) Convey that the client:

Demonstrated the ability to reframe events

Sees life through a new set of lenses.
Dared to see yourself as ...
Rejected the possibility of putting yourself down or being treated as ...
Resisted the temptation of feeling (self-hate, loneliness) ... of sinking into the past.
Reauthored your life.
Rewrote your own story.
Fully experience and know what happened then, but with the resources and understanding that you have now and that you are developing, you can come to a new understanding and an appreciation of your history.
Transcend wounds of your past.
Free self from debilitating effects of ...
Draw up your personal blueprint for ...
Broke the conspiracy of silence.
In spite of betrayal, heartbreak and adversity, you demonstrated (therapist can choose from the following -- inner strength, perseverance, dedication to your own healing, amazing tenacity, compassion, the ability to block out the pain of the moment and do whatever was needed to be done, the ability to utilize an inner strength, the ability to find a generative path, the determination to make the unknowable known, the unspeakable speakable). **Have the client give examples so these phrases don't become mere epithets.**
Recognize that you are not controlled by predetermined past choices, not stuck by your previous history.
Let go of X and not have to hide from the past.
Understand that just because someone has a disease, it does not mean they have to be sick.
Learned that you can live in spite of the wounds that will never heal.
Appreciate that a trauma can create havoc at all levels of who you are, but that you can go on ... that trauma can create rage, an inner warfare that can consume someone from the inside and that you have done things (give examples such as seeking isolation, avoiding) to maintain control. (Help the client appreciate how previous behaviors were self-protective acts.)
Recognize that you cannot undo history, but can influence the present and future.
Recognize that there is a part of you that X and another part of you that Y.

Demonstrated the ability to put things in perspective and see choices

Realized have opportunities (choices). Became aware of the possibilities of change.
Legitimated yourself by ...
Decided to develop a more comfortable relationship with yourself.
Decided to tell the rest of the story (like the radio commentator Paul Harvey who says, "And now for the rest of the story.").
Find (give) meaning to your experience.
Create purpose by ...
Validate yourself.
Put the past in the past, where it belongs.
Leave behind those things that should be left behind.
Engage in a new reconciliation with the past.

__Demonstrated the ability to exert self-control -- to stop yourself reflexively__

Behaviorally

> Took initiative to ...
> Take back power.
> Confront past traumas.
> Pleased yourself by ...   Appreciated yourself by ...
> Became a consultant for others.
> Got rid of excess baggage.
> Liberated your life.
> Found soul-mates (name social supports).

Cognitively

> You were able to notice ... catch ... plan ... recognize options ... recognize you have choices
>> ... read between the lines ... defuse the situation ... stake out a middle ground ... not give
>> in ... avoid falling into the same behavioral rut ... play a different CD in your head ... talk
>> to yourself differently ... relax (soothe) yourself ... play detective ... empower yourself ...
>> short-circuit the conflict ... redirect the situation ... not let someone else dictate (direct) how
>> you will feel or what you will do ... choose not to let someone else get you into trouble
>> ("pull your chime") ... organize yourself ... nudge your memory ... freeze frame the scene
>> and analyze what your options are ... identify reasonable goals ... take charge ... take a
>> time out ... seek help ... call upon your own personal ally by ... talk yourself out of ...
>> checked it out.
> Discovered to your satisfaction that ...
> Used your inquiring mind.
> Recognized that time boundaries are erased (in flashbacks, dreams).
> Realized many of your capabilities.
> Developed a healing theory.
> Recognized that forgiveness is for yourself, as much as for anyone else.
> Recognized you were living his/her (name perpetrator) story. Now you have begun to live
>> your own story.
> Do the work that is needed to be done -- remember resolve, forget, heal. Did whatever you
>> needed to do.
> Reconcile and connect in a way that is meaningful to you.
> Outsmarted the effects of the past.

__Demonstrated the ability to manifest self-control,__
__self-determination and survival instincts__

Recognize that the unconscious cannot tell time so at times when flashbacks occur your memories
> are not only remembered, they are relived, as if the events were occurring right now. Time
> becomes "then" and "now" together.
Find solace in the now.
Determined to see yourself through this.
Made yourself into the person you want to become.
Choose your own path (game plan).
Inspired yourself with hope.
Exerted survival skills.
Challenged the popular myth that ...
Nurtured hope, noting the benchmarks in your life.
Transformed a house of pain into a house of hope.
Transformed personal pain and despair into contributions to yourself as well as to other's lives.

<u>Negotiated</u> with immortality.

<u>Bore</u> witness.

<u>Decided</u> to leave a legacy.

<u>Mobilized</u> a healing force.

<u>Marshalled</u> great strengths.

<u>Demonstrated</u> a bedrock capacity to cope.

<u>Found</u> the resources you needed in order to resolve things in a way that is right for you.

<u>Discovered</u> that deep inside you there is (was) a strength and resilience in the midst of what looked like (fragility, victimization, suffering, pain, hopelessness, helplessness, despair -- tailor to client).

<u>Discovered</u> that there were so many things you knew how to do, but you just didn't know that you knew them.

Finally, the **critical feature** of this social discourse is whether clients begin to incorporate these expressions into their own narrative. Do clients take ownership and interject "metacognitive" verbs into their narratives? In therapy, I monitor the degree to which clients spontaneously, and of their own initiative, make statements like:

"You know, I now know how I can drive myself crazy."

"I actually caught myself."

"I changed what I said to myself."

"I know myself a little bit differently than I have in the past."

"I feel my life is slowly coming under more of my control. I realize I can take more control by taking less control. I realize I don't always have to be in charge all the time. I have choices."

"It is almost like a different path I have decided to take."

"There are more things I am looking forward to."

"I can tame and use past horrors with current experiences, integrate the past and present."

"These memories are reminders of work I need to do on myself."

"I am now a more whole person."

This type of reflexive thinking (what psychodynamic folks characterize as an "observing ego") reflects the changes and progress clients are making. In short, they are becoming their own therapist.

Treatment of Clients Diagnosed with Borderline Personality Disorder (BPD)

As noted in Section I on comorbidity, $1/3$ of BPD patients fulfill the criteria for PTSD, approximately 75% of whom are women. A history of sexual or physical abuse is in the developmental background of approximately 60% to 75% of clients with BPD. In fact, BPD occurs as a single diagnosis in only 3 to 10% of cases (Barley et al., 1993). There is a good deal of controversy, however, about the proposed DSM-IV criteria for BPD (e.g., Taylor, 1993) and about possible stigmatization attached to the diagnostic label of BPD. Herman (1992) has admonished clinicians not to label clients "borderline" since the label of BPD is pejorative, degrading and stigmatizing. Given the victimization experience of many BPD patients, **PTSD would appear to be a more appropriate diagnostic label**. Pearlman and Saakvitne (in press) have voiced a similar sentiment, "Borderline diagnosis often carries with it blame, shame and hopelessness, making the process of diagnosis harmful and abusive." (p. 12). Despite this controversy, a good deal of clinical treatment activity has been directed at the BPD population (Barley et al., 1993; Linehan, 1993). Before we consider the specific features of these interventions, we will briefly consider the clinical concerns raised about BPD.

The central features of BPD cover such areas as instability of self-image, intense interpersonal conflicts, lack of interpersonal effectiveness, frequent crises, sudden mood swings and vacillation of affect (Herman & van der Kolk, 1987). Clients diagnosed with BPD avoid seemingly intolerable affect by means of impulsive acting out. Adler (1993) has noted that central to the borderline disorder is also a feeling of "aloneness" that are associated with recurrent traumatic experiences throughout childhood and adolescence. Such feelings are often triggered at times of separation. They also evidence difficulty tolerating dysphoric feelings such as sadness and anger. Interpersonally, they experience distrust. Out of a desire to compensate they may be perceived as being "manipulative" which may lead to social rejection. As part of this transactional process the individual with BPD may feel a sense of personal "badness" and "worthlessness", and thus, the cycle continues. This interpersonal pattern often plays itself out in the therapeutic setting. The therapist needs to help the client become aware of this transactional pattern and help her to "notice", "catch" and "alter" this pattern with more adaptive coping and interpersonal skills.

While there is some general agreement on the clinical profile of BPD, there is marked disagreement on the specific diagnostic classification of this disorder. For example, Taylor (1993) has challenged the usefulness of the DSM-IV categorical classification of BPD, and instead, proposes that a dimensional model of borderline characteristics be employed, reflecting the basic dimensional manifestation of extreme neuroticism.

Whatever the controversy over the diagnostic label BPD, there is a sizable clinical subpopulation (some 19% of psychiatric inpatients) who evidence marginal adjustment with accompanying parasuicidal behaviors and poor interpersonal relations. They also frequently have a history of victimization (Barley et al., 1993).

A number of diverse interventions have been offered for the treatment of clients diagnosed BPD. These range from pharmacological to psychodynamic to cognitive-behavioral. In the pharmacological domain Soloff (1992) has concluded that "the overall efficacy of medication for BPD is **modest at best**. Residual symptoms are the rule. Pharmacotherapy does not adequately address the interpersonal domain." (p. 265). The general treatment strategy has been to select medications for specific target symptoms. (See Soloff, 1994). For example:

> MAO antidepressants and lithium for the treatment of mood-related affective
> dyscontrol
> Low dosage neuroleptics for anger/hostility and schizotypal features
> Carbamazepine for impulsive aggressive behaviors

A psychodynamic perspective has been offered in the manualized treatment approach of Kernberg and Clarkin (1992) and Yeomans et al. (1993). This approach focuses on the analysis of transference in the therapeutic setting. Treatment begins with defining a clear behavioral contract (as described below) which serves a limit-setting function. Given the emphasis on interpretation, the psychodynamic treatment seems limited to moderate to high level functioning BPD patients (Soloff, 1993).

A different treatment approach has been developed by Marsha Linehan and her colleagues at the University of Washington who have formulated a cognitive behavioral intervention for clients with BPD called Dialectical Behavior Therapy (DBT) (Linehan, 1993a,b; Heard & Linehan, 1994). The treatment targets the self-destructive behavior (parasuicidal behavior) that BPD patients evidence and teaches alternative coping skills. This is especially significant when we learn that BPD individuals who report a history of childhood sexual abuse engage in parasuicide that was more lethal than that of women who did not report abuse (Wagner & Linehan, 1994). The central features of the intervention include:

1. a year-long outpatient weekly manualized treatment that combines individual psychotherapy and group skills training;

2. the group sessions are held weekly ($2^{1}/_{2}$ hour sessions). The focus is on problem-solving training, interpersonal skills training, distress tolerance and emotional regulation skills. "The weekly sessions focus on motivational issues and skill strengthening and balances behavioral strategies with supportive validating strategies aimed at providing acceptance." (Linehan, 1994, p. 3). (There is a detailed workbook for both therapists and clients, Linehan, 1993b.) The central theme is to encourage balance between acceptance and change ("accept things as they are in order to facilitate change");

3. during the initial stage of therapy the treatment targets include the reduction of suicidal and therapy interfering behaviors. At the end of the treatment year, the BPD patients are required to take a 2-month "vacation" from their individual therapist, after which they could resume individual psychotherapy.

4. the group skills training is supplemented with individual psychotherapy sessions (1 per week) which is conducted by a therapist who is not involved in the group sessions;

5. the client is asked to keep a record of all alcohol and drug use (both prescribed and non-prescribed), to rate the degree of suicidal "urges" and the level of depression, and to record any self-injurious behaviors. (As Linehan notes the intervention is quite demanding and requires a good deal of motivation.);

6. in group, clients discuss and analyze specific parasuicidal episodes and examine choice points between impulse and action. They also examine the connections between thoughts, feelings and behaviors in a rather didactic and directive fashion. Given the high incidence of parasuicidal behavior in this population, an important target behavior is the client's level of hopelessness;

7. a recurrent theme in the group sessions is the examination of therapy interfering behaviors. This point is underscored by the finding that patients with BPD have a **high dropout rate from psychotherapy**, up to 67% after 3 months (Yeomans et al., 1993). As Gunderson and Chu (1993) observe, "most patients with BPD drop out of psychotherapy even when it is provided by expert and experienced therapists, and long-term hospitalizations resulted in only the same profile of improvement as short-term hospital care." (p. 75);

8.   an integrated team approach which includes individual psychotherapy, a skills training group for clients, planned telephone contact with clients, and supervision or group consultation for therapists;

9.   in addition, additional treatment components may include psychotropic medication, day treatment, vocational counseling, inpatient hospitalization and involvement in Alcoholic Anonymous.

Results: The initial results with severely dysfunctional chronically parasuicidal BPD female clients of this extensive cognitive behavioral intervention program are quite promising. Over the entire year, 64% of the subjects in the DBT group, as compared to 96% of the "treated as usual" BPD patients evidenced parasuicidal episodes (i.e., intentional self-inflicted injury) (Linehan, 1993a). At a 6-month and 12-month follow-up the DBT had "significantly higher Global Assessment Scale scores, and better work performance throughout the follow-up year. During the initial 6 months of the follow-up, the DBT subjects (relative to a treatment as usual group) had significantly less parasuicidal behavior, less anger and better self-reported social adjustment, while during the final 6 months DBT subjects had significantly fewer psychiatric inpatient days and better interviewer-rated social adjustment." (Linehan et al., 1994, p. 2).

Barley and his colleagues (1993) have recently extended DBT to an inpatient treatment program for BPD patients, and similarly decreased parasuicidal behavior. Their 3-month cycle group treatment program consisted of 3-week units that are designed to teach specific skills such as emotional regulation and interpersonal effectiveness. Clients were given worksheets, diary cards, and audiotapes of the sessions to review. The assignments covered such areas as practicing nonjudgmental thinking of own and other's behavior, observing and describing emotions, using self-soothing techniques during crises, and protecting self-respect when interacting with others. Generalization was emphasized as clients had an opportunity to practice their skills in the treatment milieu. Progress through a privilege level system was tied into homework compliance.

Both the Linehan and Brady outcome studies are to be applauded for their innovative work with a difficult and challenging clinical population (also see Langley, 1993). Their results are consistent with the observations of Gunderson and Chu (1993) who noted that highly structured here-and-now groups that limit detailed discussion of past traumas and focus on coping skills and practical solutions to current problems have been most helpful with BPD patients. In this tradition, Farrell and Shaw (1994) have used experiential exercises to increase the level of emotional awareness in clients with borderline personality disorders (BPD). They propose that **Emotional Awareness Training**[1] provides the basis for emotional stability in BPD clients. The skills-oriented awareness training is followed by training in distress reduction, emotional regulation, and in identifying and challenging early maladaptive cognitive schemas.

Turner, Becker and DeLoach (1994) describe a dynamic cognitive behavioral therapy approach (DCBT) that lasts 6 months to 1 year. During the first 3 months, the treatment involves sessions 3 times a week. This is followed by twice weekly sessions and with progress once a week. The DCBT involves 6 phases. These include:

(1)   containment of self-harm, parasuicidal behavior, and brief psychotic episodes

(2)   problem assessment

---

[1] An Emotional Awareness Training manual is available from Dr. Joan Farrell, Psychology Dept., Larue Carter Memorial Hospital, 1315 W. 10th St., Indianapolis, IN 46202.

(3)   cognitive-dynamic case formulation

(4)   intensive intervention

(5)   termination

(6)   supportive therapy booster sessions.

In addition, frequent telephone contact is maintained with the client. Such telephone contacts are structured, as clients are told that the calls are limited to 10 minutes. The therapist conveys to the client that 10 minutes is ample time to define a problem and generate interim solutions.

Clearly, more work is needed on improving these innovative intervention programs and in determining the relative contributions of the various features of this complex treatment package. An interesting clinical issue is how directive and didactic the therapist needs to be when running these skills-oriented groups with BPD clients. An examination of the Linehan workbooks reflect the use of "mnemonics" that are given to BPD clients at each step of the intervention. Clients need to be allowed and encouraged to take on more and more responsibility, to take ownership, to independently apply skills in new areas, and to describe (put into words) the strategies they are learning. The therapist needs to "scaffold" instruction (fade out supports) and not act as a **"surrogate frontal lobe"**, or as a **"metacognitive prosthetic device"** for their clients in order to increase the likelihood of treatment "generalization" and "internalization".

As in other forms of treatment with challenging clients there is the possibility of combining diverse interventions. But no matter what form of intervention there is a need to establish a good working relationship and nurture client-therapist alliance. There is also a need to solicit motivation and commitment to attend treatment sessions and to conduct homework. A promising way to accomplish these treatment objectives has been outlined by Yeomans et al., 1992. They highlight the role of a contract-setting phase of intervention with BPD clients. The contract provides a framework for outlining both the client's and the therapist's responsibilities and examines possible barriers or obstacles that might get in the way of the client following through. See Yeomans et al. (1992), Linehan (1993), and Meichenbaum and Turk (1987) for a discussion of how such contracts can be included in treatment. Also see Beck et al. (1993), Fleming and Pretzer (1990), Katz and Levendusky (1990), Layden et al. (1993), and Newman et al. (1993) for discussions of how cognitive therapy procedures can be used with clients with personality disorder.

Finally, I will take the liberty of sharing a personal observation of some skepticism about Axis II personality disorders. Except for antisocial personality, there is a great deal of controversy about the statistical adequacy of drawing reliable differential diagnoses of the various personality disorders, as reviewed by Zimmerman (1994). I am prone to view the clients "personality style" (if one can use such a term) as a way of coping, as a form of adaptation. At the time when the client had to deal with various stressors these ways of coping represented "survival solutions". It is not that our clients have a so-called "personality disorder" (can a personality be "disordered"), but rather the client is continuing to respond to current situations in ways that may have "worked" in the past, but do not "work" now in achieving the client's goals. If one views the clients from this "stuckiness" perspective, or "overgeneralized response set" perspective, then it de-pathologizes our clients and questions the basis of Axis II. One should maintain a critical stance toward the "hype" surrounding personality disorders. It is not clear that clients with so-called different personality disorders hold different beliefs, engage in different thinking styles, and the like. It would be "tidy" if we could pigeon-hole our clients and draw up differential treatments. As George Kelly observed, "Clinicians should be cautious about the hardening of their categories".

Treatment of Comorbidity Problems of Addictive Behavior
(Alcoholism) and PTSD
(See the separate Reference Section on Treatment of Alcoholism in Section VIII for more detail.)

As noted in Section I, a major challenge for clients with PTSD (and PTSD plus DES) is the high incidence of comorbidity (dual diagnosis) of PTSD and alcohol abuse (and other addictive substances). It has been estimated that anywhere from **60% to 80% of PTSD clients abuse alcohol or other addictive substances.**[1] The likelihood of comorbidity is further increased if the client has a developmental history of aggressive antisocial behavior, or has a history of, or is presently experiencing, panic attacks. With regard to panic attacks it has been estimated that a sizable minority (up to 25%) of current alcoholics may have used alcohol as a form of self-medication to treat their anxiety disorder and the anxiety-related features of PTSD symptomatology. In the case of PTSD, the use of alcohol may be a means of self-imposed psychic numbing and dissociation. Steele (1990) has conducted a series of studies to demonstrate the **myopic effects of alcohol** that enhances the importance of self-evaluations, bolsters social responses and relieves dysphoric emotions such as anxiety and depression. Baumeister (1991) has discussed how alcohol can help the individual **escape from self.** As part of the education process with dual diagnosed clients, it is important to teach them about the **mental narrowing effects of alcohol.**

The clinical challenge of working on comorbidity problems was brought home to me when I was asked to consult and present at both inpatient and outpatient **dual diagnosis** settings (PTSD and addictive behaviors). I was asked to present on the potential contributions of a cognitive-behavioral treatment approach, and especially, asked to address the issues of treatment nonadherence and patient noncompliance which are rampant in this population (see Meichenbaum and Turk, 1987 for a discussion of ways to **Facilitate Treatment Adherence**, Plenum Press). In my presentation I decided to cover the following topics:

1. The nature of treatment outcome and nonadherence data for addictive disorders, especially alcohol abuse.[2]

2. Assessment issues, the role of motivational interviewing, highlighting the importance of therapeutic alliance.

3. The role of **metaphors** to enhance the client's commitment to change.

4. An overview of cognitive-behavioral and other treatment approaches.

5. The need for **continuity of care** in the form of a **case manager approach,** especially with a chronic inpatient population.

This Section will follow this general outline. Obviously, one could collate an entire Handbook just on the treatment of addictive behaviors *(see references in Section VIII)*, but the present objective is to sensitize clinicians who work with PTSD clients to the need to address this critical comorbidity problem. As Aboytes (1993) observes, alcohol abuse often creates a new set of symptoms.

---

[1] It has been estimated that 2 out of 10 Americans are social users of alcohol and drugs, 5 are misusers, 1 is alcohol or chemically dependent (Blau et al., 1994). The NVVRS study of Vietnam veterans indicated a 20% coexistence between Substance Abuse Disorder and PTSD and in inpatient populations an even higher incidence of comorbidities (55% to 70%). The incidence of alcohol disorder to drug disorders was 5 to 1 (11% to 2%), with many individuals being polysubstance abusers.

[2] The National Center for PTSD has made a videotape on "PTSD/Alcoholism Comorbidity: Veterans Couldn't Wish It on Their Worst Enemy". Available from VA libraries: Call number WM/170/P975a/1992.

I. The Nature of the Problem of Alcohol Abuse

1. Most individuals who have problems with alcohol (and other addictive behaviors) do <u>not</u> receive treatment. Of the estimated 18 million Americans with alcohol abuse problems, less than 15% receive any form of treatment. Marlatt et al. (1993) estimate that there are approximately 10 million untreated alcoholics in the US.

2. Of those clients with problems of addiction who do receive treatment, how successful are such interventions? **The news is mixed.** While the long range outcome data (to be reviewed) highlight the difficulty clients with a drinking problem have in remaining abstinent, there is also data to suggest that **<u>well</u> planned brief interventions (1 to 3 sessions) can have a considerable favorable impact,** and be relatively effective when compared to more extensive treatment of alcohol problems. After reviewing this literature, Miller and Rollnick (1992) concluded that the **primary impact of brief intervention with those who have addiction problems is primarily motivational, namely to trigger a decision and commitment to change.** Moreover, they report on their research findings that $2/3$ of the variance in predicting drinking outcome could be predicted from the degree of empathy shown by the therapist during treatment. The use of **motivational interviewing procedures** facilitated both treatment relationship factors and drinking outcome data. We will consider these motivational interviewing procedures below. But first let us consider the challenge that clinicians face in working with dual diagnosis clients (PTSD and addiction problems). Consider the following **outcome data.**

   a. Alcoholics who have been treated:

% Abstinent	Follow-up Period
$1/2$	3 months
$1/3$	6 months
$1/8$	12 months
$1/10$	18 months

   b. Among those persuaded to enter treatment, only approximately 20% maintain abstinence at 1 year after treatment.

   c. i) 70% relapse during the first 3 months after discharge
      ii) 3 month abstinence is a favorable prognostic sign for long term abstinence

   d. i) 50% drop out of treatment within the first month
      ii) 70% of those who complete aftercare treatment will be abstinent at 9 months <u>versus</u> only 23% abstinent of those who drop out of aftercare treatment
      iii) 75% attrition rate from various treatment programs
      iv) Of alcoholics put on lithium carbonate, 48% are nonadherent within 6 months

3. In the treatment of <u>addictive behaviors</u>, in general, such as smoking, heroin, as well as alcohol, <u>60%</u> of those <u>successfully</u> treated revert to prior behavior patterns within 3 months, increasing to 70% at 6 months, 75% at 12 months. The relapse rates for addictions are in the range of 50-90%. The relapse rates for various addictions (heroin, smoking, alcoholism) stabilize within 3 months.

4. Most relapse for treatment of alcoholism occurs within the first 90 days post detoxification. Nearly all those patients who relapse do so before 6 months expire.

5. 80% of treatment providers base their treatment on the philosophy and principles of Alcoholic Anonymous' (AA) 12-step program. Hickey (1994) has characterized AA as a form of religion that many alcoholic clients reject. In fact, it has been estimated that only 20% of persons with alcohol problems who are referred to AA ever attend meetings. Estimates of the effectiveness of those who do attend AA vary from 12% to 25% after 3 years (Hickey, 1994). While some individuals who accept the religious orientation of AA benefit, most do not.

6. It is also possible to have relapse even after long periods of abstinence. Such relapse or what Marlatt and Gordon (1984) call the Abstinence Violation Effects (AVE) are tied to high risk situations. Their research indicates that:

   a)   35% of all relapse is due to -- negative emotional states (frustration, anger, anxiety, depression, boredom)

   b)   20% relapse is due to -- social pressure to drink again

   c)   16% relapse is due to -- interpersonal conflicts (marriage, friendship, family, work)

   These percentages generally hold across addictive behaviors (smokers, heroin, gamblers, overeaters, and alcoholics).

7. If you treat "non-addicted" problem drinkers (i.e., low dependence, no familial history of alcoholism), younger, male, unmarried clients, then they can be taught controlled moderation drinking usually with favorable outcome, 60-70% (Miller, 1983).

8. Finally, it is important to keep in mind Peele's (1991, p. 1409) admonition that "more individuals have quit addictions on their own than have been successfully treated by even the best therapies".

9. An additional concern in working with clients who have problems with addictive behaviors is the **high attrition or drop out of treatment data.** Consider the following observation about attrition offered by Stark (1992, p. 111).

   "Whereas, clients in community mental health treatment often show improvements even if they drop out after a few sessions, substance abusers do not manifest long term gain unless they participate in treatment episodes lasting at least several months."

   Stark goes on to suggest that efforts to reduce attrition and improve treatment retention should include:

   a)   more conveniently located smaller decentralized clinics;

   b)   higher clinical staff ratios;

   c)   more per capita expenditures;

   d)   clients should receive rapid initial response with continual reminders such as telephone calls and personal letters;

   e)   individual attention;

   f)   continuity of care;

   g)   use of smaller groups in friendly, comfortable environments.

Cognitive Behavioral Interventions

Given the challenging clinical picture, in terms of relapse and treatment nonattendance, what can be done? The following outline provides an overview of how I have addressed these issues in my consultation and workshops. I will convey some of the highlights in this section.

1. Assessment, motivational interviewing, building a therapeutic alliance, use of analogies and metaphors, use of behavioral contracts and therapy groups.

2. Identify treatment goals, high risk situations, look for early warning signs, prodromal therapy.

3. Self-monitor urges, coping responses and whether or not urges are followed by addictive acts.

4. Teach coping skills -- stress-inoculation training, problem-solving, relaxation skills, behavioral skills training (use instruction modeling, behavioral rehearsal, coaching, feedback) and leisure activity training.

5. Bolster self-efficacy -- have client rate degree of temptation experienced in high risk situations and ability to control such urges.

6. Use cognitive restructuring procedures.

7. Use relapse prevention models (imagery and behavioral rehearsal techniques). Use sobriety scripts and couples intervention. (See Rawson et al., 1993 and Ruzek et al., 1993 for a discussion of how various relapse prevention models can be used in substance abuse treatment.)

8. Use attribution retraining.

9. Use case manager and community care for "chronic" clients.

10. Employ booster sessions and follow-up procedures.

II. Developing a Therapeutic Alliance

Levy (1973) has highlighted the critical role of developing a therapeutic alliance with clients, especially in the case of dual diagnosis clients where denial may be an operative force. He notes that "insisting on abstinence before a therapeutic relationship has been developed is bound to fail" (p. 500). There is a need for the clinician to explore with clients the potential functions addictive behaviors serve for them. These may include:

a) giving the client a sense of identity;
b) provide the client with a peer group;
c) relieve troubled affective states and interpersonal conflicts;
d) ways of coping with distressing symptoms ("take the memories away") and reduce emotional pain (intrapersonal conflicts);
e) provide means of denying mental illness.

It is in the context of a therapeutic relationship that the client can trust enough to share his/her drug use, examine the consequences of drug use, establish goals or reasons to stop using. "Until a good reason to stop chemical use is established, the notion of stopping simply carries no purpose." (Levy, 1993, p. 501). Thus, the suggestion is to accept the clients "where they are at" and to find out what the clients want, what should the goal of treatment be, **"as stated by the client"**. Penk (1993) has suggested a useful beginning point is to explore the client's physical health and what can be done to enhance health. Once such goals are stated, once the clients are in touch with their "pain", then the therapist can help the clients draw a link between their drug use and how their chemical use interferes with their health and their lives. Fals-Stewart (1994) has used a medical analogy to help clients with alcohol problems appreciate the nature and impact of addictive behaviors. He helps his clients address the question, "What kind of disease is alcoholism?" In answering this question, the **disease of "hypertension" is offered as an analogy** whose occurrence is influenced by genetic and psychosocial factors. This multi-determined disorder can be treated by various different approaches, the choice of which depends on the nature and severity of the problem. Reframing chemical dependence within a hypertension model results in the "patients becoming less rigid about what they believe is the "right treatment" and the choice of intervention becomes a much more a **negotiated process** (p. 204). Levy's and Fals-Stewart's suggestions are consistent with the entire emphasis of this **Handbook**, on establishing a **collaborative working relationship**. Assessment and motivational interviewing procedures can be used to further nurture such collaboration.

III. Assessment and Motivational Interviewing *(See discussion of motivational nterviewing in Section III.)*

Any effort at intervention needs to begin with an examination of assessment issues (what drugs are taken, how often, what functions they serve). In Section III, I enumerated the variety of measures available to assess drinking behaviors and associated psychosocial correlates. It is suggested that any time a diagnosis of PTSD is being considered that a careful **sequential** assessment approach of addictive behaviors be included. The term **sequential** is highlighted because it is being suggested that interviewers begin with simple short-form assessments and then follow it with more detailed comprehensive measures. Moreover, the inclusion of psychosocial measures can be used as a means of providing feedback to clients (e.g., self-efficacy measures, social support measures, etc.).

By now it should be apparent that from a cognitive-behavioral perspective assessment and treatment are highly interconnected (see description below). This is most clearly indicated in the **motivational interviewing** procedures described by Miller and Rollnick (1991). Since motivation to change is a critical feature of intervention there is a need to enhance the client's awareness that there is a "problem", without being confrontational, which might lead to psychological reactance. The motivational interviewing attempts to move clients through several stages of readiness to change, namely, an initial commitment to change, to getting started, to keeping changes they have made. The following illustrative questions and interviewing procedures convey the **collaborative manner of such motivational interviewing**.

Initial Interview - Using Motivational Interviewing Procedures

Miller and Rollnick (1991) in describing motivational interviewing offer the following 5 general principles as general guidelines.

1. Express empathy
2. Develop discrepancy
3. Avoid argumentation
4. Roll with resistance
5. Support self-efficacy

The following illustrate some specific examples of these principles. Note that these general guidelines provide a useful **collaborative approach** for all counseling, not only with clients who have problems with addiction problems.

"What things have you noticed about your drinking that concern you, or that you think might become problems?"

In response to the client's answer the therapist might reply:
   "I can see how that might concern you."
   "It must be difficult for you to be realizing that."

"What else have you noticed?"

"What makes you think you should do something about your drinking?" *(Help place responsibility on the client for seeing the need for treatment.)*

"Is that all? Anything else?"

Use mildly paradoxical procedures, judiciously. For example, the therapist may comment that:

"This program is one that requires a lot of individual motivation, and frankly one concern that I have in talking to you is that I am not sure whether you really have enough motivation." *(Such comments encourage the client to take responsibility for the positive side of the argument.)*

If the client conveys denial, for example,
   "My problem isn't so bad because ..."
   "I can't be an alcoholic because ..."
   "I can control my drinking sometimes."
   "I don't lose control when I drink."
then the therapist can acknowledge the client's comments, but then refocus attention and nurture dissonance.

For example:
   "I imagine that's confusing for you. On the one hand you can see there are serious problems developing around alcohol use, but on the other hand it seems like the label 'alcoholic' doesn't quite fit because things don't look that bad."

This approach adopts a "Columbo" non-confrontational inquiry style that was described in Section III. The therapist goes public with the data and uses being perplexed as a means of putting the client in a helper role.

Another means of employing a collaborative assessment approach has been suggested by Horvath (1994). He proposes that the therapist conduct a **cost-benefits analysis** with the client when assessing addictive behavior. Only after a thorough assessment of the benefits ("What do you like about drinking?") does the therapist shift to a consideration of the costs ("What problems has drinking caused?") For instance, Horvath (1994, p. 100-101) uses the following introduction to tap the costs of addictive behavior.

   "We've been talking about what you like about drinking. If you think we have pretty much covered that topic, then I'm also curious about whether there are some things you don't like about drinking: whether it's caused any problems for you. As you know, just about everything in life has pros and cons to it, and I'm curious now about the cons."

The **cost-benefits analysis** also considers how the addictive behavior helps the client cope, as well considers any uncharacteristic behaviors that the client may have noticed arising from his/her addictive behavior. The client, with the help of the therapist can then consider the conclusions that he/she might draw after comparing the costs and benefits.

In addition, to a consideration of a cost-benefit analysis there is a need to assess the client's expectations. As noted in the Assessment of Alcohol Behavior (Section III), a critical feature to assess is the client's expectations concerning the impact of alcohol. The client's performance on Alcohol Expectancy Scales and related measures can be examined collaboratively with the client. As Goldman (1994) observes, the "assessment of expectancies may serve as one 'window' for judging the risk for relapse" (p.140). Based on such assessments, a multi-component intervention program can be developed including ongoing monitoring of urges, expectancy analysis, skills training to deal with high risk situations, spouse involvement, and relapse prevention plans, as described below. Note that the assessment process is the initial step in the intervention program. Thus, a critical feature of the therapeutic process is providing feedback based on the assessment.

Provide Feedback on Assessment Measures

1. Help the client understand his or her situation.

    Provide the client with feedback about their drinking patterns, risks, and beliefs about alcohol effects. Suggestions for risk reduction are offered (see Marlatt et al., 1994). Horvath (1994) suggests that the client and therapist generate a problem list during the initial assessment. The therapist can note that not all problems on the list need to be addressed at this point or stage of treatment, but it is helpful to generate the list in order to monitor progress. As Horvath (1994), p. 102) comments to the client:

    > "This is not an issue you are interested in addressing right now, but I am concerned that it may complicate our other work. I want to put it on the problem list, so we don't lose sight of it. This is like your family doctor making a note about a mole you have; it's not something you want to take care of right now, but we need to check on it from time to time."

2. Convey choice and empowerment to the client by including comments that allow him/her to accept or reject findings. For example,

    > "I do not know whether this is of any concern."
    > "This may or may not matter to you."

3. Ask, "What do you make of all this?

4. Summarize.

    > "Let me see if I can put together everything that we have talked about so far. You have expressed a lot of concerns to me, and I respect you for that. Let me try to put these all together so we can see where we go from here."
    > "Is my summary complete? Is there anything I have missed?"

    The therapist should include positive motivational statements as well as any doubts that the client has mentioned in the summary.

5. Therapist can also include the description of Prochaska and DiClemente's stage model of change (precontemplation, contemplation, action, maintenance stages). *(See Section III on assessment of alcoholism.)* The therapist can help the client explore where the client is operating in terms of the various stages of motivation to change. Explore and negotiate with the client where to begin the process of behavior change.

6. In a subsequent session consider alternatives with the client:

    a) Ask the client to consider anticipating what would occur if his/her drinking continued unchanged.

    b) Ask the client what he or she <u>believes should be done</u>? (Client has indicated that there is a problem, the focus now shifts to what to do about it.)

    c) The therapist can suggest additional alternatives.

7. Ask the client if he or she has any questions of the therapist.

<u>Address Concerns about Abstinence Attempts</u> -- consider the following questions from Amodeo and Kurtz, 1990. (Also see Meichenbaum and Fong, 1993, for a discussion of the variety of reasons clients offer for not complying with treatment recommendations and for not abstaining. The nature of the reasons offered has implications for the treatment interventions to be followed.)

"Describe your life just before you stopped drinking in terms of how it affected the various aspects of your life.

Describe the circumstances (or precipitants) of the last drinking episode.

Why and how did you stop?

Was there anything that made this last time different from other drinking episodes?

What circumstances (thoughts, feelings, significant persons and events) contributed to your stopping? (Review one at a time with the client.)

Can you recall a specific decision you made, or an awareness that you had come to, that you would remain abstinent (stop drinking) over the long term, or that you would try to never drink again?

Did such a decision or awareness occur at a specific point or emerge gradually over time?

Why do you feel this attempt at abstinence was effective?

How was this attempt different from other attempts to stop?

Have you experienced serious temptations to drink since the initiation of your stopping?"

Also see A.M. Ludwig (1988) (<u>Understanding the alcoholic mind: The nature of craving and how to control it</u>. New York: Oxford University Press) for a discussion of the various ways alcoholics offer answers to questions about their drinking behavior. Amodeo and Kurtz (1990) have provided a useful summary of these answers as well (as noted on the next page). The therapist can review these "reasons" with the client in order to enhance his/her motivation to change by engaging in more "change-engendering" attributions.

The types of answers that patients are likely to offer when discussing abstinence episodes
have been described by Amodeo and Kurtz (1990)

Precipitants to Abstinence

Reached Personal Bottom
Threat of Death
Physical Incapacitation
Spiritual Experience
Placating Others

Reasons to Maintain Abstinence

Felt supported by family and friends
Knew I would lose my family
Lost the urge or desire
Totally made up my mind to stop/wanted desperately to stop
Spiritual experience/divine intervention
Saw deteriorated alcoholics -- negative power of examples
Fear brain damage
Fear of dying
Self-esteem -- I knew I was capable of more
Physical aversion, felt allergic to alcohol
Fear of job loss

Temptations to Drink

Stressful event (e.g., interpersonal conflict)
Dysphoric state (depressed, bored)
Social event with much drinking (social pressure)
No particular trigger

How to Handle Temptations

Return to treatment
Talk it over with friends and family
Remove self from the situation
Prayer
Concentrate so remove urge from my mind
Contrast manageable temptations from situations that are likely to precipitate relapse
         (serious temptation versus close call)

Attribution Retraining

The therapist needs to be sensitive to the patient's attributions that are offered to explain lapses and
         relapse. Listen for attributions that are "internal, stable, and global" such as the lack of
         willpower, internal guilt, conflict, power of urges" -- help the client shift away from
         characterological and biological explanations to situational and behavioral attributions.

Also insure that the client "takes credit" for successes. Help the clients attribute success to their
         motivation, persistence, insight, strength, desire to change, and to new found abilities to
         "notice, catch, interrupt, use game plan, etc." Clients are encouraged to take responsibility
         for having accomplished change. (See Section VI on problem-solving for a discussion of
         other self-regulatory skills that clients can be encouraged to employ.)

IV. The Use of Metaphors

Consistent with the constructive narrative perspective offered in Section II, therapists working with clients who have problems with addictive behaviors often use metaphors to describe the change process. The following list of metaphors provide a "menu" of options that can be selectively sampled, individually tailored, and judiciously employed by the therapist. Each metaphor is designed to help clients reframe their drinking behavior and their motivation to change. The art of using such metaphors is not only to offer the metaphor, but to use it as a scheme to explore the implications for change.

See Miller, Marlatt & Fromme; Marlatt & Gordon; Wallace, Padesky, Meichenbaum & Turk; Ludwig, Romig & Gruenke, for a discussion of possible metaphors that can be used in the treatment of clients with addictions. The following list comes from these authors. The therapist can use these metaphors to make specific points or to help the client engage in a discovery process. For instance, the client's addictive behavior may be compared to a form of "self-medication", and a relapse prevention plan may be compared to a "personal journey". The following list provides multiple examples of possible metaphors.

Type of metaphor	Function
1. Self-medication	- patient has been own doctor, own therapist/coach *(using alcohol as a form of treatment)*
2. Porcelain vase	- how protect a precious vase - how protect self *(what would one do to protect a vase? apply these same principles to protect self)*
3. Duffel bag	- stuff painful feelings, carry with them, albatross *(explore what is impact, toll and price of doing this)*
4. Bucket of water	- heal self, how difficult the task depends on how many buckets carried
5. Being 31 at age 13 -- "child within"	- dysfunctional families, premature parenting, now act like rebellious adolescent
6. Water faucet	- turn on and off anger, fear, pain, "as if" emotions were a water faucet
7. Back of mind tell "little white lies"	- encourage client to ask, "What's in the back of his/her mind?"
8. Balloon	- overinflated, all puffed up, king of the hill - lose air -- deflated, rather develop a balance of self-esteem *(explore what the advantages are of a more balanced approach)*
9. Looking good syndrome	- hiding problems
10. Slip versus a fall	- icy pavement example - "beat up" on self leads to depression, anxiety, anger, leads to self-medication

11. Set self up for failure
- discuss immediate gratification and cognitive distortions that set one up for lapse

12. Gate/gatekeeper
- if client uses the phrase "gate" then the therapist can suggest that there must be a "gatekeeper" *(note that the gatekeeper can engage in a number of problem-solving efforts -- notice, decide, etc.)*

13. Prejudice
- know someone who is prejudice about self
- totalitarian frame of mind *(see discussion of this metaphor in Section VI on cognitive restructuring)*

14. Need a plumber? a mechanic? where do you go?
- choose help carefully

15. Fail inspection -- drive red corvette, lacks muffler but it looks good on outside
- discuss different forms of social support *(discuss how to decide who is going to be a good helper)*

16. Not judge book by cover
- discuss how people cover up feelings

17. Explain craving; game plan
- normal, expected
- discuss impact of anniversary dates
- talk honestly about cravings with patient

18. Fire-extinguisher
- prevent or put out small fires
- ounce of prevention worth pound of cure

19. Battle plan in war on addiction
- "We are giving you tools, a shield, a sword, to use in battle when you return to the war on addiction."
- concept of being prepared

20. Back-injury metaphor
- imagine recovery processes as someone who is vulnerable to reinjury or pain
- compare hanging around drinking spots or carrying large amount of money for drug user is like carrying a heavy suitcase after leaving the hospital with a back-injury
- encourage attempts at easy tests before undertaking hard tests

21. Regain trust from others, gradually
- gradual process
- anticipate ambivalence from significant others

22. Shoot self in the foot
- describe self-destructive behaviors

23. Imagining X-ray machine
- imagine being able to watch your brain as it makes a decision; what would you see *(describe the process of the "mental steps")*

24. Delicate task of balancing (convey concept of the client restoring balance -- use teeter-totter, scale, or thermostat)
- therapist's job is to place weights on positive change-seeking side of scales and gently remove weights and obstructions from negative change-avoiding side of the balance

25. Electrical circuitry
- dissonance sends a voltage through system, require channeling, use resistors and capacitors to solidly ground terminal solution
- "Obviously Healthy Motivation" or "Ohms" (Miller, 1983) *(use metaphor only with someone familiar with electricity)*

26. Check-up -- become own "maintenance" man
- describe the role of booster and follow-up sessions

27. Learn to drive standard shift car in England (wrong side of road)
- trial and error learning
- unlearn old habits
- with each error learn something new
- allow for errors (lapses)

28. Lapse is a fork in the road (not want the lapse to "snowball" into a relapse)
- notion of choice

29. I "owe" myself a drink
- highlight how client talks to himself/herself

30. Taking drugs is like driving a car (or any relevant skill) such as learning to ride a bike (first need training wheels), or teaching a child to walk (safe-proof environment)
- use analogy of learning any skill with accompanying slips, errors, etc.

31. Describe urges or cravings as an ocean wave
- a wave that arises, crests and subsides as it washes up on shore; client views self as surfer, acquires skills of balance and rides wave gracefully without being wiped out in the process
- also Samurai warrior constantly on guard against threats

32. Convey stories (imaginary other) about how others have overcome problem

33. Blueprint for change
- game plan idea

34. Lapse is an error that one can benefit from. The therapist can ask, "when does one learn most?" -- often when one fails
- learn to ride bike, experiment not work

35. Tell the story of the man who tried to train a snake (see Marlatt & Fromme, 1988)
- he kept lid on ("external willpower"); when he opened the lid, snake bit him (not be tempted)

* 36. Journey metaphor (Marlatt & Gordon, 1985) -- one of the more effective metaphors
- Discuss with the client what trips he/she may have taken; what are the different phases to the journey. Allow the client to generate the different steps. Four important stages to any journey: a)

preparation, b) departure, c) the trip itself, d) reflecting on the journey
- <u>preparation</u> involves activities such as picking a destination or goal, finding suitable vehicle, locate map
- some may postpone or delay the trip, some ambivalent
- premature departure may lead to setbacks (move from "Tobacco Road to Freedom Mountain")
- some may take several tries to succeed, zig zag journey of change
- every successful period of recovery begins with the end of the last lapse (prolapse or fall forward as compared to back-sliding which is relapse)
- journey filled with warning signals, detours, crossroads, and slippery curves
- in any journey there are long-term (distal) goals -- in this case abstinence; first have short-term or proximal goals; review map and prepare route prior to leaving on the journey

37. Use myths

- Midas and Bacchus (Dionysus) the god of wine
- Daedalas and Icarus
- Pandora's Box
- make sure client knows the story and its purpose or symbolic meaning

V. Use of Contracts

Another means of increasing the client's motivation and commitment to change is to use some form of **behavioral contract**. In Meichenbaum and Turk (1987) and in Miller (1990) there are explicit discussions on how to collaboratively formulate and use contracts. At this point, I will only enumerate the major features of such a contract

Contract-elements include:

1. A clear statement of purpose.

2. A statement of concrete achievable goals.

3. Description of mutual responsibilities.

4. Procedures for modifying the contract.

5. Conditions that will lead to the discontinuance of services.

6. A statement of means to be used to achieve goals.

VI. Treatment Interventions: Relapse Prevention Procedures[1]

A marked variety of treatment approaches have been offered to clients with addiction problems ranging from abstinence to controlled drinking, from relapse prevention to harm reduction (see Marlatt et al., 1993; Miller & Hester, 1980; Peele, 1989, 1991; Rawson et al., 1993). As De Jong (1994) has observed, the treatment objectives are to help clients:

(a)   sustain their own recovery by learning self-management skills, ways to cope with drug cravings and ways to handle social pressures to use drugs;

(b)   become integrated into a new drug-free social network;

(c)   find new ways of responding to emotional stress and physical pain.

(d)   To be added to this list as treatment objectives is the notion of **harm reduction** or **harm minimization** as a gradual step-down approach to reduce harmful consequences. Marlatt et al. (1993, p. 496) observe:

> "Harm-reduction methods are based on the assumption that habits can be placed along a continuum ranging from beneficial to harmful consequences."

The goal of harm-reduction is to help the individual with addictive problems "to begin to take steps in the right direction to reduce harmful consequences." While abstinence may be an ideal, treatment is designed to promote any movement in this direction, even if abstinence is not attained. To illustrate their point, Marlatt et al. cite Mark Twain

> "Habit is habit and not to be flung out of the window by any man, but coaxed downstairs one step at a time."

The cognitive-behavioral treatment approach, as proposed by De Jong (1994), Marlatt et al. (1994), Gordon (1985), McAuliffe and Chien (1980), Ruzek et al. (1993), and Sandez-Craig and Wilkinson (1987), teach clients how to:

(a)   **self-monitor and establish goals**

(b)   **identify cues that trigger relapse** (e.g., emotions such as negative feelings, feelings of boredom; thoughts such as negative self-statements, preoccupations with drugs, a belief that drugs or alcohol are needed to have fun, and behaviors that accompanied previous drug use).

(c)   identify and practice procedures to **avoid high-risk situations**

(d)   **cope with unavoidable high-risk situations** by such means as leaving the situation, using relaxation skills, repeating motivational statements, writing down thoughts and feelings in a journal, calling someone such as a sponsor, therapist, support person, reviewing reasons for quitting, reflecting on progress made to date,

---

[1] Moreover, in considering treatment outcome with alcoholics I am reminded of the observation reported by Miller (1993). "The secret of being a successful alcoholism treatment center is being the place where people come when they finally decide to stop drinking." (p.1479) The controversy and efficasy concerning **"controlled drinking"** interventions will not be reviewed in this manual. Since many alcoholics express a preference for such a "controlled drinking" treatment alternative, the reader should look at the fine article by Marlatt et al. (1993) on "Harm reduction for alcohol problems: Moving beyong the controlled drinking controversy" (Behavior Therapy, 24, 461-504).

using positive mental imagery, using reminder cards, and throwing away drug paraphernalia

(e)   **manage lapses** by warning clients that lapses are possible without implying that they are inevitable, educating clients that they have to take "slips" seriously

(f)   **enlist social supports** by taking an active role in securing and maintaining beneficial social supports (e.g., use family-oriented therapy, family support groups, and family education). (See the discussion below and relapse prevention training with couples.)

(g)   **establish new social relationships** (e.g., use "buddy" system, self-help groups, social skills training plus being paired with a drug-free volunteer, and the introduction to new drug-free social networks)

(h)   **engage in lifestyle changes** that involve new interests, activities, and productive roles in the community (e.g., remedial education, job training, life-skills training, healthy recreational activities). Marlatt and Gordon (1985) highlight the need to train clients to learn to manage negative emotional states due to stress, disappointment, and interpersonal conflicts. They also stress the need for clients to establish a favorable ratio between obligations (the things they feel the "should" do) and enjoyable activities (the things they feel they "want" to do). If there are too many "shoulds" in one's life then the client may feel deprived and feel that only satisfying feelings of craving by abusing drugs will help.

As DeJong observes, key elements of these relapse prevention intervention programs include:

(a)   the mix of educational and motivational features

(b)   the use of group meetings and group sponsored social activities and community service projects

(c)   the emphasis placed on developing and implementing concrete individualized action plans

(d)   the use of adjunctive procedures when indicated (e.g., pharmacotherapies, twelve step programs)

(e)   the emphasis on learning how to cope with "slips". Namely, learning how to take immediate action if a "slip" should occur including the stopping of drug intake, removing oneself from the situation, calling someone for support, employing one's action plan, analyzing what happened and what he/she can lean from the lapse experience, and recommitting to abstinence and recovery.

A useful means to accomplish these objectives is have clients develop **sobriety scripts**. In order to help clients to anticipate high risk temptation situations and to reduce the likelihood that lapses will escalate into full blown relapses, Ruzek et al. (1993) have used group treatments and what they called the **sobriety script**. In order to teach clients to "think through the drink" each client is asked to put together in written form a carefully prepared, personalized script of self-statements that can be used by individuals in recovery to talk themselves through temptations and to initiate active coping. In the script clients are asked to:

a)   identify their most important reasons for abstaining;

b) enumerate the benefits gained from sobriety;

c) describe where and how they will use specific coping actions to deal with high risk situations and lapses ("I am going to leave this situation and find some of my sober buddies");

d) describe how to deal with "cognitive and affective slips" (e.g., "No one understands me or what I went through", "Once an alcoholic, always an alcoholic", "It is an addictive disease, there is nothing I can do".) Remind clients of the myopic effects of alcohol.

e) describe powerful and personal negative consequences of past and future use of alcohol;

f) describe some personal benefits already gained from sobriety;

g) include statements of personal commitment to change ("I decided to stay clean and sober this time and I'm damn well going to stick to my decision", "It's my choice", "I am in control")

Clients are asked to say and practice these personalized scripts in front of the groups, eventually from memory. The therapist can help the group to eventually "challenge" the client of when, where, how and why the client will use this "sobriety script". What may get in the way of its use and effectiveness? In this way a paradoxical challenge can be used, for example, "Come on, are you telling us, are you saying to yourself that when you are with all your drinking buddies and your feeling lonely, and experiencing triggers of your trauma experience, you are going to produce and follow your script? How are you going to do that? Why would you pass up the chance to just hang one on?" By having clients provide the reasons for treatment adherence, especially to the whole group, this increases the likelihood of the client following through. (See Beck et al. (1993), Fromme et al. (1994), for additional examples of how cognitive-behavioral interventions have been employed in treating Harvath (1994) clients with substance abuse.) Their suggestions include:

(1) conducting cost-benefit analysis

(2) assigning the client to self-monitor addictive behavior and also "cravings" or "urges" -- their frequency, intensity and duration

(3) developing alternative behaviors and activities including activity scheduling

(4) suggesting a brief trial of abstinence or moderation

(5) encouraging support group attendance

(6) involving family participation

(7) teaching alternative ways to cope, use social problem solving and cognitive restructuring procedures

(8) engaging in relapse prevention training including script writing and imaginal and behavioral rehearsal.

O'Farrell et al. (1993) have explored the usefulness of **relapse prevention with couples**.[1] Building on prior work on marital family therapy with alcoholics (see O'Farrell, 1989, 1994) they found that:

a) working with nonalcoholic family members can motivate an initial commitment to change in the alcoholic;

b) that marital therapy can stabilize relationships that can support improvement both during and after treatment (i.e., outcome is better when the spouse is involved);

c) couples therapy should combine a focus on drinking with an instigation of positive couples and family activities, as well as teaching communication and conflict resolution skills; and,

d) adding marital therapy to individual alcoholism counseling enhanced outcome.

The value of including the spouse in treatment is highlighted by O'Farrell et al. (1993) who reported that "events in the marriage and factors involving the spouse were reasons most frequently cited by alcoholics as the cause of relapse" (p.653).

Following the suggestions of McCrady (1989), Marlatt & Gordon (1985), and Whisman (1990), O'Farrell et al. (1993) developed a couples' relapse prevention (RP) treatment package. It consisted of fifteen 50-75 minute maintenance sessions which were spread out over 12 months: (specifically every 2 weeks for the first 3 months, then every 3 weeks for the next 2 months, and every 4 weeks for the next 3 months, and every 6 weeks for the last 3 months). In addition, crisis sessions were used as needed. The focus of these sessions was to develop and rehearse individually tailored **relapse prevention (RP) plans**. Based on prior individual (6 to 8 weekly sessions) and 10 weekly group couples sessions, an individually tailored RP plan was formulated. It may include following an Antabuse contract in which the alcoholic client takes Antabuse each day while the spouse observes, the use of specific skills that were taught in group sessions (communication, conflict resolution), attending AA meetings if the participants chose this option, and other interpersonal recreational activities.

A 22-item Couples Behavior Questionnaire was administered throughout treatment in order to monitor treatment adherence. In addition, the RP plan included identifying high-risk situations and early warning signs for relapse, and planning how to deal with any drinking that might occur.

O'Farrell et al. (1994) note that those who dropped out of treatment tended to be younger, have an earlier onset of alcoholism, be more violent, and have a history of arrests and job losses. (Moreover, clients who had serious concurrent psychopathology or drug abuse were not included in the O'Farrell et al., 1994 study.) They found that providing an intensive, multifaceted, maintenance intervention program over a relatively prolonged period (12 months) was the most effective treatment. **The inclusion of RP training is central to all forms of cognitive-behavioral interventions.**

Another way to use multiple group interventions with a PTSD substance abuse disorder unit has been offered by Aboytes (1993). He highlights the need to tap the veteran's pre-military history, to address war trauma, to teach relapse prevention skills such as identifying warning signs or "red flags", and coping skills designed to handle tempting situations ("What if you did something different other than drinking? How would you do it?"), drink refusal skills and

---

[1] A report on marital and family therapy in alcoholism treatment and a Leader's Manual are available from T. O'Farrell, Alcohol and Family Studies Laboratory, VA Medical Center (116B), 940 Belmont Street, Brockton, Mass. 02401.

problem-solving, decision making skills. ("I can make it better or I can make it worse. I can make a conscious decision"). The involvement of significant other (spouse) in identifying the interpersonal scripts that contribute to alcohol intake can also prove helpful.

A somewhat different approach toward the treatment of clients with alcohol and drug problems has been offered by Berg and Muller (1992) and Muller (1994). They adopt a **solution-focused approach** that uses the "art of questioning" in order to help clients "mobilize" the motivation and skills to develop control. They propose the use of 4 types of questions as a means of intervention. These include:

(1)   Outcome questions

(2)   Instance/exception questions

(3)   Scaling questions

(4)   Endurance and/or externalization questions

I will try to convey the flavor of this approach by including illustrative type questions (See Miller, 1994 for details).

Outcome Questions -- these questions ask clients what will be different when the problems that brought them into treatment have been successfully resolved.

They often include the "miracle" question -- namely, if a "miracle" came and your problem was solved, what would change?

Expectation questions -- What would you realistically expect to happen 6 months ("minimally different", "smallest sign", "first sign", "doing instead", "others see" that would tell you that our work here has been successful? What do you know about yourself that would lead you to believe that this could happen?

Suppose for a moment that our work here together was successful, what will be different in your life?

What would have to be different in your life that would tell you that coming here was a good idea?

Distance/Exception Questions -- follow outcome questions and focuses when desirable behavior is already occurring.

When was the last time X occurred? When did you already do X? When does the problem not occur? Who noticed X? What did he/she say about this? How did it happen? What do you need to do make it occur more often?

Scaling Questions -- use client-determined rating system for assessing progress and goals.

On a scale of 1 to 10, where 10 is day after the "miracle" when the problem that brought you here is gone, and 1 is the worst situation, where are things now?

What will be different when you move up (or down) scale? What would it take for you to move from your present rating of 4 to say a rating of 6?

Endurance/Externalization Questions -- questions designed to elicit how the client was able to cope; endure, overcome problems.

Given X (strong urges, cravings, stressful events) how manage ... fight off ... overcome ... kept things from becoming worse ... find strength?

This approach focuses on what the client was doing to be successful prior to the setback and how he/she managed to overcome the lapse or setback once it did occur. For example, Miller (1994), p. 102) suggests the following type questions be used:

How will you be successful in dealing with X prior to the setback?

How did you manage to be successful so long?

What would others say you were doing to be successful?

What have you learned from this episode that you will use in the future?

Finally, it should be noted that alcohol and drugs represent frequent avoidance measures used by clients with PTSD to reduce intrusive thoughts and painful effects of memories. Once substance abuse is reduced, there may be a reemergence of traumatic memories (Penk, 1993). The client and therapist should anticipate this possibility and "normalize" such reactions should they occur. In fact, the client may come to view such reemergence of PTSD symptoms as a "sign of progress" (i.e., now beginning to gain control of addictive behavior). In turn, the client can consider what are the things he/she did to control drinking behaviors that he/she can use in the control of "triggers", intrusive thoughts and emotional aftermath. Thus, there is a need for careful systematic monitoring throughout treatment.

The treatment of dual diagnosis (PTSD and alcohol abuse) should begin with abstinence training. In summary, the treatment of the comorbidity problem of addictive behavior is critically important, but it can be a complicated and demanding intervention. The challenge is greater when the alcohol abuse has been long-term, with possible accompanying cognitive impairment.

Space does not permit a more detailed description of these diverse treatment procedures, but a useful summary of this literature has been offered by Hollon and Beck (1993). They also observe that while there is encouraging data for the cognitive behavioral relapse prevention treatment model, there is also an important role for pharmacological interventions (see O'Malley et al., 1992; Jaffe et al., 1992; and Volpicelli et al., 1992).

These clinical observations apply to mainly outpatient clients. As I noted, I have been asked to consult on possible treatment procedures for inpatient dual diagnosis clients who have a chronic history of PTSD and addictive behaviors. My reading of the literature and clinical experience has suggested that a **case manager treatment approach** that emphasizes **continuity of care** and **in vivo advocacy across various settings for clients** is the most promising approach (Hunt & Azrin, 1973; Mallams et al., 1982; Miller & Hester, 1986; Sisson & Azrin, 1989; Sullivan et al., 1992). A key feature of these community-oriented treatment approaches is for the **case manager not to "advocate for" the client, but to "advocate with" the client,** sharing responsibility, relinquishing ownership, and nurturing problem-solving skills and feelings of self-efficacy in clients. The following list describes the wide range of activities and functions of case managers. An examination of these activities indicate that an **ecologically-based treatment approach** that addresses each of the "social niches" that the client encounters is often required.

Case Manager Community Approach -- Monitor After Discharge

Need to address post discharge factors that influence both abstinence and adjustment. These include:

1. employment
2. residential stability
3. family functioning/cohesion
4. use of leisure time
5. as well as, drinking behaviors

Functions of case manager

1. Assessment

2. Case formulation

3. Continuity of care -- "human link" with the treatment program

4. Procure and orchestrate services (help patient move through the system)

5. "Advocate with" and act as friendly advisor

6. Track and evaluate

7. Provide daily contact with client's potential employer, recreation leader, treatment staff, family member (can fade or "scaffold" support)

8. Arrange for booster sessions and follow-up

The treatment program described by Seidel et al. (1994, Psychotherapy, 31, 67-78) illustrates how cognitive-behavioral techniques, relapse prevention procedures, and an inpatient-outpatient program can be developed for dual diagnosed (PTSD + addictive behaviors) Vietnam veterans. Also see Abueg, F.R., & Kriegler, J.A. (1988). Eight session treatment manual for relapse prevention training in PTSD/alcoholics. (Available from National Center for PTSD, Dept. Veterans Affairs Medical Center, Palo Alto, CA, 94304). This relapse prevention program thoughtfully includes PTSD symptoms and "set-up events" such as isolation and reminders such as anniversary dates as high-risk triggers in learning coping skills. In summary, the present section highlights the need for a comprehensive multifaceted treatment approach.

FAMILY-BASED INTERVENTIONS

The epidemiological data reviewed in Section I indicated that the presence of PTSD in one family member can perpetuate and exacerbate a dysfunctional family system, as well as engender stress in nondysfunctional family members. As noted, families with PTSD Vietnam veterans, had more marital and parenting problems, wives who were less happy and less satisfied than did families of non-PTSD veterans (Figley, 1994). This was replicated in families of Israeli soldiers with PTSD. As Solomon (1994) observed, there is a **strong association between the level of family dysfunction and chronicity of PTSD**. In short, families are likely to be significantly affected by traumatic events. Their reactions may inadvertently help to maintain the PTSD condition. For example, Ford et al. (1993) propose a transactional model where PTSD in one family member can engender marital discord and familial distress with resultant emotional and interpersonal distancing as the PTSD member may "shutdown" (engage in avoidance behavior and emotional numbing). This leads to further familial reactions that inadvertently contribute to progressive deterioration and chronicity. In addition to these dyadic stressors, traumatic events like natural disasters, accidents and violent events can cause additional undue stressors and maladaptive coping responses (e.g., an increased use of alcohol). As discussed in the next section on post-disaster interventions, traumatic events can cause significant losses of resources that contribute to and exacerbate stress. There is a clear need to **explore** trauma-related distress **among all family members** whether their exposure was direct or indirect and there is a need to **debrief** family members. There is also a need to assess and mobilize **the family into playing a role in the recovery process**. Charles Figley (1988), who is a pioneer in helping families with trauma, has noted that family members can promote recovery by:

(1) **detecting signs of traumatic stress** given their feel for the normative behavior of fellow family members (e.g., note changes in characteristic patterns of behavior);

(2) **confronting the trauma** by pointing out a connection, directly or indirectly, between reactions and traumatic events;

(3) **urging and facilitating recapitulation or reevaluation of the trauma** by reviewing and reconsidering the circumstances of the traumatic event and the attached meanings. According to Figley, the recapitulation process covers such questions as:

   i)   "What happened?

   ii) Why did it happen?

   iii) Why did I and others act as we did, then (during) and since the ordeal?

   iv) If something like this happens again, how will we be able to cope more effectively?"

(4) **facilitating resolution of the conflicts** by helping the family reframe or offer alternative ways of viewing the highly stressful event and event-related consequences in a more positive or optimistic fashion. In this way the family develops a "healing theory" or a new perspective through which to view the situation. The therapist may help the family remember[1] (share stories about) past familial struggles and achievements, correct distortions, nurture more "generous" perspectives of events and reactions, clarify insights and discoveries about family members' strengths, accept

---

[1] Herman (1992) describes how Yael Danieli in her group work with survivors of the Nazi Holocaust assigns each family member the task of reconstructing a "family tree" as a way to help the survivors to reflect and share the past in a structured controlled fashion.

feelings, effectively manage memories, find meaning, memorialize both events and individuals, develop a more optimistic vision of improved coping if a similar event were to recur. The therapist helps the family "work through" conflicts raised by memories of traumatic events and develop a more positive view of improved coping if similar events were to happen again.

In order to accomplish these therapeutic goals a number of different models have been proposed. Charles Figley (1988, 1994), who is one of the leaders in this approach, has offered a **5 phase family-based treatment approach.** These phases include:

1. **Building commitment** to the therapeutic objectives -- develop a therapeutic alliance of rapport and trust; establish the therapist's role as a consultant, facilitator, helper, and guide;

2. **Framing the problem** -- allow family members to tell their stories, exchange information, "assemble the pieces of the puzzle", assess the family's response patterns to trauma, identify the attempted solutions, formulate treatment goals;

3. **Reframing the problem** -- develop, implement and evaluate the treatment plan, including family supportiveness skills (viz., communication, problem-solving and conflict resolution); ensure that family members have an opportunity to report how others effectively encourage, advise, help, and support;

4. **Developing a consensus view or a "healing theory"** that "fits" for them -- recapitulate experiences and feelings in as much detail as possible; each member tells how he/she experienced the traumatic event and its aftermath and develop a new perspective;

5. Closure and preparedness for future difficulties -- namely, what was overcome and learned from the ordeal, "make peace with the past" and be prepared to face current and future challenges; nurture the family's feeling of "being stronger" as a result of facing the traumatic events.

As part of framing the problem, Figley (1988) suggests the use of a **"round table testimonial"**, whereby each family member has an opportunity to talk briefly (5 to 8 minutes) about "what the traumatic event means to him/her as a person and how his/her life has been disrupted". (In short, each person discusses what happened and what it had meant to him/her.) Ensure that the testimonials are given in a positive fashion and do not lapse into a "blaming" session. The therapist focuses on the participant's feelings by asking, "And how did that make you feel?"

This round table discussion moves into a consideration of a "healing theory" -- reframing of the problem (discuss what happened, why each family member behaved as he/she did during and following the event), and moving toward an optimistic scenario of what could happen if stressful events should occur in the future.

The success of these family sessions may be mitigated by the "pile-up" of demands and the "backlog" of problems that the family had before the present stressful event (e.g., prior strains, family conflicts, etc.) (See McCubbin & Patterson, 1983; Lavee & Ben-David, 1993.)

Harris (1991) provides a further framework to consider how family processes can be employed. The key elements include:

1)   Establishing psychological contact with the family

2)   Exploring the dimensions of the family's problems where all family members are provided an opportunity to describe their perceptions and reactions

3)   Examine possible solutions in terms of what has been tried so far and what can be done with the family's help

4)   Assist in taking concrete action

5)   Provide follow-up

In implementing these steps, it is important to keep in mind that "dysfunctional" families may evidence constricted intimacy and restricted expressiveness, overt hostility and unpredictable verbal and physical aggressiveness, with a history of recurrent crises. In spite of these barriers, there is a need to focus on what "strengths", what hurdles and barriers, the family has overcome. *(See potential questions a therapist can use, as noted in Section III.)* The problem-solving questions and techniques described in this Section can also be employed.

TEST YOUR EXPERTISE

Section VI - Treatment Procedures

1. a) What are the critical elements to include when educating clients and their family members about PTSD?

    b) Role play how you would educate clients about PTSD, without being didactic.

2. Tape record a session in which you are educating a client about PTSD or some other aspect of treatment (e.g., flashbacks, intrusive thoughts, etc). Now compare how you went about this educational process versus the guidelines included in this Section.

3. Indicate the procedural steps you would follow in treating clients with flashbacks. how would you
    a) educate the client about flashbacks
    b) strengthen their coping skills (e.g., identify triggers, "get grounded", cope more effectively)
    c) help the client change or reappraise his/her memories

    Role play the treatment steps you would use. Tape record a session and compare it to the enclosed procedural checklist.

4. A colleague is going to attend a conference on multiple personality disorder (MPD). He knows you have demonstrated the "perspicacity" of reading the **Handbook/Manual on PTSD**. He/She asks you to help him answer the following questions before he attends.

    a) How explicit are the diagnostic criteria for MPD?
    b) How do we assess MPD and how valid are the self-report scales?
    c) What are the iatrogenic (therapist induced) dangers of the assessment and treatment procedures?
    d) What are the specific dangers in calling forth and working with the "alters" in treatment?
    e) How can a therapist treat clients who define themselves as MPD without having to deal with "alters"?
    f) What other specific questions should I raise at the MPD conference?

5. Master the procedural steps of Direct Therapy Exposure (DTE) so you can now teach them to someone in a role play situation.

    a) How did you assess the nature of the client's ruminations? What questions did you ask?

    b) What metaphors did you use in explaining DTE to clients?

    c) How did you combine the relaxation and exposure features?

    d) How did you prepare clients to do the "homework" of listening to the audiotapes of the traumatic event?

    Try DTE with a client and compare your audiotaped sessions with the enclosed procedural checklist (Table 1).

6.   What are the contra-indications or "warning signs" to use DTE? (Recall your Section V answer to this question -- worth repeating).

7.   Have you used guided imagery procedures in your treatment of PTSD clients? What has been your experience? What are the various ways guided imagery has been used in the treatment of traumatized clients? What is your opinion of the various guided imagery procedures? With what type of PTSD clients would you "experiment" in using these procedures?

8.   Describe the procedural steps involved in conducting:

        a)   stress inoculation training (SIT)
        b)   cognitive restructuring
        c)   cogitive processing therapy
        d)   problem-solving interventions (What questions work best for you?)

        As in the case of DTE, role play, teach, and practice using these procedures. Then compare your audiotaped sessions with the enclosed guidelines. For example, demonstrate how you would use:

        a)   SIT with a client who has problems with anger control;
        b)   cognitive restructuring with a depressed "victimized" client;
        c)   social problem-solving with a client (combat veteran) who has chronic PTSD

9.   Demonstrate in role playing, and then in your therapy sessions, how you would use specific cognitive behavioral techniques:

        a)   use of metaphors (e.g., "prejudice" metaphor)
        b)   downward arrow technique
        c)   treating guilt reactions by means of cognitive restructuring
        d)   engaging clients in performing personal experiments

10.   Outline how you presently structure your therapy session. Compare the structure that you use with that included in this Section. What are the differences? Are these differences important or trivial? Are there any suggestions about structuring sessions that would be worth adding to your treatment approach? For instance, how are agendas now set in your sessions? Do clients provide session summaries? Ask clients what they have learned?

11.   Why does having clients talk about their trauma experience help? What are the implications of these findings for how we conduct treatment with PTSD clients?

12.   Experiment in writing a letter to a PTSD client that would foster change. Compare your letter with that proposed in the present Section. What metaphors and "key verbs" and "phrases" did you include? How can you incorporate these into your social discourse with clients? What phrases and metaphors from the present Section do you like best? How will you use them?

13.   What are your favorite metaphors that you use in treatment with PTSD clients? (Send a copy of these to Don Meichenbaum.)

14.   What is the "state of the art" in treating clients with borderline personality disorder (BPD)? Describe how psychoeducational procedures can be used with BPD?

15. a) Outline specific intervention procedures that can be used in treating clients with problems with addiction.

     b) You have been asked to establish a harm-reduction and a relapse-prevention program for clients with addiction problems. What specific procedures would you propose? What are the goals and techniques you would use? How would you use family members in treatment? Be specific in indicating how you would employ assessment feedback and intervention techniques.

16. What is motivational interviewing? Set up a role play situation with one individual being a PTSD client with addiction problems. The therapist should use motivational interviewing techniques, solution focused questions, and "healing" metaphors, as part of the intervention. This is a difficult task and will require much assistance from the commentator who has the enclosed checklists and examples available. Take turns.

     Now try these procedures with a client. Take your audiotape back to your role-playing group to evaluate or share it with colleagues.

17. Have you used family-based interventions with PTSD clients? How can the present brief account on family-based interventions be elaborated? What is the data that indicates that it is critical to involve family members in the treatment of PTSD clients? Describe how you could conduct such family-based assessments and interventions.

18. Figley (1988) has pointed out that traumatized families may be affected in four ways: (a) **simultaneous effects** when natural disaster strikes an entire community; (2) **vicarious effects** when a family member is the victim of the trauma, and the response of the other family members results in the experience of trauma, as in hostage situations, (3) **chiasmal effects** as when the traumatic stress actually "infects" other members of the family; and (4) **intrafamilial trauma** as when the family is the source of the trauma. Discuss how the nature of your family interventions would differ in each instance. In what ways would your treatment approach be the same. Role play a family-based intervention. How can you adapt some of the cognitive-behavioral procedures (e.g., problem-solving, cognitive restructuring) to family-based interventions? What metaphors do the family members use? How can you use them therapeutically? How can you use "circular questioning" (ala Tomm) with the family *(see Section III on Assessment)*? What new "healing theory" and skills (ala Figley) have you helped the client develop? How have you incorporated relapse prevention procedures in your treatment plan?

19. This Section is clearly the most content-filled in terms of specific intervention techniques. As you reflect upon what you have read and practicied, what two things stand-out most? How do you intend to apply this information in your day-to-day clinical practice?

20. Which colleague (student) do you think would benefit most from the material included in this Section? How would you plan to bring this to his/her attention?

SECTION VII

POST DISASTER INTERVENTIONS[1]

Goals of Section VII

Another target population are individuals who have experienced traumatic events or "disasters," either due to natural, technological, or the result of intentional human design (or some combination of these). PTSD and other forms of emotional distress such as anxiety and depression can be engendered by traumatic events such as floods, earthquakes, large fires, airplane crashes, car accidents, as well as moderate-size natural disasters. We will now consider various forms of **Post Disaster Interventions including Crisis Intervention, Debriefing, and Defusing** procedures that have been used with both victims and those responsible for providing emergency relief services.

In Section I, I reviewed the widespread incidence of disasters that underscore the critical need for post-disaster interventions. In several large household probability samples in North America approximately one-third of adults report exposure to a natural disaster during their life span (Freedy & Kilpatrick, 1994). These statistics are further underscored by Pynoos et al. (1994) who reported that over the past two decades, natural disasters have taken the lives of 3 million people worldwide and have adversely affected the lives of 800 million more. They go on to point out that the impact of such disasters is much worse in developing than in developed countries. For example,

> "Between 1960 and 1987 there were 109 major disasters worldwide. 41 of these disasters occurred in developing countries killing 758,000 people, compared to 11,441 killed in 68 disasters that occurred in developed countries".

As noted, for the survivors disasters can cause a variety of psychological problems beside PTSD. The sense of powerlessness and loss of control that is experienced at the time of the trauma can contribute to a sense of constant threat, with accompanying overreactions to minor threats, a heightened sensitivity and vulnerability, a loss of a sense of safety and trust.

Over time, **for some "survivors"** of disasters their reactions may take the form of anger, embitterment and alienation. In considering the scope of the problem it is also important to keep in mind that most studies indicate a **PTSD prevalence rate of under 20% following disasters** (McFarlane, 1994). Most adults (approximately 90%) will not experience a major mental health disorder as a result of exposure to a major natural disaster. Of those who do develop such a disorder a full psychological **recovery may be expected within 12 to 24 months** following the exposure (Freedy & Kilpatrick, 1994). In this Section, we will consider the factors that have been suggested as distinguishing those who develop and do not develop PTSD and related signs of distress as a result of exposure to a disaster.

I have been involved with various crisis intervention teams. In my capacity, I have been asked how can mental health workers be of most help after such traumatic events as an earthquake, a flood, after school and workplace shootings, and after war experiences, and with emergency relief teams. Moreover, given our work on stress inoculation training, I have been asked how to prepare individuals for possible disasters, as well as for impending stressors (as illustrated in my recent consultation in Hong Kong). This Section is the handout that I use in training mental health care workers. Note that many of the suggestions included in this handout can be used on a

---

[1] See the Spring 1994 issue of the NCP Clinical Quarterly which is devoted to post-disaster interventions and Dattilio and Freeman's (1994) edited volume Cognitive-behavioral strategies in crisis intervention, New York: Guilford. Also see American Psychiatric Association Fact Sheet "When disaster strikes" (FSS 006 $1 each). Order from APA/Division Public Affairs, Dept IN, 1400 K Street, N.W. Washington, DC 20005.

preventive, anticipatory basis, before a disaster occurs (e.g., see Williams, Solomon & Bartone, 1988).

Overview of Section VII

I   A Brief Overview of the Post-Disaster Literature

II   Assessment Issues: Who Is The Most Vulnerable To Develop PTSD Following A Disaster?
       Table 1: Possible Vulnerability Factors

III   Guidelines to Follow When Providing Post-Disaster Interventions

IV   What Is Critical Incident Stress Debriefing?

       A.   A Model of Critical Incident Stress Debriefing (CISD)
       B.   A Critical Evaluation of CISD
       C.   Goals of CISD
       D.   Format of CISD

V   How to Conduct Debriefing Sessions? -- Description of CISD Phases

VI   Alternative Modes and Models of Post-Trauma Interventions

       A.   Peer support
       B.   Outreach model
       C.   Debriefing on an individual basis
       D.   Debriefing children and families following a disaster: PTSD in children
             Expressive Art as a Form of Prevention and Treatment of PTSD with Children
       E.   Postvention intervention
       F.   School-based interventions
       G.   Military applications: Soldiers, POWs and Hostages
       H.   Additional models

VII   Disaster Relief Guidebooks

VIII   Role of Rituals and Religion

IX   Workplace Traumas: The Value of Followup Debriefings

        As a result of working your way through this Section you should be able to answer the following 4 questions:

        (1) What is it I need to know before I intervene in this post-disaster situation?

        (2) What are the "vulnerability" factors for developing PTSD and related distress?

        (3) What can I do not to make this situation worse?

        (4) What can I do to help?

**POST DISASTER INTERVENTIONS: CRISIS INTERVENTION
CRITICAL INCIDENT STRESS DEBRIEFING, DEFUSING, AND
POSTVENTION**

I   A Brief Overview of the Post-disaster Literature

The literature on post-disaster interventions is quite extensive as reflected in the following reference list. (See Allen 1993; American Red Cross, 1991; Austin, 1992; Baum et al., 1983; Berke et al., 1993; Bolin, 1985; Brom & Kleber, 1989; Brom et al., 1989; Bromet, 1989; Dyregrov, 1988, 1989; Gleser et al., 1981; Granot & Brender, 1991; Green, 1982; Green & Lindy, 1994; Hartsough & Garaventa-Myers, 1985; Hodgkinson & Stewart, 1991; Krystal, 1968; Lindy et al., 1981; Lystad, 1985; Mangelsdorff, 1985; Meyers, 1989; Mitchell, 1983, 1987, 1988; Mitchell & Bray, 1989; Mitchell & Dyregrov, 1993; Peuler, 1988; Raphael, 1986; Rubonis & Bickman, 1991; Solomon, 1992; Spitzer, 1992; Spitzer & Burke, 1993; Wenckstern & Leenaars, 1993; and Wilson & Raphael, 1993).

One can also obtain additional information from the:

a)   International Critical Incident Stress Foundation which is located at 5018 Dorsey Hall Drive, Suite 104, Elliott City, Maryland, 21042),

b)   American Psychological Association Disaster Response Network which consists of approximately 1000 psychologists from 32 state and provincial psychological associations,

c)   American Red Cross who provide disaster relief training to mental health workers.

d)   Interntional Association of Trauma Counselors, La Posada Drive, #220, Austin, Texas, 78752 - 3880, (512) 454-8626.

When a disaster occurs the local American Red Cross chapter may directly contact the state psychological association disaster chairperson who, in turn, mobilizes teams of psychologists to the site, as needed. There is often a registry of the skills and qualifications of volunteer mental health workers.

One post-disaster model that has received most attention is **Critical Incident Stress Debriefing (CISD)**, as offered by Jeffrey Mitchell and George Everly (1992, 1994). Omer (1994) notes that there have been 75 CISD teams established in the U.S. during the last 6 years. There are also CISD teams in Australia, Canada, Germany, Israel and Norway. Given the widespread popularity of this approach we will consider CISD in some detail. **ALTHOUGH THERE IS GREAT INTEREST IN CISD, IT SHOULD BE NOTED THAT THERE IS A VERY LIMITED EMPIRICAL BASIS FOR CISD** (as discussed below).

A second model that has received a good deal of attention is that offered by Hobfoll and his colleagues. Hobfoll (1988, 1989, 1991) has provided a useful **Conservation of Resources (COR) model** to describe the potential impact of disasters on individuals and on communities. Hobfoll et al (1994) propose that natural and technological disasters can attenuate **four sources of resource**, namely:

"a)   **objects** include material things such as home, car, possessions and at a community level includes roads, communal shelters, emergency equipment;

b)   **conditions** include social structures and circumstances that apply to an individual, group, or community. These may include social ties and roles (employment, parenthood, marriage) as reflected in the loss of secure work, good health, and supportive relationships. At a community level it may include the availability of employment, the level of emergency services, and the quality of ties between community organizations.

c) **personal characteristics** or internal resources are attributes of individuals that are either esteemed in their own light or that facilitate the creation or protection of other resources (e.g., levels of self-esteem and self-efficacy, and a sense of meaning and purpose, social skills, having a skilled occupation). At a community level it refers to group attributes such as communal pride and sense of community, and community competence.

d) **energies** refer to resources such as money, food, knowledge, time and credit. These energies may be exchanged or used to obtain or protect other resources. On a community level they include government financing, knowledge of how to act in a crisis, transportation and fuel reserves."

The more aggregate and rapid the resources lost the greater the likelihood of elevated psychological distress (Freedy et al., 1992). When resources are lacking, lost, or when invested without consequent gain, people can become vulnerable to psychological and physical disorders and to debilitated functioning (Hobfoll & Jackson, 1991). The COR model highlights that not only are there the acute reactions to the disaster that must be addressed, but there is a need to meet ongoing demands and ensuing stressful life events. Following from the COR model, Freedy et al. (1992) propose certain guidelines in conducting post-disaster interventions. These guidelines include:

1. Disaster interventions need to be broadly based involving multiple agencies. A critical feature of the disaster management is the provision of prompt and accurate transmission of information concerning death tolls, accident and destruction estimates, evacuation sites, continuous monitoring of the likelihood of recurrence, and provision of services.

2. Interventions should be targeted at multiple levels (individual, group and community) covering the victims, friends, and bereaved family members, and disaster workers (for example, first responders such as fire fighters and police officers, as well as body handlers and morgue workers). Williams et al. (1988) note that emergency workers are particularly vulnerable if they see themselves as similar to the victims and if they form a personal identification with the victims.

3. Interventions should address the **hierarchy of needs**, initially **physical and safety needs** (information about relatives and friends, establish a communication clearing house, provide shelter, food, financial support), then the **social needs** of identification of bodies, grieving, being reintegrated, and finally **needs related to self-evaluation** (self-esteem, self-control) can be looked after. In each instance, loss prevention strategies should be implemented (Hobfoll & Lilly, 1993).

4. There is a need to **assess the level of loss of resources** that individuals and communities have experienced. Several resource loss measures have been developed, for example, a 52-item Resources Questionnaire or a shorter 19 item scale (Freedy et al., 1993). (These scales are available from the Crime Victim's Research and Treatment Center, Department of Psychiatry and Behavioral Sciences, Medical University of South Carolina, 171 Ashley Avenue, Charleston, South Carolina, 29425-0742.)

II Assessment Issues: Who Is Most Vulnerable to Develop PTSD Following Disaster

The discussion of the Resources Questionnaires raises the issue of assessment, in general. There is a need to evaluate stressors precisely and to determine detailed information about the nature of the individual's experience in the disaster. The assessment should cover:

1. the characteristics of the "disaster;"

2. the characteristics of the individual's and group's perceptions of and reactions to the disaster;

3. the characteristics of the community's response to the disaster;

4. as well as indicate the time when the post-disaster adjustment is being assessed.

In terms of the **time line of adjustment**, an empirically useful distinction has been drawn between **0-3 months** post disaster, **3 to 18 months**, and **18 months plus**. As noted below, each of these time frames have been identified as being critical demarcation points in the adjustment process (Green & Solomon, 1994). It is proposed that the vulnerability factors that predict adjustment at each of these 3 time periods may differ. For example, disaster characteristics and the survivor's immediate disaster response may be more predictive of adjustment 0-3 months than at other periods. As one moves further out from the time of the disaster recovery factors and premorbid factors may take on more significance. For instance, Baum et al. (1993) reported that intrusive ideation was more predictive of adjustment at 4 years post-disaster than at 2 years post-disaster. The adjustment to disaster is a dynamic process that changes over time and we should expect different classes of variables to be predictive of adjustment over a changing time course.

In terms of **disaster characteristics** a number of investigators (e.g., Gleser, Green & Winget, 1978; Green, 1982, Giel, 1990; Vogel & Vernberg, 1994; Wilson et al. 1985) have identified several variables that should be considered in evaluating the potential impact of a disaster. These variables include:

1. type of disaster (human made, natural, combination) and public or private

2. scope of impact or proportion of the community affected (e.g., amount of destruction of property and associated losses of life and number of casualties)

3. whether the disaster is peripheral or central (Did the disaster leave the physical setting and social supports intact? Is the event atypical and have little relevance for the rest of the survivor's life?)

4. speed of onset and amount of warning

5. magnitude, intensity, duration of impact (identifiable beginning and end) and degree of exposure -- the impact may continue for a long time, or even indefinitely, resulting in subsequent additional trauma, changes, and disruptions

6. degree of personal impact (e.g., loss of a loved one, degree of life-threat, amount of threat to survival). (For instance, the severity of post-disaster depression is related to the degree to which the individual witnesses death and experiences personal injury and material losses, Green et al., 1990)

7. preparedness of the community (e.g., history of previous exposure or experience)

8. perceived degree of predictability, controllability, and responsibility for traumatic

events

9.   potential for reoccurrence (e.g., frequency of occurrence, prospect of future occurrence)

10.   control over future impact, loss of trust, feelings of isolation, loneliness, and alienation

In terms of the **community response** or **recovery environment** one can ascertain the degree to which the traumatic events have contributed to breakdowns in transportation , communication, and social codes and activities, disillusionment, and a lost sense of community, disruption of social supports, perhaps resulting in prolonged relocation in a new and unfamiliar environment. Moreover, one can also assess the degree to which the community has prepared for such possible disasters, have means to mobilize informal and formal social supports, self-help groups, outreach programs, public service announcements, and formal treatment services. For example, Orner (1994) observes the potential value of creating temporary communities near disaster sites for victim's family so they can receive support, be given necessary information, and be treated for shock and grief by professional staff. Quarantelli (1985) and McFarlane (1994) have both noted that **the post disaster environment may be as important in the maintenance of PTSD symptoms as the traumatic event itself.** To illustrate their point, consider the impact of the post disaster environment on the victims of the Buffalo Creek disaster where a dam burst. Erikson (1976), in her perceptive account, observes that following the disaster, the survivors were accommodated in emergency quarters without consideration for existing relationship between relatives and neighbors, so community ties were further disrupted. McFarlane (in press) reports that the level of adjustment of survivors of a major fire was influenced more by financial difficulties and difficulty rebuilding, than due to exposure to the fire per se. **"Post-disaster environment may be as important in the maintenance of the posttraumatic symptoms as the enduring memories of the trauma."**

A good example of the important role of the community in reducing stressful reactions was offered by Milgram (1993). He described how the Israeli community responded to the stress that accompanied the Persian Gulf War. For instance, the media played a role in providing "stress-inoculating" radio and television programs, conveying needed information, but also providing descriptive material on possible coping efforts. The mental health community helped establish telephone hot lines, provided newspaper articles, and guided outreach programs.

The importance of the post-disaster environment is further underscored by Pennebaker and Harber (1993) who studied people's reactions to the Loma Prieta earthquake in California. They studied how often individuals had an opportunity to talk about their reactions with others and how many times they thought about the earthquake. They discovered that during the initial first two or three weeks after the earthquake (or what they called the emergency phase), as expected, individuals were preoccupied with thoughts about the upheavel. At the same time, social contacts increased and people were able to openly express their anxieties, thoughts and feelings to others. Moreover, during this initial time, negligible changes in health problems, nightmares and social conflicts occurred. Between 3 weeks and 6 weeks after the earthquake an inhibition phase was evident during which there was a significant drop in talking about the upheaval, but many individuals continued to have thoughts about it. It is during the inhibition phase that social conflict, dreams and health problems surfaced. It was during this inhibition phase when significant others did not want to hear other people talk about the earthquake, although many still wished to talk about it. This inhibitory style was epitomized by the sale of T-shirts that read, "Thank you for not sharing your earthquake experience." After 6 weeks, an adaptation phase emerged where for most individuals the psychological upheaval was over and signs of distress receded.

While the specific time markers of 3 and 6 weeks likely vary from disaster to disaster, the Pennebaker and Harber results highlight **the need "for interventions to continue through the inhibition phase, which may not surface for 2-3 weeks after the disaster. ...**

Yet, just when a trauma becomes old news is when a second wave of adverse affects begins to crest" (p. 35). Psychological interventions may be needed most one or two months following the disaster, after more immediate needs have been met and when social support systems wear down.

In addition to collecting information about the disaster and assessing the community 's response, there is a need to **assess the "victims" of the disaster**. For example, the poor are most negatively affected by disasters due to lack of resources. The need to **assess the individual's reaction** to the disaster is further underscored by the findings that an individual's immediate reaction to a disaster is often predictive of subsequent levels of adjustment (Spiegel & Cardena, 1992). For example, recent studies by Marmar and Spiegel (American Journal of Psychiatry, in press) indicate that individuals who respond in a **dissociative fashion** at the time of the trauma (e.g., earthquake, fire, combat) may be at particular risk for subsequent maladjustment. Individuals who responded with an **apparently unwarranted calm, inappropriate composure**, and who appeared **unfazed** by the stressful circumstances may be particularly prone to develop posttraumatic problems like severe anxiety, sleep disruptions and flashbacks, which may not surface until a later period of time. At the time of the disaster they may be inclined to put themselves and others in danger because they ignore the riskiness of the situation. They continue to react as if nothing unusual were occurring. Their dissociative response may take the form of a lack of emotional reaction, a feeling that events are unreal, as well as feel disoriented. They may "shut out" reality, blank out during the traumatic event, have feelings that time has slowed down, or feel as if they are watching themselves from afar, or in slow motion. They may report "being in a daze" and manifest highly inappropriate emotional reactions, as well as feel disoriented. They may report, "I felt outside of my conscious experience.", or "I felt like I was watching myself on television or in a movie." Because of the outward appearance of "calm", individuals who are dissociating may be overlooked or ignored by rescue workers or by debriefers. Such dissociating may reflect the individual's attempt to avoid and/or control disconcerting feelings of panic or reflect ways to keep feelings to themselves. Whatever, the exact function of the dissociative response there is a need to have everyone who is willing undergo debriefing, not only those in emotional turmoil.

But dissociating is only one aspect of survivor's reactions to traumatic events. Weisaeth (1994) reports marked sensitivity in identifying victims vulnerable to developing PTSD 7 months post-disaster. The 1 week measures used included anxiety level (as assessed by Spielberger's STAI), traumatic sleep disturbance, presence of startle reactions, fear/phobia of the scene of the trauma, and degree of social withdrawal. Weisaeth reports that he was able to identify 96% of those who developed PTSD at 7 months post-disaster using these indicators. These impressive findings need to be replicated across disaster settings and types. Another critical source of information concerns the survivors exposure to prior stressors (Green, 1994). But these are only a few of the multiple vulnerability variables that have been implicated by researchers. In fact, I am continually asked,

> **"What should debriefers be looking for and listening for in order to determine who is at most "high risk" for future difficulties?"**

In order to answer this question I have put together the following list of proposed factors and possible accompanying questions that can be raised. The questions included in **Table 1** reflect a mental checklist that health care providers can keep in mind as they listen to "victims" tell their stories. As the victims and near-victims describe and explain what happened, the health care provider can sensitively sample from this list of questions, identifying which individuals are at most "high "risk", who are most vulnerable to subsequent stressful reactions, and who are most likely to evidence an impaired capacity to recover.

The questions in Table 1 reflect a personal compendium that I derived from the post-disaster literature (e.g., Adams & Adams, 1984; Baum et al., 1993; Freedy et al., 1993; Green, 1993, 1994; Green et al., 1991; McFarlane, 1993; Pennebaker & Harber, 1993; Pynoos et al.,

1994; Vogel & Vernberg, 1993). These questions cover both objective and subjective disaster characteristics, reactions during and after the disaster, and pre-disaster characteristics. Moreover, it should be noted that it is not clear whether these vulnerability factors should be considered within an additive model, or as a threshold model, or as a configural model. Should each factor be weighted the same, no matter what disaster one deals with? Disasters vary in terms of impact, property loss, level of threat/danger, losses sustained, length of impact, ensuing adversities, continual threats, and the like (McFarlane, 1994). Moreover, it is important to keep in mind that **the specific questions included in Table 1 have not been validated** and should be viewed as an "educated hunch" of what makes an individual, group, or community more "vulnerable" to the long-term negative effects of having lived through a disaster. For example, these questions are designed to assess the individual's appraisal of the disaster, its context, and its perceived meaning. The questions are worded in such a way that the more positive "yes" responses, the greater the likelihood that the individual is at "risk" for current and future psychological distress. In considering the questions in Table 1, it is important that they should not be raised in any form of cross-examination investigatory style. Instead, they represent a framework or template for the health care provider to use in identifying potentially "high-risk" individuals.

Table 1

Possible Vulnerability Factors:
Who is at "High Risk" for Developing PTSD and Other Forms of Maladjustment?

The vulnerability factors and accompanying questions are divided into three categories:

(i)   Characteristics of the disaster (essentially **within disaster** characteristics)
      a) Objective (factors that can be independently corroborated such as degree of trauma exposure)
      b) Subjective (based primarily on individual's or group's perceptions and cognitive appraisal of exposure related to perceived control, predictability, threat and responsibility)

(ii)   Characteristics of the **post-disaster** response and environmental recovery factors
      a) Reactions of the individual and group
      b) Reactions involving others

(iii)   Characteristics of the individual and group (**pre-disaster** characteristics)
      a) Demographics, previous traumatization, recent life events, psychiatric history, coping and social support

First the factor is highlighted and then it is framed in the form of a "yes", "no" questions that can be directed to the "victim(s)". The more **"yes"** answers, **the greater** the proposed **risk** for developing PTSD and related forms of distress.

I. Characteristics of the Disaster

Objective factors directly affecting the "victim" and "significant others"

1.	**Proximity to disaster and duration of the stressor**	Was the individual close or "relatively" close to the site of the disaster? Did the individual experience a "narrow escape?" (The greater the proximity, intensity and duration, the poorer the level of adjustment).
2.	**Degree of physical harm or injury to the "victim".**	Was the individual physically injured?
3.	**Intentionality of injury or harm along a "continuum of deliberateness"**	Was the individual injured "on purpose"?
4.	**Witness violence**	Did the individual witness physical violence?
5.	**Witness violent or sudden death of others -- like one's loved one or of a child or a friend**	Did the individual witness the death of a "significant other"? Was there violent or sudden death to loved ones? Has the parent lost a child? Did the individual helplessly witness such deaths?

6. **Exposure to grotesque or mutilating deaths of others -- exposure to mass deaths or human remains**

Was the individual exposed to grotesque sights, sounds and smells, (e.g., mutilated and severed bodies)? Was the individual exposed to scenes of death and destruction? If there was injury or death, was there disfigurement, mutilation and other grotesque sights? Was the individual exposed to mutilated or burned bodies? Was the individual exposed to mass deaths or mass dying? Was the individual exposed to traumatic events that were vivid and emotionally powerful? Were children among the injured and dead? Does the individual identify with the victims?

7. **Degree of property damage to "victim" and others ($5,000+)**

Did the individual experience a substantial degree of property damage to the point where his/her home is uninhabitable? Is the individual living in make-shift quarters? Was there sudden and severe property loss to others, as well? Will the property damage take a long time to repair? Is the landscape devastated?

8. **Learning of one's exposure to further potential threats**

Is the individual or group at continued "high risk" for future stressors?

9. **Irreversibility of resource losses (prolonged environmental disruption)**

Is the individual, family, group unable to reverse losses (i.e., failure to recover lost possessions, property, job, income, and other personal losses)? Is there continual displacement? Is there loss of both home and job or livelihood?

10. **Escape blocked or experience impossible choices**

Was escape blocked for the individual? Was the individual faced with impossible choices such as help others at great risk to one's own survival?

11. **Constant reminders -- remain in or near epicenter**

Are there constant reminders of the accident or traumatic event? Is the individual(s) chronically exposed to reminders of the traumatic events? Is there an absence of a "safety signal?"

12. **Signs of injury**

Is the impact of the traumatic event evident to the individual, but "invisible" or not readily noticeable to others?

13. **Involve noxious agents**

Was the individual or loved ones exposed to noxious agents or experienced continuing threat from potential toxicity or radiation? Are there continuing concerns and uncertainty about possible long-term health consequences?

14. **Degree of physical injury and death to others and loved ones**

Was there violent, sudden or severe injury or death to a "loved one," or friend or neighbor (e.g., number of friends killed)? Did the individual have to wait a prolonged period to hear about the fate of loved ones?

15. **How information of death was conveyed**

If there was death that was not witnessed was the news of the death conveyed in a non-supportive fashion? Not told why he/she cannot view body of significant other?

16. **Description of social supports -- both immediate and long-term**

(i) Was the individual separated from family members during or immediately after the disaster?
(ii) Was there significant disruption of social supports and kin networks with accompanying loss of proximity to friends and relatives?

"Subjective" factors related to the "victim" and "significant others"

17. **Perception of the disaster**

(i) Was the disaster viewed as unexpected, unpredictable, sudden, as compared to a predictable disaster (e.g., seasonal flooding)?
(ii) Was the threat not known to exist?

18. **Perception of the "intensity" of threat to life or bodily integrity to self or family**

Did the disaster cause "threat" to life survival or to physical integrity? Is the traumatic event perceived as being continually threatening to one's life or well-being or to his/her loved ones?

19. **Perception of "psychological" and "physical" demands**

Did the disaster cause excessive demands and entail extended exposure?

20. **Perception of cause of the disaster**

Did the individual(s) perceive the disaster as being due to callousness ... irresponsibility ... greed ... stupidity? Does the individual(s) feel the disaster was preventable and controllable? Is there someone to blame?

21. **Perception of preparation**

Did the individual(s) feel unprepared for the disaster? Was there lack of training for such disasters? Was there an opportunity to warn potential victims ahead of time, so they could take precautions, but the warning was not given? Were the potential victims unable to take precautions after the warning? Did the individual fail to respond to anticipatory warnings? Could the event have been prevented or the injury/destruction reduced?

22. **Perception of lack of personal control**

Does the individual feel a loss of control over social processes that are generally perceived as being in control? ... Does the disaster represent a breakdown in a "system" that is not supposed to falter? Does the individual experience a loss of personal control?

23. **Perception of assistance offered**

Did the individual offer assistance to others that proved to be unhelpful ... futile ... or even made things worse (e.g., further property loss)?

24. **Perception of personal responsibility -- blame self**

Does the individual see himself/herself as being in a role that resulted in injury or death to others because of what he/she did or failed to do?

25. **Perception of social supports**

Does the individual(s) feel he/she has no, or few, family members, friends, neighbors to turn to for help? Did the disaster interfere with peer support?

II. Characteristics of the Post-disaster Response

Reactions of the Individual

26. **Intense initial emotional reactions to disaster. For example, symptomatic response/panic anxiety/dissociation/sadness/ depression**

In the immediate aftermath of the traumatic event did the individual develop high levels of anxiety and/or evidence dissociative reactions? In children did they evidence being sad, grieving over potential and realized losses, feel alone during and immediately after the traumatic event? Does the individual experience the "pressure" of PTSD symptoms?

27. **Feelings of helplessness**

Did the individual experience terror and feel helpless and powerless during and after the event?

28. **Symptomatic responses/sleep disturbance/insomnia/agitation**

In subsequent weeks following the disaster, did the individual evidence insomnia or agitation?

29. **Presence of continual intrusive ideation**

a) Does the individual have persistent intrusive thoughts, images, dreams, nightmares of the traumatic experience?

b) Does the individual continue to repetitively "relive" and reexperience the event and its aftermath? (Note, **3 months** following the event is usually taken as a guidepost when such intrusive symptoms should become less frequent and less disruptive)

30. **Degree of bereavement**

Is the individual acquainted with the victims? Is the individual grieving the loss of significant others?

31. **Presence of evidence to "work through" and "resolve" trauma**

Is the individual having difficulty "integrating" or constructing "a new world view," or having difficulty "moving beyond" this event (i.e., a constructive resolution)? Does the individual, family or group <u>lack</u> a coherent framework (e.g., religious or philosophical outlook) that would help make sense of what has happened? Is the individual continuing to "search for meaning" by pursuing the answer to "why" questions, for which there are no acceptable answers?

32. **Self-disclosure opportunities**

Is the individual unable or unwilling to talk with others about the trauma and his/her reactions?

<u>Reactions involving significant others -- environment recovery factors</u>

33. **Opportunity for self-disclosure, working through and resolution**

Does the individual think about the upheaval a good deal, but have limited access or opportunity to share his/her feelings and thoughts with others?

34. **Lack of social support**

Are kin or neighbors/friends unavailable to provide material and social support? Has the family failed to share their different experiences about the disaster?

35. **Extent of dislocation or displacement (move often and move furthest away against one's will - involuntary relocation)**

Was (Is) the individual and his/her family placed in an unfamiliar environment due to the disaster (dislocated)? Is the nuclear family still apart? Does the relocation plan fail to take into consideration family or neighbourhood patterns and wishes? Was relocation done arbitrarily? (What is the length of time in so-called "temporary housing?")

36. **Disruption social support**

Was there significant disruption of social support and kin networks with accompanying loss of proximity to friends and relatives?

37. **Impact of disaster on social support providers**

Are the kinfolk or neighbors/friends who are providing support also "victims" of the disaster or "victims" of its aftermath?

38. **Stress of receiving social support**

Has the evacuee individual or family "worn out his/her welcome" with the host family (e.g., stayed longer than 1 month)?

39. **Resumption of normal routines -- exposure to continued adversities such as financial strain, lack of transportation, residential displacement, jobless)**

Has the individual and his/her family and community been unable to reestablish "normal" routines (e.g., sleeping arrangements, communication, transportation arrangements, work and school schedules)? Is there still dislocation and unemployment? Has the individual or group failed to engage in any proactive actions (e.g., attempts to change things)?

40. **Stress reactions of significant others**

Did the parent(s) evidence exaggerated emotional response at the time of the disaster or at the reunion? Do "significant others" (e.g., parents) evidence continual distress? Is the individual exposed to a social network of negative rumors that acts like a stress contagion or what has been called a "pressure cooker effect"? Are parents intolerant of their child's proclivity to engage in regressive behavior?

41. **Community efforts at rebuilding and social support -- evidence of community solidarity, group cohesion and a common purpose and rapid disaster relief**

Has the community failed to organize efforts to rebuild or cope in some <u>acceptable</u> fashion? Does the community evidence little concern and lack a supportive response? Is there absence of any temporary community near the disaster site for victim families? Has the group or community <u>failed to</u> engage in any group bereavement or memorial service (i.e., did <u>not</u> provide ritual healing ceremonies)? Is there disruption in community life and routines? Is there a shortage of food and petrol and health care services? Is there a lack of counseling?

42. **Nature of information**

Is the information following the disaster seen as confusing, inconsistent or contradictory? Is there an absence of an ascribed individual or designated group who gathers and disseminates information to combat negative rumors?

43. **Nature of designated leadership**

Are the authorities in charge seen as being untrustworthy, secretive, and inconsistent, and as a result suffering from a loss of credibility, leading to general mistrust?

44. **Mitigating factors to recovery**

Is the recovery process being hampered by extensive media coverage, litigation hearings, difficulty over insurance claims, unavailability of contractor or unscrupulous behaviors by contractors/repairmen/storekeepers, dispute with authorities about recovery procedures such as decontamination, lack of information about permanent housing, long term loans, and the like?

45. **How community views victim(s) -- stigmatization**

Does the community (society) view the individual ("victim") who has gone through the traumatic events in a "negative" fashion? Is there a "stigma" attached to asking for help? Does the individual fail to feel part of the community at large?

46. **Secondary victimization**

Did the individual experience "secondary victimization" (e.g., from agencies such as police, doctors, courts, insurance companies)? Has the individual experienced a loss in the market value of his/her home as a result of the disaster?

III. Characteristics of the Individual and Group

47. **High risk factors -- Is the individual a member of a group who lives on the "margin" of society or is likely to be "over-looked" or "forgotten" (e.g., geographically isolated, frail and elderly, homeless, physically or mentally ill, lack financial or social resources.**

Is the individual at particular risk because he/she is a single parent, middle aged with responsibility to both children and parents, frailed elderly, or from a lower SES level, or a child separated from his/her family as an immediate aftermath of the disaster? Is the individual or parent unemployed or work for low wages? Is the individual single, widowed, divorced? Is the child of a single, divorced or separated parent? Does the child not reside with family members?

48. **Prior history of adjustment problems to stressors and other traumatic events**

Did the individual and family members adjust poorly to prior major losses or stressors?

49. **Prior history of mental illness (e.g., anxiety, depression, substance abuse)**

Does the individual have a history of mental illness? For example, is there a personal or family history of anxiety disorders? In children is there evidence of high trait anxiety prior to the disaster?

50. **Presence of comorbidity**

Is the individual evidencing anxiety, phobias, depression, addictive behaviors and somatization?

51. **Prior exposure, to traumatic events, anniversary effects, reactive unresolved conflicts (e.g., prior violent crime victimization)**

Were there prior stressors that influenced the present reactions to the disaster (e.g., anniversary effects), or exposure to prior stressful events? Did the events reactivate prior unresolved conflicts and reactions from prior victimization?

52. **Premorbid evidence marital and familial distress**

Was there marital or familial discord prior to the disaster?

53. **Family vulnerability**

Is the family "vulnerable" as evident in the "pile-up" of family life changes and demands? Does the family have a history of irritability with each other, depression, despair and family instability?

54. **Family style of communicating**

Do the family members engage in what are called "hot reactions," tending to blow-up small events into larger crises, use language that is blaming, critical, inflames reactions, and other similar "high expressed emotional" behaviors (e.g., being overprotective unwittingly reinforcing overdependent behaviors)?

55. **Exposure to sustained anticipatory alerts**

Was the individual or group exposed to a sustained anticipatory alerts?

56. **Degree of preparedness**

Does the individual/group/community lack experience and/or training in dealing with such traumatic events (disasters)? Has the individual been assigned (as compared to volunteering) for this recovery work or involuntarily assigned to live in this residential area? Is the individual or group unable to use rescue skills that he/she was trained for?

57. **Exposure to low magnitude pre-existing non-traumatic, stressful life events in the last year**

Was the individual (family, group) exposed to a series of low magnitude stressful events in the last year?

58. **Exposure to traumatic events over the course of a lifetime.**

Was the individual (family, group) exposed to a series of traumatic events over the course of a lifetime?

In summary, I have been able to identify from the disaster literature some **58 general vulnerability factors** (each of which can be further subdivided). Surely, the health care provider cannot keep these all in mind, but he/she can review this list at critical periods during and following the disaster. These represent a "mental template" that can influence what the health care worker might "ask about" or "listen for" when engaging in active outreach. Surely, Table 1 can be developed into a behavioral checklist that can be systematically evaluated. The importance of attending to both objective and subjective vulnerability factors is illustrated by the following research examples.

Cardena and Spiegel (1993), Smith et al. (1990), and Weisaeth (1989, 1992), found that how individuals coped immediately with trauma (during the impact stage) played an important role in influencing the course of later PTSD. Maladaptive disaster behavior such as the amount of perceived helplessness, the perception of intensity of death threat, the amount of physical injury, witnessing death, and experiencing situations that posed incompatible choices, as well as stress reactions of dissociation were correlated with later incidence of PTSD.

As McFarlane (1993) observed, **"victims with high levels of acute distress should be targeted [for subsequent interventions]"** (p. 16). A sensitive way to have individuals **share their reactions** has been suggested by Goenjian (1993) who studied the effects of the Armenian earthquake which caused close to 20,000 deaths, almost 2/3 of whom were children and adolescents. He noted that "an effective way of engaging the survivors of the Armenian earthquake was to ask them about the behavior of their children and how their children's reactions affected them, or ask the parents about both their children and their own sleep patterns. Such questions were not perceived as threatening and they facilitated discussion of psychological problems" (p. 234). Goenjian highlights the need to provide a supportive environment where survivors can tell their stories at their own pace and mental health workers can listen for possible vulnerability factors and coping responses. For example,

a)   Has the individual(s) successfully managed various life stressors before the disaster?

b)   Does the individual or group have a history of coping resources and coping behaviors (e.g., social supports, direct action problem-solving and emotional palliative coping skills)?

c)   See Freedy et al. (1993) for examples of the interview instrument used with adult victims of Hurricane Hugo to identify individuals vulnerable to PTSD.

As noted, there is also a need to assess the extent of maladjustment following the disaster, keeping in mind that such distress may take the form of anxiety, depression, grief, anger, dissociation, guilt, self-blame, and jealousy of those survivors who have escaped unscathed. If diagnosable symptoms persist after 3 months then the individual may require professional or additional interventions. As Vernberg and Vogel (1993) observe, "a number of studies have found **3 months post trauma to be a dividing point between acute versus chronic PTSD symptomatology**" (p. 494). This is further underscored by Baum (1990) who reported that the amount of intrusive ideation following a disaster is a particularly sensitive indicator of poor adjustment, especially when the intrusive ideation increases as the time elapsed from the disaster increases. This relationship is particularly significant when there is exposure to toxic wastes and other technological disasters (e.g., nuclear accidents and landfill site exposure) that can cause continual uncertainties with accompanying long-term physiological and psychological distress (see Baum et al., 1993). Similarly, Goenjian (1993) reported that intrusive symptoms and hyperarousal symptoms (such as startle reactions and hypervigilance) were most resistant to treatment.

Finally, it is important to keep in mind the admonitions offered by Silver and Wortman (1980) and Wortman (1983) that at this point researchers do not know what specific behaviors constitute adaptive adjustment to traumatic events. While it is often assumed that certain behaviors such as minimizing distress, continuing to function and maintaining a positive attitude, are signs of initial "effective coping," they may not always be associated with the best long-term adjustment. Thus, without the normative data of how people initially respond to traumatic events and the long-term consequences, clinicians need to be circumspect in defining and training specific modes of coping.

Now that we have considered the factors that put individuals at risk, we can turn our attention to what can be done to reduce the risk of developing PTSD and associated disorders.

III   Guidelines to Follow When Providing Post-Disaster Interventions

The assessment and intervention strategies included in this Section are designed to reduce the likelihood that post-traumatic reactions will escalate to the point of becoming PTSD or some other psychiatric disorder. When providing post-disaster interventions a number of guidelines have been offered in the literature (e.g., see American Red Cross 1982, 1991; Cohen & Ahearn, 1980; Freedy & Kilpatrick, 1994; Hartsough & Myers, 1985; Meyers, 1994; Norris & Thompson, 1994; Weiseath, 1994; WHO, 1992). Many of these suggestions fall under the general heading of **crisis counseling**[1] or **crisis intervention**. A brief consideration of these guidelines sets the stage for a more detailed consideration of Critical Incident Stress Debriefing. These guidelines include:

---

[1] Information about crisis counseling can be obtained from Emergency Services and Disaster Relief Branch, Center for Mental Health Services, Room 13-103, 5600 Fishers Lane, Rockville, Md. 20857.

(1) There is a need to first **address the more immediate and basic needs** (food, water, shelter and the dissemination of accurate information) and **security** before mental health programs are implemented. As Freedy & Kilpatrick (1994, p.7) observe, "Maslow was right, there is a hierarchy of needs! Taking care of basic needs provides a bedrock for positive mental health." Similarly, Norris and Thompson (1994) observe that outreach programs for victims are most effective when they take the form of assisting survivors with the variety of practical problems that arise during the impact phase (e.g., beginning a search for loved ones still unaccounted for).

(2) There is a need to engage in **active outreach interventions** which may take many different forms (e.g., provision of public education, meeting "victims" on site in impacted neighborhoods, disaster shelters, Disaster Application Centers, in churches, meal sites, hospitals, schools, and community centers. As Myers (1994) describes, there is a need to "aggressively hang out", and in these settings provide both practical help, as well as counseling. As Weisaeth (1994) observes, those most in need often do not seek help. "The resistance or avoidance of the traumatized person to seek help is a major problem in preventative work."

   a) One barrier contributing to disaster victims seeking help is the **"stigma"** attached to meeting with mental health workers. Myers (1994) admonishes mental health workers to eschew the titles of "Dr.", "Psychotherapist", which tend to focus on psychopathology. Instead, mental health workers should refer to themselves as "crisis workers", and their services as "assistance", "support", or "talking", rather than as "counseling" or as "psychotherapy". Similarly, the American Red Cross refer to their mental health workers as "disaster stress relief workers" and they ask professionals to avoid using their titles when interacting with disaster survivors (Vernberg & Vogel, 1993). As Solomon (1992) reminds us, disaster victims are known to shun any services or procedures that are labeled "mental health" because of the possible associated stigma.

   b) In addition, there is a need to "normalize" the survivor's reactions so the post traumatic stress **process** (not labeled a "disorder") and accompanying grief are seen as a "normal, natural, adaptive responses" to an "abnormal" situation. Freedy and Kilpatrick (1994) suggest that this educational process can occur at public group meetings that may take place all the way to 12 months post disaster. Gist and Stolz (1982) describe how the media can be used after a disaster to educate the public and to publicize the availability of practical services.

(3) There is a need to view **disasters as a longitudinal process** requiring different interventions at different phases. As McFarlane (1994) observes, the health care provider may be called upon to engage in different roles with victims and their families at different phases. There is also a need to evaluate one's intervention efforts by monitoring short-term and long-term consequences.

(4) There is a need for health care providers not to do for survivors what they can do for themselves. The object of providing help is to **empower** and **enable "victims"** so they come to see themselves as "survivors". There is a need **not to label families as victims**, which may contribute to their feelings of estrangement from the rest of the community. As noted previously, it is also critical not to become a "surrogate frontal lobe" for survivors. As Freedy and Kilpatrick (1994) suggest, to the extent possible, encourage people to become involved in collective self-help efforts, mobilize and strengthen social networks beyond the family, use indigenous self-help groups, and where indicated, train and supervise nonprofessionals to provide help. In a collaborative manner, advocate for survivors with insurance companies, bureaucratic agencies, and

the legal system. Bring individuals together at the neighborhood or worker levels in order to address concrete practical issues.

(5) There is a need to **assess and engage community resource personnel.** As Norris and Thompson (1994) highlight, it is important that professional supports do <u>not</u> replace natural helping networks. There is also value in helping victims help each other by forming self-help groups. For example, even at the individual level, Weisaeth (1994) describes how he sets up an Information Support Centre at a disaster site where survivors can be asked to meet with family members of victims who have died or who have been severely injured (e.g., at the site of an airplane crash). Both family members and victims benefit from such interchanges.

(6) In formulating such intervention de Jong (1994) has highlighted the value of **establishing a focus/advisory group of survivors** who represent a specific cultural or ethnic group in order to obtain their input on the nature of the proposed interventions. This is especially critical when providing help in a different culture. There is also a need to **conduct a network analysis** in order to determine which group in that society is most critical for gaining entry and in providing help. For example, Gist and Stolz (1982) describe how they trained natural caregivers (e.g., ministers) to be the major outreach group. Pynoos (1994) describes how critical it was to work with the school principals after the California earthquakes. Principals turned out to be the critical linch-pin to teachers, pupils and parents. Providing services at the school was also the most natural way to conduct the outreach program.

(7) The post-disaster interventions need to focus <u>not only</u> on victims, but also on **critical decision makers** in the society (e.g., government officials, journalists). As Pynoos (1994) and Weisaeth (1994) observe, how officials react to the disaster and to the continuing adversities that follow can exacerbate or reduce the stress level of the community. For example, how and when officials offer consolation sttements, solicit and convey expert information...or let the expert do the talking; allow time for proper burial and commemorative funerals, remove bodies and other reminders, don't make false promises, help control rumors, avoid unnecessary separation of family, friends, neighborhoods, can affect the recovery process. Such decision makers need to be included in any outreach program.

(8) A number of possible **"overlooked"** or "forgotten" **groups need to be included** in any post-disaster interventions (e.g., frailed elderly, geographically isolated, mentally and physically ill, emergency relief staff, and the like). An active case finding approach should be adopted. These groups should also receive some form of crisis intervention and follow-through.

(9) **Crisis intervention** is designed to deal with the traumatic situation as soon as possible, and whenever possible, resolve the issues that provoked the crisis. Key elements of crisis intervention may include:

    (a) Identifying the needs of victims, including notification of family members, providing transportation, shelter, etc.
    (b) attending to medical and basic practical needs
    (c) connecting victims with appropriate referrals and resources
    (d) helping them clarify factual information about the disaster and ways to negotiate legal, medical, and governmental services
    (e) advocating for victims
    (f) nurturing natural social support services
    (g) referring when psychiatric consulation is indicated
    (h) helping victims share experiences and reactions

(10) Green and Lindy (1994) note that mny aspects of disaster are open to mental health interventions. For example, mental health workers can help by

    (a)   making warnings more precise
    (b)   buffering news of traumatic loss
    (c)   minimizing exposure to grotesque aspects of death and injury
    (d)   educating the public about stress reactions
    (e)   monitoring and influencing the media
    (f)   mobilizing indigenous support networks
    (g)   helping develop new support systems (e.g., neighborhood grieving activities)
    (h)   helping implement group constructive activities
    (i)   providing therapeutic interventions ranging from debriefing to various forms of psychotherapy

Let us now consider the nature of debriefing in more detail.

IV   What is Critical Incident Stress Debriefing (CISD)?

Debriefing is usually a facilitator led group-oriented intervention in which major elements of a trauma are reviewed by the participants shortly after the event, when they are out of immediate danger. Although debriefing is especially recommended for survivors of group traumas (e.g., disasters, combat, accidents, etc.), the focus is usually on individuals and their reactions, and not on the group per se. The technique of debriefing is usually applied to groups of professionals (e.g., firefighters, emergency workers, police personnel, soldiers, body handlers, etc.) who have been "briefed" beforehand. The review of traumatic events by non-trained or non-briefed survivors may follow some of the same guidelines, but it tends to be characterized as generally more supportive (e.g., the debriefing of individual hostages reported below). A central feature of this support is providing an opportunity for victims to talk about what happened to a sympathetic, nonjudgmental listener. It helps if the listener is familiar with the specific trauma, and if possible, someone who has gone through a similar trauma. The retelling of the "story" should include emotional reactions, but the affect should not become overwhelming, nor disorganizing.

The development of debriefing procedures has a long history in the military (Salmon, 1919; Marshall, 1944) and it has been recently adapted and modified for civilian purposes. One variant of this procedure is **Critical Incident Stress Debriefing (CISD)** that was developed by Jeffrey Mitchell in the 1970's at the University of Maryland Emergency Health Services Program. It was initially designed to provide support for emergency health care workers and rescuers.[1] It is a group method that helps the workers to process and defuse their emotional reactions by means of educational, preventative, and supportive processes. It is designed to prevent unnecessary complications that follow from exposure to "disasters". Mitchell and Everly (1994) reported that there are 300 formal traumatic response teams world-wide that have used the CISD model in the prevention of PTSD. Since its inception CISD has been employed with a wide array of diverse populations. **The Mitchell model of CISD is only one such model** and other groups (e.g., American Red Cross) have developed their own version of debriefing. Variations on the Mitchell CISD model have also been offered by Armstrong et al. (1981, 1991), Berman and Queen (1986), Dunning and Silva (1980), Griffin (1987), Jones (1985), Raphael (1986), and Wagner (1979). These debriefing models differ in terms of goals, content, and techniques. I do not know of any research that has compared one debriefing model with another. Since the Mitchell model

---

[1] Rescue workers such as firefighters, disaster workers, body handlers, and other emergency personnel may have acute and chronic reactions including vivid reexperiencing, intrusive thoughts, feelings of helplessness and guilt reactions, as well as physiological hyperreactivity (Scotti et al., 1994; Sutker et al. 1994). When such teams are well prepared for victim recovery events, they evidence low levels of psychological distress and few lasting negative sequelae. As part of their training (as a form of "stress inoculation") debriefing teams have been shown videotapes on what to expect prior to their entry into the disaster area.

has received most attention, I will describe it in some detail and critique it. Keep in mind that no two disasters are alike, and thus, flexibility is required.

A. A Model of Critical Incident Stress Debriefing (CISD)

Most Critical Incident Stress Debriefing (CISD) programs employ a **phase model** that can be flexibly implemented. The number and labels of the proposed intervention phases vary, but they usually include: *(described in detail below)*

1. **Introductory phase** that provide ground rules
2. **Fact phase** -- establish what happened
3. **Thought (Cognition) phase** -- discuss thoughts about what happened
4. **Reaction (Feeling) phase** -- discuss emotions associated with the event
5. **Symptom phase** -- review signs and symptoms of distress
6. **Teaching (Educational) phase** -- "normality" is emphasized along with information about useful coping strategies
7. **Re-entry (Wind-down) phase** -- discuss outstanding issues, offer summary statements and any additional advice

As noted, while the Mitchell CISD model involves moving participants through the various phases in a systematic fashion, the debriefing process can also be conducted in a more flexible fashion as participants share their stories, often combining features of the various phases. The debriefing facilitator may follow the lead of the participants addressing their reactions, feelings, cognitions, and symptoms as they emerge, rather than operate in a sequentially prescribed fashion.

B. A Critical Evaluation of CISD (The best review of this area has been offered by Raphael, McFarlane and Meldrum, 1994. It is a must!)

Should one follow the prescribed sequence of debriefing as outlined by Mitchell and Everly or should one use one of the other debriefing models? Moreover, what is the evidence that CISD, in fact, reduces stress reactions and prevents stressful reactions? Should debriefing be applied to all forms of disasters, or to just those that are characterized as "critical incidents"? Should the debriefing intervention be conducted in a similar fashion for emergency workers who have been "briefed" beforehand, as well as for nontrained "victims"? How should debriefing be altered depending upon the nature of the disaster? Is it possible that debriefing could make some survivors worse?

Given the widespread use of debriefing and its strong advocacy by some, you would expect that a data-base would exist to address these important questions. Unfortunately, that is not the case. In fact, **there is limited research evaluating the outcome effectiveness of CISD,** nor research on the relative benefits of different training formats or debriefing models (Williams et al, 1988). In most instances, when research on CISD has been conducted it usually compares a group who receive the extensive CISD involvement versus a no treatment assessment control group (e.g., Willis, 1993) or a comparison of formal CISD versus informal collegial meetings. For example, Hutton and Hasle, 1989 did not find special benefits following from formal CISD with fire-fighters. Also see Raphael, 1991. Attention placebo, dismantling, or comparative treatment group interventions are not included. Another major problem with most debriefing studies is the **lack of followup.**

To underscore the **absence of evaluative data of CISD,** consider the following quotes offered by (Orner, 1994, pages 12 and 13):

"In fact, 15 years of (CISD) practice has not generated any studies which adopt methodologies more sophisticated than that required for descriptive surveys."

"Psychological support services provided on-site or in the immediate aftermath of major incidents do not appear ever to have been subjected to systematic scrutiny."

Similarly, Shalev (1994, p.204) concludes:

"Immediate and long-term beneficial effects of debriefing have been suggested, but with little systematic evidence."

Raphel et al. (1994, p. 3) observe that

"There are no controlled studies of debriefing as a preventive intervention with the random allocation of subjects to treatment groups. Moreover, a major problem with most debriefing is the lack of followup."

McFarlane (1994, p.13) goes even further than Orner when he notes some **potential "dangers" in conducting CISD.**

"There are many victims who cope adequately and do not become symptomatic. The focus of mental health professionals on the negative outcome of these events may in itself have a detrimental effect on the communities. The few outcome studies of debriefing which have comparison groups suggest that these interventions **may worsen the outcome of some of those participating** rather than having the desired effect of lessening the distress of those involved."

McFarlane (1994, p.19) also concludes:

"The findings from all of the studies of CISD must throw open the question of the nature of debriefing and whether it has the benefits its proponents suggest and whether it may have **adverse effects** interfering with natural restoration and processing or just delaying the onset rather than preventing it. Nevertheless, these concerns must be placed alongside strong perceptions of its helpfulness."

In further support of their argument Yehuda and McFarlane (1994, unpublished manuscript) have observed that:

"The few controlled studies that have examined the preventative effect of debriefing immediately following exposure to a traumatic event have suggested a **poorer outcome** following debriefing as compared with no intervention. For example, Griffiths and Watts (1992) found that emergency service personnel who attended debriefing following a bus crash had significantly higher levels of symptoms at the 12 month followup. Kenardy et al (1993) reported that individuals who were not debriefed following the Newcastle Earthquake over a two year period showed more rapid reduction in symptoms. Others have found debriefing and preventive counseling ineffective, but not detrimental (p. 19)."

Based on this data, Yehuda and McFarlane propose that preventative short-term interventions such as debriefing may be beneficial for only a subset of individuals. In individuals whose symptoms may subside over time, interventions "may actually be harmful" (p. 20). Thus, great care[1] must be taken <u>not</u> to worsen the trauma-exposed individuals.

In a thoughtful and scholarly critique, Raphael, McFarlane and Meldram (1994, unpublished manuscript) critically evaluate acute interventions after traumatic events. They raise the possibility "that debriefing may lead to secondary traumatization ... there have been some reports of people feeling they were worse after debriefing, upset or not helped" (p. 20). Thus, while CISD is a promising intervention, there is a need for systematic evaluation.

Hiley-Young and Gerrity (1994, p.17) have also recently evaluated CISD and concluded:

> "We recognize that CISD procedures may help some disaster victims. We are concerned, however, that an **unreasonable expectation** of CISD usefulness may be developing among field practitioners".

They highlight the distinction between a "critical incident" (e.g., shooting, on-the-job accident) and a community-wide disaster that involves not only the stress of trauma exposure and initial losses, but also the variety of resulting problems and continuing adversities. They also comment that a number of people (25%) who are exposed to disasters may have a history of untreated mental illness, **"Thus further questioning the usefulness of focusing solely on the 'critical incident'"** (p.18).

Similarly, Wilson and Raphael, (1994) propose a **broader-based debriefing approach**. This more extensive approach may entail repeated debriefings over time; plus individualized counseling, or referral to specialized clinics. Such post-disaster interventions can be supplemented with predisaster education and training (Alexander and Wells, 1991). Like Hiley-Young and Gerrity, Wilson and Raphael highlight the need to go beyond the post-disaster 24 to 72 hour debriefing format. Raphael et al. (1994) also highlight the need to consider background organizational stressors that provide the context for understanding the impact of the traumatization experience as evident, in the employee shootings in the post-offices in the US.

In sum, CISD may provide some immediate opportunities for victims to talk with one another, but it is **unlikely to provide effective treatment** for complex, ongoing, or persistent problems that are the result of the disaster itself, predisaster vulnerabilities, or the variety of social conditions that surround it. **"We [Hiley-Young and Gerrity] caution against the unquestioned acceptance of CISD debriefing procedures as a sufficient intervention following community-wide disasters"** (p.18).

These concerns need to be juxtaposed with other accounts of favorable outcomes of post-disaster interventions. For example, in Armenia, Pynoos et al. (1994) report on the use of two classroom debriefings followed by three to four individual and group sessions conducted 1 1/2 years after the earthquake. The debriefing significantly reduced the severity of posttraumatic stress reactions compared to untreated controls. These results are impressive when we learn that almost 92% of the children exposed to the earthquake experienced severe or very severe posttraumatic reactions given the magnitude and

---

[1] In support of this cautionary observation, Raphael et al. (1994) note that despite timely interventions (debriefing, counseling), many high exposure workers evidenced continual disabilities and distress (e.g. Weissaeth, 1984 with survivors of a factory disaster; Smith et al., 1989 with survivors of a plane crash; Kenardy et al., in press, with earthquake survivors; and McFarlane, 1993, with firefighters). These empirical studies need to be kept in mind when considering the overall favorable perception and increasing popularity of debriefing interventions.

unremitting severity of the disaster. But in most such studies of CISD the comparison group is usually an untreated control group. With **caution in mind**, let us consider the specific features of CISD.

C. Goals of CISD (See Mitchell, 1983. 1987, 1988, for a more detailed discussion.)

1. The debriefer should insure that the participant's basic needs are met and that all needed information has been provided.

2. Have the participants share, verbally reconstruct, and ventilate the most acute, intense emotions (e.g., shock, disbelief, anxiety, fear, terror, anger, regret). Have participants tell what happened and how it affected them. Discuss the "roller coaster" of emotions that people may feel and work through "emotional overload". (Note, that while all participants are given an opportunity for ventilation of feelings, the leaders should not insist that all participants share such feelings.)

3. Have the participants explore the symbolic "meaning" of the loss.

4. The debriefer should nurture reassurance about the "normality" of the participant's intense emotions and reduce feelings of "uniqueness". The individuals' responses should be seen as "reactions" and not as "symptoms" in order not "medicalize" the process.

5. The debriefer should provide group support and enhance peer social supports: initiate the grief process within a supportive environment and improve group cohesion. While this is a worthwhile goal, Raphael et al. (1994) caution that the group setting may not always prove positive or supportive. A participant may have behaved in a manner that elicits resentment and anger and this can be exacerbated by group CISD. Such possible reactions may explain nonparticipation by some.

6. The debriefer should reduce misconceptions and correct misinformation about events and about "normal" and "abnormal" stress reactions. Reassure normalcy of reactions.

7. The debriefer should encourage, teach and reinforce coping efforts (e.g., the need that many people have to talk about their distress, to work it out physically, to help others, to do something to regain control, to identify sympathetic individuals who can provide support).

8. The group should discuss ways to reduce tension and anxiety. The debriefer should teach specific stress-reducing coping techniques, begin the grief process and prepare participants for the possible continuation of grief reactions in the subsequent months. For example, warn the participants about the possibility of the development of symptoms and prepare them for stress reactions, especially at critical points like anniversary dates or at commemorative times.

9. The debriefer should help facilitate the participant's return to routine pre-incident functioning and encourage continued group support and/or professional assistance.

10. The debriefer should screen and refer "high risk" participants for professional assistance. There is a need to continually monitor progress since delayed or long-term reactions are possible. Gerrity and Steinglass (1994) highlight the value of not only monitoring the client, but also the client's family situation. If communication breaks down, family recovery is threatened.

11. The debriefer should highlight that one purpose of the debriefing is to reconstruct what really happened so that the "group," "team," "organization", "community" benefits from the lessons learned.

D. Format of CISD

1. Debriefings usually take place in a relatively safe environment where recountings can be offered. The debriefings often range from 60 to 90 minutes or may last up to 2 to 3 hours. A shorter version, called **defusing** may take 20 to 45 minutes. The defusing meetings may range from 1 meeting to several sessions. They usually take place in settings where the individuals gather.

2. **Defusing** may be viewed as a briefer parallel version of CISD. It is usually implemented immediately, or shortly after, the traumatic event and is of a shorter duration (usually about 1 hour, as compared to 2-3 hours for CISD), and more focused. Mitchell and Everly (1994) view defusing as more flexible than CISD, involving introductory, exploration, and information phases. It is usually held with rescue or treatment specialists during protracted operations to help them deal with accumulating stress. During extended critical incidents such as a lengthy rescue operation, it may be possible to conduct several short defusings. The defusing meetings provide an opportunity to discuss events. The meetings often include:

    a) a brief description of the guidelines for the meeting;
    b) factual exploration of the incident from the perspective of each participant;
    c) advice offered about how to prevent and cope with psychological effects such as the need to recognize and "normalize" signs and symptoms, the need for self-care behaviors such as rest intervals, eating, exercise; and
    d) an examination of possible coping techniques.

3. Both debriefing and defusing are usually conducted as semi-structured group meetings consisting of 6 to 15 people who had been exposed to the trauma. Meetings are often led by trained, organized CISD team members (1 to 3 members) and selected trained peer support members or trained counsellors who are not participants in the incident for which the debriefing is to be held. CISD is essentially "peer driven." Debriefing may also be conducted on an individual basis (Pynoos & Eth, 1986).

4. Participants include anyone potentially affected by the impact of the event. The CISD may be held in subgroups if there are natural divisions such as survivors, rescuers, and relatives of casualties.

5. Usually the debriefing meetings are held within 24 to 72 hours after the critical incident. Prior to 24 hours there is usually a high degree of activity that precludes such group meetings and after 72 hours the participants begin to experience physical and emotional reactions to the stressor that may be unfamiliar and troubling. The timing of when debriefings occur depend upon the nature of the disaster. In some instances, debriefing may occur 2 to 5 days after the incident, while with extensive disasters such as floods and hurricanes, the debriefing may occur much later. In the case of earthquakes with continuing aftershocks the period for debriefing may be extended. The uncertainty of future damage and injury, the continuing reminders underscore the need for debriefings. The debriefing may be conducted at the site of the trauma or within the same organizational setting.

6. Yule (1993) has proposed that debriefing children and their parents during the first 48 hours following a disaster may be too soon. Somewhere around 7 to 14 days after the disaster seems best. In contrast, Pynoos and Eth (1986) report good responses from

children interviewed just a few hours after the traumatic events took place. Thus, experts differ on the best timing for debriefing and how debriefing should be implemented. At this point there is no data to resolve these disagreements.

7.   CISD is usually led by 2 to 4 leaders depending upon the number of people in the group. At least one leader is usually a peer coming from the local organization or area. Having co-leaders provide an opportunity for mutual support and debriefing each other. The emphasis in these meetings is on the use of peers as social support agents. The peer leaders are chosen to match the group being debriefed. The peer support personnel are often drawn from the high risk occupational group (e.g., police, fire, military, emergency medical service). (See Mitchell and Bray, 1993.) In some CISD models peer leaders are not used and mental health workers act as the assigned debriefers.

8.   At the outset, the group may be conducted so each participant has an opportunity to speak as the individuals go around the room relating their experiences. As the meeting unfolds (for example, by the fourth stage -- reaction phase) the group discussion may become more "freelance" as participants speak as they feel the urge (Mitchell & Everly, 1994). The structure of the phases should not inhibit participants from speaking at any phase and this should be conveyed to the group. In some models the "freelance" format occurs well before the fourth phase.

9.   It is more effective (and easier) to collect together the overall experience of the group before exploring individual reactions, and secondly to explore what happened, before inquiring about emotional reactions (Turnbull, 1993).

V   How to Conduct Debriefing Sessions? -- Description of CISD Phases

1.   Introductory Phase

Objective: to introduce team members, explain process, and set expectations

Debriefing staff members are introduced and the purpose of the meeting is conveyed. Introduce debriefing staff, the debriefing process and provide an overview of what will occur and how it can help. Offer debriefing rules such as the following (see Mitchell, 1988, and Spitzer & Burke, 1993, for more details).

a)   Mitchell highlights that the participants should be told about privacy and confidentiality (unless some imminent danger arises). The group is told that no disclosures will be made to superiors or to the press. Agreement by all participants to uphold privacy. No note taking or recording is allowed. Some debriefers have told me about their concerns about the "confidentiality issue," since legislation on this issue vary from state to state, and as a result the debriefers and participants may be put into a difficult position. They suggest that the confidentiality issue should not be raised with the participants.

b)   Definition of debriefing as not formal therapy, nor psychological treatment, but rather as stress management services. Debriefers are identified as "disaster stress relief workers". (Titles like "Dr." and the use of psychiatric and psychological jargon are omitted).

c)   Encouragement of participants to speak, although there is no obligation to speak during the sessions. Silent participation is acceptable. When participants speak they should speak only for themselves. The leader should thank the participants for being so open and then solicit permission to obtain more information. "Thank you for being so open. If it is okay, I would like to chat with you some more, if you would be willing". The tone conveyed should be to put the participants in charge of what and how much to self-disclose.

d) Disclosures are not used against attendees in any way. Judgment and operational critiques are not permitted. Debriefings are not situational critiques, nor performance appraisals, nor operational debriefings, nor investigations/inquiries. They allow "emotional ventilation." Turnbull (1993) provides an important **cavaet about the use of emotion in debriefing**. In discussing debriefing of relief workers after the Lockerbie air disaster he notes:

> "We also rapidly learned a cardinal rule in debriefing - **that it is <u>not</u> advisable to begin with inquiring about the emotional reactions of "exposure-hardened" individuals**. It was more effective (and easier) to **collect together the overall experience of the group before exploring individual reactions**. The correction of individual misinterpretations and misconceptions using this technique was very impressive" (p. 14).

Abueg et al. (1994) highlight the need for the leader of the debriefing to help participants manage affect. They note that if participants have been exposed to massive loss of life, or to grotesque and horrific human injury, the potential for dissociation and decompensation is high. They observe:

> "Participants may show evidence of this behavior subtly, by fixing their gaze and becoming inattentive or perseverative. Overt signs of dissociation include alterations in speech or behavior that reflects reexperiencing the original trauma in the here and now of the group. In such instances, experienced debriefers will slow or interrupt the process" (p.243).

Participants can also be provided with quick reassurances. The leader can indicate "That's okay. Everyone will space out once in a while".

e) Premature departures are discouraged and in some instances may not be permitted.

f) The group makeup may be by rank. The presence of administrators and section chiefs may make individuals feel less comfortable and inhibit self-disclosure. Individuals may fear a procedural critique. In addition, individuals often have angry feelings toward administrators which they may need to express. If the group is heterogeneous, then once it is formulated then the participants are treated equally, regardless of rank or position.

g) Remind the participants to anticipate the possible temporary worsening of reactions or symptoms following group discussion. Clarify that debriefings do <u>not</u> cause these "negative" feelings.

h) Reiterate that team members are available following the meeting to speak with participants, to provide assistance and guidance, and to act as a referral source.

i) Convey and reiterate that the purpose of the group is to acknowledge, share, empathize, reassure, and support each other throughout the process.

2. Fact Phase

Objective: to describe traumatic events from each participant's perspective, beginning at the point that is easiest to discuss -- description of facts of the incident or a detailed account of experience and losses and only subsequently ventilate affect and explore meaning.

a)   Participants are asked to tell who they are, to describe the event (what happened), where were they, and what they were doing during the critical events, what was going on, what they experienced (include sensory perceptions of sights, sounds, smells), what they witnessed, what they heard about the event and where they heard it. Ask, "What was your role?", "What did you do?", "What happened out there?" **Every person has a story to tell.**

b)   Mitchell and Everly (1994) suggest that the following general statement provides a useful opening to facilitate discussion.

> "The CISD team was not present during the incident. We only know some bits and pieces of the incident. It would be very helpful if we could get some understanding of what happened by having each of you tell us about the incident. So we would like you to tell us who you are, what your role was during the incident, and briefly, what happened from your perspective. Again, what we need to know is 'Who are you?', 'What was your job or involvement during the incident?', and 'What happened from your point of view?'" (p. 363,364).

c)   The trainer may also ask a number of additional questions. "Would you be willing to tell us what happened? What exactly happened here? To whom? For how long? Was there any warning? Were you afraid you might die or be injured? What was the most horrifying aspect of the situation? Did you feel that the actions of others could have changed what happened? Do you feel that there is someone to blame for what happened? Do you feel there is someone to blame for how it was handled?"

d)   Each person takes a turn adding details until the entire incident is described. In this way the CISD can help the participants sort out the story of what happened.

e)   If a family member was found dead, how was news obtained? What were the circumstances? What assistance was provided?

f)   If damage, what was the extent of property loss and the consequences?

3.   Thought (Cognition) Phase: Cognitive Review Phase

Objective: to allow participants to describe cognitive reactions

a)   Participants are asked to reveal the <u>first or most prominent thoughts</u> they were aware of during the incident or can recall upon reflection (tap personal aspects of the situation).

b)   The leader may ask:

> "What were your thoughts when you got to the scene and things started happening?"
> "What was going through your head?"
> "What was the first thing you thought of when you went off 'autopilot'?"
> "What do you think about the event now?"
> "What will you take away with you from this event?"
> "What will stay with you from this event?"
> "Can anything 'positive' come out of this event?"

c)   The leader can use self-disclosure by noting, "In a similar situation, I ...".

4.   Reaction (Feeling) Phase

Objective: to identify the most traumatic aspects of the event for the participants

a)   Participants are assisted in recognizing strong emotions that accompany (during and subsequent to) exposure to the incident.

b)   Participants are encouraged to discuss the effects, not just on themselves, but on those around them (friends, family, colleagues, neighbors)--so-called "ripple effects."

c)   Leader "normalizes" and "legitimizes" these feelings. "Normal response to an abnormal situation"; not a sign of "going crazy". Depending upon the nature of the disaster indicate that "no one can be trained to do what they did (e.g., walk among carnage, burning flesh and body parts) and remain unaffected.

d)   Convey the value in identifying and discussing such feelings. Commend participants that "being in touch" with such feelings is an important first step in the healing process.

e)   Wolfe (1991) and Mitchell and Everly (1994) suggest the use of the following questions:

"What was the worst thing (aspect) of the event for you personally?"
"How did you feel when it happened?"
"What was it like for you?"
"How did you react at the scene?"
"What did you feel during the event?"
"How do you feel about the event now?"
"How are you feeling now?"
"How is this affecting you physically?...emotionally?...socially?"

To this list can be added a series of questions suggested by Abueg et al. (1994). They propose asking questions that "pull for" **serial or contextual cues.** For example, the leader can ask about the survivor's **sensory experiences** at the height of the trauma. "What did you see? hear? touch? smell? They propose tapping **proprioceptive and kinesthetic cues** associated with the sensations of one's body position (being "crushed, pinned, cramped").

They also suggest assessing for the **context of the trauma** by asking about the individual'ssense of responsibility/guilt/shame? For example, "Does the individual feel as if

...he/she did _not_ do enough?
...made a mistake during the recovery phase?
...somehow was responsible for some untoward consequence?

f)   As noted, emotional responses are acknowledged and normalized.

5. Symptom Phase

Objective: to identify personal symptoms of distress

a)   This phase is initiated when participants are asked to describe any cognitive, physical, emotional, or behavioral experiences they may have had while they were at or working at the scene of the incident. They discuss symptoms of distress at the scene as well as symptoms that followed subsequently (e.g., emotional lability, sleep disturbance, depressed feelings, intrusive thoughts, substance abuse, etc.).

b) Participants are asked to trace in a chronological fashion, their reactions covering different intervals (e.g., immediately following the incident, initial 24 hours, and present time). Have participants recognize that their reactions may take various forms including behavioral, physical, emotional and cognitive. Have participants describe reactions in these different areas. Help participants appreciate that their reactions follow a time course. Have participants describe changes in their reactions.

"Has anyone experienced signs of distress since the event?"
"What are some of those signs of stress reactions?"

c) Use the phrase "stress reactions", instead of "symptoms" or "disorder" in order not to "medicalize" nor pathologize the participant's response. Stay away from psychiatric jargon.

d) Explore any particular concerns that the participants may have had. Ask the participants, "How has life changed for him/her and significant others since the stressful incident?"

6.   Teaching (Educational) Phase

Objective: to educate participants to "normal" reactions and adaptive coping processes. The military have an expression that should characterize this phase. They call it the KISS Principle--"Keep it simple, stupid."

a) Emphasis is placed on insuring that participants have accurate information about the incident and about stress reactions and patterns of recovery.

b) Educate the group about common stress responses (discuss reactions). Discuss the physiology of stress in lay terms (e.g., "fight" and "flight" responses). Help them appreciate the variety of symptoms that constitute stress reactions including constant fearful vigilance, sleep difficulties and nightmares, flashbacks and intrusive memories, preoccupying thoughts of the trauma, anxiety, anger, emotional numbness, depression with accompanying withdrawal and loss of interests.

c) Convey the expectation that people may experience stress in relation to their duties and convey the expectation that most people evidence adaptability and resilience.

d) Discuss elements of positive readjustment patterns (cognitive reframing, group cohesion and social support). Discuss the need to provide reassurance to children and constancy of care.

e) Present and discuss strategies for alleviating stress response (e.g., how to use social supports by talking about feelings and thoughts with others, and other coping responses such as relaxation procedures, exercise, proper diet and sleep, working with supervisors to initiate procedural changes).

f) Participants are taught how to be aware of the signs of stress and taught techniques that are effective in reducing excessive stress. Discuss possible "triggers" and how to handle these. Warn about possible resurgence of symptoms in the presence of reminders.

g) Participants cautioned about possible complications such as alcohol or drug abuse, interpersonal conflicts, need to avoid criticism, avoid misinforming children about the deceased, avoid being overprotective of children.

h)   Provide additional information about stressful reactions. For example, highlight that the signs of distress ("symptoms") are "normal, typical and to be expected" after the critical incident that they have experienced.

The following information may be given to individuals in a written form:

i)   Realize that symptoms are a normal response to traumatic events.

ii)   There is value in talking about the pain with others. Even tending to a pet may comfort many.

iii)   Release stress through some form of expression (e.g., exercise, art, music). Simply crying may work for some.

iv)   If symptoms become so severe to become disruptive seek professional help.

*For additional suggestions about what should be covered see the "Handout on Educating Individuals about PTSD" in this **Handbook/Manual** (Section VI).*

i)   Discuss what additional resources are available for those who wish to avail themselves of such services. Keep in mind that victims of disasters tend to avoid the use of formal agencies, preferring to turn to their informal networks for social support. But some kin may engender (rather than reduce) stress levels. Assess for the network of social supports and discuss how these can be used.

7. Re-entry (Wind-down) Phase

Objective: to clarify ambiguities, prepare for termination and assess for follow-up meetings

a)   This stage allows for questions, review, reassurances and the establishment of action plans.

b)   Provide summary statements of what has transpired in the group, reiterate commonly made points, linking member's comments to the elements of the adjustment process.

c)   Encourage participants to discuss anything they wish that would help them bring closure to the debriefing. Encouragement is also given to the participants to learn to take one day at a time.

d)   Additional referral resources are made available. For example, Goenjian (1993) noted that approximately 20% of victims of the Armenian earthquake required longer-term therapy (up to 6 months). Be sensitive to possible premorbid factors, especially prior exposure to traumatic events. Abueg et al. (1994) describe how a debriefing relationship was translated into a "brief therapeutic contract" for clients in need.

e)   Handouts are offered that reiterate information on stress reactions and coping techniques. Include accompanying versions of the handouts for significant others. Include in the handout the leaders' telephone numbers and numbers and addresses of referral sources. Keep the vocabulary in the handouts simple (see Meichenbaum & Turk, 1987, for a discussion of how such education can be conducted).

f)   The facilitator attempts to wrap up loose ends, answer remaining questions, provide reassurance, emphasize the role of communication, acknowledge competence and nurture cohesion of the group, and suggest and discuss future plans of actions *(e.g., see ritual section below)*. The client should be encouraged to use his/her **personal**

gauge as to whether or not to seek help from friends, family, or from a professional. Remind the participants that having been exposed to exceptional stress make us all vulnerable.

g)   Each CISD team member should offer a summary comment in the last few minutes of the debriefing. Invite participants to offer their observations on how the meetings have helped.

VI   Alternative Modes and Models For Post-Trauma Interventions

The CISD is only one model of post-disaster intervention. A number of alternative post-disaster intervention models have been developed. These models may focus on (1) **pre-incident educational interventions** that attempt to bolster relevant preparedness (e.g., show training films followed by stress inoculation procedures); (2) **interventions** that occur **at the time of the stressful events** such as demobilization and deescalation meetings that may be as short as 10 minutes and that emphasize "normality" of reactions and provide practical suggestions on how to cope more effectively; (3) **post-incident followup** meetings covering such variations as CISD, peer support, and individual and group counseling. Which model (or combination of models) is employed depends upon the nature of the "target" population, support staff available, and specific settings (e.g., providing help for hostage taking, bank robbery, school-based or work-setting violence, military settings). The following section (A to H) provide a brief description of some of the alternative models. Once again, note the limited empirical evaluation of these alternatives. We begin with peer support programs that may be unstructured or structured.

A. Peer support

Counseling by peers who have survived a similar incident themselves, or who can provide an account of similar traumatic stress, has been used in post-disaster interventions (Omer, 1994). The peers act as coping models as they refer to not only their experience, but also to their coping efforts. The nature of the peers self-disclosure has to be carefully calibrated in order not to overwhelm the survivors. The peer counsellors must be taught how to be good listeners, nonjudgmental and accepting, empathic and supportive without being too demanding nor intrusive. The peer counselor can help "normalize" and "validate" the survivors' experiences. The peer counselor can be taught how to be a "good helper", using Socratic questioning (*see Section III*). It is critical that the peer counselors not become **surrogate frontal lobes** for survivors, but help the survivors become empowered and feel enabled in generating coping strategies. The peer counselors can offer advice when requested, and they can screen survivors for the need for additional help. The peer counselling may be held on a structured basis with scheduled meetings, or meetings could be provided on an informal basis (1 on 1 or on small group basis). (*The material in this Handbook/Manual has been used to train peer counselors.*)

B. Outreach model

Another mode of post-trauma intervention (postvention) was offered by van der Ploeg and Kleijn (1989) who developed an **outreach treatment model** for victims of **hostage taking**. Their treatment involved:

1.   Intervention by groups of professionals including counselors and general practitioners.

2.   Outreach visits conducted at the homes of victims interested in receiving help. These visits were conducted within <u>one week</u> of release from hostage situation.

3. Encouragement for victims and family members to discuss the incident and possible coping efforts.

4. Availability of additional help.

Utterback and Caldwell (1989) describe how such an outreach program can be conducted on both a preventative and treatment basis on a college campus with the formation of a Traumatic Stress React Team (TSRT) in response to incidents of violent crimes.

C. Debriefing on an individual basis

Manton and Talbot (1990) and Talbot (1990) note the particular features of stress debriefing when the formulation of a specific group process is not feasible, as in the case of a **bank robbery** or an armed holdup where a homogeneous group does not exist. They use a series of individual sessions immediately after the incident within an hour of the event and see all staff members, usually individually. This is followed up the next day and at 2, 3, and 7 week follow-up periods. Individuals who have experienced such traumatic events are particularly concerned with "what if" questions. "What if the robber returns?; What if the robber knows who I am?, etc." These questions are carefully addressed to insure participant's safety. A key feature of the intervention is to facilitate the return of the individual to work (even for a short period, or with the in vivo support of the therapist). Follow-up is also critical. They also debrief the counsellors after the branch visits. The debriefing includes an exploration of "the roles the counsellors have filled, their frustrations and satisfactions, resources, and their feelings during and after the work." The debriefing addresses "whom did you see, what did you do, how did you perceive this person, what was the experience like for you, do you identify in any way?" (p. 269). They may use an outside person to conduct the debriefing of the counsellors. See Morton and Talbot (1988) and Raphael (1986) for more details.

Norris and Thompson (1993) have noted that the criminal justice system response can intensify or allay the victim's alienated state and influence the rate of recovery. Their work has important implications in training police and others on how to respond to victims with compassion.

D. Debriefing children and families following a disaster: PTSD in children

> *"In the US alone, based on conservative estimates the incidence of sexual and physical abuse and exposure to community and domestic violece, **more than 3 million children were exposed to traumatic events last year**" (Schwarz and Perry, 1994, p. 311)*

While this **Handbook/Manual** has focused primarily on adults it is important to recognize the need for interventions with children after disasters. This need was highlighted in the recent American Psychological Association Task Force Report on Psychological Responses of Children to Natural and Human-made Disasters. This report was published in the Journal of Clinical and Child Psychology, 1993, Volume 22, No. 4 (see Vogel & Vernberg 1993; Vernberg & Vogel, 1993). Additional useful resources on disaster and children have been offered by Saylor (1993), Schwarz and Perry, 1994; Gillis (1993), Pynoos & Nader, (1993), Yule (1993), Yule and Udwin (1993). It is from these resources, as well as from my clinical and consulting experience, that the following intervention guidelines have been formulated. Space precludes my developing this section further. For more details about possible interventions with children that could be conducted during the predisaster phase, impact phase, short-term and long-term phases, see Vernberg and Vogel, (1993).

Before we examine the nature of possible post-disaster interventions, let us first examine briefly the impact of natural disasters on children.[1] Perhaps, the most succinct summaries have been offered by Garmezy and Rutter (1985) and Belter and Shannon (1993) who observed:

Regarding the effects of stressors on children Garmezy and Rutter (1985, p. 162) conclude that:

"behavioral disturbances appear to be **less intense** than might have been anticipated; a majority of children show a moderate amount of fear and anxiety but this subsides; regressive behavior marked by clinging to parents and heightened dependency on adults appears and then moderately mild sleep disturbance persists for several months; a later less severe stressor such as a storm may lead to a temporary increase in emotional distress, although this is variable; enuresis occurs in some cases, while hypersensitivity to loud noises may be evident in others".

In the majority of cases the **disturbances are short-lived,** as reflected in the following quote from Belter and Shannon (1993).

"Diagnosable psychopathology is _not_ commonly seen in the great majority of children who experience a natural disaster ... Most children report high levels of PTSD symptoms, but this does _not_ result in widespread diagnosable psychopathology ... The acute effects diminish over time, with long-term effects for most children being minimal ... Younger children are affected to a greater degree than are older children and adolescents ... The extent to which the child's parents are negatively impacted by the disaster and have difficulty coping with it appears to be related to the impact of the disaster on the child" (p. 99-100).

Vogel and Vernberg (1993) drew similar conclusions when they observed:

"Children's symptoms typically decrease rapidly, and recovery is generally complete by 18 months to 3 years, except after severe life threat or long-term family/community disruption" (p. 461). ... Children and adolescents who exhibit the most pronounced symptoms of distress in the first few weeks after a disaster appear to be at greatest risk for developing subsequent clinical disorders" (p. 454).

They also comment on the signs of distress (PTSD symptoms) in children which may include:

a)   Sleep disturbance, nightmares, not sleep alone, problem getting to sleep.

b)   Preoccupation with the traumatic event as evident in repetitive behaviors and repeated dreams.

c)   Stereotypic play behavior and behavioral reenactments. (Children under 6 are more likely to show repetitive play and repetitive drawings.)

---

[1] There is some evidence to suggest that children are more vulnerable to less extreme stressors than those which may cause PTSD in adults, Hyman et al., 1988. See Amaya-Jackson & March, 1993, Eth & Pynoos, 1985, Johnson, 1989; March & Amaya-Jackson, 1993 and Reiss et al., 1993 for additional references on children and traumatic events.

d)   Minimal ability to enjoy themselves (e.g. in play). Thematic repetitive play is evident associated both with anxiety about a traumatic event and the reduction of that anxiety (Saylor, 1991).

e)   Numbing affect.

f)   Difficulty to relax (irritability, panic).

g)   Hyperarousal and hypervigilance (exaggerated startle response).

h)   Vacillation between withdrawal, friendliness, and aggressive outbursts (compliant, withdrawn, and aggressive).

i)   Poor peer interactions.

j)   Trauma specific fears and fears of the mundane (e.g., the darkness, strangers, being alone, being outside, animals); fear of reoccurrence.

k)   Separation difficulties, clingy, dependent behaviors.

l)   Deliberate avoidance behaviors (e.g. school absenteeism).

m)   Regressive behavior to early developmental levels, especially for children younger than 7 (e.g., enuresis).

n)   Anxiety and depression, (limited sense of the future).

o)   In older children -- substance abuse, acting out aggressive or sexual behaviours.

p)   Among adolescents -- guilt over predisaster behavior, depression, and guilt feelings related to loss of friends and loved ones, being secretive and distrusting of people.

q)   Psychogenic amnesia, intrusive flashbacks, and psychic numbing which are often seen in adult PTSD clients are **less common among children** with PTSD. Children are less likely to give adult-like descriptions of flashbacks, rather they describe intrusive specific vivid images or sounds related to the traumatic event (Pynoos & Nader, 1988). Repeated dreams are rare before age 5, while "reseeing behaviors of traumas may occur during periods of leisure or boredom" (Terr, 1994). Denial, psychic numbing and dissociative features are rarely encountered by children exposed to type I stressor. More common in exposure to Type II stressors.

r)   Presence of psychsomatic complaints, loss of appetite.

Terr (1994) has summarized these multiple signs of distress in traumatized children as consisting of:

1)   strongly visualized or repeatedly perceived memories;
2)   repetitive behaviors;
3)   trauma-specific fears and separation anxiety;
4)   changed attitudes about people, aspects of life, and the future;
5)   loss of acquired developmental skills.

Shannon et al. (1994) have reported on the 3 month followup of 5687 school-age children who had experienced Hurricane Hugo. They found that females and younger children were most vulnerable to the effects of high magnitude exposure. Lonigan et al.

(1994) describe a variety of risk factors for the development of PTSD. I have included these factors in Table 1 in this section. Interestingly, "children who reported that they experienced high levels of being sad, worried, scared, or feeling alone, were up to 5.8 times more likely to exhibit PTSD". The child's immediate reaction to trauma was found to be an important predictor of his/her recovery.

With these clinical observations in mind we can now consider the **debriefing process and other post-disaster interventions with children and their families.** Pynoos et al. (1994) have proposed that the post-disaster interventions with children may take several forms including:

a) psychological first aid
b) specialized initial debriefing interviews
c) brief therapy
d) "pulsed" interventions[1] (theray that is provided at critical junctures)
e) long term psychotherapy

These interventions may be conducted on an individual, group, family, school, and/or community basis. The goals of these interventions include the need to:

a) normalize and legitimize the children's disaster experiences
b) nurture greater tolerance of posttraumatic reactions
c) process or rework the meaning of the event and curtail rumors
d) increase recognition of and adaptation to traumatic reminders
e) ameliorate stress reactions and facilitate grief work
f) address stress that accompanies secondary adversities
g) promptly address early signs of maladaptive behavior
h) enhance responsiveness of social support network

With these treatment goals in mind we can now consider some specific treatment guidelines. Before we do so, however, we should keep in mind Vogel and Vernberg's (1993, p. 485) observation that **"relatively little evaluation of disaster-related interventions with children has been published."**

1. Children need to be **reunited** with their parents and family as soon as possible. But there is a need to help parents recognize that how they react at the time of the reunion and subsequently can have a significant impact on their children. In fact, McFarlane et al. (1989) reported that the mothers response to disaster was a better predictor of the child's response than was the child's exposure to the disaster.

2. Reestablish the school environment and regimen as soon as possible, even under adverse conditions. School can provide a **safe environment** in which a **recounting of events** can take place and a more detailed retelling of the disaster events and reactions can be offered by the children. Most groupings of children are by age and level of exposure to traumatic events. Sometimes groups are formed by sex (Vernberg & Vogel, 1993). The school setting provides a setting where such **retellings** may take place. Children may be encouraged to share, express by means of drawings, poems, plays, story telling, coloring books, where were they, what happened during the disaster, **and** what the children would like to see happen in order to make them feel safer about the disaster (e.g., earthquakes). A key feature to be highlighted in the class group discussions is the value of **including constructive activities** where children can convey by means of play, fantasy and actions some form of instrumental coping acts.

---

[1] *"Pulsed" interventions were described in Section V under the heading of the length of treatment.*

As suggested by Pynoos et al (1994), the classroom group discussions usually begin with an examination of the range of experiences and reactions that the children had, without introducing specific graphic details. The debriefing of more specific details for any specific child is usually done at a subsequent session, either individually, or in a small group, or within the larger group setting. These latter sessions can include suggestions about ways to understand and cope with post-disaster distress and the stress of additional adversities. For example, the group examines the childrens' feelings of helplessness, loss of control, fear of reoccurrence, and reactions to reminders of traumatic events, as well as the need to communicate and share such reactions with significant others.

Also see Hiley-Young and Giles (1991) for a description of a child intervention post-disaster program. They highlight the value of helping groups of children to express thoughts and feelings about their experience and they underscore the value of having the **children be proactive** either in their story-telling (e.g., noting how their lives have changed and how the events had made them stronger, wiser, more considerate). The children may also be engaged in some activity such as planting trees after a fire, writing letters to other victims, collecting food, toys to share with less fortunate.

3.   During the preliminary debriefing session children are encouraged to describe and share their post-disaster reactions. Children are also encouraged to share feelings with a family member, friend, teacher, pet, or self, (drawing, writing). For example, discuss with the group of children, "When you have feelings, who do you talk to?" The therapist models, "When bad things happen to me, sometimes I feel X (afraid). Sometimes I get Y (mad). That is okay. I need to take care of myself. I do Z (talk to someone about how I feel.") Ask group members, what they do? Who do they talk to? Pynoos et al. (1994) provide examples of other age-appropriate statements that can be offered to children. These include:

   a)   "If you see something terrible happen to someone you may see pictures of it in your mind for longer than you think."

   b)   "It is pretty hard to concentrate as well right after going through something as frightening as this."

   c)   "It is hard not to have your mommy or daddy be able to get to you right away when the earthquake started."

   d)   "It is hard to walk by that building that fell down without thinking about what happened during the earthquake."

   e)   "We are all likely to get more afraid the next time there is a high wind."

   f)   "It's okay if things don't seem as much fun as they used to, for now; this is a lot to go through."

   g)   "It helps to let someone know when something reminds you of what happened, because even your mommy or daddy taking your hand at that moment can make you feel better."

   h)   "If you are having bad dreams, it helps to let your parents know."

   i)   "If you are having pictures of what happened bother you at school which make it hard for you to learn, it will help to let your teacher know."

4.   It may be necessary to also assess for possible victimization in children. Schwarz and
     Perry (1994, p. 319) suggest the following questions:

> Have you ever been hurt by anyone? ... touched in a way you didn't like? ...
>   treated in a way you didn't like?
> Have you ever seen something that really scared you?
> Have you ever had nightmares? ... got real jumpy?

5.   Survivors need to talk over what happened in order to get the sequence of events clear,
     as well as to master feelings that recall engenders. This guideline applies to not only
     the children, but also to the children's principals, teachers, and parents. Pynoos et al.
     (1994) highlight the need to work with and enlist the cooperation of **school
     principals** who may be seen individually or in groups in order to address their
     emotional needs and to develop collaboratively a flexible intervention problem-solving
     plan. With the principal on-board the **teachers** can be seen in groups in order to
     address their disaster experiences and those of their family members. The teachers can
     be invaluable helpers as they learn about what to expect from their students during the
     post disaster period and how to "screen" children for possible further interventions.
     The teachers can be taught how to conduct group sessions. In fact, the leader who is
     running the teacher's group meeting is modeling ways to run such meetings. The
     group leader can ask the teachers to:

     a)   describe what happened to them and those around them (help them sort out the
          order of events)

     b)   describe initial reactions and actions and note the range of experience

     c)   describe their "worst moments" (Ask "When did you first feel out of danger
          following the X?)

     d)   examine the presence and reactions to reminders of traumatic events

     e)   discuss how to explain post disaster reactions to students in age-appropriate
          language

     f)   examine how to acknowledge, understand and tolerate dysphoric feelings in
          themselves and their students including anger and guilt reactions ("normalize"
          and "legitimize" reactions). Students may describe disturbing dreams.

     g)   consider how to help students deal with ensuing adversities at school and at
          home (dislocation, parental unemployment, disruption of routines and social
          network)

     h)   note how to screen for lingering symptoms in children, especially depression

     i)   highlight how critical it is to reintroduce school routines as soon as possible,
          but to do so in a flexible fashion, altering the educational demands to meet the
          needs of the students. Teachers need to recognize how post-disaster reactions
          can interfere with children's abilities to concentrate on school work and the role
          of intrusive ideation.

     Pynoos et al. (1994) offer several additional comments about the school setting that are
     worth noting. These include:

    a)   those teachers who have been assigned first aid duty or morgue duty for a possible disaster should be given preparation beforehand.

    b)   great caution should be followed when assigning older students (e.g., adolescents) to a helper role as a debriefer.

    c)   efforts to teach children coping procedures should be considered and their impact and effectiveness should be monitored carefully. For example, relaxation exercises which are often used may inadvertently be accompanied by increased vividness of traumatic imagery.

    d)   develop evacuation plans for possible future disasters, especially ways to reunite family members with their children as soon as possible after a disaster

6.   Group sessions provide an opportunity to "legitimatize" and "normalize" the children's feelings and reactions, dispel myths of "uniqueness", and note that others often have similar reactions. The group meetings also provide an opportunity to share mutual concerns; increase peer tolerance for disturbing emotions and behaviors, addressing difficulties in peer relationships, especially for children who are usually neglected or rejected; normalize grief responses; and engage in group proactive coping efforts. Illustrative of this approach are two large group interventions with adolescents that were reported by Stewart et al. (1992) and Weinberg (1990). Stewart et al. used large and small groups in a single 2 1/2 hour session that involved education, physical activity, and group enhancement procedures. Weinberg used a large school assembly to address traumas that occurred within school (e.g., accidents, suicides). A main feature of the meeting was a discussion of the natural processes of grieving.

7.   Have a separate session with parents and teachers. Engage them in their own debriefing, highlighting that one of the best predictors of their children's' reactions is their own levels of distress. If separated, highlight the importance of parent's reactions at the reunion. Help parents deal with their own trauma reaction in order to be of most help to their children. Educate parents and teachers about possible symptoms that the children may evidence (fears, anxiety, nightmares, fear of going to sleep, fatigue, poor concentration, regressive behaviors, grief and mourning responses, etc.). Indicate that children may evidence a high frequency of symbolic reenactment of the disaster, even one year after the traumatic event, (Saylor et al., 1992). Also, highlight for parents what children need from them: constancy of care; facts, not misinformation; shared feelings; support and extra time; patience; and help doing things with others, as well as by themselves in order to take back or exert some control, to rebuild beliefs in safety and trust. Comment also on the dangers of parents being overprotective. Parents need to learn how to talk about their own disaster-related feelings (e.g., fears and anxieties) with their children with the goal of acknowledging such feelings as being natural and normal, (FEMA, 1989). Furman (1979) describes a "filial therapy" in which parents are counseled by a therapist to provide help for their children.

8.   Bring children and parents together to share their feelings. Have each family member share his/her experience during and after the disaster since it is likely to be somewhat different. In this way they can become more understanding and tolerant of each family member's reaction. Interview child with parents present. Note, parents may underestimate children's distress (Yule & Williams 1990). Milgram (1993) reports, however, a study by Rosenbaum and Ronen that indicates that with repeated exposure, parents (especially mothers) were quite perceptive and accurate in judging their child's level of distress. The one reservation about involving parents in the interview with their own children is that children may be overprotective of their parents and inhibit reports of their own distress. Also noteworthy, is the finding that parents report more distress in traumatized children than do the children's teachers.

9. Since the level of distress in parents is predictive of the level of disorders in children, there is a need to undertake a proactive psychoeducational outreach program with parents. The format of the program may include:

    a) telephone hotlines

    b) group meetings for parents

    c) written material about post-disaster reactions, and recovery, ways to reduce the impact of traumatic reminders, how to tolerate reactions to such reminders and other symptomatology, need to reinstitute "normal" routines such as sleeping arrangements; highlight the need for communication.

10. Educate the children and parents about possible triggers and how to deal with resultant anxiety (e.g., 6 months, anniversary, holidays). Emphasize the need to learn to take one day at a time. Encourage clean-up to remove reminders.

11. Another format for providing post-disaster interventions is to use **home visiting**. For example, following the recent Los Angeles earthquake FEMA sponsored Project COPE where a group of counselors provided brief (6 to 8 sessions) family-based home interventions. The initial family contact was usually through the schools or preschools because their child was evidencing adjustment difficulties such as sleep disturbance, regressive behaviors, general fearfulness, and the like. While the ascribed entry for help was the child, usually the child's behavioral symptoms were a reflection of more familial systemic difficulties that had been in place before the disaster had occurred. The disaster exacerbated preexisting difficulties. Those who establish such home visiting programs would benefit from the practical guidelines suggested by Barbara Wasik, Donna Bryant and Claudia Lyon's (1990) in their book Home visiting: Procedures for helping families (Sage Publications). Also see Section VI on family-based interventions.

12. Whatever the form of the intervention there is a need to refer more seriously affected children for subsequent small group or individual treatment (namely, those instances where symptoms last 6 weeks or longer). Medication such as Clonidine and Propranolol have been used effectively in alleviating symptoms in children and adolescents (Pynoos, et al., 1994).

13. Gillis (1993) highlights the value of having the children simply meet in groups together without the debriefer present. During such sessions the children do not have to talk about the traumatic incident. Rather provide an opportunity to have the group of children experience the positive sense of being together. There is a need to prevent withdrawal and isolation by children.

14. Have the children use a variety of expressive activities in order to convey and master their feelings (e.g., coloring books about the event, art work, puppet play, psychodrama, mutual story telling, and the like.) Can also use debriefing, traumatic dream script rewriting, and in vivo flooding or graduated reexperiencing, as well as, have children engage in instrumental and commemorative activities that bolster their sense of control. Art expression can prove to be a valuable tool to help children express feelings, gain perspective, and exert control, as described below. For instance, children may be asked to draw a picture of "what happened and how it made them feel?" A second picture is elicited that reflects, "how they are now wiser, more prepared, or stronger for what they have been through." They are all "survivors" and can draw a picture of what they have learned to be prepared for a similar event, should it reoccur. Children can also be asked to draw themselves before and after the disaster.

Processing such pictures with the children can prove diagnostically helpful in identifying children who are at "high risk." The children can be asked to describe their pictures to the class, especially the one's that reflect their efforts in becoming "wiser" and "stronger". This can be followed by an authentic art exhibit of the children's work.

15. Nader (1994) highlights the therapeutic value of directly questioning children regarding their traumatic experiences, especially soon after the exposure. She observes that traumatic material becomes less accessible after the first 3-6 months after exposure. The **debriefing** covers such areas as the children relating any

   a)   horrifying images
   b)   extremely frightening moments
   c)   extreme sensory moments (sounds, smells, etc.)
   d)   moments of intense helplessness

"The degree of directness in conducting these interviews is, of course, adjusted to the tolerance and needs of the child" (Nader, 1994, p. 188). Other treatment guidelines for debriefing offered by Nader (1994) include:

   (1)   insuring that the therapist is well-informed about the nature of the trauma
   (2)   ensuring adequate self-care for the children
   (3)   a willingness to hear everything
   (4)   using occasional "time outs" from direct traumatic work.

A useful way to have children tell their stories is to use various forms of expressive art.

Expressive Art as a Form of Prevention and Treatment of PTSD with Children

"Art is a process of self-healing"
"Art helps the chaos inside come out in a creative form"

Golub, 1994, p. 33.

I have taken the liberty of sharing several "stops" in my journey consulting on the topics of stress and coping. One of the more memorable was an invitation to visit the Stress Centre at the University of Haifa, in Israel. This picturesque campus overlooks the nearby mountainside. The meeting room in which I was to present had a magnificient vista, but it was what was inside the room that most moved me. Whatever comments on stress and coping that I had to offer were "dwarfed" by the art that hung about the room. These were sketches and paintings created by concentration camp inmates while they had been in the camps. Most of these artists did not survive the Holocaust. Their images, their symbols, their pictures, captured, more poignantly, the content of what I had planned to present. Golub (1994) has described and reviewed a number of books of children's images of trauma. She notes that "making art makes whole what has been shattered", especially when expressed by children. This premise has been central to several of the projects to be described.

The therapeutic aspects of expressive art forms, and of the creative process, have long been recognized, but only of late have they been systematically studied. Many diverse art forms have been used with individuals who have experienced traumatic events including drawing, painting, music expression, poetry, journal writing, writing essays, story-telling, drama, movement, dance, pantomime, sculpture, ritual, sand play, and the collection of objects of remembrance[1] in the form of a personal collage (Ayalon, 1989, Kazanis, 1991). These expressive works help individuals transform their emotional pain, internal conflicts, and feelings into words and other forms of expression. For example, by asking individuals who have experienced traumatic events to draw what they are feeling, by asking them to use self-selected objects of remembrance to artistically create their own "small alters", Kazanis (1991) was able to help them on their "personal journey of healing" and their "ceremonies of transition and completion". As we will see art forms not only serve as outlets for expression and transformation, they also provide metaphoric means of creating new narratives. Perhaps, this is most evident in the most ambitious **structured art therapeutic program** by Dr. Arpad Barath with **children in war-torn Bosnia** and in the expressive art therapy program **Art from Ashes** by Zelmut and Metrick, who worked with school children in Oakland, California, after the devastating fires of October, 1991, as well as some of the other child and adolescent-based interventions.

Helping the Children in Bosnia. Dr. Arpad Barath who is at the University of Zagreb Medical School in the Department of Health Psychology is the director of an extensive prevention and intervention program to decrease PTSD among school children in Croatia. The program has reached 40,000 children between the ages of 6 to 14, has involved 1000 teachers and 40 school psychologists. More than 100 teams consisting of a psychologist and an art teacher have worked together in local schools to provide art expressive therapy, to undertake screening for PTSD and to produce educational materials (handouts, audiotapes, worksheets), as well as training.

The need for such a program is quite evident when we learn that the war in Croatia has created 2 to 3 million refugees, 55% of whom are children and adolescents. The death toll has been estimated at 150,000 and those who survive have witnessed the horrendous sights of war and have felt direct threats to their lives. Barath reports that 35% of the children experience severe

---

[1] Kazanis (1991) reminds us of the many moving personal remembrances that have been left at the Vietnam Memorial in Washington, each with its own poignant and highly idiosyncratic personal meaning. Why do such commemorative behaviors aide "healing"?

forms of PTSD. More girls than boys report the negative psychological aftereffects of war that include general fear and anxiety, worry about family members, separation anxiety, depression over losses. Bloch (1993) reports that the Barath art-structured program significantly reduced children's scores on standardized measures of PTSD (N = 5823), relative to their preintervention levels and relative to control groups.

The structured art program called **"Images of my childhood in Croatia since 1991"** moves each child through seven expressive stages of images of life before war, through feelings of fear and anger felt during the war, and finally, through stages expressing hope, love, and "messages to the world". In order to help the children overcome fear and their sense of powerlessness and to nurture feelings and beliefs in the future, the program uses painting, poetry and music as expressive forms. More specifically, the seven thematic expressive stages included:

1. Memories -- Paths to my childhood.
2. Time -- What happened to me since the Summer of 1991?
3. Space -- Where I am now?
4. Fear -- What I am afraid of and how?
5. War -- What color, touch and smell is the war?
6. Peace -- If I were a white dove ...
7. Love -- If I were a magician ...

For each thematic topic the children were exposed to a relevant piece of music, a form of art (e.g., Picasso's Guernica when the topic of war was introduced), and a guided visualization activity that included a prepared audiotaped exercise). Interestingly, the children's poetry and art works from this Croatia project will be touring the U.S. (Cinncinati, Philadelphia, and other cities) some time next year. Inquiries about the Croatia Project can be directed to Dr. Ellen Bloch (515-221-8545) (Also see, Bloch, 1993).

Shaw & Harris (1994) describe an intervention program for "children of war and children at war: child victims of terrorism in Mozambique". In the context of an overall intervention regimen, they describe how expressive forms of art can be used therapeutically. They asked children to draw pictures of the "worst moment", of the moment when they were freed from captivity, and "what you would like to be in the future".

Helping the Children in the Oakland Firestorm. A somewhat different form of expressive arts therapy was developed by Zelmut and Metrick (1992) whose **Art from Ashes** project consisted of 8 to 10 week sessions of approximately 60 minutes each, that combined the talents of psychologists, artists, and teachers. Through a variety of creative expressive activities the children who had to deal with the massive Oakland firestorm were invited to participate in school in group and individual art projects that provided an opportunity and outlet to get "in touch" with their feelings of anxiety and fear and to do so in a supportive environment that nurtured cooperation and a sense of mastery. Illustrative projects included the following: (See Zelmut and Metrick, 1992 for information on how to obtain more detail on the **Art from Ashes** guidebook).

a) Create a "this is me" collage -- cover before and after traumatic event. Create a collage of positive and negative consequences of the trauma.

b) Use of creative art to honor animals and pets that were lost in the fire.

c) Draw pictures of the fire, what happened now, and make cardboard shields as means of expressing control. (Use symbol of the Phoenix as a symbol of the bird who rose from the ashes). The teacher also asked children to draw pictures of what they had learned, what they could do to feel better and safer, what they could do to be better prepared for future stressors, how they have changed.

d) Paint time lines of their lives to put the episode of the firestorm in perspective.

e) Read stories that are illustrative of coping (e.g., Winnie the Pooh story which conveys that each ending is just another beginning) and that convey a sense of moving forward.[1]

f) Journal making, puppetmaking and doll making. The doll making came from the Guatemalan custom of using a tiny "worry" doll to whom one turned over one's concerns and burdens.

g) Use "safe-place" imagery and meditation -- an imaginary safe-place to which the child could enter. The child could invite a special protector or guardian angel to enter this place with the child and answer any questions or protect him/her.

At the end of the art projects the children had an art display for the other students, teachers and parents so this became a "healing ritual" of "authentic" products.

Helping the Children of the Loma Prieta Earthquake. Spoffard and his colleagues (1992) describe a school intervention program that serviced 25,000 individuals over a 16 month period following the Loma Prieta earthquake (Oct., 1989) in Santa Cruz, California. A detailed handout describing the program is available.[2] Their program includes the use of children's art work, children group meetings, parent drop-in, and other activities. Consistent with the suggestions offered by other clinicians, Spoffard et al. employed the children's "art work" as a way of nurturing a sense of their "personal empowerment". Following their initial expression of art that reflected what they had experienced, the children were encouraged to:

(1) Draw themselves as being **more prepared** for another earthquake.

(2) Share (tell) the group of fellow students about their picture. Children were also encouraged to take their picture home to share with family members. An art display was set up.

(3) The art work was used as a **catalyst for discussion.** For example, "share one thing each child could do to prepare for any future earthquakes (after shocks)?"; "What is something positive that the child has learned about him/herself?"; "What was a favorite thing that you were glad was okay?"; "How did your pet respond?"; "What could the child do to comfort his/her pet (or younger sibling) should there be another tremor?" Put each child in a "helper" role.

In a psychotherapeutic setting a number of clinicians have described how expressive forms can be used with children who have been traumatized. For example, Rhue and Lynn (1991) have described how storytelling, imagination and fantasy can be used to help children who have been sexually abused. They ask the child his/her favorite tale, story character, and/or super hero. They then ask the child to build a "safe place" in his/her fantasy and to fill it with the trappings or creatures that can help protect him/her. The child is asked how he/she can feel even better or safer in this place? For example, add a gate, use magic words, make special wishes, use certain coping responses (e.g., relaxation responses, things to say to him or herself). They supplement this imagery procedure with story-telling. Brooks (1981) uses storytelling with creative characters to help traumatized children. The metaphorical stories usually include a representative of the child (e.g., an angry tornado, a hurt puppy), a representative of the therapist (e.g., a wise owl, a teacher, a detective), a representative of a moderator (e.g., a newscaster who interviews both

[1] An illustration of this process was evident when I visited the public school in LaGuna Beach, California where they had experienced the devastating fires due to arson. The children had placed a large sign at the entrance that said, "You can't have a rainbow unless you first have a storm."

[2] Spoffard, C.J. (1992) School intervention following a critical incident. Available from Community Mental Health Services, Project COPE, P.O. Box 962, 1060 Emeline Ave., Santa Cruz, CA, 95062.

parties and elucidates issues). The stories are usually **brief** and linked to the child's real life situation. This story-telling approach is to be contrasted with the lengthy and somewhat complex metaphorical stories offered by Davis (1990). Whatever the nature of the metaphorical stories used with children, the critical feature is the ability of the child to **generalize** what is learned in the story to his/her outside real-life situations. Deblinger et al. (1990) and Ruma (1994) have described how **cognitive-behavioral play therapy** can be used successfully with victimized children. (*See the Additional Reference List on PTSD in children and Adolescents in Section VIII*).

Helping the Children of an Italian Earthquake. Galante and Foa (1986) used a 7 session school-based small group intervention for children in grades 1-4 following an earthquake. Each session had a cognitive, emotional and activity component (e.g., drawing pictures while listening or role playing). Children could express fears freely and "irrational" fears and misinformation could be corrected. Various coping skills were practiced.

E. Postvention Interventions

Wenckstern and Leenaars (1993) describe a <u>postvention</u> program that can be used in schools following a trauma such as a suicide or after a serious accident. The elements of their intervention program include:

1. Consultation with the school administration, school staff, students and pupils led by a postvention coordinator

2. Crisis intervention

3. Community linkage

4. Assessment and counseling

5. Education

6. Liaison with the media

7. Follow-up

They also describe the value of establishing a Traumatic Events Response Team (TERT) under the direction of a postvention coordinator.

F. School-Based Intervention[1]

Schools provide a unique setting for providing help to children. There is a need to debrief teachers about their reactions to the disaster before they, in turn, debrief their students. Teachers need to understand what are the signs of distress in themselves and in children and learn how to conduct the debriefing (For example, see the booklet). A guide for teachers: How to help children after a disaster" published by Alameda County Mental Health Services in California and "School intervention following a critical incident" available from The Santa Cruz Mental Health Services.

Klingman (1993) also has described how disaster relief intervention programs can work through the schools. He highlights the need to conduct anticipatory interventions before disasters strike. Such interventions should:

1. take place as soon as possible after the appearance of the symptoms (immediacy)

2. be given as close a possible to the scene of the disaster, in the natural setting (proximity)

3. include all those similarly affected in a group setting (psychological sense of community)

4. create and convey a sense of the traumatized individuals being able to recover soon and resume their roles and routines soon (expectancy).

5. ensure that steps will be taken to preserve and restore a person's or an organization's functional, historical, and interpersonal continuities, while actual or potential breaches caused by the disruptive events are being repaired (principle of continuity is maintained) (Klingman, 1993, p. 192).

---

[1] A worthwhile videotape entitled "Children and Trauma: The school's response" is available (see Videotape Information - Section VIII).

G. Military application: Soldiers, POWs and Hostages

As noted before, the initial impetus for debriefing came from the pioneering work of Salmon (1919) and was further developed by Marshall (1944). For example, Marshall (1944) provided a prototype of how soldiers can benefit from reconstructing the battle in uncovering and sharing the events in sequential order. As Shalev (1994) describes, Marshall highlighted the need for the interviewer "to never cut witnesses short, nor disbelieve their accounts". Moreover, the interviewer should try to obtain as full an account as possible indicating not only what the soldiers did in the battle, but also what they felt and said. The group processing of such accounts facilitates the debriefing processes. Modern-day versions of the Salmon and Marshall guidelines have been offered by the Department of Army, 1986; Hausman & Rioch, 1967; Cozza & Hales, 1991; Ford et al. 1993; Pontrus, 1993; Shalev, 1994; Solomon & Benbenishty, 1986. The common steps to these approaches usually consist of:

   a)   <u>Proximity</u> -- immediate and timely temporal removal to a safe, but not too distant site from the stressor
              -- implement the treatment as close as possible to the battle line or to the place where his or her breakdown occurred

   b)   <u>Immediacy</u>[1] -- provide intervention and a protective setting as soon after the onset of symptoms, based on early detection of "high risk" individuals
              -- provide rest, sleep and replenishment (adequate food, opportunity to talk) as immediately as possible
              -- provide relief from the source of stress and meet immediate needs.
              -- treatment should be initiated as quickly as possible

   c)   <u>Expectation</u> -- caregivers convey the expectation that the "client" will recover and return to combat. This expectancy is conveyed by all who are involved in treatment.
              -- promote social support that will allow for reintegration.
              -- and maintain close professional monitoring and remove from the unit as a last resort.

   d)   <u>Simplicity</u> -- treatment should be as simple as possible

Pontrus (1993) in describing guidelines for treating mass-casualty survivors from the Persian Gulf war highlight the value of providing unit-based assessments and interventions. Under the guise of unit based interventions many heavily traumatized survivors "could justify volunteering for treatment because participating would help their friends" (p. 5). The inclusion of swift intervention with clear goals, the characterization and normalization of combat stress reactions as **Battle Fatigue (BF)**, the provision of rest and replenishment along with the opportunity for ventilation or debriefing, with the purpose and expectation that the soldier will return to duty in 3-5 days were also critical features of the intervention. "The debriefing process does <u>not</u> imply illness: it is preventive in nature, although it affords the opportunity for the identification of disorders if they exist" (Lehman, 1993, p. 11). It is interesting to note that in spite of the availability of a sophisticated treatment regimen, in the Lebanon war, only 7% of Israeli soldiers with combat stress reactions received frontline care (Solomon & Shalev, 1994).

---

[1] The **value of "immediacy"** is <u>not</u> limited to military application. For instance, the significance of early intervention in reducing the likelihood of survivor's developing PTSD was illustrated by Herlofsen (1992) with survivors of an avalanche, by Alexander (1991) with police officers following exposure to recovery efforts from an oil platform disaster, and Weisaeth (1989) with survivors of an industrial accident.

Turnbull (1992) has described how **debriefing can be conducted with POWs and released hostages**. He highlights that the psychological debriefing has two phases. The first phase attempts to help the POW or hostage address the question:

a)   WHAT HAPPENED TO YOU?

The second phase addresses the question:

b)   WHAT DO YOU FEEL ABOUT WHAT HAPPENED TO YOU?

Turnbull highlights the need to meet with primary relatives before and during the debriefing, to have an assigned debriefing team leader, to build in flexibility and predictability, to use a controlled, safe environment for the debriefing, and to provide support (conduct debriefing for the debriefers). The debriefing experience for the hostage is labeled a "reentry" process which is "survivor-centered."

As Turnbull (1994) notes, the initial step is to achieve security in a protective area, to control press and media access, to provide a medical examination, to control alcohol intake, and to provide psychological debriefing. A technique used to facilitate the assimilation and integration of the traumatic experience is called **"lines and ladders" exercises**. The **"lines" exercises** is similar to what Dolan (1991) calls **a "time line"** approach. The "lines" exercise involves the plotting of a chronological map of the survivor's life. Significant high and low points are noted with positive and negative events plotted on a vertical axis, including a neutral midway point representing zero. On the horizontal axis age in years is represented. The survivor is asked to include the whole of their lifetime experiences in addition to the period of time when they were exposed to the traumatic experience. If treatment is provided on a group basis then this graphical map of each participant's life could be presented to the group. "The lines exercise brings into perspective positive and negative coping mechanisms used in the past and also during the trauma ... also a sense of continuity and the identification of adaptive and maladaptive coping efforts" (Turnbull, 1993, p.13).

The **"ladders" exercise** is designed to shift the focus to the future in a stepwise fashion. The aim is to help the survivor to make plans for the future by identifying short, intermediate, and long-term goals which can be presented to the group. A "ladder" with several rungs are drawn on large sheet of paper or on a board. On the top rung is placed the survivor's long-term goal and on the lowest rung is the lowest point in their lives (e.g., it may involve the experience surrounding the current trauma). The intermediate rungs are filled in by the survivor as steps that should be taken in order to achieve his/her ultimate goal. The survivors in the group help each individual develop a structured plan. *(The various steps discussed in Problem-Solving in Section VI can be used to facilitate this ladder's exercise).* See Turnbull (1994) for a more detailed description of the debriefing procedures with POW's and their families.

Another useful guide is the Department of Army (1991) <u>Combat Stress Behaviors: Risk Factors and Leader Actions</u>. It highlights the value of labeling the soldier's reaction as "battle fatigue" or "stress fatigue" or "field fatigue." These labels imply that with rest a positive outcome will ensue. In fact, 50% to 85% of soldiers given the diagnosis of "fatigue" return to duty following 1 to 3 days of "restoration" treatment, provided they are kept in the vicinity of their units. Recovered cases have no increased risk of relapse. 10% to 30% of "fatigue" soldiers do <u>not</u> recover within 72 hours, but do return to some duty within 1 to 2 weeks, provided they continue in a structured positive therapy at a nonhospital facility in the combat zone. Only about 5 % of "fatigue" soldiers fail to improve sufficiently and have to be removed from the combat zone.

     Morale, unit cohesion, and good leadership are mediating factors in reducing the likelihood of "fatigue" reactions (see Gal & Mangelsdorf, 1991). The ability of soldiers and commanders to recognize signs of stress in each other (e.g., buddy pairs) is valuable diagnostically, as well as therapeutically. The Army guidebook provides a list of leader behaviors that can be followed to reduce combat stress reactions and "fatigue" conditions.

     The value of **unit cohesion and group involvement** was illustrated by Herlofen (1994) who reported <u>no cases of PTSD</u> at the follow-up of survivors of a snow avalanche that killed 55% of a military unit. The close involvement of a social network of comrades at all phases of the disaster and the rescue and recovery process was seen as a buffer against the development of PTSD. The support from colleagues was seen as most critical to recovery and to the prevention of PTSD.

     Also, recall the description from Section I of the Ford et al. (1993) study in which they debriefed veterans of Operation Desert Storm and their spouse, either on a couples' or group basis. Each soldier "walked through" with his/her mate parallel accounts of war and home front experiences and the resultant impact. This post-combat military conjoint debriefing was effective in reducing the likelihood of prolonged stress responses.

     Another interesting means of addressing distress **at a community level** during a military operation was described by Lomranz (1994). He described how the Israeli government during the Gulf War SCUD Missle attacks used frequent television and news broadcasts to help the populace cope. The news accounts conveyed that the government had the power to respond forcefully and decisively, at any time, and that they were choosing for the time being to delay a response. These messages were designed to provide reassurance and convey a measure of control, even by their inaction. It was not only what the government did, but how it was presented that was critical.

H. Additional models

1.   Figley (1991) proposed an intervention model (RISE) that emphasizes:

     a)   <u>R</u>espect
     b)   <u>I</u>nformation
     c)   <u>S</u>upport
     d)   <u>E</u>mpowerment

2.   Brom and Kleber (1989) emphasize a model that includes:

     a)   Providing practical help and information

     b)   Support

         i)   provide safe and quiet environment signaling that the traumatic event is over
         ii)   help the client explore his/her experience and label emotions
         iii) help the client mobilize his/her own social support network, and if the participant wishes draw attention to his/her situation and feelings

     c)   "Reality testing" - helping participants understand that their symptoms may change and how their situation has changed.

     d)   Confrontation with the experience - reliving the trauma

     e)   Maintain contact with participants over a longer period

f)   Early recognition of disorders and referral for treatment.

VII Disaster Relief Guidebooks

Additional intervention guidelines have been suggested in a number of disaster relief guidebooks: for example, American Psychological Association Disaster Response Project (1991), American Red Cross (1982, 1994), Aquilera & Messich (1986), Cohen & Ahearn (1980), Cohen et al. (1983), Ewing (1978), Faberow (1978), Faberow & Frederick (1978), Faberow & Gordon (1981), FEMA (1989), Fraser & Spicka (1981), Frederick (1977), Hartsough & Meyers (1985), Joyner & Swenson (1993), Klingman (1993), Lindy et al. (1981), Lystad (1985), Meyers (1994), Mitchell (1983), NIMH (1985), Quarentelli (1978), Raphael (1986), Roberts (1990), Seroka et al. (1986), Slaikeu (1990), Tierney & Baisden (1983). A number of these programs use outreach interventions and self-help groups (e.g., Peuler, 1988). NIMH has produced a number of useful pamphlets for emergency medical personnel and workers and team managers. (See NIMH, 1985, for order information.) Common to many of these guidebooks is some form of assessment of the degree to which the relief workers are prepared for the disaster tasks, identify with the victims, and have their own traumatic experiences "reawakened". For example, the questions covered may include:

"How have you been prepared for this work?"
"Have you ever imagined how you would have coped if you had been one of the victims yourself?"
"Has this work reminded you of earlier unhappy events or memories?"

These programs that are designed for both adults and children use an array of community-wide techniques including outreach counseling, bibliotherapy distribution of booklets and fact sheets, coloring books, and other literature, parent guidance, crisis telephone hotline services (e.g., see Blaufarb & Levine, 1972), support groups, songs, plays, art expressions, story telling, puppet play, sociodramatic enactments, role playing, free writing, self-calming exercises, school and church programs, field trips and media presentations. These programs are often proactive in accessing hard-to-reach populations. For example, see Goenjian (1993) booklets for children who experienced the Armenian earthquake.

These educational measures usually include information about:

a)   the likely or expected course of reactions and psychological symptoms

b)   normalizing and legitimizing reactions

c)   cautions about possible complications such as abuse of alcohol, interpersonal (marital) conflict

d)   various ways to cope more effectively with their problems

VIII Role of Rituals and Religion[1]

At the end of Steven Spielberg's movie Schindler's List the survivors who were saved from the furnaces at Auschwitz gather in Israel, and each one lays a stone on Schindler's grave site. A moving ceremony of commemoration and community. In Tampa Florida, a similar ceremony was conducted for three employees who were shot to death on the job by a fellow worker. As reported in the St. Petersburg Times (Jan. 28, 1993), the workers gathered to pay homage to their deceased

---

[1] Other examples of rituals as part of the healing process were offered in Section V. With regard to religion Victor Frankl provided the definition that religion reflects a belief in a "final meaning."

colleagues by each placing a stone at the foot of a commemorative oak tree. The mourners were told:

> ... The stone is a symbol,
> of earth and repose
> That speaks to us, in our bones.
> It is a symbol that speaks from the sand
> to the soul of each of us.
>
> ... when you are ready, we invite you to take the stone, which you have held and which is a symbolic container for the energy of any suffering you wish to let go of. If you choose, you may bury the stone, or lay it to rest on the earth around the tree, all that you wish to say goodbye to.

(Barbara Kazanis)

Rituals are about symbols and metaphors; they convey the power of belief. As Jay (1994) observes, rituals, holidays and tradition provide a template for interpretation. They also provide a powerful sense of group identity, group cohesion and a sense of belonging, as evident in periodic reunions of military units (see Elder & Clipp, 1988). Consider the following example of a disaster that struck a small Southern town in the U.S. and the role of "healing" metaphors, rituals and religious services.

The small Southern town in Piedmont, Alabama is used to storms and destruction, but on Palm Sunday of March, 1994, no one was ready for the tornado that tore through the Goshen Methodist Church, which was filled with parishioners. The storm killed 20, including the minister's four year old daughter. As reported in the New York Times (April 3, 1994), the surviving parishioners used their faith and religious rituals to cope; these acted like **"anchors in a turbulent sea"**. The survivors struggled with such questions as "But why? Why a church? Why those little children? Why? Why? Why?"

As reported, this incident hurt them in a place usually safe from hurt, it was like a **"bruise on the soul."** The minister noted that while their **faith is shaken it is not the same as losing it"**. Events like this only strengthen one's faith as one church-goer commented, **"those who die inside any church will find the gates of heaven open wide."** Another resident noted, "As long as we have our faith, we are strong. Because no matter how dark it is, **if I have faith, I have a song in the night.** Our beliefs trembled, but did not break." In response to the persistent questions of "why", the Reverend noted: "There is no reason. Our faith is not determined by reason. **Our faith is undergirded by belief, where there is no reason"**.

For many, if not most, when disaster strikes, when stressors that meet criterion A of DSM-IV are experienced, it is religion and ritual, it is a coherent belief system that represents the central means of coping. Religion and rituals provide powerful culturally accepted metaphors and a framework to construct a new adaptive narrative. Religion provides a plausible way to cognitively reframe events and a means to provide guidance for healing. Such rituals come in many forms, including religious.

As Vernberg and Vogel (1993) observe, rituals serve several important psychological functions including:

1)   "opportunities for public expressions of shared grief and mutual support;

2)   reassurance that disaster victims are remembered;

3)   a recapitulation and an interpretation of disaster experiences;

4)   a degree of closure on a painful period" (p. 496).

Rituals can play an important role in the recovery process[1] (e.g., grieving, talking through stress, restoring positive memories, finding meaning by taking actions such as bearing witness, publishing memories, engaging in educational missions, commemorative ceremonies, and taking political action). For example, Hoyt (1994) describes how a ritual was used with a client who "emotionally divorced" her abusive father in a ceremony she conducted at the therapist's office. With the help of her husband she read a prepared biographical statement, played carefully selected music, and burned her father's photograph. A "decree of divorce" was signed and witnessed, followed by a brief celebration. "She felt as if she had completed a chapter in her life" (p.150). Such ceremonial rituals convey the power of constructing a new narrative.

Another occasion for finding meaning are anniversaries of the event. An anniversary of the traumatic event can provide an opportunity to look back, "take stock" of how far individuals/group/community have come since the disaster. Such ceremonial efforts provide opportunities for bonding and solidarity and a means for constructing a new narrative.

A number of specific rituals and reconstructive efforts may prove helpful (e.g., plaques, memorials, scholarship funds, commemorative and purifying activities, self-help group formation, educational attempts, and the like). For instance, consider the therapeutic value of the Vietnam memorial, the return trip to the site of the battle, or a visit to the concentration camps, or the arrival commemorative holidays. Consider why a soldier feels compelled to visit the family of his buddy who he killed accidentally in "friendly fire". Why does this "ritual" help to heal? How do these acts help to rewrite the soldier's and family's stories and contribute to the construction of their new narrative. But individuals do not only tell new stories, they also work "hard" at constructing new narratives. Traumatic events are so dramatic in punctuating our life stories, that individuals often need to engage in commensurate "dramatic" rituals in order to put these traumatic events into some perspective.

Taylor (1983) has proposed that the **search for meaning** is one of the most important themes in the coping process. Rituals, and as we will consider, religious/philosophical belief systems, help traumatized individuals find meaning. In considering these healing efforts, it is important to keep in mind the broader community. For instance, Tyler and Gifford (1991) note that when a disaster strikes there is often a "hierarchy of bereavement" based on the relative closeness of the survivors to the deceased. Those providing help should be sensitive to this implicit, unspoken social structure. There is also a need to insure that leaders and those members who were away from their unit or workplace at the time of the traumatic incident (e.g., hospitalized) also eventually receive care and support.

Finally, these rituals should be culturally sensitive and collaboratively generated with members of the "victimized" community. For example, in one school setting where children were shot and some killed, the local Buddhist priests were brought in to purify the school playground of "evil spirits," given the large Buddhist student population. One must be cautious in selecting arbitrarily from a book of rituals a procedure that may not fit with cultural and religious beliefs.

Another example of a ritual ceremony I have been involved with concerned four teenage boys who were playing "Russian Roulette" with a loaded gun. Sadly, one of the boys killed himself. The deceased boy's family did not allow the three surviving boys to attend their friend's funeral. I suggested to the boys' therapist that he explore with them any ways they could have their own

---

[1] Omer (1994) notes historically the therapeutic value of Greek tragedies in serving as transitional rituals for the general populace.

memorial service for their dead friend. In short, it was important for the therapist to see the value and need of rituals as part of the therapy process.

Perhaps, there is no more significant mode of ritual that has been institutionalized than that of **formal religion.** McIntosh et al. (1993), Meichenbaum and Fitzpatrick (1993), and Pargament et al. (1990) and Propst (1988)[1] have discussed how religious beliefs can play a critical role in the "healing" process. **Prayer and faith reflect the most widely used method of coping with traumatic life events.** For instance, Propst (1988) estimates that between 42% and 60% of people who have emotional problems turn first to clergy. Meichenbaum and Fitzpatrick (1993) have analyzed religion from a constructive narrative perspective, while McIntosh et al (1993) have viewed religious belief and activity as a means of accessing a supportive social network and as a form of information processing. They propose that religious beliefs can act as a **schema** through which individuals can process and integrate with their prior basic assumptions, the data from traumatic negative experiences, as well as find meaning in misfortune. The research on stress, coping and religion suggests that clinicians should ask clients about their religious, philosophical or world view. For example, the therapist can ask:

1) "How important is religion in your life?"

2) "How often do you attend religious services?"

3) Have you been able to make any sense or find any meaning in what has happened to you? (Be specific in noting the loss --- death of X, illness, destruction of your home, break-up of a relationship, etc.)?

4) Has your religion or faith helped you cope or handle the emotional aftermath of what you have been through?

5) Does your religious belief or faith help you make sense or find meaning in what happened?

6) Do you see any possible way that your religious belief could be of help?

In short, no matter what the therapist's view of religion may be, there is a need to be respectful of the client's belief, and then, to collaboratively explore whether there are beliefs and rituals that the client can use to cope more effectively, to "remember", to "work through", "come to terms with", "resolve", "find meaning" and "move on."

The importance of religious belief in facilitating coping was highlighted by Jeffrey Jay (1994) in a thoughtful article entitled, "Walls for wailing". Jay, who is the director of the Center for PTSD in Washington D.C., examines the role of prayer and ritual, tradition and holidays, within the Jewish religion as a prototype for possible "healing" activities. As he notes, "Anyone's life after trauma becomes a struggle to give meaning to the terrible truth of memory" (p. 31). The value of religion (in this case Judaism) is that it helps the individual redeem the memory within the context of a supportive community. Jay observes that while some forms of psychotherapy attempt to help traumatized clients **move beyond memory**, in Judaism one **moves toward memory.** "Thou shalt remember", becomes a central tenent, where memory is to be honored. To remember is an obligation to bear witness and seek an accounting. The religious client may find comfort in Jay's admonition, "One must have the courage of memory because through it, one can seek God". He reminds the reader of Elie Weisel's observation that, "I belong to a people whose suffering is the most ancient in the world. I belong to a people whose memory keeps the suffering alive ...

---

[1] Propst (1988) has described how various forms of cognitive-behavioral interventions such as stress inoculation training can be conducted within a religious framework.

Just as all the days were created for one day alone, the sabbath, all other words were created and given for one word alone: 'Remember'."

Thus, the efforts of victimized clients to "exile" from their memories the terrible pictures of trauma, the Weisel quote conveys that memories are not obstacles to be obliterated, removed, escaped from (for these efforts will fail), but rather these memories are a **bridge** from the past to the present and to the future. Memories are not to be forgotten, but **contained** and **sanctified**. But such mourning over the past needs to be "paced" and grief needs to be "titrated". As Jay (1994 p. 33) describes in a series of healing metaphors:

"Rituals cyclically connect personal tragedy with the rhythm of religious life as the ceremonies stitch and restitch a tear that can never fully be mended and that needs constant repair."

"Prayer binds one's particular loss to the losses of a people. One's personal trauma - becomes resonant with history and part of a life cycle of recovery."

"Trauma shatters the connection between one's soul and one's world". By recalling, one can "mend", "repair" and "transform", "bringing together shattered pieces".

"Trauma should not occur in isolation, nor should its suffering".

We need a "wall for wailing", for the "aching hurt of trauma"; "a place for the offering of memory"; the "declaration of self-hood" and the needed "response of others". We need a place and a way for individuals to give "further voice to their knowledge of dread, instead of hearing it alone in nightmares".

Trauma brings out the poet in our clients and in those who attempt to help "victimized" clients. The constructive narrative perspective highlighted in this **Handbook** emphasizes the important role of language, metaphor, ritual, religion, and psychotherapy in fostering change. Therapists, among their many other roles (being a listener, a trainer, a coach, etc.), are also **collaborators in the co-construction of new narratives**.

IX Workplace Traumas: The Value of Followup Debriefings

The model of debriefing that I have discussed thus far is usually implemented immediately, or soon after, a specific traumatic event. The need for a more extensive and repeated form of debriefing, as well as psychotherapeutic interventions, was highlighted when I was asked to consult on the prevention of PTSD for individuals who experience work-related traumatic events, (e.g., subway and train drivers who have to deal with the trauma of railway suicides, oil refinery workers who have to deal with industrial accidents, and policemen and soldiers who are in peace keeping roles).

The seriousness of the railway suicide was underscored when I learned that there is a 1 in 8 chance that any one train driver will be involved in a suicide incident each year (Tang, 1994). In Sweden, Karlehagen et al. (1993) estimate that during a 2 year period 3-5% of train drivers may experience on-the-track accidents. Such drivers have to deal with the aftermath of visual exposure to accident victims, deal with distressed passengers, interrogation by police, journalists, supervisors, fellow workers and family members. The impact of such on-the-track accidents is complicated by the job stress of subway drivers working alone, in the dark, on shift work, including frequent night time job assignments.

The immediate and long-term impact of major railway accidents were studied by Malt et al. (1993) and Karlehagen et al. (1993). They found that intrusive symptoms were more predictive of PTSD than were avoidance symptoms. They also reported that premorbid and non-accident related variables are important in predicting both immediate and long-term (one year) psychological outcome to on-the-track accidents. The experience of previous accidents (more than two) invoked a feeling of vulnerability in drivers and a risk expectancy that was predictive of outcome. At the one month and one year followups symptoms of distress were reduced most among the drivers with no preaccident risk experience. Thus, there is a need to obtain a history of prior accidents and related incidents in identifying which drivers are at most high risk. This data is consistent with the findings of Theorell et al. (1992) who found that subway-train drivers who had experienced a "person under train incident" evidenced both immediate psychophysiological reactions (up to 3 weeks post event) and longer term (one year) increased rates of absenteeism and depression.

What can be done to help such workers deal with such occupational stressors and how can one help drivers when such accidents occur? The following recommendations are consistent with those proposed by Meichenbaum (1987) and Williams et al. (1994). A **five-prong approach** was suggested.

1.   Provide prompt debriefing, crisis intervention or **psychological first aide** to the drivers within 24 hours of the suicide incident. The focus of the debriefing should be to allow the driver to give "full expression" to the feelings of what he/she is experiencing. These feelings may include shock, fear, anger, helplessness, sadness, guilt, and shame. These feelings are "given voice" as the driver retells in detail what happened. The debriefing procedures provide a structured way for the individual to talk through his/her experience. In the context of debriefing the driver is also helped to make sense of what happened (namely, a consideration of the circumstances of the suicide). The driver needs some time to let the ramifications of the event become apparent and reflect on what has happened. The driver is also encouraged to check with fellow workers as to how they have handled such experiences. The seriousness of the incident is underscored and the driver is educated about the signs of PTSD. As noted, an important feature is to "normalize" the driver's reactions by indicating that it is "normal" to be distressed by death. As Williams et al. (1994) comment, "It is all right, not to be all right" (p. 485). In this context the therapist may help the client make sense of symptoms, forewarn the driver about maladaptive ways of coping, such as the use of alcohol, drugs, and avoidance behaviors, especially in response to the fear that it might happen again.

2.   The second major thrust of both the immediate and long-term debriefing is some form of cognitive reframing (or consistent with the theme of this **Handbook**, the co-creation or construction of a more adaptive narrative). The sense of helplessness and powerlessness that the driver's feel is often expressed by the question: "Does the driver drive the train, or does the train drive the driver?" (Williams et al., 1994). With the support of the therapist, the driver can re-examine his/her sense of personal responsibility and may even come to reframe the incident; as one driver observed, "I was most likely doing the suicide victim a favor." Various other ways that a client's feelings of guilt can be addressed therapeutically were examined in Section VI. Yet another way to help the driver cope more effectively with this incident is to put his/her reactions in some context. It is worth examining with the driver possible other workplace stressors and to examine collaboratively the potential impact that they may have had on the driver's present reactions. Any discussion of the negative impact of the stressor should be accompanied by a parallel consideration and recognition of "signs of recovery" and adjustment. Remember, as noted earlier, there is a need to obtain "the rest of the story." Overall, there is a need to consider the memory of the traumatic event in relation to the specific life context of the driver.

3.   In vivo desensitization or the use of accompanied drivers represent an important element in the therapeutic or reacclimation effort, especially in the early period after the incident. An accompanied driver on the first trips after the incident, particularly over the route of the incident, is an important feature in the intervention. These accompanied drivers need to

receive training on how best to be supportive and how to fade supports, "scaffold" [1] or relinquish responsibility, how to help the "victimized" driver take ownership, express confidence, and experience self-efficacy, as part of the in vivo experience. Videotape modeling films, feedback training, and the debriefing of the accompanying drivers can facilitate the recovery process.

4. **Debriefing** meetings should be conducted **over a prolonged period of time.** Williams et al. (1994) suggest that at least 4 meetings be planned, namely,

    a. immediately following the incident
    b. on return to work
    c. before an inquest or internal inquiry (3-6 months)
    d. at 1 year after the incident (around the anniversary period)

    At these subsequent meetings, the therapist's probes focus on the driver's general level of adjustment, and in particular, on the role of intrusive ideation. For example, as Williams et al. suggest the driver is asked:

    "When do you still think about the incident?"
    "What is it like for you to remember what happened?"
    "What if it happened again?"

    The response to these questions, as well as other more formal modes of assessment, can be used to determine if more extensive interventions are required. Whatever the driver's response, the therapist should convey an "open door policy" for the driver to receive additional help. *The variety of other cognitive-behavioral interventions described in Section VI can be employed.*

5. The final, critical feature in making this approach work is to have these steps become **formal company policy** and part of the transportation company's **standard procedure** for **all** drivers who experience a railway suicide. If this becomes the standard mode of operation it "destigmitizes" and "depathologizes" the seeking of help. It also underscores the company's recognition of the seriousness of such incidents. The driver's view of "being too macho", not needing help, and the like, are less likely to be elicited under these formal company circumstances. This approach can be further reinforced if these issues and procedures are included as part of the **training of new drivers,** and as **part of ongoing training of experienced drivers.** When such a protocol is in place, issues of noncompliance and nonadherence are greatly reduced (see Meichenbaum & Turk, 1987). An example of such a program was offered by Foss (1994) as a form of **"mental first aid".** This approach was used after serious transportation accidents, robberies, and assaults. In his article, Foss provides an Addendum describing how early intervention can be used in a transportation company for drivers who have had serious accidents involving injury and death. The intervention begins with preparatory presentations to drivers (before accidents occur) of possible reactions and intervention procedures. A "safety ombudsman" is sent to the sight of the accident as soon as possible to provide necessary support.

    The reason I have reviewed this program in such detail is that it can also be used with other occupational groups. For example, I have worked with pilots and stewardesses who have been in plane crashes and policemen who have been involved with killings. A variation of this preventative program can be employed with many diverse occupational groups (e.g., see "inoculation training" with mortuary workers and emergency relief workers -- McCarroll et al. 1993; Dyregrov & Mitchell, 1992).

---

[1] "Scaffolding" is a metaphor offered by Jerome Bruner and David Wood to describe the tutoring process, whereby the tutor fades supports and structure (like removing parts of a scaffold) as the tutee develops skills.

But such intervention programs should be preceded by a systematic behavioral analysis (see D'Zurilla & Goldfried, 1992). Illustrative of this analytic approach is Ursano et al.'s (1994, p.52) study of body handlers. They used the following questions to assess how mortuary workers deal with the stress of their job. These questions could be altered for other populations:

"What type of bodies are the most troublesome to you?";

"What is it about dead bodies that affects your functioning or that of others?";

"How do you get yourself through rough spots?";

"How long does it take and how do you prepare yourself to go back to work after an exposure?";

"How do you deal with the stress of such incidents?";

"Have you seen people who are unable to function in the field? What seemed to happen to them?"

"What advice, if any, would you have to help these people cope with their distress, as well as, get back to work?"

(Note, that handling of children's bodies were particularly distressing, as well as handling the personal effects of victims). Such "what" and "how" type questions could be raised with other occupational groups.

The concern about work-site debriefings has taken on increasing urgency in the US. With the recent spate of shootings in the post office and in other work sites there is a need to use interventions to inform, reassure, and communicate with workers and family members. There is also a need to educate survivors about the phenomenology/experience and stressful reactions that may be experienced and the type of "ripple effects" such traumatic events may have. There is a need to help participants see how some "meaningful" change in the "system" can result from such traumatic incidents. The intervention should result in procedural and structural changes in the work setting.

As the Chinese note, in their written form for the word "crisis," there is not only the sign for "crisis", but there is also included a sign for "change" and "growth." Health care providers must work with administrators to ensure that something positive comes from the violence. What is critical for those exposed to workplace traumas is the need for the participants to see that their perceived grievances are being heard and solutions are being implemented.

TEST YOUR EXPERTISE

Section VII - Post-disaster Interventions

1. What is the Conservation of Resources model and what are the implications for assessing the impact of disasters and in providing post-disaster interventions?

2. What factors have been identified in influencing people's reactions to disasters? What are the implications for screening, treatment, and prevention?

3. You have volunteered to conduct debriefing after a disaster. One of your tasks will be to identify individuals and communities who are most "vulnerable" to the negative effects of exposure. What specific high risk factors will you be looking for? Compare your list with that offered in Table 1. As an "expert", can you readily enumerate the "high risk" factors that have been identified in the literature?

4. What posttrauma environmental factors are most important to assess for following a disaster? What are the implications of these factors for how you provide interventions.

5. A colleague is going to attend a conference or workshop on Critical Incident Stress Debriefing (CISD). What critical questions would you encourage him/her to raise at the CISD session? In offering your suggestions, critically evaluate the strengths and weaknesses of CISD.

6. Describe the specific steps (goals and questions) you would use in debriefing according to the Mitchell model? How would you alter or supplement CISD? What are the alternative debriefing models?

7. What are the PTSD characteristics in children? How do these differ from PTSD characteristics in adults? What is the course of PTSD symptoms in children who have been exposed to disasters? What are the implications for assessment and treatment?

8. Describe how you would conduct debriefing with children and their families. How would you involve school personal in your community-wide interventions? How can you use expressive art forms in interventions with children? Be specific.

9. What are the primary intervention principles that have emerged from the treatment of soldiers? Describe how these principles have been used with other populations (e.g., school-based and workplace interventions).

10. Describe how debriefing has been conducted with hostages. What can we learn from these procedures that can be used with other populations?

11. What is the role of rituals and religion in the treatment of disaster victims? How can you explain why these interventions prove effective? What theoretical models might be used to explain such changes when they occur? Have you used "rituals" as part of your treatment with PTSD clients? In what ways? How did they turn out? What lessons, if any, did you learn from this experience?

12. What are two things that you have learned from this Section? How will you incorporate this knowledge and skills into your day-to-day clinical practice?

EPILOGUE: A LOOK INTO THE FUTURE OF CLINICAL TRAINING

It has been quite a journey. I have tried to share with you the lessons that I have learned, the knowledge that I have gleaned from the literature, and the clinical skills that I have obtained from "expert" clinicians. While I feel my own level of expertise has improved, I am reminded of Sigmund Freud's observation (as cited by McFarlane, in press), that the effects of traumatic stress represent "a disorder which we are far from understanding". Hopefully, the present **Handbook/Manual** has highlighted what we know and how much more we have to learn. I welcome your feedback, as you put the enclosed guidelines into clinical practice. I hope your level of "expertise" has also improved.

I believe that some time in the future this **Handbook/Manual** will be computerized and there will be accompanying videodisks with interactive systems. You will be able to sit at a computer console and play videodisks of "experts" demonstrating each of the specific techniques discussed in this **Handbook/Manual**. In turn, cases will be presented and at critical points the videodisk will stop and invite you to offer clinical decisions. You will be able to compare your response to that of so-called "experts". Moreover, you will be able to retrieve on your computer console any assessment measure with accompanying instructional manuals that you wish to examine. Potential therapist letters to clients will be on disks so you can experimentally manipulate letters that you can send to clients. Also available will be meta-analysis of various treatment approaches that will be summarized in a succinct "user-friendly" fashion. Thus, before you use a specific treatment (e.g., EMD/R, Stress Inoculation, Direct Therapy Exposure, Cognitive Restructuring, Pharmacological interventions, CISD, and the like) you will be able to access this information. This information will also be available at conference sites before you enter workshops on that subject. Note, similar **Handbooks/Manuals** could be written for treating panic disorder patients, depression, schizophrenia, pain patients, and other groups of clients.

Moreover, this material will be available internationally, so clinicians worldwide will be able to access needed information. With Internet and the PILOTS project, beginning steps have already been taken. There is a need to provide updated ongoing input to practicing clinicians. There is a need to bridge the "gap" between clinical research and clinical practice. Hopefully, the **Institute of Clinical Excellence** will contribute to fulfilling this dream. I thank you for your support. Please bring this **Handbook/Manual** to the attention of colleagues and students.

SECTION VIII

Information Sheet and References

A.   Information Sheet -- Where Clients Can Obtain More Information

B.   Inspirational Poems

C.   Videotape Information

D.   References

     1.   As editor of the Plenum Press Series on Stress and Coping I have taken the liberty of including this list of books, many of which are quite relevant to the topic of PTSD.

     2.   PTSD adult.

     3.   PTSD adult assessment.

     4.   Possible iatrogenesis and memory: Some cautionary observations.

     5.   Alcoholism and other addictions.

     6.   PTSD: Children and adolescents.

E.   Subject Index

WHERE CLIENTS CAN OBTAIN MORE INFORMATION?

The American Psychiatric Association puts out an educational lay pamphlet, "Let's talk facts about -- Posttraumatic stress disorder" which was revised in 1992. Order from American Psychiatric Association, 1400 K St. N.W., Washington, D.C. 20005 (Pamphlet No. 2258).

Matsakis (1992) provides a valuable list of resources to obtain additional help and information on PTSD. The following sample list comes from her book. (See her fine book for a more detailed description.)

Battering

Association for Women in Psychology, Feminist Therapist Roster, 1200 17th. NW, Washington, DC 20036 (for a list of feminist counselors).

Center for Women Policy Studies, 2000 P St. NW, Suite 508, Washington DC 20036; 202-872-1770.

The International Society for Traumatic Stress Studies, 435 North Michigan Ave., Suite 1717, Chicago, IL 60611; 312-644-0828.

Military Family Resource Center, 4015 Wilson Blvd., Suite 903, Arlington, VA 22203; 800-336-4592 or 703-638-6388.

National Coalition Against Domestic Violence, P.O.Box 15127, Washington, DC 20003; 800-333-7233.

National Domestic Violence Hotline, P.O.Box 7032, Huntington Woods, MI 48070; 800-333-SAFE or for the hearing impaired, 800-873-6363.

National Organization for Victims Assistance (NOVA), 1757 Park Rd., NW, Washington, DC 20010; 202-232-6682.

Parents Anonymous, 6733 South Sepulveda Blvd., Suite 2701, Los Angeles, CA 90045; 800-755-1134 or 213-388-6685.

Dr. Lisa McCann, Treatment Innovations Task Force, Women's Trauma Recovery Center, 7600 West 110th St., Overland Park, KS 66210 (referrals for women).

Incest

Incest Survivors Anonymous, P.O.Box 5613, Long Beach, CA 90805; 213-422-1632.

International Society for the Study of MPD--Dissociative Disorders, 5700 Old Orchard Rd., 1st Flr., Skokie, IL 60077; 708-966-4322.

Child Abuse

American Professional Society on the Abuse of Children (APSAC), 332 S. Michigan Ave., Suite 1600, Chicago, IL 60604; 312-554-0166.

Childhelp USA, c/o NSCAAP, P.O. Box 630, Hollywood, CA 90028; 800-422-4450.

National Child Abuse Hotline, Childhelp USA; 800-4-A-CHILD or 800-422-4453

International Association of Trauma Counselors (IATC), P.O. Box 38706, Denver, CO 80238; 512-795-0051.

National Council on Child Abuse and Female Violence, 1155 Connecticut Ave. NW, Suite 400, Washington, DC 21136; 800-222-2000 or 202-429-6695.

Dr. David Niles, Post-Traumatic Response Network (PTRN), 5999 Stevenson Ave., Suite 404, Alexandria, VA 22304; 703-823-6102.

VOICES in Action, INC. (Victims of Incest Can Emerge Survivors). P.O.Box 148309, Chicago, IL 60614; 312-327-1500.

Crime

National Organization for Victim Assistance, 1757 Park Road NW., Washington DC, 20010 (202) 232-6682 (24-hour victim hotline).

Newsletters

The advisor: Newsletter of the American professional society on the abuse of children. Treating abuse today: The international newsjournal of abuse, survivorship and therapy.

Other

AA World Service (Alcoholic Anonymous), P.O.Box 459 Grand Central Station, New York, NY 10163; 212-686-1100. Check local listings as well.

Al-Anon Family Group Headquarters and **Alateen** (both for the families of alcoholics), Work Service Office, P.O.Box 862, Midtown Station, New York, NY 10018; 212-302-7240. Check local listings as will.

National Association for Children of Alcoholics, 31582 Coast Highway, Suite B, South Laguna, CA 92877; 714-835-3830.

Federal Emergency Management Agency (FEMA) (regarding natural catastrophes), 800-462-9029.

Group Project for Holocaust Survivors and Their Children, 345 East 80th St., New York, NY 10021; 212-737-8524.

Alliance of Information and Referral Services (AIRS), P.O.Box 3456, Joliet, IL 60434. Send a stamped, self-addressed envelope to receive a list of support groups in your area.

National Self-Help Clearinghouse, 25 West 43rd St., Rm.620, New York, NY 10036; 212-840-1259.

Disabled American Veterans, 807 Maine Ave. S.W., Washington, D.C. 20024.

Some clients have shared inspirational poems that they have found helpful. These are two examples:

Survivor Psalm by F.M. Ochberg

I have been victimized.
I was in a fight that was not a fair fight.
I did not ask for the fight I lost.
There is no shame in losing such fights, only in winning.
I have reached the stage of survivor and
am no longer a slave of victim status.
I look back with sadness rather than hate.
I look forward with hope rather than despair.
I may never forget, but I need not constantly remember.
I was a victim.
I am a survivor.

Elegy by W.H. Auden

Why **then**, why **there**
Why **thus**, we cry, did he die?
The heavens are silent.
What he was, he was:
What is fated to become
Depends on us.
Remembering his death,
How we choose to live
Will decide its meaning.
When a just man dies,
Lamentation and praise,
Sorrow and joy are one.

VIDEOTAPE INFORMATION

In my workshops on PTSD I show excerpts of interviews with Maya Angelou, the poet laureate. She poignantly tells the story of how as a child she was raped and spoke the name of her perpetrator. She reports that he died and she did not speak again for several years. The interviews illustrate how she found her voice again. I have shown these interviews to victimized clients and Maya Angelou's story has become a useful model and healing metaphor for the clients.

Maya Angelou: Rainbow in the Clouds is available from: PBS Videos
                                                              1320 Braddock Place
                                                              Alexandria, VA
                                                              22314-1698
                                                              (703)739-5380
                                                              (800)424-7963

Creativity with Bill Moyers that has an interview with Maya Angelou available from:

                                        Pacific Arts Video Publishing
                                        50 N. La Cienga Blvd.
                                        Beverly Hills, CA
                                        90211

Staying sober, keeping straight is a videotape on relapse prevention for addictive behaviors and is available from:

                                        Gerald Rogers Productions
                                        5225 Old Orchard Rd.
                                        Suite 23
                                        Skokie, Il
                                        80077
                                        (312-907-8080)

Children and trauma: The school's response is a videotape on how schools can coordinate services for children who have been exposed to traumatic events. It was produced by:

                                        Assistant District Coordinator
                                        California Department of Mental Health
                                        1600 9th Street, Suite 250
                                        Sacramento, CA 95814
                                        U.S.A.

Overcoming Adversity is a videotape that draws on J. Charles Plumb's experience as a POW in Vietnam (cost is $50, 1 hour in length). Order from 805-683-1969. Also see Surviving the Hanoi Hilton address listed in Assessment Section under "Positive Adjustment Following Trauma".

Priority POW follows a Korean War POW -- see Lehman (1994).

PTSD/Alcoholism Comorbidity: Veterans couldn't wish it on their worst enemy. Available from VA libraries: Call number WM/170/P975a/1992.

THE PLENUM SERIES ON STRESS AND COPING
Series Editor: Donald Meichenbaum

Appley, M.H., & Trumbull, R. (Eds.) (1986). Dynamics of stress: Physiological, psychological, and social perspectives.

Avison, W.R., & Gotlib, I. (Eds.) (1994). Stress and mental health.

Eckenrode, J. (Ed.) (1991). The social context of coping.

Eckenrode, J., & Gore, S. (Eds.) (1990). Stress between work and family.

Everly, G.S., Jr. (1989). A clinical guide to the treatment of human stress response.

Everly, G.S., Jr., & Lating, J.M. (1994). Psychotraumatology: Key papers and core concepts in posttraumatic stress.

Frankenhaeuser, M., Lundberg, U., & Chesney, M. (Eds.) (1991). Women, work, and health: Stress and opportunities.

Freedy, J.R., & Hobfoll, S.E. (Eds.) (in press). Traumatic Stress: Theory to practice.

Gottlieb, B.H. (Ed.) (1994). Coping with chronic stress.

Kahana, B., Harel, Z., & Kahana, E. (in preparation). Survivors of the Holocaust: Late life adaptation it extreme stress.

Kiesler, C.A., & Simpkins, C.G. (1993). The unnoticed majority in psychiatric inpatient care.

Koslowsky, M., Kluger, A.N., & Reich, M. (in press). Commuting stress: Causes, effects, and methods of coping.

Lin, N. (in press). Life stress and well-being: Resources and stressors.

Miller, D.J. (Ed.) (in press). Handbook of post-traumatic stress disorders.

Moos, R.H. (Ed.) (1986). Coping with life crises: An integrated approach.

Peterson, K.C., Prout, M.F., & Schwarz, R.A. (1991). Posttraumatic stress disorder: A clinician's guide.

Sarason, I.G., Sarason, B.R., & Pierce, G. (in press). Handbook of social support and the family.

Snyder, C.R., & Ford, C.E. (Eds.) (1987). Coping with negative life events: Clinical and social psychological perspectives.

Solomon, Z. (1993). Combat stress reaction: The enduring toll of war.

Solomon, Z. (1994). Coping with war-induced stress: The Gulf War and the Israeli response.

Stanton, A.L., & Dunkel-Schetter, C. (Eds.) (1991). Infertility: Perspectives from stress and coping research.

Wilson, J., & Raphael, B. (Eds.) (1993). International handbook of traumatic stress syndromes.

Wilson, J., Harel, Z., & Kahana, B. (Eds.) (1988). Human adaptation to extreme stress: From the Holocaust to Vietnam.

References
Posttraumatic Stress Disorder (PTSD) - Adult

Abe, J., Zane, N., & Chan, K. (1994). Differential responses to trauma: Migration-related descriminants of post-traumatic stress disorder among Southeast Asian refugees. Journal of Community Psychology, 22, 121-135.

Abueg, F., & colleagues (1991). Operation Desert Storm Clinician Packet 0DS-CP. National Center for PTSD (Andreas Bollinger, National Center for PTSD, Palo Alto VAMC/MPT- 323 E, 3801 Miranda Ave, Palo Alto, CA, 94304).

Abueg, F. R., Drescher, K. D., & Kubany, E. S. (1994). Natural disasters. In F. Dattilio & A. Freeman (Eds.), Cognitive-behavioral strategies in crisis intervention. New York: Guilford.

Acierno, R., Hersen, M., Van Hasselt, V.B., Tremont, g., & Meuser, K.T., (1994). Review of the validation and dissemination of eye movement desensitization and reprocessing: A scientific and ethical dilemma. Clinical Psychological Review, 14, 287-299.

Adams, P. R., & Adams, Z. R. (1984). Mount Saint Helen's ashfall: Evidence of a disaster stress reaction. American Psychologist 39, 252-260.

Agger, I., & Jensen, S. B. (1994). Determinant factors for countertransference reactions under state terrorism. In J. P. Wilson, & J. D. Lindy (Eds.), Countertransference in the treatment of PTSD. New York: Guilford.

Agger, I., & Jensen, S.B. (1990). Testimony as ritual and evidence in psychotherapy for political refugees. Journal of Traumatic Stress, 3, 115-130.

Aldwin, C.M. (1993). Coping with traumatic stress. PTSD Research Quarterly, 4, 1-7.

Alexander, D.A. (1993). The Piper Alpha oil rig disaster. In J.P. Wilson & B. Raphael (Eds.)., International handbook of traumatic stress. New York: Plenum.

Alexander, D.A., & Wells, A. (1991). Reactions of police officers to body handling after a major disaster. British Journal of Psychiatry, 159, 547-555.

Alexander, P., & Neimeyer, G.J. (1984). Constructivism and family therapy. International Journal of Personal Construct Psychology, 2, 111-121.

Alexander, P.C. (1992). Application of attachment theory to the study of sexual abuse. Journal of Consulting and Clinical Psychology, 60, 185-195.

Alexander, P.C., Neimeyer, R.A., Follette, V.M., Moore, M.K., & Harter, S. (1989). A comparison of group treatments of women sexually abused as children. Journal of Consulting and Clinical Psychology, 57, 479-483.

Alford, J., Mahane, A., & Fielstein, E.A. (1988). Cognitive and behavioral sequelae of combat conceptualization and implications for treatment. Journal of Traumatic Stress, 1, 485-501.

Allen, R.D. (Ed.) (1993). Handbook of post-disaster interventions. A special issue of the Journal of Social Behavior and Personality, 8(5) (488pp $30: Order from Select Press, P.O.Box 37, Cori Madera, CA, 94976-0037 Phone: 415-924-1612)

Allen, S. N., & Bloom, S. L. (1994). Group and family treatment of post-traumatic stress disorder. In D. A. Tomb (Ed.), The Psychiatric Clinics of North America, 8,425-438.

Allodi, F. D. (1994). Post-traumatic stress disorder in hostages and victims of torture. In D. A. Tomb (Ed.) The Psychiatric Clinics of North America, 8, 279-288.

American Psychiatric Association (1980). Diagnostic an statistical manual of mental disorders. (Third Edition). Washington, D.C.

American Psychiatric Association (1987). Diagnostic and statistical manual of mental disorders. (Third Edition - revised) Washington, D.C.

American Red Cross (1982). Providing Red Cross disaster health services (ARC3076-A).

American Red Cross (1991). Coping with disaster: Emotional health issues for victims. (ARC Publication No. 4475, Dec. 1991).

American Red Cross (1991, Nov). Disaster services regulations and procedures: Disaster mental health services.

Amick-McMullan, A., Kilpatrick, D. G. & Veronen, L. J. (1989a). Family survivors of homicide victims: A behavioral analysis. Behavior Therapist 12,75-79.

Amick-McMullen, A., Kilpatrick, D. G., et al. (1989b). Family survivors, of homicide victims. Theoretical perspectives and an exploratory story. Journal of Traumatic Stress, 1,21-35.

Amnesty International: Report on Torture. (1975) (rev. ed.). London Duckworth and A. I. Publications.

Andreason, N.C. (1980). Postraumatic stress disorder. In H. I. Kaplan, A. M. Freedman, & B. J. Sadock (Eds.), Comprehensive textbook of psychiatry. Baltimore, MD: Williams & Wilkins.

Andreason, N.C. (1985). Postraumatic stress disorder. In H.I. Kaplan and B.J. Sadock (Eds.), Comprehensive textbook of psychiatry. 4th Edition. Baltimore: Williams and Wilkins.

Angelou, M. (1970). I know why the caged bird sings. New York: Random House.

Antonovsky, A., (1979). Health, stress and coping. San Francisco, CA: Jossey-Boss.

Archibald, H.D., & Tuddenham, R.D. (1965). Persistent stress reactions after combat. Archives of General Psychiatry, 12, 475-481.

Armstrong, K., O'Callahan, W., & Marmar, C. (1991). Debriefing Red Cross disaster personnel: The Multiple Stressor Debriefing Model. Journal of Traumatic Stress, 4, 581-594.

Armsworth, M.W. (1989). Therapy of incest survivors: Abuse or support. Child Abuse and Neglect, 13, 546-564.

Arnold, A.L. (1985). Diagnosis of post-traumatic stress disorder. In S.M. Sonnenberg, A.S. Blank, J.A., and Talbot (Eds.), The trauma of war: Stress and recovery of Vietnam Veterans. Washington, D.C.: American Psychiatric Press

Ateson, B., Calhoun, D., et al. (1982). Victims of rape: Repeated assessment of depressive symptoms. Journal of Consulting and Clinical Psychology, 50, 96-102.

Austin, L.S. (Ed.)(1992). Responding to disaster: A guide for mental health professionals. Washington, D.C.: American Psychiatric Association.

Averill, J.R. Catlin, G., & Chon, K.K. (1990). Rules of hope. New York: Springer-Verlag.

Barath, A., Matel, D., & Marenic, J. (1993). Images of my childhood in Croatia since summer 1991. (Unpublished manuscript, University of Zagreb Medical School).

Bard, M., & Sangrey, D. (1979). The crime victim's book. New York: Basic Books.

Barocas, H.S., & Barocas, C.B. (1979). Wounds of the fathers: The next generation of Holocaust victims. International Review of Psychoanalysis, 6, 331-340.

Barsky, A.J., Wool, C., Barnett, B.A., & Cleary, P.D. (1994). Histories of childhood trauma in adult hypochondriacal patients. American Journal of Psychiatry, 151, 397-401.

Bartlett, F.C. (1932). Remembering: A study in experimental and social psychology. London: Cambridge University Press.

Basoglau, M. (Ed.), (1992). Torture and its consequences: Current treatment approaches. New York: Cambridge University Press.

Basoglu, M., Parker, M., et al. (1994). Psychological effects of torture: A comparison of tortured and nontortured political activists in Turkey. American Journal of Psychiatry, 151, 76-81.

Bass, E. & Davis, L. (1988). The courage to heal: A guide for women survivors of child sexual abuse. New York: Harper and Row.

Bass, E., & Thornton, L. (1983). I never told anyone: Writings by women survivors of child sexual abuse. New York: Harper & Row.

Batres, A. (1992). Physically disabled veterans working group. NCP Clinical Newsletter, 2, 6-8.

Baum, A. (1990). Stress, intrusive imagery and chronic stress. Health Psychology, 9, 653-675.

Baum, A., & Fleming, I. (1993). Implications of psychological research in stress and technological accidents. American Psychologist, 48, 665-672.

Baum, A., Cohen, L., & Hall, M. (1993). Control and intrusive memories as possible determinants of chronic stress. Psychosomatic Medicine, 55, 274-286.

Baum, A., Fleming, R., & Davidson, L.M. (1983). Natural disaster and technological catastrophe. Environment and Behavior, 15, 333-354.

Baumeister, R.F., Stillwell, A.M., & Heatherton, T.F. (1994). Guilt: An interpersonal approach, Psychological Bulletin, 115, 243-267.

4667) or from CTIE, 2522 Highland Ave., Cincinnati, Ohio, 45219 (Telephone 513-221-8545; FAX 513-321-8405).

Bolen, J.D. (1993). The impact of sexual abuse on women's health. Psychiatric Annals, 23, 446-453.

Bolin, R. (1988). Response to natural disasters. In M.L. Lystad (Ed.), Health response to mass emergencies: Theories and practice. New York: Brunner/Mazil.

Bollerud, K. (1990). A model for the treatment of trauma-related syndromes among chemically-dependent inpatient women. Journal of Substance Abuse Treatment, 1, 83-87.

Borus, J.T. (1973). Reentry III. Facilitating healthy readjustment in Vietnam veterans. Psychiatry, 36, 428-439.

Boudewyns, P.A. & Hyer, L. (1990). Physiological responses to combat memories and preliminary treatment outcome in Vietnam Veteran PTSD patients treated with direct therapeutic exposure. Behavior Therapy, 21, 63-87.

Boudewyns, P.A., Hyer, L., et al. (1990). PTSD among Vietnam veterans: An early look at treatment outcome using direct therapy exposure. Journal of Traumatic Stress, 3, 359-368.

Boudewyns, P.A., Hyer, L., Woods, M.G., Harrison, W.R., & McCranie, E. (1990). PTSD among Vietnam veterans: An early look at treatment outcome with direct therapeutic exposure. Journal of Traumatic Stress, 3, 359-368.

Boudewyns, P.A., Stwertka, S.A., Hyer, L.A., Albrecht, J.W., & Sperr, E.V. (1993). Eye movement desensitization for PTSD of combat: A treatment outcome pilot study. The Behavior Therapist, 16, 29-33.

Boudewyns, P.A., Woods, M.G., et al. (1991). Chronic combat-related PTSD and concurrent substance abuse: Implications for treatment of this frequent "dual diagnosis". Journal of Traumatic Stress, 4, 549-560.

Boulanger, G. (1986). Predisposition to post-traumatic stress disorder. In G. Boulanger & C. Kadushin (Eds.), The Vietnam veteran redefined: Fact and fiction. New Jersey: Erlbaum.

Bourne, P. G. (1970. Men, stress and Vietnam. Boston: Little Brown.

Bradshaw, S.L., Ohlde, C.D., & Horne, J.B. (1993). Combat and personality change. Bulletin of Menninger Clinic, 57, 466-478.

Brady, K. (1979). Father's days: A true story of incest. New York: Pull.

Brandt, L.M. (1989). A short-term group therapy model for treatment of adult female survivors of childhood incest. Group, 13, 74-82.

Braun, B.G. (Ed.) (1980). Treatment of multiple personality disorder. Washington, D.C.: American Psychiatric Press.

Braza, J., & Braza, K., (1991). War and its aftermath. Hawthorne, NJ: Career Press.

Breger, L., & McGaugh, J. (1965). Critique and reformulation of "learning theory": Approaches to psychotherapy and neurosis. Psychological Bulletin, 63, 338-358.

Bremner, J.D., Scot, T.M. et al. (1993). Deficits in short-term memory in posttraumatic stress disorder. American Journal of Psychiatry, 150, 1015-1019.

Bremner, J.D., Smithwick, S.M., et al. (1993). Childhood physical abuse and combat-related postraumatic stress disorder in Vietnam veterans. American Journal of Psychiatry, 150, 235-239.

Brende, J.O. (1981). Combined individual and group therapy for Vietnam veterans. International Journal of Group Psychotherapy, 31, 367-378.

Brende, J.O., & McDonald, E. (1989). Posttraumatic spiritual alienation and recovery in Vietnam combat veterans. Spirituality Today, 41, 4.

Brende, J.O., & Parson, E.R. (1985). Vietnam veterans: The road to recovery. New York: Plenum.

Brenner, P., Roskies, E., & Lazarus, R.S. (1982). Stress and coping under extreme conditions. In J.E. Dimsdale (Ed.), Survivors, victims, and perpetrators: Essays on Nazi holocaust. New York: Hemisphere Publishing Co.

Breslau, N., & Davis, G.C. (1992). Posttraumatic stress disorder in an urban population of young adults: Risk factors for chronicity. American Journal of Psychiatry, 149, 671-675.

Beck, A. (1994). Workshop on cognitive therapy of personality disorders. Evolution of psychotherapy conference. Hamburg, Germany.

Becker, D. (in press). The deficiency of the PTSD concept when dealing with victims of human rights violations. In R.J. Kleber et al. (Eds.), Beyond trauma. New York: Plenum.

Becker, J.V., & Skinner, L. (1983). Assessment and treatment of rape-related sexual dysfunctions. The Clinical Psychologist, 36, 102-105.

Becker, J.V., & Skinner, L. (1984). Behavioral treatment of sexual dysfunctions in sexual assault survivors. In I. Stuart and J. Jreer (Eds.), Victims of sexual aggression. New York: Van Nostrand Reinhold.

Beesley, S.W. (1989). Vietnam: The heartland remembers. New York: Berkeley Books.

Beitchman, J.H., Zucker, J.J., et al. (1992). A review of the long-term effects of child sexual abuse. Child Abuse and Neglect, 16, 101-118.

Ben-David, A., & Lavee, Y. (1992). Families in the sealed room: Interaction patterns of Israeli families during scud missile attacks. Family Process, 31, 35-44.

Bentley, S. (1991). A short listing of PTSD: From Thermopylae to Here. The Viceran, January.

Bergman, L.H., & Queen, T. (April, 19-86). Critical incident stress: Part 1. Fire Command, 52-56.

Berke, P.R., Kartex, J., & Wenger, D. (1993). Recovery after disaster: Achieving sustainable development, mitigation, and equity. Disasters, 167, 93-109.

Best, C.L. (1994). Accident injury: Approaches to assessment and treatment. In J.R. Freedy & S.E. Hobfoll (Eds.), Traumatic stress: From theory to practice. New York: Plenum.

Best, C.L., Amick, A.E., Veronen, L.J., & Kilpatrick, D.G. (1987). Manual for stress inoculation training treatment for rape victims. Medical University Press, Charleston, SC.

Bettelheim, B. (1943). Individual and mass behavior in extreme situations. Journal of Abnormal Psychology, 38, 417-452.

Bettelheim, B. (1979). Surviving and other essays. New York: Vintage.

Bettelheim, B. (1984). Afterword. In C. Vegh, I didn't say good-bye. New York: E. P. Dutton.

Beutler, L.E., & Hill, C.E. (1992). Process and ontionic research in the treatment of adult victims of childhood sexual abuse: Methodological issues. Journal of Consulting and Clinical Psychology, 60, 204-212.

Black, M. Dubowitz, H., & Harrington D. (1994). Sexual abuse: Developmental differences in children's behavior and self-perception. Child Abuse and Neglect, 18, 85-95.

Blackman, J. (1989). Intimate violence: A study of injustice. New York: Columbia University Press.

Blake, D.D. (1993). Treatment outcome research on PTSD NCP Clinical Newsletter, 3, 14-17.

Blake, D.D., Albano, A.M., & Keane, T.M. (1992) Twenty years of trauma: Psychological Abstracts 1970 through 1989. Journal of Traumatic Stress, 5, 477-484. (They have compiled a bibliography of 1596 articles. Available from Dr. Dudley Blake, Dept. of Veterans Affairs, National Center for PTSD, Medical Center, 3801 Miranda Ave., Palo Alto, California, 94304).

Blanchard, E.B., Hickling, E.J. et al. (1994). Psychological morbidity associated with motor vehicle accidents. Behaviour Research and Therapy, 32, 283-290.

Blank, A. (1992). Readjustment counseling service. NCP Clinical Newsletter, 2, 1-8.

Blank, A. S. (1994). Clinical detection, diagnosis, and differential diagnosis of post-traumatic stress disorder. In D. A. Tomb (Ed.), The Psychiatric Clinics of North America, 8, 351-384.

Blau, G.M., Whewell, M.C., et al. (1994). The prevention and treatment of child abuse in households of substance abusers: A research demonstration progress report. Social Work, 17, 16-19.

Blaufarb, H., & Levine, J. (1972). Crisis intervention in Croatia work to ease trauma among young war victims. Child Welfare League of America, 73, 83-94.

Bloch, E.L. (1993). Psychologists in Croatia work to ease trauma among, young war victims. Psychology International, Sumner. (Published by APA) (Inquiries about the Croatia project can be directed to Dr. Ellin Bloch, Center for Traumatic Information and Education, (CTTE), P.O. Box 55409, Cinncinati, Ohio 45254-0409, (Phone 513-321-

Breslau, N., Davis, G.C., Andereski, P., & Peterson, E. (1991). Traumatic evens and post-traumatic stress disorder in an urban population of young adults. Archives of General Psychiatry, 48, 216-222.

Brett, E.A., & Ostroff, R. (1985). Imaging and posttraumatic stress disorder: An overview. American Journal of Psychiatry, 142, 417-424.

Brett, E.A., Spitzer, R.L. & Williams, J.B.W. (1988). DSM-III-R criteria for posttraumatic stress disorder. American Journal of Psychiatry, 145, 1232-1236.

Breuer, J., & Freud, S. (1957). Studies on hysteria. New York: Basic Books.

Brewer, W. (1974). There is no convincing evidence for operant or classical conditioning in adult humans. In W. Weimer & D. Palermo (Eds.), Cognition and the Symbolic Processes. New York: Halsted Press.

Brewin, C. R., Andrews, B., & Gotlib, I. H., (1993). Psychopathology and early experience. Psychological Bulletin, 113, 82-98.

Brewin, C.R., & Shapiro, D.A. (1984). Beyond locus of control: Attributions of responsibility for positive and negative outcomes. British Journal of Psychology, 75, 43-49.

Breznitz, S. (1993). Memory fields. New York: Alfred Knopf.

Briere, J. (1989). Therapy for adults molested as children: Beyond survival. New York: Springer.

Briere, J. (1992). Methodological issues in the study of sexual abuse affects. Journal of consulting and Clinical Psychology, 60, 196-203.

Briere, J., & Conte, J. (1993). Self-reported amnesia for abuse in adults molested as children. Journal of Traumatic Stress, 6, 21-31.

Briere, J., & Runtz, M. (1987). Post sexual abuse trauma: Data and implications for clinical practice. Journal of Interpersonal Violence, 3, 367-379.

Briere, J., & Runtz, M. (1993). Childhood sexual abuse: Long-term sequaelae and implications for psychological assessment. Journal of Interpersonal Violence, 8, 312-330.

Briere, J., & Zaidi, Y. (1989). Sexual abuse histories and seqiv? in female psychiatric room patients. American Journal of Psychiatry, 146, 1602-1606.

Brom, D., & Kleber, R.J. (1989). Prevention of post-traumatic stress disorders. Journal of Traumatic Stress, 2, 335-351.

Brom, D., & Witzium, E. (1992). Recent trauma in psychiatric outpatients. American Journal of Orthopsychiatry, 62, 545-557.

Brom, D., Kleber, R.J., & Defares, P.B. (1989). Brief psychotherapy for posttraumatic stress disorders. Journal of Consulting and Clinical Psychology, 57, 607-612.

Brom, D., Kleber, R.J., & Hofman, M.C. (1993). Victims of traffic accidents: Incidence and prevention of post-traumatic stress disorder. Journal of Clinical Psychology, 49, 131-139.

Bromet, E.J. (1989). The nature and effects of technological failures. In R.Gist & B. Lubin (Eds.), Psychosocial aspects of disaster. New York: Wiley.

Brooks, J.S., & Scarano, T. (1985). Transcendental meditation in the treatment of post-Vietnam adjustment. Journal of Counseling and Adjustment, 64, 212-215.

Brooks, R. (1981). Creative characters: A technique in child therapy. Psychotherapy, 18, 131-139.

Browne, A. (1993). Violence against women by male partners. American Psychologist, 48, 1077-1087.

Bruhn, A.R. (1990). Earliest childhood memories: Vol. 1. Theory and application to clinical practice. New York: Praeger.

Bruner, J. (1990). Acts of meaning. Cambridge, MA: Harvard University Press.

Budman, S.H., Hoyt, M.F., & Friedman, S. (Eds.) (1992). The first session in brief therapy. New York: Guildford.

Buechler, D. (1992). Bringing together women Vietnam veterans. NCP Clinical Newsletter, 2, 7-11.

Bulman, R., & Wortman, C.B. (1977). Attributions of blame and coping in the "real world": Severe accident victims react to their lot. Journal of Personality and Social Psychology, 35, 351-363.

Burge, S.K. (1988). Post-traumatic stress disorder in victims of rape. Journal of Traumatic Stress, 1, 193-210.

Burgess, A., W., & Baldwin, B.A. (1981). Crisis intervention theory and practice: A clinical handbook. New York: Prentice Hall.

Burgess, A.W. & Holmstrom, L.L. (1979). Adaptive strategies and recovery from rape. American Journal of Psychiatry, 136, 1278-1236.

Burgess, A.W., Groth, A., et al. (1978). Sexual assault of children and adolescents. Lexington, MA: Lexington Books.

Burgess, A.W., Holmstrom, L.L., & McCausland, M.P. (1978). Counseling young victims and their parents. In A.W. Burgess, A.N. Groth, & L.L. Holmstrom (Eds.), Sexual assault of children and adolescents. Lexington: Lexington Books.

Burnam, M.A., Stein, J.A. et al. (1988). Sexual assault and mental disorders in a community population. Journal of Consulting and Clinical Psychology, 56, 843-850.

Burnstein, A. (1986). Treatment of noncompliance in patients with posttraumatic stress disorder. Psychosomatic Medicine, 27, 37-40.

Burt, M. (1980). Cultural myths and support for rape. Journal of Personality and Social Psychology, 38, 215-226.

Burt, M.R., & Katz, B.L. (1987). Dimensions of recovery from rape: Focus on growth outcomes. Journal of Interpersonal Violence, 2, 57-81.

Butler, K. (1993). The enigma of EMDR: Too good to be true? The Family Therapy Networker, November/December, 19-31.

Butler, S. (1978). Conspiracy of silence: The trauma of incest. New York: Bantam Books.

Calhoun, K.S., & Atkeson, B.M. (1991). Treatment of rape victims: Facilitating psychosocial adjustment. Elmsford, NY: Pergamon.

Calhoun, K.S., & Resick, P.A. (1993). Post-traumatic stress disorder in D. Barlow (Ed.) Clinical handbook of psychological disorders. New York: Guilford Press.

Calof, D. (1993). Facing the truth about false memory. Networker, Sept./Oct., 39-45.

Cameron, C. (1994). Veterans of a secret war: Survivors of childhood sexual trauma compared to Vietnam war veterans with PTSD. Journal of Interpersonal Violence, 9, 117-132.

Cameron, G. (1989). Community development principles and helping battered women. In B. Pressman et al. (Eds.), Intervening with assaulted women. Hillsdale, NJ: Erlbaum.

Capacchione, L. (1979). The creative journal: The art of finding yourself. Athens, OH: Ohio University/Swallow Press.

Carroll, E.M., Rueger, d.B. et al. (1985). Vietnam combat veterans with PTSD. Journal of Abnormal Psychology, 94, 329-337.

Cardena, E., & Spiegel, D. (1993). Dissociative reactions to the San Francisco bay area earthquake of 1989. American Journal of Psychiatry, 150, 474-478.

Catherall, D.R. (1986). The support system and PTSD in Vietnam veterans. Psychotherapy, 23, 478-482.

Catherall, D.R. (1992). Back from the brink: A family guide to overcoming traumatic stress. New York: Bantam.

Catherall, D.R., & Lane, C. (1992). Symbolic recognition: Ceremony and treatment of post-traumatic stress disorder. Journal of Traumatic Stress, 5, 37-44.

Caul, D. (1984). Group and video techniques for multiple personality disorder. Psychiatric Annals, 14, 43-50.

Cavenar, J.L., & Nash, J.L. (1976). The effects of combat on the normal personality: War neurosis in Vietnam returnees. Comprehensive Psychiatry, 17 647-653.

Ceci, S.J., & Bruck, M. (1993a). Suggestibility of the child witness: A historical review and synthesis. Psychological Bulletin, 113, 403-439.

Ceci, S.J., & Bruck, M. (1993b). Child witnesses: Translating research into policy. Social Policy Report of SBCD, 7, 1-29.

Ceci, A.J., & Loftus, E.F. (1994). "Memory work": A royal road to false memories. Applied Cognitive Psychology, 8, 351-364.

Centers for Disease Control Vietnam Experience Survey (VES) (1988). Psychosocial characteristics. Journal of American Medical Association, 259, 2701-2707.

Creamer, M. (in press). A cognitive processing formulation of posttrauma reactions. In R.J. Kleber et al (Eds.), Beyond trauma. New York, Plenum.

Creamer, M., Buckingham, W.J., & Burgess, P. (1991). A community based mental health response to a multiple shooting. Australian Psychologist. 26. 2.

Creamer, M., Burgess, P., & Pattison, P. (1990). Cognitive processing in post-trauma reactions: Some preliminary findings. Psychological Medicine. 20. 597-604.

Cressman, B., Cameron, G. & Rothery, M. (1989). Intervening with assaulted women: Current theory, research and practice. Hillsdale, N.J.: Erlbaum.

Dahl, S. (1993). Rape: A hazard to health. Oslo: Scandinavian University Press.

Daly, R. J. (1983). Samuel Pepys and post-traumatic stress disorder. British Journal of Psychiatry. 143. 64-68.

Dancu, C.V., & Foa, E.B. (1992). Post traumatic stress disorder. In A. Freeman and F. Dattilio (Eds.), Comprehensive casebook of cognitive therapy. New York: Plenum Press.

Daneli, Y. (1988). Confronting the unimaginable: Psychotherapists reactions to victims of the Nazi Holocaust. In J. Wilson, Z. Harel, & B. Kahana (Eds.), Human adaptation to extreme stress. New York: Plenum.

Daneli, Y. (1994). As survivors age. Clinical Quarterly. 4. 3-7.

Daneli, Y. (1994). Countertransference, trauma and training. In J. P. Wilson, & J. D. Lindy (Eds.), Countertransference in the treatment of PTSD. New York: Guilford.

Danica, E. (1988). Don't. London: The Women's Press.

Danieli, Y. (1982). Families of survivors of the Nazi Holocaust: Some short- and long-term effects. In C.D. Spielberger, I.G. Sarason, & N.A. Milgram, (Eds.), Stress and anxiety. Washington, DC: Hemisphere.

Danieli, Y. (1988). Treating survivors and children of survivors of the Nazi Holocaust. In F.M. Ochberg (Ed.), Post-traumatic therapy and victims of violence. New York: Frunner/Mazel.

Danieli, Y. (1994). As survivors age: Part II. NCP Clinical Quarterly. 4. 20-24.

Dar, R., Serlin, R.C., & Omer, H. (1994). Misuse of statistical tests in three decades of psychotherapy research. Journal of Consulting and Clinical Psychology. 62. 75-82.

Dasberg, H. (1987). Psychological distress of Holocaust survivors and offspring in Israel, Forty years later: A review. Israel Journal of Psychiatry. 24. 243-256.

Dattilio, F. M., & Freeman, A. (Eds.). (1994). Cognitive-behavioral strategies in crisis intervention. New York: Guilford.

Davidoff, D.A., Laibstain, P.F., et al. (1988). Neurobehavioral sequelae of minor head injury: A consideration of post-concussive syndrome versus post-traumatic stress disorder. Cognitive Rehabilitation. 6. 8-13.

Davidson, J.R. (1992). Drug therapy of post-traumatic stress disorder. British Journal of Psychiatry. 160. 309-314.

Davidson, J.R., & Fairbank, J.A. (1992). The epidemiology of posttraumatic stress disorder. In J.R. Davidson & E.B. Foa (Eds.), Posttraumatic stress disorder: DSM-IV and beyond. Washington, DC: American Psychiatric Press.

Davidson, J.R., & Foa, E.B. (1993). Posttraumatic stress disorder: DSM-IV and beyond. Washington D.C.: American Psychiatric Press

Davidson, J.R., Kundler, H., Saunders, W., & Smith, R. (1990). Symptom and comorbidity patterns in World War II and Vietnam veterans with posttraumatic stress disorder. Comprehensive Psychiatry. 31. 162-170.

Davidson, J.R., Kundler, H.S., et al. (1993). Predicting response to Amitriptyline in posttraumatic stress disorder. American Journal of Psychiatry. 150. 1024-1029.

Davidson, L.M., & Baum, A. (1993). Predictors of chronic stress among Vietnam veterans: Stressor exposure and intrusive recall. Journal of Traumatic Stress. 6. 195-212.

Davidson, L.M., & Baum, A. (1994). Psychophysiological aspects of chronic stress following trauma. In R.J. Ursano, B.G. McCaughey, and C.S. Fullerton (Eds.)., Individual and community responses to trauma and disaster. New York: Cambridge University Press.

Davis, C. G., Lehman, D. R. et al . (in press). The undoing of traumatic life events. Personality and Social Psychology Bulletin.

Charney, D.S., Deutch, A.Y., et al. (1993). Psychobiologic mechanisms of PTSD. Archives of General Psychiatry. 50. 294-305.

Chemtob, C.M., & Heriot, M.G. (1994). Post-traumatic stress disorder as a sequela of a Guillain-Barre syndrome.

Chemtob, C., Roitblat, H.C., Hamada, R.S., Carlson, J.G. & Twentyman, C.T. (1988). A cognitive action theory of post-traumatic stress disorder. Journal of Anxiety Disorders. 2. 253-275.

Chester, B., & Jaranson, J. (1994). The context of survival and destruction. Conducting psychotherapy with survivors of torture. Clinical Quarterly. 4. 17-20.

Chu, J. (1990). Ten traps for therapists in the treatment of trauma survivors. Dissociation. 1. 24-32.

Cienfuegos, A.J., & Monelli, C. (1983). The testimony of political repression as a therapeutic instrument. American Journal of Orthopsychiatry. 53. 43-51.

Clark, L.F. (1993). Stress and cognitive-conversational benefits of social interaction. Journal of Social and Clinical Psychology. 12. 25-55.

Classen, C., Koopman, C., & Spiegel, D. Trauma and dissociation. (1993). Bulletin of Menninger Clinic. 57. 178-194.

Classen, C.C., Koopman, C., & Spiegel, D. (1993). Trauma and dissociation. Bulletin of the Menninger Clinic. 57. 1-16.

Cleland, M. (1980). Strong in the broken places. Lincoln, VA: Chosen Books.

Cohen, L.J., & Roth, S. (1987). The psychological aftermath of rape: Long-term effects and individual differences in recovery. Journal of Social Clinical Psychology. 5. 525-534.

Cohen, R.E., & Aheam, F.L. (1980). Handbook for mental health care of disaster victims. Baltimore: John Hopkins University Press.

Cole, C.L. (1985). A group design for adult female survivors of childhood incest. Women and Therapy. 4. 71-82.

Coles, R. (1989). The call of stories. Boston: Houghton Miffin.

Coons, P.M., & Milstein, V. (1986). Psychosexual disturbances in multiple personality: Characteristics, etiology and treatment. Journal of Clinical Psychiatry. 47. 106-110.

Cooper, N.A., & Clum, G.A. (1989). Imaginal flooding as a supplementing for PTSD in combat veterans: A controlled study. Behavior Therapy. 20. 381-391.

Cote, I. (1994). Current perspectives on multiple personality disorder. Hospital and Community Psychiatry. 45. 827-829.

Courchaine, K. E., Dowd, E. T. (1994). Group approaches. In F. Dattilio & A. Freeman (Eds.), Cognitive-behavioral strategies in crisis intervention. New York: Guilford.

Courtois, C.A. (1993). Adult survivors of child sexual abuse. Milwaukee: Families International.

Courtois, C., & Sprei, J. (1988). Retrospective incest therapy. In L.E. Walker (Ed.), Handbook of sexual abuse of children. New York: Springer.

Courtois, C.A. (1979). The incest experience and its aftermath. Victimotology. 4. 337-347.

Courtois, C.A. (1988). Healing the incest wound: Adult survivors in therapy. New York: W.W. Norton.

Courtois, C.A. (1992). The memory retrieval process in incest survivor therapy. Journal of Child Sexual Abuse. 1. 15-31.

Courtois, C.A. (1993). Vicarious traumatization of the therapist. NCP Clinical Newsletter. 3. 8-9.

Coyne, J. C., Wortman, C. B., & Lehman, D. R., (1988). The other side of support: Emotional over - involvement and miscarried helping. In B. H. Gottlieb (Ed.), Social support: Formats processes and effects. Newbury, CA: Sage.

Cozza, K.L., & Hales, R.E. (1991). Psychiatry in the Army: A brief historical perspective and current developments. Hospital and Community Psychiatry. 42. 413-418.

Creamer, M., Burgess, P., & Pattison, P. (1992). Reaction to trauma: A cognitive processing model. Journal of Abnormal Psychology. 101. 453-459.

Davis, G. C., & Breslau, N. (1994). Post-traumatic stress disorder in victims of civilian trauma and criminal violence. In D. A. Tomb (Ed.), The Psychiatric Clinics of North America. 8, 289-300.

Davis, N. (1990). Once upon a time ... Therapeutic stories to heal abused children. (Psychological Associates. G178 Oxon Hill Rd., Suite 306, Oxen Hill, MD. 20745)

de Jong, J. (1994). Prevention of the consequences of man-made or natural disaster at the (inter)national, community, family and individual levels. Paper presented at NATO conference on community and disaster in Bonos, France.

de Shazer, S. (1985). Keys to solution in brief therapy. New York: Norton.

de Shazer, S. (1988). Clues: Investigating solutions in brief therapy. New York: Norton.

de Shazer, S. (1991). Putting differences to work. New York: W.W. Norton.

de Shazer, S., & Molnar, A. (1984). Four useful interventions in brief family therapy. Journal of Marital and Family Therapy. 10, 297-304.

Deahl, M.P., Farnshaw, N.M., & Jones, N. (1994). Psychiatry and war. British Journal of Psychiatry. 164, 441-442.

Deblinger, E., & Heflin, A. H. (1993). Child sexual abuse. In F. Dattilio & A. Freeman (Eds.), Cognitive-behavioral strategies in crisis intervention. New York: Guilford.

Deblinger, E., McLeer, S., & Henry, D. (1990). Cognitive behavioral treatment for sexually abused children suffering post-traumatic stress: Preliminary findings. Journal of the American Academy of Child Psychiatry. 29, 747-752.

Deitz, J. (1986). Time -limited psychotherapy for posttraumatic stress disorder: The traumatized ego and its self-reparative function. American Journal of Psychotherapy 40, 290-299.

DePanfilis, D., & Brooks, G. (1989). Child maltreatment and women abuse. Washington, DC: National Women Abuse Prevention Project.

Department of the Army, (1986). Management of stress in army operations: Field Manual 26-2, Washington, D.C. Author.

Dept. of Veterans Affairs (1991). Program evaluation of the Department of Veterans Affairs Post Traumatic Stress Disorder (PTSD) Programs. Available from The National Technical Information Service, Springfield, VT 22161. Report No. REPT-90-04.

Deriega, V.J., Hendrick, S.S., Winstead, B.A., & Berg, J.H. (1991). Psychotherapy as a personal relationship. New York: Guilford.

Des Pres, T. (1980). The survivor: An anatomy of life in the death camps.

Dew, M.A., Bromet, E., & Schulberg, H.C. (1987). A comparative analysis of two community stressors' long-term mental health effects. American Journal of Community Psychology. 15, 167-184.

Dew, M.A., Bromet, E.J., et al. (1987). Mental health effects of the Three Mile Island nuclear reactor restart. American Journal of Psychiatry. 144, 1074-1077.

Dhara, V.R., & Krebel, D. (1993). An exposure-response method for assessing the long term health effects of the Bhopal gas disaster. Disasters. 17, 281-290.

Diekstra, R. F., Engels, G. ., & Methorst, C. M. (1981). Cognitive therapy of depression: A means of crisis intervention. Crisis. 9, 32-44.

DiGiuseppe, R., Tafrate, R., & Eckhardt, C. (1994). Critical issues in the treatment of anger. Cognitive and Behavioral Practice, 1,111-132.

Dillon, J. T. (1990). The practice of questioning. London: Routledge.

Dirkstern, L.J., Hinz, L.D., & Spencer, E. (1991). Treatment of sexually abused children and adolescents. In A. Tasman & S.M. Goldfinger (Eds.), Review of psychiatry: Vol 10. Washington, DC: American Psychiatric Press.

Doctor, R. (1994). Tired of EMDR. The Behavior Therapist. 17, 202.

Dolan, Y.M. (1991). Resolving sexual abuse: Solution-focused therapy and Ericksonian hypnosis for adult survivors. New York: W.W. Norton.

Domash, M.D., & Sparr, L.F. (1992). Post-traumatic stress disorder masquerading as paranoid schizophrenia. Case report. Military Medicine. 147, 772-774.

Donovan, D.M. and McIntyre, D. (1990). Healing the hurt child: A developmental contextual approach. New York: Norton.

Downs, F. (1984). Aftermath. New York: Norton.

Downs, W. (1993). Developmental considerations for the effects of childhood sexual abuse. Journal of Interpersonal Violence. 8, 331-345.

Draucker, C.B. (1992). Counseling survivors of childhood sexual abuse. Newburg, CA: Sage.

DSM-IV Options Book: Work in progress. Task Force on DSM IV Washington: American Psychiatric Association, July 1991.

Duckworth, D.H. (1987). Post-traumatic stress disorder. Stress Medicine. 3, 175-183.

Dunning, C. (1988). Intervention strategies for emergency workers. In M. Lystad (Ed.), Mental health response to mass emergencies. New York: Brunner / Mazel.

Dunning, C. (1994). Trauma and countertransference in the workplace. In J. P. Wilson, & J. D. Lindy (Eds.), Countertransference in the treatment of PTSD. New York: Guilford.

Dunning, C., & Silva, M. (1980). Disaster-induced trauma in rescue workers. Victimology. 5, 287-297.

Dutton, M.A. (1992) Empowering and healing the battered women: A model for assessment and intervention. New York: Springer.

Dutton, M.A., Burghardt, K.J. et al. (1994). Battered women's cognitive schemata. Journal of Traumatic Stress. 7, 237-255.

Dyck, M.J. (1993). A proposal for a conditioning model of eye movement desensitization treatment for PTSD. Journal of Behavior Therapy and Experimental Psychiatry. 24, 201-210.

Dyregrov, A., (1988). Critical incident stress debriefings. Unpublished manuscript, Research Center for Occupational Health and Safety.

Dyregrov, A. (1989). Caring for helpers in disaster situations: Psychological debriefing. Disaster Management. 2, 25-30.

Dyregrov, A., & Mitchell, J.T. (1992). Work with traumatized children - Psychological effects and coping strategies. Journal of Traumatic Stress. 5, 5-17.

Eberly, R.E., & Engedahl, B.E. (1991). Prevalence of somatic and psychiatric disorders among former Prisoners of War. Hospital and Community Psychiatry. 42, 807-813.

Efran, J., Lukens, R., & Lukens, M. (1983, September - October). Constructivism: What's in it for you? Family Therapy Networker, pp 27-35.

Egendorf, A., (1975). Vietnam veterans rap groups and themes of post war life. Journal of Social Issues. 31, 111-124.

Egendorf, A., Kadushin, C., Laufer, R., Rothbart, G., & Sloan, L. (1981). Legacies of Vietnam: Comparative adjustment of veterans and their peers. New York: Center for Policy Research.

Eisen, M.R. (1992-93). The victim's burden: Guilt, shame, and abuse. Imagination, Cognition and Personality. 12, 69-88.

Ekman, P., & O'Sullivan, M. (1991). Who can catch a liar? American Psychologist. 46, 913-920.

Elder, G. H., & Clipp, E. C. (1988). War time losses and social bonding: Influences across 40 years in men's lives. Psychiatry. 51, 177-197.

Elder, G. H., Shanaham, M. J., & Clipp, E. C. (1994). When war comes to men's lives: Life-course patterns in family, work and health. Psychology and Aging, 9, 5-16.

Elder, G., & Clipp, E.C. (1989). Combat experience and emotional health: Impairment and resilience in later life. Journal of Personality. 57, 311-341.

Ellenson, G.S. (1985). Detecting a history of incest: A predictive syndrome. Social Casework. 66, 525-532.

Ellis, K.M. (1983). A review of empirical rape research: /victim reaction and response to treatment. Clinical Psychology Review. 3, 473-490.

Ellis, L.F., Black, L.D., & Resick, P.A. (1992). Cognitive behavioral treatment approaches for victims of crime. In P.A. Killer, & S.R. Heyman (Eds.), Innovations in clinical practice: A source book. Sarasota, FL: Professional Resource Exchange.

Ellsworth, R.B., Collins, J.F., Casey, N.A., and colleagues (1994). Some characteristics of effective psychiatric treatment programs. Journal of Consulting and Clinical Psychology. 54, 698-702.

Falsetti, S.A., & Resnick, H.S. (1994). Helping the victims of violent crimes. In J.R. Freedy & S.E. Hobfoll (Eds.), Traumatic stress: From theory to practice. New York: Plenum.

Farrell, J. M., & Shaw, I. A. (1994). Emotional awareness training: A prerequisite to effective cognitive-behavioral treatment of borderline personality disorder. Cognitive and Behavioral Practice, 1, 71-92.

Fawcett, J., Epstein, P., et al. (1987). Clinical management imipramine/placebo administration manual. Psychopharmacological Bulletin, 23, 309-324.

Federal Emergency Management Agency (FEMA) (1989). Coping with children's reactions to hurricanes and other disasters. (Document No. 1989 0-941-091). Washington, DC: U.S. Government Printing Office.

Felsen, I., & Erlich, H.S. (1990). Identification of patterns of offspring of Holocaust survivors with their parents. American Journal of Orthopsychiatry, 60, 506-520.

Fenster, A. (1993). Reflections on using group therapy as a treatment modality - why, now, for whom and when. Group, 17, 84-100.

Fierman, E.J., Hunt, M.F., et al. (1993). Trauma and posttraumatic stress disorder in subjects with anxiety disorders. American Journal of Psychiatry, 150, 1872-1874.

Figley, C.R. (1977). The American Legion Study of Psychological Adjustment among Vietnam veterans. Lafayette, IN: Purdue University.

Figley, C.R. (1978). Stress disorders among Vietnam veterans: Theory, research, and treatment. New York: Brunner/Mazel.

Figley, C.R. (1983). Catastrophes: An overview of family reactions. In C.R. Figley & H.T. McCubbin (Eds.), Stress and the family, Vol II. New York: Brunner/Mazel.

Figley, C.R. (1987). A five-phase treatment of post-traumatic stress disorder in families. Journal of Traumatic Stress, 1, 127-141.

Figley, C.R. (1989). Helping traumatized families. San Francisco: Jossey-Bass.

Figley, C.R. (1991). Gulf war veteran families: Struggles on the home front. In A. Bollinger (Ed.), Operation Desert Storm Clinician Packet. Palo Alto, CA: National Center for PTSD.

Figley, C.R. (1993). Coping with stressers in the home front. Journal of Social Issues, 49, 51-72.

Figley, C.R. (1994). Systemic post-traumatic stress disorder: Family treatment experiences and implications. In G. Everly and J. Lating (Eds.), Post-traumatic stress. New York: Plenum Press.

Figley, C.R. (Ed.) (1985). Trauma and its wake: The study and treatment of posttraumatic stress disorder. New York: Brunner/Mazel.

Figley, C.R. (Ed.) (1989). Treating stress in families. New York: Brunner/Mazel.

Figley, C.R. and McCubbin, H.I. (Eds.) (1983). Stress and the family. Volume II: Coping with catastrophe. New York: Brunner/Mazel.

Figley, C.R., & Leventman, S. (1980). Strangers at home: Vietnam veterans since the war. New York: Praeger.

Fine, M. (1985) (1985). Coping with rape: Critical perspectives on consciousness. Imagination, Cognition and Personality, 3, 249-267.

Finkelhor, D. (1990). Early and long-term effects of child sexual abuse: An update. Professional Psychology, 21, 325-330.

Finkelhor, D., & Dzuiba-Leatherman, J. (1994). Victimization of children. American Psychologist, 3, 173-183.

Finkelhor, D., Gelles, R.J., & Hotaling, G.T. (1983). The dark side of families. Beverley Hills, Calif.: Sage Publications.

Finkelhor, D., Hotaling, G., Lewis, I.A., & Smith, C. (1984). Sexual abuse in a national survey of adult men and women: Prevalence, characteristics, and risk factors. Child Abuse and Neglect, 14, 19-28.

Fisch, R. (1994). Basic elements in the brief therapies. In M. Hoyt (Ed.), Constructive therapies. New York: Guilford.

Fischer, W.J. (1991). Combat exposure and the etiology of postdischarge substance abuse problems among Vietnam veterans. Journal of Traumatic Stress, 4, 251-278.

Engdahl, B.E. (1994). Prisoner of war research: an overview with implications for refugee mental health. In R. Mollica & T. Bornemann (Eds.). Science of refugee mental health.

Engdahl, B.E., & Eberly, R.E. (1994). The course of chronic posttraumatic stress disorder. In T.W. Miller (Ed.). Stressful life events (2nd Ed.). New York: International Universities Press.

Engdahl, B.E., & Eberly, R.E. (1994). The effects of torture and other maltreatment: Implications for psychology. In P. Suedfeld (Ed.) Psychology and torture. Washington, DC: Hemisphere Press.

Engel, C.C., Engel, A.L. et al. (1993). Posttraumatic stress disorder symptoms and precombat sexual and physical abuse in desert storm veterans. Journal of Nervous and Mental Disease, 181, 683-688.

Engels, G.I., Garnefski, N. & Diekstra, R.F. (1993). Efficacy of rational-emotive therapy: A quantitative analyses. Journal of Consulting and Clinical Psychology, 61, 1083-1090.

Epstein, H. (1974) Children of the holocaust: Conversations with the sons and daughters of survivors. New York: G. P. Putman.

Epstein, S. (1987). Implications of cognitive self-theory for psychopathology. In N. Cheshire & N. Thomas (Eds.). Self, symptoms and psychotherapy. New York: Wiley.

Epstein, S. (1991). The self-concept, the traumatic neurosis, and the structure of personality. In D. Ozer, J.M. Healey, and R.A. Stewart (Eds.), Perspectives on personality (Vol. 3). Greenwich, CONN.: JAI Press.

Epstein, S., & Erskine, N. (1983). The development of personal theories of reality. In D. Magnusson & V. Allen (Eds.), Human Developments: An interactional perspective. New York: Academic Press.

Epston, D., White, M. & Murray, K. (1992). A proposal for a re-authoring therapy: Rose's revisioning of her life and a commentary. In S. McNamnee & K.J. Gergen (Eds.), Therapy as social construction. Newbury Park, CA: Sage.

Erickson, M., & Rossi, E. (1976). Two level communication and microdynamics of trance. American Journal of Clinical Hypnosis, 18, 153-171.

Ericsson, K.A., & Charness, N. (1994). Expert performance: its structure and acquisition. American Psychologist, 49, 725-747.

Erikson, K. (1976). Everything in its path: Destruction of community in the Buffalo Creek flood. New York: Simon & Schuster.

Ersland, S., Weisaeth, L., & Sund, A. (1989). The stress upon rescuers involved in an oil rig disaster: "Alexander L. Kielland, 1980". Acta Psychiatrica Scandinavia, 335, 38-49.

Ettedgui, E., & Bridges, M. (1985). Posttraumatic stress disorder. The Psychiatric Clinics of North America, 8, 89-103.

Everly, G.S. (1989). A clinical guide to the treatment of the human stress response. New York: Plenum Press.

Evert, K. (1987). When you're ready: A woman's healing from childhood physical and sexual abuse by her mother. Walnut Creek, CA: Launel Press.

Ewing, C. L. (1978). Crisis intervention as psychotherapy. New York: Oxford University Press.

Faberow, N.L. (1978). Training manual for human service workers in major disasters. (DHHS Publication No. ADM 86-1070). Washington, DC: U.S. Government Printing Office.

Fairbank, J.A. & Keane, T.M. (1982). Flooding for combat-related stress disorders: Assessment of anxiety reduction across traumatic memories. Behavior Therapy, 13, 499-510.

Fairbank, J.A., & Nicholson, R.A. (1987). Theoretical and empirical issues in the treatment of posttraumatic stress disorder in Vietnam Veterans. Journal of Clinical Psychology, 43, 44-55.

Fairbank, J.A., Gross, R.T., & Keane, T.M. (1983). Treatment of posttraumatic steress disorder: Evaluation of outcome with a behavioral code. Behavior Modification, 7, 557-568.

Fairbank, J.A., Hansen, D.J., & Fetterling, J.M. (1991). Patterns of appraisal and coping across different stressor conditions among former prisoners of war with and without posttraumatic stress disorder. Journal of Consulting and Clinical Psychology, 59, 274-281.

Fraser, J.S. (1989). The strategic rapid intervention approach. In C.R. Figley (Ed.), Treating stress in families. New York: Brunner/Mazel.

Fraser, S. (1987). My father's house: A memoir of incest and of healing. New York: Harper and Row.

Fred, H. (1990). Fragments of a life: The road to Auschwitz (Translated by M. Meyer). London: Robert Hale.

Frederick, C.J. (1987). Psychic trauma in victims of crime and terrorism. In G.R. Vanderbos and B.K. Bryant (Eds.), Cataclysms, crises and catastrophy. Washington, D.C.: American Psychological Association.

Fredrich, W. (Ed.), (1991). Casebook of sexual abuse treatment. New York: Norton.

Freedy, J.R., & Hobfoll, S.E. (1994). Traumatic stress: From theory to practice. New York: Plenum.

Freedy, J.R., & Kilpatrick, D.G. (1994). Everything you ever wanted to know about natural disasters and mental health (well, almost). NCP Clinical Quarterly, 4, 6-8.

Freedy, J.R., Kilpatrick, D.G., & Resnick, H.S. (1993). Natural disasters and mental health. Journal of Social Behavior and Personality, 8, 49-103.

Freedy, J.R., Resnick, H.S. & Kilpatrick, D.G. (1992). Conceptual framework for evaluating disaster impact: Implications for clinical intervention. In L.S. Austin (Ed.), Responding to disaster: A guide for mental health professionals. Washington, D.C.: American Psychiatric Press.

Freedy, J.R., Saladin, M.E., Kilpatrick, D.G., Resnick, H.S., & Saunders, B.E. (1994). Understanding acute psychological distress following natural disaster. Journal of Traumatic Stress, 7, 257-274.

Freedy, J.R., Shaw, D.L., Jarrell, M.P., & Masters, C.R., (1992). Toward an understanding of the psychological impact of disasters: An application of the Conservation Resources Stress Model. Journal of Traumatic Stress, 5, 441-454.

Freeman, A., & Reinecke, M. (1993). Cognitive therapy of suicidal behavior. New York: Springer.

Friday, N. (1973). My secret garden. New York: Trident.

Fried, H. (1990). Fragments of a life: The road to Auschwitz (Translated by M. Meyer). London: Robert Hale.

Friedman, M. J., Schnurr, P. P., & McDonagh-Coyle, A. (1994). Post-traumatic stress disorder in the military veteran. In D. A. Tomb (Ed.), The Psychiatric Clinics of North America, 8, 265-278.

Friedman, M.J. (1988). Toward rational pharmacotherapy for PTSD. An interim report. American Journal of Psychiatry, 145, 281-285.

Friedman, M.J. (1991). Biological approaches to the diagnosis and treatment of post-traumatic stress disorder. Journal of Traumatic Stress, 4, 67-91.

Friedman, M.J. (1991). Biological approaches to the diagnosis and treatment of PTSD. Journal of Traumatic Stress, 4, 1-8.

Friedman, M.J. (1991). Current trends in PTSD research. NCP Clinical Newsletter, 2, 1-11.

Friedman, M.J. (1994). New directions. Clinical Quarterly, 4, 10-11.

Friedman, M.J., & Charney, D.S. (1991). Psychopharmacotherapy for recently evaluated military casualties. In A. Bollinger (Ed.), Operation Desert Storm Clinician Packet. Palo Alto, CA: National Center for PTSD.

Friedman, S. (1992). Constructing solutions. In S.H. Budman & M.F. Hoyt (Eds.), The first session in brief therapy. New York: Guilford Press.

Furman, E. (1979). Filial therapy. In J. Noshpitz (Ed.), Basic handbook of child psychiatry, Vol 3. New York: Basic Books.

Gadow, K.N. (1991). Clinical issues in child and adolescent psychopharmacology. Journal of Consulting and Clinical Psychology, 57, 842-852.

Gal, R. (1986). A portrait of the Israeli soldier. Westport CT: Greenwood Publishing.

Gal, R., & Mangelsdorf, A.D. (1991). Handbook of military psychology. New York: John Wiley.

Galdston, R. (1971). Violence begins at home. Journal of the American Academy of Child Psychiatry, 10, 336-350.

Fitzpatrick, K.M., & Boldizar, J.P. (1993). The prevalence and consequences of exposure to violence among African-American Youth. Journal of American Academia of Child and Adolescent Psychiatry, 32, 424-430.

Flannery, R.B. (1990). Social support and psychological trauma: A methodological review. Journal of Traumatic Stress, 3, 593-612.

Flannery, R.B. (1992). Posttraumatic stress disorder: The victim's guide to healing and recovery. New York: Crossroad

Flannery, R.B., Perry, & Harvey, M.C. (1993). A structured stress reduction group approach modified for victims of psychological trauma. Psychotherapy, 30, 646-650.

Fleming, B., & Pretzer, J. L. (1990). Cognitive behavioral approaches to personality disorder. Dr. M. Hersen, R. M. Eisler, & P. M. Miller, (Eds.), Progress in Behavior Modification. Vol. 21. Newbury Park, CA: Sage.

Fly, C.L. (1973). No hope but God. New York: Hawthorne.

Foa, E. B., & Kozak, M. J. (1986). Emotional processing of fear: Exposure to corrective information. Psychological Bulletin, 99, 20-35.

Foa, E.B., Rothbaum, B.O., & Steketee, G.S. (1993). Treatment of rape victims. Journal of Interpersonal Violence, 8, 256-276.

Foa, E.B., Rothbaum, B.O., Riggs, D.S., & Murdock, T.B. (1991). Treatment of posttraumatic stress disorder in rape victims: A comparison between cognitive-behavioral procedures and counseling. Journal of Consulting and Clinical Psychology, 59, 715-723.

Foa, E.B., Steketee, G., & Olasov-Rothbaum, B. (1989). Behavioral/cognitive conceptualizations of post-traumatic stress disorder. Behavior Therapy, 20, 155-176.

Fontana, A., Rosenheck, & Brett, E. (1992). War zone traumas and posttraumatic stress disorder symptomobiology. Journal of Nervous and Mental Disease, 180, 748-755.

Ford, J.D., Shaw, D., et al. (1993). Psychosocial debriefing after Operation Desert Storm: Mental and Family assessment and intervention. Journal of Social Issues, 49, 73-102.

Forman, B.D. (1980). Cognitive modification of obsessive thinking in a rape victim: A preliminary study. Psychological Reports, 47, 819-822.

Foss, O.T. (1994). Mental first aid. Social Science and Medicine, 38, 479-482.

Fox, S.S., & Scherl, D. (1972). Crisis intervention with victims of rape. Social Work, 17, 37-42.

Foy, D.W. (Ed.). (1992). Treating PTSD: Cognitive-behavioral strategies. New York: Guilford Press.

Foy, D.W., Donahoe, C.P., Carroll, E.M., Gallers, J., & Reno, R. (1987). Posttraumatic stress disorder. In L. Michelson & L.M. Ascher (Eds.), Anxiety and stress disorders. New York: Guilford.

Foy, D.W., Resnick, H.S., & Carroll, E.M. (1990). Behavior therapy with PTSD. In A.S. Bellack & M. Hersen, (Eds.), Handbook of Comparative treatments. New York: Wiley.

Foy, D.W., Sipprelle, R.C., Rueger, D.B., & Carroll, E.M. (1984). Etiology of posttraumatic stress disorder in Vietnam veterans: Analysis of premilitary, military, and combat exposure influences. Journal of Consulting and Clinical Psychology, 52, 79-87.

Frank, E., Anderson, B., Stewart, B.D., Dancu, C., Hughes, C., & West, D. (1988). Efficacy of cognitive behavior therapy and systematic desensitization in the treatment of rape trauma. Behavior Therapy, 19, 403-420.

Frank, J. (1961). Persuasion and healing. Baltimore: John Hopkins University Press.

Frank, J.B., Koster, T.R., Giller, E.C. & Ian, E. (1990). Antidepressants in the treatment of posttraumatic stress disorder. In M.E. Wolf and A.D. Mosnaim (Eds.), Post traumatic stress disorder: Etiology, phenomenology, and treatment. Washington, D.C.: American Psychiatric Press.

Frank, J.D. (1987). Psychotherapy, rhetoric and hermeneutics: Implications for practice and research. Psychotherapy, 24, 292-302.

Frankel, F.H. (1976). Hypnosis: Trance as a coping mechanism. New York: Plenum.

Frankenthal, K. (1969). Autohypnosis and other aids for survival in situations of extreme stress. International Journal of Clinical and Experimental Hypnosis, 17, 153-159.

Frankl, V. E. (1962). Man's search for meaning. New York: Simon & Schuster.

Goldstein, G., van Kammen, W., et al. (1987). Survivors of imprisonment in the Pacific Theater during World War II. American Journal of Psychiatry, 144, 1210-1213.

Golub, D. (1985). Symbolic expression in post-traumatic stress disorder: Vietnam combat veterans in art therapy. Arts Psychotherapy, 12, 285-296.

Golub, D. (1994). Special media review: Children's images of trauma. Journal of Traumatic Stress, 7, 329-333.

Goncalves, O. F. (1994). Cognitive narrative psychotherapy: The narrative construction of alternative meanings. Journal of Cognitive Psychotherapy, 8, 105-126.

Good, B. & Kleinman, A. (1985). Epilogue: Culture and depression. In A. Kleinman & B. Good (Eds.), Culture and depression. Berkeley: University of California Press.

Goodman, J.M., & Talwar, N. (1989). Group psychotherapy for victims of incest. Psychiatric Clinics of North America, 12, 279-283.

Goodman, LA, Koss, M., & Russo, N.F. (1993). Violence against women: Physical and mental health effects. Part I. Research findings. Applied and Preventive Psychology, 2, 79-89.

Goodman, L.A., Koss, M.P., et al. (1993). Male violence against women. American Psychologist, 48, 1054-1058.

Goodwin, J. (1988). Post-traumatic symptoms in abused children. Journal of Traumatic Stress, 1, 475-488.

Goodwin, J.M. & Talwar, N. (1989). Group psychotherapy for victims of incest. Psychiatric Clinics of North America, 12, 279-283.

Goolishian, H., & Anderson, H. (1990). Understanding the therapeutic process: From individuals and families to systems in language. In F. Kaslow (Ed.), Voices in family psychology. Newburg Park, CA: Sage.

Gossette, R.L., & O'Brien, R.M. (1992). The efficacy of rational-emotive therapy in adults: Clinical facts or psychiatric artifact? Journal of Behavior Therapy and Experimental Psychiatry, 23, 9-24.

Granot, H., & Breader, M. (1991). A behavior-response wheel for training and field use by civil defense officers at emergency sites. Journal of Traumatic Stress, 4, 223-232.

Greaves, G.B. (1992). Alternative hypotheses regarding claims of satanic cult activity: A critical analysis. In D. Salzheim & S. Devine (Eds.), Out of darkness: Exploring satanism and ritual abuse. Toronto: Maxwell Macmillan.

Green, A.H. (1980). Child maltreatment: A handbook for mental health professionals. New York: Jason Aronson.

Green, B. (1994b). Traumatic stress and disaster: Mental health effects and factors influencing adaptation. In F. Llehmac & C. Nadelson (Eds.). International Review of Psychiatry (Vol. II). Washington, DC: American Psychiatric Press.

Green, B. L. & Lindy, J. D. (1994). Post-traumatic stress disorder in victims of disasters. In D. A. Tomb (Ed.). The Psychiatric Clinics of North America, 8, 301-310.

Green, B.L. (1982). Assessing levels of psychological impairment following disaster: Consideration of actual and methological dimensions. Journal of Nervous and Mental Disease, 170, 544-550.

Green, B.L. (1990). Defining trauma: Terminology and generic stressor dimensions. Journal of Applied Psychology, 20, 1632-1642.

Green, B.L. (1994). Long-term consequences of disasters. Paper presented at the NATO conference on stress, coping and disaster in Bonas, France.

Green, B.L. (1994a). Psychosocial research in traumatic stress: An update. Journal of Traumatic Stress, 7, 341-362.

Green, B.L., Grace, M.C. et al. (1994). Children of disaster in the second decade: A 17-year follow-up of Buffalo Creek survivors. Journal of American Child and Adolescent Psychiatry, 33, 71-79.

Green, B.L., Grace, M.C., et al. (1990). Risk factors for PTSD and other diagnosis in a general sample of Vietnam veterans. American Journal of Psychiatry, 147, 729-733.

Green, B.L., Korol, M.G., et al. (1991). Children and disaster: Age gender, and parental effects of PTSD symptoms. Journal of American Academy of Child and Adolescent Psychiatry, 30, 945-951.

Gallers, J., Foy, D.W., Donohue, C.R., & Goldfarb, J. (1992). Post-traumatic stress disorder in Vietnam combat veterans: Effects of traumatic violence exposure and military adjustment. Journal of Traumatic Stress, 1, 181-192.

Ganaway, G.K. (1989). Historical versus narrative truth: Clarifying the role of exogenous trauma in the etiology of MPD and its variants. Dissociation, 2, 205-220.

Ganaway, G.K. (1989). Historical versus narrative truth: Clarifying the role of exogenous trauma in the etiology of MPD and its variants. Dissociation, 2, 201-205.

Garbarino, J., Dubrow, N., Kostelny, K., & Pardo, C. (1992). Children in danger: Coping with the consequences of community violence. San Francisco: Jossey Bass.

Garbarino, J., Kostelny, K., & Dubrow, N. (1991). No place to be a child: Growing up in a war zone. New York: Lexington/MacMillan.

Gardner, R.A. (1992). True and false accusations of child sexual abuse. Cresskill; N.J.: Creative Therapeutics.

Garmezy, N., & Rutter, M. (1985). Acute reactions to stress. In M. Rutter, & L. Hersov (Eds.), Child and adolescent psychiatry: Modern approaches. Oxford: Blackwell.

Gayford, J.J. (1975). Wife-battering: A preliminary survey of 100 cases. British Medical Journal, 1, 154-157.

Gelinas, D. (1983). The persisting negative effects of incest. Psychiatry, 46, 312-332.

Gergen, K. (1985). The social constructivist movement in modern psychology. American Psychologist, 40, 266-275.

Gerrity, E.T., & Steinglass, P. (1994). Relocation stress following natural disasters. In R.J. Ursano, B.G. McCaughey, and C.S. Fullerton (Eds.). Individual and community responses to trauma and disaster. New York: Cambridge University Press.

Getzel, G., & Masters, R. (1983). Serving families of homicide victims. Social Work Groups, 8, 81-94.

Gibbs, M.S. (1989). Factors in the victim that mediate between disaster and psychopathology: A review. Journal of Traumatic Stress, 2, 537-542.

Giel, R. (1990). Psychosocial processes in disasters. International Journal of Mental Health, 19, 7-20.

Gillespie, R.D. (1942). Psychological effects of war on citizen and soldier. New York: W.W. Norton.

Gillis, H.M. (1993). Individual and small-group psychotherapy for children involved in trauma and disaster. In C.F. Saylor (Ed.), Children and disasters. New York: Plenum Press.

Gist, R. & Stolz, S.B. (1982). Mental health promotion and the media: Community response to the Kansas City hotel disaster. American Psychologist, 37, 1136-1139.

Gleaves, D.H. (1994). Behavior therapy and traditional chemical dependency treatment. The Behavior Therapist, 17, 79-83.

Gleser, G., Green, B.L., & Winget, C.P. (1981). Prolonged psychosocial effects of disaster. A study of Buffalo Creek. New York: Plenum.

Gleser, G.C., Green, B.L., & Winget, C.N. (1978). Quantifying interview data in psychic impairment of disaster survivors. Journal of Nervous and Mental Disease, 166, 209-216.

Goenjian, A. (1993). A mental health relief programme in Armenia after the 1988 earthquake: Implementation and clinical observations. British Journal of Psychiatry, 163, 230-239.

Gold-Steinberg, S., & Buttenheim, M.C. (1993). "Telling one's story" in an incest survivor's group. International Journal of Group Psychotherapy, 43, 173-189.

Goldberger, L., & Breznitz, S. (Eds.). (1993). Handbook of stress.: Theoretical and clinical aspects. (Second edition) New York: Free Press.

Goldstein R., & Scharr, J.K. (1982). The long term impact of man made disaster: An examination of a small town in the aftermath of the Three Mile Island nuclear reactor accident. Disaster, 6, 10-19.

Goldstein, E., & Farmer, K. (1992). Confabulations: Creating false memories - Destroying families. Boca Raton, FL: SIRS Books.

Green, B.L., Lindy, J. & Grace, M. (1985). Posttraumatic stress disorder: Toward DSM-IV. Journal of Nervous and Mental Disease, 173, 406-411.

Green, B.L., Lindy, J.D. et al. (1990). Buffalo Creek survivors in the second decade: Stability of stress symptoms. American Journal of Orthopsychiatry, 60, 43-54.

Green, B.L., Lindy, J.D., & Grace, M.C. (1994). Psychological effects of toxic contamination. In R. Ursano et al. (Eds.), Trauma and disaster. new York: Cambridge University Press.

Green, B.L., Lindy, J.D., Grace, M.C., & Gleser, G. (1989). Multiple diagnosis in posttraumatic stress disorder: The role of war stressors. Journal of Nervous and Mental Disease, 177, 320-335.

Green, B.L., Lindy, J.D., Grace, M.C., & Leonard, A.C. (1992). Chronic post-traumatic stress disorder and diagnostic comorbidity in a disaster sample. Journal of Nervous and Mental Disease, 180, 760-766.

Green, B.L., Wilson, J.P., & Lindy, J. (1985). Conceptualizing post-traumatic stress disorder: A psychosocial framework. In C. Figley (Ed.), Trauma and its wake. (pp. 53-73). New York: Brunner/Mazel.

Greening, T. (1990). PTSD form the perspective of existential-humanistic psychology. Journal of Traumatic Stress, 3, 323-326.

Griffin, C.A. (1987). Community disasters and PTSD: A debriefing model for response. In T. Williams (Eds.), PTSD: A handbook for clinicians. Cincinnati: American Disabled Veterans Publication.

Grinker, R.P., & Spiegel, J.P. (1945). Men under stress. Philadelphia: Blakeston.

Grubman-Black, S.D. (1990). Broken boys/mending men. Blue Ridge Summit, PA: Tals Books.

Guerney, B.G. (1977). Relationship enhancement: Skill training programs for therapy, problem prevention and enrichment. San Francisco: Jossey-Boss.

Guiao, I.Z. (in press). Cultural analysis of research findings on the political stability in the Philippines. In R.J. Kleber et al. (Eds.), Beyond trauma. New York: Plenum.

Gunderson, J.G., & Chu, J.A. (1993). Treatment implications of past trauma in borderline personality disorder. Harvard Review of Psychiatry, 1, 75-81.

Gunderson, J.G., & Sabo, A.N. (1993). The phenomenological and conceptual interface between borderline personality disorder and PTSD. American Journal of Psychiatry, 150, 19-27.

Haaga, D.A., & Davison, G.C. (1989). Outcome studies of rational-emotive therapy. In M.E. Bernard & R.D. DiGuiseppe (Eds.), Inside rational-emotive therapy. San Diego, CA: Academic Press.

Haaga, D.A., & Davison, G.C. (1993). An appraisal of rational-emotive therapy. Journal of Consulting and Clinical Psychology, 61, 215-221.

Haaken, J., & Schlaps, A. (1991). Incest resolution therapy and objectification of sexual abuse. Psychotherapy, 28, 35-47.

Hackman, H.W. & Ziegler, B.L. (1994). Enhanced coping as an alternative treatment for PTSD. Unpublished manuscript. VA Medical Center, Sheridan Wyoming.

Hales, R.E. (1992). Psychiatric lessons from the Persian Gulf war. Hospital and Community Psychiatry, 43, 769.

Haley, S. (1974). When the patient reports atrocities. Archives of general Psychiatry, 30, 191-196.

Hamada, R. (1991). PTSD treatment and the Asian American/Pacific Islander Vietnam veteran. NCP Clinical Newsletter, 1, 4.

Hamberger, L. K., & Holzworth-Munroe, A. (1994). Partner violence. In F. M. Dattilio & A. Freeman (Eds.), Cognitive-behavioral strategies in crisis intervention. New York: Guilford.

Hamilton, B., & Coates, J. (1993). Perceived helplessness and use of professional services by abused women. Journal of Family Violence, 8, 313-324.

Hammerberg, M., & Silver, S.M. (1994). Outcome of treatment for post-traumatic stress disorder in a primary care unit serving Vietnam veterans. Journal of Traumatic Stress, 7, 195-216.

Hammond, D.C. (Ed.) (1990). Handbook of hypnotic suggestions and metaphors. New York: W.W. Norton.

Hammond, K.W., Scurfield, R.M., & Risse, S.C. (1993). Posttraumatic stress disorder. In D.I. Dunner (Ed.), Current psychiatric therapy. New York: Saunders.

Hansen, M. & Harway, M. (Eds.) (1993). Battering and family therapy. Newbury, Park: Sage.

Haritous-Fatouros, M. (1988). The official torturer: A learning model for obedience to the authority of violence. Journal of Applied Social Psychology, 12, 1107-1120.

Harmond, J., Starkey, T., & Ashlock, L. (1987). A follow-up of Miami model graduates 6-12 months afterward. Vet Center Voice, 8, 8-9.

Harris, C.J. (1991). A family crisis intervention model for the treatment of post-traumatic stress reaction. Journal of Traumatic Stress, 4, 195-208.

Hart, B., & Stuehling, J. (1992). Personalized safety plan. Unpublished manuscript, Pennsylvania Coalition Against Domestic Violence, Redding, PA.

Hartman, C. L., & Jackson, H. (1994). Rape and the phenomenon of countertransference. In J. P. Wilson, & J. D. Lindy (Eds.), Countertransference in the treatment of PTSD. New York: Guilford.

Hartsough, D.M. (1985). Measurement of the psychological effects of disaster. In J. Laube & S.A. Murphy (Eds.), Perspectives on disaster recovery. Norwalk, CT: Appelton-Century-Crafts.

Hartsough, D.M. (1988). Traumatic stress as an area for research. Journal of Traumatic Stress, 1, 145-154.

Hartsough, D.M., & Garaventa-Myers, D.G. (1985). Disaster work and mental health: Prevention and control of stress among workers. (DHHS Publication No. ADM 85-1422) Washington, DC: U.S. Government Printing Office.

Hartsough, D.M., & Myers, P.G. (1985). Disaster work in mental health: Prevention and control of stress among workers. Rockville, MD: NIMH.

Harvey, J. H. (1989). People's naive understanding of their close relationships. International Journal of Personal Construct Psychology, 2, 37-48.

Harvey, J.H., Flanary, R. & Morgan, M. (1986). Vivid memories of vivid loves gone by. Journal of Social and Personal Relationships, 3, 359-373.

Harvey, J.H., Orbuch, T.L., Chwaliz, K.D., & Garwood, G. (1991). Coping with sexual assault: The role of account making and confiding. Journal of Traumatic Stress, 4, 515-532.

Harvey, J.H., Orbuch, T.L., Weber, A.L., Merback, N., & Alt, R. (1992). House of pain and hope: Accounts of loss. Death Studies, 16, 99-124.

Harvey, J.H., Weber, A.L., & Orbuch, T.L. (1990). Interpersonal accounts: A social psychological perspective. Oxford, England: Basil Blackwell.

Harvey, M.R. (1990). An ecological view of psychological trauma. Unpublished manuscript. Cambridge Hospital, Cambridge: Mass.

Harvey, M.R., & Herman, J.L. (1992). The trauma of sexual victimization. PTSD Research Quarterly, 3, 1-7.

Hassard, A. (1993). Eye movement desensitization of body image. Behavioral Psychotherapy, 21, 157-160. (Also see his protocol for eye movement desensitization.)

Hauff, E., & Vaglum, P. (1983). Vietnamese boat refugees. Acta Psychiatrica Scandinavia, 88, 162-168.

Haugaard, J.J., Reppucci, N.D., Laird, J., & Nauful, T. (1991). Children's definitions of the truth and their competency as witnesses in legal proceedings. Law and Human Behavior, 15, 253-271.

Hausman, W., & Risch, D.K. (1967). Military psychiatry. Archives of General Psychiatry, 16, 727-739.

Heard, H.L., & Linehan, M.M. (1994). Dialectred behavior therapy: An integrative approach to the treatment of borderline personality disorder. Journal of Psychotherapy Integration, 4, 55-82.

Helzer, J.E., Robins, L.N., & McEvoy, I. (1987). Posttraumatic stress disorder in the general population. New England Journal of Medicine, 317, 1630-1634.

Henden, H., & Haas, A.P. (1991). Suicide and guilt as manifestations of PTSD in Vietnam combat veterans. American Journal of Psychiatry, 148, 586-591.

Hendsen, H., & Haas, A.P. (1988). Post traumatic stress disorder. In C.G. Last & M. Hersen (Eds.), Handbook of anxiety disorders. New York: Pergamon.

Herbert, J.D., & Musar, K.T. (1992). Eye movement desensitization: A critique of the evidence. Journal of Behaviour Therapy and Experimental Psychiatry, 23, 169-174.

Herlofsen, P. (1994). Group reactions to trauma: An avalanche accident. In R.J. Ursano, B. McCaughey, & C.S. Fullerton (Eds.), Individual and community responses to trauma and disaster. New York: Cambridge University Press.

Herman, J. (1981). Father-daughter incest. Cambridge, MA: Harvard University Press.

Herman, J. L., & Schatzow, E. (1987). Recovery and verification of memories of childhood sexual trauma. Psychoanalytic Psychology, 4, 1-14.

Herman, J.L. (1992). Complex PTSD: A syndrome in survivors of prolonged and repeated trauma. Journal of Traumatic Stress, 5, 377-391.

Herman, J.L. (1992). Trauma and recovery. New York: Basic Books.

Herman, J.L. (1993). Sequelae of prolonged and repeated trauma evidence for a complex postraumatic syndrome (DESNOS). In J.R. Davidson & E.B. Foa (Eds.), Posttraumatic stress disorder: DSM IV and beyond. Washington, D.C. American Psychiatric Association.

Herman, J.L., & Schatzow, E. (1984). Time-limited group therapy for women with a history of incest. International Journal of Group Psychotherapy, 34, 605-616

Herman, J.L., & van der Kolk, B.A. (1987). Traumatic antecedents of borderline personality disorder. In B.A. van der Kolk (Ed.), Psychological trauma. Washington, DC: American Psychiatric Association.

Hickey, P. (1994). Behavior therapy and traditional chemical dependency treatment. The Behavior Therapist, 17, 79-83.

Hilberman, E., & Munson, M. Sixty battered women. Victimology, 2, 460-461.

Hiley-Young, B. (1992). Trauma reactivation and assessment: Integrative case examples. Journal of Traumatic Stress, 5, (4), 545-555.

Hiley-Young, B., & colleagues (1993). Post-traumatic stress syndrome and disorder information packet (4th Edition). A publication of the National Center for PTSD Education Division. (3801 Miranda Ave., MPD 323 E 112, Palo Alto, CA, 94304).

Hiley-Young, B., & Gerrity, E.T. (1994). Critical Incident Stress Debriefing (CISD): Value and limitations in disaster response. NCP Clinical Quarterly, 4, 17-19.

Hindman, J. (1989). Just before dawn. Ontario, OR: AlexAndria Associates.

Hobfoll, S.E. & Lilly, R.S. (1993). Resource conservation as a strategy for community psychology. Journal of Community Psychology, 21, 128-148.

Hobfoll, S.E. (1988). The ecology of stress. New York: Hemisphere.

Hobfoll, S.E. (1989). Conservation of resources: A new attempt at conceptualizing stress. American Psychologist, 44, 513-524.

Hobfoll, S.E. (1991). Traumatic stress: A theory based on rapid loss of resources. Anxiety Research, 4, 187-197.

Hobfoll, S.E., & Jackson, A.P. (1991). Conservation of resources in community intervention. 19, 111-121.

Hobfoll, S.E., Briggs, S., & Wells, J. (1994). Community stress and resources: Actions and reactions. Paper presented at the NATO conference on stress, coping and disaster in Bonas, France.

Hodgkinson, P.E., & Stewart, M. (1991). Coping with catastrophe: A handbook of disaster management. London: Routledge.

Hogancamp, V.E., & Figley, C.R. (1983). Bringing the battle home. In C.R. Figley & H.I. McCubbin (Eds.), Stress and the family. Vol. 2. Coping with catastrophe. New York: Brunner/Mazel.

Holin, C.K., & Howells, K. (1992). Clinical approaches to sex offenders and their victims. Chichester, England: John Wiley.

Holloway, H.C., & Ursano, R.J. (1984). The Vietnam veteran: Memory, social context and metaphor. Psychiatry, 47, 103-108.

Holmes, D. (1990). The evidence for repression: An examination of sixty years of research. In J. Singer (Ed.), Repression and dissociation: Implications for personality theory, psychopathology and health. Chicago: University of Chicago Press.

Horn, J.A. & Solomon, R.M. (1992). Peer support: A key element for coping with trauma. Police Stress, 25.

Horowitz, M.J. (1986). Stress-response syndromes (2nd ed.). Northvale, NJ: Aronson.

Horowitz, M.J. (1986). Stress-response syndromes: A review of post-traumatic and adjustment disorder. Hospital and Community Psychiatry, 37, 241-249.

Horowitz, M.J., & Wilner, N. (1981). Life events, stress and coping. In L. Poon (Ed.), Aging in the 80s. Washington, D.C. American Psychological Association.

Horowitz, M.J., Bonanno, G.A., & Holen, A. (1993). Pathological grief: Diagnosis and explanation. Psychosomatic Medicine, 55, 260-273.

Howard, G.S. (1989). A tale of two stories: Excursions into a narrative approach to psychology. Notre Dame, IN: Academic Publications.

Howard, G.S. (1991). Cultural tales: A narrative approach to thinking, cross-cultural psychology, and psychotherapy. American Psychologist, 46, 187-197.

Howard, K.I. et al. (1983). The dose-effect relationship in psychotherapy. American Psychologist, 41, 159-164.

Howard, K.I., Lueger, R.J., et al. (1993). A phase model of psychotherapy outcome: Causal mediation of change. Journal of Consulting and Clinical Psychology, 61, 678-685.

Howes, M., Siegel, M., & Brown, F. (1993). Early childhood memories: Accuracy and affect. Cognition, 47, 95-119.

Hoyt, M. (Ed.) (1994). Constructive therapies. New York: Guilford.

Hunter, E.J. (1982). Families under the flag: A review of military family literature. New York: Praeger.

Hurton, A.L., Johnson, B.L., Roundy, L.M., & William, D. (Eds.) (1990). The incest perpetrator: A family member no one wants to treat. Newbury Park, CA: Sage.

Hyer, L., McCranie, E.W., & Peralme, L. (1993). Psychotherapeutic treatment of chronic PTSD. PTSD Research Quarterly, 4, 1-7.

Hytten, K., & Hasle, A. (1989). Firefighters: A study of stress and coping. Acta Psychiatria Scandinavica, 80, 50-55.

Hytten, K., Jensen, A., & Skauli, G. (1990). Stress inoculation training for smoke divers and free fall lifeboat passengers. Aviation Space Environment and Medicine, 19, 983-988.

Ibarra, P., Bruehl, S.P. et al. (1994). An unusual reaction to opioid blockade with Naltrexone in a case of post-traumatic stress disorder. Journal of Traumatic Stress, 7, 307-309.

Imber-Black, E., Roberts, J., & Whiting, R. (1988). Rituals in families and family therapy. New York: Norton.Isley, P.J. (1992). A time-limited group therapy model for men sexually abused as children. Group, 16, 233-246.

Irwin, M. (1982). Literature review. In J.L. Schulman & M. Irwin. Psychiatric hospitalization of children. Springfield, IL: Charles C. Thomas.

Isely, P.J. (1992). A time limited group therapy model for men sexually abused as children. Group, 16, 235-246.

Jaffe, J.H., Kranzler, H.R., & Ciraulo, D.A. (1992). Drugs used in treatment of alcoholism. In J.H. Mendelson & N.K. Mello (Eds.), Medical diagnosis in Treatment of alcoholism. New York: McGraw-Hill.

James, B., & Nasjleti, M. (1983). Treating sexually abused children and their families. Palo Alto, CA: Consulting Psychologists Press.

Janet, P. (1919) Psychological healing. Vol. 1. (Transl. E, Paul and . Paul). New York: MacMillan.

Janoff-Bulman, R. (1985). The aftermath of victimization: Rebuilding shattered assumptions. In C.R. Figley (Ed.), Trauma and its wake (pp. 15-35). New York: Brunner/Mazel.

Janoff-Bulman, R. (1989). Assumptive worlds and the stress of traumatic events: Applications of the schema construct. Social Cognition, 7, 113-136.

Janoff-Bulman, R. (1992). Shattered assumptions: Towards a new psychology of trauma. New York: Free Press.

Janoff-Bulman, R., & Frieze, I.H. (1983). A theoretical perspective for understanding reactions to victimizations. Journal of Social Issues, 39, 1-17.

Janoff-Bulman, R., & Lang-Gunn, L. (1988). Coping with disease, crime and accidents: The role of self-blame attributions. In L. Y. Abramson (Ed.), Social cognition and clinical psychology: A synthesis. New York: Guilford.

Jay, J. (1994). Walls for wailing. Common Boundary, May/June, 30-35.

Jehu, D. (1994). Patients as victims: Sexual abuse in psychotherapy and counselling. New York: John Wiley.

Jehu, D. (1988). Beyond sexual abuse: Therapy with women who were childhood victims. New York: John Wiley.

Jehu, D., Klassen, C., & Gazan, M. (1985). Cognitive restructuring of distorted beliefs associated with childhood sexual abuse. Journal of Social Work and Human Sexuality, 4, 1-35.

Jellinek, J.M. & Williams, T. (1984). Post-traumatic stress disorder and substance abuse in Vietnam combat veterans: Treatment problems, strategies, and recommendations. Journal of Substance Abuse and Treatment, 1, 87-97.

Jensen, J.A. (1994). An investigation of Eye Movement Desensitization and Reprocessing (EMD/R) as a treatment of posttraumatic stress disorder (PTSD) symptoms of Vietnam combat veterans. Behavior Therapy, 25, 311-325.

Jensen, P.S., & Shaw, J. (1993). Children as victims of war: Current knowledge and future research needs. Journal of American Academy of Child and Adolescent Psychiatry, 32, 697-708.

Johnson, D.P. (1987). The role of creative arts therapies in the diagnosis and treatment of psychological trauma. Arts in Psychotherapy, 14, 7-13.

Johnson, D.R., Feldman, S.C. et al. (1994). The concept of second generation program in the Treatment of post-traumatic stress disorder among Vietnam veterans. Journal of Traumatic Stress, 7, 217-231.

Johnson, M.K., Hashtroudi, S., & Lindsay, D.S. (1993). Source monitoring. Psychological Bulletin, 114, 3-28.

Jones, D.R. (1985). Secondary disaster victims: The emotional impact of recovery and identifying human remains. American Journal of Psychiatry, 142, 303-307.

Jones, J.C., & Barlow, D.H. (1990). The etiology of posttraumatic stress disorder. Clinical Psychology Review, 10, 299-328.

Jordan, B.K., Schlenger, W.E. et al. (1991). Lifetime and current prevalence of specific psychiatric disorders among Vietnam veterans and controls. Archives of General Psychiatry, 48, 207-271.

Jordan, C.E., & Walker, R. (1994). Guidelines for handling domestic violence cases in community mental health centres. Hospital and Community Psychiatry, 45, 147-151.

Joseph, S., Andrews, B., Williams, R., & Yule, W. (1992). Crisis support and psychiatric symptomatology in adult survivors of the Jupiter cruise ship disaster. British Journal of Clinical Psychology, 31, 63-73.

Joseph, S., Williams, A., & Yule, W. (1993). Changes in outlook following disaster: The preliminary development of a measure to assess positive and negative responses. Journal of Traumatic Stress, 6, 271-280.

Justice, R., & Justice, B. (1990). Crisis intervention with abusing families. In A. R. Roberts (Ed.), Crisis intervention handbook. Belmont, CA: Wadsworth.

Kaniasty, K. & Norris, F.H. (1992). Social support and victims of crime: Matching event, support and outcome. American Journal of Community Psychology, 20, 211-241.

Kardiner, A. (1941). The traumatic neuroses of war. New York: Hoeber.

Kardiner, A., & Spiegel, H. (1974). The traumatic neuroses of war. New York: Paul Hoeber.

Karlehagen, S., Malt, U.F., et al. (1993). The effect of major railway accidents on the psychological health of train drivers--II. A longitudinal study of the one-year outcome after the accident. Journal of Psychosomatic Research, 37, 807-817.

Kathriner, S.R. (1991). Art therapy: An effective tool in dealing with PTSD. NCP Clinical Newsletter, 1, 9-10.

Katz, S. E., & Levendusky, P. G. (1990). Cognitive behavioral approaches to treating borderline and self - mutilating patients. Bulletin of the Menninger Clinic, 54, 398-404.

Kaufman, J., & Zigler, E. (1987). Do abused children become abusive parents? American Journal of Orthopsychiatry, 57, 186-191.

Kazanis, B. (1991). Finding and respecting our own way of grieving. Creation Spirituality, November/December 42-43.

Kazdin, A. E., & Kagan, J. (1994). Models of dysfunction in developmental psychopathology. Clinical Psychology, 1, 35-52.

Keane, T.M. (1989a). Mini-series on post-traumatic stress disorder: Current states and future directions. Behavior Therapy, 20. (See entire Spring issue).

Keane, T.M. (1989b). Post-traumatic stress disorder: Current states and future directions. Behavior Therapy, 20, 149-153.

Keane, T.M. (1990). The epidemiology of post traumatic stress disorder: Some comments and concerns. PTSD Research Quarterly, 1, 1-7.

Keane, T.M., & Kaloupek, D.G. (1982). Imaginal flooding in the treatment of posttraumatic stress disorder. Journal of Consulting and Clinical Psychology, 50, 148-140.

Keane, T.M., & Wolfe, JA. (1990). Comorbidity in post-traumatic stress disorder: An analysis of community and clinical studies. Journal of Applied Social Psychology, 20, 1776-1788.

Keane, T.M., Fairbank, JA., Caddell, J.M., & Zimering, R.T. (1989). Impulsive (flooding) therapy reduces symptoms of PTSD in Vietnam combat veterans. Behavior Therapy, 20, 245-260.

Keane, T.M., Gerardi, R.J., Lyons, J.A., & Wolfe, J. (1988). The interrelationship of substance abuse and posttraumatic stress disorder: Epidemiological and clinical considerations. Recent Developments in Alcoholism, 6, 27-48.

Keane, T.M., Gerardi, R.J., Quinn, S.J., & Litz, B.T. (1992). Behavioral treatment of posttraumatic stress disorder. In S.M. Turner, K.S. Calhoun and H.E. Adams (Eds.), Handbook of Clinical behavior therapy. Second Edition. New York: Wiley.

Keane, T.M., Zimering, R.T. & Caddell, J.M. (1985). A behavioral formulation of post-traumatic stress disorder in Vietnam veterans. The Behavior Therapist, 8, 9-12.

Kearney-Cooke, A., & Striegal-Moore, R.H. (1994). Treatment of childhood sexual abuse in anorexia nervosa and bulimia nervosa: A feminist psychodynamic approach. International Journal of Eating Disorders, 15, 305-319.

Keilson, H. (1992). Sequential traumatization in children. Jerusalem: Magness Press.

Kelly, G.A. (1955). The psychology of personal constructs. New York: Norton.

Kelly, W.E. (1985). Post-traumatic therapy and victims of violence. New York: Brunner-Mazel.

Kelly, W.E. (Ed.) (1985). Post-traumatic stress disorder and the war veteran patient. New York: Brunner/Mazel.

Kempe, R.S., & Kempe, C.H. (1984). The common secret: Sexual abuse of children and adolescents. New York: Freeman.

Kernberg, O.F., & Uarkin, J.F. (1992). The development of a disorder-specific manual: The treatment of borderline personality disorder. In N.E. Miller, J. Douhery & L. Luborsky (Eds.), Psychodynamic treatment research. New York: Basic Books.

Kfir, N., (1989). Crisis intervention verbatim. Washington D.C.: Hemisphere Publishing.

Kilpatrick, A.C. (1992). Long-term effects of child and adolescent sexual experiences: Myths, moves and menaces. Hillsdale, NJ: Erlbaum.

Kilpatrick, D.G. & Calhoun, K.S. (1988). Early behavioral treatment for rape trauma: Efficacy or artifact? Behavior Therapy, 19, 421-427.

Kilpatrick, D.G. (1983). Rape victims: Detection, assessment & treatment. The Clinical Psychologist, 36, 92-95.

Kilpatrick, D.G., & Best, C.L. (1984). Some cautionary remarks in treating sexual abuse victims with implosion. Behavior Therapy, 15, 421-423.

Kilpatrick, D.G., Edmunds, C.N., & Seymour, A.K. (1992). Rape in America: A report to the nation. Arlington, VA: National Victim Center.

Kilpatrick, D.G., Saunders, B.E. et al. (1987). Criminal victimization: Lifetime prevalence, reporting to police and psychological impact. Crime and Delinquency, 33, 479-489.

Kilpatrick, D.G., Saunders, B.E., et al. (1989). Victim and crime factors associated with the development of crime-related post-traumatic stress disorder. Behavior Therapy, 20, 199-214.

Kilpatrick, D.G., Veronen, L.J., & Best, C.L. (1985). Factors predicting psychological distress in rape victims. In C. Figley (Ed.), Trauma and its wake. New York: Brunner/Mazel.

Kingsbury, S.J. (1992). Strategic psychotherapy for trauma: Hypnosis and trauma in context. Journal of Traumatic Stress, 5, 85-94.

Kinney, J., Haapala, D., & Booth, c. (1991). Keeping families together: The homebuilders model. New York: Aldine.

Kinzie, J. D. (1994). Countertransference in the treatment of Southeast Asian refugees. In J. P. Wilson, & J. D. Lindy (Eds.), Countertransference in the treatment of PTSD. New York: Guilford.

Kinzie, J.D. & Fleck, J. (1987). Psychotherapy with severely traumatized refugees. American Journal of Psychology, 41, 82-94.

Kinzie, J.D. (1989). Therapeutic approaches to traumatized Cambodian refugees. Journal of Traumatic Stress, 2, 75-91.

Kinzie, J.D., & Leung, P.K. (1989). Clonidine in Cambodian patients with posttraumatic stress disorder. Journal of Nervous and Mental Disorders, 177, 546-550.

Kipper, D.A. (1976). The desensitization of war-induced fears. Current Psychiatric Therapies, 16, 41-47.

Kirk, S.A. & Kutchins, H. (1992). The selling of DSM: The rhetoric of science in psychiatry. New York: Aldine de Gruyter.

Kirschner, C., Kirschner, D.A., & Rappaport, R.L. (1993). Working with adult incest survivors: The healing journey. New York:

Kirschner, D.A., & Kirschner, S. (1980). Comprehensive family therapy. New York: Brunner/Mazel.

Kleber, R.J., Brom, D., & Defares, P.B. (1992). Coping with trauma: Theory, prevention and treatment. Amsterdam: Swets & Zeetlinger.

Kleber, R.J., Figley, C.R., Gersons, B.P. (in press). Beyond trauma: Cultural and societal dynamics. New York: Plenum.

Kleinknecht, R.A. (1993). Rapid treatment of blood and injection phobias with eye movement desensitization. Journal of Behavior Therapy and Experimental Psychiatry, 24, 211-218.

Kluft, R. P. (1993). Basic principles in conducting the psychotherapy of multiple personality disorder. In R. P. Kluft , & C. C. Fine (Eds.), Clinical perspectives on multiple personality disorder. Washington DC: American Psychiatric Press.

Kofoed, L.L., Friedman, M.G., & Peck, R. (in press). Alcoholism and drug abuse in patients with PTSD. Psychiatric Quarterly.

Kolb, L.C. (1985). The place of narcosynthesis in the treatment of chronic and delayed stress reactions of war. In S.M. Sonnenberg, A.S. Blank, & J.A. Talbott, (Eds.), The trauma of war stress and recovery in Vietnam veterans. Washington, D.C.: American Psychiatric Press.

Kolb, L.C. (1987). A neurophysiological hypothesis explaining posttraumatic stress disorders. American Journal of Psychiatry, 144, 989-995.

Kolb, L.C. (1989). Letter to the editor. American Journal of Psychiatry, 146, 811-812.

Kolb, L.C. (1993). The psychobiology of PTSD: Perspectives and reflections on the past, present and future. Journal of Traumatic Stress, 6, 293-304.

Koller, P., Marmar, C.R., Kanas, N. (1992). Psychodynamic group treatment of posttraumatic stress disorder in Vietnam veterans. International Journal of Group Psychotherapy, 42, 225-246.

Koopman, C., Classen, C., & Spiegel, D. (1994). Predictors of posttraumatic stress symptoms among survivors of the Oakland/Berkeley, Calif. firestorm. American Journal of Psychiatry, 15, 888-894.

Kornfeld, E.L. (in press). The development of treatment approaches for victims of human rights violations in Chile. In R.J. Kleber et al (Eds.), Beyond trauma. New York: Plenum.

Koss, M.P. (1993). Detecting the scope of rape: A review of prevalence research methods. Journal of Interpersonal Violence, 8, 198-222.

Koss, M.P. (1993). Rape: Scope, impact, interventions and public policy responses. American Psychologist, 48, 1062-1065.

Koss, M.P., & Harvey, M.I. (1991). The rape victim: Clinical and community approaches to treatment. (Revised Edition). San Francisco, CA: Sage.

Krell, R. (1985). Therapeutic value of documenting child survivors. American Academy of Child Psychiatry, 85, 397-400.

Krell, R. (1993). Child survivors of the Holocaust: Strategies of adaptation. Canadian Journal of Psychiatry, 38, 384-389.

Krystal, H. (1968). (Ed.). Massive psychic trauma. New York: Random House.

Kubany, E.S. (1994). A cognitive model of guilt typology in combat-related PTSD. Journal of Traumatic Stress, 7, 3-19.

Kubler-Ross, E. (1966). On death and dying. New York: MacMillan.

Kuch, K., & Cox, B.J. (1992). Symptoms of PTSD in 124 survivors of the Holocaust. American Journal of Psychiatry, 149, 337-340.

Kudler, H., & Davidson, J.R. (1994). General principles of biological intervention following trauma. In J.R. Freedy & S.E. Hobfoll (Eds.), Traumatic stress: From theory to practice. New York: Plenum.

Kuenning, D.A. (1991). Life after Vietnam: How veterans and their loved ones can heal the psychological wounds of war. New York: Paragon.

Kulka, R., Schlenger, W. Fairbank, J., Hough, R., Jordan, K., Marmar, C. & Weiss, D. (1990). Trauma and the Vietnam war generation: The findings of the National Vietnam veterans readjustment study. New York: Brunner/Mazel.

Kulka, R.A., Fairbank, J.A., Hough, R.L., et al. (1990). Trauma and the Vietnam generation: Findings from the National Vietnam Veterans readjustment study. New York: Brunner/Mazel.

Kulka, R.A., Schlenger, W.E., & Fairbank, J.A. (1988). National Vietnam Veteran Readjustment Study. Research Triangle, North Carolina.

Kunzman, K.A. (1990). Healing from childhood sexual abuse: A recovering woman's guide. Center City, MN: Hazelden Educational Materials.

Kunzman, K.A. (1990). The healing way: Adult recovery from childhood sexual abuse. Center City, MN: Hazelden Educational Materials.

Laird, J. (1989). Women and stories: Restoring women's self-constructions. In M. McGoldrick, C. Anderson, & C. Walsh (Eds.), Women in families. New York: Norton.

Lakoff, G., & Johnson, M. (1980). Metaphors we live by. Chicago: University of Chicago Press.

Landecker, H. (1992). The role of childhood sexual trauma in etiology of borderline personality disorder: Diagnosis and treatment. Psychotherapy, 29, 234-242.

Lang, P. (1979).A bio-informational theory of emotional imagery. Psychophysiology, 6, 495-571.

Langer, L.L., (1991). Holocaust testimonies. New Haven: Yale University Press.

Langley, M.H. (1993). Self-management therapy for borderline personality disorder. New York: Springer.

Lanktree, L.B., Briere, J., & Zaidi, L.Y. (1991). Incidence and impact of sexual abuse in a child outpatient sample: The role of direct inquiry. Child Abuse and Neglect, 15, 447-453.

Lavee, Y., & Ben-David, A. (1993). Families under war: Stresses and strains of Israeli families during the Gulf War. Journal of Traumatic Stress, 6, 235-254.

Layden, M. A., Newman, C. F., Freeman, A., & Morse, S. B. (1993). Cognitive therapy of borderline personality disorder. Boston: Ally & Bacon.

Lazarus, R.S., & Folkman, S. (1984). Stress, appraisal, and coping. New York: Springer.

Lebowitz, L., & Roth, S. (1994). "I felt like a slut": The cultural context and women's response to being raped. Journal of Traumatic Stress, 7, 366-390.

Lebowitz, L., Harvey, M.R., & Herman, J.L. (1993). A stage-by-dimension model of recovery from sexual trauma. Journal of Interpersonal Violence, 8, 378-391.

Lees, S.W. (1981). Guidelines for helping female victims and survivors of incest. Cambridge, MA: Incest Resources.

Lehman, D.R. (1993). Continuing the tradition of research in war: The Persian Gulf war. Journal of Social Issues, 49, 1-15.

Lehman, D.R., Wortman, C.B. & Williams, A.F. (1987). Long-term effects of losing a spouse or child in a motor vehicle crash. Journal of Personality and Social Psychology, 52, 218-231.

Lehman, P.R., Ellard, J.H., & Wortman, C.B. (1986). Social support for the bereaved: Recipients' and providers' perspectives on what is helpful. Journal of Consulting and Clinical Psychology, 54, 438-446.

Lehmann, L. (1993). VA's role in the treatment of acute PTSD. National PTSD Center Clinical Newsletter, 3, 11-13.

Lehmann, L. (1994). PTSD perspectives. Clinical Quarterly, 4, i 12.

Lerner, A. (1978). Poetry in the therapeutic experience. New York: Pergamon Press.

Levi, D. (1987). If this is a man: The truce. London: Sphere Books.

Levy, M. (1993). Psychotherapy with dual diagnosis patients: Working with denial. Journal of Substance Abuse Treatment, 10, 499-504.

Lew, M. (1988). Victims no longer. New York: Harper & Row.

Lifton, J. (1979). The broken connection. New York: Simon & Schuster.

Lifton, R.J. (1967). Death in life: Survivors of Hiroshima. New York: Random House.

Lifton, R.J. (1973). Home from the war: Vietnam veterans. New York: Basic Books.

Lifton, R. (1986). The Nazi doctors: Medical killing and the psychology of genocide. New York: Basic Books.

Lifton, R.J. (1988). Understanding the traumatized self. In J.P. Wilson, J.P. Harel, & B. Kahana (Eds.), Human adaptation to extreme stress. New York: Plenum.

Lifton, R.J. & Olson, E. (1976). The human meaning of total disaster: The Buffalo Creek experience. Psychiatry, 39, 1-18.

Lindemann, E. (1944). Symptomatology and management of acute grief. American Journal of Psychiatry, 101, 141-148.

Lindy, F.D., Grace, M. C., & Green, B.L. (1981). Survivors: Outreach to a relevent population. American Journal of Orthopsychiatry, 31, 468-478.

Lindy, J.D. (1985). The trauma membrane and other clinical concepts derived from psychotherapeutic work with survivors of natural disasters. Psychiatry Annual, 15, 153-160.

Lindy, J.D. (1986). An outline for the psychoanalytic psychotherapy of posttraumatic stress disorder. In C.R. Figley (Eds.), Trauma and its wake. New York: Brunner/Mazel.

Lindy, J.D. (1988). Vietnam: A casebook. New York: Brunner/Mazel.

Lindy, J.D. (1993). Focal psychoanalytic psychotherapy of posttraumatic stress disorder. In J.P. Wilson & B. Raphael (Eds.), International handbook of traumatic stress syndromes. New York: Plenum.

Lindy, J.D., Green, B.L., Grace, M., & Titchener, J. (1983). Psychotherapy with survivors of the Beverly Hills Supper Club fire. American Journal of Psychotherapy, 37, 593-610.

Lindsay, D.S., & Read, J.D. (1994). Psychotherapy and memories of childhood sexual abuse: a cognitive perspective. Applied Cognitive Psychology, 8, 281-338.

Linehan, M.M. (1993). Cognitive-behavioral treatment of borderline personality disorder. New York: Guilford.

Linehan, M.M., Heard, H.L., & Armstrong, H.E. (1993). Naturalistic follow-up of a behavioral treatment for chronically parasuicidal borderline patients. Archives of General Psychiatry, 50, 971-974.

Liporsky, J.A. (1992). Assessment and treatment of posttraumatic stress disorder in child survivors of sexual assault. In D.W. Foy (Ed.), Treating PTSD: Cognitive-behavioral strategies. New York: Guilford Press.

Lipton, M.I. (1994). Postraumatic stress disorder: Additional perspectives. Springfield, ILL: Charles C. Thomas Publishers.

Lisak, D. (1994). The psychological impact of sexual abuse: Content analysis of interviews with male survivors. Journal of Traumatic Stress, 7, 525-548.

Litz, B.T. & Keane, T.M. (1989). Information processing in anxiety disorders: Application to the understanding of post-traumatic stress disorder. Clinical Psychology Review, 9, 243-257.

Litz, B.T. (1992). Emotional numbing in combat-related post-traumatic stress disorder: A critical review and reformulation. Clinical Psychology Review, 12, 417-432.

Litz, B.T., Blake D.D., Gerardi, R.G., & Keane, T.M. (1990). Decision making guidelines for the use of direct therapeutic exposure in the treatment of post-traumatic stress disorder. The Behavior Therapist, 13, 91-93.

Loftus, E.F. (1993). The reality of repressed memories. American Psychologist, 48, 518-537.

Loftus, E.F. Polonsky, S. & Fullilove, M.T. (1994). Memories of childhood sexual abuse. Psychology of Women Quarterly, 18, 67-84.

Lohr, J.M., Kleinknecht, R.A., Conley, A.T., Dalcarro, S., Schmidt, J., & Sontag, M.E. (1993). A methodological critique of the current status of eye movement desensitization (EMD). Journal of Behaviour Therapy and Experimental Psychiatry, 23, 159-167.

Lomranz, J. (1990). Long-term adaptation to traumatic stress in light of adult development and aging perspectives. In M.A. Parris, et al. (Eds.), Stress and coping in later life families. Washington, D.C.: Hemisphere.

Lonigan, C.J., Shannon, M.P. et al. (1994). Children exposed to disaster: II. Risk factors for the development of post-traumatic symptomatology. Journal of American Child and Adolescent Psychiatry, 33, 94-105.

Lonsway, F. A., & Fitzgerald, L. F. (1994). Rape myths. Psychology of Women Quarterly, 18, 133-164.

Loo, C.M. (1993). An integrative sequential treatment model for posttraumatic stress disorder: A case study of the Japanese American internment and redress. Clinical Psychology Review, 13, 89-118.

Loo, C.M. (1994). Race-related PTSD: The Asian American Vietnam veteran. Journal of Traumatic Stress, 7, 637-656.

Ludwig, A.M., Brandsma, J.M., et al. (1972). The objective study of a multiple personality. Archives of General Psychiatry, 26, 298-310.

Lundberg-Love, P.K. (1990). Adult survivors of incest. In R.T. Ammerman & M. Hersen (Eds.), Treatment of family violence: A sourcebook. New York: Wiley.

Lundin, T. (1994). The treatment of acute trauma: Post-traumatic stress disorder prevention. In D.A. Tomb (Ed.), The Psychiatric Clinics of North America, 8, 38392.

Luntz, A. & Widom, C. (1994). Childhood sexual abuse and antisocial personality. American Journal of Psychiatry, 151, 670-674.

Lynch, M.A., & Roberts, J. (1982). Consequences of child abuse. New York: Academic Press.

Lyons, J.A., & Krane, T.M. (1989). Implosive therapy for the treatment of combat-related PTSD. Journal of Traumatic Stress, 2, 137-152.

Lystad, M. (1985). Innovations in mental health services to disaster victims. (DHHS Publication No. ADM 85-1390). Washington, DC: U.S. Government Printing Office.

Mahoney, M., & Lyddon, W. (1988). Recent developments in cognitive approaches to counseling and psychotherapy. Counseling Psychologist, 16, 190-234.

Mair, M. (1977). Metaphors for living. In A.W. Landfield (Ed.), Nebraska Symposium on Motivation, 1976. Lincoln: University of Nebraska Press.

Mair, M. (1988). Psychology of story-telling psychology. International Journal of Personal Construct Psychology, 2, 1-14.

Mair, M. (1989). Between psychology and psychotherapy. London: Routledge.

Mair, M. (1990). Telling psychological tales. International Journal of Personal Construct Psychology, 3, 121-135.

Malinoksy-Rummell, R. & Hansen, D.J. (1992). Long-term consequences of childhood physical abuse. Psychological Bulletin, 114, 68-79.

Malt, U.F. (1994). Traumatic effects of accidents. In R.J. Ursano, B.G. McCaughey, and C.S. Fullerton (Eds.), Individual and community responses to trauma and disaster. New York: Cambridge University Press.

Malt, U.F., Karlehagen, S., et al. (1993). The effect of major railway accidents on the psychological health of train drivers--I. Acute psychological responses to the accident. Journal of Psychosomatic Research, 37, 793-805.

Maltz, W., & Holman, B. (1987). Incest and sexuality: A guide to understanding and healing. Lexington, MA: Lexington Books.

Mangelsdorff, A.D. (1985). Lessons learned and forgotten: The need for prevention and mental health interventions in disaster preparedness. Journal of Community Psychology, 13, 239-257.

Mann, D., Sumner, J., Dalton, J., & Berry, D. (1990). Working with incest survivors. Psychoanalytic Psychotherapy, 4, 271-281.

Manton, M., & Talbot, A. (1988). Crisis intervention after an armed hold-up: Guidelines for counselors. State Bank Victoria, Staff Counseling, P.O.Box 267D, Melbourne, 3000 Australia.

Manton, M., & Talbot, A. (1990). Crisis intervention after an armed hold-up: guidelines for counselors. Journal of Traumatic Stress, 3, 507-522.

Marafiote, R.A. (1993). On EMDR and controlled outcome studies. The Behavior Therapist, 17, 22-24.

March, J.S. (1990). The nosology of posttraumatic stress disorder. Journal of Anxiety Disorders, 4, 61-82.

March, J.S. (1993). What constitutes a stressor? The criterion "A" issue. in J.R. Davidson & E.B. Foa (Eds.), Posttraumatic stress disorder: DSM IV and beyond. Washington, D.C.: American Psychiatric Press.

Marks, I.M. (1986). Behavioral psychotherapy: Maudsly Pocket Book of Clinical Management. Wright, Bristol.

Markus, H, & Nurius, P. (1986). Possible selves. American Psychologist, 41, 954-969.

Marlatt, G.A. & Gordon, J.R. (Eds.), (1985). Relapse prevention: Maintenance strategies in the treatment of addictive behavior. New York: Guilford Press.

Marlatt, G.S., Larimer, M.E. et al. (1993). Harm reduction for alcohol problems: Moving beyond the controlled drinking controversy. Behavior Therapy, 24, 461-504.

Marmar, C.R. (1991). Brief dynamic psychotherapy of posttraumatic stress disorder. Psychiatric Annals, 21, 405-414.

Marmar, C.R., & Freeman, M. (1988). Brief dynamic psychotherapy of post-traumatic stress disorders: Management of narcissistic regression. Journal of Traumatic Stress, 1, 323-337.

Marmar, C.R., & Horowitz, M.J. (1988). Diagnosis and phase-oriented treatment of post-traumatic stress disorder. In J. Wilson, Z. Harel, & B. Kahana (Eds.), Human adaptation to extreme stress: From the holocaust to Vietnam. New York: Plenum Press.

Marmar, C.R., Foy, D., Kagan, B., & Pynoos, R.S. (1993). An integrated approach for treating postraumatic stress. In J.M. Oldham, M.B. Riba, & A. Tasman (Eds.), Review of psychiatry. Washington, D.C.: American Psychiatric Press.

Marquis, J.N. (1991). A report of seventy-eight causes treated by eye movement desensitization. Journal of Behavior Therapy and Experimental Psychiatry, 20, 211-217.

Marsella, A. J., Friedman, M., Gerrity, E., & Scurfield, R. M. (Eds.) (in press). Ethnocultural aspects of post-traumatic stress disorders. Washington, DC: American Psychological Association.

Marshall, S.L.A. (1944). Island victory. New York: Penguin Books.

Mason, S. (1986). Johnny's song poetry of a Vietnam veteran. Toronto: Bantam.

Masters, R., Friedman, L.N., & Getzel, G. (1988). Helping families of homicide victims: A multidimensional approach. Journal of Traumatic Stress, 1, 109-125.

Matsakis, A. (1988). Vietnam wives. Kensington, MD: Woodbine.

Matsakis, A. (1991). When the bough breaks. Oakland, CA: New Habinger.

Matsakis, A. (1992). I can't get over it: A handbook for trauma survivors. Oakland, CA: New Harbinger Publications.

Matter, J., & Michelson, L.K. (1993). Theoretical, clinical, research and ethical constraints of the age movement desensitization reprocessing technique. Journal of Traumatic Stress, 6, 413-417.

Maxwell, M.J., & Sturm, C. (1994). Countertransference in the treatment of war veterans. In J.P. Wilson, & J.D. Lindy (Eds.), Countertransference in the treatment of PTSD. New York: Guilford.

Mayers, D. (1994). Disaster response and recovery: A handbook for mental health professionals. Rockville, Md: Center for Mental Health Services.

Mayou, R., Bryant, B., & Duthie, R. (1993). Psychiatric consequences of road traffic accidents. British Medical Journal, 307, 647-651.

McAdams, D. (1985). Power, intimacy and the life story. Homewood, IL: Dorsey Press.

McCabe, A., & Peterson, C. (1991). Developing narrative structure. Hillsdale, N.J.: Erlbaum.

McCann, D.L. (1992). Post-traumatic stress disorder due to devastating burns overcome by a single session of eye movement desensitization. Journal of Behavior Therapy and Experimental Psychiatry, 23, 319-323.

McCann, I.L. & Pearlman, L.A. (1990a). Vicarious traumatization: A framework for understanding the psychological effects of working with victims. Journal of Traumatic Stress, 3, 131-149.

McCann, I.L. & Pearlman, L.A. (1990b). Psychological trauma and the adult survivor: Theory, therapy and transformation. New York: Brunner/Mazel.

McCann, I.L., Pearlman, L.A., Sackheim, D.K., & Abramson, D.J. (1985). Assessment and treatment of the adult survivor of childhood sexual abuse within a schema framework. In S.M. Sgroi (Ed.), Vulnerable population (Vol.1). Lexington, MA: Lexington Books.

McCann, I.L., Sakheim, D.K., & Abrahamson, D.J. (1988). Trauma and victimization: A model of psychological adaptation. The Counseling Psychologist, 16, 531-594.

McCann, L., & Pearlman, L.A. (1990). Constructivist self-development theory as a framework for assessing and treating victims of family violence. In S. Stita, M. Williams, & K. Rosen (Eds.), Violence his home. New York: Springer.

McCann, L., & Pearlman, L.A. (1991). Through a glass darkly: Understanding and treating the adult trauma survivor through constructivist self-development theory. New York: Brunner/Mazel.

McCarroll, J.E., Ursano, R.J. et al. (1993). Traumatic stress of a wartime mortuary: Anticipation of exposure to mass death. Journal of Nervous and Mental Disease, 181, 545-551.

McCarthy, B. (1986). A cognitive-behavioral approach to understanding and treating sexual trauma. Journal of Sex and Marital Therapy, 12, 15-19.

McCarthy, B. (1990). Treating sexual dysfunction associated with prior sexual trauma. Journal of Sex and Marital Therapy, 16, 142-146.

McCarthy, B., & McCarthy, E. (1993a). Confronting the victim role: Healing from an abusive childhood. New York: Carroll and Graf.

McCarthy, B., & McCarthy, E. (1993b). Sexual awareness: Enhancing sexual pleasure. New York: Carroll and Graf.

McCaughey, B.G., Hoffman, K.J., & Llewellyn, C.H. (1994). The human experience of earthquakes. In R. Ursano et al. (Eds.), Trauma and disaster. New York: Cambridge University Press.

McCubbin, H., & Figley, C.R. (1983). Bridging normative and catastrophic family stress. In C.R. Figley (Ed.), Treating stress in families. New York: Brunner/Mazel.

McCubbin, M.A. & Patterson, J.M. (1983). The family stress process: The double ABCX model of adjustment and adaptation. In H.I. McCubbin, M. Sussman, & J.M. Patterson (Eds.), Advancements and developments in family stress theory and research. New York: Haworth.

McCubbin, M.A., & McCubbin, H.I. (1989). Theoretical orientations to family stress and coping. In C.R. Figley (Ed.), Treating stress in families. New York: Brunner/Mazel.

McFarlane, A. (1994). Individual psychotherapy for post-traumatic stress disorder. In D. A. Tomb (Ed.), The Psychiatric Clinics of North America, 8, 393-408.

McFarlane, A.C. (1989). The etiology of post traumatic morbidity: Predisposing precipitating and perpetuating factors. British Journal of Psychiatry, 154, 221-228.

McFarlane, A.C. (1989). The treatment of posttraumatic stress disorder. British Journal of Medical Psychology, 62, 81-90.

McFarlane, A.C. (1993). Helping the victims of natural disasters. Unpublished manuscript. University of Adelaide, Dept. Psychiatry, Southern Australia.

McFarlane, A.C. (1994). Helping victims of disasters. In J.R. Freedy & S.E. Hobfoll (Eds.)., Traumatic stress: From theory to practice. New York: Plenum.

McFarlane, A.C. (1994). Stress and disaster. Paper presented at the NATO conference on stress, coping and disaster in Bonas, France.

McFarlane, A.C. (1994). The severity of the trauma: Issues about its role in post traumatic stress disorder. Unpublished manuscript. University of Adelaide.

McFarlane, A.C. (in press). The severity of the trauma: What is its role in posttraumatic stress disorder? In R.J. Kleber et al (eds.). Beyond trauma: New York: Plenum.

McHugh, P.R. (1992). Psychiatric misadventures. The American Scholar, 61, 497-510.

McIntosh, D.N., Silver, R.C., & Wortman, C. (1993). Religious role in adjustment to a negative life event: Coping with the loss of a child. Journal of Personality and Social Psychology, 4, 812-821.

McKay, M.M. (1994). The link between domestic violence and child abuse: Assessment and treatment considerations. Child Welfare League of America, 73, 29-39.

McKeechie, W. (1974). The decline and fall of the laws of learning. Educational Researcher, 3, 7-11.

McMillin, R.E. (1986). Handbook of cognitive therapy techniques. New York: Norton.

Medeiros, M.E. & Prochaska, J.O. (1988). Coping strategies that psychotherapists use in working with stressful clients. Professional Psychology: Research and Practice, 1, 112-114.

Meek, C. L. (Ed.) (1990). Post-traumatic stress disorder: Assessment, differential diagnosis, and forensic evaluation. Sarasota, FL: Professional Resource Exchange.

Meichenbaum, D. (1985). Stress inoculation training. New York: Pergamon Press.

Meichenbaum, D. (1993). Stress inoculation training: A twenty year update. In R.L. Woolfolk and P.M. Lehrer (Eds.). Principles and practices of stress management. New York: Guilford press.

Meichenbaum, D. (1994). Disasters stress and cognition. Paper presented at the NATO conference on stress, coping and disaster in Bonas, France.

Meichenbaum, D., & Cameron, R. (1983). Stress inoculation training: Toward a general paradigm for training in coping skills. In D. Meichenbaum & M. Jaremko (Eds.)., Stress reduction and prevention. New York: Plenum.

Meichenbaum, D., & Fitzpatrick, D. (1993) A constructionist narrative perspective on stress and coping. Stress inoculation applications. In L. Goldberger and S. Breznitz (Eds.) Handbook of stress: Theoretical and clinical aspects. (Second Edition). New York: Free Press.

Meichenbaum, D., & Fong, G. (1993). How individuals control their own minds: A constructive narrative perspective. In D. M. Wegner & J. W. Pennebaker (Eds.). Handbook of Mental control. New York: Prentice Hall.

Meichenbaum, D., & Gilmore, J.B. (1984). The nature of unconscious processes: A cognitive-behavioral perspective. In K. Bowers and D. Meichenbaum (Eds.), The unconscious reconsidered. New York: Wiley.

Meichenbaum, D., & Novaco, R. (1977). Stress inoculation: A preventative approach. In C. Spielberger and I. Sarason (Eds.)., Stress and anxiety. Vol. 5. New York: Halstead Press.

Meichenbaum, D., & Turk, D. (1987). Facilitating treatment adherence: A practitioner's guidebook. New York: Plenum Press.

Meiselman, K. (1990). Resolving the trauma of incest: Reintegration therapy with survivors. San Francisco, CA: Jossey-Bass.

Meisman, K. (1978). Incest: A psychological study of causes and effects with treatment recommendations. San Francisco: Jossey-Bass.

Melick, M.E., Logue, J.N., & Frederick, C.J. (1982). Stress and disaster. In L. Goldberger & S. Breznitz (Eds.). Handbook of stress. New York: Free Press.

Mennen, F.E. & Meadow, D. (1992). Process to recovery: In support of long-term groups for sexual abuse survivors. International Journal of Group Psychotherapy, 42, 29-44.

Meyers, D.G. (1985). Helping the helper: A training manual. NIMH: DHHS Public No. ADM-85-1422. U.S. Government Printing Office. Washington, D.C.

Meyers, D.G. (1989). Mental health and disaster. In R. Gist & B. Lubin (Eds.), Psychosocial aspects of disaster. New York: Wiley.

Milgram, N.A. (1986). Stress and coping in times of war: Generalizations from the Israeli experience. New York: Brunner/Mozel.

Milgram, N.N. (1993). Stress and coping in Israel during the Persian Gulf War. Journal of Social Issues, 49, 103-124.

Milgram, N.N., Sandler, I., Sarason, I., & van der Kolk, B. (1991). War-related stress. American Psychologist, 46, 848-855.

Miller, T.W., Kraus, A.F. et al. (1993). Post traumatic stress disorder in children and adolescents of the Armenian Earthquake. Child Psychiatry and Human Development, 24, 115-123.

Miller, W.R. (1993). What really drives change? Addiction, 88, 1479-1480.

Mitchell, J.T. & Everly, G.S. (1993). Critical incident stress debriefing: An operations manual for the prevention of trauma among emergency service an disaster workers. Baltimore, MD: Chevron Publishing.

Mitchell, J.T. (1983). When disaster strikes: The critical incident stress debriefing process. Journal of Emergency Medical Services, 8, 36-39.

Mitchell, J.T. (1985). Healing the helper. In NIMH (Ed.). Role stressors and supports for emergency workers. Washington, DC NIMH.

Mitchell, J.T., & Bray, G.P. (1989). Emergency services stress. Englewood Cliffs, NJ: Prentice Hall.

Mitchell, J.T. (1987). Effective stress control at major incidents. Maryland Fire and Rescue Bulletin, June, 3-9.

Mitchell, J.T. (1988). Stress: Development and functions of a critical incident stress debriefing team. JEMS (Journal of Emergency Medical Services), Dec. 43-46. (For details of training, contact the International Critical Institute Stress Foundation, 5018 Dorsey Hall Drive, Suite 104, Ellicott City, Maryland, 21042.

Mitchell, J.T., & Dyregrov, A. (1993). Traumatic stress in disaster workers and emergency personnel: Prevention and intervention. In J.P. Wilson & B. Raphael (Eds.), International handbook of traumatic stress syndromes. New York: Plenum.

Mitchell, J.T., & Everly, G.S. (1994). Preventing work-related post-traumatic stress: The Critical Incident Stress Debriefing (CISD). In G.S. Everly & J.M. Lating (Eds.), Psychotraumatology. New York: Plenum Press.

Modlin, H.C. (1990). Forensic issues in post-traumatic stress disorder. In C. L. Meek (Ed.), Post-traumatic stress disorder: Assessment differential diagnosis and forensic evaluation. Sarasota, FL: Professional Resource Exchange.

Montgomery, E. (1992). Co-creation of meaning: Therapy with torture survivors. Human Systems: Journal of Systemic Consultation and Management, 3, 27-33.

Moore, R.H. (1993). Traumatic incident reduction: A cognitive-emotive treatment of posttraumatic stress disorder. In W. Dryden & L.K. Hill (Eds.), Innovations in rational-emotive therapy. Newbury Park: Sage.

Morris, M. (1982). If I should die before I wake. New York: Dell.

Moskovitz, S. (1983). Love despite hate: Child survivors of the holocaust and their adult lives. New York: Schocken.

Moss, D.C. (1991a). A new technique for treating post-traumatic stress disorder. British Journal of Clinical Psychology, 30, 91-92.

Moss, D.C. (1991b). The trauma trap. New York: Doubleday.

Norris, F.H., & Kaniasty, K. (1994). Psychological distress following criminal victimization in the general population: Cross sectional, longitudinal, and prospective analyses. Journal of Consulting and Clinical Psychology, 62, 111-123.

Norris, F.H., & Thompson, M.P. (1994). Applying community psychology to the prevention of trauma and traumatic life events. In J.R. Freedy & S.E. Hobfoll (Eds.), Traumatic stress: From theory to practice. New York: Plenum.

North, C.S., Smith, E.M., & Spitznagel, E.L. (1994). Posttraumatic stress disorder in survivors of a mass shooting. American Journal of Psychiatry, 151, 82-88.

Novaco, R., Cook, T.M., & Sarason, I. (1983). Military recruit training: An arena for stress-coping skills. In D. Meichenbaum & M. Jaremko (Eds.), Stress reduction and prevention. New York: Plenum.

Numeroff, R. (1983). A guide for health professionals. Rockville, MD: Aspen.

O'Brien, L.S. (1994). What will be the psychiatric consequences of the war in Bosnia? British Journal of Psychiatry, 164, 443-447.

O'Donohue, W., & Elliott, A. (1992). The current status of posttraumatic stress disorder as a diagnostic category: Problems and proposals. Journal of Traumatic Stress, 5, 421-439.

O'Hanlon, W.H. (1992). History becomes her story: Collaborative solution-oriented therapy of the after-effects of sexual abuse. In S. McNamnee & K.J. Gergen (Eds.), Therapy as social construction. Newbury Park, CA: Sage.

O'Hanlon, W.H., & Weiner-Davis, M. (1989). In search of solutions. New York: Norton.

O'Leary, K. D., Barling, J., et al. (1989). Prevalence and stability of physical aggression between spouses: A longitudinal analysis. Journal of Consulting and Clinical Psychology, 57, 263-268.

Oreiro, M.C. (1990). Toward an understanding of American Indian warriors. NCP Clinical Newsletter, 1, 9-10.

Ochberg, F.M. (1988b). Post-traumatic therapy and victims of violence. In F.M. Ochberg (Ed.). Post-traumatic therapy and victims of violence. New York: Brunner/Mazel.

Ochberg, F.M. (1991). Post-traumatic therapy. Psychotherapy, 28, 5-15.

Ochberg, F.M. (Ed.) (1988a). Post-traumatic therapy and victims of violence. New York: Brunner/Mazel.

Oei, T., Lim, B., & Hennessy, B. (1990). Psychological dysfunction in battle: Combat stress reactions and post traumatic stress disorder. Clinical Psychology Review, 10, 355-388.

Ofshe, R.J. (1992). Inadvertent hypnosis during interrogation: False confession due to dissociative state: Mis-identified multiple personality and the satanic cult hypothesis. The International Journal of Clinical and Experimental Hypnosis, 40(3), 125-156.

Oliver, J.E. (1993). Intergenerational transmission of child abuse: Rates, research and clinical implications. American Journal of Psychiatry, 150, 1315-1324.

Op Den Velde, W., W., Koerselman, G. F., & Aarts, P. G. (1994). Countertransference and World War II resistance fighters. In J. P. Wilson, & J. D. Lindy (Eds.), Countertransference in the treatment of PTSD. New York: Guilford.

Op den Velde, Falger, R. P. J., Hovens, J. E., et al. (1993). Posttraumatic stress disorder in Dutch resistance veterans from World War II. In J. P. Wilson, & B. Raphael (Eds.), International Handbook of Traumatic Stress Syndromes. New York; Plenum Press.

Opp, R. E., & Sampson, A. Y. (1989). Taxonomy of guilt for combat veterans. Professional Psychology, 20, 159-165.

Orner, R. (1994). Intervention strategies for emergency response groups: A new conceptual framework. Paper presented at the NATO conference on Stress, coping and disaster in Bonas, France.

Orner, R.J. (1992). Posttraumatic stress disorders and European war victims. British Journal of Clinical Psychology, 31, 387-403.

Osterweis, M., Solomon, F., & Green, M. (Eds.) (1984). Bereavement: Reactions, consequences, and care. Washington, DC: National Academy Press.

Motta, R.W. (1990). Personal and intrafamilial effects of Vietnam war experience. The Behavior Therapist, 13, 155-157.

Motta, R.W. (1993). Psychotherapy for Vietnam-related posttraumatic stress disorder. Psychological Reports, 73, 67-77.

Mueser, K.T., & Butler, R.W. (1987). Auditory hallucinations in combat-related Posttraumatic Stress Disorder. American Journal of Psychiatry, 144, 299-302.

Mullen, P.E., Martin, J.L. et al. (1993). Childhood sexual abuse and mental health in adult life. British Journal of Psychiatry, 163, 721-732.

Munley, P.H., Bains, D.S., et al. 1994. Inpatient PTSD treatment. Journal of Treatment Stress, Z, 319-325.

Munoz, R.F., Hollon, S.D., McGrath, E., Rehm, L, & van den Bos, G.R. (1994). On the AHCPR Depression in Primary Care Guidelines. American Psychologist, 49, 42-61.

Muran, E. M., & DiGuiseppe (1994). Rape. In F. Dattilio & A. Freeman (Eds.), Cognitive-behavioral strategies in crisis intervention. New York: Guilford.

Murray, E.J., & Segal, D.L. (1994). Emotional processing in vocal and written expression of feelings about traumatic experiences. Journal of Traumatic Stress, Z, 391-405.

Musar, K.T., & Herbert, J.D. (in press). EMDR: Caveat Emptor! The Behavior Therapist

Musicar, L. & Josefowitz, N. (1992). Understanding incest survivor's flashbacks from a cognitive-behavioral perspective. Paper presented at the Ontario Psychological Association, Toronto, Ontario.

Muss, D.C. (1991). A new technique for treating post-traumatic stress disorder. British Journal of Clinical Psychology, 30, 91-92.

Myers, D. (1994). Psychological recovery from disaster. NCP Clinical Quartery, 4, 1-5.

Nader, K.O., Pynoos, R.S. et al. (1993). A preliminary study of PTSD and grief among the children of Kuwait following the Gulf crisis. British Journal of Clinical Psychology, 32, 407-416.

Nadler, A., & Ben-Shushan, D. (1989). Forth years later: Long-term consequences of massive traumatization as manifested by Holocaust survivors from the city and the Kibbutz. Journal of Consulting and Clinical Psychology, 48, 178-182.

Nagata, D.K. (1990). The Japanese American Internment. Exploring the transgenerational consequences of traumatic stress. Journal of Traumatic Stress, 3, 47-70.

National Institute of Mental Health. (1985) Role stressors and supports for emergency workers. (DHHS Publication No. 85-1408). Washington, DC: U.S. Governemnt Printing Office (Write to the Emergency Services Branch of NIMH for obtaining such disaster related material. Address: NIMH's Office of Scientific Affaires, Public Inquires Branch, Room 15c-05, 5600 Fischers Lane, Rockville, MD, 20857. Ask for ADM 78-540 on medical workers, 86-1390 on emergency medical personnel, 87-1496 on team managers and 81-956 by Frederick on aircraft accidents.)

Neimeyer, R., & Feixas, G. (1990). Constructivist contributions to psychotherapy integration. Journal of Integrative and Cognitive Psychotherapy, 9, 4-20.

Neimeyer, R.A. (1988). Clinical guidelines for conducting interpersonal transaction groups. International Journal of Personal Construct Psychology, 1, 181-190.

Neimeyer, R.A. (1993). Constructivist approaches to the measurement of meaning. In G.J. Neimeyer (Ed.), Constructivist assessment. Newbury Park, CA: Sage.

Newman, F. et al (1993). Cognitive therapy of personality disorder. New York: Guilford.

Nikelly, A.G. (1992). Can DSM-III-R be used in the diagnosis of Non-Western patients? International Journal of Mental Health, 21, 3-22.

Noel, B. & Watterson, K. (1993). You must be dreaming. New York: Poseidon Press.

Norman, E. (1990). Women at war. Philadelphia: University of Pennsylvania Press.

Norman, M. (1990). These good men: Friendships forged from war. New York: Crown.

Norris, F.H. (1992). Epidemiology of trauma: Frequency and impact of different potentially traumatic events on different demographic groups. Journal of Consulting and Clinical Psychology, 60, 409-418.

Norris, F.H. (1994). Frequency and impact of traumatic life events in the older population. Clinical Quarterly, 4, 8-9.

Perez, F., (1991). Combat, chaos, and the human spirit: The roles of ritual and ceremony as healing tools. In A.D. Mangelsdorff (Ed.), Proceedings of the Eight Users' Stress Workshops. Fort Sam Houston, TX: US Army Health Command. (Proceedings of the stress workshop can be ordered from the US Department of Commerce, National Technical Information Services, 5285 Port Royal Rd., Springfield, VA, 22161. Phone: 703-487-4600.

Perry, R.W., & Lindell, M.K. (1978). The psychological consequences of natural disaster: A review of research on American communities. Mass Emergencies, 3, 105-115.

Persons, J. (1989). Cognitive therapy in practice: A case formulation approach. New York: Norton.

Peskin, H. (1981). Observations on the first international conference of children of Holocaust survivors. Family Process, 20, 391-394.

Peterson, K.C., Prout, M.F., & Schwarz, R.A. (l991). Posttraumatic stress disorder: A clinician's guide. New York: Plenum.

Pettinati, H.M. (Ed.) (1988). Hypnosis and memory. New York: Guilford.

Peuler, J. (1986). Family and community outreach in times of disaster: The Santa Cruz experience. In B.J. Sowder & M. Lystad (Eds.), Disasters and mental health. Washington, D.C.: American Psychiatric Press.

Peuler, J.N. (1988). Community outreach after emergencies. In M. Lystad (Ed.), Mental health response to mass emergencies: Theory and practice. New York: Brunner Mazel.

Piper, A. (1994). Multiple personality disorder. British Journal of Psychiatry, 164, 600-612.

Pitman, R.K., Altman, B., Greenwald, E., Longpre, R.E., Macklin, M.L., Poire, R.E., & Steketee, G.S. (1991). Psychiatric complications during flooding therapy for posttraumatic stress disorder. Journal of Clinical Psychiatry, 52, 17-20.

Pitman, R.K., Orr, S.P., et al. (1993). A controlled study of EMDR treatment for PTSD. Paper presented at the American Psychiatric Association Annual Meeting, Washington, DC.

Pogrebin, M.R., Poole, E.D., & Martinez, A. (1992). Accounts of professional misdeeds: The sexual exploitation of clients by psychotherapists. Deviant Behavior, 13, 229-252.

Polkinghorne, D. P. (1988). Narrative psychology. Albany, N. Y.: SUNY Press.

Pollock, D.A., Rhodes, M.S. & Boyle, C.A. (1990). Estimating the number of suicides among Vietnam veterans. American Journal of Psychiatry, 147, 772-776.

Pontius, E.B. (1993). Acute traumatic stress: Guidelines for treating mass casualty survivors from the Persian Gulf War. National PTSD Center Clinical Newsletter, 3, 1-5.

Pope, K.S., & Garcia-Peltoniemi, R.E. (1991). Responding to victims of torture: Clinical issues, professional responsibilities and useful resources. Professional Psychology, 22, 269-276.

Pope, K.S., Sonne, J.L., & Holroyd, J. (1993). Sexual feelings in psychotherapy. Washington, D.C.: American Psychological Association.

Powell, R. A., & Boer, D. P. (1994). Did Freud mislead patients to confabulate memories of abuse. Psychological Reports, 74, 1283-1298.

Prazoff, M., Joyce, A. S. & Azim, H. F. (1986). Brief crisis in group psychotherapy. Group, 10, 34-40.

Pribor, E.F., Yutzy, S.H., Dean, J.T., & Wetzel, R.D. (1993). Briquet's syndrome, dissociation and abuse. American Journal of Psychiatry, 150, 1507-1511.

Propst, R. (1988). Psychotherapy and religious famework. New York: Human Sciences.

Puk, G. (1994). EMDR: The utility of clinical observation. The Behavior Therapist, 17, 201-202.

Putnam, F.W., Guroff, J.J., et al. (1986). The clinical phenomenology of multiple personality disorder: Review of 100 recent cases. Journal of Clinical Psychiatry, 47, 285-293.

Putnam, F.W. (1989). Diagnosis and treatment of multiple personality disorder. New York: Guilford Press.

Putnam, F.W. (1991a). Dissociative phenomena. In A. Tasman (Ed.) Annual Review of Psychiatry. Washington, D.C.: American Psychiatric Press.

Putnam, F.W. (1991b). Recent research on multiple personality disorder. Psychiatric Clinics of North America, 14, 489-502.

Padesky, C. (1993). Socratic questioning: Changing minds or guiding discovery? Unpublished manuscript, Center for Cognitive Therapy, Newport Beach, CA. There is also an audiotape of this conference paper available.

Padesky, C.A. (1990). Schema as self-prejudice. International Cognitive Therapy Newsletter, 6, 16-17.

Page, A.C., & Crino, R.D. (1993). Eye-movement desensitization: A simple treatment for post traumatic stress disorder? Australian and New Zealand Journal of Psychiatry, 27, 288-293.

Page, W.F. (1992). The Health of Former Prisoners of War. National Academy of Sciences, Institute of Medicine, Washington, D.C.: National Academy Press.

Palmer, L. (1987). Shrapnel in the heart. New York: Random House.

Pantony, K.L., & CoplAn, P.J. (1991). Delusional dominating personality disorder: A modest proposal for identifying some consequences of rigid masculine socialization. Canaidan Psychology, 32, 120-133.

Pargament, K.I., Ensing, D.S., et al. (1990). God help me: Religious coping efforts as predictors of the outcomes to significant negative life events. American Journal of Community Psychology, 18, 793-824.

Parkes, K.R. (1984). Locus of control, cognitive appraisal and coping in stressful episodes. Journal of Personality and Social Psychology, 46, 655-668.

Parlatz, R.D. (1990) Trauma pastoral care. In A.D. Mangelsdorff (Ed.) Proceedings Seventh Users' Workshops on Combat Stress. Fort Sam Houston, TX: US Army Health Command.

Parson, E.R. (1988). Post-traumatic self disorders (PTsD): Theoretical and practical considerations in psychotherapy of Vietnam War veterans. In J. Wilson, Z. Harel, & B. Kahana (Eds.) Human adaptation to extreme stress: From the holocaust to Vietnam. New York: Plenum Press.

Pearlman, L.A., & Saakvitre, K.W. (in press). Treating vicarious traumatization in therapists of adult survivors of childhood sexual abuse. In C. Figley (Ed.) Trauma and its wake (Vol III). New York: Brunner Mazel.

Peebles-Kleiger, M.J., & Kleiger, J.H. (1994). Re-integration stress for Desert Storm families: Wartime deployments and family trauma. Journal of Traumatic Stress, 7, 173-191.

Peniston, E.G. (1986). EMG biofeedback-assisted desensitization treatment for Vietnam combat veterans post-traumatic stress disorder. Clinical Biofeedback and Health, 9, 35-41.

Penn, P. (1982). Circular questioning. Family Process, 21, 267-280.

Penn, P. (1985). Feed-forward: Future questions, future maps. Family Process, 24, 299-310.

Pennebaker, J.W. (1989). Confession, inhibition, and disease. In L. Berkowitz (Ed.), Advances in experimental social psychology. Vol. 22. Orlando, FL: Academic Press.

Pennebaker, J.W. (1990). Opening up: The healing power of confiding in others. New York: Avon.

Pennebaker, J.W. (1993). Putting stress into words: Health, linguistic, and therapeutic implications. Behavior Research and Therapy, 6, 539-548.

Pennebaker, J.W., & Francis, M.E. (1994). Cognitive emotional and language processes in writing: Health and adjustment to college. Unpublished manuscript, Sourthern Methodist University, Dallas, TX.

Pennebaker, J.W., & Harber, K.D. (1993). A social stage model of collective coping: The Loma Prieta Earthquake and the Persian Gulf War. Journal of Social Issues, 49, 125-146.

Pennebaker, J.W., & Susman, J. (1988). Disclosure of traumas and psychosomatic processes. Social Science and Medicine, 26, 327-332.

Pennebaker, J.W., & Watson, D. (1991). The psychology of somatic symptoms, In L.J. Kirmayer & J.M. Robbins (Eds.), Current conceptions of somatization. Washington, DC: American Psychiatric Press.

Perconte, S.T. (1989). Stability of positive treatment outcome and symptom relapse in postraumatic stress disorder. Journal of Traumatic Stress, 3, 185-201.

Putnam, F.W., & Loewenstein, R.J. (1993). Treatment of multiple personality disorder: A survey of current practices. American Journal of Psychiatry, 150, 1048-1052.

Putnam, F.W., Guroff, J.J., Silberman, E.K., Barban, L., & Post, R.M. (1986). The clinical phenomenology of multiple personality disorder: Review of 100 recent cases. Journal of Clinical Psychiatry, 47, 285-293.

Pynoos, R.S., & Eth, S. (1986). Witness to violence: The child interview. Journal of the American Academy of Child Psychiatry, 25, 306-315.

Pynoos, R.S., & Nader, K. (1989). Children's memory and proximity to violence. Journal of the American Academy of Child and Adolescent Psychiatry, 28, 236-241.

Pynoos, R.S., Goenjian, A. & Steinberg, A.M. Strategies of disaster intervention for children and adolescents. Paper presented at the NATO conference on stress, coping and disaster in Bonos, France.

Pynoos, R.S., Goenjian, A. et al. (1993). Post-traumatic stress reactions in children after the 1988 Armenian Earthquake. British Journal of Psychiatry, 163, 239-247.

Rachman, S. (1980). Emotional processing. Behavior Research and Therapy, 18, 15-60.

Rachman, S. (1989). Fear and courage. Second Edition. New York: W.H. Freeman.

Raphael, B. (1986). When disaster strikes: A handbook for the caring professions. London: Hutchinson.

Raphael, B. (1991). Psychological problems of rescuers and other disaster emergency personnel. British Medical Journal, 159, 533-560.

Raphael, B., & Meldrum, L. (1993). The evaluation of mental health responses and research in Australian disasters. Journal of Traumatic Stress, 6, 65-90.

Raphael, B., & Wilson, J. P. (1994). When disaster strikes: Managing emotional reactions in rescue workers. In J. P. Wilson, & J. D. Lindy (Eds.). Countertransference in the treatment of PTSD. New York: Guilford.

Raphael, B., Singre, B. et al. (1983-1984). Who helps the helpers? The effects of disaster on rescue workers. Omega, 14(1).

Raphael, B., McFarlane, A.C., & Meldrum, L. (1994). Acute interventions after traumatic events. Unpublished manuscript, Dept. of Psychiatry, Royal Brisbane Hospital, University of Queensland, Herston 4029, Australia

Ravin, J., & Boal, C.K. (1989). Post-traumatic stress disorder in work setting: Psychic injury, medical diagnosis, treatment and litigation. American Journal of Forensic Psychiatry, 10, 5-23.

Rawson, R.A., Obert, J.L., et al. (1993). Relapse prevention models for substance abuse treatment. Psychotherapy, 30, 284-298.

Read, J.R., & Lindsay, D.S. (1994). Moving toward a middle ground in the "False Memory Debate" Applied Cognitive Psychology, 8, 407-435.

Regier, D.A., Boyd, J.H., et al. (1988). One-month prevalence of mental disorders in the United States. Archives of General Psychiatry, 45, 977-986.

Reiss, A. & Roth, J. (1993). Understanding and preventing violence. Washington, DC: National Academy Press.

Resick, P.A. & Schnicke, M.K. (1993). Cognitive processing therapy for rape victims. New York: Sage.

Resick, P.A. (1993). The psychological impact of rape. Journal of Interpersonal Violence, 8, 223-255.

Resick, P.A., & Schnicke, M.K. (1990). Treating symptoms in adult victims of sexual assault. Journal of Interpersonal Violence, 5, 488-506.

Resick, P.A., & Schnicke, M.K. (1992). Cognitive processing therapy for sexual assault victims. Journal of Consulting and Clinical Psychology, 60, 748-756.

Resick, P.A., Jordan, C.G., et al. (1988). A comparative outcome study of behavioral group therapy for sexual assault victims. Behavior Therapy, 19, 385-401.

Resnick, H.S., & Newton, T. (1992). Assessment and treatment of posttraumatic stress disorder in adult survivors of sexual assault. In D.W. Foy (Ed.), Treating PTSD: Cognitive-behavioral strategies. New York: Guilford Press.

Resnick, H.S., Kilpatrick, D.G. et al. (1993). Prevalence of civilian trauma and posttraumatic stress disorder on a representative sample of women. Journal of Consulting and Clinical Psychology, 61, 984-991.

Resnick, H.S., Kilpatrick, D.G., Best, C.L. & Kramer, T.L. (1992). Vulnerability-stress factors in development of posttraumatic stress disorder. Journal of Nervous and Mental Disorder, 180, 424-430.

Resnick, H.S., Kilpatrick, D.G., Dansky, B.S., Saunders, B.E., & Best, C.L. (1993). Prevalence of civilian trauma and posttraumatic stress disorder in a representative sample of women. Journal of Consulting and Clinical Psychology, 61, 984-991.

Resnick, P.A., Jordan, C.G., Girelli, S.A., Hunter, C.K., & Marhoefer-Dvok, S. (1988). A comparative outcome study of behavioral group therapy for sexual assault victims. Behavior Therapy, 19, 385-401.

Reynolds, C.F. (1989). Sleep disturbance in posttraumatic stress disorder: Pathogenic or epiphenomenal? American Journal of Psychiatry, 146, 695-696.

Rheault, B. (1980). Outward bound as an adjunct to therapy in the treatment of Vietnam veterans. In T. Williams (Ed.), Post-traumatic stress disorders: A handbook for clinicians. Cincinnati: Disabled American Veterans.

Rhue, J.W., & Lynn, S.J. (1991). Storytelling, hypnosis and the treatment of sexually abused children. International Journal of Clinical and Experimental Hypnosis, 39, 198-214.

Richards, D.A., Lovell, K., & Marks, I.M. (1994). Post-traumatic stress disorder: Evaluation of a behavioral treatment program. Journal of Traumatic Stress, 7, 669-680.

Rickels, K. (1968). Non-specific factors in drug therapy. Springfield, IL: Charles C. Thomas.

Rimsza, M.E., Berg, R.A., & Locke, C. (1988). Sexual abuse: Somatic and emotional reactions. Child Abuse and Neglect, 12, 201-208.

Riney, S., Abueg, F., & Gusman, F. (Eds.) (1991). Operation Desert Storm clinical packet. Palo Alto, CA: VA National Center for PTSD, Clinical Lab and Educational Division, VAMC Palo Alto. (Menlo Park Division)

Roberts, W.R., Penk, W.E. Gearing, M.I., Rabinowitz, R., Dolan, M.P., & Patterson, E.T. (1982). Interpersonal problems of Vietnam combat veterans with symptoms of posttraumatic stress disorder. Journal of Abnormal Psychology, 91, 444-450.

Robins, L.N. (1993). Vietnam veterans' rapid recovery from heroin addiction: A fluke or normal expectation. Addiction, 88, 1041-1054.

Robinson, R.C., & Mitchell, J.T. (1993). Evaluation of psychological debriefings. Journal of Traumatic Stress, 6, 367-382.

Rogers, M.L. (Ed.) (1992). Special Issue: Satanic ritual abuse: The current state of knowledge. Psychology and Theology, 20(1).

Rose, S.,D. (1989). Working with adults in groups. San Francisco: Jossey-Boss.

Rosen, G.M. (1992). A note to EMDR critics: The Behavior Therapist, 15, 216.

Rosen, K.H., & Stith, S.M. (1993). Intervention strategies for treating women in violent dating relationships. Family Relations, 42, 427-433.

Rosenheck, R. (1986). Impact of post-traumatic stress disorder of World War II on the next generation. Journal of Nervous and Mental Disorder, 174, 319-327.

Rosenheck, R., & Fontana, A. (1994). A model of homelessness among male veterans of the Vietnam war generation. American Journal of Psychiatry, 151, 431-427.

Rosenheck, R., & Fontana, A. (1994). Long-term sequelae of combat on World War II, Korea and Vietnam: A comparative study. In R.J. Ursano, B.G. McCaughey, and C.S. Fullerton (Eds.), Individual and community responses to trauma and disaster. New York: Cambridge University Press.

Rosenheck, R., & Nathan, P. (1985). Secondary victimization in the children of Vietnam veterans with posttraumatic stress disorder. Hospital Community Psychiatry, 36, 538-539.

Rosenheck, R. (1993). Returning Persian Gulf troops: First year findings. NCP Clinical Newsletter, 3, 18-19.

Rosenthal, D., Sadler, A., & Edwards, W. (1987). Families and post-traumatic stress disorder. In D. Rosenthal (Ed.), Family stress. Aspen, CO: Aspen.

Ross, C.A. (1989). Multiple personality disorder: Diagnosis, clinical features, and treatment. New York: Wiley.

Ross, M. (1993). Validating memory. Paper presented at conference on Memory for Everyday and Emotional Events, University of Waterloo, Ontario. (Unpublished manuscript).

Saigh, P.A. (Ed.), (1992). Posttraumatic stress disorder. Behavioral assessment and treatment. Elmsford, N.Y.: Maxwell Press.

Saks, E. R. (1994). Does multiple personality disorder exist?: The belief, the data, the law. International Journal of Law and Psychiatry, 17, 43-78.

Sales, E., Baum, M., & Shore, B. (1984). Victim readjustment following assault. Journal of Social Issues, 40, 117-136.

Salmon, T.W. (1919). The war neuroses and their lesson. New York State Journal of Medicine, 51, 993-994.

Salter, A.C. (1992). Epidemiology in child sexual abuse. In W.O. Donohue & J.H. Geer (Eds.). The sexual abuse of children. Hillsdale, NJ: Lawrence Erlbaum.

Saporta, J.A., & Case, J. (1993). The role of medications in treating adult survivors of childhood trauma. In P.L. Paddison (Ed.), Treatment of adult survivors of incest. Washington, DC: American Psychiatric Association.

Saporta, J.A., & van der Kolk, B.A. (1992). Psychobiological consequences of severe trauma. In M. Basoglu (Ed.), Torture and its consequences. New York: Cambridge University Press.

Sarason, I. (1994). Stress and social support. Paper presented at the NATO conference in Bonas, France on Stress, coping, and disaster in Bonas, France.

Sarbin, T.R. (1986). The narrative as a root metaphor for psychology. In T.R. Sarbin, Narrative psychology. New York: Praeger.

Satre, J.P. (1964). The works. New York: Brazillen.

Saylor, C.F. (Ed.) (1993). Children and disasters. New York: Plenum Press.

Schafer, R. (1992). Retelling a life. New York: Basic Books.

Schatzow, E. & Herman, J.L. (1989). Breaking secrecy: Adult survivors disclose to their families. Psychiatric Clinics in North American, 12, 337-350.

Schepple, K.L. & Burt, P.B. (1983). Through women's eyes: Defining danger in the wake of sexual assault. Journal of Social Issues, 39, 63-81.

Scherer, M. (1992). Still loved by the sun: A rape survivor's journal. New York: Simon & Schuster.

Schlenger, W.E., Kulka, R.A., et al. (1992). The prevalence of PTSD in the Vietnam generation: A multimethod multisource assessment of psychiatric disorder. Journal of Traumatic Stress, 5, 333-363.

Schmitt, J.M., & Nocks, J.J. (1984). Alcoholism treatment of Vietnam veterans with post-traumatic stress disorder (PTSD). Journal of Substance Abuse Treatment, 1, 179-189.

Schnurr, P.P. (1994). The long-term course of PTSD. Clinical Quarterly, 4, 15-16.

Schurr, P.P. (1991). PTSD and combat-related psychiatric symptoms in older veterans. PTSD Research Quarterly, 2, 1-7.

Schwarz, L.S. (1990). A biopsychosocial treatment approach to post-traumatic stress disorder. Journal of Traumatic Stress, 3, 221-238.

Schwarz, E.D., & Kowalski, J.M. (1992). Malignant memories: Reluctance to utilize mental health services after a disaster. Journal of Nervous and Mental Disease, 180, 767-772.

Schwarz, R.A., & Prout, M.F. (1991). Integrative approaches in treatment of posttraumatic stress disorder. Psychotherapy, 28, 364-373.

Scott, M.J., & Stradling, S. J. (1992). Counseling for post-traumatic stress disorder. Newbury Park, CA: Sage.

Scott, M.J., & Stradling, S.G. (1994). Post-traumatic stress disorder without the trauma. British Journal of Clinical Psychology, 33, 71-74.

Scotti, J.R., Brach, B.K., et al. (1994). The psychological impact of accidental injury. In J.R. Freedy and S.E. Hobfoll (Eds.), Traumatic stress: From theory to practice. New York: Plenum.

Scrignar, C.B. (1984). Post-traumatic stress disorder. Diagnosis, treatment and legal issues. New York: Praeger.

Scurfield, R.M. & Tice, S. (1991). Acute psycho-social intervention strategies with medical and psychiatric evacuees of Operation Desert Storm and their families. In A.R.

Ross, R.J., Ball, W.A., et al. Sleep disturbance as the hallmark of posttraumatic stress disorder. American Journal of Psychiatry, 146, 697-707.

Rossi, P.H., Weight, J.D., et al. (1983). Victimization by natural hazards in the United States, 1970-1980: Survey estimates. International Journal of Mass Emergency Disasters, 1, 467-482.

Roth, A. & Newman, E. (1991). The process of coping with sexual trauma. Journal of Traumatic Stress, 4, 279-297.

Roth, S., & Lebowitz, L. (1988). The experience of sexual trauma. Journal of Traumatic Stress, 1, 79-109.

Roth, S., & Newman, E. (1991). The process of coping with sexual trauma. Journal of Traumatic Stress, 4, 279-297.

Roth, S., & Newman, E. (1993). The process of coping with incest for adult survivors. Journal of Interpersonal Violence, 8, 363-377.

Roth, S., Dye, E., & Lebowitz, L. (1988). Group therapy for sexual-assault victims. Psychotherapy, 25, 82-93.

Roth, W.T. (1988). The role of medication in post-traumatic therapy. In F.M. Ochberg (Ed.), Posttraumatic therapy and victims of violence. New York: Brunner/Mazel.

Rothbaum, B.O., & Foa, E.B. (1992). Exposure therapy for rape victims with post-traumatic stress disorder. The Behavior Therapist, 15, 219-222

Rothbaum, B.O., & Foa, E.B. (1993a). Subtypes of postraumatic stress disorder and duration of symptoms. In J.R. Davidson & E.B. Foa. (Eds.), Posttraumatic stress disorder: DSM-IV and beyond. Washington, D.C.: American Psychiatric Press.

Rothbaum, B.O., & Foa, E.B. (1993b). Cognitive-behavioral treatment of posttraumatic stress disorder. In P.A. Saigh. (Ed.), Posttraumatic stress disorder: A behavioral approach to assessment and treatment. New York: Pergamon Press.

Rowan, A.B., & Foy, D.W. (1993). PTSD in child sexual abuse: A literature review. Journal of Traumatic Stress, 6, 3-19.

Royce, J.R. (1964). The encapsulated man: An interdisciplinary march for meaning. Princeton, N.J.: Van Nostrand.

Royce, J.R. & Powell, A. (1983). Theory of personality and individual differences: Factors, systems, and processes. Englewood Cliffs, NJ: Prentice-Hall.

Rubin, Z., & Peplau, L.A. (1975). Who believes in a just world? Journal of Social Issues, 31, 65-89.

Rubonis, A.V., & Bickman, L. (1991). Psychological impairment in the wake of disaster: The disaster -psychopathology relationship. Psychological Bulletin, 109, 384-399.

Ruma, C.D. (1993). Cognitive behavior play therapy with sexual abused children. In S.M. Knell (Ed.), Cognitive behavioral play therapy. Northvale, NJ: Jason Aronson.

Ruma, C.D. (1994). Cognitive-behavioral play therapy with sexually abused children.

Rumbaut, R.G. (1985). Mental health and the refugee experience. In T.C. Owan (Ed.), Southeast Asian mental health. Rockville, MD: NIMH

Rundell, J.R., Ursano, R.J. et al. (1989). Psychiatric responses to trauma. Hospital and Community Psychiatry, 40, 68-74.

Rush, F. (1980). The best kept secret: Sexual abuse of children. Englewood Cliffs, NJ: Prentice-Hall.

Russell, D.E. (1983). The incidence and prevalence of intrafamilial and extrafamilial sexual abuse of female children. Child Abuse and Neglect, 7, 133-146.

Russell, D.E. (1984). Sexual exploitation. Rape, child sexual abuse and sexual harrassment. Beverely Hills; CA.: Sage.

Russell, D.E. (1987). The secret trauma: Incest on the lives of girls and women. New York: Basic Books.

Russell, D.E. (in press). The trauma, prevalence and socio-cultural causes of incestuous abuse of females. In R.J. Kleber et al. (Eds.), Beyond trauma. New York: Plenum.

Ryan, R. (1994). Posttraumatic stress disorder in persons with developmental disabilities. Community Mental Health Journal, 30, 45-54.

Safran, J.D., & Segal, Z.V. (1990). Interpersonal process in cognitive therapy. New York: Basic Books.

Shaver, F. G. (1985). The attribution of blame: Causality, responsibility and blame worthiness. New York: Springer-Verlag.

Shay, J. (1992). Fluoxetine reduces explosiveness and elevates mood of Vietnam vets with PTSD. Journal of Traumatic Stress, 5, 97-101.

Sheikh, J.I., Swales, P.J., et al. (1994). Childhood abuse in older women with panic disorder. American Journal of Geriatric Psychiatry, 2, 75-77.

Sherman, R.T., & Anderson, C.A. (1987). Decreasing premature termination from psychotherapy. Journal of Social and Clinical Psychology, 5, 298-312.

Shilony, E., & Grossman, F.K. (1993). Depersonalization as a defense mechanism in survivors of trauma. Journal of Traumatic Stress, 6, 119-128.

Siegel, J.A., Williams, L., Meyer, & Jackson-Graves, J. (1993). Adult's reports of documented child sexual abuse: Implications for retrospective research. Paper presented at the annual meeting of The American Society of Criminology, Phoenix, Az. (Reprints available from: Dr. Linda Meyer Williams, Family Research Laboratory, University of New Hampshire, 126 Horton Social Science Center, Durham, New Hampshire 03824).

Silon, B. (1992). Dissociation: A symptom of incest. Individual Psychology, 48, 155-164.

Silver, J.M., Sandberg, D.O., & Hales, R.E. (1990). New approaches in the pharmacotherapy of posttraumatic stress disorder. Journal of Clinical Psychiatry, 51, 33-38.

Silver, R.L., & Wortman, C.B. (1980). Coping with undesirable life events. In J. Garber & M.E.P. Seligman (Eds.), Human helplessness: Theory and applications (pp.279-340). New York: Academic Press.

Silver, R.L., Boon, C., & Stones, M.H. (1983). Searching for meaning in misfortune: Making sense of incest. Journal of Social Issues, 39, 81-102.

Silver, S.M., & Wilson, J.C. (1988). Native American healing and purification rituals for war stress. In J. Wilson, Z. Harel & B. Kahana (Eds.), Human adaptations to extreme stress: From the holocaust to Vietnam. New York: Plenum Press.

Simpson, M.A. (in press). Social and cultural dynamics of diagnostic and ethical problems in dealing with the effects of torture and repression: The South Africa experience. In R.J. Kleber et al (Eds.), Beyond trauma. New York: Plenum.

Sinclair, N.D. (1993). Horrific traumata: A pastoral response to post-traumatic stress disorder. New York: Haworth.

Singer, K. (1989). Group work with men who experienced incest. American Journal of Orthopsychiatry, 59, 468-472.

Sledge, W.H., Boydstin, J.A., & Rahe, A.J. (1980). Self-concept changes related to war captivity. Archives of general psychiatry, 37, 430-443.

Slovenko, R. (1993). False memories/Broken families. American Academy of Psychiatry and the Law, 18, 39-50.

Slovenko, R. (1994). Legal aspects of post-traumatic stress disorder. In D. A. Tomb (Ed.), The Psychiatric Clinics of North America, 8, 439-447.

Smith, E.M. North, C.S., & Price, P.C. (1988). Response to technological accidents. In M.L. Lystad (Ed.), Health response to mass emergencies: Theories and practice. New York: Brunner/Mazil.

Smith, E.M. North, C.S., McCool, R.E., & Shea, J.M. (1990). Acute postdisaster psychiatric disorders: Identification of persons at risk. American Journal of Psychiatry, 147, 202-206.

Smith, F. (1990). To think. New York: Teachers College, Columbia University Press.

Smith, J.R. (1985). Rap groups and group therapy for Vietnam veterans. In A.S. Blank, S.M. Sonnenberg, and J. Talbott (Eds.), Psychiatric problems of Vietnam veterans. Washington, DC: American Psychiatric Press.

Smith, J.R. (1985). Rap groups and group therapy for Vietnam veterans. In S. Sonnenberg, M. Blank, & J.A. Talbott (Eds.), The trauma of war: Stress and recovery in Vietnam veterans. Washington, D.C.: American Psychiatric Press.

Smith, M.L., Glass, G.V., & Miller, T.I. The benefits of psychotherapy. Baltimore, MD: John Hopkins Univ. Press.

Solkoff, N. (1992). Children of survivors of the Nazi Holocaust: A critical review of the literature. American Journal of Orthopsychiatry, 62, 342-358.

Bollinger (Ed.), Operation Desert Storm Clinician Packet. Palo alto, CA: National Center for PTSD.

Scurfield, R.M. (1985). Post-trauma stress assessment and treatment: Overview and formulation. In C.R. Figley (Ed.), Trauma and its wake: The study and treatment of post-traumatic stress disorder. New York: Brunner/Mazel.

Scurfield, R.M. (1992). Interventions with medical and psychiatric evacuees and their families: From Vietnam through the Gulf War. Military Medicine, 157, 88-97.

Scurfield, R.M. (1992). The collusion of sanitization and silence about war: An aftermath of "Operation Desert Storm." Journal of Traumatic Stress, 5, 505-512.

Scurfield, R.M. (1993). Treatment of PTSD among Vietnam veterans. In J.P. Wilson & B. Raphael (Eds.), The International handbook of traumatic stress syndromes. Stress and coping series. New York: Plenum Press.

Scurfield, R.M., Corker, T.M., & Gongla, P.A. (1984). Three post-Vietnam "rap therapy" groups: An analysis. Group, 8, 3-21.

Scurfield, R.M., Kenderdine, S.K., & Pollard, R.J. (1990). Inpatient treatment for war related PTSD: Journal of Traumatic Stress, 3, 185-201.

Serok, S. (1985). Implications of Gestalt therapy with post-traumatic patients. Gestalt Journal, 8, 76-89.

Sewell, J.D. (1993). Traumatic stress of multiple murder investigations. Journal of Traumatic Stress, 6, 103-119.

Shafer, R. (1981). Narration in the psychoanalytic dialogue. In W. J. Mitchell (Ed.), On narrative. Chicago: University of Chicago Press.

Shalev, A. Y. (1992). Post-traumatic stress disorder among injured survivors of a terrorist attack. Journal of Nervous and Mental Disease, 180, 505-509.

Shalev, A.Y. (1993). Post-traumatic stress disorder: A biopsychosocial perspective. Israeli Journal of Psychiatry, 30, 102-109.

Shalev, A.Y. (1994). Debriefing following traumatic exposure. In R.J. Ursano et al. (Eds.). Trauma and disaster. Cambridge: Cambridge University Press.

Shalev, A.Y. (1994). Debriefing following traumatic exposure. In R.J. Ursano, B.G. McCaughey, and C.S. Fullerton (Eds.), Individual and community responses to trauma and disaster. New York: Cambridge University Press.

Shalev, A.Y., & Rogel-Fuchs, Y. (1993). Psychophysiology of the posttraumatic stress disorder: From sulfur fumes to behavioral genetics. Psychosomatic Medicine, 55, 413-423.

Shalev, A.Y., Bleich, A., & Ursano, R.J. (1990). Posttraumatic stress disorder: Somatic comorbidity and effort tolerance. Psychosomatics, 31, 197-203.

Shannon, M.P., Lonigan, C.J., et al. (1994). Children exposed to disaster: I. Epidemiology of post-traumatic symptoms and symptom profiles. Journal of American Child and Adolescent Psychiatry, 33, 80-93.

Shapiro, F. (1989a). Efficacy of the eye movement desensitization procedure in the treatment of traumatic memories. Journal of Traumatic Stress, 2, 199-223.

Shapiro, F. (1989b). Eye movement desensitization: A new treatment for post-traumatic stress disorder. Journal of Behavior Therapy and Experimental Psychiatry, 20, 211-217.

Shapiro, F. (1991). Eye movement desensitization and reprocessing procedure: From EMD to EMDR -- A new treatment model for anxiety and related trauma. The Behavior Therapist, 14, 133-135.

Shapiro, F. (1993). Eye movement desensitization and reprocessing (EMDR) in 1992. Journal of Traumatic Stress, 6, 417-423.

Shapiro, F. (1994a). EMDR: In the eye of a paradigm shelf. The Behavior Therapist, 17, 153-156.

Shapiro, F. (1994b). Shapiro's response. The Behavior Therapist, 17, 157-158.

Shatan, C.F. (1973). The grief of soldiers: Vietnam combat veterans' self-help movement. American Journal of Orthopsychiatry, 43, 640-653.

Shatan, C.F. (1973). The guilt and grief of warriors. Human Behavior, 2, 56-61.

Shatan, C.F. (1982). The tattered ego of survivors. Psychiatric Annals, 12, 100-104.

Soloff, P. H. (1994). Is there any drug treatment of choice for the borderline patient. Acta Psychiatrica Scandinavica, 89, 50-55.

Soloff, P.H. (1993). Commentary on Yeamans, Selzer and Clarkin. Psychiatry, 56, 264-267.

Solomon, A., Neria, Y., et al. (1994). PTSD among Israeli former prisoner of war and soldiers with combat stress reaction: A longitudinal study. American Journal of Psychiatry, 151, 554-559.

Solomon, S.D. (1986). Mobilizing social support networks in times of disaster. In C. Figley (Ed.), Trauma and its wake. Vol. 2. New York: Brunner/Mazel.

Solomon, S.D. (1992). Mobilizing social support networks in times of disaster. In C. Figley (Ed.), Trauma and its wake. II. New York: Brunner/Mazel.

Solomon, S.D., & Green, B.L. (1992). Mental health effects of natural and human made disasters. PTSD Research Quarterly, 3, 1-7.

Solomon, S.D., & Smith, E.M. (1993). Social support and perceived control as moderators of responses to dioxin and flood exposure. In R. Ursano, B. McCaughey, & C. Fullerton (Eds.). Individual and community responses to trauma and ?

Solomon, S.D., & Smith, E.M. (1994). Social support and perceived control as moderators of responses to dioxin and flood exposure. In R. Ursano et al. (Eds.), Trauma and disaster. New York: Cambridge University Press.

Solomon, S.D., Gerrity, E.T., & Muff, A.M. (1992). Efficacy of treatments for posttraumatic stress disorder: An empirical review. Journal of the American Medical Association, 268, 633-638.

Solomon, Z. (1990). Does the war end when the shooting stops? The psychological toll of war. Journal of Applied Social Psychology, 20, 1733-1745.

Solomon, Z. (1993). Combat stress reactions: The enduring toll of war. New York: Plenum Press.

Solomon, Z. (1994). Coping with the Gulf War. New York: Plenum Press.

Solomon, Z., & Benbenishty, R. (1986). The role of proximity, immediacy and expectancy in frontline treatment of combat stress reactions among Israelis in the Lebanon War. American Journal of Psychiatry, 143, 613-617.

Solomon, Z., & Shalev, A. (1989). Physical and mental consequences of combat stress: A study of Israeli soldiers in the Lebanon war. Israel Journal of Psychiatry, 23, 3-8.

Solomon, Z., & Shalev, A.Y. (1994). Helping victims of military trauma. In J.R. Freedy & S.E. Hobfoll (Eds.), Traumatic stress: From theory to practice. New York: Plenum.

Solomon, Z., Bleich, A., Koslowsky, M., Kron, S., & Lerer, G. (1991). Post-traumatic stress disorder: Issues of comorbidity. Journal of Psychiatric Research, 25, 84-94.

Solomon, Z., Bleich, A., Shohom, S., Nardi, C., & Kotler, M. (1992). The "koach" project for treatment of combat related PTSD: Rationale, arms, and methodology. Journal of Traumatic Stress, 5, 175-193.

Solomon, Z., McKulincer, M., & Jakob, B.R. (1987). Exposure to recurrent combat stress reactions among Israeli soldiers in the Lebanon war. Psychological Medicine, 17, 433-440.

Solomon, Z., Waysman, M., et al. (1992). From front line to home front: A study of secondary traumatization. Family Process, 31, 289-301.

Somnier, F., Vesti, P., et al (1993). Psychosocial consequences of torture: Current knowledge and evidence. In M. Basoglu (Ed.), Torture and its consequences: Current treatment approaches. Cambridge: Cambridge University Press.

Sonnenberg, S.M. et al. (1985). The trauma of war: Stress recovery in Vietnam veterans. Washington, DC: American Psychiatric Press.

Sorenson, G. (1985). A twelve-step program for combat veterans. Vietnam Veterans Newsletter.

Sorenson, S.B., & Golding, J.M. (1990). Depressive sequelae of recent criminal victimization. Journal of Traumatic Stress, 3, 337-350.

Southwick, S. M., Bremner, D., Krystal, J. H., & Charney, D. (1994). Psychobiological research in post-traumatic stress disorder. In D. A. Tomb (Ed.), The Psychiatric Clinics of North America, 8, 251-264.

Spanos, N.P. (1994). Multiple identity enactments and multiple personality disorder: A sociocognitive perspective. Psychological Bulletin, 116, 143-166.

Spence, D. (1982). Narrative truth and historical truth: Meaning and interpretations in psychoanalysis. New York: Norton.

Spiegel, D. (1981). Vietnam grief work using hypnosis. American Journal of Clinical Hypnosis, 24, 33-40.

Spiegel, D. (1988). Dissociation and hypnosis in post-traumatic stress disorders. Journal of Traumatic Stress, 1, 17-33.

Spiegel, D., & Cardena, E. (1990). New uses of hypnosis in the treatment of posttraumatic stress disorder. Journal of Clinical Psychiatry, 51, 39-43.

Spitzer, W.J. (1992). Critical incident stress: The role of hospital-based social work in developing a state-wide intervention system for first-responders delivering emergency services. Social Work in Health Care, 18, 39-57.

Spitzer, W.J., & Burke, L. (1993). A critical incident stress-debriefing program for hospital-based health care personnel. Health and Social Work, 18, 149-156.

Spring, D. (1985). Symbolic language of sexually abused chemically dependent women. American Journal of Art Therapy, 24, 13-21.

Spurrell, M.T., & McFarlane, A. C. (1993). Post-traumatic stress disorder and coping after a natural disaster. Social Psychiatry and Psychiatric Epidemiology, 28, 194-200.

Stark, E., & Flitcraft, A. (1988). Personal power and institutional victimization: Treating the dual trauma of woman battering. In F.M. Ochberg (Ed.), Posttraumatic therapy and victims of violence. New York: Brunner/Mazel.

Staub, E. (1989). The roots of evil: The origins of genocide and other group violence. Cambridge, England: Cambridge University Press.

Steketee, G., & Foa, E. (1987). Rape victims and posttraumatic stress responses and their treatment: A review of the literature. Journal of Anxiety Disorders, 1, 69-86.

Steketee, G., & Goldstein, A.J. (1994). Reflections on Shapiro's reflections: Testing EMDR within a theoretical context. The Behavior Therapist, 17, 156-157.

Stokes, A.B. (1945). War strains and mental health. Journal of Nervous and Mental Disease, 101, 215-219.

Stone, A.M. (1993). Trauma and affect: Applying the language of affect theory to the phenomenon of traumatic stress. Psychiatric Annals, 23, 567-576.

Straker, G., & Moosa, F. (1994). Interacting with trauma survivors in contexts of continuing trauma. Journal of Traumatic Stress, 7, 457-465.

Strelau, J. (1994). Temperament and stress. Paper presented at the NATO conference on stress, disasters and coping in Bonos, France.

Stretch, R., & Figley, C. (1984). Combat and Vietnam veteran: Assessment of psychosocial adjustment. Armed Forces Society, 10, 311-319.

Stretch, R.H. (1990). Post-traumatic stress disorder and the Canadian Vietnam veteran. Journal of Traumatic Stress, 3, 265-278.

Sullivan, C.M., Tan, C., et al. (1992). An advocacy intervention program for women with abusive partners: Initial evaluation. American Journal of Community Psychology, 20, 309-332.

Summit, R. (1983). The child sexual abuse accommodation syndrome. Child Abuse and Neglect, 7, 177-193.

Sutherland, S. M., & Davidson, J. R. T. (1994). Pharmacotherapy for post-traumatic stress disorder. In D. A. Tomb (Ed.), The Psychiatric Clinics of North America, 8, 409-424.

Sutker, P.B., Uddo, M. et al. (1994). Psychopathology in war-zone deployed and nondeployed Operation Desert Storm troops assigned graves registration duties. Journal of Abnormal Psychology, 103, 383-390.

Sutter, P.B., Uddo, M., et al (1993). War-zone trauma and stress-related symptoms in Operation Desert Shield/Storm (ODS) returnees. Journal of Social Issues, 49, 33-50.

Talbot, A. (1990). The importance of parallel process in debriefing crisis counsellors. Journal of Traumatic Stress, 3, 265-278.

Talbot, A., Manton, M., & Dunn, P.J. (1992). Debriefing the debriefers: An intervention strategy to assist psychologists after a crisis. Journal of Traumatic Stress, 5, 45-62.

Tang, D. (1994). Psychotherapy for train drivers after railway suicide. Social Science and Medicine, 38, 477-478.

Tavris, C. (1993). Beware the incest-survivor machine. New York Times Book Review. January 3, 1-17. (Also see the replies—letters to the editor in the January 10 issue).

Taylor, S.E. (1983). Adjustment to threatening events: A theory of adaptation. American Psychologist, 38, 1161-1173.

Taylor, S.E. (1990). Positive illusions. New York: Basic Books.

Taylor, S.E., & Brown, J. (1988). Illusion and well-being: A social psychological perspective on mental health. Psychology Bulletin, 103, 193-210.

Taylor, S.E., Wood, J., & Lichtman, R. (1983). It could be worse: Selective evaluation as a response to victimization. Journal of Social Issues, 39, 719-740.

Terr, L.C. (1981). Psychic trauma in children: Observations following the Chowchilla school bus kidnapping. American Journal of Psychiatry, 138, 14-19.

Terr, L.C. (1988). What happens to early memories of trauma? A study of twenty children under age five at the time of documented traumatic events. Journal of American Academy of Child and Adolescent Psychiatry, 27, 96-104.

Terr, L.C. (1989). Treating psychic trauma in children: Preliminary discussion. Journal of Traumatic Stress, 2, 3-20.

Terr, L.C. (1994). Unchained memories: True stories of traumatic memories, lost and found. New York: Basic Books.

Teter, H., & Arcellana, N. (1994). Where there is no therapist: A mental health manual for oppressed communities. Coalition to Aid Refugee Survivors of Torture and War Trauma. San Francisco.

Theorell, T., Leymann, H., et al. (1992). "Persons under train" incidents: Medical consequences for subway drivers. Psychosomatic Medicine, 54, 480-488.

Thompson, S.C., & Ianigian, A. (1988). Life schemes: A framework for understanding the search for meaning. Journal of Social and Clinical Psychology, 7, 260-280.

Thrash, S.M., Dalgesh, T., & Yule, W. (1994). Information processing in posttraumatic stress disorder. Behaviour Research and Therapy, 32, 247-253.

Timerman, J. (1988). Prisoner without a name: Cell without a number. New York: Vintage.

Timms, R., & Connors, B. (1992). Embodying healing: Integrating bodywork and psychotherapy in recovery from childhood sexual abuse. Brandon, VL: Safer Society Press.

Tinnin, C., & Bills, L. (1994). Time-limited trauma therapy. Gargoyle Press, P.O. Box 438, Bruceton Mills, WV. 26525.

Tomb, D.A. (1994). The phenomenology of post-traumatic stress disorder. In D. A. Tomb (Ed.), The Psychiatric Clinics of North America, 8.

Tomm, K. (1985). Circular interviewing: A multifaceted clinical tool. In D. Campbell & R. Draper (Eds.), Applications of systemic family therapy: The Milan model. New York: Grune & Stratton.

Trepper, T.S., & Berrett, M.J. (1989). Systematic treatment of incest. New York: Brunner/Mazel.

Trickett, P.K., & Putnam, F.W. (1993). Impact of child sexual abuse in females. Toward a developmental, psychobiological integration. Psychological Science, 4, 81-87.

Trimble, M.R. (1985). Post traumatic stress disorder: History of a concept. In C.R. Figley (Ed.), Trauma and its wake. New York: Brunner/Mazel.

Trimble, M.R. (1981). Post-traumatic neurosis: From railway spine to the whiplash. New York: Wiley.

True, W.R., Rice, J., et al. (1993). A twin study of genetic and environmental contributions to liability for posttraumatic stress symptoms. Archives of General Psychiatry, 50, 257-264.

Tsai, M., & Wagner, N. (1978). Therapy groups for women sexually molested as children. Archives of Sexual Behavior, 7, 417-427.

Turnbull, G. (1992). Debriefing British POWs after the Gulf War and released hostages from Lebanon. WISMIC, 4, 4-6

Turnbull, G.J. (1994). Acute treatments. In B. van der Kolk, S.M. Farlane, & L. Weiseath (Eds.), PTSD handbook. New York: Guilford.

Turnbull, G.J. (1994). Debriefing of released British hostages from Lebanon. Clinical Quarterly, 4, 21-22.

Turner, R. M., Becker, L., & DeLoach, C. (1994). Borderline personality. In F. M. Dattilio & A. Freeman (Eds.), Cognitive-behavioral strategies in crisis intervention. New York: Guilford.

Turner, S.W. (1989). Working with survivors. Psychiatric Bulletin, 13, 173-176.

Turner, S.W., & Gorst-Unsworth, C. (1990). Psychological sequence of torture. British Journal of Psychiatry, 157, 475-480.

Tutty, L.M., Bidgood, B.A., & Rothery, M.A. (1993). Support groups for battered women: Research on their efficacy. Journal of Family Violence, 8, 325-343.

Tyler, M.P., & Gifford, R.K. (1991). Fatal training accidents: The military unit as a recovery context. Journal of Traumatic Stress, 4, 233-250.

Ursano, R.J., Kao, T.C., & Fullerton, C.S. (1992). Posttraumatic stress disorder and meaning: Structuring human chaos. Journal of Nervous and Mental Disease, 180, 756-759.

Ursano, R.J., McCaughey, B.G., & Fullerton, C.S. (1994). Individual and community responses to trauma and disaster. The structure of human chaos. New York: Cambridge University Press.

Ursano, R.J., Wheatley, R. et al. (1986). Coping and recovery styles in the Vietnam Era prisoner of war. Journal of Nervous and Mental Disease, 174, 707-714.

Usher, J.A., & Neisser, U. (1993). Childhood amnesia and the beginnings of memory for four early life events. Journal of Experimental Psychology: General, 122, 155-165

Uttershack, J., & Caldwell, J. (1989). Proactive and reactive approaches to PTSD in the aftermath of campus violence: Forming a Traumatic Stress React Team. Journal of Traumatic Stress, 2, 171-184.

van Benschoten, S.C. (1990). Multiple personality disorder and satanic ritual abuse: The issue of credibility. Dissociation, 8, 22-30.

van den Bout, J., Havenaar, J. & Meijler-Iljina, L. (in press). Trauma in Eastern Europe: Radiation attributed health problems in areas contaminated by the Chernobyl disaster. In R.J. Kleber et al (Eds.), Beyond trauma. New York: Plenum.

van der Hart, O., Brown, P., & van der Kolk, B. (1989). Pierre Janet's treatment of post-traumatic stress. Journal of Traumatic Stress, 2, 379-396.

van der Kolk, B. (1983). Psychopharmacological cases in post-traumatic stress disorder. Hospital and Community Psychiatry, 34, 683-691.

van der Kolk, B. (1984). Post traumatic stress disorder: Psychological and biological sequelae. Washington, DC: American Psychiatric Press.

van der Kolk, B. (1987). Psychological trauma. Washington, DC: American Psychiatric Association.

van der Kolk, B. (1987). The drug treatment of post-traumatic stress disorder. Journal of Affective Disorders, 13, 203-213.

van der Kolk, B.A. (1987). The role of the group in the origin and resolution of the trauma response. In B.A. van der Kolk (Ed.), Psychological trauma. Washington, DC: American Psychiatric Press.

van der Kolk, B.A. (1994). The body keeps the score: Memory and the evolving psychology of post traumatic stress. Harvard Review of Psychiatry, 1, 253-265.

van der Kolk, B.A. (1989). Compulsion to repeat the trauma: Re-enactment, revictimization and masochism. Psychiatric Clinics of North America, 12, 389-411.

van der Kolk, B.A., & van der Hart, O. (1991). The intrusive past: The flexibility of memory and the engraving of trauma. American Images, 48, 425-454.

van der Kolk, B.A., Roth, S., Pelcovitz, D. & Mandel, F.A. (1993). Complex post traumatic stress disorder. Results from the DSM IV field trial of PTSD. Unpublished manuscript, Harvard Medical School.

van der Ploeg, H.M., & Klein, W.C. (1989). Being held hostage in the Netherlands: A study of long-term aftereffects. Journal of Traumatic Stress, 2, 153-169.

van der Veer, G., et al. (1992). Counseling and therapy with refugees: Psychological problems of victims of war, torture and repression. Chichester: Hohn Wiley.

Walter, J.L., & Peller, J.E. (1992). Becoming solution-focused in brief therapy. New York: Brunner/Mozel.

Watson, I.P. (1993). Post-traumatic stress disorder in Australian prisoners of the Japanese: A clinical study. Australian and New Zealand Journal of Psychiatry, 27, 20-29.

Weathers, F.W., Keane, T.M., & Litz, B.T. (1994). Military trauma. In J.R. Freedy & S.E. Hobfoll (Eds.), Traumatic stress: From theory to practice. New York: Plenum Press.

Wegner, D. (1989). White bears and other unwanted thoughts: Suppression, obsession, and the psychology of mental control. New York: Viking.

Weisaeth, L. (1989). A study of behavioral responses to an industrial disaster. Acta Psychiatrica Scandinavia, 80, 13-24.

Weisaeth, L. (1989). The stressors and post-traumatic stress syndrome after an industrial disaster. Acta Psychiatrica Scandinavica, 80, 25-37.

Weisaeth, L. (1991). The information and support centre: Preventing the after-effects of disaster trauma. In T. Sorenson, O. Abrahamsen, S. Morgerson (Eds.). Psychiatric disorders in social domain. Oslo: Norwegian University Press.

Weisaeth, L. (1992). Prepare and repair: Some principles in prevention of psychiatric consequences of traumatic stress. Psychiatria Fennica, 23, 11-18.

Weisaeth, L. (1994). Preventive intervention. Paper presented at Bonas NATO Conference.

Weisaeth, U., & Eitinger, L. (1991). Research on PTSD and other post-traumatic reactions: European Literature. PTSD Research Quarterly, 2, 1-7.

Weisel, E. (1965). One generation after. New York: Avon Books.

Weisel, E. (1960). Night. Translated by S. Rodway. New York: Hill and Wong.

Weisman, A.D. (1986). The coping capacity. New York: Human Sciences Press.

Weiss, D.S., & Marmar, C.R. (1993). Teaching time -- linked dynamic psychotherapy for post traumatic stress disorder and pathological grief. Psychotherapy, 30, 587-591.

Weiss, J. (1993). How psychology works. New York: Guilford.

Weiss, R.S. (1975). Marital separation. New York: Basic Books.

Weissberg, M. (1993). Multiple personality disorder and iatrogenesis: The cautionary tale of Anna O. International Journal of Clinical and Experimental Hypnosis, 41, 15-34.

Welch, S.L., & Fairburn, C.G. (1994). Sexual abuse and bulimia nervosa. American Journal of Psychiatry, 15, 402-407.

Westermeyer, J.F., Harrow, M., & Morengo, J. (1991). Risk for suicide in schizophrenia and other psychotic and nonpsychotic disorders. Journal of Nervous and Mental Disease, 179, 259-266.

White, M., & Epston, D. (1990). Narrative means to therapeutic ends. New York: Norton.

White, P., & Faustman, W. (1989). Coexisting physical conditions among inpatients with posttraumatic stress disorder. Military Medicine, 154, 66-71.

Widom, C.S. (1989). Does violence beget violence? A critical examination of the literature. Psychological Bulletin, 106, 3-28.

Williams, C.L., Solomon, S.D., & Bartone, R. (1988). Primary prevention in aircraft disasters. American Psychologist, 43, 730-739.

Williams, C.M. (1980). The veteran system with a focus on womaan partners: Theoretical considerations, problems and treatment strategies. In T. Williams (Ed.), Post-traumatic stress disorders of Vietnam veterans. Cincinnah: disabled American Veterans.

Williams, C.M., Miller, J., Watson, G., & Hunt, N. (1994). A strategy for trauma debriefing after railway suicides. Social Science and Medicine, 38, 483-487.

Williams, E.C. (1983). The mental foxhole: In Vietnam veteran's search for meaning. American Journal of Orthopsychiatry, 53, 4-17.

Williams, L. Meyer (1992). Adult memories of childhood abuse: Preliminary findings from a longitudinal study. The Advisor, 19-21. (Published by the American Professional Society on the Abuse of Children, Chicago)

Williams, L. Meyer (1993). Recall of childhood trauma: A prospective study of women's memories of child sexual abuse. Paper presented at meeting of American Society of Criminology, Phoenix, Az.

van der Veer, G. (in press). Psychotherapeutic work with refugees. In R.J. Kleber et al. (Eds.), Beyond trauma. New York: Plenum.

van Devanter, L., & Furey, J.A. (1991). Visions of war, dreams of peace. New York: Warner Books, Inc.

van Putten, T., & Emory, L.O. (1973). Traumatic neuroses in Vietnam returnees. Archives of General Psychiatry, 29, 695-698.

Vanderlinden, J., Vandereycken, W., Van Dyck, R., & Vertommen, H. (1993). Dissociative experiences and trauma in eating disorders. International Journal of Eating Disorders, 13, 187-193.

Vargas, M.A., & Davidson, J. (1993). Post traumatic stress disorder. Psychiatric Clinics of North America, 4, 737-748.

Vargas, M.A., & Davidson, J. (1993). Post-traumatic stress disorder. Psychopharmacology, 16, 737-748.

Vaughan, K., & Tarrier, N. (1992). The use of image habituation training with post-traumatic stress disorders. British Journal of Psychiatry, 161, 658-664.

Veltkamp, L. J., Miller, T. W., & Silman, M. (1994). Adult non-survivors: The failure to cope of victims of child abuse. Child Psychiatry and Human Development, 24, 231-243.

Vernberg, E.M., & Vogel, J.M. (1993). Interventions with children after disasters. Journal of Clinical Child Psychology, 22, 485-498.

Veronen, L.J., & Kilpatrick, D.G. (1983). Stress management for rape victims. In D. Meichenbaum & M.E. Jaremko (Eds.), Stress reduction and prevention. New York: Plenum Press.

Vessey, J.T., & Howard, K.I. (1993). Who seeks psychotherapy? Psychotherapy, 30, 546-553.

Vesti, P., & Kastrup, M. (1994). Treatment of torture survivors: Psychosocial and somatic aspects. In J.R. Freedy & S.E. Hobfoll (Eds.), Traumatic stress: From theory to practice. New York: Plenum.

Vietnam Veterans' Administration (1985). The physician's guide for disability evaluation and examination. Washington: Department of Medicine and Surgery.

Viorst, J. (1986). Necessary losses. New York: Fawcet Gold Medal.

Vogel, J.M., & Vernberg, E.M. (1993). Children's Psychological responses to disasters. Journal of Clinical Child Psychology, 22, 464-484.

Vrana, S., & Lauterbach, O. (1994). Prevalence of traumatic events and post-traumatic psychological symptoms in a nonclinical sample of college students. Journal of Traumatic Stress, 7, 289-302.

Vyner, H. (1987). Invisible trauma: The psychosocial effects of invisible environmental contaminants. D.C. Heath: Lexington, KY.

Wagner, A.W., & Linehan, M.M. (1994). Relationship between childhood sexual abuse and topography of parasuicide among women with borderline personality disorder. Journal of Personality Disorders, 8, 1-9.

Wagner, M. (1979). Airline disaster: A stress debriefing program for police. Police Stress, 2, 16-20.

Wakefield, H., & Underwager, R. (1992). Recovered memories of alleged sexual abuse: Lawsuits against parents. Behavioral Sciences and the Law, 10, 483-507.

Wali, S. (1992). Helping victims of rape in their communities. In J. de Jong & L. Clarke (Eds.), Refugee mental health manual. WHO/UNHCR, Geneva.

Walker, E.A., Katon, W.J., Nerras, K., Jemelka, R.P., & Massoth, D. (1992). Dissociation in women with chronic pelvic pain. American Journal of Psychiatry, 149, 534-537.

Walker, L. E. (1994). Abused women and survivor therapy: A practical guide for the psychologist. Hyattsville, MD: American Psychological Association.

Walker, L.E. (1979). The battered woman. New York: Harper and Row.

Walker, L.E. (1984). The battered woman syndrome. New York: Springer.

Walker, L.E. (1991). Post-traumatic stress disorder in women: Diagnosis and treatment of battered woman syndrome. Psychotherapy, 28, 21-29.

Walsh, B. W., & Rosen, P. M. (1988). Self-mutilation. New York: Guilford.

Williams, T. (1987). Diagnosis and treatment of survival guilt. In T. Williams (Ed.), Post-traumatic stress disorders: A handbook for clinicians. Cincinnati, OH: Disabled American Veterans.

Williams, T.(Ed.) (1987). Posttraumatic stress disorders: A handbook for clinicians. Cincinnati, Ohio: Disabled American Veterans, (P.O. Box 14301, Cincinnati, Ohio, 45214).

Williams-Keeler, L., & Jones, B. (1993). Is there a relation between post-traumatic stress disorder and schizophrenia? Unpublished manuscript, Royal Ottawa Hospital, Ottawa, Ontario.

Willis, R.O. (1993). An examination of critical incident stress debriefing for emergency service providers: A quasi-experimental field study. Unpublished doctoral dissertation, University of Maryland.

Wilmer, H.A. (1987). The healing nightmare: A study of war dreams of Vietnam combat veterans. In R. Williams (Ed.), Unwinding the Vietnam war. Seattle: Real Combat Press.

Wilson, J.P., Harel, Z., & Kahana, B. (Eds.) (1988). Human adaptation to extreme stress: From the holocaust to Vietnam. New York: Plenum Press.

Wilson, J.P. & Raphael, B. (Eds.) (1993). International handbook of traumatic stress syndromes. New York: Plenum Press.

Wilson, J.P. (Ed.) (1990). Trauma transformation and healing. New York: Brunner/Mazel.

Wilson, J.P., & Krauss, G.E. (1985). Predicting post-traumatic stress disorder among Vietnam veterans. In W.C. Kelly (Ed.), Post-traumatic stress disorder and the war veteran patient. New York: Brunner/Mazel.

Wilson, J.P., & Lindy, J.D. (1994). Countertransference in the treatment of PTSD. New York: Guilford.

Wilson, J.P., Smith, W.K., & Johnson, S.K. (1985). A comparative analysis of PTSD among various survivor groups. In C. Figley (Ed.), Trauma and its wake. New York: Brunner/Mazel.

Wilson, T.D., & Brekke, N. (1994). Mental contamination and mental correction: Unwanted influences on judgments and evaluations. Psychological Bulletin, 116, 117-142.

Winfield, I., George, L.K. et al. (1990). Sexual assault and psychiatric disorders among a community sample of women. American Journal of Psychiatry, 147, 335-341.

Wolfe, D.A. & Wekerle, C. (1993). Treatment strategies for child physical abuse and neglect. Clinical Psychology Review, 13, 473-500.

Wolfe, J. (1990). Women Veterans: Updates and Trends. NCP Clinical Newsletter, 1, 9-10.

Wolfe, J. (1991). Applying principles of critical incident debriefing to the therapeutic management of acute combat stress. In A. Bollinger (Ed.), Operation Desert Storm Clinician Packet ODS-CP. Palo Alto, CA: National Center for PTSD.

Wolfe, J., Brown, P.J., & Kelley, J.M. (1993). Reassessing war stress: Exposure and the gulf war. Journal of Social Issues, 49, 15-32.

Wolfe, J., Furey, J., & Sandecki, R. (1989). Women's war-time exposure scale. (Available from Dr. Jessica Wolfe, National Center for PTSD (116B), Boston VA Medical Center, 150 S. Huntington Ave., Boston, MA, 02130).

Wolfe, J., Keane, T.M., & Kaloupek, D.G., Mora, C.A., & Wine, P. (1993). Patterns of positive readjustment in Vietnam combat veterans. American Journal of Traumatic Stress, 6, 179-194.

Wolfe, V., Gentile, C., & Wolfe, D. (1989). The impact of sexual abuse on children: A PTSD formulation. Behavior Therapy, 20, 215-228.

Wolff, R. (1987). Systematic desensitization and negative practice to alter the effects of a rape attempt. Journal of Behavioral Therapy and Experimental Psychiatry, 8, 423-425.

Wollman, D. (1993). Critical incident of stress debriefing and crisis groups: A review of the literature. Group, 17, 70-83.

World Psychiatric Association (1993). International Symposium Stress, Psychiatry and War. Paris: World Psychiatric Association.

Worman, C.B. & Silver, R.C. (1987). Coping with irrevocable loss. In G.R. Van den Bos, & B.K. Bryant (Eds.), Cataclysms, crises and catastrophes. Washington, D.C.: American Psychological Association.

Wortman, C.B. (1983). Coping with victimizations: Conclusions and implications for research. Journal of Social Issues, 39, 155-222.

Wortman, C.B., & Silver, R.C. (1989). The myths of coping with loss. Journal of Consulting and Clinical Psychology, 57, 349-357.

Wright, L. (1993). Remembering Satan - Part I and II. The New Yorker, May 17 and May 24.

Wyatt, G.E., & Peters, S.D. (1986). Methodological consideration in research on the prevalence of child sexual abuse. Child Abuse and Neglect, 10, 241-251.

Wylie, M.S. (1993). The shadow of a doubt. Networker, Sept./Oct., 18-32.

Yalom, I.D. (1985). The theory and practice of group psychotherapy. New York: Basic Books.

Yapko, M. (1993). The seductions of memory. Networker, Sept./Oct., 31-37.

Yarom, N. (1983). Facing death in war - An existential crisis. In S. Breznitz (Ed.), Stress in Israel. New York: Van Nostrand Reinhold.

Yassen, J. (1993). Groupwork with clinicians who have a history of trauma. NCP Clinical Newsletter, 3, 10-11.

Yates, A. (1991). False and mistaken allegations of sexual abuse. In A. Tasman & S.M. Goldfinger (Eds.), Review of psychiatry: Vol 10. Washington, DC: American Psychiatric Press.

Yates, J.L., & Nasby, W. (1993). Dissociation, affect, and network models of memory: An integrative proposal. Journal of Traumatic Stress, 6, 305-326.

Yates, M., & Pawley, K. (1987). Utilizing imagery and the unconscious to explore and resolve the trauma of sexual abuse. Art Therapy, 4, 36-41.

Yates, W.R., Booth, B.M. et al. (1993). Descriptive and predictive validity of a high-risk alcoholism relapse model. Journal of the Studies of Alcoholism, 54, 645-651.

Yehuda, R., Resnick, H., Kahana, & Giller, E.L. (1993). Long-lasting hormonal alterations to extreme stress in humans: Normative or maladaptive? Psychosomatic Medicine, 55, 287-297.

Yeomans, F., Selzer, M., & Clarkin, J. (1992). Treating the borderline patient: A contract-based approach. New York: Basic Books.

Yeomans, F., Selzer, M., & Clarkin, J. (1993). Studying the treatment contract in intensive psychotherapy with borderline patients. Psychiatry, 56, 254-263.

Young, J.E. (1970). Cognitive therapy for personality disorders. Sarasota, Fl.: Professional Resources Press.

Young, M.A., Fogg, L.E., Schettner, W.A., & Fawcett, J.A. (1994). Interactions in risk factors in predicting suicide. American Journal of Psychiatry, 151, 434-435.

Young, W.C., Sachs, R.G., Braun, B.G., & Watkins, R.T. (1991). Patients reporting ritual abuse in childhood: A clinical syndrome of 37 cases. Child Abuse and Neglect, 15, 181-189.

Yule, W., & Udwin, O. (1991). Screening child survivors for post-traumatic stress disorders: Experiences from the "Jupiter" sinking. British Journal of Clinical Psychology, 30, 131-138.

Yule, W., & Williams, R.M. (1990). Posttraumatic stress reactions in children. Journal of Traumatic Stress, 3, 279-295.

Zaidi, L.Y. (1994). Group treatment of adult male inpatients abused as children. Journal of Traumatic Stress, 7, 719-728.

Zaidi, LJ., & Foy, D.W. (1994). Childhood abuse experiences and combat-related PTSD. Journal of Traumatic Stress, 7, 33-42.

Zelman, D., & Merrick, S. (1992). Art from Ashes. (Available from Bay Area Arts Relief Project, c/o Cultural Arts Division, 474 14th Street, Suite 1130, Oakland, Cazlifornia, 94612).

Zettle, R.D., & Hayes, S.C. (1980). Conceptual and empirical status of rational-emotive therapy. Progress in Behavior Modification, 9, 125-166.

References
Assessment Measures for Adults

Abidin, R.R. (1992). The determinants of parenting behavior. Journal of Clinical Child Psychology, 21, 407-412.

Aldwin, C. M., Levenson, M. R., & Spiro, A. (1994). Vulnerability and resilience to combat exposure: Can stress have lifelong effects? Psychology and Aging, 9, 36-44.

Allen, J.G., & Smith, W.H. (1993). Diagnosing dissociative disorders. Bulletin of the Menninger Clinic, 57, 328-343.

Allen, S. N. (1994). Psychological assessment of post-traumatic stress disorder: Psychometrics, current trends, and future directions. In D. A. Tomb (Ed.), The Psychiatric Clinics of North America, 8, 327-350.

Allodi, F., & Cowgill, G. (1982). Ethical and psychiatric aspects of torture: A Canadian study. Canadian Journal of Psychiatry, 27, 98-102.

Andreasen, N.C., Endicott, J., Spitzer, R.L., & Winokur, G. (1977). The family history method using diagnostic criteria. Archives of General Psychiatry, 34, 1229-1235.

Armor, D.J., & Polich, J.M. (1982). Measurement of alcohol consumption. In E.M. Pattison & E. Kaufman (Eds.), Handbook of alcoholism. New York: Gardner Press.

Banyard, V.L., & Graham-Bearmann, S.A. (1993). Can women cope? A gender analysis of theories of coping with stress. Psychology of Women Quarterly, 17, 308-318.

Barrera, M., Sandler, I.N., Ramsey, T.B. (1981). Preliminary development of a scale of social support. American Journal of Community Psychology, 9, 435-447.

Barsky, A.J., Wyshak, G., & Klerman, G.L. (1990). The Somatosensory Amplification Scale and its relationship to hypochondriasis. Journal of Psychiatry Research, 24, 323-334.

Barbone, P.T., Ursano, R.J., et al. (1989). The impact of a military unit disaster on the health of assistance workers: A prospective study. Journal of Nervous and Mental Disease, 177, 317-328.

Battle, C.C., Imber, S.D., Hoehn-Saric, R., Stone, A.R., Nash, E.R., & Frank, J.D. (1966). Target complaints as criteria of improvement. American Journal of Psychotherapy, 20, 184-192.

Baum, A., Fleming, R., & Davidson, L.M. (1983). Emotional, behavioral and physiological effects of chronic stress at Three Mile Island. Journal of Consulting and Clinical Psychology, 51, 565-572.

Beck, A., Kovacs, M., & Weisman, A. (1979). Assessment of suicidal ideation: The scale for suicidal ideation. Journal of Consulting and Clinical Psychology, 47, 343-352.

Beck, A.T. (1972). Measurement of depression: The Depression Inventory. In A.T. Beck (Ed.), Depression: Causes and treatment. Philadelphia: University of Pennsylvania Press.

Beck, A.T., Epstein, N., Brown, G., & Steer, G.A. (1988). An inventory for measuring clinical anxiety: Psychometric properties. Journal of Consulting and Clinical Psychology, 56, 893-897.

Beck, A.T., Rush, A.J., Shaw, B.F., & Emery, G. (1979). Cognitive therapy of depression. New York: Guilford.

Beck, A.T., Ward, C.H., Mendelson, M., Mock, J. & Erbaugh, J. (1961). An inventory for measuring depression. Archives of General Psychiatry, 4, 561-571.

Beck, A.T., Weissman, A., Lester, D., & Trexler, L. (1974). The measurement of pessimism: The Hopelessness Scale. Journal of Consulting and Clinical Psychology, 42, 861-865.

Belle, D. (1987). Gender differences in the social moderators of stress. In R. Barnett, I. Biener & G. Baruch (Eds.), Gender and stress. New York: Free Press.

Berger, A.M., Knutson, J.M., Mehm, J.G., & Perkins, K.A. (1988). The self-report of punitive childhood experiences of young adults and adolescents. Child Abuse and Neglect, 12, 251-262.

Bernstein, E.M., & Putnam, F.W. (1986). Development, reliability, and validity of a dissociation scale. Journal of Nervous and Mental Disease, 174, 727-735.

Biaggio, M. K., Supplee, K., & Curtis, N. (1981). Reliability and validity of four anger scales. Journal of Personality Assessment, 45, 639-648.

Blake, D. (1994). Rationale and development of the clinician-administered PTSD scales. PTSD Research Quarterly, 5, 1-3.

Blake, D.D. (1993). Psychological assessment and PTSD: Not just for researchers. National PTSD Center Clinical Newsletter, 3, 16-19.

Blake, D.D., Weathers, F.W., Nagy, L.M., Kaloupek, G., Charney, L., & Keane, T.M. (1990). A clinician rating scale for assessing current and lifetime PTSD: The CAPS-I. The Behavior Therapist, 13, 187-188.

Blanchard, E. B., Hickling, E. J., et al. (1994). The psychology of motor vehicle accident related post-traumatic stress disorder. Behavior Therapy, 25, 453-468.

Blanchard, E.B., Gerardi, R.J., Kolb, L.C., & Barlow, D.H. (1986). The utility of the Anxiety Disorders Interview Schedule (ADIS) in the diagnosis of posttraumatic stress disorder (PTSD) in Vietnam veterans. Behaviour Research and Therapy, 24, 577-580.

Blanchard, E.B., Kolb, L.C., & Prins, A. (1991). Psychophysiological responses in the diagnosis of postraumatic sterss disorder in Vietnam veterans. Journal of Nervous and Mental Disease, 179, 97-101.

Blanchard, E.B., Kolb, L.C., Pallmeyer, B.A., & Gerardi, R.J. (1982). A psychophysiological study of posttraumatic stress disorder in Vietnam veterans. Psychiatric Quarterly, 54, 220-229.

Bollinger, A.R. (1992). Trauma Query Questionnaire and Related Assessment Battery used at Menlo Division of National VA Center on PTSD (Address: National Center (NC-PTSD), VAMC 323E-MD, 3901 Miranda Ave, Palo Alto, CA, 94304. Phone: 415-493-5000 ext.2978)

Bongar, B. (1991). The suicidal patient: Clinical and legal standards of care. Washington, DC: American Psychological Association.

Boon, S., & Draijer, N. (1993). Multiple personality disorder in the Netherlands: A clinical investigation of 71 patients. American Journal of Psychiatry, 150, 489-494.

Bowlby, J. (1980). Attachment and loss. Vol. 3: Loss sadness and depression. New York: Basic.

Bradburn, N.M. (1969). The structure of psychological well-being. Chicago: Aldine.

Brassard, M.R., Hart, S.N., & Hardy, D.B. (1993). The psychological maltreatment rating scales. Child Abuse and Neglect, 17, 715-730.

Bremner, J.D., Southwick, L.N. et al. (1993). Childhood physical abuse and combat-related postraumatic stress disorder in Vietnam veterans. American Journal of Psychiatry, 150, 235-239.

Bremner, J.D., Steinberg, M., et al.(1993). Use of the Structured Clinical Interview for DSM-IV Dissociative Disorders for systematic assessment of dissociative symptoms in postraumatic stress disorder. American Journal of Psychiatry, 150, 1011-1014.

Bremner, J.K., Scott, T.M., et al. (1993). Deficits in short-term memory in posttraumatic stress disorder. American Journal of Psychiatry, 150, 1015-1019.

Briere, J. (1991). The Trauma Symptom Inventory. Unpublished psychological test, University of Southern California School of Medicine, Los Angeles, CA.

Briere, J., & Runtz, M. (1989). The Trauma Symptom Checklist (TSC-33). Early data on a new scale. Journal of Interpersonal Violence, 4, 151-163.

Brodman, K., Erdmann, A.J., & Wolff, H.G. (1949). Cornell Medical Index - Health Questionnaire Manual. New York: Cornell University Medical College.

Brown, G.W., & Harris, T. (1978). The social origin of depression: A study of psychiatric disorder in women. London: Tavistock.

Buschbaum, D.G., Buchanan, R.G., Centor, R.M., Schnoll, S.H., & Lawton, M.J. Screening for alcohol abuse using CAGE scores and likelihood ratios. Annals of Internal Medicine, 115, 774-777.

Costello, E., & Borkovec, T.D. (1992). Generalized anxiety disorder. In A. Freeman and F.M. Dattilo (Eds.), Comprehensive casebook of cognitive therapy. New York: Plenum Press.

Craske, M.G., & Craig, K. (1984). Musical performance anxiety: The three-systems model and self-efficacy theory. Behaviour Research and Therapy, 22, 267-280.

Creamer, M., Burgess, P., & Pattison, P. (1992). Reaction to trauma. A cognitive processing model. Journal of Abnormal Psychology, 101, 452-459.

Curlette, W.L., Aycock, D.W., Matheny, D.B., Pugh, J.L., & Taylor, H.F. (1989). Coping Resources Inventory for Stress Manual. Atlanta, GA: Health ?? Inc.

Cutrona, E.E., & Russell, D. (1987). The provisions of social relationships and adaptation to stress. In W.H. Jones & D. Perlman (Eds.), Advances in personal relationships. Greenwich, CT: JAI Press.

D'Zurilla, F.J., & Nezu, A. (1990). Development and preliminary evaluation of the Social Problem Solving Inventory. Journal of Consulting and Clinical Psychology, 2, 156-163.

Dansky, B.S., Roth, S., & Kronenberger, W.G. (1990). The Trauma Constellation Identification Scale: A measure of the psychological impact of a stressful event. Journal of Traumatic Stress, 3, 557-572.

Davidson, F., Smith, R., & Kudler, H. (1989). Validity and reliability of the DSM III criteria for postraumatic stress disorder: Experience with a structured interview. Journal of Nervous and Mental Disease, 177, 336-341.

Davis, J.M., & Sandoval, J. (1991). Suicidal youth. School based intervention and prevention. San Francisco: Jossey-Boss.

de Beurs, E., Lange, A., et al. (1993). Goal attainment scaling: An idiosyncratic method to assess treatment effectiveness. Journal of Psychopathology and Behavioral Assessment, 15, 357-373.

Derogatis, L.R. (1975). The Affects Balance Scale. Baltimore: Clinical Psychometric Research.

Derogatis, L.R. (1977). SCL-90: Administration scoring and procedure manual -- I for the R (revised) version. Baltimore: John Hopkins University School of Medicine. Available from the author, Adolph Meyer Bldg., Rm. 200, John Hopkins Hospital, 600 N. Wolfe St., Baltimore, MD, 21205.

Derogatis, L.R. (1983). SCL-90-R Version: Manual I. Baltimore, MD: John Hopkins University.

Derogatis, L.R. (1983). SCL-90R. Administration, scoring and procedures manual. Towson, MD: Clinical Psychometric Research.

Derogatis, L.R., & Melisaratos, N. (1979). The DFSI: A multidimensional measure of sexual functioning. Journal of Sex and Marital Therapy, 5, 244-281.

Derogatis, L.R., & Spencer, P.M. (1982). The brief symptom inventory (BSI): Administration scoring and procedures manual -- I. Baltimore, MD: John Hopkins University.

Derogatis, L.R., Lipman, R.S., et al. (1974). The Hopkins Symptom Checklist (HSCL): A self-report symptom inventory. Behavioral Science, 19, 1-15.

DiNardo, P.A., & Barlow, D.H. (1988). Anxiety Disorders Interview Schedule Revised (ADIS-R). Order from Dr. David Barlow, Center for Stress and Anxiety Disorders, 1535 Western Avenue, Albany, New York, 12203.

Dolan, Y.M. (1991). Resolving sexual abuse. New York: Norton.

Donaldson, M.A. (1983). Incest years after. Putting the pain to rest. Fargo, ND: The Village Family Service.

Downs, W.R, Miller, B., & Panek, D.D. (1993). Differential patterns of partner-to-women violence. Journal of Family Violence, 8, 113-135.

Dutton, M.A. (1992). Assessment and treatment of postraumatic stress disorder among battered women. In D.W. Foy (Ed.), Treating PTSD: Cognitive-behavioral strategies. New York: Guilford Press.

Dutton, M.A. (1992). Empowering and healing the battered woman. New York: Springer.

Eaton, W.W., Kessler, R.C., Wittchen, H.U., & Magee, W.J. (1994). Panic and panic disorder in the United States. American Journal of Psychiatry, 157, 413-420.

Buschsbaum, H.K., Toth, S.L., Clyman, R.B., Cicchetti, D., & Emde, R.N. (1992). The use of a narrative story stem technique with maltreated children: Implication for theory and practice. Development and Psychopathology, 4, 603-625.

Buss, A.H., & Durkee, A. (1957). Aggression/Hostility Scale. Journal of Consulting Psychology, 21, 343-349.

Buydens-Branchey, L., Noumair, D., & Branchey, M. (1990). Duration and intensity of combat exposure and post-traumatic stress disorder in Vietnam veterans. Journal of Nervous and Mental Disease, 178, 582-587.

Buysee, D.J., Reynolds, C.F., et al. (1989). The Pittsburgh Sleep Quality Index. Psychiatry Research, 28.

Caprarag, V., Barbaranelli, C. et al. (1993). The "Big Five Questionnaire": A new questionnaire to assess the five factor model. Personality and Individual Differences, 15, 281-288.

Carlson, E.B., & Rosser-Hogan, R. (1994). Cross-cultural response to trauma: A study of traumatic experiences and postraumatic symptoms in Cambodian refugees. Journal of Traumatic Stress, 7, 43-58.

Carlson, E.B., Putnam, F.W., et al. (1993). Validity of the dissociative Experiences Scale in screening for multiple personality disorder: A multicenter study. American Journal of Psychiatry, 150, 1030-1036.

Carr, A.C., Ancill, R.J. et al. (1981). Direct assessment of depression by microcomputer. Acta Psychiatrica Scandinavia, 64, 415-422.

Carroll, E.M., Foy, D., Cannon, B.J., & Zwier, G. (1991). Assessment issues involving the families of trauma victims. Journal of Traumatic Stress, 4, 25-40.

Carver, C.S., Scheier, M.F., & Weintraub, J.K. (1989). Assessing coping strategies: A theoretically based approach. Journal of Personality and Social Psychology, 56, 267-283.

Carver, D.S., & Scheier, M.F. (1994). Situational coping and coping dispositions in a stressful transaction. Journal of Personality and Social Psychology, 66, 184-195.

Chambless, D.L., Caputo, G.C., Bright, P., & Gallager, R. (1984). Assessment of fear in agoraphobics: The Body Sensations Questionnaire and the Agoraphobic Cognitions Questionnaire. Journal of Consulting and Clinical Psychology, 52, 1090-1097.

Chambless, D.L., Caputo, G.C., Jasin, S.E., Gracely, E.J., & Williams, C. (1985). The Mobility Inventory for agoraphobics. Behaviour Research and Therapy, 23, 35-44.

Clum, G.A., & Curtin, L. (1993). Validity and reactivity of a system of self-monitoring suicide ideation. Journal of Psychopathology and Behavioral Assessment, 15, 375-386.

Cohen, S., Kamenmarck, J., & Mermelstein, R. (1983). A measure of perceived stress. Journal of Health and Social Behavior, 24, 385-396.

Cohen, S., Mermelstein, R., Kamarck, T., & Hoberman, H.N. (1985). Measuring the functional components of social support. In I. Sarason and B. Sarason (Eds.), Social support: Theory research and applications. Dordecht, The Netherlands: Martinus Nijhoff.

Colligan, R.C., Davis, J.J., & Morse, R.M. (1988). The self-administered alcoholism screening test (SAAST): A user's guide. Rochester, MN: Mayo Clinic, Department of Psychiatry and Psychology. Rochester, Minnesota 55905, (507) 284-2944.

Conte, J.R., & Shuerman, J.R. (1987). Factors associated with an increased impact of child sexual abuse. Child Abuse and Neglect, 11, 201-211.

Cook, W.W., & Medley, D.M. (1954). Proposed hostility and pharisaic-virtue sczies for the MMPI. Journal of Applied Psychology, 38, 414-418.

Coons, P.M., Cole, C., et al. (1990). Symptoms of postraumatic stress and dissociation in women victims of abuse. In R.P. Kluft (Ed.), Incest-related syndromes of adult psychopathology. Washington, DC: American Psychiatric Association.

Costa, P.T. Jr., & McCrae, R.R. (1992). Revised NEO Personality Inventory (NEO-PI-R) and NEO Five-Factor Inventory: Professional manual. Odessa, FL: Psychological Assessment Resources.

Costa, P.T. Jr., & Widiger, T.A. (Eds.). (1993). Personality disorders and the five-factor model of personality. Washington, DC: American Psychological Association.

Edwards, J.A., & Baglioni, A.J. (1993). The measurement of coping with stress: Construct validity of The Ways of Coping Checklist and The Cybernetic Coping Scale. Work and Stress, 7, 17-31.

Eliot, D.M., & Briere, J. (1991). Studying the long-term effects of sexual abuse: The Trauma Symptom Checklist (TSC) Scales. In A.W. Burgess (Ed.), Rape and sexual assault III: A research handbook. New York: Garland.

Eliot, D.M., & Briere, J. (1992). Sexual abuse trauma among professional women: Validating the trauma symptom checklist - 40. (TSC-40). Child Abuse and neglect, 16, 391-398.

Endicott, J., & Spitzer, R.L. (1972). What? Another rating scale? The Psychiatric Evaluation Form. Journal of Nervous and Mental Disease, 154, 88-104.

Endler, N.A., & Parker, J.D. (1990). Coping Inventory for Stressful Situations Manual. Toronto: Multi-Health System.

Escobar, J.I. (1987). Cross-cultural aspects of the somatization trait. Hospital and Community Psychiatry, 38, 174-180.

Everly, G. & Sobelman, S. (1987). Assessment of the human stress response. New York: AMS Press.

Fairbank, J., McCaffery, R., & Keane, T. (1985). Psychometric detection of fabricated symptoms of PTSD. American Journal of Psychiatry, 142, 501-503.

Falk, B., Hersen, & Van Hasselt, V. B. (1994). Assessment of post-traumatic stress disorder in older adults: A critical review. Clinical Psychology Review, 14, 383-416.

Falsetti, S.A., Resnick, H.S., Kilpatrick, D.G. & Freedy, J.R. (1994). A review of the "Potential Stressful Events Interview (PSEI)". A comprehensive assessment instrument of high and low magnitude stressors. The Behavior Therapist, 17, 66-68. (Copies of the PSEI can be obtained by writing to Dr. Heidi Resnick, Medical University of South Carolina, Crime Victims Research and Treatment Center, 171 Ashley Ave., Charleston, South Carolina, 29425-0742).

Falsetti, S.A., Resnick, H.S., Resick, R.A., & Kilpatrick, D.G., (1993). The Modified PTSD Symptom Scale: A brief self-report measure of posttraumatic stress disorder. The Behavior Therapist June, 161-162. (Copies of the scale can be obtained from Dr. Sherry Falsetti, Medical University of South Carolina, Crime Victims Research and Treatment Center, 171 Ashley Ave., Charleston, SC, 29425).

Famularo, R., Kinscherf, R., & Fenlon, T. (1990). Symptom differences in acute and chronic presentation childhood post-traumatic stress disorder. Child Abuse and Neglect, 14, 439-444.

Figley, C.R. (1989). Helping traumatized families. San Francisco, CA: Jossey-Bass. (Purdue measures available from Dr. Charles Figley, Florida State University, 103 Sandels Bldg. (R86E), Tallahassee, FL, 32306).

Finkelhor, D. (1979). Sexually victimized children. New York: Free Press.

Fisher, P., & Kranzler, E. (1990). Post-traumatic stress disorder: Supplemental module for the DISC 2.1. New York: Division of Child and Adolescent Psychiatry, New York State Psychiatric Institute.

Foa, E.B., Feske, U., et al. (1991). Processing of threat-related material in rape victims. Journal of Abnormal Psychology, 100, 156-162.

Foa, E.B., Riggs, D.S., Dancu, C.V., Rothbaum, B.O. (in press). Reliability and validity of a brief instrument for assessing posttraumatic stress disorder. Journal of Traumatic Stress. (Order from Dr. Edna Foa, Medical College of Pennsylvania, 3200 Henry Avenue, Eastern Pennsylvania Psychiatric Institute, Philadelphia, PA 19129).

Folkman, S., & Lazarus, R.S. (1980). An analysis of coping in a middle-aged community sample. Journal of Health and Social Behavior, 21, 219-239.

Folkman, S., Lazarus, R.S., Dunkel-Schetter, C., DeLongis, A., & Green, R.J. (1986). Dynamics of a stressful encounter: Cognitive appraisal, coping, and encounter outcomes. Journal of Personality and Social Psychology, 50, 992-1003.

Fontana, A., & Rosenheck, R. (1994). A short form of the Mississippi Scale for measuring change in combat-related PTSD. Journal of Traumatic Stress, 7, 407-414.

Fontana, A., Rosenheck, R., & Brett, E. (1992). War zone traumas and posttraumatic stress disorder symptomatology. Journal of Nervous and Mental Disease, 180, 748-755.

Foy, D.W., Sipprelle, R.C., Rueger, D.B., & Carroll, E.M. (1984). Etiology of posttraumatic stress disorder in Vietnam veterans: Analysis of premilitary, military and combat exposure influences. Journal of Consulting and Clinical Psychology, 52, 79-87.

Freedy, J.R., & Hobfoll, S. (1994). Stress inoculation for reduction of burnout: A conservative of resources approach. Anxiety, Stress and Coping, 6, 311-325.

Freeman, A., & Reinecke, M. (1993). Cognitive therapy of suicidal behavior. New York: Springer.

Friedman, N.J., Schneiderman, M.A., et al. (1986). Measurement of combat exposure, post-traumatic stress disorder and life stress among Vietnam combat veterans. American Journal of Psychiatry 143, 537-539.

Frisch, M.B. (1992). Use of Quality of Life Inventory in problem assessment and treatment planning for cognitive therapy of depression. In A. Freeman and F.M. Dattilio (Eds.), Comprehensive casebook of cognitive therapy. New York: Plenum Press. (Copies of QOLI materials are available from Michael Friesch, Psyology Dept., P.O.Box 97334, Waco, TX, 76798-7334).

Frisch, M.B, Cornell, J., Villanueva, M., & Retzlaff, P.J. (1992). Clinical validation of the Quality of Life Inventory: A measure of life satisfaction for use in treatment planning and outcome assessment. Psychological Assessment, 4, 92-101.

Frischolz, E.J., Braun, B.G. et al. The Dissociative Experience Scale: Further replication and validation. Dissociation, 3, 151-153.

Fromuth, M.E. (1986). The relationship of childhood sexual abuse with later psychological and sexual adjustment in a sample of college women. Child Abuse and Neglect, 10, 5-15.

Gallagher, R.E., Flye, B.L., Hurt, S.W., Stone, M.H., & J.W. Hull (1992). Retrospective assessment of traumatic experience (RATE). Journal of Personality Disorders, 6, 99-108

Garbarino, J. (1993). Challenges we face in understanding children and war: A personal essay. Child Abuse and Neglect, 17, 787-793.

Garner, Q.M., Olmstead, M.P., & Polivy, J. (1983). Development and validation of a multidimensional eating disorder inventory for anorexia nervosa and bulimia. International Journal of Eating Disorders, 2, 15-34.

Gidycz, C.A., & Koss, M.P. (1989). The impact of adolescent sexual victimization: Standardized measures of anxiety, depression, and behavioral deviancy. Violence and Victims, 4, 139-149.

Giller, E.L. (Ed.) (1990). Biological assessment and treatment of post-traumatic sterss disorder. Washington, DC: American Psychiatric Press.

Gold, S.R., Milan, L.D. et al. (1994). A cross validation study of the Trauma Symptom checklist. Journal of Interpersonal Violence 9, 12-26.

Goldberg, D.P. (1972). The detection of psychiatric illness by questionnaire. London: Oxford University Press.

Goldberg, D.P., & Hillier, V.F. (1979). A scaled version of the General Health Questionnaire. Psychological Medicine, 9, 139-145.

Goldman, H.H., Skodol, A.E., Lave, T.R. (1992). Revising Axis V for DSM-IV: A review of measures of social functioning. American Journal of Psychiatry, 149, 1148-1156.

Green B.L. (1993). Identifying survivors at risk: Trauma and stressors across events. In J. Wilson & B. Raphael (Eds.), International handbook of traumatic stress syndromes. New York, NY: Plenum Press.

Green, B.L. (1991). Evaluating the effects of disasters. Journal of Consulting and Clinical Psychology, 3, 538-546.

Green, B.L. (1993). Disasters and posttraumatic stress disorder. In J.R. Davidson and E.B. Foa (Eds.), Posttraumatic stress disorder: DSM-IV and beyond. Washington, D.C.: American Psychiatric Press.

Gunderson, J.G., & Zanarini, M.C. (1983). Diagnostic Interview for Borderlines (Revised). Available from authors at McLean Hospital, Psychological Research Program, 115 Mill Street, Belmont, MA 02178.

Hamilton, M. (1959). The assessment of anxiety states by rating. British Journal of Medical Psychology, 32, 50-55.

Keane, T.M. (1989). Civilian Mississippi Scale of PTSD. Available from the author. National Center for PTSD, Behavioral Science Division, VA Medical Center, Boston, MA.

Keane, T.M., Caddell, J.M., & Taylor, K.L. (1988). The Mississippi scale for combat-related PTSD: Three studies in reliability and validity. Journal of Consulting and Clinical Psychology, 56, 85-90.

Keane, T.M., Fairbank, J.A., Caddell, J.M., Zimering, R.T., & Bender, M.S. (1985). A behavioral approach to assessing and treating post-traumatic stress disorder in Vietnam veterans. In C.R. Figley (Ed.), Trauma and its wake. New York: Brunner/Mazel.

Keane, T.M., Fairbank, J.A., Caddell, J.M., Zimering, R.T., Taylor, K.L., & Mora, C.A. (1989). Clinical evaluation of a measure to assess combat exposure: Psychological assessment. Journal of Consulting and Clinical Psychology, 1, 53-55.

Keane, T.M., Malloy, P.F., & Fairbank, J.A. (1984). Empirical development of an MMPI subscale for the assessment of combat-related posttraumatic stress disorder. Journal of Consulting and Clinical Psychology, 52, 888-891.

Keane, T.M., Weathers, F.W., & Kaloupek, D.G. (1992). PTSD Research Quarterly, 3, 1-7.

Keane, T.M., Wolfe, J., & Taylor, K.L. (1987). Postraumatic stress disorder: Evidence for diagnostic validity and methods of psychological assessment. Journal of Clinical Psychology, 43, 32-43.

Kendrick, M.J., Craig, K.D., Lawson, & Davidson, P.O. (1982). Cognitive and behavioral therapy for musical performance anxiety. Journal of Consulting and Clinical Psychology, 50, 353-362.

Kihlstrom, J.F., Glisky, M.L., Angiulo, M.J. (1991). Dissociative tendencies and dissociative disorders. Journal of Abnormal Psychology, 103, 117-124.

Kilpatrick, D.G. (1988). Rape Aftermath Symptom Test. In M. Hersen and A.S. Bellack (Eds.), Dictionary of behavioral assessment techniques. Elmsford, N.Y.: Pergamon Press.

Kilpatrick, D.G., Resnick, H.S., & Freedy, J.R. (1991). High and Low Magnitude Stressor Events Structured Interview. Charleston, SC: Crime Victims Treatment and Research Center, Medical University of South Carolina.

Kilpatrick, D.G., Resnick, H.S., Saunders, B.E., & Best, C.L. (1989). The National Women's Study PTSD Module. Unpublished instrument. Charleston SC: Crime Victims Research and Treatment Center, Medical University of South Carolina.

Kirmayer, L.J., Robbins, J.M., & Paris, J. (1994). Somatoform disorders: Personlaity and the social matrix of somatic distress. Journal of Abnormal Psychology, 103, 125-136.

Kleber, R.J., & Brom, D. (1992). Coping with trauma: Theory, prevention and treatment. Amsterdam: Swets & Zeitlinger.

Kolb, J., & Gunderson, J. (1980). Diagnosing borderline patients with a structured interview. Archives of General Psychiatry, 37, 37-41.

Kolb, L.C. (1993). The psychology of PTSD: Perspectives and reflections on the past, present, and future. Journal of Traumatic Stress, 6, 293-304.

Koss, M.P. (1993). Detecting the scope of rape. Journal of Interpersonal Violence, 8, 178-222.

Koss, M.P., & Gidycz, C.A. (1985). Sexual experiences survey: Reliability and validity. Journal of Consulting and Clinical Psychology, 53, 422-423.

Koss, M.P., & Oros, C.J. (1982). Sexual experience survey: A research instrument investigating sexual aggression and victimization. Journal of Consulting and Clinical Psychology, 53, 422-423.

Krystal, J. H., Giller, E. L., & Cicchetti, D. V. (1986). Assessment of Alexithymia in post-traumatic stress disorder and somatic illness: Introduction of a reliable measure. Psychosomatic Medicine, 48, 84-94.

Kubany, E.S., Gino, A., Denny, N.R., & Torigoe, R.Y. (1994). Relationships of cynical hostility and PTSD among Vietnam veterans. Journal of Traumatic Stress, 7, 21-31.

Kulka, R.A., Schlenger, W.E., Fairbank, J.A., Hough, R.L., Jordan, B.K., Marmar, C.R., & Weiss, D.S. (1988). National Vietnam Veterans Readjustment study: Description current status, and initial PTSD prevalence estimates. Research Triangle Park, NC: Research Triangle Institute.

Hammer, A.L. (1988). Coping Resouces Inventory. Palo Alto, CA: Consulting Psychologist Press.

Hammer, A.L., & Marting, M.S. (1985). Manual for coping resources inventory. Palo Alto, CA.

Hammerberg, M. (1992). Penn Inventory for posttraumatic stress disorder. Psychometric properties. Psychological Assessment, 4, 67-76. (Complete inventory from author at University of Pennsylvania, Department of American Civilization, 301A College Hall, Philadelphia, PA 19104-6303.) (A copy also appears in Scott & Stradling, 1992.)

Hawton, K., & Catalan, J. (1982). Attempted suicide: A practical guide to its nature and management. Oxford, England: Oxford University Press.

Hendrix, C.C., & Schumm, W. (1990). Reliability and validity of the abusive violence scale. Psychological Reports, 66, 1251-1258.

Hendrix, C.C., Anelli, L.M. et al. (1994). Validation of the Purdue Post-Traumatic Stress Scale on a sample of Vietnam veterans. Journal of Traumatic Stress, 7, 311-318.

Hindman, J. (1989). Sexual victim trauma assessment. Alexandria Associates, 911 W. 3rd St. Ontario, Oregon, 97914 (Phone: 503-889-8938).

Hobfoll, S.E., Lilly, R.S., & Jackson, A.P. (1992). Conservation of social resources and the self. In H. Veiel & U. Baumann (Eds.), The meaning and measurement of social support. Washington, DC: Hemisphere.

Holahan, C.J., & Moos, R.H. (1983). The quality of social support: Measures of family and work relationships. British Journal of Clinical Psychology, 22, 157-162.

Hollon, S.D., & Kendall, P.C. (1980). Cognitive self-statements in depression: Development of an automatic thoughts questionnaire. Cognitive Therapy and Research, 4, 383-395.

Horowitz, L.M., Rosenberg, S.E., et al. (1988). Inventory of Interpersonal Problems. Journal of Consulting and Clinical Psychology, 56, 885-892.

Horowitz, M., Wilner, N., & Alvarez, W. (1979). Impact of Event Scale: A measure of subjective stress. Psychosomatic Medicine, 41, 209-218.

Hovens, J.E., Folger, P.R., De Velde, W.O., Meyer, P., De Green, J.H., & Duijn, H.V. (1993). A self-rating scale for the assessment of postraumatic stress disorder in Dutch resistance veterans of W.W.II. Journal of Clinical Psychology, 49, 196-203.

Hovens, J.E., Folger, P.R., et al. (1992). Occurrence of current post traumatic stress disorder among Dutch WWII resistance veterans according to SCID. Journal of Anxiety Disorders, 6, 147-157.

Hurt, R.D., Morse, R., Swenson, W.M. (1980). Diagnosis of alcoholism with a self-administered alcoholism screening test. Mayo Clinic Proceedings, 55, 365-370.

Hyler, S., Ruder, R, et al. (1982). The personality diagnostic questionnaire (PDQ). New York: New York State Psychiatric Institute.

Jackson, A.L., & Sears, S.J. (1992). Implications of an Africentric worldview in reducing stress for African American women. Journal of Counseling and Development, 71, 184-190.

Jacobson, A., & Richardson, B. (1987). Assault experience of 100 psychiatric inpatients: Evidence of the need for routine inquiry. American Journal of Psychiatry, 144, 908-913.

Jacobson, G.R. (1989). A comprehensive approach to pretreatment evaluation I. Detection, assessment, and diagnosis of alcoholism. In R.K. Hesler & W.R. Miller (Eds.) Handbook of alcoholism treatment approaches. New York: Pergamon.

Jehu, D. (1989). Beyond sexual abuse: Therapy with women who were childhood victims. Chichester: John Wiley.

Jones, R.T., & Ribbe, D.P. (1991). Child, adolescent and adult victims of residential fire: Psychosocial consequences. Behavior Modification, 15, 560-580.

Joseph, S., Yule, W. et al. (1993). The Herald of Free Enterprise Disaster: Measuring symptoms 30 months on. British Journal of Clinical Psychology, 32, 327-331.

Joseph, S., Yule, W., et al. (1993). Increased substance use in survivors of the Herald Free Enterprise disaster. British Journal of Medical Psychology, 66, 185-191.

Journal of Applied Social Psychology (1990), Vol. 20. Devoted to the assessment of Postraumatic Stress Reactions.

Marsella, A.J., Chemtob, C., & Hamada, R. (1991). Ethnocultural aspects of PTSD in Vietnam war veterans. In A. Bollinger (Ed.), Operation Desert Strom Clinical Packet. Palo Alto, CA: National Center for PTSD.

Marsella, A.J., Friedman, M.J., & Spain, E.H. (1992). A selective review of the literature on ethnocultural aspects of PTSD. PTSD Research Quarterly, 3, 1-7.

Martin, J., Anderson, J.C., et al. (1993). Asking about child sexual abuse: Methodological implications of a two stage survey. Child Abuse and Neglect, 17, 383-392.

Mason, J.W., Kosten, T.R., Southwick, S.M., & Giller, E.L. (1990). The use of psychoendocrine strategies in the aftermath of post-traumatic stress disorder. Journal of Applied Social Psychology, 20, 1822-1846.

Mavisskalian, M. (1986). The Fear Questionnaire: A validity study. Behaviour Research and Therapy, 24, 83-85.

McCaffrey, R.J., Hickling, E., & Marrazzo, M. (1989). Civilian related post traumatic stress disorder: Assessment related issues. Journal of Clinical Psychology, 45, 72-75.

McCellan, A.T., Luborsky, A., et al. (1985). New data from the Addiction Severity Index: Reliability and validity in three centers. Journal of Nervous and Mental Disease, 173, 412-423.

McGoldrick, M., & Gerson, R. (1985). Genograms in family assessment. New York: W.W. Norton.

McNally, L.J. (1990). Psychological approaches to panic disorder: A review. Psychological Bulletin, 108, 403-419.

McNally, R.J. (1991). Assessment of posttraumatic stress disorder in children. Journal of Consulting and Clinical Psychology, 3, 531-537.

McNally, R.J., English, G.E., & Lipke, H.J. (1993). Assessment of intrusive cognition in PTSD: Use of the modified Stroop paradigm. Journal of Traumatic Stress, 6, 33-42.

McNally, R.J., Kaspi, S.P., et al. (1990). Selective processing of threat cues in post-traumatic stress disorder. Journal of abnormal Psychology, 99, 398-402.

Meyer, T.J., Miller, M.L., Metzger, R.L., & Borkovec, T.D. (in press). Development and validation of the Penn State Worry Questionnaire. Behaviour Research and Therapy.

Miller, A.M. (1987). Monitoring and blunting: Validation of a questionnaire to assess styles of information seeking under threat. Journal of Personality and Social Psychology, 24, 237-253.

Miller, I, Kabacoff, R. I., et al. (1994). The development of a clinical rating scale for the McMaster model of family functioning. Family Process, 33,53-69.

Miller, I.W., Norman, W.H., et al. (1986). The Modified Scale for Suicidal Ideation: Reliability and validity. Journal of Consulting and Clinical Psychology, 54, 724-725.

Miller, W.R. (1983). Motivational interviewing with problem drinkers. Behavioral Psychotherapy, 11, 147-172.

Millon, T. (1987). Manual for the MCMI-II. Minneapolis, MN: National Computer Systems.

Milner, J.S. The Child Abuse Potential Inventory: Manual (2nd Ed.). Webster, NC: Psytec Corporation.

Mollica, R.F., Caspi-Yavin, Y. et al. (1992). The Harvard Trauma Questionnaire: Validating a cross-cultural instrument for measuring torture, trauma, and post traumatic stress disorder in Indochinese refugees. Journal of Nervous and Mental Disease, 180, 111-126.

Mollica, R.F., Wyshak, G., et al. (1987). Indochinese versions of the Hopkins Symptom Checklist - 25: A screening instrument for the psychiatric care of refugees. American Journal of Psychiatry, 144, 457-500.

Moos, R.H., & Moos, B.S. (1986). Family Environment Scale Manual. Palo Alto, CA: Consulting Psychologists Press.

Neal, L., Busuttil, W., & Herepath, R. (1993). Development and validation of the computerized clinician administered post traumatic stress disorder scale - 1 - revised. Unpublished manuscript, RAF Hospital Wroughton, Swindon, Wiltshire, SN4 OQJ, England.

Neimeyer, R. A., & Feixas, G. (1990). The role of homework and skill acquisition in the outcome of cognitive therapy for depression. Behavior Therapy, 21, 281-292.

Lambert, M.J., Hatch, D.R., Kingston, M.D., & Edwards, B.C. (1986). Zung, Beck, and Hamilton rating scales as measures of treatment outcome: A meta-analytic comparison. Journal of Consulting and Clinical Psychology, 54, 54-59.

Lange, A. (1990). Questionnaire of sexual experiences in the past. Unpublished manuscript, Free University of Amsterdam.

Lating. J.M., Zeichner, A., & Keane, T.M. (1994). Psychological assessment of PTSD. In G.S. Everly & J. M. Lating (Eds.), Psychotraumatology. New York, NY: Plenum Press.

Laufer, R.S., Frey-Wouters, E., et al. (1981). Post-war trauma: Social and psychological problems of Vietnam veterans in the aftermath of the Vietnam war. In A. Egendorf et al. (Eds.), Legacies of Vietnam. U.S. Government Printing Office, Washington, D.C.

Lazarus, R.S., & Folkman, S. (1984). Stress, appraisal and coping. New York: Springer.

Leary, M.R. (1983). A brief version of the Fear of Negative Evaluation Scale. Personality and Social Psychology Bulletin, 9, 371-375.

Lee, E., & Lu, F. (1989). Assessment and treatment of Asian-American survivors of mass violence. Journal of Traumatic Stress, 2, 93-120.

Ley, R. (1985). Blood, breath and fears: A hyperventilation theory of panic attacks and agoraphobia. Clinical Psychology Review, 5, 271-285.

Lipchik, E., & de Shazer, S. (1986). The purposeful interview. In W.L. Lipchik (Ed.), Interviewing. Rockville, MD: Aspen.

Litz, B.T. (1991). Psychometrically-based measures of combat related PTSD. In A. Bollinger (Ed.), Operation Desert Storm Clinical Packet. Palo Alto, CA: National Center for PTSD.

Litz, B.T., Knight, J., Wolfe, J., & colleagues. (1991). Semi-structured initial interview for Desert Storm War-zone personnel. In A. Bollinger (Ed.), Operation Desert Strom Clinical Packet. Palo Alto, CA: National Center for PTSD.

Litz, R.T., Penk, N.E. Gerardi, R.J., & Keane, T. M. (1992). The assessment of post-traumatic disorder. In P. Saigh (Ed.), Post-traumatic stress disorder. New York, NY: Pergamon.

Locke, H.J., & Wallace, K.M. (1959). Short marital adjustment and prediction tests: Their reliability and validity. Journal of Marriage and the Family, 21, 251-255.

Loranger, A.W. (1988). Personality disorder examination. Yonkers, NY: D.V. Communications.

Lucas, R.W., Mullin, P. et al. (1977). Psychiatrists and a computer as interrogators of patients with alcohol related illness: A comparison. British Journal of Psychiatry, 131, 160-167.

Lund, M., Foy, D. et al. (1984). The combat exposure scale: A systematic assessment of trauma in the Vietnam veteran. Journal of Clinical Psychology, 40, 1323-1328.

Lyons, J.A. (1991). Special Issue on the assessment of PTSD. Journal of Traumatic Stress, January Issue. Vol. 4, No. 1.

Lyons, J.A. (1991). Strategies for assessing the potential for positive adjustment following trauma. Journal of Traumatic Stress, 4, 93-112.

Lyons, J.A., Caddell, J.M. et al. (1994). The potential for faking on the Mississippi Scale for combat-related PTSD. Journal of Traumatic Stress, 7, 441-445.

Lyons, J.A., Gerardi, R.J., Wolfe, J., & Keane, R.M. (1988). Multidimentional assessment of combat-related PTSD: Phenominological, psychometric and psychophysiological considerations. Journal of Traumatic Stress, 1, 373-394.

Malloy, P.F., Fairbank, J.A., & Keane, T.M. (1983). Validation of a multimethod assessment of posttraumatic stress disorders in Vietnam veterans. Journal of Consulting and Clinical Psychology, 51, 488-494.

Mangeledorff, A.D (1991). Unit Cohesion Scale. (Address: US ARMY Health Care, Health Services Command (Atn: HSHN-T) Fort Sam Houston, TX, 78234-6060).

Maris, L.W., Berman, A.L., Maltsberger, J.T., & Yufit, R.I. (1992). Assessment and prediction of suicide. New York: Guilford Press.

Marks, I.M., & Mathews, A.M. (1979). Brief standard self-rating scale for phobic patients. Behaviour Research and Therapy, 17, 263-267.

Pitman, R.K., Orr, S.P., Forgue, D.F., et al. (1987). Psychophysiologic assessment of posttraumatic stress disorder imagery in Vietnam combat veterans. Archives of General Psychiatry, 44, 970-975.

Polaino, A., & Senra, C. (1991). Measurement of depression: Comparison between self-reports and clinical assessments of depressed outpatients. Journal of Psychopathology and Behavioral Assessment, 13, 313-324.

Psychological Assessment: Journal of Consulting and Clinical Psychology. Volume 3. Guilford.

Putnam, F. (1989). Diagnosis and Treatment of multiple personality disorder. New York: Guilford.

Putnam, F.W., Helmers, K., & Trickett, P.K. (1993). Development, reliability and validity of a child dissociation scale. Child Abuse and Neglect, 17, 731-741.

Quarantelli, E.E. (1985). An assessment of conflicting views on mental health: The consequences of traumatic events. In C.R. Figley (Ed.) Trauma and its wake. New York: Brunner/Mazel.

Quarantelli, E.L. (1985). An assessment of conflicting views of mental health: The consequences of traumatic events. In C.R. Figley (Ed.). Trauma and its wake. New York: Brunner/Mazel.

Radloff, L.S. (1975). Sex differences in depression: The effects of occupation and marital status. Sex Roles, 1, 245-265.

Rasmussen, N.H., & Avant, R.E. (1989). Somatization disorder in family practice. Practical Therapeutics, 40, 206-214.

Reaves, M.E., Callen, K.E., & Maxwell, M.J. (1993). Vietnam veterans in the general hospital: Seven years later. Journal of Traumatic Stress, 6, 343-350.

Reich, W., & Welner, Z. (1988). DICA-C-R (DSM-III-R version), revised version 5-R. St Louis: Washington University Press.

Reinecke, M. A. (1994). Suicide and depression. In F. Dattilio & A. Freeman (Eds.), Cognitive-behavioral strategies in crisis intervention. New York: Guilford.

Reiss, A., Peterson, R.A., Gursky, D.M., & McNally, J. (1986). Anxiety sensitivity, anxiety frequency, and the prediction of fearfulness. Behaviour Research and Therapy, 24, 1-8.

Resnick, H.S., & Newton, T. (1992). Assessment and treatment of postraumatic stress disorder in adult survivors of sexual assault. In D.W. Foy (Ed.), Treating PTSD: Cognitive-behavioral strategies. New York: Guilford Press.

Resnick, H.S., Falsetti, S.A., et al. (1994). Assessment of rape and other civilian trauma-related PTSD. In T.W. Miller (Ed.). Stressful life events (2nd Ed.). International Universities Press.

Resnick, H.S., Kilpatrick, D.G., & Lipovsky, J. (1991). Assessment of rape-related posttraumatic stress disorder: Stressor and symptom dimensions. Psychological Assessment, 4, 561-572.

Robins, L.N., & Helzer, J.E. (1985). NIMH Diagnostic Interview Schedule Version III Revised. St.Louis, MO: Washington University.

Robins, L.N., & Smith, E.M. (1983). Diagnostics Interview Schedule Disorder Supplement. St. Louis, MO: Washington University School of Medicine.

Robins, L.N., Helzer, J.E., Croughan, J., & Ratcliff, K.S. (1981). National Institute of Mental Health Diagnostic Interview Schedule: Its history, characteristics, and validity. Archives of General Psychiatry, 38, 381-389.

Robins, L.N., Helzer, J.E., et al. (1981), NIMH Diagnostic Interview Schedule, Version III. Rockville, MD (Publication No. ADM-T-42-3; 5-81, 8-81).

Robins, L.N., Helzer, J.F., & Croughan, J. (1982). NIMH Diagnostic Interview Schedule - DIS Wave II. St. Louis: Washington University School of Medicine.

Rodenburg, F.A., & Fantuzzo, J.W. (1993). The measure of wife abuse: Steps toward the development of a comprehensive assessment technique. Journal of Family Violence, 8, 203-228.

Rosenberg, M. (1989). Society and adolescent self-image. Middletown, CT: Wesleyan University Press.

Rosenheck, R. (1990). War Stress Inventory. West Haven, CT: Dept. Veterans Affairs. Northeast Program Evaluation Center.

Newman, C.F., & Wright, F. D. (1994). Substance abuse. In F. Dattilio & A. Freeman (Eds.), Cognitive-behavioral strategies in crisis intervention. New York: Guilford.

Newsome, R.D., & Ditzler, T. (1993). Assessing alcoholic denial. Journal of Nervous and Mental Disease, 181, 689-694.

Norris, F. (1990). Screening for traumatic stress. Journal of Applied Social Psychology, 20, 1704-1718.

Norris, F.H., & Uhl, G.A. (1993). Chronic stress as a mediator of acute stress: The case of Hurricane Hugo. Journal of Applied Social Psychology, 23, 1263-1284.

North, C.S., Smith, E.M., & Spitznagel, E.L. (1994). Violence and the homeless: An epidemiologic study of victimization and aggression. Journal of Traumatic Stress. Z, 95-110.

Olson, D.H., Russell, C.S., & Sprenke, D.H. (1983). Circumplex model VI: Theoretical update. Family Process, 22, 69-83.

Orr, S.P. (1994). An overview of psychophysiological studies of PTSD. PTSD Research Quarterly, 5, 1-6.

Osman, A., Barrios, F.X., & Osman, J.R. (1994). The Reasons for Living Inventory. The Behavior Therapist, 17, 112-114.

Osman, A., Barrios, F.X., et al., (1993). The Beck Anxiety Inventory. Psychometric properties in a community population. Journal of Psychopathology and Behavioral Assessment, 15, 287-297.

Pallmeyer, T.P., Blanchard, E.B., & Kolb, L.C. (1980). The physiology of combat induced post-traumatic stress disorder in Vietnam veterans. Behavior Research and Therapy, 24, 636-652.

Parkes, K.R. (1984). Locus of control, cognitive reappraisal and coping in stressful episodes. Journal of Personality and Social Psychology, 46, 655-668.

Paul, G. (1966). Insight vs. desensitization in psychotherapy. Stanford, CA: Stanford University Press.

Peacock, E.J., & Wong, P.T. (1990). The Stress Appraisal Measure (SAM): A multidimensional approach to cognitive appraisal. Stress Medicine, 6, 227-236.

Pearlin, L.I., & Schooler, C. (1978). The structure of coping. Journal of Health and Social Behavior, 19, 2-21.

Pelcovitz, D., van der Kolk, B.A., et al. (1993). Development and validation of the structured interview for measurement of Disorders of Extreme Stress. Journal of Traumatic Stress.

Penk, W.A., & Allen, I.M. (1991). Clinical assessment of PTSD among American minorities who served in Vietnam. Journal of Traumatic Stress, 4, 41-66.

Pennebaker, J.W., & Susman, J.R. (1988). Disclosure of traumas and psychosomatic processes. Social Science and Medicine, 26, 327-332.

Perconte, S., & Wilson, A. (1994). Self-report versus observer ratings of distress and pathology in Vietnam veterans with PTSD. Journal of Traumatic Stress, Z, 129-134.

Peterson, C., Prout, M., & Schwarz, R. (1993). Post traumatic stress disorder: A clinician's guidebook. New York: Plenum.

Peterson, D. (1968). The clinical study of social behavior. New York: Appleton-Century-Crofts.

Peterson, R.A., & Heilbronner, R.L. (1987). The Anxiety Sensitivity Index. Journal of Anxiety Disorders, 1, 117-121.

Philgren, E.M., Gidycz, C.A., & Lynn, S.J. (1993). Impact of adulthood and adolescent rape experiences on subsequent sexual fantasies. Imagination, Cognition, and Personality, 12, 321-339.

Pierce, G.R., Sarason, I.G., & Sarason, B.R. (1991). General and relationship-based perceptions of social support: Are two constructs better than one? Journal of Personality and Social Psychology, 61, 1028-1039.

Pilowsky, I. (1967). Dimensions of hypochondria. British Journal of Psychiatry, 51, 131-137.

Pitman, R., & Orr, S. (1993). New test for PTSD. Psychiatric New, June 4, 14.

Rosenheck, R., & Fontana, A. (1991). War Stress Interview for Operation Desert Storm. In Operation Desert Storm Clinical Packet. ODS-CP. National Center for PTSD, Dept. Veterans Affairs.

Ross, C. (1989). Multiple personality disorder: Diagnosis, clinical factors, and treatment. New York: John Wiley.

Ross, C., Heber, S., & Norton, G. (1989). The Dissociative Disorders Interview Schedule: A structured interview. Dissociation, 2, 169-189.

Rothbaum, B.O., Dancu, C.V., Riggs, D., & Foa, E.B. (1990). The PTSD symptom scale. Presented at European Behaviour Therapy Conference, Paris.

Rowan, A.B., Foy, D.W., Rodriquez, N., & Ryan, S. (1994). Posttraumatic stress disorder in a clinical sample of adults sexually abused as children. Child Abuse and Neglect, 18, 51-61.

Rubin, B. (1967). Depression Adjective Check Lists: Manual. San Diego, CA: Educational and Industrial Testing Service.

Sanders, M.R., & Lawton, J.M. (1993). Discussing assessment findings with families: A guided participation model of information transfer. Child and Family Behavior Therapy, 15, 5-35.

Sanders, S. (1986). The Perceptual Alteration Scale: A scale measuring dissociation. American Journal of Clinical Hypnosis, 29, 95-102.

Saporta, J.A., & Van der Kolk, G.A. (1992). Psychobiological consequences of severe trauma. In M. Basoglu (Ed.) Torture and its consequences. New York: Cambridge University Press.

Sarason, I.G., Johnson, J.H., & Siegel, J. (1978). Assessing the impact of life changes: Development of the Life Experiences Survey. Journal of Consulting and Clinical Psychology, 46, 932-946.

Sarason, I.G., Levine, H.M., Basham, R.B., & Sarason, B.R. (1983). Assessing social support. The Social Support Questionnaire. Journal of Personality and Social Psychology, 46, 932-946.

Sarason, I.G., Sarason, B.R., Shearin, E.N., & Pierce, G.R. (1987). A brief measure of social support: Practical and theoretical implications. Journal of Social and Personal Relationships, 4, 457-510.

Saunders, B.E. Arath, C.M., & Kilpatrick, D.G. (1990). Development of a crime-related Post-traumatic Stress Disorder Scale for women within the Symptom Checklist-90-Revised. Journal of Traumatic Stress, 3, 439-448.

Saunders, B.E. Kilpatrick, D.G. et al. (1989). Brief screening for lifetime history of criminal victimization at mental health intake. Journal of Interpersonal Violence, 4, 267-277.

Saunders, B.E., Kilpatrick, D.G., et al. (1989). Brief screening for lifetime history of criminal victimization at mental health intake. Journal of Interpersonal Violence, 4, 267-277.

Saunders, B.E., Mandoki, K.A., & Kilpatrick, D.G. (1990). Development of a crime related posttraumatic stress disorder scale within the Symptom Checklist-90-Revised. Journal of Traumatic Stress, 3, 439-448.

Schaeffer, M.T., & Olson, D. (1984). Assessing intimacy: The PAIR Inventory. Journal of Marital and Family Therapy, 7, 47-60.

Schlenger, W.E., & Kulka, R.A. (1989). PTSD scale development for the MMPI-2. Research Triangle Park, NC: Research Triangle Institute.

Schwarz, R.A., & Prout, M.F. (1991). Integrative approaches in the treatment of stress disorder. Psychotherapy, 28, 364-373.

Schwarzer, R, & Schwarzer, C. (1993). A critical survey of coping instruments. In M. Zeidner & N.S. Endler (Eds), Handbook of coping. New York: NY: Wiley.

Schwarzwald, J., Solomon, Z., Weisenberg, M., & Mikulincer, M. (1987). Validation of the impact of Event Scale for psychological sequaelae of combat. Journal of Consulting and Clinical Psychology, 55, 251-256.

Scott, M.J., & Stradling, S.G. (1992). Counseling for posttraumatic stress disorder. London: Sage.

Scurfield, R.M., & Blank, A.S. (1985). A guide to obtaining a military history from Vietnam veterans. In S.M. Sonnenberg, A.S. Blank, & J.A. Talbott (Eds.), The trauma of war:

Stress and recovery in Vietnam veterans. Washington, DC: American Psychiatric Press.

Shalev, A.Y., Orr, S.P., & Pitman, R.K. (1993). Psychophysiological assessment of traumatic imagery in Israeli civilian patients with posttraumatic stress disorder. American Journal of Psychiatry, 150, 620-624.

Sheikh, J., Bail, G. et al. (1990). The Childhood Trauma Questionnaire. Stanford, CA: Laboratory for Geriatric Anxiety Research.

Sher, K.J., & Trull, T.J. (1994). Personality and disinhibitory psychopathology: Alcoholism and antisocial personality disorder. Journal of Abnormal Psychology, 103, 92-102.

Siegal, J. M. (1985). The measurement of anger as a multidimensional construct. In M. A. Chesney & R. H. Rosenman (Eds.), Anger and hostility in cardiovascular and behavioral disorders. Washington, DC: Hemisphere.

Sledge, W.H., Boydstun, J.A., & Rabe, F.J. (1980). Self-concept changes related to war captivity. Archives of General Psychiatry, 37, 430-443.

Smilkstein, G. (1980). The Family APGAR. Seattle: University of Washington.

Smith, G.R. & Brown, F.W. (1990). Screening indexes in DSM-III R Somatization disorder. General Hospital Psychiatry, 12, 148-152.

Smith, J. (1985). Brecksville Psychological Assessment Manual. Unpublished manuscript.

Snaith, R.P. et al. (1978). A clinical scale for the self-assessment of irritability. British Journal of Psychiatry, 132 164-171.

Snaith, R.P., & Zigmond, A.S. (1983). The Hospital anxiety and depression scale. Acta Psychiatrica Scandenavia, 67, 361-370.

Solomon, S. D., & Canino, G. J. (1990). Appropriateness of DSM-III-R criteria for post-traumatic stress disorder. Comprehensive Psychiatry, 31, 227-237.

Solomon, Z. (1993). Combat stress reaction: The enduring toll of war. New York: Plenum Press.

Solomon, Z., Benbenishty, R. et al. (1993). Assessment of PTSD: Validation of the Revised PTSD Inventory. Israeli Journal of Psychiatry, 30, 110-115.

Solomon, Z., Waysman, M.A., et al. (1993). Psychological growth and dysfunction following war captivity. Unpublished manuscript. Tel Aviv University.

Spanier, G.B. (1976). Measuring dyadic adjustment: New scales for assessing the quality of marriage and similar dyads. Journal of Marriage and Family, 38, 15-28.

Spiegel, D. (1993). Stanford Acute Stress Reaction Questionnaire. Unpublished Manuscript.

Spiegel, D., & Cardena, E. (1990). New uses of hypnosis in the treatment of post traumatic stress disorder. Journal of Clinical Psychiatry, 51, 39-43.

Spiegel, H., & Spiegel, D. (1978). Trance and treatment. New York: Basic Books.

Spielberger, C.D. (1988). State-trait Anger Expression Inventory: Odessa, FL: Psychological Assessment Resources.

Spielberger, C.D., Gorsuch, R.L., & Lushene, R.F. (1970). Manual for State-Trait Anxiety Inventory. Palo Alto, CA: Consulting Psychologists Press.

Spitzer, R., & Endicott, J. (1977). The SADS-Change Interview. New York: New York State Psychiatric Institute.

Spitzer, R., Williams, J., & Gibbon, M. (1987). Structured Clinical Interview for DSM-III-R Personality Disorder (SCID-II). Biometrics Research Department New York State Psychiatric Institute.

Spitzer, R.C. Williams, J.B., Gibbon, M., & First, M.B. (1989). Structured clinical interview for DSM-III-R. New York: Biometrics Research Department, New York State Psychiatric Institute.

Spitzer, R.L. & Williams, J.B. (1983). Structured Clinical Interview for DSM-III. New York: New York State Psychiatric Institute.

Spitzer, R.L., & Williams, J.B. (1986). Structured Clinical Interview for DSM-III-R-Patient and Nonpatient Versions. New York: Biometrics Research Dept., New York State Psychiatric Institute.

Spitzer, R.L., Williams, J.B., & Gibbon, M. (1987). Instruction manual for the Structured Clinical Interview for DSM-III-R. New York: New York State Psychiatric Institute.

Vitaliano, P., Russo, J., et al. (1993). The Dimensions of Stress Scale: Psychometric properties. Journal of Applied Social Psychology, 23, 1847-1870.

Vitaliano, P.P., Maiuro, R.D., Russo, J., & Becker, J. (1987). Raw versus relative scores in the assessment of coping strategies. Journal of Behavioral Medicine, 10, 1-18.

Vitaliano, P.P., Russo, J., Carr, J.E., Mairuo, R.D., & Becker, J. (1985). The Ways of Coping Checklist -- Revision and psychometric properties. Multivariate Behavioral Research, 20, 3-26.

Vitousek, R., & Manke, F. (1994). Personality variables and disorders in anorexia nervosa and bulimia nervosa. Journal of Abnormal Psychology, 103, 137-147.

Watson, C.G. (1990). Psychometric postraumatic stress disorder measurement techniques: A review. Psychological Assessment, 2, 460-469.

Watson, C.G., Brown, D., Kucala, T., Juba, M., Davenport, S.C., Anderson, D. (1993). Two studies of reported pretraumatic stressors' effect on postraumatic stress disorder severity. Journal of Clinical Psychology, 49, 311-318.

Watson, C.G., Juba, M., & Anderson, P.E. (1989). Validities of five combat scales. Journal of Consulting and Clinical Psychology, 1, 98-102.

Watson, C.G., Juba, M.P., Manifold, V., Kucala, T., Anderson, P.E. (1991). The PTSD interview: Rationale, description, reliability, and concurrent validity of a DSM-II-Based technique. Journal of Clinical Psychology, 47, 179-189.

Watson, C.G., Kucala, T., & Manifold, V. (1986). A cross validation of the Keane and Penk MMPI scales as measures of postraumatic stress disorder. Journal of Clinical Psychology, 42, 727-732.

Watson, D., & Friend, R. (1969). Measurement of social evaluative anxiety. Journal of Consulting and Clinical Psychology, 33, 448-457.

Watson, E.G., Plemel, D., et al. (1994). A comparison of four PTSD measures' convergent validities in Vietnam veterans. Journal of Traumatic Stress, 7, 75-82.

Watts-Jones, D. (1990). Toward a stress scale for African-American women. Psychology of Women Quarterly, 14, 271-275.

Weathers, F.W., Huska, J.A., & Keane, T.M. (1991). The PTSD Checklist - Military Version (PCL-M). Boston, MA: National Center for PTSD.

Webster-Stratton, C. & Herbert, M. (1993). What really happens in parent training? Behavior Modification, 17, 407-456.

Weisaeth, L. (1985). Post-traumatic stress disorder after an industrial disaster. In P. Pichot et al. (Eds.), Psychiatry - The state of the art. New York: Plenum Press.

Weisaeth, L. & Eitinger, L. (1991). Research on PTSD and other post-traumatic reactions: European literature (Parts I and II) PTSD Research Quarterly 2, Nos. 2 & 3; 1-7.

Weiss, D.S., Horowitz, M.J., & Wilner, N. (1984). The Stress Response Rating Scale: A clinician's measure for rating the response to serious life events. British Journal of Clinical Psychology, 23, 202-215.

Weiss, R.L., Hops, H., & Patterson, G.R. (1973). A framework for conceptualizing marital conflict, a technology for altering it and some data for evaluating it. In L.A. Hamerlynck, L.C. Handy, & E.J. Mash (Eds.), Behavior change: Methodology, concepts, and practice. Champaign, Il: Research Press.

Weissman, M.M. (1991). Panic disorder: Impact on quality of life. Journal of Clinical Psychiatry, 52, 6-8.

Weissman, M.M., & Bothwell, S. (1976). Assessment of social adjustment by patient self-report. Archives of General Psychiatry, 33, 1111-1115.

Weissman, M.M., & Paykel, E.S. (1974). The depressed woman: A study of social relationships. Chicago, IL: University of Chicago Press.

Wolfe, J., & Charney, D.S. (1991). Use of neuropsychological assessment in postraumatic stress disorder. Psychological Assessment, 3, 573-580.

Wolfe, J., Keane, T.M., Lyons, J.A., & Gerardi, R.J. (1987). Current trends and issues in the assessment of combat-related post-traumatic stress disorder. The Behavior Therapist, 10, 27-32.

Wolpe, J. (1973). The practice of behavior therapy. New York: Pergamon.

Steinberg, M. (1993). Structured Clinical Interview of DSM-IV Dissociative Disorders (SCDID-D). Washington, D.C.: American Psychiatric Press.

Steinberg, M., Rounsaville, B., & Cichetti, D.V. (1990). The Structured Clinical Interview for DSM-III-R Dissociative Disorders: Preliminary report on a new diagnostic interview. American Journal of Psychiatry, 147, 76-82.

Steinberg, M., Rounsaville, B., et al. (1992). The mini-structured clinical interview for DSM-IV dissociative disorders. Unpublished manuscript, Yale University.

Straus, M.A. (1979). Measuring intrafamily conflicts and violence: The Conflict Tactics (CT) Scales. Journal of Marriage and Family, 41, 75-88.

Straus, M.A. (1990). The Conflict Tactics Scale and its Critics: An evaluation and new data on validity and reliability. In M.A. Straus & R.J. Gelles, (Eds.), Physical violence in American families. New Brunswick: Transaction Publication.

Streiner, D.L. (1993). A checklist for evaluating the usefulness of rating scales. Canadian Journal of Psychiatry, 38, 140-148.

Stretch, R.H. (1991). Psychosocial readjustment of Canadian Vietnam veterans. Journal of Consulting and Clinical Psychology, 39, 188-189.

Stuart, M.R. & Lieberman, J.A. (1986). The fifteen minute hour. New York: Preager.

Swartz, M., Hughes, D., et al. (1986). Developing a screening index for community studies of somatization disorder. Journal of Psychiatric Research, 20, 335-343.

Tallis, F., Eysenck, M., & Mathews, A. (1992). A questionnaire for the measurement of nonpathological worry. Personality and Individual Differences, 13, 161-168.

Tambs, K., & Moum, T. (1993). How well can a few questionnaire items indicate anxiety and depression? Acta Psychiatry Scandinavia, 87, 364-367.

Tanaka-Matsumi, J., & Higginbotham, V.N. (1994). Clinical application of behavior therapy across ethnic and cultural boundaries. The Behavior Therapist, 17, 123-126.

Taylor, G.J., Bagby, R.M. et al. (1990). Validation of the alexithymia construct: A measurement-based approach. Canadian Journal of Psychiatry, 35, 390-297.

Taylor, J.J., Ryan, D.P., & Bagby, B.M. Toward the development of a new self-report alexithymia scale. Psychotherapy and Psychosomatics, 44, 191-199.

Thompson, S.C. (1985). Finding positive meaning in a stressful event and coping. Basic and Applied Social Psychology, 6, 275-285.

Thrasher, S.M., Dalgeish, T., & Yule, W. (1994). Information processing in post-traumatic stress disorder. Behaviour Research and Therapy, 32, 247-254.

Tobin, D.L., Holroyd, K.A., & Reynolds, R.V. (1984). User's manual for the coping strategies inventory. Unpublished manuscript, Ohio University, Department of Psychology, Athens.

Tolman, R. (1989). The development of a measure of psychological maltreatment of women by their male partners. Violence and Victims, 4, 159-177.

Tomm, K. (1985). Application of systematic family therapy. New York: Grane & Stratton.

Trepper, T.S., & Barrett, M.J. (1989). Systemic family treatment of incest. New York: Brunner/Mazel.

Uddo, M., Vasterling, J.J., Bradey, K., & Sutker, P.B. (1993). Memory and attention in combat-related post-traumatic sterse disorder (PTSD). Journal of Psychopathology and Behaviorial Assessment, 15, 43-52.

Van der Kolk, B.A., Pelcoviz, D., Roth, S., & Mandel, f. (in press). Disorders of Extreme Stress: Results of the DSM-IV field trials for PTSD. British Journal Psychiatry.

van der Kolk, B.A., Perry, J.C., & Herman, J.L. (1991). Childhood origins of self-destructive behavior. American Journal of Psychiatry, 148, 1665-1671.

Vanderlinden, J., Van Dyck, R., Vertommen, H., & Vandereycken, W. (1992). Development and characteristics of a dissociation questionnaire. Nederlands Tijdschrift voor Psychologie, 47, 134-147.

Vanderlinden, J., VanDyck, R. et al. (1991). Dissociative experiences in the general population: A study with the Dissociation Questionnaire (DES-Q). Dissociation, 4, 180-184.

Veronen, L.J., & Kilpatrick, D.G. (1980). Self-reported fears of rape victims: A preliminary investigation. Behavior Modification, 4, 383-396.

References

Possible Iatrogenesis and Memory:
Some Cautionary Observations

Berliner, L., & Williams, L.M. (1994). Memories of child sexual abuse: A response to Lindsay and Read. Applied Cognitive Psychology, 8, 379-387.

Bliss, E.L. (1986). Multiple personality, allied disorders and hypnosis. New York: Oxford University Press.

Brewin, C. R., Andrews, B., & Gotlib, I. H., (1993). Psychopathology and early experience. Psychological Bulletin, 113, 82-98.

Briere, J., & Conte, J. (1993). Self-reported amnesia for abuse in adults molested as children. Journal of Traumatic Stress, 6, 21-31.

Bruhn, A.R. (1990). Earliest childhood memories: Vol 1. Theory and application to clinical practice. New York: Praeger.

Ceci, S.J., & Bruck, M. (1993). Suggestibility of the child witness: A historical review and synthesis. Psychological Bulletin, 113, 403-439.

Dirkstem, L.J., Hinz, L.D., & Spencer, E. (1991). Treatment of sexually abused children and adolescents. In A. Tasman & S.M. Goldfinger (Eds.), Review of psychiatry: Vol 10. Washington, DC: American Psychiatric Press.

Femina, D.D., Yaeger, C.A., & Lewis, D.O. (1990). Child abuse: Adolescent records vs. adult recall. Child Abuse and Neglect, 14, 227-231.

Freyd, J.J. (1994). Betrayal trauma: Traumatic amnesia as an adaptive response to childhood. Ethics and Behavior, 4, 1-30.

Ganaway, G.K. (1989). Historical versus narrative truth: Clarifying the role of exogenous trauma in the etiology of MPD and its variants. Dissociation, 2, 205-220.

Gold, S.N., Hughes, & Hohnecker, L. (1994). Degrees of repression of sexual abuse memory. American Psychologist, 49, 441-442.

Goldstein, E., & Farmer, K. (1992). Confabulations: Creating false memories – Destroying families. Boca Raton, FL: SIRS Books.

Greaves, G.B. (1992). Alternative hypotheses regarding claims of satanic cult activity: A critical analysis. In D. Salzheim & S. Devine (Eds.), Out of darkness: Exploring satanism and ritual abuse. Toronto: Maxwell Macmillan.

Haugaard, J.J., Reppucci, N.D., Laird, J., & Nauful, T. (1991). Children's definitions of the truth and their competency as witnesses in legal proceedings. Law and Human Behavior, 15, 253-271.

Herman, J. L., & Schatzow, E. (1987). Recovery and verification of memories of childhood sexual trauma. Psychoanalytic Psychology, 4, 1-14.

Holmes, D. (1990). The evidence for repression: An examination of sixty years of research. In J. Singer (Ed.), Repression and dissociation: Implications for personality theory, psychopathology and health. Chicago: University of Chicago Press.

Howes, M., Siegel, M., & Brown, F. (1993). Early childhood memories: Accuracy and affect. Cognition, 47, 95-119.

Johnson, M.K., Hashtroudi, S., & Lindsay, D.S. (1993). Source monitoring. Psychological Bulletin, 114, 3-28.

Jones, P.H. (1992). Interviewing the sexually abused child. London: Gaskell.

Kihlstrom, J.F. (1993). The recovery of memory in the laboratory and clinic. Unpublished manuscript, Yale University.

Loftus, E.F. (1993). The reality of repressed memories. American Psychologist, 48, 518-537.

Merskey, H. (1992). The manufacture of personalities: The production of multiple personality disorder. British Journal of Psychiatry, 160, 327-340.

Ofshe, R.J. (1992). Inadvertent hypnosis during interrogation: False confession due to dissociative state: Mis-identified multiple personality and the satanic cult hypothesis. The International Journal of Clinical and Experimental Hypnosis, 40(3), 125-156.

Woody, G.E., Cottler, L.B., & Cacciola, J. (1993). Severity of dependence. Data from the DSM-IV field trials. Addiction, 88, 1573-1579.

World Health Organization (1990). Composite International Diagnostic Interview (CIDI). Version 10. Geneva, WHO.

Yarrow, M.R., Campbell, J.D., & Barton, R.V. (1970). Recollections of childhood: A study of retrospective method. Monograph of the Society for Research in Child Development, 138-305 (5). Washington, DC: National Institute of Mental Health.

Yeung, A.S., Lyons, M.J., et al. (1993). The relationship between DSM-III Personality Disorders and the Five Factor Model of personality. Comprehensive Psychiatry, 34, 227-234.

Zanarini, M.C., Gunderson, J.G., & Frankenberg, F.R. (1989). The revised diagnostic interview for borderlines. Journal of Personality Disorders, 3, 10-18.

Zeitlin, S.B., McNally, R.J., & Cassiday, K.L. (1993). Alexithymia in victims of sexual assault: An effect of repeated traumatization. American Journal of Psychiatry, 150, 661-663.

Zilberg, N.J., Weiss, D.S., & Horowitz, M. (1982). Impact of Events Scale: A cross-validation study. Journal of Consulting and Clinical Psychology, 50, 407-414.

Zimering, R. Caddell, F.M., Fairbank, J.A., & Keane, T.M. (1993). Post-traumatic stress disorder in Vietnam veterans: An experimental validation of the DSM-III diagnostic criteria. Journal of Traumatic Stress, 6, 327-342.

Zimmerman, M. (1994). Diagnosing personality disorders. Archives of general psychiatry, 51, 225-245.

Zuckerman, M., Lubin, B., et al. (1964). Measurement of experimentally-induced affects. Journal of Consulting and Clinical Psychology, 28, 418-421.

Zung, W.W. (1975). A rating instrument for anxiety disorders. Psychometrics, 12, 371-379.

References

Alcoholism and Other Addictions

Assessment of Drinking Behavior

Allen, J.P., & Litten, R.Z. (1993). Psychometric and laboratory measures to assist in the treatment of alcoholism. Clinical Psychology Review, 13, 223-239.

Allsop, S., & Saunders, B. (1989). The effectiveness of relapse programmes. In B.F. Grenyer and N. Solowy (Eds.), National Drug and Alcohol Research Centre: Cognitive behavioral approaches to the treatment of drug and alcohol problems. Sydney: University of New South Wales.

Annis, H.M. (1982). Situational Confidence Questionnaire. Toronto: Addiction Research Foundation.

Babor, T.F., Korner, P. Wilber, C., & Good, S.P. (1987). Screening and intervention strategies for harmful drinkers: Initial lessons from the Amethyst Project. Australian Drug and Alcohol Review, 48, 410-424.

Barbor, T.F., Kranzler, H.R., Lauerman, R.J. (1989). Early detection of harmful alcohol consumption: Comparison of clinical laboratory and self-report screening procedures. Addictive Behaviors, 14, 139-157.

Brown, S.A., Goldman, M.S., Inn, A., & Anderson, L.R. (1980). Expectations of reinforcement from alcohol: Their domain and relation to drinking patterns. Journal of Consulting and Clinical Psychology, 48, 419-426.

Burling, I.A., Reilly, P.M. Moltzen, J.O. & Ziff, D.C. (1989). Self-efficacy among inpatient drug and alcohol abusers: A predictor of outcomes. Journal of Studies on Alcohol, 50, 354-360.

Buschbaum, D.G., Buchanan, R.G., Centor, R.M., Schnoll, S.N., & Lawton, M.J. (1991). Screening for alcohol abuse using CAGE scores and likelihood ratios. Annals of Internal Medicine, 115, 774-777.

Carroll, J. (1983). Substance abuse problem checklist. Eagleville, PA: Eagleville Hospital.

Claussen, B., & Asland, O.G. (1993). The Alcoholism Use Disorders Identification Test (AUDIT) in a routine health examination of long-term unemployed. Addiction, 88, 363-368.

Colligan, R.C., Davis, L.J., & Morse, R.M. (1988). The self-administered alcoholism screening test (SAAST): A user's guide. Dept. of Psychiatry and Psychology, Mayo Clinic, Rochester, Minnesota 55905, (507) 284-2944.

Collins, R.L., & Lapp, W.M. (1992). The Temptation and Restraint Inventory for measuring drinking restraint. British Journal of Addictions, 87, 625-633.

Collins, R.L., Parks, G.A., & Marlatt, G.A. (1985). Social determinants of alcohol consumption: The effects of social interactions and model status on the self-administrator of alcohol. Journal of Consulting and Clinical Psychology, 53, 189-200.

DiClemente, C.C., & Hughes, S.O. (1990). Stages of change profiles in outpatient alcoholism treatment. Journal of Substance Abuse, 2, 217-235.

Drummond, O.C. (1990). The relationship between alcohol dependence and alcohol related problems in a clinicl population. British Journal of Addictions, 85, 357-366.

Embree, B.G., & Whitehead, P.C. (1993). Validity and reliability of self-reported drinkingbehavior: Dealing with the problem of response bias. Journal of Studies of Alcohol, May, 334-344.

Ende, L.E. (1991). Management of alcohol withdrawal syndrome with selected PRN medications. The Provider, November, 168-171.

Ewing, J.A. (1984). Detecting alcoholism: The CAGE questionnaire. Journal of the American Medical Association, 252, 1905-1907.

Frisch, M.B., Cornell, J., Villanueva, M. & Retzlaff, P.J. (1992). Clinical validation of the Quality of Life Inventory: A measure of life satisfaction for use in treatment planning and outcome assessment. Psychological Assessment, 4, 92-101.

Pyncos, R.S., & Nader, K. (1989). Children's memory and proximity to violence. Journal of the American Academy of Child and Adolescent Psychiatry, 28, 236-241.

Reich, W. (1994). The monster in the mists. The New York Times Book Review, May 15.

Rogers, M.L. (Ed.) (1992). Special Issue: Satanic ritual abuse: The current state of knowledge. Psychology and Theology, 20(1).

Ross, M. (1993). Validating memory. Paper presented at conference on Memory for Everyday and Emotional Events, University of Chicago. (University of Waterloo, Ontario, Unpublished manuscript).

Russell, D. (1986). The secret trauma: Incest in the lives of girls and women. New York: Basic Books.

Sales, B.D., Shuman, D.W., & O'Connor, M. (1994). In ta dim light: Admissibility of child sexual abuse memories. Applied Cognitive Psychology, 8, 399-406.

Schwarz, N., & Sudman, S. (1994). Autobiographical memory and the validity of retrospective reports. New York: Springer-Verlag.

Tavris, C. (1993). Beware the incest-survivor machine. New York Times Book Review, January 3. (Also see the replies--letters in the January 10 issue).

Terr, L. (1988). What happens to early memories of trauma? A study of twenty children under age five at the time of documented traumatic events. Journal of American Academy of Child and Adolescent Psychiatry, 27, 96-104.

Terr, L.C. (1991) Childhood traumas: An outline and overview. American Journal of Psychiatry, 148, 10-20.

Terr, L. (1994). Unchained memories. New York: Basic Books.

Usher, J.A., & Neisser, U. (1993). Childhood amnesia and the beginnings of memory for four early life events. Journal of Experimental Psychology: General, 122, 155-165

Waganaar, W.A., & Groeneweed, J. (1990). Memory of concentration camp survivors. Applied Cognitive Psychology, 4, 77-87.

Wakefield, H., & Underwager, R. (1992). Recovered memories of alleged sexual abuse: Lawsuits against parents. Behavioral Sciences and the Law, 10, 483-507.

Weissberg, M. (1993). Multiple personality disorder and iatrogenesis: The cautionary tale of Anna O. International Journal of Clincial and Experimental Hypnosis, 41, 15-34.

Williams, L. M. (1992). Adult memories of childhood abuse: Preliminary findings from a longitudinal study. The Advisor, 19-21.

Wright, L. (1993). Remembering Satan - Part I and II. The New Yorker. May 17 and May 24.

Wright, L. (1994). Remembering Satan. New York: Knopf

Yapko, M.D. (1994). Suggestions of abuse. New York: Simon & Schuster.

Yates, A. (1991). False and mistaken allegations of sexual abuse. In A. Tasman & S.M. Goldfinger (Eds.), Review of psychiatry: Vol 10. Washington, DC: American Psychiatric Press.

Yates, J.L., & Nasby, W. (1993). Dissociation, affect, and network models of memory: An integrative proposal. Journal of Traumatic Stress, 6, 305-326.

Rounsaville, F.J., Bryant, K., Babor, T., Kranzler, H., & Kadden, R. (1993). Cross system agreement for substance use disorders. DSM-III-R, DSM-IV, and ICD-10. Addiction, 88, 337-348. (Copies of the composit structured interview and accompanying scoring algorithms are available from Bruce Rounsaville, Yale University School of Medicine, Substance Abuse Treatment Unit, 27 Sylvan Ave, New Haven, 06519).

Schmidt, P.M. & Cooney, N.L. (1992). Implementing an alcohol screening program. The Behavior Therapist, 15, 192-195.

Selzer, M.L. (1971). The Michigan Alcoholism Screening Test (MAST): The quest for a new diagnostic instrument. American Journal of Psychiatry, 127, 1653-1658.

Skinner, H. A. (1992). The drug abuse screening test. Addictive Behaviors, 7, 363-371.

Skinner, H. A., & Allen, B. A. (1982). Alcohol dependence syndrome: Measurement and validation. Journal of Abnormal Psychology, 91, 199-209.

Skinner, H.A., & Horn, J.L. (1984). Alcohol Dependence Scale user's guide. Toronto: Addiction Research Foundation.

Stockwell, T., Hodgson, R., Edwards, G., Taylor, C., & Rankin, H. (1979). The development of a questionnaire to measure severity of alcohol dependence. British Journal of Addictions, 74, 87-89.

Swenson, W.M., & Morse, R.M. (1975). The use of a self-administered alcoholism screening test (SAAST). Mayo Clinic Proceedings, 50, 214-218.

Thiagarajan, S. (1989). The role of efficacy expectations in the treatment of drug and alcohol problems. In B.F. Grenyer and N. Solovij (Eds.), National Drug and Alcohol Research Centre Monograph 7: Cognitive-behavioural approaches to the treatment of drug and alcohol problems. Sydney: University of New South Wales.

Wanberg, R., Horn, J., & Foster, E. (1977). A differential assessment model of alcoholism: The scales of the alcohol use inventory. Journal of Studies of Alcohol, 38, 512-543.

White, H.Rl., & Laborive, E.W. (1989). Towards the assessment of problem drinking. Journal of Studies on Alcohol, 50, 30-37.

Weick, A., Ropp, C., Sullivan, W.P., & Kisthardt, W. (1989). A strengths perspective for social work practice. Social work, 34, 350-354.

Young, R.McD., & Knight, R.G. (1989). The Drinking Expectancy Questionnaire: A revised measure of alcohol related beliefs. Journal of Psychopathology and Behavioral Assessment, 11, 99-112.

Young, R.McD., Oei, T.P., & Crook, G.M. (1991). Development of a drinking self-efficacy questionnaire. Journal of Psychology and Behavioral Assessment, 13, 1-15.

Cognitive, Motivational and Social Correlates of Drinking Alcohol

Amodea, M., & Kurz, N. (1990). Cognitive processes and abstinence in a treated alcoholic population. International Journal of Addictions, 25, 983-109.

Baumeister, R. (1991). Escaping the self. New York: Basic Books.

Gorman, D.M., & Brown, G.W. (1992). Recent developments in life-event research and their relevance for the study of addictions. British Journal of Addictions, 87, 837-849.

Gorski, T., & Miller, M. (1982). Counseling for release prevention. Independence, Mo.: Independence Press.

Ludwig, A. (1985). Cognitive processes associated with "spontaneous" recovery from alcoholism. Journal of Studies of Alcoholism, 46, 53-58.

Ludwig, A.M. (1988). Understanding the alcoholic's mind: The nature of craving and how to control it. New York: Oxford University Press.

Miller, W.R. & Rollnick, S. (Eds.) (1991). Motivational interviewing: Preparing people to change addictive behaviors. New York: Guilford.

Miller, W.R. (1985). Motivation for treatment: A review with special emphasis on alcoholism. Psychological Bulletin, 98, 84-107.

Fromme, K., Kivlaken, D.R., & Marlatt, G.M. (1986). Alcohol expectancies, risk identification and secondary prevention with problem drinkers. Advances in Behaviour Research and Therapy, 8, 237-251.

Grant, B.F. (1992). Prevalence of the proposed DSM-IV alcohol use disorders: United States, 1988. British Journal of Addiction, 87, 309-316.

Greenfield, T.K. (1986). Quantity per occasion and consequences of drinking: A reconsideration and recommendation. International Journal of Addictions, 21, 1059-1079.

Guydish, J., & Greenfield, T.K. (1990). Alcohol-related cognitions: Do they predict treatment outcome? Addictive Behaviors, 15, 423-430.

Hurt, R.D., Morse, R., Swanson, W.M. (1980). Diagnosis of alcoholism with a self-administered alcoholism screening test.

Jellinek, E.M. (1952). Phases of alcohol addiction. Quarterly Journal of Studies of Alcohol, 13, 673-684.

Leonard, K.E., & Blane, H.T. (1992). Alcohol and marital aggression in a national sample of young men. Journal of Interpersonal Violence, 7, 19-30.

Mann, R.E., Sobell, L.C., et al. (1985). Reliability of a family tree questionnaire for assessing family history of alcohol problems. Drug and Alcohol Dependence, 15, 61-67.

Mayer, J., & Filstead, W.J. (1979). Adolescent Alcohol Involvement Scale (AAIS). Journal of Studies on Alcohol, 40, 291-300.

McLellan, A.T., Erdlen, F.R., Erdlen, D.L., & O'Brien, C.P. (1981). Psychological severity and response to alcoholism rehabilitation. Drug and Alcohol Dependence, 8, 23-35.

Miller, P.J., Ross, S., Emmerson, R.Y., & Todt, E.H. (1989). Self-efficacy in alcoholics: Clinical validation of the Situational Confidence Questionnaire. Addictive Behaviors, 14, 217-229.

Miller, W.R. (1983). Motivational interviewing with problem drinkers. Behavioural Psychotherapy, 11, 147-172.

Miller, W.R., & Marlatt, G.A. (1984). Manual for the comprehensive drinker profile. Odessa, Florida: Psychological Resources.

Miller, W.R., & Marlatt, G.A. (1984). The Comprehensive Drinker Profile. Psychological Assessment Resources, P.O.Box 98, Odessa, Florida, 33556. There are a number of follow-ups and related measures by these authors and by Miller and his colleagues.

Miller, W.R., Sovereign, R.G., & Krege, B. (1988). Motivational interviewing with problem drinkers II: The drinker's checkup is a preventive intervention. Behavioral Psychology, 16, 251-268.

Poplin, C., Kannenberg, C., Lacey, J., & Waller, P. (1988). Assessment of classification instruments designed to detect alcohol abuse. US Dept. of Transportation, Washington.

Prochaska, J.O., & DiClemente, G.C. (1986). Toward a comprehensive model of change. In W.R. Miller and N. Heather (Eds.), Treating addictive behaviors: Processes of change. New York: Plenum Press.

Radert, E.R., (Ed.) (1991). The adolescent assessment/referral system manual. US Dept. Health and Human Services: ADAMHA: US Govt. Printing Office.

Robins, L.N., Helzer, J.E., Croughan, J., & Ratcliff, K.S. (1981). National Institute of Mental Health Diagnostic Interview Schedule: Its history, characteristics and validity. Archives of General Psychiatry, 38, 381-389.

Robins, L.N., Helzer, J.E., Ratcliff, K.S., & Seyfried, W. (1982). Validity of the Diagnostic Interview Schedule, Version II: DSM-III diagnosis. Psychological Medicine, 12, 855-870.

Rollnick, S., Heather, N., Gold, R., & Hall, W. (1992). Development of a short readiness to change questionnaire for use in brief, opportunistic interventions among excessive drinkers. British Journal of Addiction, 87, 743-754.

Roosa, M.W., Sandler, I.N., Gehring, M., Beals, J., & Cappo, L. (1988). The children of alcoholics life-events schedule: A stress scale for children of alcohol-abusing parents. Journal of Studies on Alcohol, 49, 422-429.

Kopp (1971). Guru: Metaphors from psychotherapist. Palo Alto: Science and Behavior Books.

Lindstrom, L. (1992). Managing alcoholism: Matching clients to treatment. London: Oxford University Press.

Mallams, J.H., Godley, M.D., Hall, G.M., & Meyers, R.A. (1982). A social systems approach to resocializing alcoholics in the community. Journal of Studies on Alcohol 43, 1115-1123.

Marlatt, G.A. & Fromme, K. (1988). Metaphors for addiction. In S. Peele (Ed.), Visions of addiction. Lexington, Mass: Lexington Books.

Marlatt, G.A., Larimer, M.E., et al. (1993). Harm reduction for alcohol problems: Moving beyond the controlled drinking controversy. Behavior Therapy, 24, 461-504.

McAuliffe, W. E., & Chien, J. M. (1986). Recovery training and self-help: A relapse prevention program for treatment of addicts. Journal of Substance Abuse Treatment 3, 9-20.

McCrady, B.S. (1989). Extending relapse prevention models to couples. Addictive Behavior, 14, 69-74.

Meyer, R. and Institute of Medicine (1992). Prevention and treatment of alcohol-related problems: Research opportunities. Journal of Studies on Alcohol, 53, 5-16.

Miller, L. (1990). The formal treatment contract in the inpatient management of borderline personality disorder. Hospital and Community Psychiatry, 41, 985-987.

Miller, W.R. & Hester, R.K. (1980). The effectiveness of alcoholism treatment: What research reveals. In W.R. Miller and N.K. Heather (Eds.), Treating addictive behaviors: Processes of change. New York: Plenum.

Miller, W.R., & Hester, K. (1986). Inpatient alcoholism treatment. American Psychologist, 41, 749-805.

Miller, W.R, Leckman, A.L., Delancy, H.D., & Tinkcim, M. (1992). Long term followup of behavioral self-control training. Journal of Studies in Alcohol 83, 249-261.

O'Farrell, T.J. (1989). Marital and family therapy in alcoholism treatment. Journal of Substance Abuse and Treatment 6, 23-29.

O'Farrell, T.J. (Ed.), (1994). Treating alcohol problems: Marital and family interventions. New York: Guilford.

O'Farrell, T.J., Choquette, K.A. et al. (1993). Behavioral marital therapy with and without additional couples relapse prevention sessions for alcoholics and their wives. Journal of Studies of Alcohol 54, 652-666.

Peele, S. (1989). Diseasing of America: Addiction treatment out of control. Lexington, MA: Lexington Books.

Peele, S. (1991). What works in addiction treatment and what doesn't: Is the best therapy no therapy? International Journal of Addictions, 25, 1409-1419.

Romig, C.A., & Gruenke, C. (1991). The use of metaphor to overcome inmate resistance to mental health counseling. Journal of Counseling and Development, 69, 414-418.

Rosenberg, H. (1993). Prediction of controlled drinking by alcoholics and problem drinkers. Psychological Bulletin, 113, 129-139.

Sandiez-Craig, M., & Wilkinson, D.A. (1987). Treating problem drinkers who are not severely dependent on alcohol. In M. Sobell & C. Sobell (Eds.), Drugs and society. New York: Haworth Press.

Sisson, R.W., & Azrin, N.H. (1989). The community reinforcement approach. In R.K. Hester & W.R. Miller (Eds.), Handbook of alcoholism treatment approaches: Effective alternatives. New York: Pergamon.

Sullivan, W.P., Wolk, J.L., & Hartman, D.J. (1992). Case management in alcohol and drug treatment: Improving client outcomes. Families in Society: Journal of Contemporary Human Services, 21, 195-203.

Thom, B., Brown, C., Drummond, C., Edwards, G., Mullan, M., & Taylor, C. (1992). Engaging patients with alcohol problems in treatment: The first consultation. British Journal of Addiction, 87, 601-611.

Tucker, J.A., Vuchinich, R.E., & Downey, K.K. (1992). Substance abuse. In S.M. Turner, K.J. Calhoun and H.E. Adams (Eds.), Handbook of clinical behavior therapy. New York: Wiley.

Steele, C.M., & Josephs, R.A. (1990). Alcohol myopia: Its prized and dangerous effects. American Psychologist, 45, 921-933.

Vaillant, G., & Milofsky, E. (1982). Natural history of male alcoholism. Archives of General Psychiatry, 39, 127-133.

Weist, M.O., & Prinz, R.J. (1987). Parental alcoholism and childhood psychopathology. Psychological Bulletin, 102, 204-218.

Relapse Prevention Model

Beer, J.S., Marlatt, G.A., Kivlahan, D.R., Fromme, K., Larimer, M. & Williams, E. (in press). An experimental test of three methods of alcohol risk-reduction with young adults. Journal of Consulting and Clinical Psychology.

Brownell, K.D., Marlatt, G.A., Lichtenstein, E., & Wilson, G.T. (1986). Understanding and preventing relapse. American Psychologist 41, 765-782.

Chaney, E.F., O'Leary, M.R., & Marlatt, G.A. (1978). Skill training with alcoholics. Journal of Consulting and Clinical Psychology, 46, 1092-1104.

Kivlahan, D.R., Marlatt, G.A., Fromme, K., Coppel, D.B., & Williams, E. (1990). Secondary prevention with college drinkers: Evaluation of an alcohol skills training program. Journal of Consulting and Clinical Psychology, 58, 805-810.

Marlatt, G.A., & George, W.H. (1984). Relapse prevention: Introduction and overview of the model. British Journal of Addiction, 79, 261-273.

Marlatt, A., & Gordon, J. (1985). Relapse prevention: Maintenance strategies in the treatment of addictive behaviors. New York: Guilford Press.

Nathan, P.E., & Skinstad, A. (1987). Outcomes of treatment for alcohol problems: Current methods, problems and results. Journal of Consulting and Clinical Psychology, 55, 332-340.

Sanchez-Craig, M., Annis, H.M., Bornet, A.R., & MacDonald, K.R. (1984). Random assignment to abstinence and controlled drinking: Evaluation of a cognitive-behavioral program for problem disorders. Journal of Consulting and Clinical Psychology, 52, 390-403.

Wilson, G.T. (1987). Cognitive studies in alcoholism. Journal of Consulting and Clinical Psychology, 55, 325-331.

Treatment of Alcoholism

Barker, G. (1985). Using metaphors in psychotherapy. New York: Brunner/Mazel.

Botvin, G.J., Baker, & Dusenbury, L., Torru, S., & Botvin, G.M. (1990). Preventing adolescent drug abuse through multimodal cognitive-behavioral approach: Results of a 3-year study. Journal of Consulting and Clinical Psychology 58, 437-447.

Botvin, G.J., & Wills, T.A. (1985). Personal and social skills training: Cognitive-behavioral approaches to substance abuse prevention. In C. Bell and R. Battjis (Eds.), Cognitive-behavioral Prevention research. Deterring drug use among children and adolescents. NIDA Research Monograph, Washington, D.C.

Brickman, P., Rabinowitz, V.C., Karuza, J., Coates, D., Cohen, S., & Kidder, L. (1982). Models of helping and change. American Psychologist 37, 368-384.

DeJong, W. (1994). Relapse prevention: An emerging technology for promoting long-term drug abstinence. International Journal of Addictions, 29, 681-705.

Heather, N., & Roberson, I. (1981). Controlled drinking. London: Methuen.

Hester, R.K. & Miller, W.R. (Eds.), (1989). Handbook of alcoholism treatment approaches: Effective Alternates. New York: Pergamon.

Hollon, S.D., & Beck, A.T. (1993). Cognitive and cognitive-behavioral therapies. In S.L. Garfield and A.E. Bergin (Eds.), Handbook of psychotherapy and behavior change. An empirical analysis (4th ed.). New York: Wiley.

Hunt, G.M., & Azrin, N.H. (1973). A community reinforcement approach to alcoholism. Behaviour Research and Therapy, 13, 1115-1123.

References

Post-Traumatic Stress Disorder (PTSD) - Children and Adolescents

Alexander, P.C. (1992). Introduction to special section on adult survivors of childhood sexual abuse. Journal of Consulting and Clinical Psychology, 60, 165-166. (See entire issue.)

Amaya-Jackson, L. & March, J. (1993). Post traumatic stress disorder in children and adolescents. In H.L. Leonard (Ed.). Child psychiatric clinics of North America: Anxiety disorders. New York: Saunders.

Ayalon, O. (1983). Coping with terrorism: The Israeli Case. In D. Meichenbaum and M. Jaremko (Eds.), Stress reduction and prevention. New York: Plenum.

Beitchman, J.H., Zucker, K.J., Hood, J.E., DaCosta, G.A., Akman, D., & Cassavia, E. (1992). A review of the long-term effects of child sexual abuse. Child Abuse and Neglect, 16, 105-118.

Belter, R.W., & Shannon, M.P. (1993). Impact of natural disasters on children and families. In C.F. Saylor (Eds.), Children and disasters. New York: Plenum Press.

Benedick, E.P. (1985). Children and disaster: Emerging issues. Psychiatry Annals, 15, 168-172.

Bergner, R. M., Delgado, L. K., & Graybell, D. Finkelhor's risk factor checklist: A cross validation study. Child Abuse and Neglect, 18, 331-340.

Black, D. (1982). Children and disaster. British Medical Journal, 285, 989-990.

Blom, G. (1986). A school disaster: Intervention and research aspects. Journal of the American Academy of Child Psychiatry, 25, 336-345.

Briere, J.N. (1992). Child abuse trauma: Theory and treatment of the lasting effects. Newbury Park, CA: Sage.

Brooks, R. (1981). Creative characters: A technique in child therapy. Psychotherapy, 18, 131-139.

Cahill, C., Llewelyn, S.P., & Pearson, C. (1991). Long-term effects of sexual abuse which occurred in childhood: A review. British Journal of Clinical Psychology, 30, 117-130.

Caplan, N., Whitemore, J.K., & Choy, M.H. (1989). The boat people and achievement in America. Ann Arbor: University of Michigan Press.

Cicchetti, D., & Lynch, M. (1993). Toward an ecological/transactional model of community violence and child maltreatment: Consequences for children's development. Psychiatry, 56, 96-117 (See Psychiatry 1993 Issue on Children and Violence).

Cole, P. M., & Putman, F. W. (1994). Effect of incest on self and social functioning: A developmental psychopathology perspective. Journal of Consulting and Clinical Psychology, 60, 174-184.

Davis, N. (1990). Once upon a time... Therapeutic stories to heal abused children. Published by Psychological Associates of Oxon Hill, 6178 Oxon Hill Road, Suite 306, Oxon Hill, Maryland 20745 (Telephone 301-567-9297).

Deblinger, E., McLeer, S.V., & Henry, D. (1990). Cognitive behavioral treatment of sexually abused children suffering post-traumatic stress: Preliminary findings. Journal of American Academy of Child and Adolescent Psychiatry, 29, 747-752.

Doris, J. (Ed.) (1993). The suggestibility of children's recollections: Implications for eyewitness testimony. Washington, D.C.: APA Books.

Dyregrov, A., & Mitchell, J.T. (1992). Working with traumatized children: Psychological effects and coping strategies. Journal of Traumatic Stress, 5, 5-17.

Elliott, A.N., O'Donohue, W.T., & Nickerson, M.N. (1993). The use of sexually anatomically detailed dolls in the assessment of sexual abuse. Clinical Psychology Review, 13, 207-222.

Wallace, B.C. (1989). Relapse prevention in psychoeducational groups for compulsive crack cocaine smokers. Journal of Substance Abuse Treatment, 6, 229-239.

Whisman, M.A. (1990). The efficacy of booster maintenance sessions in behavior therapy: Clinical Psychology Review, 10, 155-170.

Attrition

Baekeland, F., & Lundwall, L. (1975). Dropping out of treatment: A critical review. Psychological Bulletin, 82, 738-783.

Chafetz, M.E., Blane, H.J., & Hill, M.J. (1970). Frontiers of alcoholism. New York: Science House.

Leigh, G., Ogborne, A.C., & Cleland, P. (1984). Factors associated with patient dropout from an outpatient alcoholism treatment service. Journal of Studies in Alcohol, 45, 359-367.

Meichenbaum, D., & Fong, G.T. (1993). How individuals control their own minds: A constructive narrative perspective. In D.M.Wegner and J.W. Pennebaker (Eds.), Handbook of mental control. New York: Prentice Hall.

Meichenbaum, D., & Turk, D.C. (1987). Facilitating treatment adherence: A practitioner's handbook. New York: Plenum.

Stark, M.J. (1992). Dropping out of substance abuse treatment: A clinically oriented review. Clinical Psychology Review, 12, 93-116.

Chemical Treatment of Alcoholism - Naltrexone -- opioid antagonist

Beck, A. T., Wright, F. D., Newman, C. F., & Liese, B. S. (1993). Cognitive therapy of substance abuse. New York: Guilford.

Berg, I. K., & Miller, S. D. (1992). Working with the problem drinker: A solution -focused approach. New York: Norton.

Fals-Stewart, W. (1994). Behavior therapy and the disease model of chemical dependence. The Behavior Therapist, 17, 202-204.

Horvath, A. T. (1994). Comorbidity of addictive behavior and mental disorder: Outpatient practice guidelines (For those who prefer not to treat addictive behavior). Cognitive and Clinical Practice, 1, 93-110.

Institute of Medicine. (1990). Broadening the base of treatment of alcohol problems. Washington, DC: Natural Academy Press.

Miller, S. D. (1994). Some questions (not answers) for the brief treatment of people with drug and alcohol problems. In M. Hoyt (Ed.), Constructive therapies. New York: Guilford.

O'Malley, S.S., Jaffe, A.J., Chang, G., Schottenfeld, R.S., Meyer, R.E., & Rounsaville, B. (1992). Naltrexone and coping skills therapy for alcohol dependence: A controlled study. Archives of General Psychiatry, 49, 881-887.

Volpicelli, J.R., Alterman, A.I., Hayashida, M., & O'Brien, C.P. (1992). Naltrexone in the treatment of alcohol dependence. Archives of General Psychiatry, 49, 876-880.

Relapse Prevention Film

Staying sober -- keeping straight -- Gerald T. Rogers Production, 5225 Old Orchard Road, Suite 23, Skokie, Illinois 60077. (312-967-8080).

Embry, D.D. (1990a). I get support from friends: A story/workbook to help young people of active duty, reserve, and national guard families affected by Desert Storm. Tucson, AZ: Project Me.

Embry, D.D. (1990b). They're coming home: The story/workbook stars your child, and your child cope with problems that might arise when a loved one returns from deployment. Tucson, AZ: Project Me.

Embry, D.D. (1991). They're coming home: A guide for parents and infants and toddlers affected by deployment. Tucson, AZ: Project Me.

Eth, S., & Pynoos, R.S. (Eds.). (1985). Posttraumatic stress disorder in children. Washington, D.C.: American Psychiatric Press.

Finkelhor, D. (1979). Sexually victimized children. New York: Free Press.

Finkelhor, D. (1984). Child sexual abuse: New theory and research. Beverly Hills, CA: Sage.

Finkelhor, D. (1986). A sourcebook on child sexual abuse: New theory and research. Beverly Hills, CA: Sage.

Finkelhor, D. (1994). The international epidemiology of child sexual abuse. Child Abuse and Neglect, 18, 409-417.

Frederick, C. (1985). Children traumatized by catastrophic situations. In S. E. Eth & R. Pynoos (Eds.), Post-traumatic stress disorder in children. Washington DC: American Psychiatric Assoc.

Frederick, C.J. (1985). Children traumatized by catastrophic situations. In S.Eth & R.S. Pynoos (Eds.) Post-traumatic stress disorder in children. Washington, DC: American Psychiatric Press.

Galante, R., & Foa, D. (1986). An epidemiological study of psychic trauma and treatment effectiveness for children after a natural disaster. Journal of Clinical Psychiatry, 25, 357-363.

Garbarino, J., Dubrow, N. Kostelny, K., & Pardo, C. (1992). Children in danger: Coping with the consequences of community violence. San Francisco: Jossey-Bass.

Garbarino, J., Kostelny, K., & Dubrow, N. (1991). What children can tell us about living in danger. American Psychologist, 46, 376-383.

Garrison, E.G. (1987). Psychological maltreatment of children. American Psychologist, 42, 157-159.

Gillis, H.M. (1993). Individual and small-group psychotherapy for children involved in trauma and disaster. In C.F. Saylor (Eds.), Children and disasters. New York: Plenum Press.

Giorretto, H. (1982). A comprehensive child sexual abuse treatment program. Child Abuse and Neglect, 6, 263-278.

Gross, A.B., & Keller, H.R. (1992). Long-term consequences of childhood physical and psychological maltreatment. Aggressive Behavior, 18, 171-185.

Handford, H., Mayes, S., Mattison, R., Humphrey, F., Bagnato, S., Bixler, E., & Kales, J. (1986). Child and parent reaction to Three Mile Island nuclear accident. Journal of the American Academy of Child Psychiatry, 25, 346-356.

Harkness, L. (1991). The effect of combat-related PTSD on children. NCP Clinical Newsletter, 2, 12-13.

Hiley-Young, B., & Giles, S. (1991). Secondary prevention with high risk children in elementary school. NCP Clinical Newsletter, 2, 4-8.

James, B. (1984). Treating traumatized children. Lexington, MA: Lexington Books.

Johnson, K. (1989). Trauma in the lives of children. Claremont, CA: Hunter House.

Kashami, J., Anasserli, E.D., Dandry, A.C., & Holcomb, W.R. (1992). Family violence: Impact on children. Journal of American Academy of Child and Adolescent Psychiatry, 31, 181-189.

Kazdin, A.E. (1992). Child and adolescent dysfunction and paths toward maladjustment: Targets for intervention. Clinical Psychology Review, 12, 795-817.

Kempe, R.S., & Kempe, C.H. (1984). The common secret: Sexual abuse of children and adolescents. New York: W.H. Freeman.

Keppel-Benson, J.M., & Ollendick, T.H. (1993). Posttraumatic stress disorder in children and adolescents. In C.F. Saylor (Ed.), Children and disasters. New York: Plenum Press.

Klingman, A. (1987). A school-based emergency crises intervention in a mass school disaster. Professional Psychology: Research and Practice, 18, 604-612.

Klingman, A. (1992a). School psychology services: Community based first-order crisis intervention during the Gulf War. Psychology in the Schools, 29, 376-384.

Klingman, A. (1992b). Stress reactions of Israeli youth during the Gulf War. A quantitative study. Professional Psychology, 23, 521-527.

Klingman, A. (1993). School-based intervention following a disaster. In C.F. Saylor (Ed.), Children and disasters. New York: Plenum Press.

Klingman, A., & Eli, Z.B. (1981). A school community in disaster: Primary and secondary prevention in situational crises. Professional Psychology, 12, 523-533.

Klingman, A., Koengsfeld, E., & Markman, D. (1987). Art activity with children following disaster: A preventive oriented crisis intervention modality. Arts in Psychotherapy, 14, 153-166.

Kotowitz, A. (1991). There are no children here. New York: Double Day.

Leavitt, L.A., & Fox, N.A. (Eds.) (1992). Psychological effects of war and violence on children. New York: Erlbaum.

Liporsky, J.A. (1992). Assessment and treatment of posttraumatic stress disorder in child survivors of sexual assault. In D.W. Foy (Ed.), Treating PTSD: Cognitive-behavioral strategies. New York: Guilford Press.

Lorion, R.P. (Ed.) (1990). Protecting the children: Strategies for optimizing emotional and behavioral development. New York: Haworth Press.

Lyons, J.A. (1987). Post-traumatic stress disorder in children and adolescents: A review of the literature. Journal of Developmental Behavioral Pediatrics, 8, 349-356.

Lystad, M.H. (1984). Children's responses to disaster: Family implications. International Journal of Family Psychiatry, 5, 41-60.

Malinosky-Rummell, R., & Hansen, D.J., (1993). Long term consequences of childhood physical abuse. Psychological Bulletin, 14, 68-79.

March, J.S., & Amaya-Jackson, L. (1993). Post-traumatic stress disorder in children and adolescents. PTSD Research Quarterly, 4, 1-7.

Martin, H.P., & Beezley, P. (1977). Behavioral observations of abused children. Development of Medical Clinical Neurology, 19, 373-387.

Mason, O. (1990). Why is daddy like he is? A book for kids about PTSD. (Patience Mason, P.O.Box 1517, High Springs, FL, 23643).

McLeer, S.V., Deblinger, E., Atkins, M.S., Foa, E.B., & Ralphe, D.L. (1988). Posttraumatic stress disorder in sexually abused children. Journal of American Academy of Child and Adolescent Psychiatry, 27, 650-684.

Milner, J.S. (1993). Social information processing and physical child abuse. Clinical Psychology Review, 13, 275-294.

Nader, K. (1994). Countertransference in the treatment of acutely traumatized children. In J. P. Wilson, & J. D. Lindy (Eds.), Countertransference in the treatment of PTSD. New York: Guilford.

Parson, E. R. (1994). Inner city children of trauma: Urban violence traumatic stress syndrome (U-VTS) and therapists' responses. In J. P. Wilson, & J. D. Lindy (Eds.), Countertransference in the treatment of PTSD. New York: Guilford.

Pynoos, R.S. Frederick, C., Nader, K., Arroyo, W., Steinberg, A., Eth, S., Nunez, F., & Fairbanks, C. (1987). Life threat and posttraumatic stress in school-age children. Archives of General Psychiatry, 44, 1057-1063.

Reiss, D., Richters, J.E. et al. (Eds.), (1993). Children and violence. New York: Guilford.

Rhue, J.W., & Lynn, S.J. (1991). Story telling, hypnosis, and the treatment of sexually abused children. International Journal of Clinical and Experimental Hypnosis, 39, 198-214.

Rosenblatt, R. (1983). Children at war. Garden City, NJ: Anchor Press.

Rozensky, R.H., Sloan, I.H., Schwarz, E.D., & Kowalski, J.M. (1993). Psychological response of children to shootings and hostage situations. In C.F. Saylor (Ed.), Children and disasters. New York: Plenum Press.

Rubenstein, A., & Embry, D.D. (1990a). How to support our children during Operation Desert Storm. Tucson, AZ: Project Me.

Rubenstein, A., & Embry, D.D. (1990b). They're coming home: Project Me.

Rubenstein, A., & Embry, D.D. (1991). They're coming home: A guide for friends and relatives, schools, employers, co-workers, and the community. Tucson, AZ: Project Me.

Rymer, R. (1993). Genie: An abused child's flight from silence. New York: Harper Collins.

Saigh, P.A. (1987a). In vitro flooding of a childhood post-traumatic disorder. Professional School Psychology Review, 16, 203-211.

Saigh, P.A. (1987b). In vitro flooding on an adolescent's post-traumatic stress disorder. Journal of Clinical Child Psychology, 16, 147-150.

Saigh, P.A. (1989a). The development and validation of the Children's Posttraumatic Stress Disorder Inventory. International Journal of Special Education, 4, 75-84.

Saigh, P.A. (1989b). The use of in vitro flooding in the treatment of traumatized adolescents. Journal of Behavioural and Developmental Pediatrics, 10, 17-21.

Salzinger, S., Feldman, R.S., Hammer, M., & Rosario, M. (1993). The effects of physical abuse on children's social relationships. Child Development, 64, 169-187.

Saylor, C.F. (1993a). Children and disasters: Clinical and research issues. In C.F. Saylor (Ed.), Children and disasters. New York: Plenum Press.

Saylor, C.F. (Ed.) (1993b). Children and disasters. New York: Plenum Press.

Schwarz, e. D., & Perry, B. D. (1994). The post-traumatic response in children and adolescents. In D. A. Tomb (Ed.), The Psychiatric Clinics of North America, 8, 311-326.

Sgroi, S.M. (Ed.) (1982). Handbook of clinical intervention in child sexual abuse. Lexington, MA: D.C. Health.

Shaw, J.A. & Harris, J.J. (1974). Children of war and children at war: Child victims of terrorism in Mozambique. In R. Ursano et al. (Eds.), Trauma and disaster. New York: Cambridge University Press.

Sorenson, T., & Snow, B. (1991). How children tell: The process of disclosure in child sexual abuse. Child Welfare, 70, 3-15.

Spaccarelli, A. (1994). Stress, appraisal and coping in child sexual abuse: A theoretical and empirical review. Psychological Bulletin, 116, 340-362.

Stewart, J. S., Hardin, S. B., et al. (1992). Group protocol to mitigate disaster stress and enhance social support in adolescents exposed to Hurricane Hugo. Issues in Mental Health, 13, 105-119.

Swenson, C.C., & Klingman, A.(1993). Children and war. In C.F., Saylor (Ed.), Children and disasters. New York: Plenum Press.

Terr, L.C. (1983). Chowchilla revisited: The effects of psychic trauma four years after a school bus kidnapping. American Journal of Psychiatry, 140, 1543-1550.

Terr, L.C. (1985). Psychic trauma in children and adolescents. Psychiatric clinics of North America, 8, 815-835.

Varma, V.P. (Ed.) (1992). The secret life of vulnerable children. New York: Routledge.

Weinberg, R. B. (1990). Serving large numbers of adolescent victim-survivors: Group interventions following trauma at school. Professional Psychology, 21, 271-278.

Wenckstern, S., & Leenaars, A.A. (1993). Trauma and suicide in our schools. Death Studies, 17, 151-171.

Yule, W. (1993). Technology-related disasters. In C.F. Saylor (Ed). Children and disasters. New York: Plenum Press.

Yule, W., & Udwin, O. (1991). Screening child survivors for post-traumatic stress disorders: Experiences from the "Jupiter" sinking. British Journal of Clinical Psychology, 30, 279-295.